A Practical Guide to
Using Repo Master Agreements

A Practical Guide to
Using Repo Master Agreements

Paul C. Harding and Christian A. Johnson

Published by
Euromoney Institutional Investor Plc
Nestor House, Playhouse Yard
London EC4V 5EX
United Kingdom

Tel: +44 (0) 20 7779 8999 or USA +1 800 437 9997
Fax: +44 (0) 20 7779 8300
www.euromoneybooks.com
E-mail: hotline@euromoneyplc.com

Copyright © 2004 Euromoney Institutional Investor Plc

ISBN 1 84374 120 2

This publication is not included in the CLA Licence and must not be copied without the permission of the publisher.

All rights reserved. No part of this publication may be reproduced or used in any form (graphic, electronic or mechanical, including photocopying, recording, taping or information storage and retrieval systems) without permission by the publisher.

This publication is designed to provide accurate and authoritative information with regard to the subject matter covered. In the preparation of this book, every effort has been made to offer the most current, correct, and clearly expressed information possible. The materials presented in this publication are for informational purposes only. They reflect the subjective views of authors and do not necessarily represent current or past practices or beliefs of any organisation. In this publication, neither the authors, their past or present employers, the editor or the publisher is engaged in rendering accounting, business, financial, investment, legal, tax, or other professional advice or services whatsoever and is not liable for any losses, financial or otherwise, associated with adopting any ideas, approaches or frameworks contained in this book. If investment advice or other expert assistance is required, the individualized services of a competent professional should be sought.

Printed and bound in Great Britain by
CPI Antony Rowe, Chippenham and Eastbourne

Disclaimer

This book is intended to provide an informational and illustrative overview of its subject mainly to non-lawyers. It should in no way be relied upon, for any reason, including but not limited to the provision of legal or tax advice in respect of any particular situation, contractual relationship or contemplated transaction. Users of this book must consult such legal and other advisers as they deem appropriate in the preparation and negotiation of repo documentation.

Any examples given herein are illustrative only, and neither the authors of this book nor the publisher assumes any responsibility for any use to which standard repo documentation, or any definition or provision set forth in this book, may be put.

Contents

	Foreword	viii
	Preface	x
	About the authors	xii
	Acknowledgements	xiii
Chapter 1:	**Introduction to the repo markets**	**1**
	Origins and size of the repo market	1
	Nature and types of repo	2
	Typical uses of repo	7
	Buy/sellbacks	9
	Differences between repos and securities loans	11
	Risks with repos	12
Chapter 2:	**Legal issues affecting repos**	**14**
	English perspecive	14
	Legal nature of a repo transaction	14
	Other applicable laws	17
	The Sykes opinion	17
	The TBMA/ISMA GMRA English law opinion	18
	ISMA legal opinions	18
	US Perspective	18
	Introduction	18
	Enforcement of New York choice of law	19
	Enforceability of the Master Repurchase Agreement	20
	Recharacterisation of a repo as a secured loan	20
	US bankruptcy and banking insolvency law	22
	Capacity	28
	Severability	29
	Use of employee plan assets	29
Chapter 3:	**Commentary on the TBMA/ISMA Global Master Repurchase Agreement**	**31**
	Evolution of the TBMA/ISMA GMRA	31
	Structure of the TBMA/ISMA GMRA	32

	Paragraph-by-paragraph analysis of the TBMA/ISMA GMRA	33
	Paragraphs 1–5	33
	Paragraphs 6–10	58
	Paragraphs 11–15	80
	Paragraphs 16–21	85
	TBMA/ISMA GMRA Annex I	89
	Additional provisions appearing in Annex I negotiations	96
	TBMA/ISMA GMRA Annex II	107
	Other annexes	108
Chapter 4:	**The European Master Agreement**	**117**
	Background	117
	Structure of the European Master Agreement	118
	Clause-by-clause analysis of the EMA	121
	General Provisions	121
	Product Annex for Repurchase Transactions	152
	Margin Maintenance Annex	165
Chapter 5:	**Commentary on the Master Repurchase Agreement (September 1996 version)**	**176**
	Evolution of the Agreement	176
	Structure of the Agreement	177
	Paragraph-by-paragraph analysis of the Agreement	177
	Paragraphs 1–5	178
	Paragraphs 6–10	192
	Paragraphs 11–15	196
	Paragraphs 16–20	207
	Annex I	213
	Additional provisions appearing in Annex I negotiations	214
	Other Annexes	222
	Annex II	222
	Annex III	222
	Annex IV	235
	Annex V	240
	Annex VI	243
	Annex VII	245
	Annex VIII	251
	Annex IX	259
Chapter 6:	**Tri-party Custodial Agreements**	**262**
	Introduction	262
	Paragraph-by-paragraph commentary	262
	Paragraphs 1–5	264

	Paragraphs 6–11	283
	Schedules I–IV	298
	Appendices	303
	Recitals	263
Chapter 7:	**New developments**	308
	European Repo Council half-yearly survey	308
	Form of mini close-out notice	308
	Shaping of deal tickets for settlement purposes	308
	ISMA's buy-in rules	309
	Bibliography	310
Appendix 1:	**TBMA/ISMA Global Master Repurchase Agreement**	313
	Reproduced with the kind permission of the International Securities Market Association and The Bond Market Associiation	
Appendix 2:	**Amendment Agreement to a PSA/ISMA Global Master Repurchase Agreement**	351
	Reproduced with the kind permission of the International Securities Market Association and The Bond Market Associiation	
Appendix 3:	**The European Master Agreement**	361
	Reproduced with the kind permission of the European Banking Federation	
Appendix 4:	**Master Repurchase Agreement**	407
	Reproduced with the kind permission of The Bond Market Association	
Appendix 5:	**Custodial Undertaking in Connection with Master Repurchase Agreement (April 2003 version)**	449
	Reproduced with the kind permission of The Bank of New York	
	Index	477

Foreword

Christopher Georgiou
Partner, Securities and Structured Finance, Ashurst

When I first encountered the repo market in 1993, I didn't know what a repo was, and neither did anyone I knew. As a young lawyer starting out in the business of advising repo desks on the documentation of their deals, I thought the easiest way in would be to read a book on the subject. I couldn't find any. There was no alternative but to read the agreement! At that time, it was the 1992 version of the Global Master Repurchase Agreement (GMRA), which was not an easy read. Full of jargon and specialist concepts, and confusingly using terminology that was different from the commercial jargon actually used by traders in the market, it also had a little annex at the back with lots of blanks to complete with the parties' elections and any desired supplemental terms. With no practical experience of the commercial issues or market practice, I sat nervously by the phone waiting for calls from experienced traders or negotiators, ready to be baffled by expert arguments and instantly be discovered for my ignorance.

I imagine that this is the position that many people find themselves in today. Of course the market today is much more mature than it was back then. It has seen spectacular growth. Volumes traded have increased significantly, the range of typical underlying assets has expanded, the range of applications of the repo instrument has increased from flow capital markets and money markets business to complex structured finance transactions, and emerging economies throughout the world are developing repo markets using technology and experience gleaned from the more mature US and European repo markets. As a result of this maturity and continued growth, there has been a corresponding material increase in the number of new personnel entering the market, comprising traders; brokers; corporate treasurers; fund managers; governments and central banks; credit officers; operations teams; collateral management functions; regulators; tax advisers; service providers; and, of course, legal, compliance and documentation professionals. Amongst these, many will be complete innocents who share my initial trepidation at entering a new market and who quickly need to familiarise themselves with the market, its standards and its documentation.

What all of these players have in common, whether new or experienced, is a need for a practical guide that renders the dry and somewhat formidable standard market contracts comprehensible and accessible – and, more importantly, one that provides reassurance that they understand and are not out of step with widely accepted customs of market practice (no one enjoys that rookie feeling of not knowing what they're talking about!). Paul Harding and Christian Johnson's excellent book fulfils this need. Written in clear and concise language, the book sets out and explains every provision of the three principal market standard repo agreements, as well as one of the most widely-used tri-party agreements. Even the annexes for negotiation are to be feared no longer, as the book provides helpful hints and tips on the most commonly seen provisions. There is also a very useful comparative analysis between the

GMRA and the European Master Agreement, and between the GMRA and the Master Repurchase Agreement. Some institutions will come across all three in their dealings and it is instructive to understand the differences in approach of each.

This book lives up to its title as a practical, informative and hands-on guide for practitioners in the repo markets, considerably helping to lift the cloak of obscurity that continues to shroud the market and its documentation. Paul and Christian have achieved their aim, and I congratulate them on a work that I am sure will serve as an invaluable 'bible' for the market for years to come.

September 2004

Preface

There is a 1984 movie called *Repo Man*. Set in the United States, it concerns the repossession of vehicles in a kind of bounty-hunting fashion. It has been described as: "an offbeat punk fable with a little of everything: action, comedy, urban decay, police drama, mystery, governmental conspiracy and UFOs". It did not immediately remind us of the TBMA/ISMA Global Master Repurchase Agreement or the Master Repurchase Agreement: more's the pity, but we liked the bit about the punk fable.

Repo is a huge business: we estimate the current global volume of the market to be equivalent to US$7,900 billion. In most countries repos are classified as a money-market product because the vast majority of maturities are less than 364 days. In fact, in Europe nearly two thirds of them are for less than one month. They combine liquidity with security. In the United States overnight repos are an enormous part of the market.

In this book we have concentrated on repo master agreements in English. There are significant repo master agreements in French and German, which are much used in those markets, but regrettably the authors' deficiencies in those languages prevent their inclusion here.

This book also does not deal with tax, regulatory or accounting issues, except where they touch on documentation. Readers should therefore refer to more specialist literature for commentaries on these matters.

This book comprises seven chapters and five appendices.

Chapter 1 sets the scene, and describes the market and products in general, as well as explaining the differences among them.

Chapter 2 describes the legal issues surrounding repos both in Europe and in the United States.

Chapters 3, 4 and 5 provide, we hope, clear but detailed commentary on the TBMA/ISMA Global Repurchase Master Agreement, the European Master Agreement and the US Master Repurchase Agreement respectively. Our aim with these chapters is to provide clarity and avoid any comments such as Byron's condemnation of Coleridge: "Explaining metaphysics to the nation. / I wish he would explain his explanation."

In Chapter 6 we emphasise the growing importance of tri-party repo by dissecting the standard Custodial Undertaking used by The Bank of New York.

Chapter 7 is a summary of various new developments in the repo market over the past two years.

Terms used in the commentaries may have capitalisation or minor spelling differences in different chapters to match the corresponding documentation.

Finally, the five appendices provide practical information in one place for easy reference. They are:

Appendix 1: A facsimile of the TBMA/ISMA Global Master Repurchase Agreement (reproduced with the kind permission of the International Securities Market Association and The Bond Market Association).

Appendix 2: A facsimile of the Amendment Agreement to the TBMA/ISMA Global Master Repurchase Agreement (reproduced with the kind permission of the International Securities Market Association and The Bond Market Association).

Appendix 3: A facsimile of the European Master Agreement (reproduced with the kind permission of the European Banking Federation).

Appendix 4: A facsimile of the Master Repurchase Agreement and its Annexes (reproduced with the kind permission of The Bond Market Association).

Appendix 5: A facsimile of the Bank of New York Custodial Undertaking (reproduced with the kind permission of The Bank of New York).

We believe that this book has something to offer to seasoned practitioners and "rookies" alike.

We hope that you enjoy it and find it useful.

Paul A. Harding and Christian C. Johnson
June 2004

About the authors

Paul C. Harding is a graduate of the University of London, and has worked in several UK and foreign banks in London, in credit, marketing and documentation roles. Since 1990 he has been involved with derivatives documentation. He was a well-known negotiator in the City of London with Barclays Capital Securities Limited and Hill Samuel Bank Limited, where he was Head of Treasury Documentation.

In February 1997 he founded Derivatives Documentation Limited, a derivatives consultancy and project management company, based in the City of London and providing negotiation, recruitment and in-house training services in derivatives documentation (website: www.derivsdocu.com). Its clients include many of the world's leading banks.

In November 2001 Paul's book *Mastering the ISDA Master Agreement* was published by Financial Times–Prentice Hall. This was followed by his *Mastering Collateral Management and Documentation*, written in conjunction with Christian Johnson, which was published by Financial Times–Prentice Hall, in November 2002.

His book on the 2002 ISDA Master Agreement was published in December 2003 also by Financial Times–Prentice Hall, and in June 2004 his *A Practical Guide to the 2003 ISDA Credit Derivatives Definitions* was published by Euromoney Books.

Christian A. Johnson is an associate law professor at Loyola University Chicago School of Law, where he teaches courses on derivatives, banking and taxation. He graduated from Columbia Law School and was the Executive Editor of the *Columbia Law Review*. He practised law with Milbank Tweed Hadley & McCloy in New York and Mayer Brown Rowe & Maw in Chicago before teaching.

Christian Johnson has published extensively on corporate finance and banking. He has published more than 25 articles on banking, corporate finance and derivatives, and wrote and published *Over-the-Counter Derivatives Documentation: A Practical Guide for Executives* in 2000.

Christian is also a frequent speaker and panellist on corporate finance and banking issues, and has served as an expert witness in these areas. Finally, he brings more than 14 years in negotiating and documenting repurchase transactions and over-the-counter derivatives, having represented several large money centre banks, Federal Home Loan Banks and hedge funds in negotiations.

His previous collaboration with Paul Harding was in 2002, when he co-wrote *Mastering Collateral Management and Documentation*, which was published by Financial Times–Prentice Hall.

Acknowledgements

Paul C. Harding

I should like to thank my wife, Sheila, for all her encouragement and patience in what is the fifth technical book I have written or co-written in the past four years. Our dining-room table is now empty of drafts and research materials, which appeals to her minimalist tendencies. I thank her for all her sacrifices over the past four years.

My grateful thanks are due to our daughters, Alex and Isabelle, for typing assistance well beyond the call of duty. Another daughter, Abby, worked like a Trojan to edit out idiosyncrasies in the various chapters with all the skill of a technological titan.

Christian Johnson and I should like to thank the International Securities Market Association and The Bond Market Association for kindly permitting the reproduction of their documentation in Appendices 1, 2 and 4 of this book. We are also grateful to the European Banking Federation for permission to reproduce their European Master Agreement in Appendix 3 and to The Bank of New York for permission to reproduce their Custodial Undertaking in Appendix 5. All these institutions gave their permissions most readily and we are pleased to express our grateful thanks to them here.

I would like to thank all those who kindly read proofs of this book and made comments, in particular:

    Kurt Crommelin, Bayerische Hypo und Vereinsbank AG
    Jane Lawidsen, Danske Bank A/S
    Wilfried Schuette, DZ- Deutsche Genossenschaft Bank AG
    Keith Spiller, UBS Investment Bank
    Leeanne Robb, National Australia Bank Limited, who made useful comments on Chapter 3.

Any errors remain my own.

We are also very grateful to Christopher Georgiou for writing the foreword to this book. Christopher was the author of a widely used book on the PSA/ISMA Global Master Repurchase Agreement (1995).

We should like to thank the editorial staff at Euromoney Books for all their excellent editing and support. Special thanks are due to Elizabeth Gray, Managing Editor, Johanna Geary and Kim Gross.

Finally, it has been a real pleasure to work with Christian Johnson on another book. To my mind, Christian is a teacher with a real love of imparting knowledge, a characteristic that has enhanced this book enormously.

Christian A. Johnson

I begin by thanking my lovely wife Cori for her patience with me and the late nights as the book progressed and took shape.

I would also like to thank Gary A. Buki, Managing Counsel from The Bank of New York, for his patience in answering endless questions about the finer points of tri-party custodial

ACKNOWLEDGEMENTS

agreements, and Gail Shanley from Citigroup, for answering questions about market practice and the Master Repurchase Agreement. I should like to thank Omer Oztan, former Assistant General Counsel of The Bond Market Association (and now of Cantor Fitzgerald) for answering questions about the repo market, The Bond Market Association, and the Master Repurchase Agreement. Any errors in the book, however, are all my own.

I extend special thanks to Dean Nina Appel and the faculty of Loyola University Chicago School of Law for providing me with financial and moral support. I would also like to thank my research assistants, Debra Ostvig, Colleen Bryan and Sharon Nowakowski, for able research assistance, and help in editing and proof reading the manuscript.

Finally, I want to thank Paul Harding for inviting me to work with him on this book. This book is Paul's brainchild, and he brought tremendous energy, enthusiasm and work to completing it. He was also tremendously helpful in editing my contributions regarding the BMA Master Repurchase Agreement, The Bank of New York tri-party custodial agreement, and the effect of US federal and New York law on the agreements. It has been an honour to collaborate with one of the most prolific and able commentators on repurchase agreements and derivatives.

Chapter 1

Introduction to the repo markets

Origins and size of the repo market

The first repurchase transactions (almost universally known as a repo or a reverse repo) were transacted by the US Federal Reserve in 1918 for institutions that could not legally borrow or lend securities, but could buy or sell them. Since then repo has become the main market intervention tool of many central banks (including the Bank of England and the European Central Bank) for their daily liquidity open market operations. Open market operations drain cash from the system when a central bank thinks that there is too much of it and pour it in when liquidity is low.

The European market

The Italian repo market, which started in 1970, is the oldest repo market in Europe. Repo began in the London market in the mid-1980s, when investment banks started to use repo to finance their bond positions. Repo markets in France, Germany and Spain also started in the 1980s, and today the repo market in Europe is enormous.

In its half-yearly survey of 69 financial institutions on 10 December 2003, ISMA's European Repo Council reported total outstandings of €3.788 trillion (€3,788 billion). This was a 12 per cent increase on the corresponding figure of €3,377 billion at the end of 2002. Tri-party repo accounted for about €425 billion of this.

Nearly 64 per cent of repo transactions in the European financial markets mature in less than one month and so the market is very short-term in nature. Of total transactions, 73 per cent are denominated in euros and just under 10 per cent in sterling. The European market splits into 81 per cent classic repos and 19 per cent buy/sellbacks, according to the survey.

The US market

The Bond Market Association in the United States publishes quarterly figures of the average daily outstanding amount in the US repo market. As of 31 December 2003 it estimated average daily outstandings of US$4.041 trillion (US$4,041 billion).

Total market size

Therefore, as at the end of December 2003 the total estimated daily outstandings in the European and US repo markets was approximately equivalent to US$7.9 trillion (US$7,900 billion). This is not the notional value of transactions, as in the derivatives markets. Based on latest ISDA figures as at 31 December 2003, the estimated aggregate notional values of interest rate swaps and options and currency swaps was US$142 trillion. However, consultants consider that only between 1 per cent and 2 per cent of this figure is really at risk. Taking the higher 2 per cent figure, this would represent US$2.840 trillion. Therefore, the repo market is, on this basis, arguably much larger in real risk terms.

The growth of the market

The repo market does not function in isolation. It links together money markets, bond markets, futures markets and OTC derivatives markets.

Active repo markets thrive on active bond markets. The repo market's rapid growth in the past 10 years has been due to the following main factors:

- a global increase in non-bank funding;
- an expansion in global public debt;
- repo's liquidity and flexibility;
- the high quality of collateral used (ie, government debt);
- arbitrage opportunities between the cash and futures markets; and
- as an alternative to bank deposits or unsecured products such as commercial paper or certificates of deposit.

Apart from central banks, the main players in the repo market are securities houses, investment banks, insurance companies, fund managers, hedge funds, broker-dealers, corporate treasurers and even local authorities.

Almost all major money markets now have an established repo market. Even emerging markets are starting to set them up.

Repo now covers government bonds, supranational bonds, agency bonds, corporate bonds, Eurobonds, Brady bonds, mortgage-backed securities, Treasury bills and equities.

Repo trading is conducted over the telephone, with rates displayed on screens supplied by brokers. There is growing use of electronic dealing systems, with live dealing rates displayed on screens and trades being conducted at the click of a mouse. There are also fully automated trading systems. A further factor that has encouraged the growth of repo is the development of centralised clearing and netting systems, such as RepoClear run by the London Clearing House. Here the bilateral relationship between the two contracting parties is novated (transferred) by each party so that the clearing house is its counterparty in respect of individual transactions. All trade confirmations and details are matched.

Repos are generally considered to be a money-market instrument in most countries because transactions are for less than one year. In fact, 64 per cent of transactions are for less than one month.

However, repos are now also occasionally transacted for periods of more than one year.

Nature and types of repo

What is a repo?

Repo is short for the word "repurchase", and refers to a contract for the sale and repurchase of securities. These securities are normally fixed-rate bonds, but in recent years equities have also been repurchased or repoed.

Exhibit 1.1 illustrates a typical repo transaction.

Exhibit 1.1
Typical repo transaction

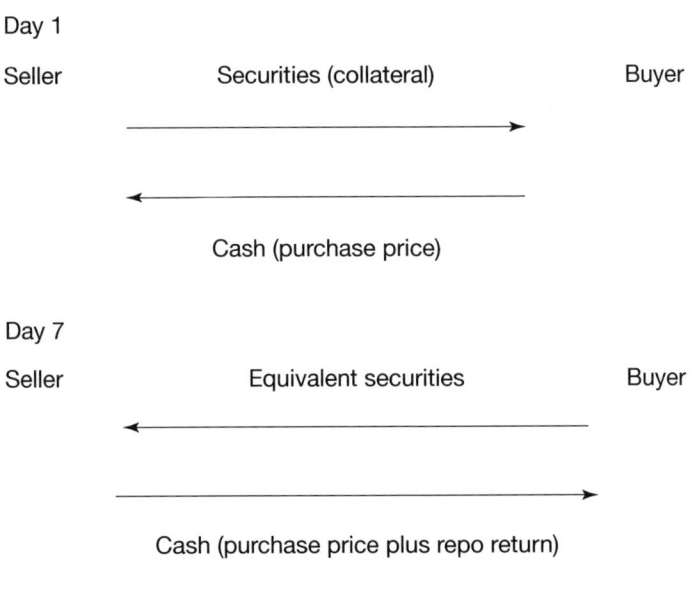

Source: Authors' own

What happens is that a Seller sells bonds to a Buyer for an agreed cash price and commits at the same time to buy back equivalent bonds of the same issuer on an agreed future date for the same cash price plus a rate of return, which is called the repo rate. This remains fixed during the life of the repo. It is called the Pricing Rate in the TBMA/ISMA Global Master Repurchase Agreement (the "TBMA/ISMA GMRA").

The basic repo, therefore, combines a spot sale and a forward purchase. It represents a temporary transfer of assets. Looking at it another way, the Seller delivers securities and receives cash from the Buyer on a delivery-versus-payment basis (the safest method) after a written Confirmation has been agreed. Upon maturity, the Buyer returns the securities and receives back its cash plus a financing charge called the repo rate from the Seller.

All transactions are fully collateralised, as the bonds secure the Buyer's cash and the cash secures the Seller's bonds. The bonds are revalued daily and, if their value has fallen, the Seller transfers additional bonds to the Buyer. Repo therefore reduces counterparty risk.

During the trade legal title to the bonds passes to the Buyer, which may deal with them as it sees fit. Its only obligation is to sell back equivalent bonds (ie, those issued by the same issuer, of the same issue and the same nominal value) to the Seller on the "Repurchase Date".

During the trade the Seller no longer owns the bonds, but has full title to the cash received for them and can use that cash as it sees fit. The Seller is only obligated to pay the "Repurchase Price" (including the repo rate) for the equivalent bonds on the Repurchase Date.

The economic intention behind a repo is that the market risk and reward of the underlying securities remain with the Seller, although the legal structure of a repo involves an outright transfer of ownership in each case. Whatever happens to the market value of the bonds during the repo's life, the Seller has to repurchase them at the price originally agreed (the Purchase Price plus the repo return). So, during the term of the repo, the Seller will mark to market (value) the securities each business day. A fall in value would be an unrealised loss in its daily profit-and-loss account while a rise in value would be an unrealised gain.

What has just been described is called a "classic repo" and is viewed from the Seller's perspective. This description might make a repo sound like a secured loan, but this is not the case, as will be shown in Chapter 2 when legal issues are examined.

Types of repo

There are a number of different types of repo:

- reverse repo;
- flex repo;
- general collateral repo;
- special repo;
- hold-in-custody or "trust me" repo;
- open or "on demand" repo;
- overnight repo;
- term repo;
- cross-currency repo;
- tri-party repo;
- syndicated repo; and
- equity repo.

Reverse repo
As mentioned before, a classic repo is viewed from the Seller's perspective. A reverse repo is seen from the Buyer's viewpoint. Like a car backing into a garage, it reverses securities into its business, in return for cash. So a reverse repo is the mirror image of a classic repo – it is a purchase and resale transaction.

Flex repo
A flex repo is a repo with a fixed term and repo rate, which allows the Seller to sell bonds on a phased basis according to an agreed schedule in return for cash from the Buyer. Repurchase of the bonds is also made on a phased basis.

General collateral repo
This is a transaction in which the Seller is selling bonds just to raise cash. The Buyer will charge a higher repo rate than for a special repo (see below), but the rate will probably still be LIBID (the London Interbank Bid Rate) or below as the repo is a secured transaction. Such repos are described by the market as "cash driven".

Special repo
With a special repo, a Buyer is buying particular bonds that it needs, for example, to cover a forward sale that it has made with a third party. To obtain these bonds it is willing to charge the Seller a lower repo rate on the cash that it pays to the Seller. This allows the Seller to make a profit on the cash, as it will redeposit it elsewhere at a higher rate during the repo term. The

key thing for the Buyer is to get the bonds. If a bond is special it pushes the repo rate downwards. Zero rates and even negative rates are possible when dealing in specials. The Seller therefore benefits from a reduced repo rate and a lower Repurchase Price. Such repos are described by the market as "stock driven".

Specials are often delivered to settle futures contracts.

Hold-in-custody repo
This is also called a "trust me" repo and is more common in the United States. It involves the Seller transferring beneficial, but not legal, title to the bonds to the Buyer and holding them in a segregated account in its own books as custodian for the Buyer. The Seller therefore retains possession and control of the purchased bonds, and the Buyer has to rely on the Seller to keep the securities segregated so as to retain beneficial ownership. This form of repo would only be used when the Seller is a far better credit risk than the Buyer, or where the Buyer is not a financial institution and lacks the operational infrastructure to transfer securities. The advantage to the Seller, of course, is that it saves on transfer and substitution costs, as the securities do not physically move.

However, the risks are that a dishonest Seller could repo the same securities out again on the same basis; could fail to return margin when its exposure is reduced; or could become insolvent, leaving the Buyer potentially as an unsecured creditor if the Seller failed to segregate the securities.

Open repo
In an open repo the term of the transaction is not agreed in advance, but it may be terminated at any time by either party giving notice to the other. Settlement usually takes place one Business Day after notice of termination is given.

This type of repo is also called an "on demand" repo.

Overnight repo
An overnight repo is simply a repo entered into on one Business Day and terminated on the next.

Term repo
This is a repo for more than one Business Day and for which a termination date is agreed, although it could be brought forward by mutual agreement of the parties. Normally the term of a repo will not exceed 364 days. Most trades are for one month or less. In the European repo market 37 per cent of total trades are for one week or less.

Cross-currency repo
This is a type of repo where the currencies of the cash and securities are different. Valuation takes into account the exchange rate between the two currencies. This can, of course, open up the transaction to foreign exchange risk and result in the Buyer being temporarily under-collateralised.

Tri-party repo
A tri-party repo involves the Seller and Buyer as well as a third-party securities clearing system, such as Euroclear or Clearstream, which handles the administrative aspects of repo between the Seller and Buyer (eg, marking to market, checking collateral eligibility, cus-

tody of securities, cash management, transferring the bonds and cash (following a sale or margin call) simultaneously between accounts, and dealing with corporate actions).

For a Buyer a tri-party repo is the easiest way of transacting a repo and receiving the bonds. It is also the safest because it avoids the risks of hold-in-custody repo. The operational support of the securities clearing system comes at a price, but provides the benefits of reduced administration, simple collateral movement and possible reduced funding costs.

Under a tri-party agreement the securities dealer delivers collateral to a custodian (eg, Euroclear), which will place it into a segregated account. The securities dealer controls which securities are in the account and the custodian confirms to the investor on each business day that its cash remains fully collateralised by pre-agreed eligible securities.

The custodian will settle transactions on their Repurchase Date, provided that the necessary levels of cash and securities are in the parties' accounts with the custodian.

Smaller market players like tri-party arrangements because they avoid setting up in-house administrative facilities to deliver and collect collateral.

The costs of the tri-party repo arrangement are normally borne by the seller.

In tri-party repo in the European market the Buyer and Seller enter into a repo transaction (probably under the PSA/ISMA Global Master Repurchase Agreement or the TBMA/ISMA Global Master Repurchase Agreement), and also make the Transaction subject to the terms of a service agreement between the three parties, which will define the precise role and functions of the tri-party repo service provider.

Similarly, in the United States the Buyer and Seller will also enter into a repo transaction (probably under the BMA Master Repurchase Agreement), and will also make the Transaction subject to the terms of a tri-party custodial agreement, using a large financial institution such as The Bank of New York or JP Morgan Chase as the custodian.

Syndicated repo

Repos have also been used as a syndicated financing technique, particularly in connection with international securities. A number of structures, eg, club, sub-participation and trusts, have been used, each with its pros and cons. In considering syndicated repo it is necessary to make international legal and tax analyses. Banks also need to examine their regulatory capital position prior to entering into such transactions.

Equity repo

Investment banks use equity repo like debt repo to fund their long positions and cover their short positions (please see next section below for the meaning of these terms). Because the Purchased Securities are equities, they are invariably lower quality as collateral for the Buyer's cash and normally the repo rate on that cash is higher than for investment-grade bond collateral.

The equity repo market has operated in London since the early 1990s. Trades are often conducted with a basket of stocks, which might be customised to a client's requirements or be constituent stocks in an index such as the FTSE 100. Where a stock falls out of an index, it will be substituted by a stock joining that index.

Equity repo has the following main differences from debt repo:

- greater participation rights in the issuer's business with equities;
- greater scope of voting rights;
- wider range of corporate actions, eg, rights issues, takeover offers etc;
- issues of bonus shares rather than cash dividends are possible with equities;
- notification requirement if more than 3 per cent of the shares in a UK publicly listed company are held;
- equities can be partly paid; and
- stamp duty is more likely than with debt securities.

One big repo-type product not mentioned in the above list is the buy/sellback transaction. This is because they are a subject in themselves (which we will examine after the next section on typical uses of repos).

Typical uses of repo

The uses of repo transactions can best be seen from the respective viewpoints of the Seller and the Buyer.

Seller's viewpoint

Cheaper financing

Repo is a relatively cheap way of financing for a securities firm. Unlike banks they cannot use the competitively priced interbank deposit market, but they do have large pools of securities that can be used as collateral to secure cash received from Buyers. This reduces their financing costs, because the money they receive is on a secured rather than unsecured basis, thus reducing default risk. However, because repo is only a temporary transfer of assets it gives Sellers access to cash without liquidating their bond positions. They can receive any coupons due and benefit from any increases in market value for the securities.

Financing a long position

A long position is where an investor wants to hold on to particular securities because it believes that the market price will rise. So a securities house could use a repo to refinance the purchase price of the securities that it has transferred to the Buyer. Therefore, the cash received from the Buyer for the securities is used by the Seller to pay for these same securities that it has previously bought from a third party. This will be cheaper than finance raised on an unsecured basis.

Leveraging

Hedge funds frequently leverage their positions in the bond market. This is done by a hedge fund entering into a repo by selling securities for cash. That cash can then be used to purchase more of the same securities, which can then be sold under another repo. The cash from that second repo can then be used to purchase more securities, which can also be repoed out. Alternatively the cash can be used to repurchase the first securities sold under the repo. Leveraging allows parties to take larger positions in financial markets, which could add to systemic risk.

Buyer's viewpoint

Lending
A Buyer generally views repo as a form of lending that is more secure than making an unsecured loan to a borrower. The largest Buyers are banks that have surplus liquidity arising from their customer deposits. The wider the range of securities they are willing to take, the higher the repo rates they can earn.

Opportunity for higher returns
Institutional investors and corporate treasurers often find that they can get better returns on repos than on other short-term money-market instruments. The return reflects the risks that the Buyer runs, namely that the Seller may default on its repurchase obligations. There is also the risk that the price of the securities held by the Buyer may fall in the meantime, although their value would be topped up by margin calls when this occurs.

Covering short positions
A short position is one where a dealer sells a security that he does not own because he believes that market prices will fall before the delivery date. Bond dealers and institutions frequently use repos to hedge their trading positions, by buying securities under a repo transaction and delivering them on the appropriate date to meet the short position. Sometimes, if a Seller is funding a long position or a Buyer is covering a short position, it might not want to go directly into the market itself to transact. Instead it will use a specialist broker as an intermediary to screen a potentially sensitive position from the market.

Within a bank a repo desk will be connected to cash traders, who want to know financing costs; to the fixed-income sales force, who may use repo as a tool to offer higher yields or cheaper financing to customers; to proprietary trading desks, where it is a source of financing and hedging; and to syndicated loan desks, where repo is a lending tool.

The repo markets in government bonds are by far the biggest, because they are very liquid and have a high volume of transactions. However, repos have also been transacted with Eurobonds, Brady bonds, agency securities and mortgage-backed securities. In the United States there is also a major equity repo market.

As mentioned before, central banks use repos to help to control a country's money supply through open-market operations. Gilt repo became part of the Bank of England's open-market operations in March 1997. Almost invariably the market's position is one of a shortage of liquidity (ie, a need to increase the supply of sterling), which the Bank of England relieves via open market operations conducted at a fixed official interest rate. The Bank of England's operation in this case is actually a reverse repo. The Bank will reverse in gilts and eligible bills, and pay out cash. In the rare event of excess liquidity in the market, the Bank of England will sell bills to mop up this surplus.

The reason central banks choose repo as the money-market instrument to relieve shortages is because it combines security (government debt is the collateral) with liquidity to trade in large volumes.

The duration of such transactions will vary, but is usually between two and four weeks. As well as controlling market liquidity, central banks' open-market operations are also done to send a signal to the market on the intended direction of short-term interest rates.

Buy/sellbacks

A buy/sellback is a contractual commitment between two parties first to sell securities (bonds, bills or notes) and then to buy them back at an agreed future date. The Buyer receives a return on its cash which represents the difference between the original sale and future repurchase prices of the securities.

The Repurchase Price is determined between the coupon income accrued during the buy/sellback's life on the nominal amount of the bonds and a return based on the implied "interest" rate or repo rate on the cash advanced. So, like a classic repo, a buy/sellback involves a contract to sell securities and repurchase them on an agreed future date.

However, it is important to realise that the forward price has nothing to do with the actual market price of the collateral at the time of the forward trade. It is just an accounting mechanism for the "interest" element inherent in the trade, which, in the case of a buy/sellback, is implied in the forward price.

To say that repos and buy/sellbacks are similar but different is not a helpful way to distinguish between them.

Differences between repos and buy/sellbacks

While they both achieve the same economic effect, the differences between a buy/sellback and a repo can be explained as detailed below.

Documentation

Buy/sellbacks are simple as far as documentation is concerned. The Buyer simply writes two deal tickets – the spot purchase and forward sale tickets. So, effectively, there are two separate transactions, while a repo is typically structured as one.

Moreover, with a standard buy/sellback there is no master agreement such as a TBMA/ISMA GMRA, which a repo requires. However, the absence of the TBMA/ISMA GMRA means that the advantages of margining, close-out netting and substitution are lost to a buy/sellback. It could be documented under the Buy/Sell Back Annex of the TBMA/ISMA GMRA, but then it would lose its documentation simplicity.

Absence of close-out netting

Parties to a buy/sellback have no contractual rights when an Event of Default occurs. Where two parties have several buy/sellback transactions outstanding between them, if a counterparty defaults on one deal, the other party must simply wait until the scheduled maturity dates of the other buy/sellbacks to see if it will happen again. Under a classic repo documented under a repo master agreement all transactions could be terminated.

Margining

One reason a repo needs more extensive documentation than a buy/sellback is margining. The repoed securities are regularly valued or marked to market. By comparing the value of the securities against the amount of cash payable, the parties can calculate which will suffer a loss if the other defaults and that party can call for margin in cash or securities in an amount that will remove or reduce its risk exposure on the other party. If this risk exposure happens again, because either the market value of the securities falls or the amount due from the Seller increases as a result of the daily accrual of the repo rate, then the margin requirement is recalculated and more margin is transferred. If the Buyer holds too much margin, it has to return a portion of the securities or cash to the Seller.

So, repo transactions have required longer documentation to set out these margining provisions, and to deal with non-compliance and the application of margin in default and insolvency situations.

Until recently some institutions (eg, small continental banks, particularly in Italy) preferred not to have margin mechanisms, as they lacked the internal controls to monitor and operate margining provisions. Historically, where a counterparty risk exposure arose buy/sellback transactions were repriced (ie, terminated and a new buy/sellback transaction entered into).

Insolvency risk
Because a buy/sellback is documented as two separate transactions, there is a risk of a party becoming insolvent after the initial purchase but before the forward sale. In jurisdictions where "cherry picking" is possible, the absence of close-out netting in the buy/sellback transaction could seriously prejudice the solvent party, by allowing a liquidator to choose which contracts it is going to honour because they are profitable and which to enforce against the solvent party because they are unprofitable to its insolvent client. The solvent party would be left as an unsecured creditor for these sums.

Accounting treatment
A buy/sellback is typically treated as an outright sale so that the securities leave the Seller's balance sheet and the coupon on the securities accrues for the benefit of the Buyer.

With a repo the Seller retains the securities on its balance sheet and the coupon on the securities accrues for the benefit of the Seller.

Regulatory capital treatment
The lack of close-out netting provisions in relation to a buy/sellback transaction increases the amount of capital that a financial institution must set aside in its trading book against the possibility of loss. Without close-out netting regulators will require the institution to set aside capital based on its gross exposure to the counterparty concerned. This is because buy/sellbacks suffer from the regulatory capital disadvantage of being unable to net or margin their obligations.

For these reasons, to be able to margin and to calculate exposure on a net basis many institutions now bring buy/sellbacks within their repo documentation, particularly the PSA/ISMA GMRA or the TBMA/ISMA GMRA, whose daily marking to market, margining and close-out netting mechanism make them acceptable to regulators for regulatory capital purposes.

Other technical differences between a repo and buy/sellback are detailed below.

Purchase price
With a buy/sellback the purchase price of the buy transaction is usually the unadjusted market price of the securities. With a repo the market price of the securities is normally rounded to produce a Purchase Price, which is easier to transfer.

Sellback price
This is expressed as an absolute price for a buy/sellback (ie, it factors in an explicit repo rate in the sellback price). Any coupon received by the Buyer during the transaction's term is also factored into the Sellback Price. With a repo any coupon paid to the Buyer is separately accounted for to the Seller. A repo's Repurchase Price is expressed as the initial Purchase Price plus the daily accrual of the repo rate from the Purchase Date to the Repurchase Date.

Termination
Repos can be open or terminable on demand; buy/sellbacks cannot. This is because no forward price can be calculated unless a termination date is stipulated.

Substitution
The Seller normally has this right with a repo, but not with a buy/sellback.

Distributions
If an income or a dividend payment occurs during the repo term, the Buyer promptly pays an equivalent sum by way of a manufactured dividend to the Seller. With a buy/sellback the Buyer keeps the income payment on the securities, but normally takes it into account when calculating the sellback price, so that the income or dividend payment is part of the sellback price paid over at the maturity of the buy/sellback.

While the Buyer will usually do this, in fact the actual coupon paid is not legally recoverable, because there is no contract in place with an obligation on the Buyer to return it.

Differences between repos and securities loans

It will now be useful to distinguish repos from securities loans, which share many of their mechanics, eg, outright transfer of title, margining and the right to retransfer Equivalent Securities, as shown below.

Type of transaction

A repo is a sale and repurchase contract, while securities lending is a lending and borrowing relationship and contract.

Method of exchange

In a classic repo cash is paid by the Buyer in return for bond collateral, while in securities lending stock is given in return for collateral that may be in the form of cash, bonds, certificates of deposit or letters of credit.

Payment

In a repo the Seller pays a repo rate to the Buyer for its cash, which is accounted for on the Repurchase Date.

In a securities loan the Borrower pays a fee to the stock lender for the use of the securities based on their value. It is usually paid monthly in arrears. Interest is paid on any cash collateral. The reason for this difference is historical.

Type of securities

With a repo (unless it is a special repo) the precise nature of the securities transferred is of secondary importance, primarily being there to provide some assurance to the Buyer that the Seller will perform its obligation to pay the Repurchase Price on the Repurchase Date. With a securities loan the Borrower will be very specific about the securities that it wants to borrow, probably because it needs them to settle a transaction with a third party.

Specials

Demand for particular securities is reflected in a repo by the lower repo rate paid by the Seller, but in a securities loan it is reflected by the higher fee paid by the Borrower. In fact, one reason the securities lending market remains popular is that lenders such as fund managers and insurance companies prefer to lend stock in return for a fixed fee rather than engage in repo, which requires a dealing desk and interest rate management, and exposes the Seller to market risk.

Income

In a classic repo income is paid over to the Seller in the form of a manufactured dividend by the Buyer.

In a stock loan either the stock is recalled over the coupon date or the coupon is passed through to the lender.

Risks with repos

While the credit risk with repos is less than with unsecured transactions, it still exists in the forms detailed below.

Counterparty default

This is where a repo counterparty defaults by not returning cash or securities on the Repurchase Date. With the Buyer acquiring full title to the bonds under a repo transaction the risk is that the value of the bonds will have fallen below the Purchase Price (the cash paid) when the default occurs.

Counterparty risk can be reduced through margining and by agreeing appropriate initial margin or haircuts.

Issuer risk

This risk arises where the issuer of the securities defaults during the repo term. However, the Buyer has recourse against the Seller, which is obligated to buy the bonds back at the agreed Repurchase Price on the Repurchase Date. Before that the Buyer can call for top-up margin from the Seller. This is likely to be a real problem only if the Seller defaulted at the same time as the issuer, which is a remote possibility. Securities issued by the Seller or any of its affiliates are not acceptable in repo transactions because of the correlation risk involved.

Market risk

This is the risk that the value of a financial instrument will fall due to market price movements. With a bond this would arise where market interest rates rise.

Margining reduces the Buyer's risk in this respect. However, the Seller is still exposed to this risk because the economic effects of market risk are its and it will mark the loss on its balance sheet during the repo's life. Margin takes the form of initial margin and top-up margin (see commentary on paragraph 4 of the TBMA/ISMA GMRA in Chapter 3, pages 32–54).

The amount of margin required will be influenced by the following factors:

- the credit quality of the margin giver;
- the term of the repo (shorter is better);
- the margin's price volatility; and
- the presence of a legal agreement such as the TBMA/ISMA GMRA or the Master Repurchase Agreement.

Operational risk

This risk arises from system failure, human error, fraud, accident or natural disaster. ISDA defines it as: "the risk of direct or indirect loss resulting from inadequate or failed internal processes, people and systems and from external events". Operational risk also includes settlement risk, which is eliminated where a delivery-versus-payment system is the norm.

Legal risk

This risk arises from a failure to agree on the interpretation of a legal document, or such a document being inadequate for its purpose, or difficulty in enforcing a legal agreement when a default occurs. Fortunately, the terms of the PSA/ISMA GMRA and TBMA/ISMA GMRA are not often challenged, and their close-out netting mechanism has been proved to be effective.

If a repo master agreement is entered into by the parties and the enforceability of its close-out netting provisions is supported by a robust legal opinion from a reputable law firm in the country where the counterparty is incorporated, regulators will allow exposure to be reported on a net basis for regulatory capital purposes, which will lead to a reduction in the capital to be allocated to repos in a bank's trading book.

Chapter 2

Legal issues affecting repos

English perspective*

Historically, legal jurisdictions have either passed specific legislation covering repos (eg, as in France) or relied on general capital markets legislation, as in England.

Legal nature of a repo transaction

Legally the key feature of repos is that they are sale and repurchase agreements, not a species of secured loan.

With the sale absolute legal ownership of the securities is passed to the Buyer in return for the payment of an agreed Purchase Price. The Seller has no further claim on these securities. In respect of the repurchase leg of the Transaction the Seller has only a contractual right to repurchase the Equivalent Securities, but has no ownership interest in them if the repurchase does not occur. In those circumstances the Seller has only a right to claim cash damages.

The question has been asked if repo is actually a secured loan in disguise.

When the repo market began in the United Kingdom in the late 1980s, there was some confusion about the legal characterisation of a repo. This was due in part to:

- lack of standard documentation;
- lack of common intention between market players;
- use of repo for different business purposes; and
- similar tax, accounting and capital adequacy treatment as for a secured loan.

The introduction of market standard documentation in 1992 in the form of the PSA/ISMA Global Master Repurchase Agreement (the "PSA/ISMA GMRA"), with clear sale and repurchase language, steadied the market, and underlined its intention to create a sale and repurchase contract allowing the Buyer to deal with the bond security freely and the Seller to release all its ownership rights to it. The general legal consensus in the United Kingdom is that a standard repo is unlikely to be recharacterised as a secured loan. Recharacterisation arises when a court decides that the nature of a transaction is otherwise than it seems.

In relation to the PSA/ISMA GMRA, the market obtained and relied on an opinion from Richard Sykes, QC, which was issued in November 1995. Sykes opined that the English courts would not seek to recharacterise a repo transaction as a secured loan. However, it should be remembered that the opinion only related to "standard repos".

---

* by Paul Harding

As indicated before, under English law the nature of transactions is decided or characterised by looking at the intentions of the parties concerned, which are normally gauged from the express language of the documentation. This approach is one of "substance over form". The courts can recharacterise a repo as a secured loan if the form of the transaction does not match its substance or the conduct of the parties indicates this. Factors that the courts may consider are:

- the right to deal with the securities;
- the right to the coupon;
- the right to substitution; and
- proceeds on enforcement.

Right to deal with the securities

This right arises where legal title to the repoed securities passes from the Seller to the Buyer, which is then entitled to sell them, repo them out to a third party or hold on to them – in other words, to deal with them as it thinks fit.

Under a secured loan the lender obtains a partial ownership interest in the security, which is subject to the borrower's "equity of redemption" (ie, the right, when the loan is repaid, to the return of the very assets previously charged to the lender).

Because the Buyer does not return the selfsame securities on the Repurchase Date, but Equivalent Securities instead, this reflects the sale and repurchase nature of the repo contract.

Right to the coupon

An underlying principle of repo transactions is that the Seller should not be disadvantaged by them. An area where it potentially could be disadvantaged is in the payment of income by the bond issuer. As legal ownership of the bonds has passed to the Buyer, it is recorded as their holder in the books of the bond issuer. Therefore, it will receive any interest coupons on the bonds.

However, since a repo is only a temporary transfer of assets and a Repurchase Date is fixed at the time of entering into the Transaction, it was considered equitable that the Seller should receive equivalent income from the Buyer, which will remit a "manufactured coupon" to the Seller shortly after an interest coupon is paid on the bonds. This again reinforces the sale and repurchase nature of the repo contract.

Right to substitution

Paragraph 8 of both the PSA/ISMA GMRA and the TBMA/ISMA Global Master Repurchase Agreement (the "TBMA/ISMA GMRA") give the Seller the right to request substitution of the Purchased Securities previously delivered to the Buyer with New Purchased Securities.

Under English law it is important that the Seller does not have an automatic right to substitute securities, as this could be seen as retaining an interest in the securities that it had supposedly sold to the Buyer. The Buyer must be free to consent or not. Where the Buyer cannot veto a substitution request from the Seller, the repo could be recharacterised as a secured loan with the security interest being a floating charge because the Buyer would not have control over which assets can be disposed of or substituted. The normal way of dealing with this is for the Buyer to have an unfettered right to consent or not to the Seller's substitution requests, as it has in the PSA/ISMA GMRA and the TBMA/ISMA GMRA.

The Buyer's right to consent to substitution requests also highlights the sale and repurchase nature of the repo contract.

Proceeds on enforcement

Where, following the Seller's default or insolvency, the Buyer sells the securities on the open market and obtains less than the Repurchase Price for them, it will base its residual claim on cash damages and not refer to unpaid indebtedness. The close-out netting mechanism of paragraph 10(b)–(d) of the PSA/ISMA GMRA or the TBMA/ISMA GMRA fosters the damages concept, and again indicates the sale and repurchase nature of the repo contract.

Disadvantages of recharacterisation as a secured loan

There has been no case in an English court where a repo has been recharacterised as a secured loan. In the next section Christian Johnson refers to a US case – *In Lombard-Wall Inc. v Columbus Bank and Trust Co. 1982* – where a bankruptcy court held that the repo in that case was a secured loan for bankruptcy purposes and the court stayed the parties from liquidating holdings of securities collateral under the repo transactions. This decision led to changes in the US Bankruptcy Code that recategorised repo as a transaction where the automatic stay does not apply.

If an English court decided that a particular repo transaction was in reality a secured loan the consequences would be serious and would entail the following:

Inability to deal with securities

If the repo transaction was recharacterised as a secured loan, a Buyer who had entered into a repo to cover a short position would not be able to pass the securities unencumbered to its client (unless the Seller defaulted and could sell them) as the Seller would retain an ownership interest in them.

Enforcement formalities

If a repo transaction is simply a sale and repurchase, the Buyer as absolute owner of the securities can dispose of them at any time. However, if the Buyer holds only a security interest in them, while the Seller retains the ownership rights, then it will be able to enforce his security only in a prescribed legal procedure and may find other creditors – such as an administrator or the Inland Revenue – ahead of it. It may, in fact, be prevented from selling the securities by the Seller's liquidator because it does not have sufficient legal title to sell them.

Breach of negative pledge

A negative pledge is an undertaking by a borrower that it will not give security to any of its lenders. If a repo is recharacterised as a secured loan, it would undoubtedly breach any negative pledge given by the Seller to another lender. This would then allow the other lenders to accelerate their loans to the Seller and demand early repayment.

Administration freezes

Under English insolvency law administration is a rehabilitative process, similar to the Chapter 11 bankruptcy legislation in the United States, whereby the court allows an insolvent company breathing space to reorder its affairs under the supervision of an insolvency official called an administrator. During this period of typically three or six months, secured creditors cannot enforce their charges, but securities subject to sale and repurchase arrangements would be unaffected by administration freezes.

In England and Wales the creation of security interests requires certain formalities to perfect them, such as registration within 21 days of creation at Companies House. Failure to do this would render a security interest void against a liquidator. However, a pledge or charge over securities is not one of the registrable charges set out in Section 396 of the Companies Act 1985 and therefore for securities this would not be a drawback where a repo was recharacterised as a secured loan.

Other applicable laws

While the rights and obligations of the parties under a PSA/ISMA GMRA or a TBMA/ISMA GMRA are governed by English law, it is important to remember that certain other laws may also apply. For instance, in an insolvency proceeding it is the law of the jurisdiction where the insolvent party is incorporated that will govern and determine whether these agreements' close-out netting provisions are enforceable in the local courts.

The local law also determines a party's capacity to enter into a repo transaction in the first place. Whether a sale or repurchase of securities is valid will depend upon the law of the jurisdiction where the securities are located.

Special statutes in Belgium and Luxembourg define the co-ownership rights of depositors of securities in the Euroclear and Clearstream systems.

The Sykes opinion

As discussed above, in November 1995 Richard Sykes, QC, issued his opinion on the enforceability of the PSA/ISMA GMRA under English law. He considered that an English court would not recharacterise a repo transaction as a secured loan because the PSA/ISMA GMRA clearly states in its paragraph 6(e) that absolute title to the securities passes to the Buyer, which has only a contractual obligation to return Equivalent Securities on the agreed Repurchase Date.

Sykes also considered that Margin Transfers would not be recharacterised, and that repricing and adjustment (see Chapter 3, pages 54–57, for a description of these terms) would also be upheld.

Most importantly, Sykes was of the view that close-out netting in paragraph 10 would be upheld in an English liquidation; that set-off under Insolvency Rule 4.90 would be available; and that paragraph 10 would apply to all types of insolvency methods in England and Wales.

In Sykes's opinion, if other clauses were illegal or unenforceable this should not affect paragraph 10 (Events of Default), which is a complete code in itself.

Sykes thought that in England and Wales any type of counterparty could enter into the PSA/ISMA GMRA, although he offered no advice on local authorities probably because of the *Hammersmith and Fulham* interest rate swaps case, which resulted in a ruling that English local authorities have no legal capacity to enter into derivatives transactions.

Sykes did not consider it necessary in order for paragraph 10 to work that all Transactions should be treated as a single agreement, but, as they were, this would be upheld in the English courts, in his opinion. He also thought that the close-out netting provisions would not be affected by the insolvency laws of other jurisdictions on branches in those jurisdictions.

Sykes considered that the PSA/ISMA GMRA would be effective under English law unless the law of the jurisdiction where a foreign counterparty was incorporated prevented it from having the capacity to enter into the PSA/ISMA GMRA or Transactions under it. He did not consider there to be any advantage in automatic termination in all circumstances (except insolvency) over termination by notice under the PSA/ISMA GMRA. Finally, he considered that paragraph 10 of the PSA/ISMA GMRA was effective where a party had entered into several transactions through the same agent for a disclosed single principal.

The TBMA/ISMA GMRA English law opinion

By the time that the TBMA/ISMA GMRA was written, Richard Sykes had retired and the TBMA/ISMA GMRA legal opinion for England was written by Freshfields Bruckhaus Deringer in March 2001, and updated annually. Freshfields Bruckhaus Deringer's opinion generally supports Sykes's opinion, and covers both the PSA/ISMA GMRA and the TBMA/ISMA GMRA. It should be noted, however, that Freshfields' legal opinion was obtained only on behalf of, and for the benefit of, TBMA and ISMA members. Other participants in the market are unable to rely upon it.

ISMA legal opinions

The Bond Market Association (TBMA) and The International Securities Market Association (ISMA) have obtained legal opinions on the validity of the TBMA/ISMA GMRA, and the enforceability and effectiveness of its close-out netting provisions, in 33 jurisdictions on behalf of and for the benefit of their members. These are shown in Exhibit 2.1 below.

In order to minimise the capital allocated to repo counterparty exposure in a bank's trading book, regulators require written, reasoned, independent legal opinions from major law firms for each jurisdiction where a bank is seeking to net its exposure in respect of Transactions under Agreements with various counterparties in that country. Regulators require these legal opinions to be updated at least once a year. ISMA and TBMA update their opinions annually and regularly circularise their members with legal developments.

US perspective**
Introduction

As a practical matter the enforcement of one's rights under a repurchase transaction will be substantively similar whether the US Master Repurchase Agreement (the "Master Repurchase Agreement") or the TBMA/ISMA Global Master Repurchase Agreement is selected by the parties. However, there are important regulatory and insolvency considerations under New York law that either do not exist under English law or take a different form. When negotiating

---

** by Christian Johnson

LEGAL ISSUES AFFECTING REPOS

Exhibit 2.1
Legal opinions obtained by ISMA and TBMA jointly and individually

Jointly commissioned

Austria
Belgium
Canada
England
Finland
France
Germany
Irish Republic
Italy
Japan
Luxembourg
Netherlands
Portugal
Spain
Switzerland
United States

Commissioned solely by ISMA

Abu Dhabi
Australia
Bahamas
Bahrain
Bermuda
British Virgin Islands
Cayman Islands
Denmark
Hong Kong
Kuwait
Netherlands Antilles
New Zealand
Saudi Arabia
Singapore
South Africa
Sweden
Thailand
Turkey

Note: These opinions cover both the PSA/ISMA GMRA and the TBMA/ISMA GMRA.
ISMA has also commissioned legal opinions for Greece, Hungary and Poland.
Source: www.isma.org.

the Master Repurchase Agreement it is important to understand and appreciate those differences.

The following discussion is limited to the Master Repurchase Agreement entered into by a party with any of the following types of entities:

- banks and savings associations that are organised or chartered under federal or state law and that take FDIC-insured deposits;
- corporations, limited liability companies and partnerships organised under state law;
- broker-dealers that carry customer accounts insured by the Securities Investor Protection Corporation.

Although the legal treatment of the Master Repurchase Agreement and repurchase transactions is favourable under US Federal and New York law, the application of these legal principles to specific transactions can be complex. Experienced legal counsel should always be sought to review the specific terms of individual repurchase transactions and their relationship to the Master Repurchase Agreement.

Enforcement of New York choice of law

The Master Repurchase Agreement is governed by New York law (see its paragraph 16). Indeed, the agreement was written on the basis of the common law and statutory provisions of the State of New York. Non-US parties often question whether such a choice of law would be respected by the courts of the State of New York or the US District courts located in the State of New York ("New York courts").

This is an especially important question if the party has no contacts with New York or is not incorporated or organised under New York law. There appears to be little doubt, however, that a New York court would enforce the selection of New York law and would grant jurisdiction to the parties in the event of any litigation. New York courts are required by the laws of the State of New York to enforce the choice of New York law. The aggregate amount of obligations arising out of the contract, however, cannot be less than US$250,000 (NY General Obligation Law §5-1401(1)). Because repurchase transactions involve securities valued in the millions of dollars, the US$250,000 threshold should be easily satisfied.

New York courts are also required by the laws of the State of New York to enforce New York as the forum for litigation "for which a choice of New York has been made" (NY General Obligation Law §5-1402(1)). The aggregate amount of obligations arising out of the contract, however, cannot be less than US$1 million. Because repurchase transactions involve securities valued in the millions of dollars, the US$1 million threshold should be easily satisfied.

Enforceability of the Master Repurchase Agreement

Parties should be able to enforce their rights under the Master Repurchase Agreement, assuming that both parties are solvent. Both US federal law and New York State law should characterise a repurchase transaction governed by the Master Repurchase Agreement as a transfer of title of the securities transferred from the Seller to the Buyer. Similarly, the transfer of cash or securities under the margin maintenance provisions (paragraph 4) would also be characterised by both US federal and New York State law as a transfer of title. Finally, there is no reason to believe that any provision of the Master Repurchase Agreement would violate any public policies of the US government or the State of New York.

Unfortunately, unlike the International Swaps and Derivatives Association (ISDA), The Bond Market Association has not solicited New York law opinion on behalf of its members regarding the enforceability of the agreement. The lack of such an opinion, however, is probably indicative of market practice that such opinions are unnecessary.

Recharacterisation of a repo as a secured loan

The repo market trades and operates on the assumption that a repurchase transaction is not a secured loan. It should be noted that such a recharacterisation has been rare, and the US Congress, courts, regulators and commentators have all reacted swiftly and strongly against such a recharacterisation. Such recharacterisation is also strongly opposed to global market practice. Some commentators and courts, however, have asserted that a repurchase transaction could be recharacterised under New York State law as a secured loan.[1] More recent decisions and commentators, however, follow the widespread thinking that a repurchase transaction should not be recharacterised in such a way.[2] Although a recent bankruptcy court

---

[1] See *In Lombard-Wall Inc. v Columbus Bank & Trust Co.*, No. 82-B-11556 (Bankr. S.D.N.Y. 1982); Gary Walters, *Repurchase Agreements and the Bankruptcy Code: The Need for Legislative Action*, 52 Fordham L.Rev. 828 (April, 1984).

[2] See, eg, *In Re Bevill, Bresler & Schulman Asset Management Corp.*, 67B.R. 557 (D.N.J. 1986); *SEC v. Drysdale Sec. Corp.*, 785 F.2d 38 (2d Cir. 1986); Jeanne L. Schroeder, *Repo Madness: The Characterization of Repurchase Agreements under the Bankruptcy Code and the U.C.C.*, 46 Syracuse L.Rev. 999 (1996).

decision has introduced some ambiguity,[3] its result has been criticised and dealt with a limited factual scenario.[4]

Even if such recharacterisation occurs, the Master Repurchase Agreement is deemed to create a secured loan, providing a perfected security interest in the securities transferred by the Seller (deemed to be a pledgor) to the Buyer (deemed to be a secured party).

The recharacterisation of a repurchase transaction as a secured loan would be problematic for a party, for several reasons. First, a party would be required to look to its remedies under Articles 8 and 9 of the New York Uniform Commercial Code ("NYUCC") rather than those set forth in the Master Repurchase Agreement. For example, if the Seller were to fail to repurchase securities as required under the Master Repurchase Agreement, the Buyer would be entitled to sell the securities immediately (see paragraph 11(d)(i)). If the repurchase transaction were recharacterised as a secured loan, however, the Buyer would be required to comply with the provisions of Articles 8 and 9 of the NYUCC prior to foreclosing and selling the securities.

Second, if a repurchase transaction were recharacterised as a secured loan, the Buyer would be required to comply with the attachment and perfection provisions of Articles 8 and 9 of the NYUCC if it wanted to have a valid security interest in the purchased securities. Depending upon the type of securities transferred, if Article 9 were applicable because of the recharacterisation, the Buyer may not have a perfected lien that would enable it to foreclose on the now "recharacterised" collateral. As discussed below, however, transfers of book-entry US and agency securities are generally done in such a way under the Master Repurchase Agreement as to ensure that the Buyer (as the secured party) would have a perfected security interest.

Both the agreement and market participants operate under the assumption that repurchase transactions constitute a sale followed by a repurchase and are not secured loans. Paragraph 6 states that: "the parties intend that all Transactions hereunder be sales and purchases and not loans". However, the agreement does provide some protection for the Buyer if the repurchase transaction were deemed to be (or recharacterised as) a secured loan by a court or a regulatory body. The Seller will be deemed to have pledged the Securities and granted a security interest to the Buyer (see paragraph 6). Under Federal regulations and the NYUCC the Buyer should have a perfected security interest in the Purchased Securities.

For a Buyer (deemed to be a secured party) to enforce its rights with respect to a security interest under New York law, the security interest must first attach and then be perfected. In the United States generally every state, including New York, has adopted a version of the UCC that governs the attachment and perfection of a security interest in Purchased Securities. Articles 8 and 9 govern, first, how a secured party attaches and then perfects a security interest in Purchased Securities, and, second, how it can exercise its rights with respect to the collateral.

The type of securities used in repurchase transactions such as US Treasury and agency securities are typically held by large multi-tiered financial intermediaries in book-entry form. When a party pledges that book-entry security to another, the pledgor will instruct its

---

[3] *In re: Criimi Mae, Inc.*, 251 B.R. 796 (Bankr. D. Md. 2000).

[4] Jeanne L. Schroeder, *A Repo Opera: How Criimi Mae Got Repos Backwards*, 76 Am. Bankr. L.J. 565 (Fall, 2002). Schroeder's article is important in that she criticises the Criimi Mae Court for misinterpreting her prior commentary.

financial intermediary (ie, a financial institution or broker-dealer) to transfer the security to the secured party. The pledgor's financial intermediary will then notify the Federal Reserve to move the security from its account at the Federal Reserve to the Federal Reserve account of the secured party's financial intermediary.

New York law has been amended to recognise that these types of transfers by a party through various financial intermediaries have the same effect as if the party had transferred certificated securities (see NYUCC Article 8). For example, New York law recognises that a party giving instructions to its financial intermediary (generally referred to as a securities intermediary) to transfer the Treasury security is sufficient to constitute a transfer to that person for the purposes of creating a security interest.

Under New York law, for a security interest to attach (1) there generally must be a written security agreement; (2) the pledgor must have rights in the collateral pledged; and (3) the secured party must give the pledgor value. Once the security interest has attached to the collateral, then the secured party may exercise its rights against the pledgor with respect to the collateral.

For a party to exercise its rights against third parties, however, the security interest must also be perfected. This typically requires the secured party, either expressly or indirectly, to give third parties notice that the security interest has attached. With respect to collateral such as cash and securities New York law requires the secured party to have possession (either directly or through an intermediary) of the collateral.

These general rules, however, are pre-empted by Federal law with respect to the attachment and perfection of security interests in US government Treasury and certain agency securities. These rules are set forth in Federal regulations commonly referred to as the "TRADES Regulations" (13 C.F.R. Part 357). The attachment and perfection of similar types of book-entry collateral, such as securities issued by Federal National Mortgage Association ("Fannie Mae") or the Federal Home Loan Mortgage Corporation ("Freddie Mac"), are also governed by the TRADES Regulations. The tri-party custodial agreement described in Chapter 6 deals primarily with these types of securities. A list of the different types of securities subject to the TRADES Regulations is attached at the end of this Chapter as Exhibit 2.2.

The TRADES Regulations, however, do not create a new method for attaching and perfecting a security interest in US government Treasury securities. Instead they specify that the attachment and perfection are governed by the securities intermediary's jurisdiction. In the case of the Master Repurchase Agreement this jurisdiction will generally be New York, especially if either The Bank of New York or JP Morgan Chase tri-party custodial agreement is used, because the securities will be held in New York.

Once the parties have entered into the **Master Repurchase Agreement** and the Seller is deemed under paragraph 6 to have pledged collateral to the Buyer by transferring the securities to the Buyer, through a securities intermediary, the Buyer will have an attached and perfected security interest in the collateral.

US bankruptcy and banking insolvency law

A principal concern for a solvent party is whether, upon the bankruptcy or insolvency of its counterparty under the Master Repurchase Agreement, the solvent party will still be able to enforce its rights under the agreement without being subject to various limitations imposed under different insolvency regimes. Such party's rights will depend upon the bankruptcy or insolvency regime that expressly applies to it. This discussion also assumes that a repurchase transaction is not recharacterised as a secured loan.

Most corporate parties organised under state law in the United States are subject to the US Bankruptcy Code. However, debtors that are financial institutions and that take federally insured deposits, such as banks and savings institutions, are not subject to the US Bankruptcy Code. Instead they are subject to insolvency rules found in the Federal Deposit Insurance Act ("FDIA"). Broker-dealers that carry customer accounts insured by the Securities Investor Protection Corporation ("SIPC") are subject to special insolvency rules in addition to those under the US Bankruptcy Code.

Apart from these three classes of parties there are other parties that are not subject to these insolvency rules. For example, insurance companies are subject to the insolvency rules of the insurance laws of the state under which they are organised. Quasi-government entities, such as Federal Home Loan Banks, have their own insolvency rules. Municipalities and other government subdivisions also have their own insolvency regimes. A discussion of these rules is beyond the scope of this chapter.

US Bankruptcy Code

The US Bankruptcy Code has special rules dealing with a bankrupt debtor (a party that has filed for its own bankruptcy) that has entered into a "repurchase agreement" with a "repo participant". These rules are very creditor-friendly and provide important protections for the creditor.

Solvent parties eligible for special treatment
A repo participant is defined under the US Bankruptcy Code as "an entity" (which includes government units) "that has an outstanding repurchase agreement with the debtor on any day during the period beginning ninety days before the date of the filing of the bankruptcy petition" (11 USC §101(46)).

Unfortunately the definition of repurchase agreement in the US Bankruptcy Code is limited to specific types of securities. They include "certificates of deposit, eligible bankers' acceptances, or securities that are direct obligations of, or that are fully guaranteed as to principal and interest by, the United States or any agency of the United States" (11 USC §101(47)). While US Treasury securities, such as Treasury bills or notes, would be included in the definition, other securities, such as those debt securities issued by Fannie Mae or other corporate issuers, would not be included. In addition, the repurchase transactions cannot have a maturity greater than one year.

Fortunately, courts have found that repurchase agreements that do not technically qualify because the securities involved do not fit into the definition of a repurchase agreement, could still be eligible for bankruptcy code protections under other similar preferential provisions. For example, a repurchase agreement transferring securities could be treated as a "securities contract" provided that the solvent party was a stockbroker, a financial institution or a securities clearing agency (11 USC §741(7)). This is an important provision because broker-dealers are among the largest participants (typically as Sellers) in the repo market.

Right to terminate and liquidate

When a debtor files for bankruptcy under the US Bankruptcy Code, the law imposes an automatic stay under its Section 11 USC §362. The stay ordinarily prevents the creditor of a bankrupt debtor from exercising the majority of its legal rights and remedies (ie, to terminate and liquidate) under the relevant contract. Generally, the automatic stay remains in effect until the case is dismissed or completed, or the judge grants relief, unless a specific exemption from the automatic stay applies.

For example, assuming that there was no relevant exemption, upon the filing of a bankruptcy petition a party to the Master Repurchase Agreement would normally be automatically stayed from exercising any of the self-help remedies found in the Master Repurchase Agreement against its bankrupt counterparty. Without a specific exemption the solvent party would be prevented from terminating and liquidating the agreement.

Congress, however, has eliminated many of these concerns. If the solvent party is a repo participant and has entered into a repurchase agreement, the termination and liquidation of the repurchase agreement cannot "be stayed, avoided, or otherwise limited by operation of any provision of this title or by order of a court or administrative agency in any proceeding under this title" (11 USC §559). The only exception is where the defaulting party is a stockbroker and such order is authorised under the Securities Investor Protection Act ("SIPA") or any statutory provision administered by the SEC. This means that a solvent party would typically not be subject to the automatic stay and could immediately exercise its rights under the Master Repurchase Agreement.

In the event that a transaction did not qualify as a repurchase agreement because non-qualifying securities were used, other provisions could still provide much the same protections as for a repurchase agreement. For example, if the insolvent party were a stockbroker, a financial institution or a securities clearing agency, a repurchase agreement has been characterised as a security contract within the broad definition of the US Bankruptcy Code. Under this characterisation as a security contract the termination and liquidation of the repurchase agreement also cannot "be stayed, avoided, or otherwise limited by operation of any provision of this title or by order of a court or administrative agency in any proceeding under this title" (11 USC §559).

Set-off rights are also protected for a solvent party under the US Bankruptcy Code. A repo participant may exercise its set-off rights under a Master Repurchase Agreement (11 USC §362(b)(7)). Similar protections are enjoyed by commodity brokers, forward contract merchants, stockbrokers, financial institutions and securities clearing agencies with respect to commodity contracts, forward contracts or securities contracts (11 USC §362(b)(6)).

As reviewed above, a solvent party's right to terminate and liquidate the Master Repurchase Agreement is limited if the defaulting party is a stockbroker or a broker-dealer. In discussions the SIPC has indicated that it will bar the immediate termination and liquidation in such situations. The SIPC, however, has indicated that in the case of a repurchase agreement (regardless of whether it meets the Bankruptcy Code definition) it would consent to its termination and liquidation if the SIPC receives a letter from the solvent party stating that (i) "it has no knowledge of any fraud involved in the transactions and that it has a perfected security interest in the underlying securities, and (ii) that the SIPC might perform the debtor's obligations under the agreement".

LEGAL ISSUES AFFECTING REPOS

Preference payments and avoiding power

A bankruptcy trustee has the power, commonly referred to as a trustee's avoiding power, to reclaim or unwind property transfers made to a creditor prior to the bankruptcy in certain situations. The avoiding power permits a trustee to reclaim preference payments made to a creditor up to 90 days prior to the filing of a bankruptcy petition (and up to one year in the case of transfers to insiders) (11 USC §547(b)). Repo participants were concerned that this avoiding power was disruptive of a party's rights under the Master Repurchase Agreement.

Congress resolved this concern by enacting Section 546(f) of the US Bankruptcy Code, which generally exempts transfers made under a repurchase agreement from a trustee's avoiding powers, particularly with respect to preference payments or constructive fraudulent transfer. Similar protections are provided to preference or constructive fraudulent transfers with respect to any margin or settlement payments made prior to the bankruptcy filing by or to a commodity broker, a forward contract merchant, a stockbroker, a financial institution or a securities clearing agency. Section 548(d)(2) of the US Bankruptcy Code also provides that a trustee cannot avoid a "fraudulent transfer" because such transfer is always deemed to be made "for value to the extent of such payment".

US banking insolvency law

Financial institutions are generally not subject to the US Bankruptcy Code. Instead they are subject to various banking law insolvency statutes, such as the Federal Deposit Insurance Act ("FDIA"), the National Bank Act or the New York Banking Law. Typically, if the party accepts insured deposits, it will be subject to the FDIA.

Parties had many of the same concerns about US banking law as they did about the US Bankruptcy Code with respect to repurchase agreements. Congress, however, has basically resolved these concerns by amending the various banking law statutes in a manner similar to the US Bankruptcy Code.

Generally, US banking law provides similar exemptions and provisions that favour the solvent counterparty with respect to "qualified financial contracts" (12 USC §1821(e)(8)). The definition of qualified financial contract includes a "repurchase agreement". A "repurchase agreement" has the same definition for FDIA purposes as it does under the Bankruptcy Code, except that it also includes mortgage-related securities, mortgage loans and interests in mortgage loans, thus broadening the reach of the provisions. Qualified financial contracts also include securities contracts, forward contracts and commodity contracts all defined for purposes of the FDIA as they are defined under the US Bankruptcy Code.

Termination

Under US banking law the solvent party is generally precluded from terminating the Master Repurchase Agreement and underlying transactions solely because of the financial institution's insolvency. The FDIA, however, provides that a qualified financial contract (ie, a repurchase agreement) can be terminated and liquidated under certain circumstances, depending upon whether the Federal Deposit Insurance Corporation ("FDIC") is appointed as a receiver or a conservator of the insolvent financial institution.

The solvent counterparty of an insolvent financial institution can terminate and liquidate a qualified financial contract (ie, a repurchase agreement) upon the appointment of the FDIC as a receiver one day after such appointment (12 USC §1821(e)(8)(A)). As a receiver the FDIC has the power to liquidate (but not operate) the financial institution and wind up its affairs.

In contrast, if the FDIC is appointed as conservator of the insolvent financial institution, the solvent party will not have the right to terminate the Master Repurchase Agreement because of the insolvency of the financial institution. The FDIC, as conservator, has the right to operate the financial institution as a going concern. The FDIC essentially steps into the shoes of the insolvent institution. To terminate the Master Repurchase Agreement upon appointment of the FDIC as a conservator, an Event of Default (other than an insolvency) or a Termination Event would have to occur (12 USC §1821(e)(8)(E)).

Under general insolvency rules the FDIC has the right to repudiate the contracts of an insolvent financial institution. This could result in the FDIC cherry picking, that is, selectively terminating or transferring the disadvantageous contracts and maintaining the advantageous ones. The FDIA, however, provides that, if the FDIC is going to transfer any qualified financial contract, it must transfer all the qualified financial contracts of a creditor to the same party (12 USC §1821(e)(9)). In addition, the FDIC may not selectively repudiate or terminate any individual transaction or contract under a Master Repurchase Agreement that the insolvent financial institution had with its counterparty; rather, it must terminate the Master Repurchase Agreement and any underlying transactions all at once if it intends to terminate any individual transaction (12 USC §1821(e)(9)).

Solvent parties have also worried in the past that the FDIC may try to avoid certain payments made before the insolvency of the financial institution as a preferential payment. Such payments, however, may not be avoided by the FDIC unless "the transferee had actual intent to hinder, delay, or defraud such institution" (12 USC §1821(e)(8)(C)). This should protect the vast majority of payments made in the normal course of business under the Master Repurchase Agreement.

It is possible that the New York Banking Law may apply to the insolvency of a financial institution. Its rules largely parallel those described above under the FDIA. Generally speaking, an insolvency that would involve the New York Banking Law would also involve the FDIC and the FDIA rules. Although it is possible that the New York Banking Law may apply alone, such a situation is more likely to occur with a New York branch of a non-US bank that does not have deposits insured by the FDIC, a situation beyond the scope of this discussion.

Pending legislation to the US Bankruptcy Code and FDIA

Although the majority of the concerns regarding US bankruptcy and banking insolvency issues were resolved in the early 1990s, participants have wanted these provisions to be strengthened and clarified, especially as repo volume has grown and the product has become more complex. The US Senate and the US House of Representatives have responded by each passing bills to resolve these issues. The provisions regarding repurchase transactions in the two bills are in most respects identical.

Unfortunately, due to concerns over consumer bankruptcy protection provisions in the two bills, the House and Senate have been unable to reconcile the bills for final passage into law. Once the controversial consumer bankruptcy provisions are resolved, it is likely that these repo provisions will be passed into law. So far this has taken more than six years. The following is a brief summary of several of the most important provisions that will be added to the bankruptcy and insolvency statutes.

Participants in the repo market have been concerned that the current definitions of repurchase agreement found in the US Bankruptcy Code and in the FDIA are too narrow. Many popular types of repo transactions are not expressly included under the statutory definition of a repurchase agreement.

The pending legislation eliminates any uncertainty by expressly including "qualified government securities" (included by regulatory authority but not by statute). It also expressly includes US agency securities from issuers such as Fannie Mae or Freddie Mac and any other obligations eligible for purchase by Federal Reserve Banks.

Increasingly, parties that enter into not only repurchase transactions with each other, but also other types of transactions, such as over-the-counter derivatives, are entering into cross-product master agreements (often referred to as "master master agreements"). Under these contractual arrangements, upon a default under one of the underlying master agreements (such as a Master Repurchase Agreement or an ISDA Master Agreement) the non-defaulting party would be able to terminate all the underlying master agreements and net out all termination payment amounts together.

There has been some concern that the different insolvency statutes would not permit such close-out netting. The pending legislation amends both the Bankruptcy Code and the FDIA in order to ensure that such cross-product netting is enforced, provided that all the underlying master agreements constitute qualified financial contracts under FDIA.

Federal Deposit Insurance Corporation Improvement Act (FDICIA)

In addition to the statutory provisions favouring creditors in both the FDIA and the US Bankruptcy Code, the US Congress enacted additional statutory provisions as part of the Federal Deposit Insurance Corporation Improvement Act of 1991 ("FDICIA") to enforce "netting contracts". FDICIA has been codified in the United States Code in Title 12, sections 4401–4406. FDICIA is important because, if a court were to find that the parties were ineligible for the repo-friendly provisions found in the US Bankruptcy Code or the FDIA, the parties could still enforce the Master Repurchase Agreement, provided that they were financial institutions.

Under FDICIA netting rights are enforceable regardless of any other provisions, statutes, regulations or judicial action. To be enforceable, however, parties must be "financial institutions" as defined in FDICIA. In addition, under FDICIA as currently codified, the Master Repurchase Agreement must also be governed by federal law or by state law (such as the laws of the State of New York).

A netting contract is defined under FDICIA as a contract that: "provides for netting present or future payment obligations or payment entitlements (including liquidation or close-out values relating to the obligations or entitlements) among the parties to the agreement" (12 USC §4402(14)(a)). The Master Repurchase Agreement should be characterised as a netting contract under FDICIA. The Margin Maintenance provisions found in paragraph 4 of the Master Repurchase Agreement are calculated on an aggregate (ie, net) basis. The remedies found in paragraph 11 also assume that the payments will be made on an aggregate (ie, net) basis. Finally, paragraph 19 (Intent) provides that both parties agree that the Master Repurchase Agreement constitutes a netting contract for the purposes of FDICIA.

The definition of financial institution includes not only financial institutions that accept federally insured deposits, but also "a broker or dealer, a depository financial institution, a futures commission merchant, or any other financial institution as determined by the Board of Governors of the Federal Reserve System" (12 USC §4402(9)). Under Federal Reserve Board regulations a financial institution also includes parties that meet quantitative and qualitative tests that generally describe the characteristics of a dealer in the repo market. The financial institution, however, does not need to be chartered or organised under US federal or state law in order to benefit from FDICIA (12 CFR Part 231).

Pending legislation

As part of the pending legislation described above, there are several additional amendments proposed to strengthen further the enforcement of netting between financial institutions under the FDICIA. First, the pending legislation makes the FDICIA applicable to bilateral netting contracts governed by non-US law (eg, English law). Previously only bilateral netting contracts governed by US law were eligible for the protections. Second, the definition of financial institutions was expanded to include uninsured national and state member banks and foreign banks (expressly rather than possibly indirectly through Regulation EE). Third, the pending legislation clarifies that the FDICIA does not override the FDIC's power to transfer a repurchase agreement or permit a party to terminate the repurchase agreement during the time period provided to the FDIC to repudiate or transfer a repurchase agreement when the FDIC is appointed as a receiver or conservator.

Capacity

As with European documentation, it is important that a US party has the capacity to enter into repurchase transactions and the Master Repurchase Agreement. Where a US entity is concerned, however, there is no precedent under New York law where a party has been found to lack the capacity to enter into repurchase transactions. Unfortunately, there are no statutory protections against *ultra vires* actions in this area, as are found in English law. In contrast to England, US parties by and large have not suggested or pushed for such legislation in the United States.

Normally, US dealers (whether they are banks or non-bank entities) take the position that such capacity is understood and that such powers are part of their business as dealers. A party can generally eliminate such concerns, however, by requesting that the counterparty deliver a secretary's certificate that verifies that its board of directors has approved such actions.

A party may want to be especially vigilant, however, when dealing with non-dealers, such as government entities, pension plans or similar entities that are governed by special statutory rules and regulations. By entering into repurchase transactions with a counterparty that may not have the corporate capacity to do so, a party risks a court finding that the transactions are unenforceable, or ordering the party to make restitution for any gains and profits from such transactions.

Although there is no case law on this particular issue, Orange County raised this argument in 1995 when it sued Merrill Lynch for losses that it suffered in the repo market.[5] Orange County sued Merrill Lynch for US$2 billion in restitution and other equitable

---

[5] In re County of Orange, Plaintiffs Complaint, Case No. SA-22272-JR (Bankr. C.C. Cal. Jan. 12, 1995) (complaint filed by Orange County against Merrill Lynch).

relief for entering into repurchase agreements with Orange County that were in violation of the California State Constitution and California statutes. These provisions and statutes restricted the type of transactions and the amount of investments that Orange County could make.

Ultimately Merrill Lynch settled the lawsuit with Orange County. Although the Orange County litigation is unusual both in its size and nature, it illustrates the possible consequences of entering into repurchase transactions with a party that lacks corporate capacity to do so.

Severability

Parties are sometimes concerned that, if one provision of the Master Repurchase Agreement is considered to be unenforceable or illegal, the entire agreement would be unenforceable. The Master Repurchase Agreement, however, expressly provides in paragraph 14 that the agreement will be enforceable even if there are provisions that are illegal or unenforceable. New York law will enforce such a clause provided that the unenforceable or illegal provisions are only incidental to the main objective of the agreement.[6]

Use of employee plan assets

The United States has stringent rules that protect employee benefit plans, pension plans and similar types of arrangements (a "Plan"), as well as certain entities in which Plans invest, from being taken advantage of by parties that have an interest or certain relationships with the Plan (a "Related Party"). The principle behind this protection is that a Related Party may have an opportunity to engage in proprietary trading or similar types of behaviour because of the special relationship it has with the Plan (eg, serving as an investment adviser). These laws define a Related Party very broadly. For example, an entity may be considered to be a Related Party merely because of its affiliation with another entity. Paragraph 18 of the Master Repurchase Agreement deals explicitly with these concerns.

In certain circumstances the law permits a Plan to avoid certain transactions with a Related Party. Parties are concerned that, if a counterparty is considered to be a Plan, the Plan may be able to avoid its obligations under the Master Repurchase Agreement if the other party is considered to be a Related Party. Because it may be difficult to determine if it is a Related Party, a party will request that its counterparty represent that it is not a Plan.

In general, a counterparty will know whether it is organised as a Plan for the purposes of US law. It is more difficult to determine if the counterparty is holding what are referred to as "plan assets", which may result in the counterparty being treated in the same manner as a Plan for purposes of the law. An entity is sometimes considered to hold plan assets if Plans have made an equity investment in the entity. If the percentage equity ownership of an entity by different Plans exceeds a certain percentage (most commonly 25 per cent), the entity itself may be treated as holding plan assets (unless the entity is an operating company or satisfies certain conditions). In particular, the assets of investment funds may inadvertently become plan assets if too many Plans have invested in them.

---

[6] See, eg, *Donnel v Stogel*, 161 A.D.2d 93, 97–98 (N.Y. App., Div. 2d Dept. 1990).

Exhibit 2.2
Securities eligible for deposit in the Federal Reserve's book-entry securities system

United States Treasury
Farm Credit Financial Assistance Corporation
Farmers Home Administration
Federal Agricultural Mortgage Corporation (Farmer Mac)
Federal Farm Credit Banks Funding Corporation
Federal Home Loan Banks
Federal Home Loan Mortgage Corporation (Freddie Mac)
Federal National Mortgage Association (Fannie Mae)
Financing Corporation
Student Loan Marketing Association (Sallie Mae)
United States Postal Service
Tennessee Valley Authority
Resolution Funding Corporation
African Development Bank
Asian Development Bank
Inter-American Development Bank
International Bank for Reconstruction and Development
International Finance Corporation

Source: The Federal Reserve's Fedwire Book-Entry Securities Transfer Service (revised December 1998)

Chapter 3

Commentary on the TBMA/ISMA Global Master Repurchase Agreement

This chapter provides a straightforward but detailed commentary on the TBMA/ISMA Global Master Repurchase Agreement (the "TBMA/ISMA GMRA"). A segment of the Agreement text is quoted first (shaded in grey) and explanatory commentary follows immediately below it in each case.

First, it might be useful to set the scene and outline the evolution of the TBMA/ISMA GMRA.

Evolution of the TBMA/ISMA GMRA

In 1986 the US-based Public Securities Association (the "PSA"), now The Bond Market Association ("TBMA"), published its prototype repurchase agreement (governed by New York Law) covering US treasuries so as to provide the repo market with a standard agreement containing a number of basic legal protections. The prototype included provisions for mark-to-market procedures; stated the rights of both parties when one of them defaulted; and sought to ensure the availability of bankruptcy protections. The PSA Master Repurchase Agreement was revised in 1987 and by the early 1990s it was the industry standard document in the US repo market.

In November 1992 the PSA, in conjunction with the International Securities Market Association ("ISMA") issued the "Global Master Repurchase Agreement" covering gross paying securities other than US treasuries and equities, and subject to English law. The Agreement was closely modelled on the standard form PSA Master Repurchase Agreement used in the US repo market.

In November 1995 the PSA and ISMA published a revised version of the 1992 Agreement motivated in part by the arrival of the new UK gilt repo market, which started on 2 January 1996.

The revisions included major changes to the margining provisions and the inclusion, for the first time, of provisions dealing with agency transactions and fully documented buy/sellback transactions. Both the revised form of the PSA/ISMA GMRA and the Gilt Repo Annex, which together formed the Gilt Repo Legal Agreement, were published in November 1995, along with the Bank of England's Gilt Repo Code of Conduct. This Code of Conduct prohibited gilt repos being traded until a PSA/ISMA GMRA or TBMA/ISMA GMRA was executed.

The success of the PSA/ISMA GMRA showed the advantages of standardised documentation in reducing risk by eliminating undocumented or poorly documented transactions, reducing documentation costs and lowering barriers to new market entrants. It was also favoured by regulators, who decide on the amount of capital to be allocated to repos in a bank's trading book, because it reduced risk.

Although an English law agreement, the PSA/ISMA GMRA, was also intended for use in the European cross-border market. It is still extensively used in countries other than the United States, sometimes in combination with country-specific annexes.

On 30 November 2000 the TBMA/ISMA GMRA was published. A study of this is offered below.

Structure of the TBMA/ISMA GMRA

The basic structure of the TBMA/ISMA GMRA is:

- a printed standard form master agreement containing provisions for all repurchase transactions between the Seller and the Buyer (a set of explanatory notes was also published and is worth reading);
- various annexes as follows:
    i) Annex I: Supplemental Terms or Conditions. This enables the parties to make choices in relation to certain provisions of the TBMA/ISMA GMRA and to tailor the document to suit their purposes and relative credit strengths. **Negotiators negotiate Annex I**;
    ii) Annex II: Form of Confirmation;
    iii) Buy/Sell Back Annex;
    iv) Agency Annex and Addendum;
    v) Product Annexes for equities, gilts and bills of exchange; and
    vi) Country Annexes for Canada, Italy, Japan, the Netherlands, South Africa and Thailand.

Parties choose which of these Annexes they want to apply to their TBMA/ISMA GMRA.

The key features of the TBMA/ISMA GMRA are that:

- repos are structured as outright sales and repurchases;
- full legal title to securities and cash is transferred;
- the Seller has an obligation to return equivalent securities;
- there is provision for initial margin and top-up margin;
- the equivalent of the coupon received from the issuer on a security is paid to the Seller on the same day; and
- legal title to collateral is robust, which overcomes doubts when an Event of Default occurs.

In essence the TBMA/ISMA GMRA includes provisions dealing with payment and transfer of securities and cash, margin maintenance, coupon payments on securities, reciprocal representations and warranties (dealing with authority, title to securities and tax), rights of substitution, reciprocal events of default (which permit close-out of all transactions that are subject to the TBMA/ISMA GMRA), and termination of individual transactions upon the occurrence of specified tax events, as well as standard "boilerplate" clauses.

The TBMA/ISMA GMRA can potentially cover repos and buy/sellbacks in equities, gross paying securities, net paying securities, US Treasury instruments, bills of exchange and certificates of deposit. The Agency Annex allows Agency Transactions to be undertaken with disclosed principals.

When the TBMA/ISMA GMRA was revised in 1999/2000 it did not undergo major, wholesale radical surgery from its predecessor, the PSA/ISMA GMRA. Rather, there was a refashioning of certain provisions inspired by market demand. This can be clearly seen by printing off the blacklined version showing the differences between the two documents from ISMA's website (www.isma.org under the Legal and Regulatory section).

This is in stark contrast to the process used in ISDA's 2001 Margin Provisions, where a radical new regime for documenting collateralised transactions was proposed, but has still not been widely taken up by the market. While parties (usually less sophisticated ones) are still entering into PSA/ISMA GMRAs, the TBMA/ISMA GMRA is in widespread use.

Paragraph-by-paragraph analysis of the TBMA/ISMA GMRA

> **2000 VERSION**
>
> **TBMA/ISMA**
>
> **GLOBAL MASTER REPURCHASE AGREEMENT**
>
> Dated as of
> _____
>
> **Between:**
>
> _____ ("Party A")
>
> **and**
>
> _____ ("Party B")

Headings and parties

The TBMA/ISMA GMRA is dated as of a certain date. This is normally the date of signing before the first trade. Banks in Europe will not trade repos unless the TBMA/ISMA GMRA is signed and in place. In the United Kingdom this is a requirement of the Bank of England's Gilt Repo Code. This differentiates it from the ISDA Master Agreement, where the agreement is often signed well after the date of the first trade and in the meantime the parties rely on the Confirmation.

There is a block where the parties state their full legal names. Usually, but not always, Party A prepares the draft of Annex I (which is what negotiators negotiate) and will produce the execution copies when all points have been agreed by the parties.

Paragraph 1

> **1. Applicability**
> (a) From time to time the parties hereto may enter into transactions in which one party, acting through a Designated Office, ("Seller") agrees to sell to the other, acting

> through a Designated Office, ("Buyer") securities and financial instruments ("Securities") (subject to paragraph 1(c), other than equities and Net Paying Securities) against the payment of the purchase price by Buyer to Seller, with a simultaneous agreement by Buyer to sell to Seller Securities equivalent to such Securities at a date certain or on demand against the payment of the repurchase price by Seller to Buyer.
> (b) Each such transaction (which may be a repurchase transaction ("Repurchase Transaction") or a buy and sell back transaction ("Buy/Sell Back Transaction") shall be referred to herein as a "Transaction" and shall be governed by this Agreement, including any supplemental terms or conditions contained in Annex I hereto, unless otherwise agreed in writing.

(a) This sub-paragragh sets out the mechanics of a classic repo transaction, and the obligations of the Buyer and Seller to each other. It also contemplates that the parties might act through branches of their respective organisations. Repo transaction may be for a particular term or on demand.

Equities and Net Paying Securities are excluded unless selected in Annex I. (Annex I and the other Annexes are discussed at the end of this chapter.)
(b) Repos and buy/sellbacks may be traded and covered under the TBMA/ISMA GMRA, and are called "Transactions" governed by it. They are also subject to the provisions of Annex I unless otherwise agreed in writing (which would be rare).

> (c) If this Agreement may be applied to
> (i) Buy/Sell Back Transactions, this shall be specified in Annex I hereto, and the provisions of the Buy/Sell Back Annex shall apply to such Buy/Sell Back Transactions;
> (ii) Net Paying Securities, this shall be specified in Annex I hereto and the provisions of Annex I, paragraph 1(b) shall apply to Transactions involving Net Paying Securities.

(c) If buy/sellbacks are to be traded under the TBMA/ISMA GMRA, this must be stated in Annex I and the provisions of the Buy/Sell Back Annex will apply to them. If either party wants to enter into Net Paying Securities under the TBMA/ISMA GMRA, this must also be stated in Annex I and Annex 1, paragraph 1(b) will apply to them.

> (d) If Transactions are to be effected under this Agreement by either party as an agent, this shall be specified in Annex I hereto, and the provisions of the Agency Annex shall apply to such Agency Transactions.

(d) If either party wants to engage in Agency Transactions on behalf of disclosed third parties, this must be stated in Annex I and the terms of the Agency Annex will apply to those transactions. If neither party wants to engage in Buy/Sell Back Transactions, Net Paying Securities or Agency Transactions, this also must be stated in Annex I.

Paragraph 2

This is an extensive Definitions Paragraph and appears much earlier in the TBMA/ISMA GMRA than it does in the ISDA Master Agreement, where it is located in Section 14, the last section of the main text.

> **2. Definitions**
> (a) "Act of Insolvency" shall occur with respect to any party hereto upon–
> (i) its making a general assignment for the benefit of, entering into a reorganisation, arrangement, or composition with creditors; or
> (ii) its admitting in writing that it is unable to pay its debts as they become due; or
> (iii) its seeking, consenting to or acquiescing in the appointment of any trustee, administrator, receiver or liquidator or analogous officer of it or any material part of its property; or
> (iv) the presentation or filing of a petition in respect of it (other than by the counterparty to this Agreement in respect of any obligation under this Agreement) in any court or before any agency alleging or for the bankruptcy, winding-up or insolvency of such party (or any analogous proceeding) or seeking any reorganisation, arrangement, composition, re-adjustment, administration, liquidation, dissolution or similar relief under any present or future statute, law or regulation, such petition (except in the case of a petition for winding-up or any analogous proceeding, in respect of which no such 30 day period shall apply) not having been stayed or dismissed within 30 days of its filing; or
> (v) the appointment of a receiver, administrator, liquidator or trustee or analogous officer of such party or over all or any material part of such party's property; or
> (vi) the convening of any meeting of its creditors for the purposes of considering a voluntary arrangement as referred to in section 3 of the Insolvency Act 1986 (or any analogous proceeding);

(a) Act of Insolvency is an important definition and is sometimes supplemented by country-specific provisions in Annex I, or even in a country Annex (eg, the South African Annex).

The events described in the definition are:

- a composition with creditors;
- a written admission of inability to pay debts when due;
- steps to appoint an insolvency official;
- presentation of a bankruptcy petition by a third party that is not dismissed within 30 days. (Please note that in (iv) there is no 30-day grace period for a third-party winding-up order, as there is in the 1992 ISDA Master Agreement);
- actual appointment of an insolvency official; and
- convening a creditors' meeting to propose a voluntary arrangement (a process allowed under the UK's 1986 Insolvency Act where a solvent party can make a composition of its debts or an arrangement of its financial affairs, if its creditors agree).

As we shall see in paragraph 10(a), there is no grace period for Acts of Insolvency or for most other Events of Default.

> (b) "Agency Transaction", the meaning specified in paragraph 1 of the Agency Annex;

(b) An Agency Transaction is one where one of the contracting parties is acting as agent for a disclosed principal.

> (c) "Appropriate Market", the meaning specified in paragraph 10;

(c) In valuing Securities for the purposes of close-out of Transactions under paragraph 10 following an Event of Default, "Appropriate Market" is the one deemed most relevant by the non-Defaulting Party for obtaining prices from dealers.

> (d) "Base Currency", the currency indicated in Annex I hereto;

(d) This definition is used in two places and possibly different currencies are appropriate in each place. It is used in paragraph 4 to calculate Net Exposure for margining purposes. Any Cash Margin payable under paragraph 4(e) must be paid in the Base Currency, unless otherwise agreed. It is also used for calculating a close-out amount in paragraph 10. The mention of the local currencies of the parties' jurisdictions is a good idea here because, if they become insolvent, it is likely that any court judgement will be awarded in a local currency. It is therefore important to consider whether to quote more general wording in Annex I to account for these different uses of Base Currency, rather than simply to nominate one particular currency. Factors likely to influence the choice of the Base Currency are the location and jurisdiction of incorporation of the parties, and the currency of the Purchase Price and Repurchase Price of the securities in repo transactions.

> (e) "Business Day" –
> (i) in relation to the settlement of any Transaction which is to be settled through Clearstream or Euroclear, a day on which Clearstream or, as the case may be, Euroclear is open to settle business in the currency in which the Purchase Price and the Repurchase Price are denominated;
> (ii) in relation to the settlement of any Transaction which is to be settled through a settlement system other than Clearstream or Euroclear, a day on which that settlement system is open to settle such Transaction;

COMMENTARY ON THE TBMA/ISMA GMRA

> (iii) in relation to any delivery of Securities not falling within (i) or (ii) above, a day on which banks are open for business in the place where delivery of the relevant Securities is to be effected; and
>
> (iv) in relation to any obligation to make a payment not falling within (i) or (ii) above, a day other than a Saturday or a Sunday on which banks are open for business in the principal financial centre of the country of which the currency in which the payment is denominated is the official currency and, if different, in the place where any account designated by the parties for the making or receipt of the payment is situated (or, in the case of a payment in euro, a day on which TARGET operates);

(e) This definition identifies a Business Day as one when particular settlement systems for settling repo transactions are open for business. The definition covers both deliveries and payments. TARGET is the market's euro payment settlement system.

> (f) "Cash Margin", a cash sum paid to Buyer or Seller in accordance with paragraph 4;

(f) If the value of the bonds sold to the Buyer falls during the life of the repo transaction, the Buyer is entitled under paragraph 4 (Margin Maintenance) to call for more bonds or for Cash Margin to maintain the value of the bonds against which it has paid out its cash at the start of the repo transaction.

> (g) "Clearstream", Clearstream Banking, société anonyme, (previously Cedelbank) or any successor thereto;

(g) Together with Euroclear, one of Europe's two major central securities depositories and settlement systems. Clearstream is now owned by Deutsche Börse.

> (h) "Confirmation", the meaning specified in paragraph 3(b);

(h) A written confirmation of a repo or buy/sellback transaction setting out its economic terms and containing the matters outlined in paragraph 3(b) and in Annex II.

> (i) "Contractual Currency", the meaning specified in paragraph 7(a);

(i) This is the currency of the Purchase Price of the securities sold by the Seller to the Buyer for cash on the Purchase Date.

> (j) "Defaulting Party", the meaning specified in paragraph 10;

(j) One of the two parties to the TBMA/ISMA GMRA that has committed one or more of the Events of Default described in paragraph 10.

> (k) "Default Market Value", the meaning specified in paragraph 10;

(k) This definition was the first one to be extensively revised from the PSA/ISMA GMRA. The definition is used for calculating the value of the securities held by the parties when, following an Event of Default, close-out netting is applied. The Default Market Value of securities is always calculated by the non-Defaulting Party. The new paragraph 10(e) provides both more time and more ways than the PSA/ISMA GMRA did in which to determine Default Market Value, as we shall see.

> (l) "Default Notice", a written notice served by the non-Defaulting Party on the Defaulting Party under paragraph 10 stating that an event shall be treated as an Event of Default for the purposes of this Agreement;

(l) This is self-explanatory.

> (m) "Default Valuation Notice", the meaning specified in paragraph 10;

(m) This is a written notice sent by the non-Defaulting Party to the Defaulting Party describing the basis on which it has calculated Default Market Value for Securities held for the purposes of close-out under paragraph 10(e).

> (n) "Default Valuation Time", the meaning specified in paragraph 10;

(n) Where an Act of Insolvency has occurred, the close of business on the fifth dealing day after the non-Defaulting Party first becomes aware of the Act of Insolvency. With other Events of Default the Default Valuation Time is the close of business on the fifth dealing day in the Appropriate Market (determined by the non-Defaulting Party) after the Event of Default occurs.

> (o) "Deliverable Securities", the meaning specified in paragraph 10;

COMMENTARY ON THE TBMA/ISMA GMRA

(o) At close-out, the securities the Defaulting Party is obligated to deliver to the non-Defaulting Party.

> (p) "Designated Office", with respect to a party, a branch or office of that party which is specified as such in Annex I hereto or such other branch or office as may be agreed to by the parties;

(p) The TBMA/ISMA GMRA requires parties to state in Annex I the branches or offices through which they will enter into Transactions. For credit and regulatory capital purposes, it is best to enter into Transactions through branches in jurisdictions favourable to the TBMA/ISMA GMRA's close-out netting provisions. Otherwise supervisors may not recognise the netting provisions of the TBMA/ISMA GMRA for regulatory capital purposes, with the result that gross exposures to counterparties may be required to be taken into account when allocating capital to cover trading book risk.

> (q) "Distributions", the meaning specified in sub-paragraph (w) below;

(q) Essentially, interest paid on securities by their issuer to their holders.

> (r) "Equivalent Margin Securities", Securities equivalent to Securities previously transferred as Margin Securities;

(r) When Margin Securities are returned by the Buyer, the securities must be of the same issuer, issue, identical type, nominal value, description and amount as those originally transferred by the Seller. They do not need to be the same identically numbered securities. They are initially transferred to the Buyer as Margin Securities and returned by him as Equivalent Margin Securities.

> (s) "Equivalent Securities", with respect to a Transaction, Securities equivalent to Purchased Securities under that Transaction. If and to the extent that such Purchased Securities have been redeemed, the expression shall mean a sum of money equivalent to the proceeds of the redemption;

(s) Equivalent Securities are to be returned by the Buyer to the Seller on the Repurchase Date. The same characteristics as for Equivalent Margin Securities apply. Wherever you see the word "Equivalent" in the TBMA/ISMA GMRA, it generally, but not always, describes an action of the Buyer in fulfilling some obligation to the Seller. The exception relates to margin maintenance in paragraph 4, where either party might need to return margin at different times.

However, in the unlikely event that the Purchased Securities have been redeemed before the Repurchase Date, Equivalent Securities shall mean the cash redemption proceeds.

> (t) Securities are "equivalent to" other Securities for the purposes of this Agreement if they are: (i) of the same issuer; (ii) part of the same issue; and (iii) of an identical type, nominal value, description and (except where otherwise stated) amount as those other Securities, provided that
> (A) Securities will be equivalent to other Securities notwithstanding that those Securities have been redenominated into euro or that the nominal value of those Securities has changed in connection with such redenomination; and
> (B) where Securities have been converted, subdivided or consolidated or have become the subject of a takeover or the holders of Securities have become entitled to receive or acquire other Securities or other property or the Securities have become subject to any similar event, the expression "equivalent to" shall mean Securities equivalent to (as defined in the provisions of this definition preceding the proviso) the original Securities together with or replaced by a sum of money or Securities or other property equivalent to (as so defined) that receivable by holders of such original Securities resulting from such event;

(t) Securities are further defined as equivalent to other Securities where they are:

- issued by the same issuer;
- part of the same issue; and

- of the identical type, nominal value, description and amount.

The definition is expanded to take account of former EU currency-denominated securities which have been redenominated into euro. It also defines securities that have been subject to a takeover, scrip issue or corporate event where the original securities have been replaced by other securities or cash.

> (u) "Euroclear", Morgan Guaranty Trust Company of New York, Brussels office, as operator of the Euroclear System or any successor thereto;

(u) Together with Clearstream, Euroclear is one of Europe's two leading central securities depositories and settlement systems. Since 2000 Euroclear's legal name has been Euroclear Bank SA/NV.

> (v) "Event of Default", the meaning specified in paragraph 10;

(v) One or more of the 10 adverse events described in paragraph 10(a).

COMMENTARY ON THE TBMA/ISMA GMRA

> (w) "Income", with respect to any Security at any time, all interest, dividends or other distributions thereon, but excluding distributions which are a payment or repayment of principal in respect of the relevant securities ("Distributions");

(w) Essentially, interest or dividends paid by an issuer of Securities to their holders. The definition specifically excludes principal payments or repayments.

> (x) "Income Payment Date", with respect to any Securities, the date on which Income is paid in respect of such Securities or, in the case of registered Securities, the date by reference to which particular registered holders are identified as being entitled to payment of Income;

(x) The date (which is usually the contractual payment date but may not be) on which an issuer pays interest or dividends on Securities that it has issued to their holders. With registered Securities it is the day up until which interest has accrued (the record date) and when the issuer announces that the amount will be paid over to holders at an agreed future date, which will be the Income Payment Date. This is a common practice with gilts. If a repo transaction matures between the record date and the Income Payment Date, the Buyer must still pay a manufactured dividend to the Seller in respect of the announced dividend. It will do this once the dividend is actually paid.

> (y) "LIBOR", in relation to any sum in any currency, the one month London Inter Bank Offered Rate in respect of that currency as quoted on page 3750 on the Bridge Telerate Service (or such other page as may replace page 3750 on that service) as of 11:00 a.m., London time, on the date on which it is to be determined;

(y) The Telerate quotation for one-month LIBOR at 11.00 a.m. on the day it is calculated. Please note that LIBOR here means one-month LIBOR.

> (z) "Margin Ratio", with respect to a Transaction, the Market Value of the Purchased Securities at the time when the Transaction was entered into divided by the Purchase Price (and so that, where a Transaction relates to Securities of different descriptions and the Purchase Price is apportioned by the parties among Purchased Securities of each such description, a separate Margin Ratio shall apply in respect of Securities of each such description), or such other proportion as the parties may agree with respect to that Transaction;

(z) This definition is used to cover any haircuts or initial margin taken in respect of any Transaction. It is common for a party dealing with a less creditworthy counterparty to require an initial margin or haircut. This means that the stronger credit receives more than the cash it gives and has a cushion or buffer of securities. So, for example, where the Seller gives initial margin of 2.5 per cent, this is expressed as a Margin Ratio of 102.5 per cent. The Buyer therefore receives 102.5 per cent in securities value for its cash. Another way of looking at this, from the Buyer's viewpoint, is collateral value divided by cash. Different Margin Ratios may apply to different securities. Credit officers calculate these, and take into account the credit quality of the counterparty supplying the collateral, the collateral's price volatility and the term of the repo. Margin guards against market risk, the risk that the value of the collateral will fall during the repo term. The Margin Ratio is fixed once and for all at the start of the repo transaction.

Unless otherwise agreed by the Buyer and the Seller, the Margin Ratio is the Market Value of the securities being purchased by the Buyer divided by the Purchase Price for the repo. A party's exposure to the other party under each repo transaction is obtained by comparing the difference between the price at which the securities are to be repurchased multiplied by the Margin Ratio and the Market Value of the securities. The ability of one party to call for margin from the other is determined by calculating, on a global basis, the Net Exposure of all the repo transaction exposures, after taking into account margin held by, and income and interest due to, each party. The failure to deliver securities either at the time of purchase or repurchase (a "fail") could be an Event of Default under the TBMA/ISMA GMRA, if the parties choose this in Annex I.

> (aa) "Margin Securities", in relation to a Margin Transfer, Securities reasonably acceptable to the party calling for such Margin Transfer;

(aa) Where the value of Securities held falls during the life of a repo transaction, a Buyer is entitled to call on the Seller for a Margin Transfer up to the value of the Purchased Securities held by it against the cash it had paid the Seller on the Purchase Date. They do not need to be the same type of Securities as the Purchased Securities. They just need to be reasonably acceptable to the Buyer. When the Buyer has excess Margin Securities (because market prices have moved in his favour), he would return Equivalent Margin Securities to the Seller, if called upon to do so.

> (bb) "Margin Transfer", any, or any combination of, the payment or repayment of Cash Margin and the transfer of Margin Securities or Equivalent Margin Securities;

(bb) A Margin Transfer may involve cash or securities and may be made by either the Buyer or the Seller, depending upon circumstances. It is governed by the provisions of paragraph 4.

> (cc) "Market Value", with respect to any Securities as of any time on any date, the price for such Securities at such time on such date obtained from a generally recognised ⟫→

> source agreed to by the parties (and where different prices are obtained for different delivery dates, the price so obtainable for the earliest available such delivery date) (provided that the price of Securities that are suspended shall (for the purposes of paragraph 4) be nil unless the parties otherwise agree and (for all other purposes) shall be the price of those Securities as of close of business on the dealing day in the relevant market last preceding the date of suspension) plus the aggregate amount of Income which, as of such date, has accrued but not yet been paid in respect of the Securities to the extent not included in such price as of such date, and for these purposes any sum in a currency other than the Contractual Currency for the Transaction in question shall be converted into such Contractual Currency at the Spot Rate prevailing at the relevant time;

(cc) This definition is used for the purposes of margining and substitution. The Market Value is typically the price (including accrued income) obtained from a reputable pricing source agreed to by the parties. Where different prices are obtained because of multiple delivery dates, the prevailing price will be the one obtained for the earliest delivery date. Bid, offer or mid-market prices are not specified, but are agreed to by dealers and occasionally referred to in Annex I.

In the case of suspended securities, the definition provides that the value of such securities (for the purposes of the margining calculations in paragraph 4 only) will be zero, so that the suspension of the Purchased Securities will or may cause a Transaction Exposure in respect of the Transaction concerned. However, it would be clearly unfair for the purposes of close-out netting or substitution for the value of such securities to be zero, so for these purposes the value is treated as the Market Value of the relevant securities on the Business Day immediately before the date of suspension plus accrued income if not already in the price. Currency conversion may be necessary in particular cases and will be undertaken at the prevailing Spot Rate defined in (rr) below.

> (dd) "Net Exposure", the meaning specified in paragraph 4(c);

(dd) A party has a Net Exposure or risk on its counterparty if the value of its repo positions (adjusted for Net Margin held from its counterparty plus any Income due to it but unpaid) is greater than the corresponding amounts calculated in respect of the counterparty. The party with the Net Exposure or risk can call for a Margin Transfer from its counterparty. Only one party can have a Net Exposure at any one time.

> (ee) the "Net Margin" provided to a party at any time, the excess (if any) at that time of (i) the sum of the amount of Cash Margin paid to that party (including accrued interest on such Cash Margin which has not been paid to the other party) and the Market Value of Margin Securities transferred to that party under paragraph 4(a)

> (excluding any Cash Margin which has been repaid to the other party and any Margin Securities in respect of which Equivalent Margin Securities have been transferred to the other party) over (ii) the sum of the amount of Cash Margin paid to the other party (including accrued interest on such Cash Margin which has not been paid by the other party) and the Market Value of Margin Securities transferred to the other party under paragraph 4(a) (excluding any Cash Margin which has been repaid by the other party and any Margin Securities in respect of which Equivalent Margin Securities have been transferred by the other party) and for this purpose any amounts not denominated in the Base Currency shall be converted into the Base Currency at the Spot Rate prevailing at the relevant time;

(ee) Net Margin comprises the net collateralised position of each party after taking into account the current market value of Margin Securities and Cash Margin (including accrued but undistributed interest on that cash) held by them, and returns of each made to the other. Currency conversion may be necessary in calculating Net Margin.

> (ff) "Net Paying Securities", Securities which are of a kind such that, were they to be the subject of a Transaction to which paragraph 5 applies, any payment made by Buyer under paragraph 5 would be one in respect of which either Buyer would or might be required to make a withholding or deduction for or on account of taxes or duties or Seller might be required to make or account for a payment for or on account of taxes or duties (in each case other than tax on overall net income) by reference to such payment;

(ff) Net Paying Securities are those on which the coupon paid by the issuer is paid net of withholding tax, as with Japanese government bonds. They were excluded from the PSA/ISMA GMRA because of uncertainty about the tax treatment of the manufactured dividend made by the Buyer (ie, the payment made by the Buyer to the Seller, which is equal to the coupon paid by the issuer). It is now possible for non-Japanese entities to be registered as foreign holders of Japanese government bonds, which will result in them receiving a gross income payment.

However, rather than focusing on the interest payment on the bond, the TBMA/ISMA GMRA concentrates on whether there is a withholding tax chargeable on the manufactured dividend from the Buyer to the Seller.

In November 1996 changes in UK tax law reduced the circumstances where withholding tax applied to manufactured dividends, with the result that most bonds became gross paying. Hence net paying securities were treated the same as gross paying ones, ie, the Buyer is now required to pay only the equivalent of the Income that it received from the issuer to the Seller.

If parties wish to enter into repos in Net Paying Securities, then this has to be stated in Annex 1 of the TBMA/ISMA GMRA.

> (gg) "Net Value", the meaning specified in paragraph 10;

(gg) The non-Defaulting Party's reasonable opinion of the value of Securities to be delivered from or to the Defaulting Party upon close-out. Transaction Costs are also accounted for in the definition of Net Value.

> (hh) "New Purchased Securities", the meaning specified in paragraph 8(a);

(hh) These are Securities that the Buyer agrees, after a request from the Seller, to substitute for the Purchased Securities or part of them. The New Purchased Securities must be of at least equal value to the Purchased Securities at the time the substitution is made.

> (ii) "Price Differential", with respect to any Transaction as of any date, the aggregate amount obtained by daily application of the Pricing Rate for such Transaction to the Purchase Price for such Transaction (on a 360 day basis or 365 day basis in accordance with the applicable ISMA convention, unless otherwise agreed between the parties for the Transaction), for the actual number of days during the period commencing on (and including) the Purchase Date for such Transaction and ending on (but excluding) the date of calculation – or, if earlier, the Repurchase Date;

(ii) In order to calculate the Price Differential for a Transaction (ie, between the Purchase Date and the Repurchase Date) the parties need to apply the Pricing Rate to the Purchase Price on a 360-day or 365-day basis in accordance with the applicable ISMA day count convention. Price Differential equals the total financing charge that has accrued to date for the repo transaction.

> (jj) "Pricing Rate", with respect to any Transaction, the per annum percentage rate for calculation of the Price Differential agreed to by Buyer and Seller in relation to that Transaction;

(jj) This is the repo rate payable by the Seller to the Buyer for the Buyer's cash. It represents the economic effect of interest without being an interest rate itself.

> (kk) "Purchase Date", with respect to any Transaction, the date on which Purchased Securities are to be sold by Seller to Buyer in relation to that Transaction;

(kk) The date on which the parties enter into the first leg of the repo transaction and the Purchased Securities are transferred to the Buyer in exchange for an agreed cash sum.

> (ll) "Purchase Price", on the Purchase Date, the price at which Purchased Securities are sold or are to be sold by Seller to Buyer;

(ll) The price at which the Purchased Securities are sold to the Buyer by the Seller on the Purchase Date.

> (mm) "Purchased Securities", with respect to any Transaction, the Securities sold or to be sold by Seller to Buyer under that Transaction, and any New Purchased Securities transferred by Seller to Buyer under paragraph 8 in respect of that Transaction;

(mm) The Securities that are the subject of the repo transaction and that, potentially, with the parties' agreement, may be substituted with New Purchased Securities under the provisions of paragraph 8.

> (nn) "Receivable Securities", the meaning specified in paragraph 10;

(nn) At close-out, the Securities the non-Defaulting Party is obligated to deliver to the Defaulting Party.

> (oo) "Repurchase Date", with respect to any Transaction, the date on which Buyer is to sell Equivalent Securities to Seller in relation to that Transaction;

(oo) The second and final leg of the repo transaction, when Securities equivalent to the Purchased Securities will be delivered to the Seller by the Buyer against a cash payment including the agreed repo return.

> (pp) "Repurchase Price", with respect to any Transaction and as of any date, the sum of the Purchase Price and the Price Differential as of such date;

(pp) The Repurchase Price is equivalent to the original Purchase Price and the repo return, and is paid by the Seller to the Buyer on the Repurchase Date.

> (qq) "Special Default Notice", the meaning specified in paragraph 14;

(qq) Paragraph 14 provides that, where it has not proved possible for the non-Defaulting Party to deliver a Default Notice in the normal course to a Defaulting Party, perhaps due to *force majeure* or other extreme circumstances, it can now send a Special Default Notice (which it composes itself). The effect is that an Event of Default is deemed to have occurred on the date stated in the Special Default Notice.

> (rr) "Spot Rate", where an amount in one currency is to be converted into a second currency on any date, unless the parties otherwise agree, the spot rate of exchange quoted by Barclays Bank PLC in the London inter-bank market for the sale by it of such second currency against a purchase by it of such first currency;

(rr) This is the foreign exchange conversion rate between two currencies. It is the relevant rate quoted by Barclays Bank PLC unless the Parties otherwise agree.

> (ss) "TARGET", the Trans-European Automated Real-time Gross Settlement Express Transfer System;

(ss) The EU-wide centralised settlement system for euro payments.

> (tt) "Term", with respect to any Transaction, the interval of time commencing with the Purchase Date and ending with the Repurchase Date;

(tt) The contractual life of an individual repo or buy/sellback transaction.

> (uu) "Termination", with respect to any Transaction, refers to the requirement with respect to such Transaction for Buyer to sell Equivalent Securities against payment by Seller of the Repurchase Price in accordance with paragraph 3(f), and reference to a Transaction having a "fixed term" or being "terminable upon demand" shall be construed accordingly;

(uu) The definition refers to the Buyer's obligation to sell Equivalent Securities to the Seller for the Repurchase Price on the Repurchase Date. It also refers to the two tenors possible for a Transaction: fixed term or terminable on demand.

> (vv) "Transaction Costs", the meaning specified in paragraph 10;

A PRACTICAL GUIDE TO USING REPO MASTER AGREEMENTS

(vv) The costs, commissions and fees due in respect of the purchase or sale of Securities at close-out in order for the parties to settle their obligations to each other.

> (ww) "Transaction Exposure", with respect to any Transaction at any time during the period from the Purchase Date to the Repurchase Date (or, if later, the date on which Equivalent Securities are delivered to Seller or the Transaction is terminated under paragraph 10(g) or 10(h)), the difference between (i) the Repurchase Price at such time multiplied by the applicable Margin Ratio (or, where the Transaction relates to Securities of more than one description to which different Margin Ratios apply, the amount produced by multiplying the Repurchase Price attributable to Equivalent Securities of each such description by the applicable Margin Ratio and aggregating the resulting amounts, the Repurchase Price being for this purpose attributed to Equivalent Securities of each such description in the same proportions as those in which the Purchase Price was apportioned among the Purchased Securities) and (ii) the Market Value of Equivalent Securities at such time. If (i) is greater than (ii), Buyer has a Transaction Exposure for that Transaction equal to that excess. If (ii) is greater than (i), Seller has a Transaction Exposure for that Transaction equal to that excess; and

(ww) The Transaction Exposure is the amount by which the value of the parties' obligations became unaligned during the repo transaction's life. If the Market Value of the securities it holds falls, the Buyer has a risk exposure on the Seller and can demand more margin. If the market value of the securities transferred to the Buyer rises, the Seller has a risk exposure on the Buyer and can demand return of margin. Technically, it is the difference between the current value of the securities held by the Buyer and the current value of cash held by the Seller multiplied by the Margin Ratio. Net Exposure is therefore the aggregate of all Transaction Exposures plus any margin received but not returned minus any margin given and not returned, taking into account any manufactured dividend owing to a party.

> (xx) except in paragraphs 14(b)(i) and 18, references in this Agreement to "written" communications and communications "in writing" include communications made through any electronic system agreed between the parties which is capable of reproducing such communication in hard copy form.

(xx) Written communications may be made through electronic systems, provided that they can be printed out as hard copies. This does not apply with paragraphs 14(b)(i) (hand-delivered communications) or 18 (communications concerning waivers).

Paragraph 3

This paragraph describes the mechanics of initiating, confirming and terminating a Transaction. The TBMA/ISMA GMRA envisages that either party may enter into a Transaction on the telephone or in writing. However, much repo trading is now done electronically or via automated trading systems such as Broker Tec or Eurex Repo.

> **3. Initiation; Confirmation; Termination**
> (a) A Transaction may be entered into orally or in writing at the initiation of either Buyer or Seller.

(a) A Transaction will normally be entered into orally over the telephone between two repo dealers in different organisations.

> (b) Upon agreeing to enter into a Transaction hereunder Buyer or Seller (or both), as shall have been agreed, shall promptly deliver to the other party written confirmation of such Transaction (a "Confirmation").
>   The Confirmation shall describe the Purchased Securities (including CUSIP or ISIN or other identifying number or numbers, if any), identify Buyer and Seller and set forth
> (i) the Purchase Date;
> (ii) the Purchase Price;
> (iii) the Repurchase Date, unless the Transaction is to be terminable on demand (in which case the Confirmation shall state that it is terminable on demand);
> (iv) the Pricing Rate applicable to the Transaction;
> (v) in respect of each party the details of the bank account[s] to which payments to be made hereunder are to be credited;
> (vi) where the Buy/Sell Back Annex applies, whether the Transaction is a Repurchase Transaction or a Buy/Sell Back Transaction;
> (vii) where the Agency Annex applies, whether the Transaction is an Agency Transaction and, if so, the identity of the party which is acting as agent and the name, code or identifier of the Principal; and
> (viii) any additional terms or conditions of the Transaction;
> and may be in the form of Annex II hereto or may be in any other form to which the parties agree.
>   The Confirmation relating to a Transaction shall, together with this Agreement, constitute prima facie evidence of the terms agreed between Buyer and Seller for that Transaction, unless objection is made with respect to the Confirmation promptly after receipt thereof. In the event of any conflict between the terms of such Confirmation and this Agreement, the Confirmation shall prevail in respect of that Transaction and those terms only.

(b) Upon agreeing to enter into a Transaction, one or both parties shall deliver a written confirmation. This is decided in Annex I. The Confirmation may be substantially in the form of

Annex II and must contain the prescribed information shown, along with any additional terms as the parties may agree.

With a buy/sellback transaction, the Buy/Sell Back Annex permits the parties to deliver either a single confirmation that relates to both legs of the buy/sellback transaction or a separate confirmation for each leg of the Transaction. The Confirmation or Confirmations relating to a buy/sellback transaction must state the Pricing Rate applicable to that Transaction.

If a Transaction is a buy/sellback transaction and/or an agency transaction, this must be stated in the Confirmation.

In the event of any conflict between the terms of a Confirmation and the TBMA/ISMA GMRA, the Confirmation shall prevail in respect of the relevant Transaction and the relevant terms only.

> (c) On the Purchase Date for a Transaction, Seller shall transfer the Purchased Securities to Buyer or its agent against the payment of the Purchase Price by Buyer.

(c) On the Purchase Date of the Transaction the Seller transfers the Purchased Securities to the Buyer on a delivery-versus-payment basis.

> (d) Termination of a Transaction will be effected, in the case of on demand Transactions, on the date specified for Termination in such demand, and, in the case of fixed term Transactions, on the date fixed for Termination.

(d) Repo transactions may be on demand, meaning that they will continue until one party calls for termination. Alternatively, they may be for a fixed term and will mature at the end of that term.

> (e) In the case of on demand Transactions, demand for Termination shall be made by Buyer or Seller, by telephone or otherwise, and shall provide for Termination to occur after not less than the minimum period as is customarily required for the settlement or delivery of money or Equivalent Securities of the relevant kind.

(e) Termination of demand Transactions may be made by either the Buyer or the Seller. Termination will occur after not less than the minimum period customarily required for settlement or delivery of cash or Equivalent Securities of the relevant kind from the date of demand.

> (f) On the Repurchase Date, Buyer shall transfer to Seller or its agent Equivalent Securities against the payment of the Repurchase Price by Seller (less any amount then payable and unpaid by Buyer to Seller pursuant to paragraph 5).

(f) On the Repurchase Date, which is the maturity date of the Transaction, the Buyer transfers to the Seller Equivalent Securities, again on a delivery-versus-payment basis.

Sub-paragraph (f) allows the Seller to deduct from the Repurchase Price any amounts that the Buyer may owe it in respect of the manufactured dividends, ie, income received from the issuer of the Purchased Securities but not yet paid over to the Seller by the Buyer.

Paragraph 4

The amount of margin or collateral required for a repo depends upon the following factors:

- the counterparty's credit standing;
- the length of the repo term – longer term is more risky;
- the tenor of the collateral – longer-term collateral is usually more volatile;
- collateral price volatility;
- scarcity of collateral; and
- its current market price.

The margin maintenance provisions of the TBMA/ISMA GMRA are designed to reduce market risk arising from changes in the value of securities during the repo term. At its most basic level, a party's exposure in a Transaction is the difference between the current value of the securities that it has bought and the current value of the cash it has paid its counterparty plus the repo return that has accrued daily on that sum. If the value of the securities is higher than the value of the cash, it has no exposure. If the value of the securities is below the value of the cash, it has an exposure equal to the difference.

The TBMA/ISMA GMRA fixes the amount of margin at the outset of each Transaction by reference to the value of the securities at the Purchase Date and the Purchase Price to give the Margin Ratio, which is defined as the Market Value of the Purchased Securities at the time when the Transaction was entered into divided by the Purchase Price. The parties may choose a different Margin Ratio for any or all Transactions entered into under the TBMA/ISMA GMRA.

If a Transaction relates to different types of securities and the parties attribute the Purchase Price among the different types, the definition of Margin Ratio allows a separate Margin Ratio to be applied to each type of security.

Credit departments set Margin Ratios and it is unusual for them to be specifically documented under the TBMA/ISMA GMRA or the PSA/ISMA GMRA or in a Confirmation, being normally agreed by dealers in the Purchase Price. Having said that, many major banks do not take haircuts on top-quality securities transferred between them, eg, gilts.

It is common practice for dealers to reduce the frequency of margin calls by setting a monetary threshold in Annex I before a margin call can be made.

Margin is calculated on a global basis for all Transactions to give an overall Net Exposure. The party that has the Net Exposure can call for a Margin Transfer.

A party has a Net Exposure if its exposure on each Transaction (calculated to reflect the margin requirements for that Transaction by applying the Margin Ratio to it) less the margin held by it **exceeds** the other party's exposure on each Transaction (again applying the appropriate Margin Ratio) less the margin held by it.

Amounts of unpaid income due to a party are also added.

Initial margin is not taken separately, but is included in the Purchase Price by way of a haircut (ie, where the amount of cash provided is less than the value of the securities).

A margin call is satisfied by making a margin transfer, which may be in the form of cash or securities. The particular combination is at the option of the party making the transfer, although any securities have to be reasonably acceptable to the other party. Where securities are provided by way of margin, there is an outright transfer of the Margin Securities and the party making the margin transfer is entitled to the return of Equivalent Margin Securities. Where the party calling for margin has also previously delivered margin that has not yet been returned, it is entitled to have that margin returned first and such returned collateral will be deducted from the amount of the margin call.

If the Seller is unable to supply more margin where required, it has to return a portion of the cash Purchase Price received from the Buyer.

Where cash is transferred, the parties may specify the currency, the interest rate and payment dates. A payment of Cash Margin will give rise to a debt to the margin giver from the margin receiver.

Like transfers of Purchased Securities, transfers of Margin Securities pass full legal title to the transferee.

> **4. Margin Maintenance**
> (a) If at any time either party has a Net Exposure in respect of the other party it may by notice to the other party require the other party to make a Margin Transfer to it of an aggregate amount or value at least equal to that Net Exposure.

(a) The parties to the repo transaction envisage that each side's net risk (Net Exposure) will be fully collateralised at all times. The Buyer expects the value of the Purchased Securities to be at least equal to the cash that it transferred to the Seller on the Purchase Date.

Conversely, the Seller will call for a return of some of the bonds if their value exceeds the value of the cash that it holds. Therefore, each party can call for a Margin Transfer to restore the balance between these two values.

> (b) A notice under sub-paragraph (a) above may be given orally or in writing.

(b) A call for a Margin Transfer may be made in writing (fax, e-mail or electronic messaging system) or by telephone.

> (c) For the purposes of this Agreement a party has a Net Exposure in respect of the other party if the aggregate of all the first party's Transaction Exposures plus any amount payable to the first party under paragraph 5 but unpaid less the amount of any
> ⟫→

COMMENTARY ON THE TBMA/ISMA GMRA

> Net Margin provided to the first party exceeds the aggregate of all the other party's Transaction Exposures plus any amount payable to the other party under paragraph 5 but unpaid less the amount of any Net Margin provided to the other party; and the amount of the Net Exposure is the amount of the excess. For this purpose any amounts not denominated in the Base Currency shall be converted into the Base Currency at the Spot Rate prevailing at the relevant time.

(c) A party has a net risk exposure on the other party if the value of its repo positions plus accrued interest due to it under paragraph 5 (but unpaid) less net collateral held by it is greater than the corresponding amounts for its counterparty. Amounts in other currencies are to be converted into the Base Currency agreed in Annex I at the prevailing Spot Rate as defined.

> (d) To the extent that a party calling for a Margin Transfer has previously paid Cash Margin which has not been repaid or delivered Margin Securities in respect of which Equivalent Margin Securities have not been delivered to it, that party shall be entitled to require that such Margin Transfer be satisfied first by the repayment of such Cash Margin or the delivery of Equivalent Margin Securities but, subject to this, the composition of a Margin Transfer shall be at the option of the party making such Margin Transfer.

(d) Where a party that calls for a Margin Transfer has previously delivered Cash Margin or Margin Securities to the other party that have not been returned, it is entitled to have these returned and they will be deducted from the amount of the margin call. Otherwise it can decide if it will meet the Margin Transfer with Cash Margin or Margin Securities or a combination of them.

> (e) Any Cash Margin transferred shall be in the Base Currency or such other currency as the parties may agree.

(e) Cash Margin will be transferred in the Base Currency selected in Annex I, unless the parties agree otherwise.

> (f) A payment of Cash Margin shall give rise to a debt owing from the party receiving such payment to the party making such payment. Such debt shall bear interest at such rate, payable at such times, as may be specified in Annex I hereto in respect of the relevant currency or otherwise agreed between the parties, and shall be repayable subject to the terms of this Agreement.

(f) From this sub-paragraph it is made clear that the recipient of Cash Margin shall owe it as a debt to its transferor. The Cash Margin will bear interest at the rate for the period held stated in Annex I or as otherwise agreed between the parties. It is also repayable subject to the terms of the TBMA/ISMA GMRA.

> (g) Where Seller or Buyer becomes obligated under sub-paragraph (a) above to make a Margin Transfer, it shall transfer Cash Margin or Margin Securities or Equivalent Margin Securities within the minimum period specified in Annex I hereto or, if no period is there specified, such minimum period as is customarily required for the settlement or delivery of money, Margin Securities or Equivalent Margin Securities of the relevant kind.

(g) Margin Transfers must be made promptly. That is why in Annex I various deadlines are agreed for the transfer of various sorts of Margin Securities. These are usually for the minimum period that is customary in the relevant market for the settlement of the relevant securities or the transfer of Cash Margin. This is also the fallback where Annex I is silent on the point.

> (h) The parties may agree that, with respect to any Transaction, the provisions of sub-paragraphs (a) to (g) above shall not apply but instead that margin may be provided separately in respect of that Transaction in which case –
> (i) that Transaction shall not be taken into account when calculating whether either party has a Net Exposure;
> (ii) margin shall be provided in respect of that Transaction in such manner as the parties may agree; and
> (iii) margin provided in respect of that Transaction shall not be taken into account for the purposes of sub-paragraphs (a) to (g) above.

(h) In sub-clause (h) the margin requirements may be disapplied for any particular Transaction in favour of alternative margin requirements. Where this happens, the Transaction will be ignored in the calculations for Net Exposure; the nature of margin to be provided will be separately agreed by the parties and the remainder of the provisions in (a)–(g) above will be disregarded in respect of that particular Transaction.

> (i) The parties may agree that any Net Exposure which may arise shall be eliminated not by Margin Transfers under the preceding provisions of this paragraph but by the repricing of Transactions under sub-paragraph (j) below, the adjustment of Transactions under sub-paragraph (k) below or a combination of both these methods.

(i) The TBMA/ISMA GMRA also includes alternative mechanisms for the elimination of exposure through its repricing and adjustment provisions in paragraphs 4(j) and (k). These provisions operate either by changing the ultimate Repurchase Price of the securities (which is described as the repricing route) or by changing the identity or the amount of the securities (which is described as the adjustment route).

If the repricing route is taken, then the Original Transaction is terminated early and replaced with a new Transaction in relation to Equivalent Securities, but at a new price. A cash sum is paid that represents the difference between the Repurchase Price under the original Transaction and the Purchase Price on the new, repriced Transaction. Accrued interest on the Original Transaction is also taken into account. Repricing was introduced to cover buy/sellbacks, which do not, *per se*, use margin transfers. Repos may now also be repriced and this is done where the parties lack a margining infrastructure.

If the adjustment route is selected, then, again, the original Transaction is terminated early and replaced with a new Transaction, but this time in respect of new securities that have a market value substantially equal to the Repurchase Price under the original Transaction and with likely changes to the other terms.

(j) Where the parties agree that a Transaction is to be repriced under this sub-paragraph, such repricing shall be effected as follows
(i) the Repurchase Date under the relevant Transaction (the "Original Transaction") shall be deemed to occur on the date on which the repricing is to be effected (the "Repricing Date");
(ii) the parties shall be deemed to have entered into a new Transaction (the "Repriced Transaction") on the terms set out in (iii) to (vi) below;
(iii) the Purchased Securities under the Repriced Transaction shall be Securities equivalent to the Purchased Securities under the Original Transaction;
(iv) the Purchase Date under the Repriced Transaction shall be the Repricing Date;
(v) the Purchase Price under the Repriced Transaction shall be such amount as shall, when multiplied by the Margin Ratio applicable to the Original Transaction, be equal to the Market Value of such Securities on the Repricing Date;
(vi) the Repurchase Date, the Pricing Rate, the Margin Ratio and, subject as aforesaid, the other terms of the Repriced Transaction shall be identical to those of the Original Transaction;
(vii) the obligations of the parties with respect to the delivery of the Purchased Securities and the payment of the Purchase Price under the Repriced Transaction shall be set off against their obligations with respect to the delivery of Equivalent Securities and payment of the Repurchase Price under the Original Transaction and accordingly only a net cash sum shall be paid by one party to the other. Such net cash sum shall be paid within the period specified in sub-paragraph (g) above.

(j) Where the parties agree upon repricing the following steps are taken:
(i) The original Transaction is terminated early by its Repurchase Date being brought forward to the date the repricing is to occur.
(ii) The parties will be considered to have entered into a new Transaction on the conditions shown in (iii) and (iv) below.

(iii) The Purchased Securities under the new repriced Transaction shall be of the same type, issue, amount and issuer as the Purchased Securities under the Original Transaction.
(iv) The Purchase Date of the new Transaction will be the date the repricing occurs.
(v) The Purchase Price of the new Transaction shall be equal to the Market Value of the Purchased Securities on the Repricing Date multiplied by the Margin Ratio that applied to the Original Transaction, in order to preserve the original haircut arrangements.
(vi) All the other terms, including the Repurchase Date, repo return and Margin Ratio, shall be identical to those in the Original Transaction. Only the Purchase Price of the Repriced Transaction has changed.
(vii) The parties' obligations under the Original Transaction (on the repurchase leg) and under the sale leg of the Repriced Transaction are netted off, and a cash sum is paid over representing the difference between the Repurchase Price under the Original Transaction and the Purchase Price under the new Repriced Transaction. This cash net sum must be paid over in the minimum customary time in the market concerned.

> (k) The adjustment of a Transaction (the "Original Transaction") under this sub-paragraph shall be effected by the parties agreeing that on the date on which the adjustment is to be made (the "Adjustment Date") the Original Transaction shall be terminated and they shall enter into a new Transaction (the "Replacement Transaction") in accordance with the following provisions –.
> (i) the Original Transaction shall be terminated on the Adjustment Date on such terms as the parties shall agree on or before the Adjustment Date;
> (ii) the Purchased Securities under the Replacement Transaction shall be such Securities as the parties shall agree on or before the Adjustment Date (being Securities the aggregate Market Value of which at the Adjustment Date is substantially equal to the Repurchase Price under the Original Transaction at the Adjustment Date multiplied by the Margin Ratio applicable to the Original Transaction);
> (iii) the Purchase Date under the Replacement Transaction shall be the Adjustment Date;
> (iv) the other terms of the Replacement Transaction shall be such as the parties shall agree on or before the Adjustment Date; and
> (v) the obligations of the parties with respect to payment and delivery of Securities on the Adjustment Date under the Original Transaction and the Replacement Transaction shall be settled in accordance with paragraph 6 within the minimum period specified in sub-paragraph (g) above.

(k) As an alternative to margining and repricing there is also the adjustment route, which involves the termination of the Original Transaction on the Adjustment Date and the entry into a Replacement Transaction involving the following steps:
(i) The parties agree the terms for terminating the Original Transaction on or before the Adjustment Date with effect from then.
(ii) With adjustment the new Securities are different from the original Purchased Securities. They are agreed by the parties on or before the Adjustment Date and their Market Value will be substantially the same as the Repurchase Price under the Original Transaction on the

Adjustment Date multiplied by the Margin Ratio applying to the Original Transaction and taking account of the Price Differential (ie, repo interest) that has accrued to the Adjustment Date.
(iii) The Replacement Transaction's Purchase Date is the Adjustment Date.
(iv) The other terms of the Replacement Transaction will be agreed by the parties on or before the Adjustment Date.
(v) The payment and delivery obligations of the parties in respect of Securities due under the Original and Replacement Transactions on the Adjustment Date are to be settled in the minimum customary time in the market concerned, and in accordance with the payment and transfer provisions of paragraph 6.

Paragraph 5

> **5. Income Payments**
> Unless otherwise agreed–
> (i) where the Term of a particular Transaction extends over an Income Payment Date in respect of any Securities subject to that Transaction, Buyer shall on the date such Income is paid by the issuer transfer to or credit to the account of Seller an amount equal to (and in the same currency as) the amount paid by the issuer;

Paragraph 5(i) provides for the payment of manufactured dividends by the Buyer to the Seller where a Transaction extends over an Income Payment Date. The amount paid equals the income paid by the issuer to the Buyer as beneficial owner of the securities and is equal to the full gross amount of the coupon.

This payment is considered fair because a repo transaction is essentially a temporary transfer of assets and the economic intention is to preserve the Seller's entitlement to income due from the issuer of the bond or equity. However, the payment means that the securities are worth less and this might lead to a margin call from the Buyer.

Please note that the Buyer does not bear the credit risk of the issuer failing to pay the coupon. The Buyer is obligated to pay the manufactured dividend to the Seller only if and when the issuer pays its coupon.

> (ii) where Margin Securities are transferred from one party ("the first party") to the other party ("the second party") and an Income Payment Date in respect of such Securities occurs before Equivalent Margin Securities are transferred by the second party to the first party, the second party shall on the date such Income is paid by the issuer transfer to or credit to the account of the first party an amount equal to (and in the same currency as) the amount paid by the issuer;
> and for the avoidance of doubt references in this paragraph to the amount of any Income paid by the issuer of any Securities shall be to an amount paid without any

> withholding or deduction for or on account of taxes or duties notwithstanding that a payment of such Income made in certain circumstances may be subject to such a withholding or deduction.

(5)(ii) Similar provisions apply to Margin Securities that are held by the Buyer over an Income Payment Date, so that there is a payment of a manufactured dividend to the party who has delivered the Margin Securities. The payment made by the issuer will be made without any deduction for withholding tax.

It is not necessary that the Buyer be entitled to receive the actual coupon because it may have repoed on the securities. In that case the Buyer must ensure that it has equivalent rights against its Buyer or a mismatch will occur.

One point to note is that, because the TBMA/ISMA GMRA is mostly intended to be used with gross paying securities when calculating the amount of the manufactured dividend, the recipient of the dividend (Buyer) may need to gross up the actual coupon paid and account for any withholding tax. It is therefore the Buyer's responsibility not to cross any Income Payment Date where a manufactured dividend may be subject to a withholding tax. It will avoid this by seeking to substitute the securities. Otherwise it will bear the risk of it.

It is this provision that may, among other things, lead to practical difficulties if the parties transact in Net Paying Securities. To do so they must amend the TBMA/ISMA GMRA to allow for these types of transactions and the payment provisions (which, read together, require a gross payment) must be amended in Annex 1.

Paragraph 6

Paragraph 6 is largely administrative in nature.

> **6. Payment and Transfer**
> (a) Unless otherwise agreed, all money paid hereunder shall be in immediately available freely convertible funds of the relevant currency. All Securities to be transferred hereunder (i) shall be in suitable form for transfer and shall be accompanied by duly executed instruments of transfer or assignment in blank (where required for transfer) and such other documentation as the transferee may reasonably request, or (ii) shall be transferred through the book entry system of Euroclear or Clearstream, or (iii) shall be transferred through any other agreed securities clearance system or (iv) shall be transferred by any other method mutually acceptable to Seller and Buyer.

(a) All money transfers shall be in cleared funds in the relevant currency. All securities transfers must be appropriately documented or may be transferred through securities clearance systems or by such other method as the parties mutually agree. Transfers through securities clearance systems are likely to be the most common route.

COMMENTARY ON THE TBMA/ISMA GMRA

> (b) Unless otherwise agreed, all money payable by one party to the other in respect of any Transaction shall be paid free and clear of, and without withholding or deduction for, any taxes or duties of whatsoever nature imposed, levied, collected, withheld or assessed by any authority having power to tax, unless the withholding or deduction of such taxes or duties is required by law. In that event, unless otherwise agreed, the paying party shall pay such additional amounts as will result in the net amounts receivable by the other party (after taking account of such withholding or deduction) being equal to such amounts as would have been received by it had no such taxes or duties been required to be withheld or deducted.

(b) The TBMA/ISMA GMRA is an international agreement and, where cross-border Transactions occur, tax authorities may impose taxes called withholding taxes on payments made under those Transactions. Where this happens and a party was due to receive a payment as payee, it would receive less than it expected. Paragraph 6(b) provides an indemnity that a payer has to increase or gross up its payment if a withholding tax is charged, so that the payee receives what it expected to receive. Generally speaking, the burden of withholding taxes usually falls on the payer.

All moneys must be paid gross, unless any withholding tax or deduction is imposed by law, whereupon the payer must gross up its payment to the payee so that the latter receives what it expected to receive.

> (c) Unless otherwise agreed in writing between the parties, under each Transaction transfer of Purchased Securities by Seller and payment of Purchase Price by Buyer against the transfer of such Purchased Securities shall be made simultaneously and transfer of Equivalent Securities by Buyer and payment of Repurchase Price payable by Seller against the transfer of such Equivalent Securities shall be made simultaneously.

(c) All transfers of Purchased Securities by the Seller on the Purchase Date and Equivalent Securities by the Buyer on the Repurchase Date must be on a simultaneous delivery-versus-payment basis on those dates.

> (d) Subject to and without prejudice to the provisions of sub-paragraph 6(c), either party may from time to time in accordance with market practice and in recognition of the practical difficulties in arranging simultaneous delivery of Securities and money waive in relation to any Transaction its rights under this Agreement to receive simultaneous transfer and/or payment provided that transfer and/or payment shall, notwithstanding such waiver, be made on the same day and provided also that no such waiver in respect of one Transaction shall affect or bind it in respect of any other Transaction.

A PRACTICAL GUIDE TO USING REPO MASTER AGREEMENTS

(d) Either party may waive the simultaneous delivery-versus-payment requirement on a transaction-by-transaction basis (no precedent is set) if market practice or practical difficulties dictate, provided that payment and delivery take place on the same day. This creates what is called "daylight risk".

> (e) The parties shall execute and deliver all necessary documents and take all necessary steps to procure that all right, title and interest in any Purchased Securities, any Equivalent Securities, any Margin Securities and any Equivalent Margin Securities shall pass to the party to which transfer is being made upon transfer of the same in accordance with this Agreement, free from all liens, claims, charges and encumbrances.

(e) The parties will do all things necessary and execute all necessary documentation to transfer absolute title to the Purchased Securities and the Equivalent Securities, and securities posted or returned as margin. Such transfers shall be free of any encumbrances. This is central to the structure of repo transactions.

> (f) Notwithstanding the use of expressions such as "*Repurchase Date*", "*Repurchase Price*", "*margin*", "*Net Margin*", "*Margin Ratio*" and "*substitution*", which are used to reflect terminology used in the market for transactions of the kind provided for in this Agreement, all right, title and interest in and to Securities and money transferred or paid under this Agreement shall pass to the transferee upon transfer or payment, the obligation of the party receiving Purchased Securities or Margin Securities being an obligation to transfer Equivalent Securities or Equivalent Margin Securities.

(f) Absolute title transfer to the transferee upon transfer or payment is basically repeated and the Buyer's/transferee's obligation to return Equivalent Securities or Equivalent Margin Securities is also recited.

> (g) Time shall be of the essence in this Agreement.

(g) This is self-explanatory. Prompt performance of obligations is expected under the TBMA/ISMA GMRA.

> (h) Subject to paragraph 10, all amounts in the same currency payable by each party to the other under any Transaction or otherwise under this Agreement on the same date shall be combined in a single calculation of a net sum payable by one party to the other and the obligation to pay that sum shall be the only obligation of either party in respect of those amounts.

(h) This provision permits settlement netting of payments of sums in the same currency due on the same day in respect of different Transactions, provided that no Event of Default in paragraph 10 has taken place. Instead of making gross payments to each other the party owing more pays the difference between the two amounts to the other.

> (i) Subject to paragraph 10, all Securities of the same issue, denomination, currency and series, transferable by each party to the other under any Transaction or hereunder on the same date shall be combined in a single calculation of a net quantity of Securities transferable by one party to the other and the obligation to transfer the net quantity of Securities shall be the only obligation of either party in respect of the Securities so transferable and receivable.

(i) Again, subject to no paragraph 10 Event of Default having taken place, this provision permits the transfer of the net amount of Securities of the same issue and currency due on the same day in respect of different Transactions. Therefore, the party with the higher number of Securities to deliver transfers the difference between the number of securities due from each side to the other party.

> (j) If the parties have specified in Annex I hereto that this paragraph 6(j) shall apply, each obligation of a party under this Agreement (other than an obligation arising under paragraph 10) is subject to the condition precedent that none of those events specified in paragraph 10(a) which are identified in Annex I hereto for the purposes of this paragraph 6(j) (being events which, upon the serving of a Default Notice, would be an Event of Default with respect to the other party) shall have occurred and be continuing with respect to the other party.

(j) Paragraph 6(j) is a new condition precedent introduced into the TBMA/ISMA GMRA. It allows a party to withhold further payments or deliveries (other than upon a termination following an Event of Default) if a potential Event of Default has occurred and continues in relation to the other party that would, if a Default Notice were given, constitute an Event of Default. The potential Events of Default are those stated in paragraph 10(a) of the TBMA/ISMA GMRA. The parties can choose in Annex I to limit the application of this provision so that it does not apply to specified potential Events of Default. Some market players have indicated, for example, that they do not wish this condition precedent to apply in the event of a failure to deliver securities (ie, the new Event of Default contained in paragraph 10(a)(ii)). Their choice might also be influenced by whether the potential Event of Default might be triggered by market rumour.

Paragraph 7

> **7. Contractual Currency**
> (a) All the payments made in respect of the Purchase Price or the Repurchase Price of any Transaction shall be made in the currency of the Purchase Price (the "Contractual Currency") save as provided in paragraph 10(c)(ii). Notwithstanding the foregoing, the payee of any money may, at its option, accept tender thereof in any other currency, provided, however, that, to the extent permitted by applicable law, the obligation of the payer to pay such money will be discharged only to the extent of the amount of the Contractual Currency that such payee may, consistent with normal banking procedures, purchase with such other currency (after deduction of any premium and costs of exchange) for delivery within the customary delivery period for spot transactions in respect of the relevant currency.

(a) All payments of the Purchase Price or the Repurchase Price shall be made in the currency of the Purchase Price (the "Contractual Currency"), except where close-out netting is involved under paragraph 10(c)(ii) and there may be Transactions in different currencies. Then conversion into the Base Currency would occur. However, the receiver of any money may accept payment in another currency, but the payer's obligations will only be discharged where the amount converted meets its full liability in the Contractual Currency.

> (b) If for any reason the amount in the Contractual Currency received by a party, including amounts received after conversion of any recovery under any judgment or order expressed in a currency other than the Contractual Currency, falls short of the amount in the Contractual Currency due and payable, the party required to make the payment will, as a separate and independent obligation, to the extent permitted by applicable law, immediately transfer such additional amount in the Contractual Currency as may be necessary to compensate for the shortfall.

(b) If the amount received after such conversion (whether in the normal course of business or after a court judgment) falls short of the amount required in the Contractual Currency, the payer will make up the shortfall.

> (c) If for any reason the amount in the Contractual Currency received by a party exceeds the amount of the Contractual Currency due and payable, the party receiving the transfer will refund promptly the amount of such excess.

(c) If, following conversion, the payee receives more than the amount owed in the Contractual Currency, it must promptly repay the surplus.

COMMENTARY ON THE TBMA/ISMA GMRA

The Contractual Currency should be distinguished from the Base Currency, which is specified in Annex I for the purpose of the TBMA/ISMA GMRA as a whole, and which is used in the calculation of close-out netting and margining.

Paragraph 8

This paragraph permits either the Seller to substitute Purchased Securities with New Purchased Securities or the Buyer to substitute Equivalent Margin Securities with New Margin Securities. Under the TBMA/ISMA GMRA substitutions are structured as contractual variations of the original repo transaction.

It is important to note that there is no right of substitution without the consent of the other party. If the party wishing to substitute had an unfettered right to substitute securities without the need for the other party's consent, then it could be argued that the party holding the securities is not holding them as absolute owner but has only a security interest in them and the other party retains ownership. In the United Kingdom this could lead a court to recharacterise the repo as a secured loan, which would have the adverse consequences referred to in Chapter 2 (pages 16–17).

If the Buyer still holds the securities and has not repoed them out, he will probably not object to the substitution.

Substitution typically allows dealers to retrieve and sell securities that have become special.

> **8. Substitution**
> (a) A Transaction may at any time between the Purchase Date and Repurchase Date, if Seller so requests and Buyer so agrees, be varied by the transfer by Buyer to Seller of Securities equivalent to the Purchased Securities, or to such of the Purchased Securities as shall be agreed, in exchange for the transfer by Seller to Buyer of other Securities of such amount and description as shall be agreed ("New Purchased Securities") (being Securities having a Market Value at the date of the variation at least equal to the Market Value of the Equivalent Securities transferred to Seller).

(a) During the life of the repo transaction the Seller may, with the Buyer's agreement, substitute New Purchased Securities of equivalent Market Value on the substitution date for all or part of the Purchased Securities originally transferred to the Buyer on the Purchase Date at the start of the repo transaction. These would be different Securities from the Purchased Securities, which the Seller may want back, for instance, to cover a short sale to a third party.

> (b) Any variation under sub-paragraph (a) above shall be effected, subject to paragraph 6(d), by the simultaneous transfer of the Equivalent Securities and New Purchased Securities concerned.

(b) Any such permitted substitution will involve a simultaneous transfer of Equivalent

A PRACTICAL GUIDE TO USING REPO MASTER AGREEMENTS

Securities for New Purchased Securities, unless a waiver is given under paragraph 6(d) if there are practical difficulties in arranging such simultaneous delivery. In that case whichever leg of the transaction is problematical will be completed later that same day.

> (c) A Transaction which is varied under sub-paragraph (a) above shall thereafter continue in effect as though the Purchased Securities under that Transaction consisted of or included the New Purchased Securities instead of the Securities in respect of which Equivalent Securities have been transferred to Seller.

(c) If a substitution takes place, the Transaction continues as if the substituted securities were the original Purchased Securities.

> (d) Where either party has transferred Margin Securities to the other party it may at any time before Equivalent Margin Securities are transferred to it under paragraph 4 request the other party to transfer Equivalent Margin Securities to it in exchange for the transfer to the other party of new Margin Securities having a Market Value at the time of transfer at least equal to that of such Equivalent Margin Securities. If the other party agrees to the request, the exchange shall be effected, subject to paragraph 6(d), by the simultaneous transfer of the Equivalent Margin Securities and new Margin Securities concerned. Where either or both of such transfers is or are effected through a settlement system in circumstances which under the rules and procedures of that settlement system give rise to a payment by or for the account of one party to or for the account of the other party, the parties shall cause such payment or payments to be made outside that settlement system, for value the same day as the payments made through that settlement system, as shall ensure that the exchange of Equivalent Margin Securities and new Margin securities effected under this sub-paragraph does not give rise to any net payment of cash by either party to the other.

(d) Sub-Paragraph (d) concerns the simultaneous substitution of Margin Securities by new Margin Securities if the transferee agrees to the transferor's request. Where this is impractical, paragraph 6(d) allows the final leg to be completed later that same day.

Paragraph 8(d) contains a provision requiring the parties to repay any cash received under settlement systems triggered by a substitution of Margin Securities. This originally related to the UK Central Gilts Office ("CGO") Assured Payment system, under which transfers of gilts automatically triggered a corresponding payment in the reverse direction equal to their value. Paragraph 8(d) effectively required the party receiving any such payment to repay it to the other party outside the CGO. This problem does not happen in Crest, which can take and make deliveries free of payment. However, it could apply to other settlement systems around the world that cannot accept deliveries free of payment.

Paragraph 9

> **9. Representations**
>
> Each party represents and warrants to the other that-
>
> (a) it is duly authorised to execute and deliver this Agreement, to enter into the Transactions contemplated hereunder and to perform its obligations hereunder and thereunder and has taken all necessary action to authorise such execution, delivery and performance;
>
> (b) it will engage in this Agreement and the Transactions contemplated hereunder (other than Agency Transactions) as principal;
>
> (c) the person signing this Agreement on its behalf is, and any person representing it in entering into a Transaction will be, duly authorised to do so on its behalf;
>
> (d) it has obtained all authorisations of any governmental or regulatory body required in connection with this Agreement and the Transactions contemplated hereunder and such authorisations are in full force and effect;
>
> (e) the execution, delivery and performance of this Agreement and the Transactions contemplated hereunder will not violate any law, ordinance, charter, by-law or rule applicable to it or any agreement by which it is bound or by which any of its assets are affected;
>
> (f) it has satisfied itself and will continue to satisfy itself as to the tax implications of the Transactions contemplated hereunder;
>
> (g) in connection with this Agreement and each Transaction–
>
> (i) unless there is a written agreement with the other party to the contrary, it is not relying on any advice (whether written or oral) of the other party, other than the representations expressly set out in this Agreement;
>
> (ii) it has made and will make its own decisions regarding the entering into of any Transaction based upon its own judgment and upon advice from such professional advisers as it has deemed it necessary to consult;
>
> (iii) it understands the terms, conditions and risks of each Transaction and is willing to assume (financially and otherwise) those risks; and
>
> (h) at the time of transfer to the other party of any Securities it will have the full and unqualified right to make such transfer and that upon such transfer of Securities the other party will receive all right, title and interest in and to those Securities free of any lien, claim, charge or encumbrance.
>
> On the date on which any Transaction is entered into pursuant hereto, and on each day on which Securities, Equivalent Securities, Margin Securities or Equivalent Margin Securities are to be transferred under any Transaction, Buyer and Seller shall each be deemed to repeat all the foregoing representations. For the avoidance of doubt and notwithstanding any arrangements which Seller or Buyer may have with any third party, each party will be liable as a principal for its obligations under this Agreement and each Transaction.

Paragraph 9 contains various important representations from the parties that, as the last sub-paragraph (h) states, are repeated on each occasion a Transaction is entered into, and on each day securities and margin are transferred.

The paragraph 9 representations made by each party to the other are:

(a) that they each have authority to enter into the TBMA/ISMA GMRA and Transactions under it, and have taken all necessary internal action to achieve this;

(b) that each party is entering into the TBMA/ISMA GMRA as principal, except for Transactions under the Agency Annex;

(c) that each person signing the TBMA/ISMA GMRA or entering into any Transaction is authorised to do so;

(d) that all governmental or regulatory authorisations to enter into the TBMA/ISMA GMRA and any Transactions have been obtained, and are in full force and effect;

(e) that the execution of the TBMA/ISMA GMRA and any Transactions do not violate any laws, rules or agreement by which one of the parties are bound or their assets affected;

(f) that each party has done and will continue to do its due diligence on the tax implications of the repo and buy/sellbacks under the TBMA/ISMA GMRA;

(g) that they enter into the "non-reliance" representation shown not relying on any advice from their counterparty; they have made their own independent decision to enter into Transactions, with or without professional advice, and they understand and are willing to assume the risks of any Transaction;

(h) that any Securities they transfer to their counterparty are transferred with full legal title free from any circumstances and the transferee will receive such Securities in that manner. This is, of course, vital, as repo transactions are based upon a sale and repurchase of the Securities.

The representations are repeated when Transactions are entered into and on each day that securities or margin are transferred.

The final sentence of the last sub-paragraph (h) protects a party if its counterparty is acting as agent for an undisclosed principal. Since the Agency Annex prohibits agency trading for undisclosed principals, such agent is here treated as if it were the principal and is liable as such.

Paragraph 10

Compared with Section 6 of the ISDA Master Agreement, the close-out netting mechanism of paragraph 10 is relatively straightforward.

The events that give rise to an Event of Default (of which there are 10) under the TBMA/ISMA GMRA cover the usual range of events, although it should be noted that there is no cross-default provision and no credit-related Event of Default. Default Notices are required except for the presentation of a winding-up petition in a bankruptcy, when termination is automatic. Events of Default can affect either party and involve the termination of all Transactions under the Agreement.

There are no grace periods for Events of Default except for the last one.

The consequences of an Event of Default are that:

- all outstanding transactions are accelerated immediately;
- securities margin held by the Defaulting Party has to be returned to the non-Defaulting Party and Cash Margin plus accrued interest becomes immediately repayable;
- the non-Defaulting Party calculates the Default Market Value of securities to be transferred;
- each party's obligations are valued and converted into a monetary figure;
- these monetary figures are set off against each other and only the net balance is payable by the party owing the higher figure; and

- the Defaulting Party will be liable for the non-Defaulting Party's expenses plus interest in connection with enforcement following the Event of Default.

Of course, an Event of Default is a serious matter and the non-Defaulting Party will carefully consider whether or not it wishes to trigger it by issuing a Default Notice (necessary in most cases). It has the option to do so, but is not compelled to do so.

Paragraph 10(a)

> **10. Events of Default**
> (a) If any of the following events (each an "Event of Default") occurs in relation to either party (the "Defaulting Party", the other party being the "non-Defaulting Party") whether acting as Seller or Buyer–
> (i) Buyer fails to pay the Purchase Price upon the applicable Purchase Date or Seller fails to pay the Repurchase Price upon the applicable Repurchase Date, and the non-Defaulting Party serves a Default Notice on the Defaulting Party; or

(a)(i) The first Event of Default concerns actions at the heart of a repo transaction. In sub-paragraph (a) an Event of Default occurs when the Buyer fails to pay the Purchase Price for the Purchased Securities on the Purchase Date, or when the Seller fails to repay the Repurchase Price for the Equivalent Securities on the Repurchase Date at the end of the repo transaction. If either of these events were to happen, the non-Defaulting Party must serve a Default Notice on the Defaulting Party to trigger the close-out process.

> (ii) if the parties have specified in Annex I hereto that this sub-paragraph shall apply, Seller fails to deliver Purchased Securities on the Purchase Date or Buyer fails to deliver Equivalent Securities on the Repurchase Date, and the non-Defaulting Party serves a Default Notice on the Defaulting Party; or

(a)(ii) This Event of Default applies to deliveries – a failure by the Seller to deliver Purchased Securities to the Buyer on the Purchase Date, or a failure by the Buyer to deliver Equivalent Securities to the Seller on the Repurchase Date. Again, a Default Notice needs to be sent by the non-Defaulting Party.

Paragraph 10(a)(ii) is optional and will apply only if the parties specifically agree to apply it in Annex 1. Some market players wanted to be able to call an Event of Default where the other party fails to deliver Securities. In the discussions leading up to the inclusion of this provision it was recognised that "settlement fails" frequently occur in the market, and that their occurrence is not generally an indicator of credit deterioration or indeed impending insolvency of the delivering party. For that reason some market players were reluctant to include this new Event of Default. Those favouring its inclusion believed strongly that there could be circumstances in which a failure to deliver is in fact a first indicator of credit deterioration or impending insolvency, although they recognised that this would not generally be the context in which a failure to deliver occurred. They wished, however, to be able to act upon the occurrence of a failure to deliver where they saw it occurring in such contexts. Please note that the mini close-out arrangements in paragraphs 10(g) and (h) remain available as an alternative to paragraph 10(a)(ii).

In fact, a similar provision to this appeared in the 1992 version of the PSA/ISMA GMRA, but was deleted from the 1995 version.

> (iii) Seller or Buyer fails to pay when due any sum payable under sub-paragraph (g) or (h) below, and the non-Defaulting Party serves a Default Notice on the Defaulting Party; or

(a)(iii) Sub-paragraphs 10(g) and (h) are the mini close-out provisions, under which individual Transactions are closed out when there is a failure to deliver. Here in (iii) any failure to make a compensatory payment under those provisions following a close-out will constitute an Event of Default and will terminate all Transactions under the TBMA/ISMA GMRA. Again, the non-Defaulting Party must send a Default Notice.

> (iv) Seller or Buyer fails to comply with paragraph 4 and the non-Defaulting Party serves a Default Notice on the Defaulting Party; or

(a)(iv) It shall be an Event of Default if the Buyer or the Seller fails to comply with the margin maintenance provisions of paragraph 4. A Default Notice is again required from the non-Defaulting Party.

> (v) Seller or Buyer fails to comply with paragraph 5 and the non-Defaulting Party serves a Default Notice on the Defaulting Party; or

(a)(v) The fifth Event of Default arises when the Buyer, or less likely the Seller, fails to comply with the manufactured dividend provisions of paragraph 5 (ie, passing on in full the equivalent of income received from the issuer of the bond or equity to the other party in respect of Purchased Securities or Margin Securities). Again, the non-Defaulting Party needs to send a Default Notice to the Defaulting Party.

> (vi) an Act of Insolvency occurs with respect to Seller or Buyer and (except in the case of an Act of Insolvency which is the presentation of a petition for winding-up or any analogous proceeding or the appointment of a liquidator or analogous officer of the Defaulting Party in which case no such notice shall be required) the non-Defaulting Party serves a Default Notice on the Defaulting Party; or

(a)(vi) An Event of Default occurs if an Act of Insolvency afflicts the Buyer or the Seller. A Default Notice is again needed from the non-Defaulting Party, except where the presentation of a winding-up petition or the appointment of a liquidator is involved. These exceptions give rise to automatic close-out under the TBMA/ISMA GMRA.

> (vii) any representations made by Seller or Buyer are incorrect or untrue in any material respect when made or repeated or deemed to have been made or repeated, and the non-Defaulting Party serves a Default Notice on the Defaulting Party; or

(a)(vii) This is a material misrepresentation Event of Default, again requiring a Default Notice from the non-Defaulting Party.

> (viii) Seller or Buyer admits to the other that it is unable to, or intends not to, perform any of its obligations hereunder and/or in respect of any Transaction and the non-Defaulting Party serves a Default Notice on the Defaulting Party; or

(a)(viii) This Event of Default occurs when the Buyer or the Seller admits that it cannot or does not intend to perform its obligations under the TBMA/ISMA GMRA or in respect of any Transaction. This would also cover repudiation of Transactions or the TBMA/ISMA GMRA. Such repudiation need not be in writing to trigger this Event of Default. Again, a Default Notice needs to be given by the non-Defaulting Party.

> (ix) Seller or Buyer is suspended or expelled from membership of or participation in any securities exchange or association or other self regulating organisation, or suspended from dealing in securities by any government agency, or any of the assets of either Seller or Buyer or the assets of investors held by, or to the order of, Seller or Buyer are transferred or ordered to be transferred to a trustee by a regulatory authority pursuant to any securities regulating legislation and the non-Defaulting Party serves a Default Notice on the Defaulting Party; or

(a)(ix) This Event of Default is triggered by the non-Defaulting Party serving a Default Notice on the Defaulting Party after the Buyer or the Seller:

- has been suspended or expelled from a stock exchange or other self-regulatory organisations; or
- has been suspended by a government agency from dealing in securities; or
- has had its assets or those of investors held by it transferred to a trustee appointed by a competent regulatory authority invoking securities regulations or law.

> (x) Seller or Buyer fails to perform any other of its obligations hereunder and does not remedy such failure within 30 days after notice is given by the non-Defaulting Party requiring it to do so, and the non-Defaulting Party serves a Default Notice on the Defaulting Party;
> then sub-paragraphs (b) to (f) below shall apply.

(a)(x) This final Event of Default catches failure by the Buyer or the Seller in performing any of its other obligations under the TBMA/ISMA GMRA and its subsequent failure to remedy this within 30 days following a notice from the non-Defaulting Party. Where such a failure occurs, the non-Defaulting Party will issue a Default Notice to the Defaulting Party.

Paragraph 10(b)

> (b) The Repurchase Date for each Transaction hereunder shall be deemed immediately to occur and, subject to the following provisions, all Cash Margin (including interest accrued) shall be immediately repayable and Equivalent Margin Securities shall be immediately deliverable (and so that, where this sub-paragraph applies, performance of the respective obligations of the parties with respect to the delivery of Securities, the payment of the Repurchase Prices for any Equivalent Securities and the repayment of any Cash Margin shall be effected only in accordance with the provisions of sub-paragraph (c) below).

With the Default Notice having been issued by the non-Defaulting Party to the Defaulting Party, the parties move into early termination of all Transactions under sub-paragraphs (b) to (f) of paragraph 10.

The effect of an Event of Default is to bring forward the Repurchase Date and terminate all transactions under the TBMA/ISMA GMRA. The date for delivery of Cash Margin (including accrued interest) and the return of Equivalent Margin Securities is also accelerated, and the performance of the parties' obligations in respect of these matters can take place only in accordance with the provisions of 10(c). The advantage of this acceleration is that the risk of adverse price movements in the Purchased Securities is reduced.

Paragraph 10(c)

> (c) (i) The Default Market Values of the Equivalent Securities and any Equivalent Margin Securities to be transferred, the amount of any Cash Margin (including the amount of interest accrued) to be transferred and the Repurchase Prices to be paid by each party shall be established by the non-Defaulting Party for all Transactions as at the Repurchase Date; and
> (ii) on the basis of the sums so established, an account shall be taken (as at the Repurchase Date) of what is due from each party to the other under this Agreement
> ⟫→

COMMENTARY ON THE TBMA/ISMA GMRA

> (on the basis that each party's claim against the other in respect of the transfer to it of Equivalent Securities or Equivalent Margin Securities under this Agreement equals the Default Market Value therefor) and the sums due from one party shall be set off against the sums due from the other and only the balance of the account shall be payable (by the party having the claim valued at the lower amount pursuant to the foregoing) and such balance shall be due and payable on the next following Business Day. For the purposes of this calculation, all sums not denominated in the Base Currency shall be converted into the Base Currency on the relevant date at the Spot Rate prevailing at the relevant time.

(c)(i) Each party's positions in respect of Equivalent Securities, Equivalent Margin Securities, Cash Margin (including accrued interest) and Repurchase Prices to be paid in respect of all Transactions between them shall be converted into a cash sum by the non-Defaulting Party, as at the Repurchase Date (ie, the date on which these close-out calculations are made). It is important to note that the parties' obligations are reduced to a net cash sum. It is not possible to set off claims for the delivery of securities against claims for the payment of money.

(c)(ii) On the basis of these calculations the non-Defaulting Party will then net off the amounts due to and from each party (on the basis of their Default Market Values), and arrive at a single net figure payable by the party with the lower valuation for its Transactions on the following Business Day. If Transactions are in different currencies, these will be converted into the Base Currency at the prevailing Spot Rate.

Effective close-out netting helps prevent "cherry picking" by the liquidator of an insolvent counterparty. Under the Insolvency Rules (1986) a liquidator may disclaim an onerous contract (for example, one that is not profitable to an insolvent Seller). This would leave a non-defaulting Buyer having a damages claim for loss (for the contract was profitable to the Buyer), which may be recovered only by proving with the other unsecured creditors in the winding-up of the Seller. Obviously the Buyer will receive only a partial payment in relation to the damages claim, as the Seller is insolvent (its assets cannot meet the claims against it).

If the liquidator can cherry pick, then it disclaims the unprofitable contracts, but requires the Buyer to perform the profitable contracts. Thus, the Buyer cannot net off its exposure under the profitable and unprofitable contracts. Because close-out netting terminates all Transactions and converts the gross obligations of the parties to a single net sum, it defeats cherry picking, which can operate only in relation to amounts under more than one Transaction.

Paragraph 10(d)

> (d) For the purposes of this Agreement, the "Default Market Value" of any Equivalent Securities or Equivalent Margin Securities shall be determined in accordance with sub-paragraph (e) below, and for this purpose –

> (i) the "Appropriate Market" means, in relation to Securities of any description, the market which is the most appropriate market for Securities of that description, as determined by the non-Defaulting Party;
> (ii) the "Default Valuation Time" means, in, relation to an Event of Default, the close of business in the Appropriate Market on the fifth dealing day after the day on which that Event of Default occurs or, where that Event of Default is the occurrence of an Act of Insolvency in respect of which under paragraph 10(a) no notice is required from the non-Defaulting Party in order for such event to constitute an Event of Default, the close of business on the fifth dealing day after the day on, which the non-Defaulting Party first became aware of the occurrence of such Event of Default;

This lists various factors determining the Default Market Value of any Equivalent Securities or Equivalent Margin Securities in accordance with paragraph 10(c). These are:

(i) Appropriate Market. This means that the non-Defaulting Party determines the most relevant market for obtaining prices from dealers for the Securities that are the subject of close-out valuation.

(ii) Default Valuation Time. Where an Act of Insolvency has occurred, this is the close of business on the fifth dealing day after the non-Defaulting Party first becomes aware of the Act of Insolvency. With other Events of Default it is the close of business on the fifth dealing day in the Appropriate Market (determined by the non-Defaulting Party) after the Event of Default happens.

Under the 1995 PSA/ISMA GMRA, in the event of a close-out following an Event of Default, for the purposes of the close-out calculation Securities were valued either at the price at which a non-Defaulting Party dealt in the two Business Days following notice of an Event of Default. or at the close of business one (or, in certain cases, two) dealing day(s) following the day on which the Event of Default occurred.

Because of concerns that these provisions were not flexible enough, the TBMA/ISMA GMRA allows the non-Defaulting Party to calculate the close-out amount by reference to an actual sale or purchase price, or, if the non-Defaulting Party chooses, the market value of the Securities, in either case at any time during the five dealing days following the occurrence of the Event of Default, if a Default Notice is served, or five dealing days after the non-Defaulting Party becomes aware of a bankruptcy Event of Default. (As with the PSA/ISMA GMRA, Transaction Costs are also taken into account.)

> (iii) "Deliverable Securities" means Equivalent Securities or Equivalent Margin Securities to be delivered by the Defaulting Party;

(iii) Deliverable Securities are Securities that the Defaulting Party has to deliver to the non-Defaulting Party on the accelerated Repurchase Date.

COMMENTARY ON THE TBMA/ISMA GMRA

> (iv) "Net Value" means at any time, in relation to any Deliverable Securities or Receivable Securities, the amount which, in the reasonable opinion of the non-Defaulting Party, represents their fair market value, having regard to such pricing sources and methods (which may include, without limitation, available prices for Securities with similar maturities, terms and credit characteristics as the relevant Equivalent Securities or Equivalent Margin Securities) as the non-Defaulting Party considers appropriate, less, in the case of Receivable Securities, or plus, in the case of Deliverable Securities, all Transaction Costs which would be incurred in connection with the purchase or sale of such Securities;

(iv) Net Value refers to Securities that are deliverable by the Buyer or the Seller on the accelerated Repurchase Date and have been valued at their fair market value reasonably determined by the non-Defaulting Party. The non-Defaulting Party may use prices for similar Securities in calculating the Net Value, if it deems this appropriate. Transaction Costs are deducted from Securities deliverable by the non-Defaulting Party to the Defaulting Party on the accelerated Repurchase Date, but they are added to Securities deliverable by the Defaulting Party to the non-Defaulting Party on the accelerated Repurchase Date.

> (v) "Receivable Securities" means Equivalent Securities or Equivalent Margin Securities to be delivered to the Defaulting Party; and

(v) Receivable Securities are those are deliverable by the non-Defaulting Party to the Defaulting Party on the accelerated Repurchase Date.

> (vi) "Transaction Costs" in relation to any transaction contemplated in paragraph 10(d) or (e) means the reasonable costs, commission, fees and expenses (including any mark-up or mark-down) that would be incurred in connection with the purchase of Deliverable Securities or sale of Receivable Securities, calculated on the assumption that the aggregate thereof is the least that could reasonably be expected to be paid in order to carry out the transaction;

(vi) Transaction Costs include costs, fees, commission or expenses reasonably chargeable in respect of the purchase of Deliverable Securities by the Defaulting Party, or incurred in the sale of Receivable Securities by the non-Defaulting Party for delivery to the other party on the accelerated Repurchase Date.

Paragraphs 10(e)(i) and 10(e)(i)(A)

> (e)(i) If between the occurrence of the relevant Event of Default and the Default Valuation Time the non-Defaulting Party gives to the Defaulting Party a written notice (a "Default Valuation Notice") which–
>
> (A) states that, since the occurrence of the relevant Event of Default, the non-Defaulting Party has sold, in the case of Receivable Securities, or purchased, in the case of Deliverable Securities, Securities which form part of the same issue and are of an identical type and description as those Equivalent Securities or Equivalent Margin Securities, and that the non-Defaulting Party elects to treat as the Default Market Value–
>
> (aa) in the case of Receivable Securities, the net proceeds of such sale after deducting all reasonable costs, fees and expenses incurred in connection therewith (provided that, where the Securities sold are not identical in amount to the Equivalent Securities or Equivalent Margin Securities, the non-Defaulting Party may either (x) elect to treat such net proceeds of sale divided by the amount of Securities sold and multiplied by the amount of the Equivalent Securities or Equivalent Margin Securities as the Default Market Value or (y) elect to treat such net proceeds of sale of the Equivalent Securities or Equivalent Margin Securities actually sold as the Default Market Value of that proportion of the Equivalent Securities or Equivalent Margin Securities, and, in the case of (y), the Default Market Value of the balance of the Equivalent Securities or Equivalent Margin Securities shall be determined separately in accordance with the provisions of this paragraph 10(e) and accordingly may be the subject of a separate notice (or notices) under this paragraph 10(e)(i)); or
>
> (bb) in the case of Deliverable Securities, the aggregate cost of such purchase, including all reasonable costs, fees and expenses incurred in connection therewith (provided that, where the Securities purchased are not identical in amount to the Equivalent Securities or Equivalent Margin Securities, the non-Defaulting Party may either (x) elect to treat such aggregate cost divided by the amount of Securities sold and multiplied by the amount of the Equivalent Securities or Equivalent Margin Securities as the Default Market Value or (y) elect to treat the aggregate cost of purchasing the Equivalent Securities or Equivalent Margin Securities actually purchased as the Default Market Value of that proportion of the Equivalent Securities or Equivalent Margin Securities, and, in the case of (y), the Default Market Value of the balance of the Equivalent Securities or Equivalent Margin Securities shall be determined separately in accordance with the provisions of this paragraph 10(e) and accordingly may be the subject of a separate notice (or notices) under this paragraph 10(e)(i));

The non-Defaulting Party may give one of a number of Default Valuation Notices to the Defaulting Party.

Under 10(e)(i)(A) such a notice will base the Default Market Value of the Transactions on the actual sale or purchase price of a transaction made in the same securities in the market by the non-Defaulting Party, and adjusted for Transaction Costs between the time the Event of Default happened and the Default Valuation Time (ie, the close of business on the fifth dealing day in the Appropriate Market after the Event of Default occurred). Receivable Securities are Securities that the non-Defaulting Party must deliver to the Defaulting Party on close-out and Deliverable Securities are those that the Defaulting Party must deliver to the non-Defaulting Party at the same time. Any balance of securities not covered by this will be dealt with separately under the close-out process. Under this arrangement the non-Defaulting Party's real market trades during this five-dealing-day period serve as a benchmark for the Default Market Value. It can use that figure for all the same securities or *pro rata* just on those that it needs to terminate. With large blocks of securities the prices obtained over those five dealing days will vary. The five dealing days are useful for liquidating large blocks of securities. A non-Defaulting Party might well sell the securities repoed to it by the Defaulting Party, in order to protect its position after an Event of Default.

Paragraph 10(e)(i)(B)

> (B) states that the non-Defaulting Party has received, in the case of Deliverable Securities, offer quotations or, in the case of Receivable Securities, bid quotations in respect of Securities of the relevant description from two or more market makers or regular dealers in the Appropriate Market in a commercially reasonable size (as determined by the non-Defaulting Party) and specifies–
> (aa) the price or prices quoted by each of them for, in the case of Deliverable Securities, the sale by the relevant market marker or dealer of such Securities or, in the case of Receivable Securities, the purchase by the relevant market maker or dealer of such Securities;
> (bb) the Transaction Costs which would be incurred in connection with such a transaction; and
> (cc) that the non-Defaulting Party elects to treat the price so quoted (or, where more than one price is so quoted, the arithmetic mean of the prices so quoted), after deducting, in the case of Receivable Securities, or adding, in the case of Deliverable Securities, such Transaction Costs, as the Default Market Value of the relevant Equivalent Securities or Equivalent Margin Securities; or

Under 10(e)(i)(B) the non-Defaulting Party would send a Default Valuation Notice to the Defaulting Party stating that it has received bid quotations for securities to be delivered by the Defaulting Party, or that it has received offer quotations for securities that it must deliver to the Defaulting Party from two or more dealers in the Appropriate Market for a commercially reasonable-sized block of such securities. The Notice will specify the quotations received and any Transaction Costs. The non-Defaulting Party then states that it will take the arithmetic mean of such quotations plus the Transaction Costs in relation to Deliverable Securities and minus them in respect of Receivable Securities.

Paragraphs 10(e)(i)(C) and 10(e)(ii)

> (C) states –
> (aa) that either (x) acting in good faith, the non-Defaulting Party has endeavoured but been unable to sell or purchase Securities in accordance with sub-paragraph (i)(A) above or to obtain quotations in accordance with sub-paragraph (i)(B) above (or both) or (y) the non-Defaulting Party has determined that it would not be commercially reasonable to obtain such quotations, or that it would not be commercially reasonable to use any quotations which it has obtained under sub-paragraph (i)(B) above; and
> (bb) that the non-Defaulting Party has determined the Net Value of the relevant Equivalent Securities or Equivalent Margin Securities (which shall be specified) and that the non-Defaulting Party elects to treat such Net Value as the Default Market Value of the relevant Equivalent Securities or Equivalent Margin Securities,
> then the Default Market Value of the relevant Equivalent Securities or Equivalent Margin Securities shall be an amount equal to the Default Market Value specified in accordance with (A), (B)(cc) or, as the case may be, (C)(bb) above.
> (ii) If by the Default Valuation Time the non-Defaulting Party has not given a Default Valuation Notice, the Default Market Value of the relevant Equivalent Securities or Equivalent Margin Securities shall be an amount equal to their Net Value at the Default Valuation Time; provided that, if at the Default Valuation Time the non-Defaulting Party reasonably determines that, owing to circumstances affecting the market in the Equivalent Securities or Equivalent Margin Securities in question, it is not possible for the non-Defaulting Party to determine a Net Value of such Equivalent Securities or Equivalent Margin Securities which is commercially reasonable, the Default Market Value of such Equivalent Securities or Equivalent Margin Securities shall be an amount equal to their Net Value as determined by the non-Defaulting Party as soon as reasonably practicable after the Default Valuation Time.

Under paragraph 10(e)(i)(C) the non-Defaulting Party may send a Default Valuation Notice to the Defaulting Party stating that, acting in good faith, it has been unable to buy or sell securities under (e)(i)(A) or obtain quotations under (e)(i)(B). Alternatively, the non-Defaulting Party may state that it believes that it would not be commercially reasonable to obtain quotations (eg, where the position is so large that this will materially affect the quotations that could be obtained), or that it is not commercially reasonable to use the quotations obtained (eg, where the securities are very illiquid and there is considerable disparity between the quotations obtained). The non-Defaulting Party may instead determine the market value to be the Net Value of the Securities. Net Value is a fair market value reasonably determined by the non-Defaulting Party, and derived from such pricing sources and based on such pricing methods as the non-Defaulting Party thinks appropriate. If the non-Defaulting Party has not given a Default Valuation Notice by the Default Valuation Time, then the Net Value of the securities at the Default Valuation Time will be used. If a commercially reasonable Net Value is still not determinable at the end of the five-day dealing period, the Net Value shall be calculated by the non-Defaulting Party as soon as reasonably practicable thereafter.

Paragraph 10(f)

> (f) The Defaulting Party shall be liable to the non-Defaulting Party for the amount of all reasonable legal and other professional expenses incurred by the non-Defaulting Party in connection with or as a consequence of an Event of Default, together with interest thereon at LIBOR or, in the case of an expense attributable to a particular Transaction the Pricing Rate for the relevant Transaction if that Pricing Rate is greater than LIBOR.

Paragraph 10(f) states that the Defaulting Party will be liable to the non-Defaulting Party for its legal and professional expenses in protecting its position following an Event of Default, together with interest at one-month LIBOR from the Event of Default date until close-out, or at the Pricing Rate for any particular Transaction if that is higher than one-month LIBOR.

Paragraph 10(g)

> (g) If Seller fails to deliver Purchased Securities to Buyer on the applicable Purchase Date Buyer may-
> (i) if it has paid the Purchase Price to Seller, require Seller immediately to repay the sum so paid;
> (ii) if Buyer has a Transaction Exposure to Seller in respect of the relevant Transaction, require Seller from time to time to pay Cash Margin at least equal to such Transaction Exposure;
> (iii) at any time while such failure continues, terminate the Transaction by giving written notice to Seller. On such termination the obligations of Seller and Buyer with respect to delivery of Purchased Securities and Equivalent Securities shall terminate and Seller shall pay to Buyer an amount equal to the excess of the Repurchase Price at the date of Termination over the Purchase Price.

Paragraphs 10(g) and (h) are the TBMA/ISMA GMRA's mini close-out provisions. Under paragraph (g), if the Seller fails to deliver securities to the Buyer on the Purchase Date the Buyer may:
(i) demand immediate repayment of the Purchase Price;
(ii) demand payment of Cash Margin if a Transaction Exposure has arisen; or
(iii) terminate the Transaction concerned by written notice to the Seller.

Mini close-out provisions may close out individual Transactions where delivery has failed to be made. Where it is agreed that a payment will be made (ie, repayment of the Purchase Price or payment of Cash Margin), but such a payment is not made, it will constitute an Event of Default under paragraph 10(a)(iii) and, with the subsequent issuance of a Default Notice by the non-Defaulting Party, would lead to termination of all Transactions under the TBMA/ISMA GMRA.

If the Buyer chooses to terminate the transaction, the Seller remains liable to account for repo interest accrued on the cash up to the date of termination, even if the Purchase Price was not actually paid.

Paragraph 10(h)

> (h) If Buyer fails to deliver Equivalent Securities to Seller on the applicable Repurchase Date Seller may
> (i) if it has paid the Repurchase Price to Buyer, require Buyer immediately to repay the sum so paid;
> (ii) if Seller has a Transaction Exposure to Buyer in respect of the relevant Transaction, require Buyer from time to time to pay Cash Margin at least equal to such Transaction Exposure;
> (iii) at any time while such failure continues, by written notice to Buyer declare that that Transaction (but only that Transaction) shall be terminated immediately in accordance with sub-paragraph (c) above (disregarding for this purpose references in that sub-paragraph to transfer of Cash Margin and delivery of Equivalent Margin Securities and as if references to the Repurchase Date were to the date on which notice was given under this subparagraph).

Paragraph 10(h) gives corresponding rights to the Seller if the Buyer fails to redeliver securities on the Repurchase Date. Then the Seller may:
(i) demand immediate repayment of the Repurchase Price if made by the Seller; or
(ii) demand payment of Cash Margin if a Transaction Exposure has arisen; or
(iii) terminate the Transaction concerned by written notice to the Buyer.
Paragraph 10(h) has been revised to clarify that, where a mini close-out occurs, the period for determining the value of the relevant securities for the purposes of the mini close-out calculation commences at the time the mini close-out notice is given.

Paragraphs 10(i) and 10(j)

> (i) The provisions of this Agreement constitute a complete statement of the remedies available to each party in respect of any Event of Default.
> (j) Subject to paragraph 10(k), neither party may claim any sum by way of consequential loss or damage in the event of a failure by the other party to perform any of its obligations under this Agreement.

The TBMA/ISMA GMRA specifically provides that it contains a complete statement of all remedies if an Event of Default occurs and that the parties waive any other legal rights they may have. Furthermore, neither party is entitled to claim any sum by way of consequential loss or damage. This provision was included in the 1995 PSA/ISMA GMRA because it was not covered in the 1992 Agreement and market players were concerned that they could face potentially unlimited liability if failures occurred along a chain of repo deals, to those further down the chain. Particular concerns related to delivery fines for futures trades where a trader expected to receive securities under a repo in order to meet an obligation under a futures contract.

Paragraph 10(k)

> (k)(i) Subject to sub-paragraph (ii) below, if as a result of a Transaction terminating before its agreed Repurchase Date under paragraphs 10(b), 10(g)(iii) or 10(h)(iii), the non-Defaulting Party, in the case of paragraph 10(b), Buyer, in the case of paragraph 10(g)(iii), or Seller, in the case of paragraph 10(h)(iii), (in each case the "first party") incurs any loss or expense in entering into replacement transactions, the other party shall be required to pay to the first party the amount determined by the first party in good faith to be equal to the loss or expense incurred in connection with such replacement transactions (including all fees, costs and other expenses) less the amount of any profit or gain made by that party in connection with such replacement transactions; provided that if that calculation results in a negative number, an amount equal to that number shall be payable by the first party to the other party.
>
> (ii) If the first party reasonably decides, instead of entering into such replacement transactions, to replace or unwind any hedging transactions which the first party entered into in connection with the Transaction so terminating, or to enter into any replacement hedging transactions, the other party shall be required to pay to the first party the amount determined by the first party in good faith to be equal to the loss or expense incurred in connection with entering into such replacement or unwinding (including all fees, costs and other expenses) less the amount of any profit or gain made by that party in connection with such replacement or unwinding; provided that if that calculation results in a negative number, an amount equal to that number shall be payable by the first party to the other party.

This paragraph was not included in the PSA/ISMA GMRA. It enables a non-Defaulting Party to claim the costs associated either with entering into replacement transactions or new hedges, or with unwinding existing hedges in respect of all transactions where there is an Event of Default, or in respect of individual Transactions in a mini close-out. The hedging cost must not exceed the cost of an appropriate replacement transaction. Where any profits are made by the non-Defaulting Party during this process, they are deducted from the costs incurred on the other replacement or hedging Transactions.

Paragraph 10(l)

> (l) Each party shall immediately notify the other if an Event of Default, or an event which, upon the serving of a Default Notice, would be an Event of Default, occurs in relation to it.

Finally, in this paragraph each party agrees to notify the other if it experiences an actual or potential Event of Default.

Paragraph 11

Paragraph 11 allows for termination of tax-affected transactions. This would be the case where a withholding tax was introduced or if a previous gross paying regime changed to a net paying regime on its securities.

> **11. Tax Event**
> (a) This paragraph shall apply if either party notifies the other that
> (i) any action taken by a taxing authority or brought in a court of competent jurisdiction (regardless of whether such action is taken or brought with respect to a party to this Agreement); or
> (ii) a change in the fiscal or regulatory regime (including, but not limited to, a change in law or in the general interpretation of law but excluding any change in any rate of tax),
> has or will, in the notifying party's reasonable opinion, have a material adverse effect on that party in the context of a Transaction.

Paragraph 11(a) applies where one party to the TBMA/ISMA GMRA notifies the other that there is a change in tax law, or any action is taken by a tax authority or court that has a material adverse effect on the notifying party in relation to a particular Transaction.

> (b) If so requested by the other party, the notifying party will furnish the other with an opinion of a suitably qualified adviser that an event referred to in sub-paragraph (a)(i) or (ii) above has occurred and affects the notifying party.
> (c) Where this paragraph applies, the party giving the notice referred to in sub-paragraph (a) may, subject to sub-paragraph (d) below, terminate the Transaction with effect from a date specified in the notice, not being earlier (unless so agreed by the other party) than 30 days after the date of the notice, by nominating that date as the Repurchase Date.

Under these sub-paragraphs the other party may request the notifying party to produce a legal or tax opinion confirming the events in paragraph 10(a)(i) or (ii) and stating how they affect the notifying party. Assuming that the notifying party's concerns are justified, whether or not an opinion is requested, the notifying party may give at least 30 days' notice to terminate that Transaction by bringing forward the Repurchase Date.

> (d) If the party receiving the notice referred to in sub-paragraph (a) so elects, it may override that notice by giving a counter-notice to the other party. If a counter-notice is given, the party which gives the counter-notice will be deemed to have agreed to indemnify the other party against the adverse effect referred to in sub-paragraph (a) so far as relates to the relevant Transaction and the original Repurchase Date will continue to apply.

If such a choice is made, the other party may override the election by giving a counter-notice, but the giving of such a counter-notice constitutes an agreement to indemnify the notifying party against the adverse effect that it has suffered insofar as it relates to the Transaction at issue. In these circumstances the original Repurchase Date remains unchanged.

> (e) Where a Transaction is terminated as described in this paragraph, the party which has given the notice to terminate shall indemnify the other party against any reasonable legal and other professional expenses incurred by the other party by reason of the termination, but the other party may not claim any sum by way of consequential loss or damage in respect of a termination in accordance with this paragraph.

If the Transaction is terminated by the notifying party, the other party has no entitlement to claim any sum for consequential loss or damage, but shall be indemnified by the notifying party against reasonable legal and professional expenses incurred by it because of the termination.

> (f) This paragraph is without prejudice to paragraph 6(b) (obligation to pay additional amounts if withholding or deduction required); but an obligation to pay such additional amounts may, where appropriate, be a circumstance which causes this paragraph to apply.

Paragraph 11 is without prejudice to the withholding tax gross up obligations of paragraph 6(b), but such obligations could in themselves bring paragraph 11 into play.

It is interesting to note that the Italian Annex specifically provides that the change for Italian bonds from a net paying regime to a gross paying regime does not trigger a Tax Event under paragraph 11.

Paragraph 12

> **12. Interest**
> To the extent permitted by applicable law, if any sum of money payable hereunder or under any Transaction is not paid when due, interest shall accrue on the unpaid sum as a separate debt at the greater of the Pricing Rate for the Transaction to which such sum relates (where such sum is referable to a Transaction) and LIBOR on a 360 day basis or 365 day basis in accordance with the applicable ISMA convention, for the actual number of days during the period from and including the date on which payment was due to, but excluding, the date of payment.

This paragraph provides for interest to accrue on late payments at the higher of the Pricing Rate or one-month LIBOR on a 360-day or 365-day count convention from, and including, the date the payment was due to, but excluding, the date it was actually paid.

Paragraph 13

> **13. Single Agreement**
> Each party acknowledges that, and has entered into this Agreement and will enter into each Transaction hereunder in consideration of and in reliance upon the fact that all Transactions hereunder constitute a single business and contractual relationship and are made in consideration of each other. Accordingly, each party agrees (i) to perform all of its obligations in respect of each Transaction hereunder and that a default in the performance of any such obligations shall constitute a default by it in respect of all Transactions hereunder, and (ii) that payments, deliveries and other transfers made by either of them in respect of any Transaction shall be deemed to have been made in consideration of payments, deliveries and other transfers in respect of any other Transactions hereunder.

This paragraph presents the single agreement concept and states that the parties have relied upon it when entering into Transactions. It also stresses that a default under any one Transaction will constitute a default with respect to all other Transactions under the TBMA/ISMA GMRA between the parties. Therefore, all Transactions are interdependent upon each other. They form a single contractual relationship and are made in consideration of each other.

This paragraph is intended to ensure that, if the close-out netting provisions are unenforceable in any jurisdiction, the non-Defaulting Party may try to prevent the liquidator concerned from cherry picking. Paragraph 13 should force a liquidator to disclaim either all or no Transactions, but it is untested in the courts.

This important provision appears late in the main text of the TBMA/ISMA GMRA. In the ISDA Master Agreement it appears in Section 1(c).

Paragraph 14

> **14. Notices and Other Communications**
> (a) Any notice or other communication to be given under this Agreement–
> (i) shall be in the English language, and except where expressly otherwise provided in this Agreement, shall be in writing;
> (ii) may be given in any manner described in sub-paragraphs (b) and (c) below;
> (iii) shall be sent to the party to whom it is to be given at the address or number, or in accordance with the electronic messaging details, set out in Annex I hereto.
> (b) Subject to sub-paragraph (c) below, any such notice or other communication shall be effective–
> (i) if in writing and delivered in person or by courier, at the time when it is delivered;
> (ii) if sent by telex, at the time when the recipient's answerback is received;
> (iii) if sent by facsimile transmission, at the time when the transmission is received by a responsible employee of the recipient in legible form (it being agreed that the burden of proving receipt will be on the sender and will not be met by a transmission report generated by the sender's facsimile machine);
> (iv) if sent by certified or registered mail (airmail, if overseas) or the equivalent (return receipt requested), at the time when that mail is delivered or its delivery is attempted;
> (v) if sent by electronic messaging system, at the time that electronic message is received;
> except that any notice or communication which is received, or delivery of which is attempted, after close of business on the date of receipt or attempted delivery or on a day which is not a day on which commercial banks are open for business in the place where that notice or other communication is to be given shall be treated as given at the opening of business on the next following day which is such a day.

These boilerplate provisions are very similar to those in Section 12 of the ISDA Master Agreement.

They state that notices will be in English and normally in writing, and will be sent to a party at the address shown in its communications details in Annex I (Annex V of the PSA/ISMA GMRA).

Communications may be sent by letter, telex, fax, certified mail or electronic messaging system. The 2002 ISDA Master Agreement definition of "electronic messaging system" makes it clear that this does not include e-mails. The TBMA/ISMA GMRA is silent on this point.

As regards a fax, its receipt is only effective on the date a responsible employee receives the fax in legible form. The sender must prove receipt; a transmission report from a fax machine is not good enough for this purpose. There is no definition of who is a responsible employee and any doubts about this could affect the timing of receipt of the notice. A permitted electronic message is effective upon receipt. If the date of delivery or receipt is not a Business Day, or takes place after close of business on a Business Day, then it will only become effective on the next following Business Day.

> (c) If–
> (i) there occurs in relation to either party an event which, upon the service of a Default Notice, would be an Event of Default; and
> (ii) the non-Defaulting Party, having made all practicable efforts to do so, including having attempted to use at least two of the methods specified in sub-paragraph (b)(ii), (iii) or (v), has been unable to serve a Default Notice by one of the methods specified in those sub-paragraphs (or such of those methods as are normally used by the non-Defaulting Party when communicating with the Defaulting Party),
> the non-Defaulting Party may sign a written notice (a "Special Default Notice") which-
> (aa) specifies the relevant event referred to in paragraph 10(a) which has occurred in relation to the Defaulting Party;
> (bb) states that the non-Defaulting Party, having made all practicable efforts to do so, including having attempted to use at least two of the methods specified in sub-paragraph (b)(ii), (iii) or (v), has been unable to serve a Default Notice by one of the methods specified in those sub-paragraphs (or such of those methods as are normally used by the non-Defaulting Party when communicating with the Defaulting Party);
> (cc) specifies the date on which, and the time at which, the Special Default Notice is signed by the non-Defaulting Party; and
> (dd) states that the event specified in accordance with sub-paragraph (aa) above shall be treated as an Event of Default with effect from the date and time so specified.
>
> On the signature of a Special Default Notice the relevant event shall be treated with effect from the date and time so specified as an Event of Default in relation to the Defaulting Party, and accordingly references in paragraph 10 to a Default Notice shall be treated as including a Special Default Notice. A Special Default Notice shall be given to the Defaulting Party as soon as practicable after it is signed.

This is a new sub-paragraph.

This provision takes into account the practical difficulties that parties experience when seeking to serve Default Notices on Defaulting Parties in extreme market conditions. The sub-paragraph provides that, where the non-Defaulting Party has made all practical efforts to deliver the Default Notice in one of the normal ways, but has not been able to do so, it may complete a Special Default Notice. This notice deems an Event of Default to occur with effect from the date and time specified in the Special Default Notice.

There is no standard form of Special Default Notice. A non-Defaulting Party would have to compose its own. It must be given to the Defaulting Party, if possible, as soon as practicable after it has been signed.

> (d) Either party may by notice to the other change the address, telex or facsimile number or electronic messaging system details at which notices or other communications are to be given to it.

This is a simple statement that a party will notify its counterparty of any changes of address or details in relation to its communications information that appears in Annex I.

Paragraph 15

> **15. Entire Agreement; Severability**
> This Agreement shall supersede any existing agreements between the parties containing general terms and conditions for Transactions. Each provision and agreement herein shall be treated as separate from any other provision or agreement herein and shall be enforceable notwithstanding the unenforceability of any such other provision or agreement.

Paragraph 15 clearly states that the TBMA/ISMA GMRA supersedes all other repo master agreements concerning the same matters. Therefore, there is no particular need to terminate a previous 1995 PSA/ISMA GMRA between the parties, although, in practice, this can now be done in Annex I (as we shall see on pages 93–94). The ISDA Master Agreement lacks this useful provision.

The severability provision is brief. Its effect is to enable the TBMA/ISMA GMRA to continue in effect even if an individual provision therein may become unenforceable.

In the 1990s some lawyers considered that including a severability provision might undermine the single agreement concept of a master agreement. However, the market no longer seems to regard this as a problem.

Paragraph 16

> **16. Non-assignability; Termination**
> (a) Subject to sub-paragraph (b) below, neither party may assign, charge or otherwise deal with (including without limitation any dealing with any interest in or the creation of any interest in) its rights or obligations under this Agreement or under any Transaction without the prior written consent of the other party. Subject to the foregoing, this Agreement and any Transactions shall be binding upon and shall inure to the benefit of the parties and their respective successors and assigns.

> (b) Sub-paragraph (a) above shall not preclude a party from assigning, charging or otherwise dealing with all or any part of its interest in any sum payable to it under paragraph 10(c) or (f) above.

(a) The rights and obligations under the TBMA/ISMA GMRA and/or any Transactions are not assignable or chargeable without the consent of the other party. It should be noted that any assignment may affect the enforceability of the close-out netting provisions if a party becomes insolvent because a third party would take over its rights and would destroy the mutuality required for set-off.

The TBMA/ISMA GMRA and any Transactions thereunder will survive any name change or takeover of one of the contracting parties.

(b) There is one exception to this transfer prohibition. Paragraph 16(b) permits a party to assign its right in a net sum payable to it following termination after an Event of Default. This is also permitted in Section 7 of ISDA Master Agreement. The party may also transfer sums due to it under paragraph 10(f) (ie, legal and professional expenses due to it).

> (c) Either party may terminate this Agreement by giving written notice to the other, except that this Agreement shall, notwithstanding such notice, remain applicable to any Transactions then outstanding.
> (d) All remedies hereunder shall survive Termination in respect of the relevant Transaction and termination of this Agreement.
> (e) The participation of any additional member State of the European Union in economic and monetary union after 1 January 1999 shall not have the effect of altering any term of the Agreement or any Transaction, nor give a party the right unilaterally to alter or terminate the Agreement or any Transaction.

(c) Paragraph 16(c) allows a party to terminate the TBMA/ISMA GMRA by written notice to the other party without prejudice to existing Transactions.

(d) This simple provision states that legal remedies available under the TBMA/ISMA GMRA and any Transactions will survive their termination.

(e) This sub-paragraph 16(e) was added to provide for continuity of contract in the event that any further member states of the European Union participate in economic and monetary union.

Paragraph 17

> **17. Governing Law**
> This Agreement shall be governed by and construed in accordance with the laws of England. Buyer and Seller hereby irrevocably submit for all purposes of or in

> connection with this Agreement and each Transaction to the jurisdiction of the Courts of England.
>
> Party A hereby appoints the person identified in Annex I hereto as its agent to receive on its behalf service of process in such courts. If such agent ceases to be its agent, Party A shall promptly appoint, and notify Party B of the identity of, a new agent in England.
>
> Party B hereby appoints the person identified in Annex I hereto as its agent to receive on its behalf service of process in such courts. If such agent ceases to be its agent, Party B shall promptly appoint, and notify Party A of the identity of, a new agent in England.
>
> Each party shall deliver to the other, within 30 days of the date of this Agreement in the case of the appointment of a person identified in Annex I or of the date of the appointment of the relevant agent in any other case, evidence of the acceptance by the agent appointed by it pursuant to this paragraph of such appointment.
>
> Nothing in this paragraph shall limit the right of any party to take proceedings in the courts of any other country of competent jurisdiction.

The TBMA/ISMA GMRA is governed by English law and the parties submit to the jurisdiction of the English courts. This is without prejudice to the ability of any party to take proceedings in courts of other countries. However, it might be useful to restrict this where one of the parties may want to bring an action in a court in a jurisdiction unsympathetic to close-out netting.

This provision for the appointment of process agents and their replacements applies where one or more parties lack a UK office. The appointments are now detailed in Annex I rather than in Annexes VI and VII in the PSA/ISMA GMRA. Evidence of the acceptance of a Process Agent appointment must be delivered to the other party within 30 days of the date of the TBMA/ISMA GMRA.

Paragraph 18

> **18. No Waivers, etc.**
> No express or implied waiver of any Event of Default by either party shall constitute a waiver of any other Event of Default and no exercise of any remedy hereunder by any party shall constitute a waiver of its right to exercise any other remedy hereunder. No modification or waiver of any provision of this Agreement and no consent by any party to a departure herefrom shall be effective unless and until such modification, waiver or consent shall be in writing and duly executed by both of the parties hereto. Without limitation on any of the foregoing, the failure to give a notice pursuant to paragraph 4(a) hereof will not constitute a waiver of any right to do so at a later date.

This is a standard provision in many market agreements. If either party chooses to waive an Event of Default, that waiver sets no precedent for other Events of Default. This flexibility recognises that the professional market may choose to overlook Events of Default or to resolve them in other ways, without prejudicing the right to call an Event of Default for subsequent breaches. Failure to give margin transfer notices will not amount to a waiver of any right to do so at a later date. All waivers must be in writing.

Paragraph 19

> **19. Waiver of Immunity**
> Each party hereto hereby waives, to the fullest extent permitted by applicable law, all immunity (whether on the basis of sovereignty or otherwise) from jurisdiction, attachment (both before and after judgment) and execution to which it might otherwise be entitled in any action or proceeding in the Courts of England or of any other country or jurisdiction, relating in any way to this Agreement or any Transaction, and agrees that it will not raise, claim or cause to be pleaded any such immunity at or in respect of any such action or proceeding.

Sovereign counterparties often seek immunity from confiscation of their assets or from being sued. This provision waives such immunity to the fullest extent permissible under the law. A similar provision appears in Section 13(d) of the ISDA Master Agreement.

Paragraph 20

> **20. Recording**
> The parties agree that each may electronically record all telephone conversations between them.

Each party consents to the tape recording of telephone calls between them. This is recommended in the UK Financial Services Authority's *Conduct of Business Rules (2001)*.

Paragraph 21

> **21. Third Party Rights**
> No person shall have any right to enforce any provision of this Agreement under the Contracts (Rights of Third Parties) Act 1999.

The Contracts (Rights of Third Parties) Act 1999 reformed an area of English law known as "privity of contract". Before it came into force, a person could only enforce a contract if they were a party to it. The new Act enables third parties to enforce contracts that are beneficial to them and that were entered into on or after 11 May 2000, provided that they are identified in the contract by name, as a class or by a particular description. While the Act has exceptions to this, many market players exclude the effect of the Act and ensure that privity of contract applies by using language similar to paragraph 21. It is also advisable to do this so that a third party does not intervene and threaten the mutuality of the close-out netting provisions.

Signing block

Authorised signatories of both parties sign the signing block. Market practice is to sign the TBMA/ISMA GMRA before allowing any trading under it.

TBMA/ISMA GMRA Annex I

Annex I presents a number of standard Supplemental Terms or Conditions for which choices need to be made. It is also the place where miscellaneous additional provisions are presented for consideration.

Part 1(a)–(c)

> **ANNEX I**
> **Supplemental Terms or Conditions**
> Paragraph references are to paragraphs in the Agreement.
> 1. The following elections shall apply
> [(a) paragraph 1 (c)(i), Buy/Sell Back Transactions [may/may not] be effected under this Agreement, and accordingly the Buy/Sell Back Annex [shall/shall not] apply.]*
> [(b) paragraph 1 (c)(ii). Transactions in Net Paying Securities [may/may not] be effected under this Agreement, and accordingly the provisions of sub-paragraphs (i) and (ii) below [shall/shall not] apply.
> (i) The phrase "other than equities and Net Paying Securities" shall be replaced by the phrase "other than equities",
> (ii) In the Buy/Sell Back Annex the following words shall be added to the end of the definition of the expression "IR": "and for the avoidance of doubt the reference to the amount of Income for these purposes shall be to an amount paid without withholding or deduction for or on account of taxes or duties notwithstanding that a payment of such Income made in certain circumstances may be subject to such a withholding or deduction".]*
> [(c) paragraph 1 (d). Agency Transactions [may/may not] be effected under this Agreement, and accordingly the Agency Annex [shall/shall not] apply.]*

1(a)–(c) of Annex I offers choices as to whether or not Buy/Sell Back Transactions, Transactions in Net Paying Securities or Agency Transactions and their relevant Annexes (in the case of Buy/Sell Back Transactions and Agency Transactions) will apply.

Transactions in Net Paying Securities do not have a separate Annex and, if they are to apply, it is recommended that the wording shown in 1(b) is included in Annex I.

It is possible to state in this part of the Annex whether or not other products and Annexes, such as the Gilts Annex, Italian Annex or the Equities Annex, are to apply.

Part 1(d)

> (d) paragraph 2(d). The Base Currency shall be: _____.

The Base Currency is the currency into which Margin Transfers are converted to calculate aggregate collateral levels for the purposes of paragraph 4 and is the currency into which all Transaction values are converted on close-out in paragraph 10.

Sometimes one currency is quoted for both matters, eg, the euro, and sometimes split Base Currencies are quoted for each paragraph, eg:

paragraph 2(d): The Base Currency shall be:
(i) for the purposes of paragraph 4 of this Agreement, US dollars and
(ii) for the purposes of paragraph 10 of this Agreement, where the Defaulting Party is Party A, US dollars and where the Defaulting Party is Party B, the euro.

This would suggest that Party A is incorporated in the United States.

Part 1(e)

> (e) paragraph 2(p). [list Buyer's and Seller's Designated Offices]

With the agreement of their counterparty, parties may list here the branches through which they wish to trade repos and buy/sellbacks. Such branches should be in jurisdictions where there is a "clean" and positive legal opinion that close-out netting under paragraph 10 is enforceable.

Part 1(f)

> (f) paragraph 2(cc), The pricing source for calculation of Market Value shall be:_____.

This is where one or more pricing sources may be named for the calculation of the Market Value of Securities. The following is a typical example of wording commonly seen in the market:

paragraph 2(cc): The pricing source for calculation of Market Value shall be:
(i) calculated in accordance with market practice in the principal market for the relevant Securities, or as otherwise agreed between Party A and Party B and stated in the relevant Confirmation; and/or
(ii) in the case of UK gilt-edged securities, GEMM's prices published by the Bank of England for Transactions over UK gilt-edged securities, or as otherwise agreed between Party A and Party B and stated in the relevant Confirmation.

Part 1(g)

> (g) paragraph 2(rr), Spot rate to be: _____.

Where one currency needs to be converted into another, this will be at the relevant spot rate for the currencies concerned quoted by Barclays Bank PLC in the London interbank market, unless the parties agree on some other rate provider or information source. Most commonly you would see the following wording:

(i) paragraph 2(rr):   Spot rate to be as defined in paragraph 2(rr).

Part 1(h)

> (h) paragraph 3(b).   [Seller/Buyer/both Seller and Buyer]* to deliver Confirmation.

This sub-paragraph designates which party will deliver a Confirmation in respect of a recently executed Transaction. Most commonly you would see:

(k) paragraph 3(b):   Both Seller and Buyer to deliver Confirmation.

Otherwise one might see just the Seller to deliver the Confirmation. Buyer only is quite rare.

Part 1(i)

> (i) paragraph 4(f), Interest rate on Cash Margin to be [ ]% for - currency.
> [ ]% for - currency,
>   Interest to be payable [payment intervals and dates].

This sub-paragraph concerns the rate of interest to be paid on Cash Margin and the frequency of such interest payments. It is not normal in fact to quote interest rates. Normally a bland clause such as the following appears in Annex I:

paragraph 4(f):   The interest rate (including the payment intervals and payment dates) on Cash Margin in respect of the relevant currency shall be as agreed by the parties at the time of each Transaction.

Sometimes there is a fallback to a relevant interest rate, for instance, on Telerate or Bloomberg, where the parties fail to agree.

This is an example of the discretion that the TBMA/ISMA GMRA gives to dealers in agreeing these matters between themselves. It is also evident in 1(f) and 1(j).

Part 1(j)

> (j) paragraph 4(g), Delivery period for margin calls to be:_____.

At this point in the Annex the parties state the deadlines for the delivery of Margin Securities following a margin call. A typical example would be:

> **paragraph 4(g):   Delivery period for margin calls to be:**
> **(i) in the case of gilt-edged securities, if notice of the call is effectively given on a day before 12 noon (London time) on that day, the same day and if such notice is effectively given after such time on that day, the next Business Day; and**
> **(ii) in all other cases paragraph 4(g) shall apply subject to a maximum delivery period of two Business Days.**

Part 1(k)

> [(k) paragraph 6(j). Paragraph 6(j) shall apply and the events specified in paragraph 10(a) identified for the purposes of paragraph 6(j) shall be those set out in sub paragraphs [ ] of paragraph 10(a) of the Agreement.]*

This is the election for paragraph 6(j) to apply. If chosen, it means that the non-Defaulting Party may withhold further payments or deliveries if a potential Event of Default has occurred to the Defaulting Party. If a party wants to apply it, it has to choose which paragraph 10(a) Events of Default it should cover. Prime candidates would be paragraph 10(a)(i) and (iii)–(x).

Part 1(l)

> (l) paragraph 10(a)(ii). Paragraph 10(a)(ii) shall apply.]*

This is where the parties can choose if failure to deliver securities shall be an Event of Default. If they select it and delivery fails to take place, then close-out of all Transactions will follow the issuance of a Default Notice from the non-Defaulting Party to the Defaulting Party. If it is disapplied, then the parties can still fall back to the mini close-out provisions of paragraphs 10(g) and (h) in respect of individual Transactions.

Part 1(m)

> (m) paragraph 14. For the purposes of paragraph 14 of this Agreement
> (i) Address for notices and other communications for Party A
> Address:
> Attention:
> Telephone:
> Facsimile:

> Telex:
> Answerback:
> Other:
> (ii) Address for notices and other communications for Party B
> Address:
> Attention:
> Telephone:
> Facsimile:
> Telex:
> Answerback:
> Other:

Parties record their relevant notice details here. It can also be subdivided into notices for the Collateral Management Department for margin maintenance and the Legal Department for notices under paragraph 10.

Part 1(n)

> [(n) paragraph 17. For the purposes of paragraph 17 of this Agreement
> (i) Party A appoints [ ] as its agent for service of process;
> (ii) Party B appoints [ ] as its agent for service of process;]*

Because the TBMA/ISMA GMRA is governed by English law, if a party is not incorporated in England (or Wales) it must appoint a Process Agent for the receipt of writs and other legal papers. This appointment is procedurally necessary to make an effective claim in the English courts and for the enforcement of foreign judgements in the English courts.

Part 2(a)

> 2. The following supplemental terms and conditions shall apply
> [Existing Transactions
> (a) The parties agree that this Agreement shall apply to all transactions which are subject to the PSA/ISMA Global Master Repurchase Agreement between them dated and which are outstanding as at the date of this Agreement so that such transactions shall be treated as if they had been entered into under this Agreement, and the terms of such transactions are amended accordingly with effect from the date of this Agreement]*

A party may use this wording to bring Transactions from a previous PSA/ISMA GMRA under the TBMA/ISMA GMRA. Alternatively, the TBMA and ISMA have issued an Amendment Agreement to enable the terms of a PSA/ISMA GMRA to be changed to conform with the TBMA/ISMA GMRA without the parties having to sign a new TBMA/ISMA GMRA. A copy of this Amendment Agreement is reproduced in Appendix 2 of this book by kind permission of the International Securities Market Association and The Bond Market Association.

Part 2(b)

> [Forward Transactions
> (b) The parties agree that Forward Transactions (as defined in sub-paragraph (i)(A) below) may be effected under this Agreement and accordingly the provisions of sub-paragraphs (i) to (iv) below shall apply.
> (i) The following definitions shall apply
> (A) "Forward Transaction", a Transaction in respect of which the Purchase Date is at least [three] Business Days after the date on which the Transaction was entered into and has not yet occurred;
> (B) "Forward Repricing Date", with respect to any Forward Transaction the date which is such number of Business Days before the Purchase Date as is equal to the minimum period for the delivery of margin applicable under paragraph 4(g).
> (ii) The Confirmation relating to any Forward Transaction may describe the Purchased Securities by reference to a type or class of Securities, which, without limitation, may be identified by issuer or class of issuers and a maturity or range of maturities. Where this paragraph applies, the parties shall agree the actual Purchased Securities not less than two Business Days before the Purchase Date and Buyer or Seller (or both), as shall have been agreed, shall promptly deliver to the other party a Confirmation which shall describe such Purchased Securities.
> (iii) At any time between the Forward Repricing Date and the Purchase Date for any Forward Transaction the parties may agree either
> (A) to adjust the Purchase Price under that Forward Transaction; or
> (B) to adjust the number of Purchased Securities to be sold by Seller to Buyer under that Forward Transaction.
> (iv) Where the parties agree to an adjustment under paragraph (iii) above, Buyer or Seller (or both), as shall have been agreed, shall promptly deliver to the other party a **Confirmation of the Forward Transaction,** as adjusted under paragraph (iii) above.
> (c) Where the parties agree that this paragraph shall apply, paragraphs 2 and 4 of the Agreement are amended as follows.
> (i) Paragraph 2(ww) is deleted and replaced by the following
> "(ww) 'Transaction Exposure' means
> (i) with respect to any Forward Transaction at any time between the Forward Repricing Date and the Purchase Date, the difference between (A) the Market Value of the Purchased Securities at the relevant time and (B) the Purchase Price;

(ii) with respect to any transaction at any time during the period (if any) from the Purchase Date to the date on which the Purchased Securities are delivered to Buyer or, if earlier, the date on which the Transaction is terminated under paragraph 10(g), the difference between (A) the Market Value of the Purchased Securities at the relevant time and (B) the Repurchase Price at the relevant time;

(iii) with respect to any Transaction at any time during the period from the Purchase Date (or, if later, the date on which the Purchased Securities are delivered to Buyer or the Transaction is terminated under paragraph 10(g)) to the Repurchase Date (or, if later, the date on which Equivalent Securities are delivered to Seller or the Transaction is terminated under paragraph 10(h)), the difference between (A) the Repurchase Price at the relevant time multiplied by the applicable Margin Ratio (or, where the Transaction relates to Securities of more than one description to which different Margin Ratios apply, the amount produced by multiplying the Repurchase Price attributable to Equivalent Securities of each such description by the applicable Margin Ratio and aggregating the resulting amounts, the Repurchase Price being for this purpose attributed to Equivalent Securities of each such description in the same proportions as those in which the Purchase Price was apportioned among the Purchased Securities) and (B) the Market Value of Equivalent Securities at the relevant time.

In each case, if (A) is greater than (B), Buyer has a Transaction Exposure for that Transaction equal to the excess, and if (B) is greater than (A), Seller has a Transaction Exposure to Buyer equal to the excess."

(ii) In paragraph 4(c)

(aa) the words "any amount payable to the first party under paragraph 5 but unpaid" are deleted and replaced by "any amount which will become payable to the first party under paragraph 5 during the period after the time at which the calculation is made which is equal to the minimum period for the delivery of margin applicable under paragraph 4(g) or which is payable to the first party under paragraph 5 but unpaid"; and

(bb) the words "any amount payable to the other party under paragraph 5 but unpaid" are deleted and replaced by "any amount which will become payable to the other party under paragraph 5 during the period after the time at which the calculation is made which is equal to the minimum period for the delivery of margin applicable under paragraph 4(g) or which is payable to the other party under paragraph 5 but unpaid".]*

* Delete as appropriate

These sub-paragraphs provide optional wording for Forward Transactions. These are defined as Transactions where the Purchase Date is more than three Business Days after the trade date. An interim Confirmation may describe the securities by class of issuer and type, but within two Business Days of the Purchase Date either the Buyer or the Seller must send the other party a Confirmation describing the exact Purchased Securities.

However, the Purchase Price or the amount of the securities may be adjusted before the Purchase Date. If they are, a new Confirmation must be issued.

There are amendments to the definition of Transaction Exposure in paragraph 2(ww) and the treatment of due but unpaid paragraph 5 Income to a party.

Forward Transactions are included in the margining mechanism of the TBMA/ISMA GMRA even before the Purchase Date. This could well lead to a margin call and a temporarily overcollateralised position before the Purchase Date.

A Forward Transaction is an obligation to have securities coming on to the Buyer's balance sheet at a certain date. It might be entered into if a particular stock is required but not needed immediately. It is therefore most likely to be used for "specials". However, if a party is confident that it can obtain the stock in the market, then there is no need to enter into a forward repo transaction. Relatively few of these Transactions have been done in the market largely because of the temporary overcollateralisation that they entail.

Additional provisions appearing in Annex I negotiations

Unlike the ISDA Master Agreement, where many different provisions are potentially negotiable in its Part 5, the type of additional provisions that occasionally appear in Annex I are more limited.

Notwithstanding this, counterparties have, in recent times, tried to import ISDA provisions, such as Default Under Specified Transaction and Cross Default (with accompanying definitions of Specified Indebtedness and Threshold Amount), into Annex I.

These provisions seem to be inappropriate here because repos and buy/sellbacks are short-term secured transactions, and wheeling in defaults from other agreements (often with different close-out regimes) begs the question whether parties should be doing business together in the first place. These approaches should be resisted.

Sometimes an indemnity clause relating to what ISDA describes as Automatic Early Termination might appear in Annex I, as follows:

> paragraph 10(m). A new paragraph 10(m) shall be inserted as follows:
> "If an Act of Insolvency occurs with respect to the Seller or Buyer and no notice is required in order for such Act of Insolvency to constitute an Event of Default for the purposes of this Agreement, then the Defaulting Party shall fully indemnify the non-Defaulting Party against all expense, loss, damage or liability that the non-Defaulting Party may incur in respect of this Agreement and each Transaction as a consequence of movements in interest, currency, exchange or other relevant rates, prices or values between the Repurchase Date and the first day (being a day on which the non-Defaulting Party is open for business in any Designated Office of such party) on which the non-Defaulting Party first becomes, or has become, aware that the Repurchase Date has occurred. The non-Defaulting Party may for this purpose convert any expense, loss, damage or liability into the Base Currency"

Although repos are short-term in nature, this may be more acceptable if the parties consider it likely to help their recoveries in an insolvency situation. It could, however, be argued that this wording might cut across the consequential loss prohibition in paragraph 10(j).

In the same vein some counterparties propose an ISDA type set-off clause in Annex I, as in the following example:

> Without prejudice to the provisions of paragraph 10 of the Agreement, each party hereby acknowledges that:
>
> Nothing in this Agreement shall affect the right of set-off or similar right to which the parties may be entitled in law. Further, in circumstances where there is a Defaulting Party, the net balance under paragraph 10(c)(ii) (the "Early Termination Amount") payable to one party (the Payee) will, at the option of the party ("X") which is not the Defaulting Party (and without prior notice to the Defaulting Party), be reduced by its set-off against any amount(s) (the "Other Agreement Amount") payable (whether at such time or in the future or upon the occurrence of a contingency) by the Payee to the Payer (irrespective of the currency, place of payment or booking office of the obligation) under any other agreement(s) between the Payee and the Payer or instrument(s) or undertaking(s) issued or executed by one party to, or in favour of, the other party (and the Other Agreement Amount will be discharged promptly and in all respects to the extent it is so set-off).
>
> For this purpose, either the Early Termination Amount or the Other Agreement Amount (or the relevant portion of such amounts) may be converted by X into the currency in which the other is denominated at the rate of exchange at which such party would be able, acting in a reasonable manner and in good faith, to purchase the relevant amount of such currency.
>
> If an obligation is unascertained, X may in good faith estimate that obligation and set-off in respect of the estimate, subject to the relevant party accounting to the other when the obligation is ascertained.
>
> Nothing in this provision shall be effective to create a charge or other security interest. This provision shall be without prejudice and in addition to any right of set-off, combination of accounts, lien or other right to which any party is at any time otherwise entitled (whether by operation of law, contract or otherwise).

In other examples the set-off is extended to the non-Defaulting Party's Affiliates. Again, the argument could be adduced that repos and buy/sellbacks are short-term secured transactions and that a set-off clause extending the close-out beyond the TBMA/ISMA GMRA is unreasonable, particularly since the Transactions are meant to be fully collateralised.

In the United Kingdom there is a mandatory right of set-off under Rule 4.90 of the Insolvency Rules (1986) between parties dealing with each other in the same capacity. A set-off clause extends beyond that right.

Whether the set-off extension is acceptable is a question of policy for each contracting party.

Sometimes counterparties seek to make any termination payment to a Defaulting Party dependent upon its having no other liabilities to the non-Defaulting Party. Such conditionality language is prejudicial to the full effectiveness of close-out netting in some jurisdictions and is best resisted.

Finally, one ISDA-type provision rarely seen in Annex I is a non-reliance provision, which is perhaps surprising given that in the United Kingdom anyone (including a natural person) can trade repos.

Scope of Agreement

One common provision that appears is one that sweeps in repos and buy/sellbacks between the parties outside a master agreement into the TBMA/ISMA GMRA. It can appear in two main forms:

> The parties agree that all transactions (whether Repurchase Transactions or Buy/Sell Back Transactions) entered into by the parties prior to the effective date of this Agreement and outstanding at the effective date of execution hereof shall be deemed to be Transactions under this Agreement entered into pursuant thereto and governed by its terms.

or

> Unless otherwise agreed in writing, the parties agree that this Agreement shall apply to all Transactions which the parties may enter into (as the term "Transaction" is defined in paragraph 1(a) and (b)), even if not so specified in the Confirmation.

In some examples the sweep-in is on the basis that the Confirmation does not expressly forbid it, which is unlikely. Buy/sellbacks are most likely to be swept in under this provision.

Single branch margining

The TBMA/ISMA GMRA provides in paragraph 4 for global margining of positions, ie, multi-branch comparison of all exposures and margin held in order to determine if a Margin Transfer needs to be made. Some counterparties may be able to margin only on a branch-by-branch basis in which case one might see the following language:

> (e) Subparagraphs (c) and (d) of paragraph 4 of the Agreement shall be replaced by the following wording:
> (c) For the purposes solely of this paragraph 4 Margin Maintenance:
> (i) Net Exposures shall be calculated separately in relation to Transactions entered into between one particular Designated Office of Party A and one particular Designated Office of Party B (collectively a "Group") and;
> (ii) one party has a Net Exposure in respect of the other party if
> (A) the aggregate of all the first party's Transaction Exposures with respect to a Group plus any amount payable to the first party under paragraph 5 with respect to such Group but unpaid less the amount of any Net Margin provided with respect to such Group to the first party exceeds;

> (B) the aggregate of all the other party's Transaction Exposures with respect to such Group plus any amount payable to the other party under paragraph 5 with respect to such Group but unpaid less the amount of any Net Margin with respect to such Group provided to the other Party;
> and the amount of the Net Exposure is the amount of the excess. For this purpose any amounts not denominated in the Base Currency shall be converted into the Base Currency at the Spot Rate prevailing at the relevant time.
> (d) To the extent that a party calling for a Margin Transfer has, with respect to the relevant Group, previously paid Cash Margin which has not been repaid or delivered Margin Securities in respect of which Equivalent Margin Securities have not been delivered to it, that party shall be entitled to require that such Margin Transfer be satisfied first by the repayment of such Cash Margin or the delivery of Equivalent Margin Securities but, subject to this, the composition of a Margin Transfer shall be at the option of the party making such Margin Transfer.

An abbreviated version of this is:

> The parties agree with regard to the provisions of sub-paragraphs 4(a) to 4(g) that margin may be calculated and provided separately for each pair of Designated Offices. Accordingly Net Exposure may only be calculated for Transactions entered into between one Designated Office of Party A and one Designated Office of Party B at a time.
>   Margin shall only be provided for Transactions entered into between one Designated Office of Party A and one Designated Office of Party B at a time.
>   Margin provided in respect of Transactions entered into between one Designated Office of Party A and one Designated Office of Party B shall not be taken into account for the purposes of Margin Maintenance for Transactions entered into between Party A and any other Designated Office of Party B.
>   For the avoidance of doubt, this paragraph 2(d) shall not affect the provisions of paragraph 10 of the Agreement which shall operate across all Designated Offices in the usual way.

FASB 125/140

The following language is still sometimes seen in TBMA/ISMA GMRAs with US counterparties:

> (*) Paragraph 8 of the Agreement is hereby amended by adding at the end of the paragraph the following sub-paragraphs (e), (f) and (g):

> "(e) In the case of any Transaction for which the Repurchase Date is not the Business Day immediately following the Purchase Date and with respect to which Seller does not have any existing right to vary the Transaction, Seller shall have the right (subject to the proviso to this sub-paragraph) by notice to Buyer (such notice to be given at or prior to 12 p.m. (London time) on that Business Day) to vary that Transaction in accordance with sub-paragraphs (a) and (b) above, provided however that Buyer may elect by close of business on the Business Day notice is received (or by close of business on the next Business Day if notice is received after 12 p.m. (London time) on that day) not to vary that Transaction. If Buyer elects not to vary the Transaction, Seller shall have the right, by notice to Buyer, to terminate the Transaction on the Business Day specified in that notice, such Business Day (unless the parties otherwise agree) not to be later than two Business Days after the date of the notice.
>
> (f) If Seller exercises its right to vary the Transaction or to terminate the Transaction under sub-paragraph (e) above, notwithstanding paragraph 10(h), Seller shall be required to pay to Buyer by close of business on the Business Day of such variation or termination an amount equal to –
>
> (i) Buyer's actual cost (including all fees, expenses and commissions) of (aa) entering into replacement transactions; (bb) entering into or terminating hedge transactions; and (cc) terminating or varying transactions with third parties in connection with or as a result of such variation or termination; and
>
> (ii) to the extent that Buyer party does not enter into replacement transactions, the loss incurred by Buyer directly arising or resulting from such variation or termination,
>
> in each case as determined and calculated in good faith by Buyer.
>
> (g) Where one party (the "Requesting Party") has requested the other party to transfer Equivalent Margin Securities to it in exchange for the transfer to the other party of new Margin Securities in accordance with paragraph 8(d) but the other party does not agree to the request, if the Requesting Party so elects by written notice specifying the Equivalent Margin Securities to be transferred and the Business Day on which those Equivalent Margin Securities are to be transferred (such Business Day (unless the parties otherwise agree) not to be later than two Business Days after the date of the notice) the other party shall, unless otherwise agreed, transfer those Equivalent Margin Securities to the Requesting Party in exchange for the transfer to the other party of Cash Margin of an amount equal to the Market Value of the Equivalent Margin Securities so transferred."

This provision relates to the after-effects of FASB 125 and needs to be used only where US counterparties are concerned.

On 28 June 1996 the US Financial Accounting Standards Board issued an accounting standard called FASB 125 *Accounting for Transfers and Servicing of Financial Assets and Extinguishments of Liabilities*. FASB 125 instituted new accounting rules for transactions involving financial assets, including repos and buy/sellbacks.

Before the full implementation of FASB 125 on 1 January 1998, securities reversed in under a repo agreement were not required to be recorded on the balance sheet of the transferee (ie, the repo buyer) and securities repoed out were not required to be identified as collateral pledged in the financial statements of the transferor (ie, the repo seller). However, with effect from 1 January 1998, depending upon the contractual agreement between the parties, FASB 125 could affect the accounting for securities under a repo.

In particular, if the repo buyer has the right to sell or repledge the repo securities, and if the repo seller does not maintain control over them (by not having the right to substitute the securities or terminate the transaction at short notice), then the repo buyer must record the securities as an asset, and also recognise its obligation to return the securities and thus gross up its balance sheet (ie, by effectively double-counting the transaction). The repo seller would generally be required to reclassify the assets from securities inventory to a receivable for securities pledged as collateral.

At that time the PSA/ISMA GMRA was the principal repo master agreement used in the European market.

Paragraph 8 of the PSA/ISMA GMRA provided that the repo parties could agree to substitute new securities for Purchased Securities by varying the terms of the Transaction. The parties could also agree to substitute New Margin Securities for Margin Securities already delivered.

TBMA and ISMA members therefore lobbied for a standard provision to be issued that would allow a repo seller to vary the terms of a Transaction under paragraph 8 by notice to the Buyer, or give the Seller the right to terminate a Transaction before its maturity if the Buyer did not agree to the variation (ie, the substitution). Furthermore, they wanted a party that had transferred Margin Securities to have the right to provide cash margin in exchange for securities equivalent to those Margin Securities if the parties disagreed over the substitution of those Margin Securities. This was because market players preferred not to alter existing trading practices and economics in the repo market.

This FASB 125 wording became very popular in the market.

On 29 September 2000 the US Federal Accounting Standards Board released FASB 140, which replaced FASB 125 in its entirety, but carried forward many of its provisions without reconsideration.

This is why FASB 125 language may still be found in Annexes I with US counterparties.

Inclusion of US Treasury repos under the TBMA/ISMA GMRA

While repos on US treasuries can be automatically transacted under the TBMA/ISMA GMRA, many counterparties like to include the language shown below. As such Transactions are cross-border in nature, US parties will often seek payee tax representations and tax documentation from their counterparties.

> In relation to Transactions involving U.S. Treasury instruments the following amendments to the Agreement shall apply.

> Paragraph 6(a) is amended, in clause (ii), by the replacement of the word "or" following the word "Euroclear" with a comma and by the addition of the words "or a U.S. Federal Reserve Bank" after the word "Clearstream".
>
> Paragraph 6(b) of the Agreement is amended by inserting "(i)" immediately after "(b)" at the beginning of the paragraph and by inserting the following new paragraph after the existing paragraph 6(b):
>
> "(ii) In the case of any payment to a party hereto ("Payee") by the other party hereto ("Payor"), Payee agrees to deliver to Payor (or, if applicable, to the appropriate tax authority) any certificate or document reasonably requested by Payor that would entitle Payee to an exemption from, or reduction in the rate of, withholding or deduction of tax from money payable by Payor to Payee."

Agency transactions

Parties are entering more frequently into agency repo transactions under the TBMA/ISMA GMRA, where one party acts as principal and the other as agent for a disclosed principal or principals. Agent-to-Agent Transactions are not possible under the TBMA/ISMA GMRA.

When deciding to enter into Agency Transactions, parties enter into the Agency Annex and possibly its Addendum (if multiple disclosed principals are involved), although the Addendum can be disapplied if the parties are not interested in entering into its pooling arrangements, as in the following example:

> (i) Paragraph 1(d) of the Agency Annex (addendum for multiple principal transactions) shall not apply to this Agreement.
>
> (ii) For the purposes of this Agreement, unless specified otherwise at the time a Transaction is entered into, each Transaction under this Agreement shall be an Agency Transaction, and accordingly, paragraph 2(a)(i) of the Agency Annex shall be deleted.
>
> (iii) Paragraph 2(a)(ii) of the Agency Annex is hereby deleted and replaced with the following:-
>
> "(ii) it enters into that Transaction on behalf of one or more Principals whose identities are disclosed to the other party (whether by name or by reference to a code or identifier which the parties have agreed will be used to refer to a specific Principal) on or before the time the Transaction is entered into."
>
> (iv) Add new Paragraph 4(e) of the Agency Annex:–
>
> "When the Agent enters into an Agency Transaction, it will allocate the Transaction either to a single Principal or to several Principals, each of whom shall be responsible for only that part of the Transaction which has been allocated to it. Where the allocation is to two or more Principals, a separate Transaction shall be deemed to have been entered into between the other party and each such Principal with respect to the appropriate proportion of the Purchased Securities."

> (v) The following is added as new paragraph 5(e) of the Agency Annex:-
> "(d) Party A may simultaneously enter into a number of such Agency Transactions, PROVIDED THAT, if required to do so by Party B, it identifies to Party B details of Transactions made in respect of each Principal on or before the time of entering into each Agency Transaction. Party A and Party B agree that Party A may at any time, and without prior notice, substitute a new Principal (the "New Principal" (which has been approved by Party B prior to trading)) in place of the existing Principal (the "Existing Principal") for an Agency Transaction (a "Substitution") whereupon simultaneously:
> (i) Party B and the Existing Principal shall be released from all of their respective obligations and liabilities to each other in respect of the Agency Transaction and the Existing Principal shall have no further rights in respect of the Agency Transaction;
> (ii) the New Principal shall assume, and undertakes to Party B to perform, the obligations and liabilities in favour of Party B identical to all of the Existing Party's obligations and liabilities under the Agency Transaction immediately prior to the Substitution; and
> (iii) Party B shall assume, and undertakes to the New Principal to perform, the obligations and liabilities in favour of the New Principal identical to all of its obligations and liabilities to the Existing Principal under the Agency Transaction immediately prior to the Substitution."

Emerging markets provisions

Repo markets are developing within emerging markets. Until recently emerging market repo was limited to Brady bonds and sovereign Eurobonds issued by countries such as Poland or Argentina. Brady bonds are popular because they are US dollar-denominated and government-backed. Settlement of international bonds is relatively straightforward through the Euroclear and Clearstream settlement systems, but where settlement is in a local market there is more risk and the local currency may not be liquid either.

Emerging markets repo centres round the government debt market, particularly in Latin America. Counterparty risk in these markets is significantly higher than in developed markets. It is not unknown for haircuts of up to 50 per cent to apply in term trades in emerging markets repo.

Often banks that trade with counterparties in these markets include provisions relating to the suspension of trading or listing of securities and enabling a contracting party to terminate a Transaction if a *force majeure* type of event occurred.

On suspension of securities from trading or listing, it is commonly provided that the value of those securities shall be treated as zero for margining purposes. The transferee of the securities may transfer equivalent securities to the original transferor or, if it cannot do so, it may hold them in trust for the original transferor.

Acceleration events are also included that give either party a right to terminate a Transaction. Such events include a national emergency declaration, the imposition of martial law or the declaration of war in the issuer's country. A fall in the Market Value of securities by more than a certain percentage from their Purchase Price may also constitute an acceleration event.

Here is an example of a detailed emerging markets provision in the form of an Annex:

ANNEX I, PART *
EMERGING MARKET SECURITIES

The following Supplemental Terms and Conditions shall apply to Transactions in Emerging Market Securities (as defined below) and references to "Securities" in this Part * of Annex I shall be interpreted accordingly:

1. Without prejudice to any other term of the Agreement (as amended or supplemented by the Annexes thereto), the parties agree that if any Securities have been suspended from their principal trading market or Buyer is unable to obtain a Market Value for such Securities from a generally recognized source and such suspension or inability to obtain a Market Value continues for a period of 5 Business Days:

1.01 their Market Value for the purpose of paragraph 4 only shall be nil; and

1.02 the Buyer shall be obligated to deliver to the Seller such suspended Securities upon delivery to the Buyer of a Margin Transfer in an amount that shall satisfy the conditions of paragraph 4.

In the event that the Buyer is, for any reason, unable to effect delivery of such suspended Securities to Seller, Buyer agrees that it will hold such suspended Securities in a separate account in the name of the Seller and on trust for the benefit of the Seller, the same constituting property of the Seller upon delivery to the Buyer of the relevant Margin Transfer.

2. If, during the course of any Transaction under this Agreement, there has occurred any of the following:

2.01 either the country of incorporation of either party hereto (the "Domicile Country") or the country of issue of the Securities (the "Issuing Country") is or becomes engaged in hostilities or there shall be a declaration of national emergency, or there shall occur a disaster or material escalation of civil unrest that would constitute a national emergency, or there shall be an imposition of martial law, or there shall be a declaration of war by the Issuing Country or by the Domicile Country and such events have a material effect on the ability of either party to this Agreement to perform its obligations hereunder; or

2.02 there shall have occurred a fall in the Market Value of the Securities of more than 35% (or such other percentage as the parties may agree with respect to a given Transaction) based on the original Purchase Price;

then, in the event that the relevant party under 2.01 above is the Seller, and in any event with respect to clause 2.02, the Buyer shall have the right, exercisable by written notice to the Seller, to accelerate the Repurchase Date to any Business Day selected by the Buyer, such date to be a date which is within five (5) Business Days of the date of such notice delivered by the Buyer to the Seller.

In the event that the relevant party in 2.01 above is the Buyer, then the Seller shall have the right to accelerate the Repurchase Date as if the above paragraph referred to the Seller instead of to the Buyer, *mutatis mutandis*.

> None of the events detailed in clause 2.01 or 2.02 shall of themselves constitute an Event of Default but failure by either party to make any payment in connection with its obligations under this clause 2 shall be an Event of Default for the purposes of paragraph 10.
> 3. Unless agreed otherwise between the parties, the pricing source for calculation of Market Value shall be the mean of the live dealing screens of any three leading brokers as selected by Party A in good faith and in a commercially reasonable manner.
> 4. In this Part * of Annex I, Emerging Market Securities shall mean any securities not issued in the countries set out below:
> Australia
> Austria
> Belgium
> Canada
> Denmark
> Finland
> France
> Germany
> Ireland
> Italy
> Japan
> Netherlands
> New Zealand
> Norway
> Portugal
> Spain
> Sweden
> Switzerland
> United Kingdom
> United States of America
> or as otherwise agreed between the parties.

A shorter version of these provisions is as follows:

> The Parties agree that in relation to any Securities where:
> (a) the Securities have been suspended from their principal trading market;
> (b) there is an inability to obtain a Market Value for such Securities from a generally accepted pricing source; or
> (c) there has been during the course of any Transaction, a fall in the value of the Securities of more than 25% based on the Purchase Price plus accrued Price Differential;

> then for each Transaction in such securities (an "Affected Transaction") the parties shall have the following rights and obligations:
> (1) the Buyer may elect, by written notice to the Seller to accelerate the Repurchase Date to any Business Day selected by the Buyer, such date to be a date which is within five (5) Business Days of the date of such notice delivered by the Buyer to the Seller; or
> (2) the Buyer may elect repricing of the Affected Transaction in accordance with paragraph 4; or
> (3) the Buyer may elect adjustment of the Affected Transaction in accordance with paragraph 4;
> (4) where the Buyer wishes to continue the Transaction the Buyer shall be obligated to deliver to the Seller such Securities upon delivery to the Buyer of New Purchased Securities in an amount which shall satisfy the conditions of paragraph 8.
>
> In the case of either (1), (2), (3) or (4) above then the Buyer shall have the right to call for Margin Transfer in accordance with paragraph 4 and it is hereby agreed between the parties that where there is an inability to obtain a Market Value for such securities from a generally accepted pricing source, the Market Value for such securities for the purpose of (a) and (b) above shall be nil.
>
> For the avoidance of doubt the value of the securities for the purpose of Sub-clause (c) above shall be the Market Value.

An additional provision sometimes seen in this context concerns the default of a Security's issuer, eg:

> If during the course of any Transaction under this Agreement there is an event of default under the terms and conditions of the Security which is the subject of a Transaction, then at the option of either party (exercised by written notice to the other party) the Repurchase Date for each such Transaction shall be deemed to have immediately occurred, and the parties shall terminate each such Transaction with settlement to occur within two business days of the date of the notice.

No consequential loss

Paragraph 10(i) states that the Agreement constitutes a complete statement of the remedies available to each party for an Event of Default and paragraph 10(i) prohibits consequential losses.

Some counterparties will seek to disapply either or both of these provisions. Whether this is acceptable is a matter of policy.

Closing documentation requirements

Finally, requirements for closing documents are starting to appear in Annex I. These include general documentation requests, such as:

> Each party shall deliver promptly to the other party evidence of signing authority (including specimen signatures) after executing this Agreement.

as well as requests for more detailed and more wide-ranging documentation:

> Each party shall deliver to the other party evidence of signing authority (including specimen signatures). In addition, Party A shall deliver Party B an independent, external legal opinion in form and substance satisfactory to Party B confirming Party A's capacity and authority to enter into the Transactions contemplated under this Agreement together with a board resolution authorising the execution of this Agreement and the entry into Transactions under it.

or

> Each party shall deliver to the other, upon request, such other documents as tax forms, financial statements, articles of incorporation, corporate resolutions, or other evidence of capacity, authority, incumbency and specimen signatures and any other relevant documents that are required by law or are reasonably requested.

Such documentation might, for instance, be required from a hedge fund counterparty.

In Chapter 5 Christian Johnson presents examples of provisions in Annex I to the Master Repurchase Agreement.

TBMA/ISMA GMRA Annex II

> **ANNEX II**
> **Form of Confirmation**
>
> To:_____
> From:_____
> Date:_____
> Subject: [Repurchase][Buy/Sell Back]* Transaction
> (Reference Number:)
> Dear Sirs,
> The purpose of this [letter]/[facsimile]/[telex], a "Confirmation" for the purposes of the Agreement, is to set forth the terms and conditions of the above repurchase transaction entered into between us on the Contract Date referred to below.
>
> ⇛

> This Confirmation supplements and forms part of, and is subject to, the Global Master Repurchase Agreement as entered into between us as of [ ] as the same may be amended from time to time (the "Agreement"). All provisions contained in the Agreement govern this Confirmation except as expressly modified below. Words and phrases defined in the Agreement and used in this Confirmation shall have the same meaning herein as in the Agreement.
> 1. Contract Date:
> 2. Purchased Securities [state type[s] and nominal value[s]]:
> 3. CUSIP, ISIN or other identifying number[s]:
> 4. Buyer:
> 5. Seller:
> 6. Purchase Date:
> 7. Purchase Price:
> 8. Contractual Currency:
> [9. Repurchase Date]:*
> [10. Terminable on demand]:*
> 11. Pricing Rate:
> [12. Sell Back Price]:*
> 13. Buyer's Bank Account[s] Details:
> 14. Seller's Bank Account[s] Details:
> [15. The Transaction is an Agency Transaction. [Name of Agent] is acting as agent for [name or identifier of Principal]]:*
> [16. Additional Terms]:*
>
> Yours faithfully,
>
> * Delete as appropriate

Annex II is a sample Confirmation. Frequently, repo confirmations do not much resemble it. Many are sent out electronically and have the appearance of contract notes. However, they must be agreed before securities and cash can be transferred between the parties.

Other annexes

TBMA and ISMA have issued a number of country and product Annexes for use with the TBMA/ISMA GMRA. They are:

Country Annexes
- Canadian Annex
- Italian Annex
- Japanese Securities Annex
- Netherlands Annex
- South African Annex
- Thai Annex

"Product" Annexes

- Agency Annex and Addendum
- Bills Annex
- Buy/Sell Back Annex
- Equities Annex
- Gilts Annex

All these Annexes are available from the websites of ISMA (www.isma.org) and TBMA (www. bondmarkets.com).

Canadian Annex

The Canadian Annex is half a page long and solely concerns annualising the Pricing Rate to conform with the requirements of Section 4 of the Interest Act (Canada).

Italian Annex

The Italian Annex is used for repos or buy/sellbacks in securities issued in Italy, whether or not the issuer is actually Italian.

The Italian Annex mainly concerns itself with three matters, viz:
- late delivery;
- withholding tax; and
- income.

In the Italian market there is no procedure for late delivery of Securities or Equivalent Securities. The Bank of Italy accepts only performance strictly in line with the agreement terms and may impose heavy sanctions, including fines, for failed or delayed delivery. Italian market players, therefore, consider it important for the party that has failed to receive delivery of Securities or Equivalent Securities to have additional remedies. Paragraph 4 of the Annex makes it clear that, where the innocent party terminates the Transaction, it is entitled to recover all costs associated with the termination, including interest lost on any deposit that the innocent party has to place with the Bank of Italy.

As an alternative to terminating the Transaction, the innocent party may choose to roll it over in whole or in part. This is achieved by terminating the original Transaction and entering into a replacement Transaction. The Pricing Rate for the replacement Transaction is minus 5 per cent, unless the parties agree otherwise. If a partial delivery is involved, the Seller can refuse delivery and roll over the undelivered part on the same terms as if it had rolled over the whole lot.

Paragraph 5 of this Annex states that an Italian withholding tax may need to be applied to the capital gains realised as a result of the Transactions in Italian securities. In such case the party that is required to pay the amount of such Italian withholding tax will be entitled to deduct such amount from the Repurchase Price or to obtain its reimbursement from the other party within 10 days of its demand. The formula contained in this paragraph reflects the calculation needed to determine the amount of such withholding tax. This paragraph also provides that the party that has made the deduction in respect of such withholding tax shall help the other party (by, for instance, providing vouchers) in obtaining any tax relief or tax credit available under any applicable tax treaty, or under the local law of the country of which such other party is a resident or out of which it is acting, by providing to it appropriate evidence of the payment of the amount deducted to the Italian tax authorities.

As far as Income is concerned, no tax event is deemed to occur if the securities cease to be Net Paying Securities. In fact, since January 1997 Italian bonds have paid their coupons gross to non-residents whose jurisdictions of incorporation have a double tax treaty with Italy containing an "exchange of information" provision. Furthermore, in the new paragraph 5(b) the Buyer may be exempt from Italian withholding tax if there is a double tax treaty in place or if it is a supranational entity.

As regards buy/sellbacks, the agreed Pricing Rate is adjusted by applying the Pricing Rate Adjustment Price to give a new Pricing Rate, which in turn establishes a new Sellback Price that takes into account the applicable withholding tax rate.

Japanese Securities Annex

The Japanese Securities Annex firstly concerns new withholding tax measures for Exempt Securities. It moves on to securities transfers, with an implied preference for them to take place through centralised clearing systems such as BOJ Net, Euroclear or Clearstream. It disapplies payment and securities netting in respect of Japanese Securities (paragraphs 6(h) and (i)). Finally, it makes termination under the Act of Insolvency Event of Default automatic without exception.

Netherlands Annex

The Netherlands Annex is used only for repo transactions involving Dutch domestic securities where both parties are Dutch. Parties no longer need it for cross-border Transactions in Dutch securities. The Annex changes the governing law to Netherlands law and provides that the Buyer can settle in cash if physical delivery is not reasonably practicable upon termination. The Annex also includes additional representations and Events of Default.

South African Annex

The South African Annex applies to parties incorporated in or acting through a branch in South Africa.

The Annex aims to amend the Act of Insolvency definition in paragraph 2(a), particularly in relation to South African concepts of insolvency, such as curatorship (a sort of administration process for banks). The Annex adds four new Events of Default to paragraph 10(a). These relate to various insolvency proceedings under South African law.

There is also a provision for overnight repo, and a representation that a South African party has obtained any South African Reserve Bank exchange control approvals needed to enter into the TBMA/ISMA GMRA and Transactions under it.

Thai Annex

The Thai Annex covers Thai domestic securities transactions. It changes the governing law to Thai law and the jurisdiction to the Thai courts. It also states that Confirmations for Transactions need to be signed by both parties.

Agency Annex and Addendum

The Agency Annex is used where a party is acting on behalf of a single disclosed Principal. The Addendum to the Agency Annex is used where it is acting on behalf of multiple disclosed Principals.

The Confirmation must state if a Transaction is an Agency Transaction.

The identity of the Principal must be disclosed in some way. This is useful for credit exposure purposes and to determine if the Principal is subject to the laws of a jurisdiction where close-out netting works.

The agent must also have actual authority to enter into Transactions for a single Principal.

Agent-to-agent Transactions are not possible under the Annex. This is because margin maintenance and close-out netting operate on a Principal-to-Principal basis.

Paragraph 3 provides that, if an agent learns that its Principal is afflicted by an Event of Default or a breach of the warranty in paragraph 5(c) of the Annex, it will inform the other party at once.

Paragraph 4 states that the TBMA/ISMA GMRA operates as a single agreement between each Principal and the other party. There is an extra Event of Default that entitles the other party to give a Default Notice to the Principal if an Event of Default occurs to the agent. This provision is important because the other party might have difficulty in enforcing rights where the agent has defaulted.

The agent gives a warranty of authority to act for the Principal in paragraph 5(c) of the Annex. If it is not in fact authorised to act on behalf of the Principal, the agent will become liable in damages.

The Agency Annex Addendum is used where the agent wants to enter into Transactions for more than one Principal or block transactions. These Principals must all be disclosed and the agent must warrant that it has actual authority to act on behalf of each Principal.

The main provisions of the Addendum are that:

- The agent must allocate Transactions between the various Principals *before* the Purchase Date and, when they have been allocated, the other party shall be deemed to have a contract with each Principal. This is to avoid legal uncertainty about the status of the Transaction if it is not allocated before the Purchase Date and the relevant Principal becomes insolvent. Until the allocation is done the risk is on the agent.
- Margin transfers are allocated *pro rata* between each Pooled Principal at the end of each Business Day according to the proportion that this represents of the aggregate Net Exposure outstanding. Therefore, margin calls may be made on a net aggregated basis. This involves an automatic rebalancing of margin between the Principals and is common practice in the fund management industry. The positions of all Principals are taken into account in aggregate rather than on an individual Principal basis. In addition, rather than making individual margin transfers from one Principal to another or from a Principal to the other party, they rebalance or reallocate margin already held by book entries rather than making actual payments or deliveries.
- The agent must maintain accounting records of the various allocations and the pooling arrangements, and promptly provide the other party with a statement of them if requested.
- The agent warrants that the information in such statement is complete and accurate; that each Principal is duly authorised to enter into Transactions and perform their obligations; and that no actual or potential Event of Default has occurred to any Principal to whom Transactions have been allocated.

Bills Annex

The Bills Annex is used for Transactions in certificates of deposit, bills of exchange, local authority bills and UK Treasury bills, all of which may also be Margin Securities.

The Annex amends the definition of "Equivalent Securities" and states that instruments must be executed by both parties acting in the same capacity (ie, principal to principal). Because they are short-term in nature (typically up to six months' tenor), their maturity date must be after the Repurchase Date. Where they are Margin Securities, they must have a maturity date at least one day beyond the Repurchase Date of the longest outstanding Transaction when the margin transfer is made.

The Seller guarantees payment of eligible bank bills and undertakes to endorse them if required. The Seller is likely to be a bank, because only its guarantee is likely to be acceptable in the market.

Buy/Sell Back Annex
Buy/sellbacks are very popular in Italy and Spain, and this Annex should be used for them where they are to be covered by the TBMA/ISMA GMRA.

The Confirmation must state if it is a buy/sellback transaction and the deal may be confirmed in one document or in two separate Confirmations detailing each leg of the transactions. The parties must agree the Sellback Price and the Pricing Rate.

The Annex amends the TBMA/ISMA GMRA to reflect differences between buy/sellbacks and repos. These are that:
- buy/sellbacks are not terminable on demand;
- the Purchase Price shall be quoted exclusive of accrued interest. This is the same with the Sellback Price;
- Buy/sellbacks are subject to repricing rather than margin maintenance; and
- manufactured dividends are not paid, but any income payments are factored into the Sellback Price.

Equities Annex
Parties use the Equities Annex when they undertake equities repo transactions or are using equities as Margin Securities. The Annex principally deals with three areas, viz:
- dividends;
- corporate actions; and
- voting rights.

While the Annex retains the standard position of a Buyer paying over a dividend to a Seller when it receives it, there is also the alternative of a Seller seeking to make a substitution of securities where it foresees that a repo transaction will cross over an Income Payment Date. Where this is desired, but the substitution cannot be made, the Seller can notify the Buyer that it wishes to terminate the Transaction concerned.

Where neither a termination nor a substitution is made, the Buyer will pay the Seller a manufactured dividend plus an amount equal to any tax benefit to which the Buyer may be entitled.

Where the Buyer fails to make reasonable efforts to deliver securities upon termination, it must indemnify the Seller against any costs (except consequential losses) incurred because of the non-delivery. It must also indemnify the Seller against any withholding tax liabilities that it could have avoided by using any tax credit to which it was entitled.

Corporate actions include such events as rights issues, scrip issues and takeover offers for a company.

With corporate actions, the Buyer must notify the Seller within a reasonable period of time after the date on which a holder of such securities would have been made aware of the corporate action by the issuer. In those circumstances the Seller may either terminate the Transaction and demand return of its securities, so that it can decide how it wishes to exercise its rights, or it may tell the Buyer that it wishes to receive Equivalent Securities in the form they take following the corporate action.

As regards voting rights, neither the Buyer nor the transferee of margin securities is obligated to exercise any voting rights on equities that have been bought under a repo or supplied as margin, unless the parties otherwise agree.

Gilts Annex
The Gilts Annex is issued by the Bank of England and not the TBMA or ISMA.

A revised Code of Best Practice has been produced. It is intended to reflect best practice that has developed over time in other repo markets as well as in the cash, gilt and stock lending markets. The Code has been recognised by the UK's Financial Services Authority. It calls for:
(i) daily marking to market;
(ii) margin to be called whenever a counterparty has a mark-to-market exposure that it considers material;
(iii) the confirmation to be sent on the trade date and checked on a timely basis; and
(iv) parties seriously to consider using the Gilts Annex and the TBMA/ISMA GMRA.

The Gilts Annex is a commonly used product Annex in the European market.

The following is a paragraph-by-paragraph commentary on the Gilts Annex, the text of which is obtainable from ISMA's website (www.isma.org).

Paragraph 1 – Interpretation
This paragraph provides four definitions and states that terms specified in the TBMA/ISMA GMRA shall have the same meanings in this Annex.

Paragraph 2 – Scope
Transactions under the TBMA/ISMA GMRA may include gilt repo transactions. The Annex's terms and conditions may also cover other securities under "Delivery by Value" transactions (see page 114).

Paragraph 3 – Crest Service
This paragraph contains provisions for the use of the Crest service through which gilts are usually held and transferred. Indeed, the rules for taxing gilt interest payments will allow payment of gross coupons only if they are held in special accounts called "STAR" accounts at Crest. Crest provides a secure settlement system for gilt-edged securities through electronic book-entry transfers in real time, with an assured payment mechanism provided by settlement banks.

The Crest system has several curiosities, two of which are the assured payment system and DBV Transactions.

CRESTCo (which operates the Crest system) is now owned by Euroclear Bank SA/NV.

Paragraph 3.2. has the first appearance of the assured payment system.

Crest's assured payment mechanism is a variation on delivery versus payment. Transfers of gilts between parties' respective Crest accounts will trigger an automatic payment obligation to the person transferring (the transferor). This is a payment obligation, not an actual payment, as far as Crest is concerned because the Crest service depends upon settlement banks. Each Crest member must name a settlement bank that undertakes to meet its payment obligations. Therefore, the assured payment obligation takes place between the transferor's and transferee's respective settlement banks, not within Crest itself.

Technically paragraph 3.2. treats the assured payment obligation as discharging the transferee's obligation to the transferor in respect of that assured payment obligation.

Paragraphs 3.3. and 3.4. deal with DBV Transactions, which use Crest's "Delivery by Value" service. This service enables Crest members to "lend" money to each other on an overnight basis, secured by the delivery of gilts to the "lender". The transactions are not structured as secured loans, but as sales and repurchases, and title to the gilts passes to the transferee, even though the Registrar does not record the transfer, because the transactions are all overnight. Because the service was designed for cash-driven transactions, the transferee cannot state which gilts it requires: these are selected automatically by Crest from those available in the transferor's account, as stated in paragraph 3.3.(c). This will usually be late in the dealing day. The transferee may, however, limit the types of stock that may be delivered to it, eg, British government or non-British government stock only, or any stock deliverable through Crest. So the Crest service also potentially contemplates the transfer of non-gilts and this was foreshadowed in paragraph 2.2. The transactions are automatically reversed by the system on the morning of the following Business Day, at the same price as the original transfer.

Paragraph 3.3.(b) states additional requirements for DBV Transaction Confirmations.

Paragraph 3.3.(d) requires that payment of repo "interest" should be made inside or outside the Crest system in same-day funds. Please note that Crest's automatic assured payment obligation on the reversal is equal only to the cash provided at the time of the transfer (ie, the Purchase Price) and does not include the parties' agreed repo rate.

Paragraph 3.3.(e) covers a failure to redeliver gilts on the Repurchase Date following an event that prevents Crest from automatically reversing the transaction. The suspension or termination of either party's Crest membership is specified as a cause of this failure.

If the Seller defaults, this is treated as a failure to pay the Repurchase Price (which entitles the Buyer to call an Event of Default under paragraph 10(a)(i) of the TBMA/ISMA GMRA). If the Buyer defaults, this is treated as a failure to redeliver securities (which would trigger paragraph 10(h) of the TBMA/ISMA GMRA or paragraph 10(a)(ii) if that applies).

Paragraph 3.3.(g) covers a position arising after an Event of Default affects a DBV Transaction. If Equivalent Securities are returned to the Seller's Crest account by the Buyer against an assured payment, these transactions must be reversed. This is because there must be certainty on whether a DBV Transaction is terminated or not by an Event of Default and the effect of the Event of Default on all other Transactions between the parties.

Paragraph 3.4. enables the parties to enter into DBV Transactions for longer than overnight – either for a fixed term (a "Term DBV Repo") or on demand (an "Open DBV Repo"). Since the transaction is made up of a series of overnight transactions, this would, in theory, require a series of separate trades and Confirmations for each trading day. But paragraph 3.4.(a) lets the parties do a single trade and send a single Confirmation. This does not change the legal structure as separate transactions or the operational mechanics. These remain the same as for separate overnight contracts.

The series of transactions would be terminated by an Event of Default under paragraph 10(a) of the TBMA/ISMA GMRA, or by a terminating event under paragraph 10(g) or (h) (ie, a mini close-out). Paragraph 3.4.(f) provides that the repo interest element of the Repurchase Price of each Transaction is deferred until the maturity of the last Transaction in the series. Please note that the rest of the Repurchase Price, which will equal the Purchase Price, is automatically paid by the daily reversals of the DBV Transaction by Crest. However, until maturity the repo interest element forms part of the exposure calculation for margining purposes under paragraph 4(c) of the TBMA/ISMA GMRA as if it were an unpaid manufactured dividend owed by the Buyer to the Seller under paragraph 5 of the TBMA/ISMA GMRA. (See paragraph 3.4.(g) of the Annex for further explanation.)

Paragraph 3.4.(h) provides for the immediate payment of repo interest if the series of DBV Transactions is terminated by an Event of Default under paragraph 10(a) of the TBMA/ISMA GMRA.

Paragraph 4 – Transactions in partly paid securities
If partly paid or nil paid securities are the subject of a gilt repo or buy/sellback and a call or instalment becomes due before maturity, it will be the Buyer (because it owns the securities on the relevant date) that will be liable to pay the call or instalment. Paragraph 4 requires that:
(a) the Seller must pay the Buyer in advance the amount of the call or instalment (paragraph 4.2.);
(b) on the Repurchase Date the Repurchase Price is not adjusted to reflect the call or instalment, or the Seller's advance payment (paragraph 4.3.); and
(c) the Buyer must redeliver Equivalent Securities in respect of which the call or instalment has been satisfied (paragraph 4.4.).

It would be normal for the securities to rise in price after the call or instalment has been paid. This should trigger a margin call from the Seller to the Buyer for a margin transfer to the Seller equal to the difference, so that it regains the money that it gave to the Buyer.

Paragraph 5 – Exercise of rights of conversion
This provision covers conversion rights arising in respect of securities that are covered by a gilt repo or buy/sellback. It essentially enables the Seller to require the Buyer to exercise those rights as required by the Seller. This works by the Seller issuing a notice to the Buyer requesting a change in the type of securities that it is entitled to receive from the Buyer at the maturity of the Transaction. So, instead of receiving back securities in the same form as originally sold to the Buyer, it may ask for securities in their converted form. Therefore, if the Buyer wishes to avoid a breach at maturity, it will need to exercise its conversion rights in accordance with the Seller's wishes or buy such securities in the market. If the Seller does not issue a notice, the Buyer may deliver the securities at maturity in their unconverted form.

Paragraph 6 – Termination of on demand Transactions
The general position for on-demand repos and buy/sellbacks in paragraph 3(e) of the TBMA/ISMA GMRA (allowing the transactions to be closed out by notice within the minimum customary settlement period for the relevant securities) is altered by requiring at least one Business Day's notice of termination or allowing same-day termination if demand is made by 10.00 a.m. London time.

Paragraph 7 – Dividend entitlements: effect on margin provisions
Paragraph 7 deals with an ex-dividend date arising with a gilt repo or buy/sellback transaction, or on gilts provided as margin and not returned. The length of the ex-dividend period for most gilt-edged securities has been reduced to seven Business Days.

An ex-dividend date entitles the current holder of a security to its dividend. This would lower the price of the gilt and usually result in the Buyer making a margin call on the Seller, and, when the dividend is paid, paying it to the Seller under the manufactured dividend provisions of the TBMA/ISMAGMRA. However, it was considered unfair for the Buyer to make a margin call in these circumstances, since it faced minimal risk, because the dividend was on a stock issued by the UK government. Instead the Seller is deemed to have paid Cash Margin to the Buyer equal to the dividend and that Cash Margin is deemed to be returned when the Transaction matures. However, this overlooks paragraph 4(f), where the Buyer is obligated to pay interest on Cash Margin. As this is deemed or theoretical Cash Margin, the Buyer has not actually received any money and so the way around this is for the parties to agree a zero interest rate for these purposes at the time of trading.

The following chapter reviews the European Master Agreement.

* Within chapters, terms used in the commentaries may have capitalisation or minor spelling differences to match the corresponding documentation.

Chapter 4

The European Master Agreement

Background

In July 1998 the Banking Federation of the European Union (the "FBE") was approached by a number of ad hoc working groups that proposed circulating a draft of the document later to become known as the European Master Agreement ("EMA") to FBE members.

The FBE circulated the document with comments requested by early 1999. During this period overtures were made to the International Swaps and Derivatives Association (ISDA) and the International Securities Market Association (ISMA) for cooperation, but to no avail.

On 5 February 1999 the FBE approved the EMA in principle, which was followed by full FBE board approval on 26 March 1999. On 30 July 1999 the FBE issued a final draft of the EMA along with an explanatory memorandum.

The EMA was officially launched at the FBE's Berlin board meeting held on 29 October 1999. The document was jointly sponsored by the FBE, the European Savings Banks Group and the European Association of Co-operative Banks. The EMA underwent minor revision in January 2001 and major revision of some of its parts in early 2004.

The full text of the EMA is available on the FBE's website (www.fbe.be). Versions are offered in seven languages (English, French, German, Greek, Italian, Portuguese and Spanish). It is reproduced as Appendix 3 of this book with the kind permission of the European Banking Federation.

Legal opinions have been commissioned from law firms in 14 countries. France and Germany were the main promoters of the EMA.

Goals and benefits of the EMA

Goals

The EMA was created to provide a common standard text there could be used in different languages and under different national laws within and outside the European Union (EU). The aim is to encourage replacement of the many domestic agreements currently in use. Initially the EMA focused on agreements covering repos and securities lending. Indeed, one goal was to use the EMA in developing a single euro-denominated repo and securities lending market. The European Central Bank has solely used the EMA since November 2001 for repo transactions with its EU and Swiss counterparties.

The EMA is designed to be a multi-product agreement like the ISDA Master Agreement. The eventual aim is to document all trading transactions under one master agreement. As mentioned above, initially the EMA covered repo and securities lending transactions, but in early 2004 this was extended to interest rate derivatives transactions, options and foreign exchange transactions, with the possibility of other products being added in the future.

The EMA is also designed to be multi-jurisdictional. This means that parties to it may choose the particular governing law under which it is to operate and its contractual language, in this way taking into account individual national legal requirements.

Benefits
The EMA:

- proposes a standard multi-product agreement with uniform Events of Default;
- aims to avoid inconsistencies among numerous single product master agreements;
- aims to speed up the negotiation process by reducing the volume of master agreements handled and the number of legal opinions required;
- typifies the single agreement approach and includes a close-out netting mechanism which reduces credit exposure and hence regulatory capital requirements for financial institutions;
- reduces the risk of "cherry picking" (which could happen where the parties may have several single product master agreements in existence in jurisdictions not amenable to close-out netting);
- could potentially reduce documentation backlogs;
- facilitates cross-product netting and margining (for those who can do it);
- simplifies and potentially reduces the number of domestic and cross-border European master agreements into one document. Ultimately, the use of the EMA could result in further harmonisation of operational provisions among the New York or English law master agreements developed by ISDA, The Bond Market Association (TBMA), ISMA and the International Securities Lending Association (ISLA). This issue is particularly relevant with respect to back-to-back transactions, where mismatches and documentation basis risk can arise through inconsistencies;
- possibly increases trading with more European counterparties that want to use an agreement that is standard in their country. This is in line with the EMA's goal to become the common basic agreement text very close to home country standard documentation;
- could offer a standard for documentation in countries lacking their own standard forms;
- offers flexibility through choice of governing law and submission to courts in agreed jurisdictions;
- may offer cost savings;
- possibly lends itself more easily to computerisation, eg, formation of databases of standard and non-standard terms; and
- could be used in the 10 countries that acceded to the EU on 1 May 2004, if not already used there.

Structure of the European Master Agreement

The EMA is composed of the following elements:

- General Provisions (which are always incorporated into the Agreement);
- Separate Product Annexes for Repurchase Transactions, Securities Loans and Derivatives. The Derivatives Annex also has three specialist Supplements for Foreign Exchange Transactions, Interest Rate Transactions and Options;

THE EUROPEAN MASTER AGREEMENT

- A Margin Maintenance Annex for Repurchase Transactions, Securities Loans and Derivatives; and
- Special Provisions (which consist of individually negotiated terms).

This structure is shown in Exhibit 4.1

Exhibit 4.1
Overview of EMA structure

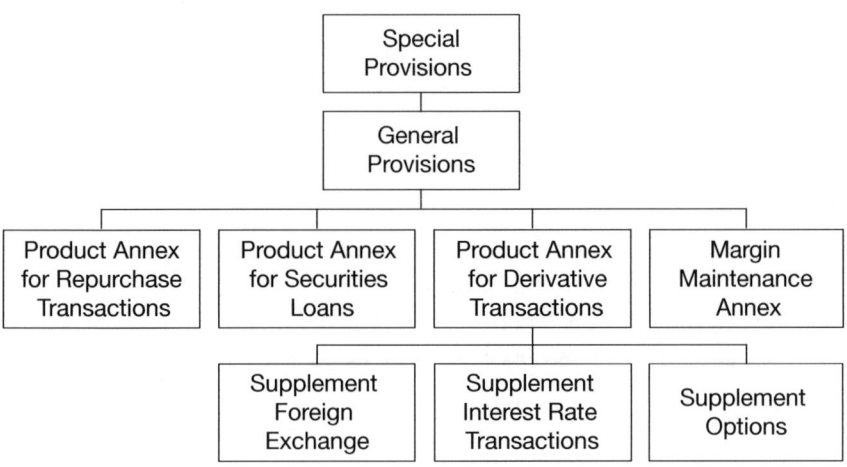

Source: Author's own

General Provisions

The General Provisions and Annexes are essentially terms of business that are not signed as such, but are incorporated into the EMA. The Special Provisions are what the parties sign. Exceptionally, the General Provisions may be incorporated into the terms of a Transaction, usually where the Special Provisions are not yet agreed and signed. In Section 1(2) the second sentence addresses such situations.

The General Provisions are a multi-product document broadly similar to an ISDA Master Agreement. They contain contractual principles common to repos, securities loans and derivatives. Duplications and inconsistencies that could arise where parties enter into different master agreements with each other are therefore avoided. A further benefit is that the Annexes that deal specifically with repos, securities loans, derivatives and margin maintenance are relatively brief and focused technical documents.

The General Provisions contain the following 11 Sections:

1. Purpose, Structure, Interpretation
2. Transactions
3. Payments, Deliveries and Related Definitions
4. Taxes

119

5. Representations
6. Termination
7. Final Settlement Amount
8. Notices
9. Booking Offices
10. Miscellaneous
11. Governing Law, Settlement of Disputes, Jurisdiction, and Arbitration.

Generally, these provisions are in line with existing market documentation standards. Where this is not so (eg, with default and no default termination events), a choice has to be made or a new approach taken.

Special Provisions

The Special Provisions are the only part of the EMA signed by the parties. It will normally constitute the Master Agreement, incorporate Product Annexes, Supplements and the Margin Maintenance Annex, and include bilaterally agreed provisions, including choice of law and any amendments and additions to terms in the General Provisions. It may be quite short if the parties are satisfied with the General Provisions of the EMA and do not amend them. It sets the scope of the contractual arrangements between the parties.

Product Annexes
The three Product Annexes apply to repos, securities lending transactions and derivatives transactions respectively, and address issues arising under them in a consistent manner, eg, definitions, deliveries and payments, corporate and other special events, subscription rights (for repos and securities loans), and market disruption.

The following comments apply to the Product Annexes for repos and securities loans.

Under these Annexes consequential damages arising from late delivery are excluded on principle, but costs incurred in borrowing substitute securities by the party entitled to receive the securities may be charged.

Generally, subscription rights will need to be transferred to the Seller or Lender of the securities, whether or not the Buyer or Borrower then holds the securities. Often the Buyer or Borrower will need to purchase subscription rights in the market in order to transfer them. The treatment of subscription rights is therefore broadly in line with the way income distributions are normally treated under repo and securities lending transactions.

Because the EMA is silent on voting rights, the person who owns the securities at the relevant time may freely exercise such rights. Unless expressly agreed, the Seller or Lender is not entitled to give voting instructions. The fact that the Buyer or Borrower may be holding securities of the same kind as those purchased at the relevant time will have no impact. (These matters will be revisited later in this chapter, where the Annexes will be examined more closely.)

Margin Maintenance Annex
The Margin Maintenance Annex for Repurchase Transactions, Securities Loans and Derivatives Transactions sets out common rules on margin provision for these types of transactions. This is a new approach in the market. The Margin Maintenance Annex states

in its Section 1(1) that margining may occur globally for all Transactions, or for each individual Transaction, or for specified groups of Transactions (eg, by distinguishing among repos, securities loans and derivatives transactions, or between equity and debt transactions) on each Business Day. It allows margin calculations to be made on a net basis for all transactions governed by the EMA.

The commentary on the EMA in this chapter will be confined to the General Provisions, the Special Provisions, the Product Annexes for Repurchase Transactions and Securities Loans, and the Margin Maintenance Annex. It will not discuss the Derivatives Annex nor its Supplements because they are not central to the subject of this book.

Clause-by-clause analysis of the EMA
General Provisions
Section 1

> **MASTER AGREEMENT**
> **FOR FINANCIAL TRANSACTIONS**
>
> **GENERAL PROVISIONS**
> Edition 2004
>
> **1. Purpose, Structure, Interpretation**
> (1) *Purpose, Applicability.* The provisions set out in this document (the "General Provisions") are intended to govern financial transactions (each a "Transaction") under any Master Agreement for Financial Transactions (each a "Master Agreement") based on the form published by the Banking Federation of the European Union ("FBE"). The provisions of a Master Agreement shall apply to the extent that they are incorporated by the parties into the terms of a Transaction or type of Transactions between them.

The broad, general sweep of the EMA is apparent in this very first sub-section. The General Provisions can govern financial transactions under any master agreement based on, but not identical to, the EMA. The provisions of such a master agreement shall apply provided that the parties specify this in the Transaction terms (ie, in any oral agreement between dealers and in the Transaction Confirmation).

> (2) *Structure.* A Master Agreement consists of (i) an agreement between the parties thereto providing a basis for Transactions between them (the "Special Provisions"),
> ⟫→

> (ii) these General Provisions, (iii) any annexes thereto (each an "Annex"), being Annexes concerning particular types of Transactions ("Product Annexes") or concerning other matters and (iv) any supplements to the Product Annexes (each a "Supplement"). If no Special Provisions have been agreed, these General Provisions (together with, if applicable, any Annexes and any Supplements thereto) shall constitute a Master Agreement governing all Transactions into the terms of which they have been incorporated. Each Master Agreement and the terms agreed in respect of all Transactions thereunder shall collectively be referred to herein as the "Agreement".

A Master Agreement comprises the Special Provisions, the General Provisions, any Product Annexes or Supplements and any other Annexes. Where no Special Provisions have been agreed, the General Provisions and any agreed Annexes will constitute a Master Agreement, which will govern all Transactions that state that it does so. The Master Agreement and the agreed Transaction terms shall be collectively referred to as the "Agreement". Note that the Confirmation is not referred to directly, but, as will be seen when discussing the General Provisions in more detail, it is an important part of the Agreement.

> (3) *Interpretation.* In the event of any conflict between different parts of the Agreement, (i) any Annex shall prevail over the General Provisions, (ii) the Special Provisions shall prevail over the General Provisions and any Annex and (iii) the terms agreed in respect of an individual Transaction shall, in respect of that Transaction only, prevail over all other terms of the Agreement. Unless otherwise specified, all references herein or in any Annex to Sections are to Sections of these General Provisions or such Annex, respectively. Certain expressions used in the Agreement are defined at the places indicated in the Index of Defined Terms published by the FBE in connection with these General Provisions.

This is primarily an Inconsistency clause. Where there is any conflict between parts of the EMA:

- any Annex shall prevail over the General Provisions;
- the Special Provisions shall prevail over the General Provisions and any Annex; and
- agreed terms for an individual Transaction shall prevail over all other terms of the EMA in respect of that Transaction only.

This hierarchy corresponds to the basic approach of the ISDA Master Agreement.

Please note that there is no Definitions Section as such in the General Provisions. Definitions appear in the body of the EMA. However, at the end of the EMA there is an Index of Defined Terms that refers to the location of definitions within it.

THE EUROPEAN MASTER AGREEMENT

> (4) *Single Agreement.* The Agreement constitutes a single contractual relationship. Accordingly, (i) each obligation of a party under any Transaction is incurred and performed in consideration of the obligations incurred and to be performed by the other party under all Transactions, and (ii) unless otherwise agreed, a failure by a party to perform an obligation under any Transaction shall constitute a failure to perform under the Agreement as a whole. The parties enter into the Master Agreement between them and each Transaction thereunder in reliance on these principles, which they consider fundamental to their risk assessment.

This single agreement wording more closely resembles that in the TBMA/ISMA Global Master Repurchase Agreement than the text in the ISDA Master Agreement.

This sub-section acknowledges that the EMA and each Transaction under it constitutes a single contractual relationship, and that, where a party fails to perform an obligation under one Transaction, this constitutes a failure to perform under the whole EMA and consequently gives grounds to close it out. Therefore all Transactions are interdependent on each other.

The final sentence emphasises that the parties have entered into the EMA and the Transactions in reliance on the above principles, which are fundamental to their risk assessment.

The purpose of the single agreement provision is to prevent liquidators cherry picking. Cherry picking is a practice where a liquidator will honour payments on those Transactions that are profitable to his insolvent client and refuse to do so on other Transactions that are not profitable to them, but will insist that the counterparty performs its obligations in respect of those Transactions.

> (5) *Modifications.* Any modification of these General Provisions or any modified or new Annex which the FBE may promulgate in the future may become effective between the parties to a Master Agreement by each party notifying its acceptance in the manner designated by the FBE.

If the FBE modifies the terms of the General Provisions, or amends or issues new Annexes in the future, parties can adhere to them by notifying each other in the manner to be prescribed by the FBE. This could be by way of an amendment agreement or even by the protocol route used by ISDA, for instance, for Economic and Monetary Union (EMU) provisions.

Section 2

> **2. Transactions**
> (1) *Form.* A Transaction may be entered into orally or by any other means of communication.

This self-explanatory clause gives some flexibility for entering into Transactions.

> (2) *Confirmation.* Upon the parties having agreed on a Transaction each party shall promptly send to the other a confirmation (a "Confirmation") of such Transaction in the manner specified in Section 8(1). The absence of either or both Confirmations shall not affect the validity of the Transaction.

This clause anticipates that both parties will promptly send each other a Confirmation of the Transaction terms by letter, telex, fax or electronic messaging system (the methods mentioned in Section 8(1)). However, the Transaction remains valid even if one or both parties fail to issue a Confirmation.

In the United Kingdom the Financial Services Authority's *Conduct of Business Rules (2001)* requires parties to exchange Confirmations no later than the following Business Day.

Section 3

> **3. Payments, Deliveries and Related Definitions**
> (1) *Date, Place, Manner.* Each party shall make the payments and deliveries to be made by it at the time, date and place and to the account agreed in respect of the Transaction concerned and in the manner customary for payments or deliveries of the relevant kind. Each payment shall be made in the currency agreed in respect thereof (the "Contractual Currency"), free of all costs and in funds which are freely available on the due date. Each party may change its account for receiving a payment or delivery by giving notice to the other at least ten Business Days prior to the scheduled date for the relevant payment or delivery, unless the other party reasonably objects to such change and gives timely notice thereof.

The EMA envisages cash payments and physical delivery, as do the TBMA/ISMA GMRA, GMSLA (Global Master Securities Lending Agreement), OSLA (Overseas Securities Lending Agreement) and the ISDA Master Agreement.

Payments and deliveries must be made punctually, to the agreed account and in the customary manner for such payments and deliveries. Each payment must be in cleared funds in the agreed currency. Either party may, by giving not less than 10 Business Days' prior notice to the other, change its account for payments or deliveries, unless the other party promptly and reasonably objects to it. A party might object, for instance, if such a change of account is to an overseas office of the first party and the change might cause a withholding tax charge to arise. It might also object to an overseas transfer of account if there were a risk of exchange controls being imposed.

THE EUROPEAN MASTER AGREEMENT

> (2) *Transfer of Title, Retransfer of Securities*
>
> *(a) Transfer of Title.* Unless otherwise agreed, any delivery or transfer of securities or other financial instruments ("Securities") or any other assets (including, in respect of Derivative Transactions, any other underlying assets of such Transactions) by a party to the other pursuant to the Agreement shall constitute a transfer to such other party of the unrestricted title to such Securities and/or assets or, if customary in the place where delivery is to be effected, of a legal position (such as a co-ownership interest in a collective holding of Securities, the position as beneficiary of a trust or another form of beneficial ownership) which is the functional equivalent of such title (including, in each case, an unrestricted right to dispose of such Securities and/or assets) and not the creation of a security interest; the use of the terms "margin" or "substitution" shall not be construed as indicating an agreement to the contrary. The transferor of any Securities and/or assets shall, accordingly, (i) not retain in respect of those Securities and/or assets any ownership interest, security interest or right to dispose and (ii) execute all documents reasonably required to effect such full transfer. As far as transfer of Securities is concerned, if registered Securities are to be transferred, the transferee may dispose of the Securities received before the transfer is entered into the relevant register; if the entry depends upon a circumstance beyond the transferor's reasonable control, the transferor does not warrant that such entry will be effected.

The provision confirms the absolute right to transfer title from the transferor to the other party in a repo, securities lending or derivative transaction. This includes any pro-rated co-ownership rights in a collective pool of securities, as in the Euroclear or Clearstream systems, or being a beneficiary under a trust, in each case with the unfettered right to dispose of such securities. It is stressed that no security interest is thereby created and the terms "margin" or "substitution" shall not in themselves cause such title transfer to be called into question.

The transferor cedes all its ownership, charging or sale rights to the transferee and agrees to execute all necessary transfer documentation. If the transfer involves registered securities, the transferee is free to sell or transfer the securities before the original transfer is recorded by the registrar. The transferor does not have to warrant that the entry will be registered if there is a circumstance beyond its reasonable control.

> *(b) Retransfer of Securities.* An obligation to return or retransfer any Securities is an obligation to transfer Securities of the same kind as such Securities. Securities are "of the same kind" as other Securities if they are of the same issuer and the same type and nominal value and represent identical rights as such other Securities; if all such other Securities have been redeemed, redenominated, exchanged, converted, subdivided,

> consolidated or been the subject of a capital increase, capital reduction, call on partly paid securities or event similar to any of the foregoing, Securities "of the same kind" means the amount of Securities, money and other property (together "Substitute Assets") received in respect of such other Securities as a result of such event (provided that if any sum had to be paid in order to receive such Substitute Assets, an obligation to transfer them shall be conditional upon payment by the transferee of such sum to the transferor).

It is stated that securities of the same type, issuer, nominal value and with equivalent rights must be retransferred in a repo or securities lending transaction — but not the identically numbered securities. This requirement also applies if the securities concerned have been subject to a corporate event, whereupon equivalent securities reflecting the corporate event must be retransferred. However, if payment is due to be made for such substitute assets, the transferee should make such payment before retransferring them to the transferor, on the basis that a repo transaction (which is a temporary transfer of assets) aims to place the transferor in the same position that it would have been in if it had held the securities and not entered into the repo.

> (3) *Conditions Precedent.* Each payment or delivery obligation of a party is subject to the conditions precedent that (i) no Event of Default or event which by the lapse of time or the giving of notice (or both) may become an Event of Default with respect to the other party has occurred and is continuing and (ii) no notice of termination has been given in respect of the relevant Transaction because of a Change of Circumstances.

This provision reflects two-thirds of a similar provision in the ISDA Master Agreement (ie, Section 2(a)(iii)). A party's payment or delivery obligations are subject to no actual or potential Event of Default having occurred and no notice of termination having been issued due to a Change of Circumstances as listed in General Provisions Section 6(2).

> (4) *Payment Netting.* If on any date both parties would otherwise be required to make payments in the same currency in respect of the same Transaction, the mutual payment obligations shall automatically be set off against each other and the party owing the higher amount shall pay to the other the difference between the amounts owed. The parties may agree that this principle shall apply in respect of two or more Transactions or one or more types of Transactions or that it shall apply also in respect

THE EUROPEAN MASTER AGREEMENT

> of mutual obligations to deliver assets which are fungible with each other. If and so long as a single currency can be expressed in different currency units (such as the euro unit and national currency units under the principles governing the transition to European Economic and Monetary Union), the principle set forth in the first sentence of this subsection shall apply only if both payments are to be made in the same unit.

This provision permits single Transaction, multiple Transaction and cross-product payment netting where only the difference is payable by the party owing the higher amount to the other party. This procedure applies to cash payments and fungible securities (ie, securities of the same type and class). Payments must occur on the same day and in the same currency. This even applied where euros and national currencies were involved, but they cannot now be set off against each other and indeed this has not been possible since 1 January 2002 in any case.

> (5) *Late Payment.* If in respect of a Transaction a party fails to make a payment to the other when due (and, for the avoidance of doubt, without being entitled to withhold such payment), interest, payable on demand, shall accrue (before and after judgment) at the Default Rate on the amount outstanding, calculated for the period from (and including) the due date to (but excluding) the day on which such payment is received. "Default Rate" means the higher of (a) the Interbank Rate and (b) the cost to the other party, as certified by it, of funding the relevant amount, in each case plus any interest surcharge which may be agreed in the Special Provisions. "Interbank Rate" means the interbank offered interest rate charged by prime banks to each other for overnight deposits at the place of payment and in the currency of the amount outstanding for each day on which interest is to be charged (being, if an amount in euros is outstanding, the Euro Overnight Index Average ("EONIA") Rate calculated by the European Central Bank).

This provision states that interest will be chargeable on overdue payments at the Default Rate from, and including, the due date to, but excluding, the date payment is received, as is the normal practice in the derivatives markets. The Default Rate is defined as the higher of the overnight interbank rate for the currency concerned (eg, EONIA for the euro) or the Non-Defaulting Party's self-certified funding cost plus any interest surcharge agreed in the Special Provisions.

> (6) *Business Day Convention.* If any payment or delivery date, any determination or valuation date, any commencement or termination date or any exercise date agreed

> between the parties which is deemed to be a Business Day is not a Business Day, payments, deliveries, determinations or valuations shall be made or, as the case may be, the commencement date, the termination date or the exercise date shall be deemed to occur, as elected in respect of the relevant Transaction, on (a) the immediately preceding Business Day ("Preceding"), (b) the immediately following Business Day ("Following"), or (c) the immediately following Business Day, unless such day falls in the next calendar month, in which case the relevant payment, delivery, determination or valuation shall be made or, as the case may be, the relevant commencement date, termination date or exercise date shall be deemed to occur on the immediately preceding Business Day ("Modified Following" or "Modified"), provided that failing such election, (b) shall apply.

A Business Day Convention must be chosen for payments and deliveries. The options are Preceding, Following or Modified Following. If no choice is made, the fallback is the Following Business Day Convention.

> (7) *Business Day Definition.* "Business Day" means (a) in relation to any payment in euros a day on which all relevant parts of TARGET are operational to effect such a payment, (b) in relation to any payment in any other currency a day (other than a Saturday or a Sunday) on which commercial banks are open for business (including payments in the currency concerned as well as dealings in foreign exchange and foreign currency deposits) in the place(s) agreed in relation to the relevant Transaction or, if not so agreed, in the place where the relevant account is located and, if different, in the principal financial centre, if any, of the currency of such payment, (c) in relation to any delivery of Securities, (i) where a Transaction is to be settled through a securities settlement system, a day on which such securities settlement system is open for business in the place where delivery of the Securities is to be effected, and (ii) where a Transaction is to be settled in a way other than (i), a day (other than a Saturday or a Sunday) on which commercial banks are open for business in the place where delivery of the Securities is to be effected, (d) in relation to any delivery of any assets other than Securities, a day (other than a Saturday or a Sunday) on which commercial banks are open for business in the place where delivery of the relevant assets is to be effected or any other day agreed between the parties in the Confirmation of the relevant Transactions or otherwise, (e) in relation to any valuation, a day on which an up-to-date valuation based on the agreed price sources can reasonably be carried out, and (f) in relation to any notice or other communication, a day (other than a Saturday or Sunday) on which commercial banks are open for business in the city specified in the address provided by the recipient pursuant to Section 8(1).

THE EUROPEAN MASTER AGREEMENT

This standard provision covers cash payments, securities transfers, valuations and notices. It defines Business Day as follows:

(a) a day when the TARGET payment system is open for euro settlements;

(b) for other currencies, a non-weekend day when commercial banks are open for foreign exchange dealings in the place where the Transaction is to be made, failing which the principal financial centre for the currency concerned;

(c) for securities, a day when the relevant securities settlement system in the place where the securities are to be delivered is open for business, failing which a non-weekend day when commercial banks are open for the delivery of securities;

(d) for other assets, a non-weekend day on which commercial banks can take delivery of other assets. The timing of their delivery may also be stated in a Confirmation between the two parties;

(e) for up-to-date valuations, a day when the necessary price sources are available for the valuation to be carried out; and

(f) for notices, a non-weekend day when commercial banks are open for business.

> (8) *Market Value.* "Market Value" means in respect of any Securities as of any time on any date, (a) the price for such Securities then quoted through and obtainable from a generally recognised source agreed to by the parties and (b) failing such agreement or such quotation (i) if the Securities are listed on a stock exchange and not then suspended, their price last quoted on such exchange; (ii) if the Securities are not so listed, but have, on the main market on which they are traded, the price published or made public by a central bank or an entity of undisputed authority on such day, such price last published or made public; and (iii) in any other case, the average of the bid and offer prices for such Securities, as of such time on such date, as established by two leading market participants other than the parties, in each of the cases listed in (a) and (b) together with (if not included in such price) any interest accrued on such Securities as of that date.

This provision concerns the valuation of securities. In the first two instances mentioned valuation shall be determined by current market prices. Otherwise an average of the bid and offer prices provided by two independent market-makers shall be used to determine the Market Value. If accrued interest is not included in the price (called a "dirty price"), it must be added to any "clean price" obtained.

Section 4

> **4. Taxes**
> (1) *Withholding Tax.* If a party is or will be obligated to deduct or withhold an amount for or on account of any tax or other duty from a payment which it is to make, it shall

> pay to the other party such additional amounts as are necessary to ensure that such other party receives the full amount to which it would have been entitled at the time of such payment if no deduction or withholding had been required. This shall not apply if the tax or duty concerned is imposed or levied (a) by or on behalf or for the account of the jurisdiction (or a tax authority of or resident in the jurisdiction) in which the Booking Office of the payee (or its place of residence, if the payee is an individual) is located, (b) pursuant to (directly or indirectly) an obligation imposed by a treaty to which such jurisdiction is a party, or by a regulation or directive enacted under such treaty, or (c) because the payee has failed to perform its obligation under Section 10(4)(b).

Compared with the ISDA Master Agreement or the TBMA/ISMA GMRA, this is a relatively brief withholding tax gross up provision. If a payer is obligated by his tax authority to withhold tax on a payment, this clause requires him to gross up his payment so that the payee receives what he expected to receive. However, the gross up will not apply where it arises in a domestic income tax situation, or where there is a failure to follow treaty obligations, or where the payee fails to provide the necessary documentation to enable the payer to make a payment free of withholding tax or at a reduced rate. Withholding tax in this Agreement only applies to cross-border situations.

> (2) *Documentary Tax.* Subject to Section 10(2), each party shall pay any stamp, documentary or similar tax or duty payable with respect to the Agreement (a "Documentary Tax") and imposed upon it in the jurisdiction in which its Booking Office or place of residence is located and shall indemnify the other party for any Documentary Tax payable in such jurisdiction and imposed upon the other party, unless the Booking Office of such other party (or its place of residence, if the other party is an individual) is also located in such jurisdiction.

This provision states that in a non-default situation each party shall pay any stamp or similar tax imposed by its local tax jurisdiction on the Agreement. However, each party shall also indemnify the other party against such taxes in such jurisdiction, provided that the first party's tax jurisdiction is not the same as the other party's tax jurisdiction.

Section 5

> **5. Representations**
> (1) *Representations.* Each party represents to the other, as of the date on which it enters into a Master Agreement and as of each date on which a Transaction is entered into, that:
> ⟫➔

> (a) *Status.* It is validly existing under the laws of its organisation or incorporation;
> (b) *Corporate Action.* It is duly authorised to execute and deliver, and perform its obligations under, the Agreement;
> (c) *No Violation or Conflict.* The execution, delivery and performance of the Agreement do not violate or conflict with any provision of law, judgment or government or court order applicable to it, or any provision of its constitutional documents;
> (d) *Consents.* All governmental and other consents which are required to be obtained by it with respect to the Agreement have been obtained and are in full force and effect;
> (e) *Obligations Binding.* Its obligations under the Agreement are legal, valid and binding;
> (f) *Absence of Certain Events.* No Event of Default or event which by the lapse of time or the giving of notice (or both) may become an Event of Default and, to its knowledge, no Change of Circumstances with respect to it has occurred and is continuing;
> (g) *Absence of Litigation.* There is not pending or, to its knowledge, threatened against it any action, suit or proceeding before any court, tribunal, arbitrator or governmental or other authority that is likely to affect the legality, validity, binding effect or enforceability against it of the Agreement or its ability to perform its obligations under the Agreement;
> (h) *No Reliance.* It has the necessary knowledge and experience to assess the benefits and risks incurred in each Transaction and has not relied for such purpose on the other party;
> (i) *Margin.* It has full title to the Securities transferred, as margin or collateral, to the other party under the Agreement and that such Securities shall be free and clear of any lien, security interest or any other right which may affect the right of the other party to dispose freely of such Securities.

The representations apply mutually, as is normal, both when the EMA is signed and each time a Transaction is executed. Items (a)–(g) are common in most types of agreements, and concern status, authority, no conflicts, consents obtained, binding obligations, absence of adverse events and litigation. Item (f) includes Change of Circumstances as well as actual and potential Events of Default. Item (g) — absence of litigation — has no explicit materiality test for the effect of the litigation, although the stated results would clearly be adverse. Item (h) is a short non-reliance provision. Item (i) represents that a collateral giver has full legal title to Securities that it is to transfer to a collateral receiver, and that it can make that transfer free and clear of any security interest, ie, unencumbered.

> (2) *Applicability to Guarantor.* If a third person specified in the Special Provisions or in a Confirmation as Guarantor (a "Guarantor") has, in an instrument specified in the Special Provisions or otherwise agreed between the parties, given a guarantee or other credit support in respect of any obligations of either party under the Agreement (a "Guarantee"), then the representations of such party in respect of itself and the Agreement pursuant to subsection 1 (a) through (i) shall *mutatis mutandis* apply also to the Guarantor and the Guarantee.

This provision extends the representations in Section 5(1) to any guarantor or credit support provider, *mutatis mutandis*. Reference to the guarantor may be made in the Special Provisions or in a Confirmation.

Section 6(1)

Ten Events of Default are specified in Section 6(1):

1. Failure to Pay;
2. Failure to Provide or Return Margin or Collateral;
3. Other Breach of Agreement;
4. Misrepresentation;
5. Default under Specified Transactions;
6. Cross-Default;
7. Restructuring Without Assumption;
8. Insolvency Events;
9. Repudiation of Obligations;
10. Guarantee Ineffective.

An Event of Default is caused by one party only and gives the right to a Non-Defaulting Party to close out all Transactions under their EMA.

> **6. Termination**
> (1) *Termination due to an Event of Default*
> (a) *Event of Default.* The occurrence of any of the following events in respect of a party shall constitute an event of default ("Event of Default"):
> (i) *Failure to Pay or Deliver.* The party fails to make, when due, any payment or delivery under the Agreement and such failure continues for three Business Days after the day on which notice of such failure is given to the party;

A three-Business-Day grace period following notice by the Non-Defaulting Party is allowed.

> (ii) *Failure to Provide or Return Margin or Collateral.* The party fails to provide or return, when due, margin or collateral required to be provided or returned by it under the Agreement;

No grace period is allowed for a party that has failed to provide or return collateral.

> (iii) *Other Breach of Agreement.* The party fails to perform, when due, any other obligation under the Agreement and such failure continues for thirty days after the day on which notice of such failure is given to the party;

This Event of Default covers a party's failure to fulfil any other obligation under the EMA. This provision allows a remedial period of 30 calendar days after the Non-Defaulting Party gives notice to the Defaulting Party.

> (iv) *Misrepresentation.* Any representation by the party in the Agreement proves to have been incorrect on the date as of which it was made and the other party determines in good faith that, as a result thereof (or of the matters of fact or law which were not correctly stated), the balance of its risks and benefits under the Agreement is materially adversely affected;

A party makes a misrepresentation that the other party judges in good faith to affect the EMA in a materially adverse way.

> (v) *Default under Specified Transactions.* If the parties have, in the Special Provisions, specified any Transactions ("Specified Transactions") to which this Section 6(1)(a)(v) will apply, the party fails to make a payment or a delivery under any such Specified Transaction and such failure (A) results in the liquidation or early termination of, or an acceleration of obligations under, such Specified Transaction or (B) continues beyond any applicable grace period (or, if there is no such period, for at least three Business Days) after the last payment or delivery date of such Specified Transaction, provided, in either case, that such failure is not caused by circumstances which, if occurring under the Agreement, would constitute a Change of Circumstances as described in subsection 2(a)(ii);

This is a concept from the ISDA Master Agreement, where essentially it means a default under an OTC derivatives-type transaction between the two contracting parties to the ISDA Master Agreement, but governed by terms outside of it, ie, possibly under a long-form Confirmation, market terms or another master agreement.

Under the EMA, the scope of Specified Transactions must be stated in the Special Provisions.

The default "tests" here are where the failure to pay or deliver results in termination or acceleration of the Specified Transaction, or where the failure occurs following the expiry of a grace period after the last payment under the Specified Transaction is due. A three-Business-Day grace period applies if none exists in the Specified Transaction documentation.

This default is deemed not to have occurred if the failure is due to Illegality or Impossibility.

> (vi) *Cross Default.* Any payment obligation of the party in respect of borrowed money (whether incurred by it as primary or secondary obligor and whether arising from one or more contracts or instruments) in an aggregate amount of not less than the applicable Default Threshold (A) has become, or may be declared, due and payable prior to the stated maturity thereof as a result of any default or similar event (however described) which has occurred in respect of the party or (B) has not been performed for more than seven days after its due date and, in either case, the other party has reasonable grounds to conclude that the financial obligations of the party under the Agreement may not be performed. "Default Threshold" means the amount specified as such in the Special Provisions in respect of a party or, in the absence of such specification, 1 per cent of such party's equity (meaning the sum of its capital, disclosed reserves and retained earnings, determined in accordance with generally accepted accounting principles applicable to that party, as reported in its most recent published audited financial statements);

This clause covers the non-repayment of borrowed money in third-party agreements above a Default Threshold stated in the Special Provisions, with a fallback to 1 per cent of the Defaulting Party's equity as defined. The Cross Default tests are (i) potential acceleration under an agreement or (ii) non-payment more than seven days after its due date, with the other party having reasonable grounds to believe that the Defaulting Party will not perform its financial obligations.

> (vii) *Restructuring Without Assumption.* The party is subject to a Corporate Restructuring and the Successor Entity fails to assume all obligations of such party under the Agreement. "Corporate Restructuring" means, with respect to such party, any consolidation or amalgamation with, or merger into, or demerger, or transfer of all or substantially all assets to, another person, or an agreement providing for any of the foregoing, and "Successor Entity" means the person which results from, survives or is the transferee in, such Corporate Restructuring;

This sub-section partly reflects the ISDA Master Agreement Merger without Assumption provision (Section 5(a)(viii)).

It states that an Event of Default will occur if a Successor Entity fails to take over all the restructured party's obligations under the EMA following a merger-type event or a substantial asset transfer.

(viii) *Insolvency Events.* (1) The party is dissolved or has a resolution passed for its dissolution (other than, in either case, pursuant to a Corporate Restructuring resulting in a solvent Successor Entity); (2) the party commences an Insolvency Proceeding against itself or takes any corporate action to authorize such Insolvency Proceeding; (3) a governmental or judicial authority or self-regulatory organisation having jurisdiction over the party in a Specified Jurisdiction (a "Competent Authority") commences an Insolvency Proceeding with respect to the party; (4) a Competent Authority takes any action under any bankruptcy, insolvency or similar law or any banking, insurance or similar law governing the operation of the party which is likely to prevent the party from performing when due its payment or delivery obligations under the Agreement; (5) a person other than a Competent Authority commences an Insolvency Proceeding against the party in a Specified Jurisdiction and such action (A) results in a Judgment of Insolvency, or (B) is not dismissed or stayed within thirty days following the action or event commencing the Insolvency Proceeding, unless the commencement of such Proceedings by such person or under the given circumstances is obviously inadmissible or frivolous; (6) the party is bankrupt or insolvent as defined under any bankruptcy or insolvency law applicable to it in a Specified Jurisdiction; (7) the party makes a general assignment for the benefit of, or enters into a composition or amicable settlement with, its creditors generally; (8) the party is generally unable to pay its debts as they fall due; or (9) the party causes or is subject to any event which, under the laws of the Specified Jurisdiction, has an effect which is analogous to any of the events specified in Nos. (1) to (8). "Insolvency Proceeding"; means a mandatory or voluntary proceeding seeking a judgment, order or arrangement of insolvency, bankruptcy, composition, amicable settlement, rehabilitation, reorganisation, administration, dissolution or liquidation with respect to a party or its assets or seeking the appointment of a receiver, liquidator, administrator or similar official for such party or for all or any substantial part of its assets under any bankruptcy, insolvency or similar law or any banking, insurance or similar law governing the operation of the party;

the expression does not include a solvent corporate reorganisation. An Insolvency Proceeding is "commenced" if a petition to conduct such proceeding is presented to or filed with, or (where no such petition is required) a decision to conduct such proceeding is taken by, a competent court, authority, corporate body or person. "Judgment of Insolvency" means any judgment, order or arrangement instituting an Insolvency Proceeding. "Specified Jurisdiction" in relation to a party means the jurisdiction of that party's organisation, incorporation, principal office or residence and any additional jurisdiction that may be specified with respect to that party in the Special Provisions;

The usual long list of insolvency events with which we are familiar from the ISDA Master Agreement and the TBMA/ISMA GMRA is recited in this clause. Three things are notable. First, in 5(1) a dissolution following a Corporate Restructuring that results in a solvent Successor Entity is not an Insolvency Event. Second, in 5(B) there is an exclusion for frivolous proceedings. Third, at the end of the definition of Specified Jurisdiction the insolvency events are limited to a party's home jurisdiction and any other jurisdiction agreed by the parties in the Special Provisions.

In contrast, insolvency provisions in other market documentation seem to suggest that insolvency proceedings in any country, irrespective of whether the party is present there or not, may trigger termination.

> (ix) *Repudiation of Obligations.* The party declares that it will not perform any material obligation under the Agreement or under any Specified Transaction (otherwise than as part of a bona fide dispute as to the existence, nature or extent of such obligation);

Apart from *bona fide* disputes, it will be an Event of Default if a party wilfully repudiates material obligations under the EMA or a Specified Transaction.

> (x) *Guarantee Ineffective.* A Guarantee given with respect to the party is not in full force and effect, except if it has ceased to be in effect (i) in accordance with its terms, (ii) upon satisfaction of all of the party's obligations secured by such Guarantee or (iii) with the consent of the other party.

It will be an Event of Default if a guarantee ceases to be effective, except where this occurs in accordance with its terms; all obligations covered by it are satisfied; or the other party agrees that the guarantee need not be in full force and effect.

> (b) *Termination.* If an Event of Default occurs with respect to a party (the "Defaulting Party") and is continuing, the other party (the "Non-Defaulting Party") may, by giving not more than twenty days' notice specifying the relevant Event of Default, terminate all outstanding Transactions, but not part thereof only, with effect as from a date (the "Early Termination Date") to be designated by it in such notice. Notwithstanding the foregoing, unless otherwise specified in the Special Provisions, all Transactions shall terminate, and the Early Termination Date shall occur, automatically in the case of an Event of Default mentioned in paragraph (a)(viii)(l), (2), (3), (5)(A) or, to the extent analogous thereto, (9) as of the time immediately preceding the relevant event or action.

This provision states that, if an Event of Default occurs, the Non-Defaulting Party may give the Defaulting Party up to 20 days' notice stating an Early Termination Date on which all Transactions under the EMA will be terminated. Automatic termination will occur with certain Insolvency Events. This process closely follows that outlined in Section 6(a) of the ISDA Master Agreement.

Section 6(2)

The Change of Circumstances events in Section 6(2) are:
(i) Tax Event;
(ii) Illegality, Impossibility; and
(iii) Credit Event Upon Restructuring.

These equate to corresponding Termination Events in the ISDA Master Agreement.

> (2) *Termination due to Change of Circumstances*
> (a) *Change of Circumstances.* The occurrence of any of the following events or circumstances in respect of a party shall constitute a change of circumstances ("Change of Circumstances"):
> (i) *Tax Event.* As a result of the entry into force of any new law or regulation or of any change in law or any other provision of mandatory effect or change in the application or official interpretation thereof occurring after the date on which a Transaction is entered into, or as a result of a Corporate Restructuring of either party not falling under subsection 1 (a)(vii), the party would, on or before the next due date relating to such Transaction, (A) be required to pay additional amounts pursuant to Section 4(1) with regard to a payment which it is obligated to make, other than a payment of interest pursuant to Section 3(5), or (B) receive a payment, other than a payment of interest pursuant to Section 3(5), from which an amount is required to be deducted for or on account of a tax or duty and no additional amount is required to be paid in respect of such tax or duty under Section 4(1), other than by reason of Section 4(1)(c);

Under the Tax Event, if a withholding tax is levied (due to a change in tax law or regulation or following a Corporate Restructuring) after a Transaction has been entered into, and that tax results in a payment having to be grossed up or a receipt being received net (except in either case where a payment of default interest is involved), a Change of Circumstances will be deemed to have occurred.

> (ii) *Illegality, Impossibility.* As a result of the entry into force of any new law or regulation or of any change in law or any other provision of mandatory effect or change in the application or official interpretation thereof or, if so specified in the Special Provisions, as a result of an Impossibility Event, in each case occurring after the date on which a Transaction is entered into, it becomes, or is likely to become, unlawful or impossible for the party (A) to make, or receive, a payment or delivery in respect of such Transaction when due or to punctually comply with any other material obligation under the Agreement relating to such Transaction or (B) to perform any obligation to provide margin or collateral as and when required to be provided by it under the Agreement; "Impossibility Event" means any catastrophe, armed conflict, act of terrorism, riot or any other circumstance beyond the party's reasonable control affecting the operations of the party;

Sub-section 6(2)(a)(ii) provides that if, following a change of law or its interpretation, it becomes unlawful or impossible for a party to make or receive payments or deliveries under the EMA, or punctually to comply with any important obligation under the EMA, including the provision of collateral, then that will also constitute a Change of Circumstances. Impossibility Events (which are defined) need to be stated in the Special Provisions.

> (iii) *Credit Event upon Restructuring.* If the party is subject to a Corporate Restructuring, the creditworthiness of the Successor Entity is materially weaker than that of the party immediately before the Corporate Restructuring.

The Credit Event Upon Restructuring event is a short-form simplified version of the similar Credit Event Upon Merger provision in the ISDA Master Agreement. It applies if the creditworthiness of the Successor Entity is far worse than that of the original contracting party before the Corporate Restructuring took place.

> (b) *Termination.* If a Change of Circumstances occurs with respect to a party (the "Affected Party"), the Affected Party in the case of paragraph (a)(i) or (ii), and the other party (the "Non-Affected Party") in the case of paragraph (a)(ii) or (iii) may, subject to the limitations set forth below, by giving not more than twenty days' notice, terminate the Transaction(s) affected by such change, with effect as from a date (the "Early Termination Date") to be designated by it in such notice, it being understood that, in the case of paragraph (a)(iii), all Transactions will be deemed so affected. If, without prejudice to any agreement between the parties on the provision of margin or collateral, either party determines that as a result of such termination its credit exposure to the other party is significantly increased, it may, not later than one week after the effective date of the notice of termination, by giving notice to the other party require such other party to provide, within one week after receipt of such last-mentioned notice, margin or collateral reasonably acceptable to it in such amount as to be at least equal to the increase in credit exposure under the Agreement, as determined by it. In the cases of paragraph (a)(i) and (ii), the right to terminate shall be subject to the following limitations: (i) the Early Termination Date may not be earlier than thirty days before the date on which the Change of Circumstances becomes effective, and (ii) the Affected Party may, unless it would otherwise be required to pay additional amounts as contemplated by paragraph (a)(i)(A), give notice of termination only after a period of thirty days has expired following a notice by it informing the other party of such event and if the situation (if capable of remedy) has not been remedied within such period (by way of an agreed transfer of the affected Transactions to another Booking Office or otherwise).

The Affected Party may give notice of a Change of Circumstances in respect of a Tax Event and either party may give notice with respect to an Illegality or Impossibility. However, only the Non-Affected Party may give notice for a Credit Event Upon Restructuring. The notice may specify that only affected Transactions, in the case of Tax Event or Illegality or Impossibility, but all Transactions with a Credit Event Upon Restructuring will be terminated on a specific Early Termination Date no later than 20 days after the notice is issued. If the

Non-Affected Party decides that its exposure is significantly increased by the proposed termination, it may give a notice to the Affected Party not later than one week after the termination notice to transfer to it, within seven days, sufficient reasonably acceptable collateral to offset the increase in credit exposure that it has calculated.

Certain other conditions also apply. The Termination Date may not be earlier than 30 days before the date on which the Change of Circumstances takes effect and, barring any obligation to gross up for a withholding tax, an Affected Party may give a termination notice only when 30 days have passed from when it advised the other party of the Tax Event or Illegality or Impossibility and if the position remains unremedied, eg, by trying to transfer affected Transactions to another of the Affected Party's Booking Offices.

Section 6(3)

> (3) *Applicability to Guarantor.* If a Guarantee has been given with respect to a party and any of the events described in subsections 1(a)(iii) through (ix) and 2(a) occurs with respect to the relevant Guarantor or such Guarantee, the occurrence of such event shall have the same effect as if it had occurred with respect to such party or the Agreement, respectively.

This provision extends the application of termination for most Events of Default or all Change of Circumstances events to a party's guarantor.

Section 6(4)

> (4) *Effect of Termination.* In the event of a termination pursuant to this Section 6, neither party shall be obligated to make any further payment or delivery under the terminated Transaction(s) which would have become due on or after the Early Termination Date or to provide or return margin or collateral which would otherwise be required to be provided or returned under the Agreement and related to the terminated Transaction(s). These obligations shall be replaced by an obligation of either party to pay the Final Settlement Amount in accordance with Section 7.

In a termination situation neither party makes any normal payments or deliveries, nor does either party transfer collateral in respect of terminated Transactions. The parties proceed to the close-out netting mechanism of Section 7 of the EMA.

Section 6(5)

> (5) *Event of Default and Change of Circumstances.* If an event or circumstance which would otherwise constitute or give rise to an Event of Default also constitutes a

> Change of Circumstances as referred to in subsection 2(a)(ii), it will be treated as a Change of Circumstances and will not constitute an Event of Default, except that any event as described in subsection l(a)(viii) will always be treated as an Event of Default and not as a Change of Circumstances.

Where an event could be deemed to be either an Event of Default, an Illegality or an Impossibility, it will be treated as an Illegality or Impossibility in line with the normal market practice of trying to mitigate the effects of such events and closing out only affected Transactions. However, any Insolvency Event will always be treated as an Event of Default.

Section 7

> **7. Final Settlement Amount**
> (1) *Calculation*
> (a) *Procedure and Bases of Calculation.* Upon termination pursuant to Section 6, the Non-Defaulting Party or, as the case may be, the Non-Affected Party or, if there are two Affected Parties, each party (each the "Calculation Party") shall as soon as reasonably possible calculate the Final Settlement Amount.
>
> "Final Settlement Amount" means, subject to subsection 2(b)(i), the amount determined by the Calculation Party to be equal to, as of the Early Termination Date, (A) the sum of all Transaction Values which are positive for it, the Amounts Due owed to it and its Margin Claims less (B) the sum of the absolute amounts of all Transaction Values which are negative for it, the Amounts Due owed by it and the Margin Claims of the other party;
>
> "Amounts Due" owed by a party means the sum of (i) any amounts that were required to be paid by such party under any Transaction, but not paid, (ii) the Default Value, as of the agreed delivery date, of each asset that was required to be delivered by such party under any Transaction, but not delivered (in either case regardless of whether or not the party was entitled to withhold such payment or delivery, by virtue of Section 3(3) or for any other reason) and (iii) interest on the amounts specified in (i) and (ii) from (and including) the due date of the relevant payment or delivery to (but excluding) the Early Termination Date at the Interbank Rate or, if Section 3(5) is applicable, the Default Rate; Margin Claims shall be disregarded for the determination of Amounts Due;
>
> "Default Value" means, in respect of any assets (including Securities or, in respect of Derivative Transactions, any other underlying assets of such Transactions) on any given date, an amount equal to (A) if the assets are or were to be delivered by the Calculation Party, the net proceeds (after deducting fees and expenses) which the Calculation Party has or could have reasonably received when selling assets of the same kind and quantity in the market on such date, (B) if the assets are or were to be delivered to the Calculation Party, the cost (including fees and expenses) which the

THE EUROPEAN MASTER AGREEMENT

> Calculation Party has or would have reasonably incurred in purchasing assets of the same kind and quantity in the market on such date, and (C) if a market price for such assets cannot be determined, an amount which the Calculation Party determines in good faith to be its total losses and costs (or gains, in which case expressed as a negative number) in connection with such assets;
>
> "Margin Claims" means, as of the Early Termination Date, the aggregate of the amount of cash paid and the Default Value of Securities transferred, as margin or collateral, by a party and not repaid or retransferred to it, plus any interest accrued on such cash at the rate agreed in respect thereof;
>
> "Transaction Value" means, with respect to any Transaction or group of Transactions, an amount equal to, at the option of the Calculation Party, (i) the loss incurred (expressed as a positive number) or gain realized (expressed as a negative number) by the Calculation Party as a result of the termination of such Transaction(s), or (ii) the arithmetic mean of the quotations for replacement or hedge transactions on the Quotation Date obtained by the Calculation Party from not less than two leading market participants. In the case of (ii), each such quotation shall be expressed as the amount which the market participant would pay or receive on the Quotation Date if such market participant were to assume, as from the Quotation Date, the rights and obligations of the other party (or their economic equivalent) under the relevant Transaction(s); the resulting amount shall be expressed as a positive number if it would be payable to the market participant, and shall otherwise be expressed as a negative number. If, in such case, no or only one quotation can reasonably be obtained, the Transaction Value shall be determined pursuant to (i),
>
> "Quotation Date" means the Early Termination Date, except that in the event of an automatic termination as provided in Section 6(1)(b), the Quotation Date shall be the date designated as such by the Non-Defaulting Party, which shall be not later than the fifth Business Day after the day on which the Non-Defaulting Party became aware of the event which caused such automatic termination.

The party or parties not at fault have the right to calculate the Final Settlement Amount.

The Final Settlement Amount is calculated as of the Termination Date by off setting the values of each party's Transactions, Margin Claims and Amounts Due (ie, cash payments or securities deliveries due, but not made because of the termination) and calculating one net figure payable one way or the other.

Each term is defined according to its various constituents.

Default Value relates to the value of Securities or assets underlying Derivative Transactions. If the assets are deliverable by the Calculation Party, the net proceeds are reduced by selling fees and expenses. If the assets are to be delivered to the Calculation Party, the purchase fees and expenses are added to the amount receivable. If the market price of assets cannot be ascertained, the Calculation Party's good faith determination of its losses and costs (minus its gains) in respect of such assets will be used to determine the Default Market Value.

Margin Claims include accrued interest on cash deposits.

Apart from Transaction losses and costs, Transaction Values take into account the cost of replacement hedging transactions (calculated by averaging two market quotations). If only one quotation is available, the calculation of Transaction Value will be made in good faith by the Calculation Party itself.

With automatic termination for an Insolvency Event, the Quotation Date may be set by the Non-Defaulting Party, but not later than the fifth Business Day after it became aware of the relevant Insolvency Event that caused the automatic termination.

> (b) *Conversion.* Any Amounts Due, Default Value, Margin Claims and Transaction Value not denominated in the Base Currency shall be converted into the Base Currency at the Applicable Exchange Rate. "Base Currency" means the euro, unless otherwise agreed. "Applicable Exchange Rate" means the arithmetic mean of the respective rates at which the person calculating or converting an amount pursuant to the Agreement is reasonably able to (i) purchase the relevant other currency with, and (ii) sell such currency for, the Base Currency on the date as of which such amount is calculated or converted.

All calculations of the constituent elements of the Final Settlement Amount are to be converted at prevailing market exchange rates into the Base Currency, which shall be the euro unless otherwise agreed in the Special Provisions.

> (2) *Payment Obligations*
> (a) *One Calculation Party.* If one party only acts as Calculation Party, the Final Settlement Amount, as calculated by it, shall be paid (i) to that party by the other party if it is a positive number and (ii) by that party to the other party if it is a negative number; in the latter case the amount payable shall be the absolute value of the Final Settlement Amount.

This provision is equivalent to the Second Method in the 1992 ISDA Master Agreement. If the Final Settlement Amount is positive, the Defaulting Party pays it to the Non-Defaulting Party. If it is negative, then the Non-Defaulting Party pays it to the Defaulting Party. In either case the full amount due must be paid over.

An easy way to remember who gets what is to view the positive and negative amounts from the Non-Defaulting Party's viewpoint. If the close-out amount is positive, the Non-Defaulting Party receives it and could be said to view the situation positively. If the close-out amount is negative, the Non-Defaulting Party has to pay it over and so views the situation negatively.

> (b) *Two Calculation Parties.* If both parties act as Calculation Party and their calculations of the Final Settlement Amount differ from each other, the Final Settlement Amount shall (i) be equal to one-half of the difference between the amounts so calculated by both parties (such difference being, for the avoidance of doubt, the sum of the absolute values of such amounts if one is positive and the other negative) and (ii) be paid by the party which has calculated a negative or the lower positive amount.

In a "no fault" termination both parties will act as Calculation Parties. It is likely that their calculations of the Final Settlement Amount will differ. In that case the amount payable is calculated as one half of the difference between the amounts calculated by them both and is paid by the party that has calculated a negative amount or a lower positive amount.

> (3) *Notification and Due Date*
> (a) *Notification.* The Calculation Party shall notify as soon as reasonably possible the other party of the Final Settlement Amount calculated by it and provide to such other party a statement setting forth in reasonable detail the basis upon which the Final Settlement Amount was determined.

The Calculation Party has a duty promptly to provide the other party with a statement showing, in reasonable detail, how it has calculated the Final Settlement Amount.

> (b) *Due Date.* The Final Settlement Amount shall be payable immediately upon receipt of the notification mentioned in paragraph (a) if termination occurs as a result of an Event of Default, and otherwise within two Business Days following such receipt, but in either case not before the Early Termination Date, It shall bear interest as from the Early Termination Date to the date on which the payment is due at the Interbank Rate and thereafter at the Default Rate.

The Final Settlement Amount shall be payable immediately upon receipt of the Calculation Party's notification of it if the termination is due to an Event of Default, or within two Business Days of its receipt if termination is due to some other reason, but in any case it will not be payable before the Termination Date. Interest is payable on the Final Settlement Amount from the Termination Date, at the rates designated. The Default Rate applies if the payment is made late.

> (4) *Set-Off.* The Non-Defaulting Party may set off its obligation (if any) to pay the Final Settlement Amount against any actual or contingent claims ("Counterclaims") which it has against the Defaulting Party on any legal grounds whatsoever (including by virtue of any financing or other contract). For the purpose of calculating the value of the Counterclaims, the Non-Defaulting Party shall, (i) to the extent that they are not payable in the Base Currency, convert them into the Base Currency at the Applicable Exchange Rate, (ii) to the extent that they are contingent or unascertained, take into account for such calculation their potential amount, if ascertainable, or otherwise a reasonable estimate thereof, (iii) to the extent that they are claims other than for the payment of money, determine their value in money and convert them into a money claim expressed in the Base Currency and (iv) to the extent that they are not yet due and payable, determine their present value (also having regard to interest claims), The provisions of this subsection 4 relating to Counterclaims against a Defaulting Party shall apply *mutatis mutandis* to Counterclaims against an Affected Party if termination occurred pursuant to Section 6(2)(a)(ii) or (iii).

Once the Final Settlement Amount has been calculated, if it is negative and the Non-Defaulting Party is obligated to pay it over to the Defaulting Party, the Non-Defaulting Party has the right to calculate and off set any Counterclaims it has against the Defaulting Party (including under other contracts). Counterclaims in other currencies can be converted into the Base Currency (eg, into euros); a reasonable estimate can be made for contingent claims; non-money claims can be converted into monetary terms in the Base Currency; and future claims can be discounted back to their net present value, having regard to interest claims.

The set-off clause also applies to Counterclaims against an Affected Party if termination is due to Illegality, Impossibility or Credit Event Upon Restructuring Change of Circumstances events.

Section 8

> **8. Notices**
> (1) *Manner of Giving Notices.* Unless otherwise specified in the Agreement, any notice or other communication under the Agreement shall be made by letter, telex, telefax or any electronic messaging system agreed to by the parties in the Special Provisions to the address (if any) previously specified by the addressee.

Notices between the parties may be made by letter, telex or fax. Any electronic messaging system agreed to between the parties must be specified in the Special Provisions.

> (2) *Effectiveness.* Every notice or other communication made in accordance with sub-section 1 shall be effective (a) if made by letter or telefax, upon receipt by the addressee, (b) if made by telex, upon receipt by the sender of the addressee's answer-back at the end of transmission, and (c) if made by an electronic messaging system, upon receipt of that electronic message, provided that if, in any such case, such notice or other communication is not received on a Business Day or is received after the close of business on a Business Day, it shall take effect on the first following day that is a Business Day.

This provision determines the timing of receipt of notices by the addressee, depending upon the medium used to communicate them. Any notices not received on a Business Day, or after close of business on it, shall be effective only from the following Business Day.

> (3) *Change of Address.* Either party may by notice to the other change the address, telex or telefax number or electronic messaging system details at which notices or other communications are to be given to it.

Changes in contact details should be notified to the other party.

Section 9

> **9. Booking Offices**
> (1) *Extent of Obligations.* If a party enters into a Transaction through a Booking Office other than its principal office, its obligations in respect of that Transaction shall constitute obligations of such party as a whole, to the same extent as if they had been entered through such party's principal office. Such party shall not be obligated, however, to perform such obligations through any of its other offices if performance through that Booking Office is unlawful or impossible by virtue of any of the events described in Section 6(2)(a)(ii).

The first sentence states that a counterparty may regard the entering into of a Transaction by a party through one of its branches as an obligation of the organisation as a whole, as though the Transaction had been entered into by the party's Head Office. However, that party is not obligated to perform such obligations through any of its other offices (including its Head Office) if performance is illegal or impossible through the Transaction's original Booking Office.

> *(2) Change of Booking Office.* Neither party may change a Booking Office without the prior written consent of the other.

Prior written consent of the other party is needed for a party to change its Booking Office. Consent is necessary because such a change could have adverse tax consequences for the other party.

> *(3) Definition.* "Booking Office" of a party means the office agreed by the parties through which such party is acting for the relevant Transaction, provided that if no such office is agreed in respect of a party, such party's principal office (or, in the absence of a principal office, such party's registered office or place of residence) shall be deemed to be the Booking Office.

The Booking Office is the office agreed by the parties in respect of the relevant Transaction and payments under it. If no Booking Office is specified, the fallback is a party's Head Office or registered office in its place of residence.

Section 10

This is a catch-all clause with 11 sub-sections.

> **10. Miscellaneous**
> (1) *Transfer of Rights and Obligations.* No rights or obligations under the Agreement may be transferred, charged or otherwise disposed of to or in favour of any third person without the prior consent of the other party given in the manner specified in Section 8(1), except that no such consent shall be required in the case of a transfer of all or substantially all assets of a party in connection with a Corporate Restructuring which does not involve a change of the tax status relevant to the Agreement and does not otherwise adversely affect the interests of the other party to any significant extent. The limitation provided in the preceding sentence shall not apply to a party's right to receive the Final Settlement Amount or to be indemnified pursuant to subsection 2.

The transfers stated in this clause are not permitted without the prior written consent of the other party. Such consent is not required where a Corporate Restructuring occurs that does not have asset reduction, tax or other significant adverse effects. No consent is necessary for a party to transfer any Final Settlement Amount due to it from the other party. This provision resembles Section 7 of the ISDA Master Agreement.

THE EUROPEAN MASTER AGREEMENT

(2) *Expenses.* A Defaulting Party and a party failing to make a payment or delivery when due shall on demand indemnify the other party for all reasonable expenses, including legal fees, incurred by the other party for the enforcement or protection of its rights under the Agreement in connection with an Event of Default or such failure.

This is an expenses indemnity for a Non-Defaulting Party or an innocent party seeking to enforce or protect its rights following an Event of Default or non-receipt of collateral.

(3) *Recording.* Each party (i) may electronically or otherwise record telephone conversations of the parties in connection with the Agreement or any potential Transaction, (ii) shall give notice of such potential recording to its relevant personnel and obtain any consent that may be legally required before permitting such personnel to conduct such telephone conversations and (iii) agrees that recordings may be submitted in evidence in any Proceedings relating to the Agreement or any potential Transaction.

This common provision is recommended by the UK Financial Services Authority's *Conduct of Business Rules (2001)*.

(4) *Documents.* So long as either party has or may have any obligation under the Agreement, each party shall, if it is reasonably able and legally in a position to do so and would not thereby materially prejudice its legal or commercial position, promptly make available to the other or to any appropriate government or taxing authority any form, certificate or other document (properly completed and, where appropriate, certified) that is either (a) specified in the Agreement, or (b) reasonably requested in writing in order to allow the other party to make a payment under the Agreement without any deduction or withholding for or on account of any tax or other duty, or with such deduction or withholding at a reduced rate.

The parties conditionally agree to provide to each other or to any government or tax authority such documents as may be stated in the EMA or requested separately to mitigate the effects of withholding tax.

(5) *Remedies.* The rights and remedies provided in the Agreement are cumulative and not exclusive of any rights and remedies provided by law.

147

This provision is inserted because termination should not be the exclusive remedy of the Non-Defaulting Party. Such party also has the options of leaving the EMA in place or of seeking specific performance of the counterparty's obligations (ie, where money damages would provide insufficient relief and delivery of securities was required).

> (6) *No Waiver.* A failure or delay in exercising (and any partial exercise of) any right or remedy under the Agreement shall not operate as a waiver (or partial waiver) of, and accordingly not preclude or limit any future exercise of that right or remedy.

This standard provision is found in many agreements. Waivers given under the EMA do not set any precedent in the future.

> (7) *Termination.* The Agreement may be terminated by either party upon the giving of not less than twenty days' notice to the other party. Notwithstanding such notice, any Transaction then outstanding shall continue to be subject to the provisions of the Agreement and to that extent the effect of the termination shall occur only when all obligations under the last such Transaction shall have been performed.

The EMA has an unusual termination provision, triggered by 20 days' notice by either party. However, this is without prejudice to existing Transactions and total termination of the EMA will occur only when the last payment has been made under the last Transaction.

> (8) *Contractual Currency.* If for any reason a payment is made in a currency other than the Contractual Currency and the amount so paid, converted into the Contractual Currency at the exchange rate prevailing at the time of such payment for the sale of such other currency against the Contractual Currency, as reasonably determined by the payee, falls short of the amount in the Contractual Currency payable under the Agreement, the party owing such amount shall, as a separate and independent obligation, immediately compensate the other party for the shortfall.

This is a standard provision setting forth obligations to make good currency conversion shortfalls. The ISDA Master Agreement extends this provision to cover return of surpluses made on currency conversions, but the EMA does not. Under both Agreements the Contractual Currency is the one stated for payments in a Confirmation.

> (9) *Previous Transactions.* Transactions entered into prior to the effective date of a Master Agreement will be subject to such Master Agreement, individually or by category, to the extent provided in the Special Provisions.

This is a scope of agreement or sweep-in clause that aims to draw in transactions outside the EMA. Such transactions need to be specified in the Special Provisions.

> (10) *Agency Transactions.*
> (a) *Conditions.* A party may enter into a Transaction, (an "Agency Transaction") as agent (the "Agent") for a third person (a "Principal") only if (i) the party has authority on behalf of that Principal to enter into the Transaction, to perform on behalf of that Principal all of that Principal's obligations and to accept performance of the obligations of the other party and receive all notices and other communications under the Agreement and (ii) when entering into the Transaction and in the relevant Confirmation the party specifies that it is acting as Agent in respect of the Transaction and discloses to the other party the identity of the Principal. If these conditions are not fully satisfied, the party shall be deemed to act as principal.

Agency Transactions are possible under the EMA, provided that the Agent is fully authorised by the Principal to act on its behalf; its agency capacity is stated in the Confirmation; and it is acting for a disclosed principal. Failure to fulfil these conditions will convert the Agent to the Principal.

> (b) *Information on Certain Events.* Each party undertakes that, if it enters as Agent into an Agency Transaction, forthwith upon becoming aware (i) of any event or circumstance which constitutes an event as described in Section 6(l)(a)(viii) with respect to the relevant Principal or (ii) of any breach of any of the representations given in Section 5 and paragraph (f) below or of any event or circumstance which has the result that any such representation would be incorrect on the date as of which it was made, it will inform the other party of that fact and will, if so required by the other party, furnish the other party with such additional information as the other party may reasonably request.

An Agent must inform the other party of any Insolvency Event affecting the Principal; or of any breach of a Section 5 representation or of the representation in sub-section 10(f) below; and of any event that would invalidate any representation as of the date it was made. The Agent also undertakes to provide any additional information sought by the other party.

> (c) *Parties.* Each Agency Transaction shall be a transaction solely between the relevant Principal and the other party. All provisions of the Agreement shall apply separately as between the other party and each Principal for whom the Agent has entered into an Agency Transaction, as if each such Principal were a party to a separate Agreement with the other party, except as provided in paragraph (d) below. A Process Agent appointed by the Agent shall be a Process Agent also for each Principal.

Effectively, an Agency Transaction is a transaction between the relevant Principal and the other party as if that Principal had entered into a separate EMA with the other party. A Process Agent appointed by the Agent shall be deemed to be a Process Agent for each Principal.

> (d) *Notice of Termination.* If an Event of Default or a Change of Circumstances as described in Section 6(2)(a)(ii) or (iii) occurs with respect to the Agent, the other party may give notice pursuant to Section 6(1)(b) or 6(2)(b), respectively, to the Principal with the same effect as if an Event of Default or Change of Circumstances, respectively, had occurred with respect to the Principal.

If an Event of Default or Illegality, Impossibility or Credit Event Upon Restructuring Change of Circumstances event occurs to the Agent, the other party may issue a termination notice to the Principal as if the above events had occurred to the Principal.

> (e) *Own Account Transactions.* The foregoing provisions do not affect the operation of the Agreement between the parties hereto in respect of any Transactions into which the Agent may enter on its own account as a principal.

The Agent may enter into transactions as a principal in its own right under the EMA, whereupon these Agency provisions would not apply to it.

> (f) *Representation.* Each party acting as Agent represents to the other in its own name and in the name of the Principal that it will, on each occasion on which it enters or purports to enter into an Agency Transaction, have the authority as described in subsection 10(a)(i) on behalf of the person whom it specifies as the Principal in respect of that Agency Transaction.

Each party, when or if acting as Agent under the EMA, reaffirms that it has the Principal's authority to act on its behalf whenever it enters into an Agency Transaction.

> (11) *Severability.* In the event that any provision of the Agreement is invalid, illegal or unenforceable under the law of any jurisdiction, the validity, legality and enforceability of the remaining provisions in the Agreement under the law of such jurisdiction, and the validity, legality and enforceability of such and any other provisions under the law of any other jurisdiction shall not in any way be affected thereby. The parties shall, in such event, in good faith negotiate a valid provision the economic effect of which comes as close as possible to that of the invalid, illegal or unenforceable provisions.

This is a standard provision found in many other agreements. It enables the EMA to remain in effect even if an individual provision therein may become unenforceable. Negotiations between the parties for a substitute provision must be conducted in good faith.

Section 11

> **11. Governing Law, Settlement of Disputes, Jurisdiction, Arbitration**
> (1) *Governing Law.* The Agreement shall be governed by and construed in accordance with the law specified in the Special Provisions or, failing such specification, the law of the country, if identical, in which both parties' principal offices are located when the Master Agreement between them is entered into.

For domestic agreements the parties' domestic law will govern, assuming that they are both in the same jurisdiction. A choice of law is necessary for cross-border transactions and must be specified in the Special Provisions. Alternatively, parties can choose the domestic law of either of them or the law of a third country agreed between them.

> (2) *Settlement of Disputes, Jurisdiction, Arbitration.* Each party irrevocably agrees that in respect of any dispute arising under or related to the Agreement (i) the courts specified in the Special Provisions shall have non-exclusive jurisdiction and each party irrevocably submits to such non-exclusive jurisdiction, or (ii) if so specified in the Special Provisions, any such dispute shall be finally settled by one or more arbitrators appointed and proceeding in accordance with the rules of arbitration specified in the Special Provisions, each party agreeing to comply with such rules. Failing either of such specifications, the courts having jurisdiction in the principal financial centre

> or, in the absence of a generally recognized financial centre, the capital city of the country whose law governs the Agreement shall have non-exclusive jurisdiction with respect to any suit, action or other proceeding relating to the Agreement (the "Proceedings") and each party irrevocably submits to such non-exclusive jurisdiction.

Non-exclusive jurisdiction is provided in this clause and each party irrevocably submits to it. The relevant courts must be stated in the Special Provisions. Arbitration proceedings are also possible and disputes may be settled by one or more arbitrators under rules specified in the Special Provisions. Where neither route is stated in the Special Provisions, the fallback is the courts having jurisdiction in the main financial centre or capital city of the country whose law governs the EMA.

> (3) *Service of Process.* If so specified in the Special Provisions, each party appoints a process agent (the "Process Agent") to receive, for it and on its behalf, service of process in any Proceedings. If for any reason a party's Process Agent is unable to act as such, such party shall promptly notify the other party and within thirty days appoint a substitute process agent which is acceptable to the other party.

Where relevant, Process Agents must be specified in the Special Provisions. Process Agents receive writs and other legal documents on behalf of contracting parties that are not incorporated in the jurisdiction whose law governs the EMA. The 30-day time limit to appoint a substitute Process Agent is normal.

> (4) *Waiver of Immunity.* The Agreement constitutes a commercial agreement. To the fullest extent permitted by applicable law, each party waives, with respect to itself and its assets, (irrespective of their use or intended use), all immunity on the grounds of sovereignty or otherwise from suit, execution or other legal process and agrees that it will not claim any such immunity in any Proceedings.

Generally, sovereigns like to have immunity from being sued and from having their assets confiscated. This right is waived here for the contracting parties. The statement that the EMA is a commercial agreement is an emphasis rarely seen in such documentation.

Product Annex for Repurchase Transactions

This Annex supplements the EMA's General Provisions. The latest edition of it was published in January 2001.

Section 1

> **MASTER AGREEMENT
> FOR FINANCIAL TRANSACTIONS**
>
> **PRODUCT ANNEX
> FOR
> REPURCHASE TRANSACTIONS**
>
> Edition January 2001
>
> This Annex supplements the General Provisions which form part of any Master Agreement for Financial Transactions based on the form published by the Banking Federation of the European Union.
>
> **1. Purpose, Applicability**
>
> (1) *Purpose.* The purpose of this Annex ("Repurchase Annex") is to govern Transactions ("Repurchase Transactions") in which one party (the "Seller") sells to the other (the "Buyer") Securities against payment of an agreed price (the "Purchase Price") and in which the Buyer sells to the Seller Securities of the same kind and quantity as such Securities against payment of another agreed price for delivery and payment at a specified later date or on demand. Any reference in this Annex to a Transaction shall be construed as a reference to a Repurchase Transaction.

This provision describes the sale and repurchase procedure for a classic repo (see commentary on paragraph 1 of the TBMA/ISMA GMRA in Chapter 3, page 34).

> (2) *Applicability.* If this Annex forms part of a Master Agreement between any two parties, such Master Agreement (including this Annex) shall apply to any Repurchase Transaction between such parties which is to be conducted by each party through a Booking Office specified in such Master Agreement in respect of Repurchase Transactions.

This provision brings under the EMA Repurchase Transactions that are subject to this Annex. Booking Offices will be specified in paragraph 5 of the Special Provisions.

Section 2

> **2. Deliveries and Payments**
>
> (1) *Purchase.* On the settlement date agreed for the purchase of Securities by the Buyer under a Transaction (the "Purchase Date"), the Seller shall transfer to the Buyer the Securities sold in that Transaction (the "Purchased Securities") against simultaneous payment of the Purchase Price.

Sale of the Securities by the Seller occurs on a delivery-versus-payment basis on the Purchase Date.

> (2) *Repurchase.* On the settlement date agreed for the repurchase of the Purchased Securities (the "Repurchase Date"), the Buyer shall transfer to the Seller Securities of the same kind and quantity as the Purchased Securities against simultaneous payment of the Repurchase Price.

The same procedure applies to the repurchase of the Securities on the Repurchase Date. The repurchased securities must be of the same class, type and issuer as the Purchased Securities, but need not be the identically numbered securities.

> (3) *Definitions, Interpretation.* "Repurchase Price" means the sum of the Purchase Price and the Price Differential. "Price Differential" means for any Transaction the aggregate amount obtained by applying the pricing rate agreed for such Transaction and expressed as a percentage per annum (the "Pricing Rate") to the Purchase Price for the actual number of days during the period from (and including) the Purchase Date to (but excluding) the Repurchase Date, on a 360-day or 365-day basis in accordance with market practice or on any other basis agreed between the parties. A payment shall be "simultaneous" if it occurs as part of a delivery- versus-payment system or, should the use of such system in the given circumstances not be customary, if it occurs on the same day as the transfer of the relevant Securities. Any reference in this Annex to the Purchased Securities or other Securities in the context of the return or retransfer thereof, or to any rights or other assets to be transferred pursuant to Section 4(4), shall be construed so as to mean a reference to Securities, rights or assets of the same kind and quantity as (also referred to below as the "Equivalent" of) such Purchased Securities or other Securities, rights or assets, respectively.

"Repurchase Price" means the sum of the Purchase Price and the financing charge (the "Pricing Rate"). These terms are familiar from the TBMA/ISMA GMRA. As usual, the charging period is from and including the Purchase Date to, but excluding, the Repurchase Date. Payments should be simultaneous (ie, delivery versus payment), but may instead be made separately on the same day if that is the custom. The equivalent nature of Securities to be returned or retransferred is emphasised.

> (4) *On Demand Transactions.* The parties may agree that Transactions are terminable on demand, in which case the Repurchase Date shall be the date specified in the demand notice sent by either party to the other, provided that the period between the taking effect of such notice and the Repurchase Date so specified shall be not less than the minimum period customarily required for the payment of money and the delivery of Securities of the relevant kind. In the absence of a demand notice, the Repurchase Date for a Transaction terminable on demand shall be the day which falls 364 days after the Purchase Date.

For an On Demand Transaction the Repurchase Date shall be the date stated in the demand notice, although the time gap between the notice taking effect and the Repurchase Date itself must be at least the normal minimum settlement time customary in the market concerned. Where no demand notice is issued, the Transaction will automatically terminate 364 days after the Purchase Date. This cut-off was included for tax and regulatory reasons in a number of jurisdictions. Such an automatic cut-off may have systems implications.

> (5) *Late Payment.* If the Purchase Price or the Repurchase Price is not paid when due, the interest payable pursuant to Section 3(5) of the General Provisions shall be calculated at the higher of the Default Rate and the Pricing Rate, without prejudice to the application of Section 6(1)(a)(i) of the General Provisions.

If the Purchase Price or the Repurchase Price is late in being paid, interest will be charged at the higher of the Default Rate and the Pricing Rate, but without prejudice to the Non-Defaulting Party's right to invoke the Failure to Pay Event of Default.

> (6) *Late Delivery*
> (a) *Failure by Seller.* If the Seller fails to transfer the Purchased Securities to the Buyer on the applicable Purchase Date, the Buyer may, at any time while such failure continues:
> (i) if it has paid the Purchase Price to the Seller, require the Seller immediately to repay the sum so paid;
> (ii) require the Seller to pay to the Buyer an amount equal to the excess, if any, of the Buyer's Borrowing Cost over the pro rata portion of the Price Differential attributable to the period of the delay, each calculated for the period from (and including) the Purchase Date to (but excluding) the earlier of the date on which the Purchased Securities are transferred to the Buyer and the Repurchase Date (which in the case of a Transaction terminable on demand shall be deemed to be the earliest date on which

> the Purchased Securities would be required to be returned following a demand by the Seller); "Borrowing Cost" of a party means the cost (including fees and expenses), as determined by such party, which such party has or would have reasonably incurred in borrowing the Equivalent of the Purchased Securities, in the market for the relevant period; and
>
> (iii) if the parties have not agreed on measures to promptly remedy the failure, give notice that the Repurchase Date shall be advanced so as to occur immediately, whereupon the mutual obligations originally agreed by the parties under the relevant Transaction shall be netted, so that no payments or deliveries are due except that the Seller shall pay to the Buyer (in addition to complying with its obligations pursuant to (i) and (ii), if applicable) an amount equal to the Price Differential for the period from (and including) the Purchase Date to (but excluding) the Repurchase Date so advanced.

If the Seller fails to transfer the Purchased Securities to the Buyer on the Purchase Date, the Buyer may:

(i) require the immediate return of the Purchase Price (if paid); or

(ii) require the Seller to pay the excess of the Buyer's cost of borrowing the Securities (including fees and expenses) over the accrued Price Differential, pro-rated for the delay. The calculation will be from, and including, the Purchase Date to, but excluding, the earlier of the date on which the Securities are transferred to the Buyer and the Repurchase Date. With On Demand Transactions the provisions of Section 2(4) of this Annex would need to be observed; or

(iii) terminate the Transaction immediately, with the Seller paying the Buyer the repo rate accrued from, and including, the Purchase Date to, but excluding, the accelerated Repurchase Date.

> (b) *Failure by Buyer.* If the Buyer fails to return the Purchased Securities to the Seller on the applicable Repurchase Date, the Seller may, at any time while such failure continues:
>
> (i) if it has paid the Repurchase Price to the Buyer, require the Buyer immediately to repay the sum so paid;
>
> (ii) require the Buyer to pay to the Seller an amount equal to the excess, if any, of the Seller's Borrowing Cost over the amount receivable if the Repurchase Price were placed on deposit at the Interbank Rate, each calculated for the period from (and including) the Repurchase Date to (but excluding) the date of actual return of the Purchased Securities or, if earlier, the date specified in the notice, if any, given pursuant to (iii); and
>
> (iii) if the parties have not agreed on measures to promptly remedy the failure, give notice requiring cash settlement in lieu of delivery on a date to be specified in such notice, whereupon the obligations of the parties originally agreed in respect of the

THE EUROPEAN MASTER AGREEMENT

> Repurchase Date shall cease, and the Buyer shall (A) pay to the Seller (in addition to complying with its obligations pursuant to (i) and (ii), if applicable) an amount equal to the excess, if any, of the Alternative Purchase Cost for such Securities over the Repurchase Price or, as the case may be, (B) be entitled to receive from the Seller the excess, if any, of the Repurchase Price over such Alternative Purchase Cost; "Alternative Purchase Cost" means the cost (including fees and expenses), as determined by the Seller, which the Seller has or would have reasonably incurred in purchasing the Equivalent of the Purchased Securities in the market on the date so specified for cash settlement.

If the Buyer fails to return the Purchased Securities to the Seller on the Repurchase Date, the Seller may:
(i) require immediate repayment of the Repurchase Price (if paid); or
(ii) require the Buyer to pay the excess of the Seller's cost of borrowing the Securities over the amount that it would have earned by placing the Repurchase Price on interbank deposit calculated for the period from, and including, the Purchase Date to, but excluding, the date the Purchased Securities are actually returned or earlier, as stated in a notice under Section 2(6)(b)(iii) of this Annex; or
(iii) terminate the Transaction, with the Buyer paying the excess of the Seller's cost of purchasing the relevant securities (the "Alternative Purchase Cost") over the Repurchase Price. If the Repurchase Price exceeds the Alternative Purchase Cost, the Seller must pay over the surplus to the Buyer.

> (c) _Remedies._ Beyond the remedies provided in this subsection 6, neither party shall, in the event of any failure by the other party to transfer or return Purchased Securities, be entitled to recover any additional damage as a consequence of such failure, and such failure shall not constitute an Event of Default under Section 6(1)(a)(iii) of the General Provisions. This paragraph (c) is without prejudice to any remedy available in the event of any failure by a party to perform any other obligation (including any obligation to make a payment under this subsection 6) when due.

Consequential damages for late delivery are excluded as a matter of principle and the EMA basically follows the TBMA/ISMA GMRA in this respect.

The failure to deliver shall not constitute another Breach of Agreement Event of Default. However, the EMA explicitly provides that the party entitled to the delivery can charge the costs of borrowing substitute securities (see Section 2(6)(a)(ii) and (b)(ii) of this Annex). Under the EMA such party has a choice between a buy-in, ie, a purchase of the securities that should have been delivered, or a borrowing of such securities. The TBMA/ISMA GMRA only provides for a buy-in.

This provision does not prevent a party from seeking any other legal remedy in respect of obligations due other than from a failure to deliver.

> (7) *Special Events.* If, during the term of a Transaction and in respect of some or all of the Purchased Securities:
>
> (i) a payment of any interest or dividend or any other distribution of money or other property by the issuer of the Purchased Securities (collectively a "Distribution", which term shall include a repayment of principal and a payment in the case of a capital reduction) would, as a result of any change in law or in the application or official interpretation thereof occurring after the date on which such Transaction is entered into, be subject to any deduction or withholding in respect of a tax or other duty or would give rise to a tax credit;
>
> (ii) a notice of early redemption has been validly given;
>
> (iii) a public redemption, exchange, conversion or compensation offer or a public purchase bid is made or announced;
>
> (iv) subscription or other rights or assets which are not freely transferable are granted or distributed to the holders; or
>
> (v) if specified in the Special Provisions, a tax credit or tax entitlement is attached to any interest or dividend paid to the holders (whether or not subparagraph (i) would otherwise apply)
>
> then, subject to any other agreement between the parties, the Repurchase Date for such Securities shall, automatically in the case of (v) and otherwise upon demand by either party, be advanced to the third Business Day before, in the case of (i), (ii) and (v), the expected payment or redemption date or before, in the case of (iii) and (iv), the last day on which such bid or offer may be accepted or the day on which such rights or assets are granted or distributed.

Subject to any other agreement, the Repurchase Date is advanced in the following cases:
(i) a change in law or its interpretation or application results in a withholding tax being levied on an interest or dividend distribution for the Purchased Securities; or
(ii) a notice of early redemption is validly issued in respect of the Purchased Securities; or
(iii) a public redemption, exchange, conversion or purchase bid is made or announced or a compensation offer is made; or
(iv) non-freely transferable subscription rights or their like are granted or distributed to Purchased Securities holders; or
(v) if stated in the Special Provisions, a tax credit or entitlement is attached to any interest or dividend paid to the Seller, whether or not there are withholding tax implications.

The acceleration or early termination is automatic in respect of (v). Otherwise it is on demand by either party, whereupon the Repurchase Date will be advanced either to three Business Days before the occurrence of the event or, in the case of (iii) or (iv), to the last day on which a bid or offer may be accepted or the day on which the assets or rights are granted.

As mentioned before, subscription rights generally will be transferred to the Seller, whether or not the Buyer then holds the Purchased Securities. Therefore, the Buyer will often need to purchase subscription rights in the market in order to transfer them. The treatment of subscription rights (if they are freely transferable) is therefore broadly in line with the normal treatment of income distributions under repos.

THE EUROPEAN MASTER AGREEMENT

Section 3

> **3. Substitution**
> (1) *General Principle.* The Seller may, at its cost and with the consent of the Buyer, substitute for any Purchased Securities other Securities ("New Securities") which at the time at which the parties agree to such substitution have a Market Value at least equal to the Market Value of the Purchased Securities for which they are substituted.

The Seller may, at its own cost and with the Buyer's consent, substitute New Securities of an equal Market Value for the Purchased Securities that it has previously transferred to the Buyer.

> (2) *No Novation.* The substitution shall have no novation effect on the relevant Transaction, and the Transaction shall continue in effect, except that the New Securities will be deemed to be Purchased Securities instead of the Securities that are replaced.

A substitution will not constitute a novation of the existing Transaction. The New Securities will be deemed to be the original Purchased Securities.

> (3) *Simultaneous Retransfer.* The substitution will be carried out by simultaneous transfer of the New Securities in exchange for the Purchased Securities to be replaced.

The substitution will be simultaneous.

Section 4

> **4. Distributions, Subscription Rights**
> (1) *Cash Distributions.* If during the term of a Transaction any Distribution of money is made by the issuer to the holders of the Purchased Securities, the Buyer shall pay to the Seller, on the date of such Distribution, an amount in the same currency as, and equal to, the amount received by the holders in respect of such Distribution.

The Buyer must pay a manufactured dividend to the Seller on income that it receives from the issuer of Purchased Securities on the same day that it receives it.

> (2) *Withholding Taxes, Tax Credits.* If a Distribution is subject to withholding tax and/or gives rise to a tax credit, the amount payable by the Buyer under subsection 1 shall be equal to the full amount to which the Seller would be entitled, as previously notified by it, in respect of such Distribution if it were the owner of the Purchased Securities, including the amount of (a) any applicable withholding tax to the extent that the Seller would be entitled to apply for an exemption from, or a refund of, such tax and (b) any tax credit available to the Seller.

If payment of a distribution is subject to a withholding tax levied on the issuer, the Buyer must gross up and pay the Seller what it would have been entitled to receive as a distribution had if it been the holder of the Securities or any tax credit available to it. However, the Seller must have previously notified the Buyer of this situation and of any other relevant tax issues.

> (3) *Subscription Rights.* If subscription rights which are freely transferable are granted with respect to the Purchased Securities, the Buyer shall transfer to the Seller, not later than on the third day on which such rights are traded, the Equivalent of the subscription rights attributable to such Purchased Securities. If the rights are not so transferred by such date, the Seller may purchase their Equivalent in the market for the account of the Buyer. Should the Seller be unable so to purchase the rights, it may require the Buyer to pay to it an amount equal to the Market Value of such rights prevailing on the next following trading day for such rights.

Subscription rights, like any other freely transferable income distribution, are to be transferred by the Buyer to the Seller. Where this is not done by the third trading day of such rights, the Seller may purchase the equivalent subscription rights in the market for the Buyer's account. If it cannot buy such rights, it can require the Buyer to pay it an amount equal to the Market Value of the subscription rights on the next Business Day.

> (4) *Non-cash Distributions.* Any freely transferable bonus shares, non-cash Distributions and ancillary rights (other than subscription rights) which are issued, made or allotted with respect to the Purchased Securities during the term of a Transaction shall be transferred to the Seller on the Repurchase Date.

Any bonus shares, scrip dividends, etc, made during the Transaction term will be transferred to the Seller on the Repurchase Date, for the sake of convenience.

> (5) *Transfer Obligations.* For the avoidance of doubt, the provisions of subsections 1 through 4 shall apply whether or not the Buyer retains the ownership of the Purchased Securities during the term of the Transaction.

The above provisions will apply whether or not the Buyer retains ownership of the Purchased Securities throughout the Transaction term.

Section 5

> **5. Specific Terms for Buy/Sell Back Transactions**
> (1) *Applicability, Definitions.* Transactions shall be subject to this Section 5 if they are identified as Buy/Sell Back Transactions. "Buy/Sell Back Transactions" are Repurchase Transactions for which the Purchase Price and the Repurchase Price are each composed of (a) a price quoted exclusive of Accrued Interest (being the "Clean Price", payable on the Purchase Date, and the "Forward Price", also called "Sell Back Price", payable on the Repurchase Date) and (b) Accrued Interest, calculated as of the Purchase Date when payable together with the Clean Price and calculated as of the Repurchase Date when payable together with the Forward Price. "Accrued Interest" means the accrued portion, as of the relevant date of calculation, of the interest (if any) payable by the issuer of the Purchased Securities in respect of such Securities.

This provision describes the components of a Buy/Sell Back Transaction. Please see commentary on Buy/Sell Back Transactions in Chapter 1 (pages 9–11).

> (2) *Interpretation.* In the event of any conflict, this Section 5 shall, with respect to Buy/Sell Back Transactions, prevail over any other terms of this Annex. For Buy/Sell Back Transactions, (a) any reference in the Agreement to the Purchase Price shall be construed as referring to the Clean Price plus Accrued Interest paid or payable on the Purchase Date and (b) any reference in the Agreement to the Repurchase Price shall, notwithstanding the definition of that term in Section 2 (3), be construed as referring to the agreed Forward Price plus Accrued Interest paid or payable on the Repurchase Date or, as the case may be, to the adjusted Forward Price calculated pursuant to subsection 5 (to which no Accrued Interest shall be added).

Where there is a conflict between terms, Section 5 of the Repurchase Annex will prevail in respect of Buy/Sell Back Transactions. Clean Prices plus Accrued Interest on the Purchase Date and Repurchase Date are defined.

> (3) *Confirmation.* The Confirmation of a Buy/Sell Back Transaction shall specify the Forward Price and the Pricing Rate.

The Confirmation will state the Forward Price and the Pricing Rate.

> (4) *Distributions.* Section 4(1) shall apply to Buy/Sell Back Transactions only if specifically so agreed.

Because it is normal for a Buyer in a Buy/Sell Back Transaction to keep any income payment on the securities but factor it into the Sell Back Price, if distributions are to be paid over to the Seller then this procedure must be specifically agreed between the parties.

> (5) *Adjusted Forward Price.* In relation to a date other than the originally agreed Repurchase Date, for example in relation to a Repurchase Date advanced in accordance with Section 2(6)(a)(iii) or Section 2(7), the Forward Price shall be equal to:
> (a) the Repurchase Price as defined in Section 2(3), less (except if the parties have agreed that Section 4 (1) shall apply)
> (b) the sum of (i) the amount of any Distribution in respect of the Purchased Securities made by the issuer on a date falling between the Purchase Date and the Repurchase Date, and (ii) the aggregate amount obtained by daily application of the Pricing Rate for the relevant Transaction to such amount from (and including) the date of the Distribution to (but excluding) such advanced or postponed Repurchase Date.

This provision describes the necessary adjustments to the Forward Price if the Repurchase Date is accelerated due to late delivery of Securities or due to a Section 2.7. Special Event. The Forward Price will equal the Repurchase Price plus any Distribution made by an issuer on the Purchased Securities together with the daily Pricing Rate on such Distribution calculated from, and including, the Distribution date to, but excluding, the accelerated or postponed Repurchase Date.

Section 6

> **6. Margin Maintenance, Repricing**
> (1) *Margin Provisions.* Any obligations of the parties to transfer cash or Securities as Margin under certain circumstances shall be performed in accordance with the provisions of the applicable Margin Maintenance Annex published by the FBE, or with any other rules to be separately agreed.

THE EUROPEAN MASTER AGREEMENT

Any obligations of the parties to transfer cash or securities margin shall be done in accordance with the EMA's Margin Maintenance Annex or according to such other rules as the parties may agree.

> (2) *Repricing.* If the parties agree on the repricing of one or more Transactions (the "Original Transactions") instead of a transfer of Margin, then
> (a) the Repurchase Date of each Original Transaction shall be deemed advanced to the date as of which the repricing is to occur (the "Repricing Date"),
> (b) a new Transaction (the "New Transaction") shall be deemed entered into under which (i) Purchased Securities shall be the Equivalent of those purchased under the Original Transaction, (ii) the Purchase Date shall be the Repricing Date, (iii) the Purchase Price shall be equal to the Market Value of such Securities on the Repricing Date divided by the Margin Ratio, if any, applicable to the Original Transaction, as agreed pursuant to the applicable Margin Maintenance Annex, and (iv) the Repurchase Date, the Pricing Rate, the Margin Ratio and, subject to the above, the other terms shall be identical to the ones of the Original Transaction, and
> (c) the obligations to pay the Purchase Price and to transfer the Purchased Securities under the New Transaction shall be discharged by setting them off against the obligations to pay the Repurchase Price and to retransfer the Equivalent of the Purchased Securities under the Original Transaction, so that only a net cash amount shall be payable by one party to the other on the Repricing Date or, if that is not practicable, on the next Business Day.

Parties may choose repricing instead of margin transfer. If they do, then:
(a) the Repurchase Date of each Original Transaction is brought forward to the Repricing Date; and
(b) a new Transaction is deemed to be entered into, under which:

- Purchased Securities shall be equivalent to those under the Original Transaction;
- the Purchase Date will be the Repricing Date;
- The Purchase Price shall be determined by dividing the Securities' Market Value on the Repricing Date by the Margin Ratio (haircut) for the Original Transaction agreed in the Margin Maintenance Annex; and
- the Repurchase Date, Pricing Rate and Margin Ratio shall be identical to those in the Original Transaction; and

(c) Repurchase Price and Purchase Price payments respectively due under the Original and New Transactions are netted off so that any payment due is paid on the Repricing Date, or the next Business Day if not practicable.

Suggested Form of Confirmation for repos and buy/sellbacks

This Confirmation template, which is shown in Appendix 3, contains the standard terms for repo transactions and buy/sellbacks. It is interesting that Margin Ratio (haircut) is specified here while it is not in the sample Confirmation in Annex II of the TBMA/ISMA GMRA.

Credit Departments set Margin Ratios and it is not normal for them to be specifically documented under the TBMA/ISMA GMRA because they are usually agreed by dealers in the Purchase Price. Nevertheless, many major banks do not take haircuts on top-quality securities transferred between them.

Product Annex for Securities Loans

As this book focuses on Repurchase Transactions, there are only brief comments on this Annex here. It is reproduced in full in Appendix 3 with the kind permission of the European Banking Federation.

Many of the provisions of this Annex are the same as for the Repurchase Annex, the differences being the following:

Terminology
"Lender" and "Borrower" for "Seller" and "Buyer"
"Loaned Securities" for "Purchased Securities"
"Delivery Date" for "Purchase Date" and "Return Date" for "Repurchase Date"

Nature of arrangement
The arrangement is a fee payable for a loan of securities and the obligation to retransfer them on the Return Date.

Failure to Transfer
If the Lender fails to transfer the Loaned Securities to the Borrower, the Borrower may:

- require the Lender to pay it the excess of its cost of borrowing the securities over the relevant portion of the Lending Fee; or
- terminate the Transaction.

If the Borrower fails to return the Loaned Securities on the Return Date the Lender may:

- require the Borrower to pay the higher of the Lender's cost of borrowing the securities and the Lending Fee for the period of the delay; or
- terminate the Transaction, with the Borrower paying the Lender its cost of borrowing the securities.

Partial deliveries
Partial deliveries are possible under Section 2(5)(c). If not agreed, termination will ensue.

Lending Fee
The Lending Fee is based upon a 360-day year and is payable monthly in arrears.

Buy/Sell Backs
There is no reference to Buy/Sell Back Transactions, of course.

Margin Maintenance Annex

This Annex adopts a new approach in the market in that it provides common margining terms for repos, securities loans and derivative transactions. It was revised in early 2004 to extend coverage to Derivative Transactions. The Annex supplements the EMA's General Provisions.

Section 1

> **MASTER AGREEMENT**
> **FOR FINANCIAL TRANSACTIONS**
> **MARGIN MAINTENANCE ANNEX**
> **Edition 2004**
>
> This Annex supplements the General Provisions which form part of any Master Agreement for Financial Transactions based on the form published by the FBE.
>
> **1. Net Exposure**
>
> (1) *General Principles.* If, at any time when Net Exposure is calculated pursuant to subsection 2, one party (the "Margin Provider") has an Adjusted Net Exposure to the other (the "Margin Recipient") resulting from any Transactions and/or from transfers of Margin pursuant to this Annex, the Margin Recipient may by notice to the Margin Provider require the same to transfer to it cash ("Cash Margin") or Securities ("Margin Securities") acceptable to the Margin Recipient and whose aggregate Market Value, when multiplied by the valuation percentage, if any, agreed between the parties ("Valuation Percentage"), shall be at least equal to the Adjusted Net Exposure. "Adjusted Net Exposure" means the sum of the Net Exposure and any supplementary amount ("Independent Amount") agreed in favour of the Margin Recipient less any Independent Amount agreed in favour of the Margin Provider. Such notice may be given orally or as provided in Section 8(1) of the General Provisions. The Net Exposure will be determined, and accordingly Margin will be required to be transferred, in respect of (a) all such Transactions, (b) specified groups of Transactions, (c) each individual Transaction or (d) otherwise, as agreed by the parties (in the Special Provisions or otherwise), provided that failing such agreement, (b) shall apply in such a manner that all Repurchase Transactions, all Securities Loans and all Derivative Transactions shall each form a separate group of Transactions to which this Annex applies. The "Market Value" of cash shall be the nominal amount thereof, converted, if not denominated in the Base Currency, in accordance with subsection 2. Any reference in this Annex to Transactions shall be construed as a reference to Repurchase Transactions and/or Securities Loans and/or Derivative Transactions.

Following calculation of Net Exposure the party at risk may call upon the other to provide acceptable cash or securities margin to cover the Net Exposure. Net Exposure is modified by adding any Independent Amount agreed in favour of the Margin Recipient and deducting any Independent Amount in favour of the Margin Provider. The result is called the Adjusted Net Exposure. The parties can choose if the margin shall cover:

(a) all repo, securities lending or derivative transactions; or

(b) specified groups of Transactions; or

(c) individual Transactions; or

(d) as otherwise agreed by the parties in the Special Provisions.

However, if the parties do not make a choice, the fallback shall be (b) (ie, repos, securities loans and derivative transactions forming separate groups).

> (2) *Calculation.* The person designated by the parties for this purpose or, failing such designation, each party (each the "Valuation Agent") shall calculate the Net Exposure on each Valuation Date by 11 a.m. Brussels time. The Net Exposure shall be expressed as a positive number if the Valuation Agent would, pursuant to its calculation, be the Margin Recipient, and shall otherwise be expressed as a negative number. All calculations shall be made in the Base Currency; any amount not denominated in the Base Currency shall be converted into the Base Currency at the Applicable Exchange Rate.

One or both parties may be the Valuation Agent (note the change from the term "Calculation Party" in the General Provisions). Net Exposure is to be calculated on each Valuation Day by 11.00 a.m. Brussels time. Intra-day valuations or margin calls are not catered for. All calculations shall be made in the Base Currency. A positive Net Exposure will entail a payment of margin to the Margin Recipient, while a negative Net Exposure will involve a payment of margin to the Margin Provider.

> (3) *Definitions.* "Net Exposure" means (I) in relation to Repurchase Transactions and Securities Loans the excess (if any), calculated pursuant to subsection 2, of the Liabilities of the Margin Provider over the Liabilities of the Margin Recipient, and (II) in relation to Derivative Transactions the Potential Final Settlement Amount, provided that (a) if the calculation is to be made pursuant to both (I) and (II), the Net Exposure shall be the aggregate of the amounts so calculated, (b) the amount of any prior Adjusted Net Exposure in respect of which a transfer of Margin has already been required, but not completed, shall be subtracted from any Net Exposure subsequently calculated and (c) if both parties act as Valuation Agent and their calculations of Net Exposure differ from each other, (i) the Net Exposure shall be one-half of the difference of the amounts so calculated by both parties (such difference being, for the avoidance of doubt, the sum

of the absolute values of such amounts if one is positive and the other negative) and (ii) the Margin Provider shall be the party which has calculated a negative or the lower positive amount;

"Liabilities" means, with respect to a party, the aggregate of

(a) the Market Values of any Securities transferred to that party under a Transaction or pursuant to this Annex 1 and not yet returned to the other party, multiplied (i) in the case of Loaned Securities, by the applicable Margin Ratio and (ii) in the case of Margin Securities, by any applicable Valuation Percentage;

(b) a cash amount equal to the sum of (i) the amount, multiplied by the applicable Margin Ratio, of that party's obligation(s) to pay the Repurchase Price in respect of any Repurchase Transaction if the relevant Valuation Date were the Repurchase Date, and (ii) the Market Value, multiplied by any applicable Valuation Percentage, of any Cash Margin transferred to and not repaid by that party (including unpaid accrued interest on such Cash Margin); and

(c) the cash amount or cash equivalent in respect of any Distribution to be paid or transferred by such party to the other party, but not yet paid or transferred;

"Margin" means either Cash Margin or Margin Securities;

"Margin Ratio" (also called "Haircut") means, with respect to each Repurchase Transaction or Securities Loan, the percentage agreed by the parties by which the Liabilities of the Seller or the Borrower in relation to the Repurchase Price and the Loaned Securities, respectively, are multiplied, as provided under "Liabilities" above, in order to determine the Net Exposure; failing an agreement to that effect, the Margin Ratio shall be equal to (a) with respect to a Repurchase Transaction, the Market Value of the Purchased Securities on the date on which the Transaction was entered into, divided by the Purchase Price, and (b) with respect to a Securities Loan (i) the Market Value, on the date on which the Transaction was entered into, of any Margin to be provided at the commencement of such Securities Loan, multiplied by the applicable Valuation Percentage and divided by the Market Value of the Loaned Securities as of such date, and (ii) if no Margin is provided at the commencement of such Securities Loan, 100 per cent., unless the parties have expressly excluded the provision of Margin for the entire term of the Transaction, in which case the Margin Ratio shall be zero until the Return Date;

"Potential Final Settlement Amount" means the amount which, at the time on each Valuation Date when Net Exposure is calculated in respect of Derivative Transactions pursuant to subsection 2, the Valuation Agent, acting as if it were the Calculation Party (as defined in Section 7(1)(a) of the General Provisions), determines to be equal to the Final Settlement Amount calculated in respect of Derivative Transactions (but excluding Repurchase Transactions and Securities Loans), if the same had to be calculated as of such time and date, such determination to be made in accordance with Section 7(1)(a) of the General Provisions, except that (a) if the determination can be made on the basis of bid and offered quotations, the arithmetic

> mean of such quotations shall be used for such determination, and (b) the amount of Margin Claims shall be adjusted so as to take into account the applicable Valuation Percentages;
>
> "Valuation Date" means, in respect of calculation of the Net Exposure, each of the dates agreed as such between the parties, and failing such agreement each Business Day.

This is a long section.

Net Exposure calculations compare the Liabilities of both parties in respect of repos and securities loans, and exclude any margin previously called for but not yet transferred. With Derivative Transactions the Net Exposure is the Potential Final Settlement Amount adjusted in the same manner. Where both parties are Valuation Agent and their Net Exposure figures differ, the difference is split and the Margin Provider will be the party that has calculated a negative amount or lower positive amount.

The definition of Liabilities takes into account the Buyer's or Borrower's obligations to retransfer equivalent securities in line with agreed haircuts and taking into account Distributions received but unpaid to the party owed them. "Margin" can mean either Cash Margin or Margin Securities. "Valuation Date" means each of the dates agreed by the parties for calculating Net Exposure or otherwise each Business Day.

Section 2

> **2. Notification of Adjusted Net Exposure and Transfer of Margin**
> (1) *Notification.* Promptly after determining the Net Exposure, the Valuation Agent shall notify each relevant party of the Adjusted Net Exposure and upon request of a party provide such party with a statement setting forth in reasonable detail the calculation basis of the Adjusted Net Exposure. The notice may be given orally or as provided in Section 8(1) of the General Provisions.

The Valuation Agent shall notify the other party of the Adjusted Net Exposure promptly and, if requested, provide a statement, in reasonable detail, showing how the Adjusted Net Exposure was calculated. The notice may be provided orally or by letter, telex, fax or electronic messaging system.

> (2) *Transfer.* The Margin Provider shall, upon receipt of the notice referred to in the first sentence of Section 1(1), transfer to the Margin Recipient Margin with an aggregate Market Value at least equal to the Adjusted Net Exposure no later than the date agreed for such transfer, and failing such agreement on the Business Day immediately following receipt of such notice, if such notice is received on a Business Day prior to 11.00 a.m., and otherwise on the second Business Day following such receipt.

When the notice is received, the Margin Provider shall transfer Margin with an aggregate value equal to the Adjusted Net Exposure. The transfer shall occur by the deadline agreed by the parties, failing which on the following Business Day, if such notice is received by the Margin Provider before 11.00 a.m. on a Business Day, and if not, on the second Business Day following receipt of the notice. This provision does not seem to take into account securities with a longer settlement cycle than two Business Days. However, this will probably not be an issue with two contracting parties in the same domestic market.

> (3) *Composition of Margin.* The Margin Provider is entitled to determine the composition of the Margin to be transferred, unless the Margin Recipient has previously paid Cash Margin which has not been repaid or transferred Margin Securities which have not been returned to it, in which case the Margin Provider shall first repay such Cash Margin or return such Margin Securities.

The Margin Provider is entitled to decide what type of margin it wishes to transfer. However, where the Margin Recipient has previously transferred cash or securities to the Margin Provider, the Margin Recipient can insist that these be returned first.

> (4) *Cash Margin.* Cash Margin shall be acceptable for the purpose of Section 1 (l) if transferred in the Base Currency or such other currency as the parties may have specified as eligible (in the Special Provisions or otherwise). A payment of Cash Margin shall give rise to a debt owing from the Margin Recipient to the Margin Provider and shall bear interest at such rate, and payable at such times, as agreed by the parties. In the absence of such agreement, that rate shall be equal to the Interbank Rate less 0.10 per cent. per annum, and the interest shall be payable at the end of each calendar month and on each date when the Margin Recipient is required to provide or return Margin.

Cash Margin is payable in the Base Currency or in a currency specified as eligible in the Special Provisions. Payment of Cash Margin represents a debt owed by the Margin Recipient to the Margin Provider. Cash Margin will bear interest at an agreed rate, failing which it shall be Interbank Rate minus 10 basis points per annum. The inclusion of a fallback interest rate is new in collateral agreements. Interest is payable at the end of each calendar month and on each date the Margin Recipient returns Cash Margin.

> (5) *Margin Securities.* Margin Securities shall be acceptable for the purpose of Section 1 (l) if Securities of the relevant kind (a) have been specified by the parties as eligible ⟫

> (in the Special Provisions or otherwise) or (b) have an original maturity of not more than five years and are issued by the central government of the country in which the Margin Recipient has its principal office or in which it is organised, incorporated or resident. A transfer of Margin Securities shall give rise to an obligation of the Margin Recipient to the Margin Provider to return such Securities as provided in this Annex.

Agreed Margin Securities should be stated in the Special Provisions. Securities with a maturity of less than five years and issued by the Margin Recipient's central government are considered acceptable Margin Securities. A transfer of Margin Securities constitutes an ultimate obligation of the Margin Recipient to retransfer them to the Margin Provider.

> (6) *Margin Thresholds.* Except in the case of a return of Margin pursuant to subsection 7, a transfer of Margin will take place only (a) to the extent that the Adjusted Net Exposure exceeds the threshold amount, if any, agreed by the parties ("Exposure Threshold") in relation to the Margin Recipient's Net Exposure and (b) if the Market Value of the Margin to be transferred exceeds the minimum amount, if any, agreed for such transfer (the "Minimum Transfer Amount"). In the absence of an agreement on either or both such amounts, such amount, or both, respectively, shall be zero.

Margin transfers may be subject to Exposure Thresholds or Minimum Transfer Amounts. Where not specified, these shall be zero.

> (7) *Return of Margin.* Upon satisfaction by a party of all its obligations under Transactions in respect of which Margin is required to be transferred as provided in the fourth sentence of Section 1(1), any Margin previously transferred and not returned shall be returned to the party which transferred it.

All Margin must be returned when the other party has fully satisfied its obligations under Transactions for which Margin was required (ie, no Net Exposure is left).

Section 3

> **3. Provisions Applicable to Margin Securities**
> The provisions of Section 3 of the Repurchase Annex (regarding substitution of Purchased Securities) and Sections 2(3), 2(5)(b)(ii) and (d), 2(6) and 3 of

THE EUROPEAN MASTER AGREEMENT

> the Securities Lending Annex (regarding interpretation, failure to return Loaned Securities, special events, Distributions and subscription rights) shall apply *mutatis mutandis* to Margin Securities transferred pursuant to this Annex, provided that (a) the consent of the Margin Recipient shall not be required for a substitution by the Margin Provider of new Margin Securities acceptable pursuant to Section 2(5) of this Annex for Margin Securities previously transferred and (b) if any of the special events referred to in terminated, but Margin acceptable pursuant to Section 2 (4) or (5) of this Annex shall be substituted for such Securities upon request of either party.

Certain provisions of the Repurchase Annex and the Securities Lending Annex shall apply, *mutatis mutandis*, to Margin Securities. However, if substituted Margin consists of cash or securities previously accepted by the Margin Recipient, their consent is not required again. The occurrence of any of the Special Events in Section 2(6) of the Securities Lending Annex will not lead to termination of the relevant Transaction, but acceptable cash or Margin Securities shall be substituted for such securities upon either party's request.

Special Provisions

The Special Provisions are the heart of the EMA and are the only part of the EMA signed by the contracting parties.

They comprise five paragraphs, viz:

Paragraph 1

> **MASTER AGREEMENT**
> **FOR FINANCIAL TRANSACTIONS**
> dated as of_____
> between
> _____ and _____
> ("Party A")   ("Party B")
>
> **SPECIAL PROVISIONS**
>
> Edition 2004
>
> **1. Nature of Agreement**
> This contractual arrangement (the "Special Provisions"), together with the General Provisions (the "General Provisions") and any annex (each an "Annex") referred to below, constitutes a master agreement (the "Master Agreement") under which the parties may enter into financial transactions.

The contractual arrangement of the EMA (ie, Special Provisions, General Provisions and the Annexes selected in Paragraph 2) is defined here.

Paragraph 2

> **2. Incorporation of Documents**
> The following documents, all in the _____ language, published by the FBE are hereby incorporated into and shall accordingly form part of the Master Agreement:
> (a) the General Provisions, Edition 2004
> (b) the following Annex[es]:
> Product Annex[es] for:
> Repurchase Transactions, Edition January 2001
> Securities Loans, Edition January 2001
> Derivative Transactions, Edition 2004
> Supplement for Foreign Exchange Transactions, Edition 2004
> Supplement for Interest Rate Transactions, Edition 2004
> Supplement for Option Transactions, Edition 2004
> Margin Maintenance Annex, Edition 2004
> Other Supplements (give details)

In Paragraph 2, the documents constituting the EMA are chosen and their language is also specified.

Paragraph 3

> **3. Addresses for notices (Section 8(1) of the General Provisions)**
> The addresses for notices and other communications between the parties are: ...

This is where the parties' addresses for notices and other communications are inserted.

Paragraph 4

> **4. Governing law, Settlement of Disputes, Jurisdiction, Arbitration (Section 11(1) and (2) of the General Provisions)**
> The law governing the Agreement is _____ law.
> Settlement of Disputes:
> Jurisdiction: The court (s) referred to in Section 11(2) is/are _____.
> Arbitration: The rules of arbitration referred to in Section 11(2) are the Rules of Arbitration of [Euro Arbitration - European Center for Financial Dispute Resolution] [the International Chamber of Commerce] §§ [other]§§ [with which each party agrees to comply].
> The parties agree to submit those disputes to [a single] [three] arbitrator[s].
> Such arbitration shall take place in _____.
> The language[s] in which arbitration shall be conducted [is] [are]_____.

THE EUROPEAN MASTER AGREEMENT

The governing law of the EMA is selected here, together with which courts will have jurisdiction. Alternatively, arbitration details may be inserted instead.

Paragraph 5

5. Other provisions

This is a miscellaneous provision and typically incorporates the matters referred to in the Appendix (Checklist), which is shown in full in Appendix 3.

The provisions most commonly negotiated are:

- Default Threshold for Cross-Default
- Whether Automatic Termination is to apply
- Transactions and groups of Transactions covered

Of course, these negotiated provisions relate to the Annexes for Repurchase Transactions and Securities Loans. As yet there is very little evidence of the most commonly negotiated issues in the Derivatives Annex.

Comparison of the EMA with the TBMA/ISMA GMRA

While we have been comparing the EMA with the TBMA/ISMA GMRA throughout this commentary, it is now useful to draw the similarities and differences together.

No chosen law

Unlike the TBMA/ISMA GMRA the EMA has no chosen law. Its General Provisions allow the parties to choose a governing law in the Special Provisions, failing which there is a fallback option. This is the law of the country, if identical, in which both parties' principal offices are located when the EMA is signed.

Documentation structure

The TBMA/ISMA GMRA has a structure comprising:

- a master agreement setting out core provisions applying to Transactions;
- a number of Annexes, some containing supplemental terms or conditions, some amending core provisions, and some covering certain transaction types and countries; and
- individual trade Confirmations.

The EMA is similar, comprising:

- the General Provisions, which correspond to the TBMA/ISMA GMRA;
- the Special Provisions to be completed with the bespoke particular requirements of the parties, including choice of law and jurisdiction; and
- supplemental Annexes to be included as the parties require. Currently the EMA offers

173

product annexes for Repurchase Transactions, Securities Loans and Derivative Transactions (with Supplements for Foreign Exchange Transactions, Interest Rate Transactions and Options), and a Margin Maintenance Annex for them.

Scope

The EMA is wider in scope than the TBMA/ISMA GMRA. It aims to consolidate, into a single set of harmonised documents, agreements covering repos, securities loans and derivative transactions. It also allows for the possibility, by the addition of new product annexes, of expanding the scope of the EMA to include other financial transactions in the future. If this aim is achieved, it would enable market players to document potentially all trading transactions under a single master agreement, in other words under a "master master agreement".

Fundamental principles

Certain fundamental principles are common to both agreements, viz:

- Each agreement constitutes a single contractual relationship explicitly affirming the mutual interdependence of each Transaction entered into under its umbrella.
- The essential legal nature of each non-Derivative Transaction is that of sale and repurchase: an absolute transfer of title rather than a secured loan.
- It follows that the obligation of the Buyer is to retransfer equivalent Securities.

Common elements in the documentation

Common elements in the documentation include:

- basic mechanics and operational details;
- provisions relating to margin maintenance, although note here that the EMA addresses this topic via the separate "Margin Maintenance Annex", which (unlike the TBMA/ISMA GMRA) sets out common rules regarding margin for repos, securities loans and derivative transactions;
- provisions regulating the treatment of income on repoed securities;
- provisions permitting substitution of repoed securities;
- representations;
- events of default and procedures to apply following a default;
- miscellaneous matters, notably governing law and jurisdiction, including:
    - English law and courts for the TBMA/ISMA GMRA; and
    - for the EMA, the requirement on the parties to make a choice in the Special Provisions essential if the fallback option (which would not work in a cross-border context) is to be avoided.

Differences

These are:

Events of Default

The TBMA/ISMA GMRA does *not* include a cross-default or a default for "restructuring without assumption". The TBMA/ISMA GMRA covers default by reason of regulatory event (ie, suspension of membership of an exchange or self-regulatory organisation, etc) and default by reason of failure to perform other obligations. It also provides for a mini close-out regime which applies to failure to perform delivery obligations in respect of securities.

The TBMA/ISMA GMRA lacks a Cross-Default provision. The EMA includes one with a materiality threshold designed to avoid technical defaults as well as a default for failure to pay or deliver. The EMA has perhaps greater latitude on grace periods than the TBMA/ISMA GMRA and a separate "Termination due to Change of Circumstances" regime, covering Tax Event, Illegality, Impossibility and Credit Event upon Restructuring.

Consequences of default

The TBMA/ISMA GMRA states that the agreement provides a complete statement of the remedies available in respect of a default. The EMA does not preclude parties from seeking legal redress through other legal means, apart from termination, but does prohibit seeking redress for consequential losses.

Tax

While the TBMA/ISMA GMRA contains a general gross up provision, the withholding tax and gross up provision in the EMA is based on the principle that a gross up should apply in a cross-border but not in a domestic context.

Choice of law

These two forms of repo agreement do not, of course, exist in a legal vacuum. The laws applicable affect the contractual obligations of the parties under the agreements.

This point needs stressing with the EMA, which leaves the choice of law to the parties' selection as one of the Special Provisions. The parties therefore need to choose a suitable law. With repo transactions, they should focus on recharacterisation risk under the chosen law. It could be disastrous if the repo was recharacterised as a secured loan. As always, legal due diligence is vital.

Despite heavy initial promotion from French and German banks, the EMA is still only gradually being used widely in Europe. The accession of 10 new countries to the European Union on 1 May 2004 may give it added impetus.

The TBMA/ISMA GMRA is certainly well ahead as far as legal opinion on its enforceability is concerned (34 versus 14) and for that reason is likely to remain the repo master agreement of choice in Europe for the time being.

However, the EMA is useful where a counterparty insists on entering into a local law agreement.

* Within chapters, terms used in the commentaries may have capitalisation or minor spelling differences to match the corresponding documentation.

Chapter 5

Commentary on the Master Repurchase Agreement (September 1996 version)

This chapter will annotate The Bond Market Association (TBMA) Master Repurchase Agreement (the "Agreement" or "MRA"). The Agreement is the market standard in the United States for repurchase transactions. As the repurchase market continues to evolve, the Agreement should be flexible enough to accommodate any variety of new repurchase transactions, structures and securities.

For each section of the Agreement the text is quoted first (shaded in grey) and explanatory commentary follows immediately below. Before presenting the paragraph-by-paragraph analysis, however, this chapter will outline the evolution and basic structure of the Agreement.

Evolution of the Agreement

As the repo market developed in the 1970s, the documentation of repos and reverse repos was relatively informal and was typically done through a letter agreement.[1] The letter agreement would name the parties and provide the basic economic terms of the Transaction. As time passed, however, market practice became even more relaxed, and parties began to rely solely upon the buy and sell confirmations that were issued as part of the Transaction.

Parties became more concerned about proper documentation, however, with the 1982 *Lombard-Wall* ruling[2] and certain bankruptcy code amendments passed in 1984. As discussed in Chapter 2, the characterisation and documentation of repos became more important, and individual parties began developing more extensive and specialised documentation.

In response to the difficulties that parties had in negotiating these individual and customised agreements, the securities industry, through the Public Securities Association (PSA) (now The Bond Market Association or TBMA), developed a standard form of repurchase agreement in February 1986 entitled the PSA Master Repurchase Agreement. This standard form was revised in its entirety in August 1987 to reflect important regulations and other issues surrounding the Government Securities Act of 1986. The repo market in the United States embraced the PSA Master Agreement and it became the market standard agreement for documenting repo transactions.

---

[1] For a more thorough discussion of the development of repo documentation see Chapter 14 of Marcia Stigum, *The Repo and Reverse Repo Markets* (New York: Dow Jones, 1989).

[2] *Lombard-Wall, Inc. v. Bankers Trust Co.*, 23 B.R. 165 (1982). *Lombard-Wall* involved the bankruptcy of a smaller repo dealer where its counterparties suffered significant losses.

Another revised version of the PSA Master Repurchase Agreement was issued in September 1996 by The Bond Market Association (the "BMA"). This is the Agreement that is still in use in the United States and that is annotated below. The revised MRA was drafted in response to three developments. First, as the repo market had grown and broadened, many believed that the 1987 Agreement was inadequate to document the new types of securities that were being used in repo transactions.

Second, the Agreement was revised to deal with counterparty insolvency concerns. It was also drafted to take into account amendments to Article 8 of the Uniform Commercial Code. Finally, the Agreement was modified so that it could be used with various supplemental annexes: for example, annexes were developed for "forward start" repos and Buy/Sellback repos.

The BMA has published on its website "Guidance Notes Summarizing Key Changes from August 1987 Version" that summarise the salient differences between the August 1987 Master Repurchase Agreement and the 1996 Agreement.

Structure of the Agreement

The Agreement's basic structure is a printed master form containing provisions for all repurchase transactions between the Seller and the Buyer. The Agreement anticipates, although it does not require, that the parties will enter into multiple repurchase transactions. The Agreement also has nine different annexes that can be negotiated and included when the Agreement is executed between the parties.

Annex I consists of the Supplemental Terms and Conditions. Here amendments to the Agreement are typically made and required information is added. For example, the parties will list under Annex I which other annexes will apply to the Agreement. It is market practice that no changes are made directly to the pre-printed Agreement form itself.

As in Annex I, each additional annex provides for the varying needs of the parties entering into the Agreement. Annex II provides a place for the parties to add their names and addresses for purposes of giving notices and communications between them. Annexes III and IIIA provide important definitions and clauses needed to enter into repos with international securities. Annex IV supplies agency provisions if a party is to act as agent in a repo for another party. Annex V offers specific provisions for using margin with forward transactions. Annex VI deals with provisions necessary for Buy/Sell Back Transactions. Annex VII deals with transactions involving regulated investment companies. Finally, Annex IX deals with transactions involving certain Japanese financial institutions.

Paragraph-by-paragraph analysis of the Agreement

Terms capitalised in this chapter have the same meaning as used in the 1996 Agreement. The discussion of the annexes also provides common amendments seen in the market. (Chapter 3, written by Paul Harding, on the TBMA/ISMA GMRA Master Agreement takes a similar approach.)

The annotations in this chapter, for illustration purposes, will assume that there is only one repurchase transaction outstanding between the Buyer and the Seller. The Seller is selling US Treasury Securities with a Market Value on the Purchase Date of US$10,000,000. The Purchase Price is US$9,800,000. The Price Rate is 5 per cent and the Repurchase Date is 30 days later. The Repurchase Price is US$9,840,833.

A PRACTICAL GUIDE TO USING REPO MASTER AGREEMENTS

> **Master Repurchase Agreement**
>
> **September 1996 Version**
> Dated as of _____
> Between: _____
> and _____

The Agreement will generally be dated as of either the first trade between the parties or the date that the Agreement is executed, whichever occurs first. It is normal to date the Agreement as of the date of the first trade between the parties, even if it is not signed until several months later. This is based on US practice, where the words "as of" mean "with effect from" a specified date.

The legal names of the parties will be entered into this first section of the Agreement. Parties will often add descriptive language, such as where they are incorporated or organised.

Paragraph 1

> **1. Applicability**
> From time to time the parties hereto may enter into transactions in which one party ("Seller") agrees to transfer to the other ("Buyer") securities or other assets ("Securities") against the transfer of funds by Buyer, with a simultaneous agreement by Buyer to transfer to Seller such Securities at a date certain or on demand, against the transfer of funds by Seller. Each such transaction shall be referred to herein as a "Transaction" and, unless otherwise agreed in writing, shall be governed by this Agreement, including any supplemental terms or conditions contained in Annex I hereto and in any other annexes identified herein or therein as applicable hereunder.

This Paragraph of the Agreement sets out the mechanics of a repurchase transaction, and the obligations of the Buyer and the Seller to each other. The Agreement is written in such a way that either party may be a "Buyer" or a "Seller", depending upon the terms of the transaction, but a party would normally act in only one of the two capacities for the duration of an executed Agreement. If the parties also enter into a tri-party custodial agreement (as will be discussed in Chapter 6), a party can be designated as a Buyer or a Seller. Paragraph 1 also implies that, when parties enter into multiple transactions, all the transactions will be governed by the same Agreement.

Neither the definition of a Transaction in Paragraph 1 nor anywhere else in the Agreement restricts the type or class of assets that can be transferred. Although the vast majority of Transactions will involve US government or agency securities, the Agreement could accommodate the transfer of any other type or class of securities. Theoretically it would also be possible to transfer non-security types of assets, although there may be practical, documentary or legal concerns in using the Agreement for such purposes. Any asset that is transferred by the Seller to the Buyer is referred to as a Security.

Although the Agreement does not restrict its use for the transfer of any particular assets, additional provisions may be required for a specific Security or type of Transaction. As explained above, The BMA has prepared supplemental annexes for particular types of Transactions, specifically Annex V for using margin with forward transactions and Annex VI for Buy/Sell Back Transactions.

Paragraph 2

Paragraph 2 contains an extensive listing of definitions. As with other typical finance agreements, each reference in the Agreement that is capitalised will have a corresponding definition either in Paragraph 2 (Definitions) or where it is first defined elsewhere in the Agreement's text.

> **2. Definitions**
> (a) "Act of Insolvency", with respect to any party, (i) the commencement by such party as debtor of any case or proceeding under any bankruptcy, insolvency, reorganization, liquidation, moratorium, dissolution, delinquency or similar law, or such party seeking the appointment or election of a receiver, conservator, trustee, custodian or similar official for such party or any substantial part of its property, or the convening of any meeting of creditors for purposes of commencing any such case or proceeding or seeking such an appointment or election, (ii) the commencement of any such case or proceeding against such party, or another seeking such an appointment or election, or the filing against a party of an application for a protective decree under the provisions of the Securities Investor Protection Act of 1970, which (A) is consented to or not timely contested by such party, (B) results in the entry of an order for relief, such an appointment or election, the issuance of such a protective decree or the entry of an order having a similar effect, or (C) is not dismissed within 15 days, (iii) the making by such party of a general assignment for the benefit of creditors, or (iv) the admission in writing by such party of such party's inability to pay such party's debts as they become due;

The definition of an Act of Insolvency is important because its occurrence to either a Buyer or a Seller (a "debtor") is an Event of Default under Paragraph 11(v) of the Agreement. The language in the definition is very broad in order to include an Act of Insolvency under any bankruptcy, insolvency or regulatory regime. (Please see the insolvency discussion in Chapter 2, pages 22–28.)

The definition identifies three types of Acts of Insolvency that may occur to a party. Clause (i) refers to a voluntary bankruptcy or insolvency. A voluntary bankruptcy or insolvency occurs when the party itself commences a bankruptcy or insolvency proceeding. The occurrence of a voluntary Act of Insolvency is relatively easy to identify and permits the nondefaulting party to exercise its remedies promptly upon being notified of the Act of Insolvency.

Clause (ii) refers to an involuntary Act of Insolvency. Most bankruptcy, insolvency or regulatory regimes provide an opportunity for creditors to force a debtor into insolvency. The definition focuses in particular on an involuntary Act of Insolvency under the provisions of the Securities Investor Protection Act of 1970 (which specifically applies to broker-dealers and provides some protections for their customers). This is done to subject the debtor to judicial or regulatory supervision in order to prevent the debtor from dissipating or wasting assets. Because many debtors are able to have an involuntary Act of Insolvency proceeding dismissed, it is often difficult for a party to determine if an involuntary Act of Insolvency has actually occurred. An Event of Default with respect to an involuntary Act of Insolvency occurs only if, first, the debtor consents to or does not contest the proceeding; second, a court or regulator issues an order of relief (thus affirming that the involuntary Act of Insolvency will not be dismissed); or third, the debtor is unable to obtain the dismissal of the proceeding within 15 days of the involuntary Act of Insolvency.

The third category is similar to a voluntary Act of Insolvency. It applies where, as described in clause (iii), a general assignment for the benefit of creditors occurs. This is in substance a voluntary liquidation outside of a formal bankruptcy or insolvency proceeding and is governed by either common law or a state statute. As described in clause (iv), this category may also apply where a debtor admits in writing that it is unable to pay its debts as they become due. This is generally viewed as one of the standard definitions of an insolvent or bankrupt party. As a practical matter, this is a relatively rare occurrence, because most debtors would have entered into a voluntary Act of Insolvency in such a situation.

> (b) "Additional Purchased Securities", Securities provided by Seller to Buyer pursuant to Paragraph 4(a) hereof;

Under Paragraph 4(a) the Seller is required to transfer additional property to the Buyer in the event that the original Securities transferred to the Buyer have declined in value (ie, their value is less than the amount of cash transferred by the Buyer to the Seller).

> (c) "Buyer's Margin Amount" with respect to any Transaction as of any date, the amount obtained by application of the Buyer's Margin Percentage to the Repurchase Price for such Transaction as of such date;

This is an amount that determines whether a Seller will have to transfer additional Securities or cash to a Buyer in the event that the market value of transferred Securities has declined. It is determined by multiplying the Buyer's Margin Percentage by the Repurchase Price for a particular Transaction.

For example, assume that the Buyer's Margin Percentage is 102 per cent and the Repurchase Price is US$9,840,833.33. The Buyer's Margin Amount would be equal to US$10,037,650.00. If the Market Value of the Purchased Securities transferred by the Seller drops below that amount, the Seller will need to transfer additional Securities or cash to the Buyer. The Buyer's Margin Amount will generally be more than the Repurchase Price, in order to ensure that the Buyer always holds Securities at least equal in value to the

Repurchase Price (ie, the amount of cash that the Seller will transfer to the Buyer at the maturity of the Transaction).

> (d) "Buyer's Margin Percentage", with respect to any Transaction as of any date, a percentage (which may be equal to the Seller's Margin Percentage) agreed to by Buyer and Seller or, in the absence of any such agreement, the percentage obtained by dividing the Market Value of the Purchased Securities on the Purchase Date by the Purchase Price on the Purchase Date for such Transaction;

The Buyer's Margin Percentage will normally be more than 100 per cent, in order to maintain an appropriate cushion with respect to the Repurchase Price. In the United States the Buyer's Margin Percentage typically is 102 per cent for US Treasury and Agency Securities. If the parties fail expressly to set forth a percentage, the Agreement assumes that the Buyer's Margin Percentage is equal to the Market Value of the Purchased Securities (those transferred to the Buyer) divided by the Purchase Price.

For example, assume that the Buyer transferred cash of US$9,800,000 to the Seller in exchange for Securities with a Market Value of US$10,000,000. The Buyer's Margin Percentage would be 102.041 per cent. Note that, because the Purchase Price is calculated (assuming a 2 per cent haircut) by subtracting 2 per cent from the Market Value, the calculation of the Buyer's Margin Percentage will differ from the designated 102 per cent.

> (e) "Confirmation", the meaning specified in Paragraph 3(b) hereof;

Please see Paragraph 3(b) for a description of a Confirmation.

> (f) "Income", with respect to any Security at any time, any principal thereof and all interest, dividends or other distributions thereon;

Under the Agreement Income is defined to include any distribution made on a security, including principal, interest and, in the case of equity securities, any dividends or other redemptions or distributions. The treatment of Income is governed by Paragraph 5 of the MRA.

> (g) "Margin Deficit" the meaning specified in Paragraph 4 (a) hereof;

A Margin Deficit occurs under Paragraph 4(a) if the Market Value of Purchased Securities declines, possibly requiring the Seller to transfer Additional Purchased Securities.

> (h) "Margin Excess", the meaning specified in Paragraph 4(b) hereof;

A Margin Excess occurs under Paragraph 4(b) if the Market Value of Purchased Securities appreciates, possibly requiring the Buyer to transfer Securities or cash to the Seller.

> (i) "Margin Notice Deadline", the time agreed to by the parties in the relevant Confirmation, Annex I hereto or otherwise as the deadline for giving notice requiring same-day satisfaction of margin maintenance obligations as provided in Paragraph 4 hereof (or, in the absence of any such agreement, the deadline for such purposes established in accordance with market practice);

The Margin Notice Deadline may be set out in the Confirmation, especially if it is a Transaction with a Maturity Date of more than a few days. If it is not set out in the Confirmation, the parties are to rely on market practice. Market practice for the Margin Notice Deadline is typically 10.00 a.m., to provide the parties sufficient time to make the required transfers.

> (j) "Market Value" with respect to any Securities as of any date, the price for such Securities on such date obtained from a generally recognized source agreed to by the parties or the most recent closing bid quotation from such a source, plus accrued Income to the extent not included therein (other than any Income credited or transferred to, or applied to the obligations of, Seller pursuant to Paragraph 5 hereof) as of such date (unless contrary to market practice for such Securities);

Market Value of a Security is generally determined by reference to a recognised source such as Bloomberg, Reuters or *The Wall Street Journal*. The price is based on a bid quotation, meaning the price at which a broker would purchase the Security. Because accrued Income (generally accrued interest) will eventually be paid on a Purchased Security (and thus increase the amount of cash held by the Buyer), the amount of such accrued Income is added to the price of the Security.

> (k) "Price Differential", with respect to any Transaction as of any date, the aggregate amount obtained by daily application of the Pricing Rate for such Transaction to the Purchase Price for such Transaction on a 360 day per year basis for the actual number of days during the period commencing on (and including) the Purchase Date for such Transaction and ending on (but excluding) the date of determination (reduced by any amount of such Price Differential previously paid by Seller to Buyer with respect to such Transaction);

Price Differential is the amount that is added to the Purchase Price to determine the Repurchase Price. The Price Differential represents the amount that the Buyer earns from the Seller for purchasing and holding the Purchased Security during the term of the Transaction.

The Price Differential is determined in much the same way as interest is calculated on a loan. The Pricing Rate (an annual percentage) is multiplied by the Purchase Price to determine an annual amount. This annual amount is then divided by 360 days to determine the amount of the Price Differential that is earned each day by the Buyer. This daily amount is then multiplied by the number of days the Purchased Securities are held by the Buyer. The number of days is calculated by including the Purchase Date but excluding the Repurchase Date (ie, the date that the Purchased Securities are transferred back to the Seller).

For example, assume that the Purchase Price is US$9,800,000, the Pricing Rate is 5 per cent and the term of the Transaction is 30 days. The Pricing Differential is calculated as follows:

$$US\$9{,}800{,}000 \times (0.05/360) \times 30 \text{ days} = US\$40{,}833.33$$

> (l) "Pricing Rate", the per annum percentage rate for determination of the Price Differential;

The Pricing Rate represents the return that the Buyer requires on its cash when it purchases the Securities. In the example, it is assumed that it would be 5 per cent per annum.

> (m) "Prime Rate", the prime rate of U.S. commercial banks as published in The Wall Street Journal (or, if more than one such rate is published, the average of such rates);

The Wall Street Journal currently publishes the Prime Rate on a daily basis. The prime rate is the "base rate on corporate loans posted by at least 75% of the nation's 30 largest banks" (*WSJ* Money Rate section).

> (n) "Purchase Date", the date on which Purchased Securities are to be transferred by Seller to Buyer;

The Purchase Date is also typically the date that the parties enter into the Transaction.

> (o) "Purchase Price", (i) on the Purchase Date, the price at which Purchased Securities are transferred by Seller to Buyer, and (ii) thereafter, except where Buyer and Seller agree otherwise, such price increased by the amount of any cash transferred by Buyer to Seller pursuant to Paragraph 4(b) hereof and decreased by the amount of any cash transferred by Seller to Buyer pursuant to Paragraph 4 (a) hereof or applied to reduce Seller's obligations under clause (ii) of Paragraph 5 hereof;

The Purchase Price is the price that the Buyer pays the Seller for the Purchased Securities. The Purchase Price would ordinarily be equal to the Market Value of the Purchased Securities less a discount (referred to as a haircut).

In the United States market practice would customarily be to apply a discount for US Treasury or Agency Securities of 2 per cent. The Market Value is multiplied by 2 per cent. That amount is then subtracted from the Market Value to determine the Purchase Price.

For example, US$10,000,000 multiplied by 2 per cent equals US$200,000. The Purchase Price would then be equal to US$9,800,000. Note that this is a different amount than would have resulted if the Purchase Price had been calculated by dividing the Market Value by 102 per cent, which would have equalled US$9,803,921.56.

With respect to transfers of Purchased Securities between a Buyer and a Seller pursuant to Paragraph 4, there are two different methods to take into account. The method set forth in the definition of Purchase Price will adjust the Purchase Price for any transfers made under Paragraph 4. Under the definition the Purchase Price is increased by any Securities or cash transferred to the Seller by the Buyer because of a Margin Excess under Paragraph 4(b). The Purchase Price is decreased by any Securities or cash transferred by the Seller to the Buyer because of a Margin Deficit under Paragraph 4(a). It is also decreased by any cash transferred by the Seller to the Buyer to reduce the Seller's obligations under Paragraph 5(ii) (Income Payments).

Under a common amendment to the repurchase agreement typically made in Annex I (see discussion on pages 216–217), the Purchase Price is not changed due to a margin maintenance transfer pursuant to Paragraph 4 of the Agreement.

> (p) "Purchased Securities", the Securities transferred by Seller to Buyer in a Transaction hereunder, and any Securities substituted therefor in accordance with Paragraph 9 hereof. The term "Purchased Securities" with respect to any Transaction at any time also shall include Additional Purchased Securities delivered pursuant to Paragraph 4(a) hereof and shall exclude Securities returned pursuant to Paragraph 4(b) hereof;

The term "Purchased Securities" is intended to include not only those Securities transferred by the Seller to the Buyer on the Purchase Date, but also any other Securities transferred to the Buyer during the term of the Transaction. Specifically, it also includes any Securities that were substituted for the Purchased Securities pursuant to Paragraph 9. It also includes any Additional Securities transferred pursuant to Paragraph 4(a) because of a Margin Deficit, but excludes any Securities that were transferred back to the Seller pursuant to Paragraph 4(b) because of a Margin Excess.

> (q) "Repurchase Date", the date on which Seller is to repurchase the Purchased Securities from Buyer, including any date determined by application of the provisions of Paragraph 3(c) or 11 hereof;

COMMENTARY ON THE MASTER REPURCHASE AGREEMENT

A Repurchase Date can materialise under three different circumstances:

- First, the Repurchase Date is the date that the Buyer will transfer the Purchased Securities back to the Seller in exchange for the Repurchase Price. In the example the Repurchase Date is 30 days after the Purchase Date.
- Second, the Repurchase Date is the date that the Buyer will transfer the Purchased Securities to the Seller in a Transaction that is terminable upon demand of the Seller under Paragraph 3(c).
- Third, the Repurchase Date is also the date that a nondefaulting party declares an Event of Default under Paragraph 11.

> (r) "Repurchase Price", the price at which Purchased Securities are to be transferred from Buyer to Seller upon termination of a Transaction, which will be determined in each case (including Transactions terminable upon demand) as the sum of the Purchase Price and the Price Differential as of the date of such determination;

The Repurchase Price is the sum of the Purchase Price and the Price Differential at the Repurchase Date.

For example, assume that the Purchase Price was US$9,800,000 and the Price Differential was US$40,833.33. The Repurchase Price would be US$9,040,833.33.

> (s) "Seller's Margin Amount", with respect to any Transaction as of any date, the amount obtained by application of the Seller's Margin Percentage to the Repurchase Price for such Transaction as of such date;

This is an amount that determines whether a Seller can call for the return of Purchased Securities in the event that the Purchased Securities have increased in Market Value above the Seller's Margin Amount. For example, assume that the Seller's Margin Percentage is 102 per cent and the Repurchase Price is US$9,840,833.33. The Seller's Margin Amount would be equal to US$10,037,650. If the Market Value of the Purchased Securities transferred by the Seller exceeds US$10,037,650, the Buyer is required to transfer the excess to the Seller.

> (t) "Seller's Margin Percentage", with respect to any Transaction as of any date, a percentage (which may be equal to the Buyer's Margin Percentage) agreed to by Buyer and Seller or, in the absence of any such agreement, the percentage obtained by dividing the Market Value of the Purchased Securities on the Purchase Date by the Purchase Price on the Purchase Date for such Transaction.

Many Sellers will have determined an amount for the appropriate Seller's Margin Percentage required in order to ensure that the Market Value of the Purchased Securities does not exceed the Repurchase Price. If the parties fail expressly to set forth that percentage, the Agreement

A PRACTICAL GUIDE TO USING REPO MASTER AGREEMENTS

deems that it is equal to the Market Value of the Purchased Securities (those transferred to the Buyer) divided by the Purchase Price on the Purchase Date. Generally, parties do not expressly set forth the Seller's Margin Percentage and instead look to the deemed percentage as set forth in paragraph 2(t).It is not unusual for the Seller's Margin Percentage and the Buyer's Margin Percentage to be identical, especially if the parties did not set out the Seller's Margin Percentage.

Paragraph 3

Paragraph 3 is one of the key operative sections of the Agreement. Paragraph 3 describes how to initiate, document and terminate a Transaction.

> **3. Initiation; Confirmation; Termination**
> (a) An agreement to enter into a Transaction may be made orally or in writing at the initiation of either Buyer or Seller. On the Purchase Date for the Transaction, the Purchased Securities shall be transferred to Buyer or its agent against the transfer of the Purchase Price to an account of Seller.

Paragraph 3(a) describes how the parties initiate a Transaction. For example, Paragraph 3(a) confirms that the industry practice of entering into a Transaction orally creates an enforceable contract, although such contracts are always followed up in writing. It is also worth noting that either party may initiate the Transaction.

The Agreement also expressly provides that the transfer of Purchased Securities is to occur simultaneously with the transfer of the Purchase Price.

> (b) Upon agreeing to enter into a Transaction hereunder, Buyer or Seller (or both), as shall be agreed, shall promptly deliver to the other party a written confirmation of each Transaction (a "Confirmation"). The Confirmation shall describe the Purchased Securities (including CUSIP number, if any), identify Buyer and Seller and set forth (i) the Purchase Date, (ii) the Purchase Price, (iii) the Repurchase Date, unless the Transaction is to be terminable on demand, (iv) the Pricing Rate or Repurchase Price applicable to the Transaction, and (v) any additional terms or conditions of the Transaction not inconsistent with this Agreement. The Confirmation, together with this Agreement, shall constitute conclusive evidence of the terms agreed between Buyer and Seller with respect to the Transaction to which the Confirmation relates, unless with respect to the Confirmation specific objection is made promptly after receipt thereof. In the event of any conflict between the terms of such Confirmation and this Agreement, this Agreement shall prevail.

Although the Transaction is entered into orally, the parties are required to deliver a Confirmation to each other. It is market practice for the Dealer to prepare the Confirmation. Typically, one party (usually the dealer) will agree to deliver the Confirmation. Alternatively, each party could deliver its own Confirmation to the other. The Confirmation may be in a computer-generated form, which, as a matter of market practice, generally does not require either the Buyer or the Seller to execute it. Often the Confirmation is quite cryptic, so it is important that the parties understand the structure and terminology used in the Confirmation and other market practices.

The Confirmation sets forth the economic terms of a Transaction. The Confirmation also identifies the parties and describes the Security to be transferred (including its CUSIP number). The Confirmation will also include the following information, although the parties may use different vocabulary:

(i) Purchase Date (often referred to as the trade date);
(ii) Purchase Price (often referred to as the principal);
(iii) Repurchase Date (often referred to as the maturity date);
(iv) Pricing Rate or Repurchase Price;
(v) any additional terms not inconsistent with the Agreement.

In addition, the Confirmation may include payment and delivery instructions. The Confirmation probably will not reference the Agreement.

Under the Agreement the Confirmation is intended to document the final terms of a Transaction. A party objecting to the terms set out in the Confirmation must object promptly. Although the Agreement does not define "promptly", parties should look to market practice with respect to the particular Security transferred or the type of Transaction.

In contrast to the ISDA Master Agreement, the terms of the Confirmation will not prevail over the terms of the Agreement. In these circumstances the Agreement will prevail. In the event that the parties want to modify the terms of the Agreement for a particular Transaction, the parties need to amend the Agreement itself. It is unclear, however, why an amendment done through a Confirmation would not be sufficient to amend the Agreement.

> (c) In the case of Transactions terminable upon demand, such demand shall be made by Buyer or Seller, no later than such time as is customary in accordance with market practice, by telephone or otherwise on or prior to the business day on which such termination will be effective. On the date specified in such demand, or on the date fixed for termination in the case of Transactions having a fixed term, termination of the Transaction will be effected by transfer to Seller or its agent of the Purchased Securities and any Income in respect thereof received by Buyer (and not previously credited or transferred to, or applied to the obligations of, Seller pursuant to Paragraph 5 hereof) against the transfer of the Repurchase Price to an account of Buyer.

Paragraph 3(c) provides how the parties terminate a Transaction or, in other words, how the repurchase occurs. Termination is effected by the Buyer transferring the Purchased Securities (and any Income not previously transferred) to the Seller against the Seller transferring the Repurchase Price to the Buyer. Where a Transaction has a designated maturity date (ie, a fixed-term repo), it is terminated on the Repurchase Date set out in the Confirmation.

In a Transaction that is terminable upon demand the Transaction terminates on the date designated by the party entitled to terminate the Transaction upon demand. The parties are to look to market practice to determine how much notice a party is required to give to terminate a Transaction. Repurchase transactions terminable upon demand are relatively uncommon in the United States. The repurchase transaction will usually be either an overnight repo or a term repo (ie, one with a fixed maturity date).

Paragraph 4

A fundamental principle behind a repurchase transaction is that the Buyer is entitled to hold Purchased Securities that have a Market Value at least equal to the Repurchase Price. This ensures that, if the Seller does not perform and repurchase the Purchased Securities, the Buyer will be able to liquidate the Purchased Securities for an amount at least equal to the Repurchase Price.

Conversely, the Seller is permitted to claw back prior to termination at least some of the Purchased Securities that it has transferred in the event that the Purchased Securities have appreciated well above the Repurchase Price. This protects the Seller from a Buyer who fails to return appreciated Purchased Securities.

> **4. Margin Maintenance**
> (a) If at any time the aggregate Market Value of all Purchased Securities subject to all Transactions in which a particular party hereto is acting as Buyer is less than the aggregate Buyer's Margin Amount for all such Transactions (a "Margin Deficit"), then Buyer may by notice to Seller require Seller in such Transactions, at Seller's option, to transfer to Buyer cash or additional Securities reasonably acceptable to Buyer ("Additional Purchased Securities"), so that the cash and aggregate Market Value of the Purchased Securities, including any such Additional Purchased Securities, will thereupon equal or exceed such aggregate Buyer's Margin Amount (decreased by the amount of any Margin Deficit as of such date arising from any Transactions in which such Buyer is acting as Seller).

Paragraph 4(a) provides the mechanics that permit a Buyer to call for Additional Purchased Securities in the event that there is a Margin Deficit. A Margin Deficit can occur if the Purchased Securities have declined in value. It is important to note that the Margin Deficit is determined by taking into account the Aggregate Market Value of all Purchased Securities, not just a Margin Deficit with respect to one particular Transaction. Aggregating deficits minimises the number of calls for Additional Purchased Securities, as Securities fluctuate in value.

The Buyer is permitted (but not required) to call for Additional Purchased Securities (in the form of either cash or Securities at the option of the Seller) sufficient to cause the Purchased Securities to equal or exceed the Buyer's Margin Amount. For example, assume that the Buyer's Margin Amount equals US$10,037,649.66, and the Market Value of the Purchased Securities is US$10,000,000. The Seller would be required to transfer to the Buyer at least US$37,649.66 in either Securities or cash. (See the definition of the Buyer's Margin Amount for a discussion of how it is calculated.)

> (b) If at any time the aggregate Market Value of all Purchased Securities subject to all Transactions in which a particular party hereto is acting as Seller exceeds the aggregate Seller's Margin Amount for all such Transactions at such time (a "Margin Excess"), then Seller may by notice to Buyer require Buyer in such Transactions, at Buyer's option, to transfer cash or Purchased Securities to Seller, so that the aggregate Market Value of the Purchased Securities, after deduction of any such cash or any Purchased Securities so transferred, will thereupon not exceed such aggregate Seller's Margin Amount (increased by the amount of any Margin Excess as of such date arising from any Transactions in which such Seller is acting as Buyer).

Paragraph 4(b) provides the mechanics to permit a Seller to claw back Purchased Securities (in the form of either cash or Securities at the Buyer's option) where there is a Margin Excess. A Margin Excess can occur if the Purchased Securities have appreciated in value. It is important to note that the Margin Excess is determined by taking into account the Aggregate Market Value of all Purchased Securities, not just a Margin Excess with respect to one particular Transaction. Again, aggregating the value minimises the number of returns of Purchased Securities that would be required.

The Seller is permitted (but not required) to call for the return of Additional Purchased Securities (in the form of either cash or Securities at the option of the Buyer) sufficient to cause the Purchased Securities to equal or exceed the Seller's Margin Amount. For example, assume that the Seller's Margin Percentage is 102 per cent and the Repurchase Price is US$9,840,833.33. The Seller's Margin Amount would be equal to US$10,037,650.00. If the Market Value of the Purchased Securities transferred by the Seller were to equal US$10,137,650.00, the Buyer would be required to transfer the excess of US$100,000 in either Securities or cash to the Seller.

> (c) If any notice is given by Buyer or Seller under subparagraph (a) or (b) of this Paragraph at or before the Margin Notice Deadline on any business day, the party receiving such notice shall transfer cash or Additional Purchased Securities as provided in such subparagraph no later than the close of business in the relevant market on such day. If any such notice is given after the Margin Notice Deadline, the party receiving such notice shall transfer such cash or Securities no later than the close of business in the relevant market on the next business day following such notice.

Paragraph 4(c) sets out the mechanics for giving notice for a call of Purchased Securities upon the occurrence of a Margin Deficit or a Margin Excess. The general rule calls for same-day delivery, provided that notice is given by the Margin Notice Deadline. If notice is given after the Margin Notice Deadline, delivery must occur by close of business on the next business day.

> (d) Any cash transferred pursuant to this Paragraph shall be attributed to such Transactions as shall be agreed upon by Buyer and Seller.

Although the calculations for a Margin Deficit or Margin Excess are computed on an aggregate basis, any cash transferred must be allocated between the Transactions as the parties agree.

> (e) Seller and Buyer may agree, with respect to any or all Transactions hereunder, that the respective rights of Buyer or Seller (or both) under subparagraphs (a) and (b) of this Paragraph may be exercised only where a Margin Deficit or Margin Excess, as the case may be, exceeds a specified dollar amount or a specified percentage of the Repurchase Prices for such Transactions (which amount or percentage shall be agreed to by Buyer and Seller prior to entering into any such Transactions).

To avoid nuisance transfers of cash or Securities between the parties, the parties may agree to a threshold amount that must be exceeded prior to requiring a transfer. The equivalent to this concept in ISDA documentation is the Minimum Transfer Amount found in the ISDA Credit Support Annexes. For example, if the parties agreed that the threshold amount would be US$500,000, a Margin Deficit or Margin Excess would have to be equal to or greater than that amount before a party is obligated to make a transfer. Once the threshold amount has been met, however, the entire Margin Deficit or Margin Excess would be required to be transferred (not just the amount greater than US$500,000).

The designation of a threshold amount is both a credit and an operational decision. The designation effectively results in the Buyer granting the Seller additional unsecured credit. For example, if the Margin Deficit did not exceed the threshold, the Buyer would not be able to recoup its Repurchase Price if it were to liquidate the Purchased Securities.

> (f) Seller and Buyer may agree, with respect to any or all Transactions hereunder, that the respective rights of Buyer and Seller under subparagraphs (a) and (b) of this Paragraph to require the elimination of a Margin Deficit or a Margin Excess, as the case may be, may be exercised whenever such a Margin Deficit or Margin Excess exists with respect to any single Transaction hereunder (calculated without regard to any other Transaction outstanding under this Agreement).

Although the calculation of Margin Deficit or Margin Excess is computed on an aggregate basis with respect to all the outstanding Transactions between the parties, Paragraph 4(f) provides that the parties may agree to apply Paragraph 4 on a Transaction-by-Transaction basis. Such a rule would result in more frequent transfers between the parties, but may be helpful if a party has credit concerns about the other party.

Paragraph 5

Although the conceptual framework and basis for the MRA is that the Seller and the Buyer are entering into an actual sale of the Purchased Securities, a repurchase transaction also provides that such Purchased Securities will be sold back to the Seller by the Buyer. Accordingly, the Agreement was drafted to provide that any interest, principal or other payments made on the Purchased Securities are to remain the property of the Seller.

COMMENTARY ON THE MASTER REPURCHASE AGREEMENT

Although Income payments are considered to be the property of the Seller, the Buyer still retains the right to vote and to give consent with respect to the Purchased Securities.

> **5. Income Payments**
> Seller shall be entitled to receive an amount equal to all Income paid or distributed on or in respect of the Securities that is not otherwise received by Seller, to the full extent it would be so entitled if the Securities had not been sold to Buyer.

Paragraph 5 provides that the Seller is entitled to receive an amount equal to any interest, principal or any other distributions made on a Purchased Security that is received by the Buyer during the time that the Buyer holds the Purchased Securities. Note that Paragraph 5 does not characterise it as a direct pass through of these amounts, but instead requires the Buyer to make a payment equal to any Income received by the Buyer.

> Buyer shall, as the parties may agree with respect to any Transaction (or, in the absence of any such agreement, as Buyer shall reasonably determine in its discretion), on the date such Income is paid or distributed either (i) transfer to or credit to the account of Seller such Income with respect to any Purchased Securities subject to such Transaction or (ii) with respect to Income paid in cash, apply the Income payment or payments to reduce the amount, if any, to be transferred to Buyer by Seller upon termination of such Transaction.

Upon the date that Income is paid or distributed, the Buyer has two options: (1) it may transfer the Income directly to the Seller or (2) it can elect, with respect to Income paid in cash, to reduce the Repurchase Price to be paid by the Seller to the Buyer. The first option is the market standard, with the second option often being eliminated by one of the optional provisions to be added in Annex I (see discussion on page 216 of the provision).

The second option has the advantage of minimising the risk that the Seller will not transfer the entire Repurchase Price. This will also affect, however, the amount of the Price Differential, since the Purchase Price has gone down.

> Buyer shall not be obligated to take any action pursuant to the preceding sentence (A) to the extent that such action would result in the creation of a Margin Deficit, unless prior thereto or simultaneously therewith Seller transfers to Buyer cash or Additional Purchased Securities sufficient to eliminate such Margin Deficit, or (B) if an Event of Default with respect to Seller has occurred and is then continuing at the time such Income is paid or distributed.

Under this clause there are two circumstances in which the Buyer is not required to make such a transfer or to reduce the Repurchase Price (as required under the preceding clause). First, the Buyer is not required to make a transfer if it would create a Margin Deficit. This is most likely to occur if the Income were a distribution of principal. The Seller has the option, however, under this circumstance simultaneously to transfer cash or Additional Purchased Securities to the Buyer if the Seller wants the Income payment to be paid to it by the Buyer.

Second, the Buyer is not required to make a transfer if an Event of Default has occurred (and is continuing) with respect to the Seller. This would provide the Buyer with additional cushion if the Buyer were able to retain the Income (in particular any interest payments) until the Repurchase Date. Of course, the Buyer on the Repurchase Date would be required to transfer the Income to the Seller against transfer of the Repurchase Price.

Paragraph 6

> **6. Security Interest**
> Although the parties intend that all Transactions hereunder be sales and purchases and not loans, in the event any such Transactions are deemed to be loans, Seller shall be deemed to have pledged to Buyer as security for the performance by Seller of its obligations under each such Transaction, and shall be deemed to have granted to Buyer a security interest in, all of the Purchased Securities with respect to all Transactions hereunder and all Income thereon and other proceeds thereof.

Paragraph 6 can best be understood as a "belt and suspenders" (or "belt and braces") provision. Historically there has been some concern that a court might recharacterise a repurchase transaction as a secured loan. (A discussion of the issue can be found in Chapter 2, pages 21–22.) Assuming that a court were to make such a recharacterisation, the Agreement provides that the Buyer will be deemed to have made a secured loan to the Seller, with the Seller granting a security interest in the Purchased Securities. Paragraph 6 provides that the Buyer should have a perfected security interest in the Purchased Securities because the Seller is deemed to have granted a security interest to the Buyer and the Buyer perfects its interest by taking possession of the pledged Purchased Securities.

Paragraph 7

> **7. Payment and Transfer**
> Unless otherwise mutually agreed, all transfers of funds hereunder shall be in immediately available funds. All Securities transferred by one party hereto to the other party (i) shall be in suitable form for transfer or shall be accompanied by duly executed instruments of transfer or assignment in blank and such other documentation as the party receiving possession may reasonably request, (ii) shall be transferred on the book-entry system of a Federal Reserve Bank, or (iii) shall be transferred by any other method mutually acceptable to Seller and Buyer.

COMMENTARY ON THE MASTER REPURCHASE AGREEMENT

Paragraph 7 is a mechanical section dealing with how cash and Securities are to be transferred. Funds (ie, cash) are to be transferred in the form of "immediately available funds", which requires a wire transfer. In a wire transfer of funds the Buyer's and Seller's respective Banks (and any intermediary banks) make offsetting entries to the respective accounts of the Buyer and Seller, giving the parties immediate access to the transferred funds.

Paragraph 7 assumes that the Purchased Securities will be either in certificate or in book-entry form. If the Purchased Securities are in certificate form, the Seller will need to provide the necessary certificates, endorsements, and other documentation required physically to transfer the Purchased Securities.

If the Seller decides to transfer using a book-entry system of a Federal Reserve Bank, the Seller can transfer US government securities or agency securities (such as Fannie Mae or Freddie Mac notes) electronically.

Paragraph 8

> **8. Segregation of Purchased Securities**
> To the extent required by applicable law, all Purchased Securities in the possession of Seller shall be segregated from other securities in its possession and shall be identified as subject to this Agreement. Segregation may be accomplished by appropriate identification on the books and records of the holder, including a financial or securities intermediary or a clearing corporation.

The first two sentences in Paragraph 8 deal with Hold-in-Custody repos, where the Seller does not transfer either possession or title to the Buyer. Instead, the Seller makes a notation on its books and records that the particular Purchased Securities identified in a Confirmation are the property of the Buyer. The obvious danger of these types of Hold-in Custody repos is the possibility that the Seller will transfer the same Purchased Securities to multiple third parties. In the event that the Seller is unable to repurchase the Purchased Securities, there would not be sufficient Purchased Securities to satisfy each of the Buyer's claims. This scenario can be avoided by using tri-party custodial agreements (as will be described in Chapter 6).

In addition, the use rights for the Buyer (explained below) would be unavailable to a Buyer in a Hold-in-Custody repo. This is because the Buyer cannot use Purchased Securities of which it does not have control or possession.

> All of Seller's interest in the Purchased Securities shall pass to Buyer on the Purchase Date and, unless otherwise agreed by Buyer and Seller, nothing in this Agreement shall preclude Buyer from engaging in repurchase transactions with the Purchased Securities or otherwise selling, transferring, pledging or hypothecating the Purchased Securities, but no such transaction shall relieve Buyer of its obligations to transfer Purchased Securities to Seller pursuant to Paragraph 3, 4 or 11 hereof, or of Buyer's

> obligation to credit or pay Income to, or apply Income to the obligations of, Seller pursuant to Paragraph 5 hereof.

Paragraph 8 also clarifies that a Buyer of Purchased Securities may use the Purchased Securities for any purpose that it chooses. For example, the Buyer could transfer the Purchased Securities in a repurchase transaction to a third party. It could also pledge or use the collateral in any other type of transaction.

These use rights however, do not excuse the Buyer from meeting its obligations under Paragraphs 3 (Termination), 4 (Margin Maintenance) or 11 (Events of Default). For example, upon termination of the Transaction the Buyer is required to transfer the Purchased Securities back to the Seller on the Repurchase Date, even if the Buyer had previously transferred the Purchased Securities in a transaction with a third party. A Buyer should take measures to ensure that it can reacquire any Purchased Securities that it had transferred in an unrelated transaction to a third party. Failure to transfer the Purchased Securities to the Seller would constitute an Event of Default under Paragraph 11.

Sellers that have transferred securities that were subject to a hedging transaction should be aware of the risk that the Buyer might not return the same Purchased Securities. Under Financial Accounting Statement 133 such failure to receive the same Securities would result in termination of the hedge, and possible income and balance sheet consequences.

> **Required Disclosure for Transactions in Which the Seller Retains Custody of the Purchased Securities**
>
> Seller is not permitted to substitute other securities for those subject to this Agreement and therefore must keep Buyer's securities segregated at all times, unless in this Agreement Buyer grants Seller the right to substitute other securities. If Buyer grants the right to substitute, this means that Buyer's securities will likely be commingled with Seller's own securities during the trading day. Buyer is advised that, during any trading day that Buyer's securities are commingled with Seller's securities, they [will]* [may]** be subject to liens granted by Seller to [its clearing bank]* [third parties]** and may be used by Seller for deliveries on other securities transactions. Whenever the securities are commingled, Seller's ability to resegregate substitute securities for Buyer will be subject to Seller's ability to satisfy [the clearing] * [any] ** lien or to obtain substitute securities-
>
> * Language to be used under 17 C.F.R. §403.4(e) If Seller Is a government securities broker or dealer other than a financial Institution.
>
> ** Language to be used under 17 C.F.R. §403.5(d) If Seller Is a financial Institution.

The above Required Disclosure is important for Buyers. In situations where the Seller is holding the Purchased Securities during the term of the repurchase transaction, a Buyer's remedies can be severely limited if the Seller commingles the Purchased Securities with its own property, grants liens on the Purchased Securities or transfers the Purchased Securities to a third party.

Paragraph 9

> **9. Substitution**
> (a) Seller may, subject to agreement with and acceptance by Buyer, substitute other Securities for any Purchased Securities. Such substitution shall be made by transfer to Buyer of such other Securities and transfer to Seller of such Purchased Securities. After substitution, the substituted Securities shall be deemed to be Purchased Securities.

Paragraph 9(a) does not grant the Seller the right to substitute other Securities for the Purchased Securities. Instead, the Buyer must expressly consent to such requests for substitutions. This can be problematic for the Seller if the Buyer does not consent. For example, the Seller itself may have acquired the Purchased Securities in an earlier repurchase transaction, and then used those securities in a new repurchase transaction. If it is required to return the Purchased Securities in the earlier repurchase transaction, it may not be able to substitute them with the Buyer if the Buyer chooses not to consent.

> (b) In Transactions in which Seller retains custody of Purchased Securities, the parties expressly agree that Buyer shall be deemed, for purposes of subparagraph (a) of this Paragraph, to have agreed to and accepted in this Agreement substitution by Seller of other Securities for Purchased Securities: provided, however, that such other Securities shall have a Market Value at least equal to the Market Value of the Purchased Securities for which they are substituted.

The rule in Paragraph 9(b) is the opposite of the rule in Paragraph 9(a). Paragraph 9(b) deals with a Hold-in-Custody repo and provides that the Seller is entitled to substitute without the consent of the Buyer. There appears to be no policy reason to prohibit substitution, given that it is the Seller rather than the Buyer that has possession of the Purchased Securities.

Paragraph 10

> **10. Representations**
> Each of Buyer and Seller represents and warrants to the other that (i) it is duly authorized to execute and deliver this Agreement, to enter into Transactions contemplated hereunder and to perform its obligations hereunder and has taken all necessary action to authorize such execution, delivery and performance, (ii) it will engage in such Transactions as principal (or, if agreed in writing, in the form of an annex hereto or otherwise, in advance of any Transaction by the other party hereto, as agent for a disclosed principal), (iii) the person signing this Agreement on its behalf is duly authorized to do so on its behalf (or on behalf of any such disclosed principal), (iv) it has obtained all authorizations of any governmental body required in connection with this Agreement and the Transactions hereunder and such authorizations are in full force
> ⟫→

> and effect and (v) the execution, delivery and performance of this Agreement and the Transactions hereunder will not violate any law, ordinance, charter, by-law or rule applicable to it or any agreement by which it is bound or by which any of its assets are affected. On the Purchase Date for any Transaction Buyer and Seller shall each be deemed to repeat all the foregoing representations made by it.

The representations required in Paragraph 10 are typical of a finance contract. The representations are important for three reasons. First, if a representation proves to be incorrect or untrue in any material respect, it constitutes an Event of Default under paragraph 11(vi) and permits the nondefaulting party to terminate the Agreement. Second, requiring a party to make a representation should limit a party's right to assert later that it did not have the authority or power, or to attempt a similar defence in the event that the party argues that the Master Repurchase Agreement is unenforceable against it. Third, the representations are a form of due diligence that serve as a checklist for a party to ensure that there are no problems or issues that would prevent it from entering into the Agreement with the other party.

As noted in the final sentence of Paragraph 10, the parties are deemed to make the representations not only upon execution of the Agreement, but also each time that they enter into an individual Transaction. This can be problematic if a party's situation has changed to such a degree that it can no longer make the representations.

The first representation is used to determine whether the parties have the necessary corporate authority and power to enter into the Transactions. If there is any concern about this issue, a party may also want its counterparty to deliver a secretary's certificate verifying board resolutions that authorised the Agreement.

The second representation will flush out undisclosed principals. For example, a party may be acting as an undisclosed agent of another party to protect such party's identity. Such a representation is useful if there is any concern by a party that it would not want to do business with the agent's principal.

The third representation affirms the authority of the party signing. A party may want to require its counterparty to deliver an incumbency certificate (with a specimen signature) that certifies that the signatory has authority to execute the agreement. The secretary's certificate, of course, should be checked against the executed agreement as additional due diligence.

The fourth representation is important if a party is doing business with a highly regulated entity, such as a utility or a broker-dealer. Many such regulated entities have restrictions regarding the type and volume of business that can be conducted.

The fifth representation covers other restrictions that may affect a party's right to enter into the Agreement. For example, there may be restrictions in the company's bylaws or charter against engaging in such a Transaction. There may be particular statues or ordinances that prohibit engaging in such transactions, particularly for a governmental entity, such as a municipality.

Paragraph 11

Paragraph 11 sets forth the Events of Default and the Buyer's or Seller's remedies upon the occurrence of an Event of Default. Although an Event of Default may have occurred with respect to only a single transaction, a party wanting to exercise its remedies must terminate all of the repurchase transactions as well as the Master Repurchase Agreement, as opposed to just the offending Transaction. Parties that want a remedy in which they can terminate a single Transaction would need to draft such a provision in Annex I.

> **11. Events of Default**
> In the event that (i) Seller fails to transfer or Buyer fails to purchase Purchased Securities upon the applicable Purchase Date, (ii) Seller fails to repurchase or Buyer fails to transfer Purchased Securities upon the applicable Repurchase Date, (iii) Seller or Buyer fails to comply with Paragraph 4 hereof, (iv) Buyer fails, after one business day's notice, to comply with Paragraph 5 hereof, (v) an Act of Insolvency occurs with respect to Seller or Buyer, (vi) any representation made by Seller or Buyer shall have been incorrect or untrue in any material respect when made or repeated or deemed to have been made or repeated, or (vii) Seller or Buyer shall admit to the other its inability to, or its intention not to, perform any of its obligations hereunder (each an "Event of Default"):

The preamble to Paragraph 11 sets out the various Events of Default that permit the nondefaulting party to exercise its remedies under the Agreement. These Events of Default are similar to those that are found in other standard finance contracts.

Clause (i). A failure to perform on the Purchase Date (ie, at the initiation of a Transaction), such as where the Seller fails to transfer the Purchased Securities or the Buyer fails to transfer the Purchase Price, is an Event of Default. There is no cure period (ie, a grace period to rectify the default) for this Event of Default.

Technical defaults unrelated to creditworthiness often occur in the repo markets. Such defaults occur because of the use of computer technology to match the transfers of the securities with the transfers of cash. Any deviation or ambiguity in the instructions will result in the computer rejecting the Transaction and causing a failure. If the Event of Default was caused by a technical failure, parties typically waive the default and resubmit the Transaction for execution.

Clause (ii). A failure to perform on the Repurchase Date (ie, at the termination of a Transaction), such as where the Buyer fails to transfer the Purchased Securities or the Seller fails to repurchase them, is an Event of Default. There is no cure period for this Event of Default. This Event of Default is also relatively common in the repo market and generally occurs because of technology's failure to match the transfers of the Purchased Securities with the transfers of cash. Again, any deviation or ambiguity in the instructions will result in the computer rejecting the transfer and causing a failure. If the Event of Default was caused by a technical failure, the parties will typically waive the default and re-execute the repurchase. There is, however, much greater risk for the nondefaulting party, due to fluctuations in the Market Value of the Purchased Securities. If the Purchased Securities have greatly appreciated in value, a Buyer may prefer to default on its obligation to return the Purchased Securities. Similarly, a Seller may prefer to retain the Purchase Price if the Market Value of the Purchased Securities has fallen.

Clause (iii). A failure to perform a party's obligations under either a Margin Deficit or Margin Excess pursuant to Paragraph 4 is an Event of Default. There is no cure period for this Event of Default. Compliance with this Paragraph 4 is important in order to maintain the proper proportion between the Repurchase Price and the Market Value of the Purchased Securities. Limiting the amount of any Margin Deficit or Margin Excess through proper application of Paragraph 4 will minimise the incentive to default based upon fluctuations in the value of the Purchased Securities.

Clause (iv). A failure to comply with the Income payment requirements found in Paragraph 5 is an Event of Default. This Event of Default can occur only with respect to the Buyer, since the Buyer would be the recipient of any Income payments on the Purchased Securities. There is a one-business-day cure period after notice before this Event of Default can be declared. Because the Event of Default is not deemed to occur until after the cure period has expired, it is important that a party promptly give notice upon such a failure. The nondefaulting party should also carefully study the notice provisions regarding how notice is to be given, to ensure that the notice complies with the Agreement's requirements. Otherwise, exercising remedies before the Event of Default has technically occurred could expose the nondefaulting party to damages if it exercises its rights to terminate prematurely.

Clause (v). The occurrence of an Act of Insolvency with respect to a Buyer or Seller is an Event of Default. The different Acts of Insolvency were discussed above under the definition of an Act of Insolvency. There is no cure period for this Event of Default. It is important that the nondefaulting party acts decisively upon the Act of Insolvency, because it is unlikely that the nondefaulting party will be able to collect damages above retention of the Purchase Price (if the nondefaulting party is the Seller) or above retention of the Purchased Securities (if the nondefaulting party is the Buyer). It is particularly important for a party to exercise its remedies before the Purchased Securities can fluctuate in value.

Clause (vi). A material misrepresentation is an Event of Default. There is no cure period for a material misrepresentation. The Agreement does not define what is meant by the term "material". One possible way to determine if a representation was "incorrect or untrue in any material respect" is to determine whether the nondefaulting party would have entered into the Agreement if it had known about the untrue or incorrect representation before executing the Agreement. It should also be remembered that a representation will be deemed to be repeated each time a party enters into a Transaction. That means that, even if a representation was correct or true on the date of execution of the Agreement, it will also have to be correct or true each time the parties enter into an additional Transaction.

Clause (vii). A party admitting to the other that it is unable to (or intends not to) perform its obligations under the Agreement is an Event of Default. This is typically referred to as an anticipatory breach of contract. If a party makes such an admission, it permits the other party to declare an Event of Default prior to the actual non-performance by the defaulting party.

> (a) The nondefaulting party may, at its option (which option shall be deemed to have been exercised immediately upon the occurrence of an Act of Insolvency), declare an ⋙→

COMMENTARY ON THE MASTER REPURCHASE AGREEMENT

> Event of Default to have occurred hereunder and, upon the exercise or deemed exercise of such option, the Repurchase Date for each Transaction hereunder shall, if it has not already occurred, be deemed immediately to occur (except that, in the event that the Purchase Date for any Transaction has not yet occurred as of the date of such exercise or deemed exercise, such Transaction shall be deemed immediately cancelled). The nondefaulting party shall (except upon the occurrence of an Act of Insolvency) give notice to the defaulting party of the exercise of such option as promptly as practicable.

The declaration of an Event of Default (except upon the occurrence of an Act of Insolvency) is at the option of the nondefaulting party. This provides the nondefaulting party with some flexibility as to whether it wants to declare an Event of Default and exercise its remedies, and when it wants to do so. The nondefaulting party, however, is required promptly to notify the defaulting party of such a declaration.

Because of the finality and effect of an Act of Insolvency on a defaulting party, an Event of Default is deemed to occur automatically.

If a Repurchase Date has not yet occurred, a Repurchase Date for each Transaction shall be deemed to have occurred on the date that an Event of Default is declared.

If a Purchase Date has not yet occurred, the Transaction shall be deemed to be cancelled.

> (b) In all Transactions in which the defaulting party is acting as Seller, if the nondefaulting party exercises or is deemed to have exercised the option referred to in subparagraph (a) of this Paragraph, (i) the defaulting party's obligations in such Transactions to repurchase all Purchased Securities, at the Repurchase Price therefor on the Repurchase Date determined in accordance with subparagraph (a) of this Paragraph, shall thereupon become immediately due and payable, (ii) all Income paid after such exercise or deemed exercise shall be retained by the nondefaulting party and applied to the aggregate unpaid Repurchase Prices and any other amounts owing by the defaulting party hereunder, and (iii) the defaulting party shall immediately deliver to the nondefaulting party any Purchased Securities subject to such Transactions then in the defaulting party's possession or control.

Upon the declaration of an Event of Default by the Buyer the following three things occur:

- First, the Seller's obligation to repurchase the Purchased Securities becomes immediately due. In other words, the Seller must repurchase the Purchased Securities regardless of when the Transaction would have terminated according to its terms.
- Second, any Income retained by the Buyer is applied against the Repurchase Price. This reduces the risk of non-payment from the Seller. It will also, however, have the effect of decreasing the Repurchase Price payable by the Seller.
- Third, the Seller must immediately deliver any Purchased Securities that it is holding. The

most likely scenario in which a Seller would be holding Purchased Securities would be in a Hold-in-Custody repo. This also illustrates the risk of a Hold-in-Custody repo for a Buyer. Upon the default of the Seller it may be difficult, if not impossible, to compel the Seller to deliver the Purchased Securities (especially if an Act of Insolvency has occurred to the Seller). In addition, the securities subject to the Hold-in-Custody repo may not have been properly identified and segregated on the Seller's books and records.

> (c) In all Transactions in which the defaulting party is acting as Buyer, upon tender by the nondefaulting party of payment of the aggregate Repurchase Prices for all such Transactions, all right, title and interest in and entitlement to all Purchased Securities subject to such Transactions shall be deemed transferred to the nondefaulting party, and the defaulting party shall deliver all such Purchased Securities to the nondefaulting party.

Upon the declaration of an Event of Default by a Seller against a Buyer the Seller is entitled, upon tender of the aggregate Repurchase Price, to the immediate return of the Purchased Securities. Although the Seller is entitled to such return, there may be several difficulties for the Buyer in performing. First, if the Buyer has exercised its use rights under Paragraph 8, the Buyer may not have possession of the Purchased Securities. For example, it may have transferred the Purchased Securities in a repurchase transaction to a third party and may not have the wherewithal to repurchase them for the Seller. Second, if an Act of Insolvency has occurred with respect to the Buyer, such retransfer would require the permission of the bankruptcy court or receiver having jurisdiction over the Buyer.

> (d) If the nondefaulting party exercises or is deemed to have exercised the option referred to in subparagraph (a) of this Paragraph, the nondefaulting party, without prior notice to the defaulting party, may:

Paragraph 11(d) deals with the most important remedy available to a party in a repurchase transaction, that of simply either retaining the Purchased Securities (in the case of the Buyer) or retaining the Purchase Price (in the case of the Seller). This right (and the credit protection that it provides to a party) is what makes repurchase transactions very popular as a financing tool.

> (i) as to Transactions in which the defaulting party is acting as Seller, (A) immediately sell, in a recognized market (or otherwise in a commercially reasonable manner) at such price or prices as the nondefaulting party may reasonably deem satisfactory, any or all Purchased Securities subject to such Transactions and apply the proceeds thereof to the aggregate unpaid Repurchase Prices and any other amounts owing by the defaulting party hereunder or

Under Clause (i)(A) the Buyer is entitled to liquidate the Purchased Securities, and thus recover the unpaid Repurchase Prices and any other amounts owing to the Buyer. The Buyer, however, must sell the Purchased Securities in a recognised market or in a commercially reasonable manner. It is important to recognise that failure to act reasonably may subject the Buyer to damages if the Buyer would have recovered greater amounts by acting reasonably. It appears that selling the Purchased Securities on a recognised market would satisfy a Buyer's obligation to act in good faith or in a commercially reasonable manner. The Buyer should also use the recognised market that is the most liquid and active for a particular type of Purchased Security.

> (B) in its sole discretion elect, in lieu of selling all or a portion of such Purchased Securities, to give the defaulting party credit for such Purchased Securities in an amount equal to the price therefor on such date, obtained from a generally recognized source or the most recent closing bid quotation from such a source, against the aggregate unpaid Repurchase Prices and any other amounts owing by the defaulting party hereunder; and

Under Clause (i)(B) the Buyer is entitled to retain the Purchased Securities and give the Seller credit against the Repurchase Price (and any other amounts owing) for an amount equal to the price that the Buyer could have obtained if it had liquidated the Purchased Securities. The credit would be equal to the price of the Purchased Securities on such date from a generally recognised source. It could also be the most recent closing bid quotation from such source. The bid quotation would be the price that such a source would be willing to pay for the Purchased Securities (which, of course, would be lower than the price at which such source would be willing to sell).

Caution should be exercised by a Buyer when using this option. The right to retain the Purchased Securities does not entitle the Buyer to retain highly appreciated Purchased Securities with a Market Value well above the Purchase Price without compensating the Seller.

> (ii) as to Transactions in which the defaulting party is acting as Buyer, (A) immediately purchase, in a recognized market (or otherwise in a commercially reasonable manner) at such price or prices as the nondefaulting party may reasonably deem satisfactory, securities ("Replacement Securities") of the same class and amount as any Purchased Securities that are not delivered by the defaulting party to the nondefaulting party as required hereunder or (B) in its sole discretion elect, in lieu of purchasing Replacement Securities, to be deemed to have purchased Replacement Securities at the price therefor on such date, obtained from a generally recognized source or the most recent closing offer quotation from such a source.

Under Clause (ii)(A) the Seller is immediately entitled to purchase Replacement Securities instead of tendering the Repurchase Price to the Buyer. The Replacement Securities must be of the same class and amount as the Purchased Securities. They must also have been purchased either in a recognised market or in a commercially reasonable manner.

Under Clause (ii)(B) the seller is entitled to retain the Purchase Price and is deemed to have purchased Replacement Securities. The credit would be equal to the price of the Purchased Securities on such date from a generally recognised source. It could also be the most recent closing offer quotation from such source. The offer quotation would be the price at which such a source would be willing to sell the Purchased Securities (which, of course, would be higher than the price at which such source would be willing to buy).

See the discussion of below Paragraph 11(e) on cases where the price for the Replacement Securities is greater than the Repurchase Price.

> Unless otherwise provided in Annex I, the parties acknowledge and agree that (1) the Securities subject to any Transaction hereunder are instruments traded in a recognized market, (2) in the absence of a generally recognized source for prices or bid or offer quotations for any Security, the nondefaulting party may establish the source therefor in its sole discretion and (3) all prices, bids and offers shall be determined together with accrued Income (except to the extent contrary to market practice with respect to the relevant Securities).

This clause in Paragraph 11(d) sets out certain agreed assumptions about the Purchased Securities upon the declaration of an Event of Default.

First, the parties agree that the Purchased Securities are Securities that are traded in a "recognised market". Market practice dictates what is meant by a recognised market for a particular Security.

Second, if there is no "generally recognised source" to determine a bid or offer quotation, the nondefaulting party may establish that source, using its sole discretion. Such a source has to be established in a reasonable manner and in good faith.

Third, the party determining prices, bids and offers must take into account accrued Income (except if it is market practice not to take that into account). Taking into account accrued Income will directly affect the above calculations by increasing the total Market Value for both Purchased Securities and Replacement Securities.

> (e) As to Transactions in which the defaulting party is acting as Buyer, the defaulting party shall be liable to the nondefaulting party for any excess of the price paid (or deemed paid) by the nondefaulting party for Replacement Securities over the Repurchase Price for the Purchased Securities replaced thereby and for any amounts payable by the defaulting party under Paragraph 5 hereof or otherwise hereunder.

A Seller is protected by clause (e) in a situation in which the Market Value of a Purchased Security has increased. If the purchase price or deemed purchase price for a Replacement Security is greater than the Repurchase Price, the Buyer (the defaulting party) is liable for such excess. This is most likely to occur where a Purchased Security has appreciated greatly in value. Clause (e) also acts as a deterrent to a Buyer that might otherwise try to benefit in such a scenario by retaining the Purchased Securities.

The Buyer is liable for any Income owing to the Seller that was not previously transferred pursuant to Paragraph 5. Finally, the Buyer is also liable for any other amounts otherwise owing to the Seller.

> (f) For purposes of this Paragraph 11, the Repurchase Price for each Transaction hereunder in respect of which the defaulting party is acting as Buyer shall not increase above the amount of such Repurchase Price for such Transaction determined as of the date of the exercise or deemed exercise by the nondefaulting party of the option referred to in subparagraph (a) of this Paragraph.

A Seller is protected by Paragraph 11. Paragraph 11(f) limits the Repurchase Price to the amount determined as of the declaration date of the Event of Default. Typically, this calculation results in a lower Repurchase Price where the Repurchase Date set out in the Confirmation has not yet occurred.

> (g) The defaulting party shall be liable to the nondefaulting party for (i) the amount of all reasonable legal or other expenses incurred by the nondefaulting party in connection with or as a result of an Event of Default, (ii) damages in an amount equal to the cost (including all fees, expenses and commissions) of entering into replacement transactions and entering into or terminating hedge transactions in connection with or as a result of an Event of Default, and (iii) any other loss, damage, cost or expense directly arising or resulting from the occurrence of an Event of Default in respect of a Transaction.

The defaulting party is not only liable for the amounts as determined above, but also for any other losses, damages, costs or expenses (collectively "Costs") incurred as a result of the Event of Default.

Clause (g)(i). The defaulting party is liable for legal Costs incurred by the nondefaulting party as a result of the Event of Default and in enforcing its rights under the Agreement.

Clause (g)(ii). The defaulting party is liable for any Costs of acquiring replacement securities. It is also liable for any Costs associated with entering into or terminating any hedges with respect to any Transactions or replacement transactions affected by the Event of Default.

Clause (g)(iii). This clause is a catch-all provision that imposes liability on the defaulting party for any other Costs incurred by the nondefaulting Party as a result of the Event of Default.

> (h) To the extent permitted by applicable law, the defaulting party shall be liable to the nondefaulting party for interest on any amounts owing by the defaulting party hereunder, from the date the defaulting party becomes liable for such amounts hereunder

> until such amounts are (i) paid in full by the defaulting party or (ii) satisfied in full by the exercise of the nondefaulting party's rights hereunder. Interest on any sum payable by the defaulting party to the nondefaulting party under this Paragraph 11(h) shall be at a rate equal to the greater of the Pricing Rate for the relevant Transaction or the Prime Rate.

The defaulting party is obligated to pay interest on any amounts that are not promptly paid to the nondefaulting party under Paragraph 11.

An amount is considered paid when it is either paid in full or deemed to be paid in full pursuant to the Agreement.

The interest to be used is either the Pricing Rate for the relevant Transaction or the Prime Rate, whichever is greater. As a practical matter the Prime Rate normally is the higher of the two interest rates.

> (i) The nondefaulting party shall have, in addition to its rights hereunder, any rights otherwise available to it under any other agreement or applicable law.

Although the nondefaulting party's remedies are laid out in great detail in paragraph 11, paragraph 11 is not intended to provide the sole remedies for the nondefaulting party. The nondefaulting party is not precluded from any other remedies that may be available under any other Agreement between the parties or under applicable law. For example, there may be common law or other statutory remedies that may more properly or easily compensate the nondefaulting party upon the declaration of an Event of Default.

Paragraph 12

> **12. Single Agreement**
> Buyer and Seller acknowledge that, and have entered hereinto and will enter into each Transaction hereunder in consideration of and in reliance upon the fact that, all Transactions hereunder constitute a single business and contractual relationship and have been made in consideration of each other. Accordingly, each of Buyer and Seller agrees (i) to perform all of its obligations in respect of each Transaction hereunder, and that a default in the performance of any such obligations shall constitute a default by it in respect of all Transactions hereunder, (ii) that each of them shall be entitled to set off claims and apply property held by them in respect of any Transaction against obligations owing to them in respect of any other Transactions hereunder and (iii) that payments, deliveries and other transfers made by either of them in respect of any Transaction shall be deemed to have been made in consideration of payments, deliveries and other transfers in respect of any other Transactions hereunder, and the obligations to make any such payments, deliveries and other transfers may be applied against each other and netted.

The mechanical application of the Agreement, and the application of the bankruptcy and insolvency statutory, regulatory or common law rules upon the occurrence of an Act of Insolvency to a party to the Agreement, are dependent upon treating the Agreement and any underlying Transactions as a single agreement. This approach permits the parties to treat their credit exposure to the other party on a net versus a gross basis, greatly increasing the volume of business that can be conducted between the parties.

First, a default under a single Transaction constitutes an Event of Default under Paragraph 11, permitting the nondefaulting party to exercise its remedies under Paragraph 11, regardless of whether the defaulting party is performing under the other Transactions.

Second, each party is permitted to set off claims and apply property held in one Transaction against obligations owing under another Transaction. Both a nondefaulting and a defaulting party are entitled to such set-off rights.

Third, payments, deliveries and other transfers between the parties may be applied against each other and netted.

In addition to the business and credit risk advantages, there are several important legal benefits of treating the Agreement and the underlying Transactions as a single agreement. For example, certain benefits of the Agreement, such as netting, are enforceable under the US Bankruptcy Code, the Federal Deposit Insurance Act, and other bankruptcy and insolvency law against certain bankrupt or insolvent parties (see Chapter 2, pages 23–27).

In addition, this clause clarifies that Paragraph 12 is a bilateral contract and therefore, the Agreement's netting provisions should be enforceable under the FDICIA as long as both parties qualify as "financial institutions" under the statute (see Chapter 2, pages 27–28).

Paragraph 13

> **13. Notices and Other Communications**
> Any and all notices, statements, demands or other communications hereunder may be given by a party to the other by mail, facsimile, telegraph, messenger or otherwise to the address specified in Annex II hereto, or so sent to such party at any other place specified in a notice of change of address hereafter received by the other. All notices, demands and requests hereunder may be made orally, to be confirmed promptly in writing, or by other communication as specified in the preceding sentence.

Because certain Events of Default can be declared only after notice has been given (and the appropriate cure period has expired), it is important that the parties understand how to give notice under the Agreement. The notice provisions are quite liberal in this respect. Notice can be given by mail, facsimile, telegraph, messenger or otherwise. It is, however, required to be given to the address specified in Annex II (or to any amended notice address received by the other party). Notice can also be given orally, provided that it is confirmed promptly in writing.

It is worth noting that a party may exercise its remedies under Paragraph 11 without giving prior notice. The nondefaulting party, however, is required to follow up with notice promptly after such exercise.

Paragraph 14

> **14. Entire Agreement; Severability**
> This Agreement shall supersede any existing agreements between the parties containing general terms and conditions for repurchase transactions. Each provision and agreement herein shall be treated as separate and independent from any other provision or agreement herein and shall be enforceable notwithstanding the unenforceability of any such other provision or agreement.

The first sentence in Paragraph 14 is a form of "integration" or "merger" clause. It provides that the Agreement will supersede any other arrangements with respect to repurchase transactions that the parties have entered into previously. The clause is intended to preclude disputes by providing that the Agreement is the controlling document with respect to any repurchase transactions then outstanding and all future Transactions, in the absence of any future Agreement between the parties to the contrary.

The second sentence is a typical severability or separability clause. It is possible that a court may find a certain provision to be unenforceable, for example, because the provision violates public policy. Some courts have invalidated an entire Agreement or contract based on finding only one clause to be unenforceable. The severability clause is intended to clarify that the parties want the court to enforce the remainder of the Agreement, regardless of the unenforceability of a single provision.

Paragraph 15

> **15. Non-assignability; Termination**
> (a) The rights and obligations of the parties under this Agreement and under any Transaction shall not be assigned by either party without the prior written consent of the other party and any such assignment without the prior written consent of the other party shall be null and void. Subject to the foregoing, this Agreement and any Transactions shall be binding upon and shall inure to the benefit of the parties and their respective successors and assigns. This Agreement may be terminated by either party upon giving written notice to the other, except that this Agreement shall, notwithstanding such notice, remain applicable to any Transactions then outstanding.

The parties may not assign either the Agreement or any underlying Transactions to a third party without the consent of the non-transferring party. The prohibition against assignments is important because the non-transferring party may have concerns about the third party transferee. For example, the non-transferring party may not have the necessary credit approvals to conduct repurchase transactions with the third party. It may even be precluded by statute from dealing with certain types of entities.

The parties may terminate the Agreement at any time by giving written notice. However, the Agreement shall continue to be binding upon the parties with respect to any outstanding Transactions entered into previously.

> (b) Subparagraph (a) of this Paragraph 15 shall not preclude a party from assigning, charging or otherwise dealing with all or any part of its interest in any sum payable to it under Paragraph 11 hereof.

Although a party is restricted from transferring its interest under subparagraph (a), such restriction shall not apply to a nondefaulting party exercising its remedies under Paragraph 11. Paragraph 15(b) permits a nondefaulting party to assign its right in a net sum that is payable to it following termination after an Event of Default.

Paragraph 16

> **16. Governing Law**
> This Agreement shall be governed by the laws of the State of New York without giving effect to the conflict of law principles thereof.

The Agreement is to be governed by New York law. New York law (including the case law interpreting its provisions) is considered to be the most sophisticated and relevant for enforcing and interpreting finance contracts such as the Agreement. As explained in Chapter 2 (page 19), New York courts will enforce the selection of New York law. If both parties agree in advance to submit to New York jurisdiction, New York courts will also agree to adjudicate disputes, even if the Transactions and the parties have no relationship with the State of New York. (For an example of a submission to jurisdiction clause, see the sample clause on pages 218–19.)

Paragraph 17

> **17. No Waivers, Etc.**
> No express or implied waiver of any Event of Default by either party shall constitute a waiver of any other Event of Default and no exercise of any remedy hereunder by any party shall constitute a waiver of its right to exercise any other remedy hereunder. No modification or waiver of any provision of this Agreement and no consent by any party to a departure herefrom shall be effective unless and until such shall be in writing and duly executed by both of the parties hereto. Without limitation on any of the foregoing, the failure to give a notice pursuant to Paragraph 4(a) or 4(b) hereof will not constitute a waiver of any right to do so at a later date.

Parties are often concerned that, by waiving a particular Event of Default, they may also be waiving other Events of Default occurring at the same time or in the future. The Agreement clarifies that a defaulting party may not make such an assumption.

Parties have a similar concern that agreeing not to exercise certain remedies may also constitute a waiver of a right to exercise other remedies. Again, the Agreement clarifies that no precedent is set thereby.

Paragraph 17 further clarifies that any amendment to the Agreement must be in writing and signed by both parties.

Finally, parties are concerned that, if they do not immediately call for the transfer of Purchased Securities upon the first occurrence of a Margin Deficit or Margin Excess, they are precluded from doing so later. The Agreement clarifies that the party calling for a transfer may do so at any time, provided that such Margin Deficit or Margin Excess is still present.

Paragraph 18

Because employee benefit plans typically hold large amounts of cash and investments in Securities, there are concerns that the provisions of the Employment Retirement Income Security Act (ERISA) may be violated if assets of an employee benefit plan are used in violation of ERISA in a repurchase transaction.

> **18. Use of Employee Plan Assets**
> (a) If assets of an employee benefit plan subject to any provision of the Employee Retirement Income Security Act of 1974 ("ERISA") are intended to be used by either party hereto (the "Plan Party") in a Transaction, the Plan Party shall so notify the other party prior to the Transaction. The Plan Party shall represent in writing to the other party that the Transaction does not constitute a prohibited transaction under ERISA or is otherwise exempt therefrom, and the other party may proceed in reliance thereon but shall not be required so to proceed.

Paragraph 18 does not prohibit assets of an employee benefit plan from being subject to a repurchase transaction. It does, however, require one party to notify the other that it intends to use such assets and that the use of such assets does not constitute a prohibited Transaction under ERISA. (See Chapter 2, page 29, for a discussion of prohibited transactions under ERISA.)

> (b) Subject to the last sentence of subparagraph (a) of this Paragraph, any such Transaction shall proceed only if Seller furnishes or has furnished to Buyer its most recent available audited statement of its financial condition and its most recent subsequent unaudited statement of its financial condition.

In addition to the representation required above, subparagraph (b) also requires the Seller to furnish its financial statements to the Buyer as an additional source of due diligence for the Buyer with respect to ERISA concerns.

> (c) By entering into a Transaction pursuant to this Paragraph, Seller shall be deemed (i) to represent to Buyer that since the date of Seller's latest such financial statements, there has been no material adverse change in Seller's financial condition which Seller has not disclosed to Buyer, and (ii) to agree to provide Buyer with future audited and unaudited statements of its financial condition as they are issued, so long as it is a Seller in any outstanding Transaction involving a Plan Party.

Subparagraph (c) requires additional representations from the Seller with respect to the ERSIA representation and requires covenants to deliver future financial statements.

Paragraph 19

To ensure that each party is treating the Agreement and each Transaction consistently, the parties agree under Paragraph 19 to characterise the Agreement and each Transaction in particular ways for various bankruptcy and insolvency rules. As the parties are not making representations in Paragraph 19, if a court disagreed with their characterisation it would not constitute a misrepresentation.

> **19. Intent**
> (a) The parties recognize that each Transaction is a "repurchase agreement" as that term is defined in Section 101 of Title 11 of the United States Code, as amended (except insofar as the type of Securities subject to such Transaction or the term of such Transaction would render such definition inapplicable), and a "securities contract" as that term is defined in Section 741 of Title 11 of the United States Code, as amended (except insofar as the type of assets subject to such Transaction would render such definition inapplicable).

The parties agree in subparagraph (a) that each Transaction should be characterised as either a "repurchase agreement" or a "securities contract" for purposes of the US Bankruptcy Code. (See Chapter 2, page 23, for a discussion of repurchase agreements and the US Bankruptcy Code.)

It is important to note that for purposes of subparagraph (a) it is not relevant whether either party is subject to the US Bankruptcy Code. The parties are only agreeing that they would characterise their repurchase transactions as such if the US Bankruptcy Code were applicable.

> (b) It is understood that either party's right to liquidate Securities delivered to it in connection with Transactions hereunder or to exercise any other remedies pursuant to Paragraph 11 hereof is a contractual right to liquidate such Transaction as described in Sections 555 and 559 of Title 11 of the United States Code, as amended.

The concept in subparagraph (b) is similar to subparagraph (a). As explained in Chapter 2 (pages 23–25), the US Bankruptcy Code provisions with respect to a contractual right to liquidate a Transaction are helpful to a Buyer or Seller if the bankrupt party is subject to the US Bankruptcy Code. Here again, the parties are only agreeing that such Code sections are applicable if the bankrupt party were subject to the US Bankruptcy Code.

> (c) The parties agree and acknowledge that if a party hereto is an "insured depository institution", as such term is defined in the Federal Deposit Insurance Act, as amended ("FDIA"), then each Transaction hereunder is a "qualified financial contract", as that term is defined in FDIA and any rules, orders or policy statements thereunder (except insofar as the type of assets subject to such Transaction would render such definition inapplicable).

The parties agree in subparagraph (c) that each Transaction should be characterised as a qualified financial contract under the Federal Deposit Insurance Act (the "FDIA"). (See Chapter 2, pages 25–27, for a discussion of repurchase agreements and FDIA.)

It is important to note that for purposes of this subparagraph it is not relevant whether either party is subject to FDIA. The parties are merely agreeing that they would characterise their repurchase transactions as such if FDIA were applicable.

> (d) It is understood that this Agreement constitutes a "netting contract" as defined in and subject to Title IV of the Federal Deposit Insurance Corporation Improvement Act of 1991 ("FDICIA") and each payment entitlement and payment obligation under any Transaction hereunder shall constitute a "covered contractual payment entitlement" or "covered contractual payment obligation", respectively, as defined in and subject to FDICIA (except insofar as one or both of the parties is not a "financial institution" as that term is defined in FDICIA).

The parties agree in subparagraph (d) that the Agreement and certain terms should be characterised as meeting several different definitions under the Federal Deposit Insurance Corporation Improvement Act of 1991 (the "FDICIA"). (See Chapter 2, pages 27–28, for a discussion of repurchase agreements and FDICIA.)

It is important to note that for purposes of subparagraph (d) it is not relevant whether either party is subject to FDICIA. The parties are only agreeing that they would characterise their repurchase transactions as such if FDICIA were applicable.

Paragraph 20

There are certain federal statutory protections given to certain types of transactions or entities. However, these protections do not extend to repurchase transactions. To avoid potential contention or dispute, Paragraph 20 requires the parties to acknowledge that their relationship or Transactions will not qualify for these protections.

> **20. Disclosure Relating to Certain Federal Protections**
> The parties acknowledge that they have been advised that:
> (a) in the case of Transactions in which one of the parties is a broker or dealer registered with the Securities and Exchange Commission ("SEC") under Section 15 of the Securities Exchange Act of 1934 ("1934 Act"), the Securities Investor Protection Corporation has taken the position that the provisions of the Securities Investor Protection Act of 1970 ("SIPA") do not protect the other party with respect to any Transaction hereunder;

The Securities Investor Protection Act of 1970 ("SIPA") was intended to protect and safeguard investors from losses caused by the failure of securities dealers (Pub. L. No. 91-598, 84 Stat. 1636 (1970) codified as amended at 15 USC §78aaa-78lll (2000)). The SIPA protections, however, do not extend to a party that is conducting a repurchase transaction with a broker or dealer registered with the SEC under Section 15 of the 1934 Act.

> (b) in the case of Transactions in which one of the parties is a government securities broker or a government securities dealer registered with the SEC under Section 15C of the 1934 Act, SIPA will not provide protection to the other party with respect to any Transaction hereunder: and

SIPA was intended to protect and safeguard investors from losses caused by the failure of securities dealers. The SIPA protections, however, do not extend to a party that is conducting a repurchase transaction with a government securities broker, or a government securities dealer, that is registered with the SEC under Section 15C of the 1934 Act.

> (c) in the case of Transactions in which one of the parties is a financial institution, funds held by the financial institution pursuant to a Transaction hereunder are not a deposit and therefore are not insured by the Federal Deposit Insurance Corporation or the National Credit Union Share Insurance Fund, as applicable.

A PRACTICAL GUIDE TO USING REPO MASTER AGREEMENTS

The definition of what constitutes an insured deposit under the Federal Deposit Insurance Act is very broad and may even encompass a letter of credit, for example. However, a repurchase transaction cannot be characterised as an insured deposit under these statutory provisions. This means that a party that has entered into a Master Repurchase Agreement with a financial institution that has FDIC-insured deposits would not benefit from the FDIC insured deposit protections.

```
         [Name of Party]                    [Name of Party]
By:_____     By:_____
Title:_____    Title:_____
Date:_____     Date:_____
```

Upon execution of the Agreement a party should verify that the person executing the Agreement on behalf of the opposing party was authorised to do so. Generally, a party establishes such authorisation by providing an incumbency certificate or a signature page from a bank's signature book.

The incumbency certificate is a verification from the party's corporate secretary that the party executing the Agreement was authorised to do so. Often the certificate will also contain a specimen signature of the person signing the Agreement.

Typically, banks will provide an extract from the bank's signature book, that is, a list of authorised signatories for the bank. The signature book will provide a specimen signature of each signatory plus a description of the types of documents that such person is authorised to sign.

To complete this section of the chapter it might be useful to summarise the main differences between the TBMA/ISMA GMRA and the Master Repurchase Agreement in Exhibit 5.1 below.

Exhibit 5.1

Main differences between the TBMA/ISMA GMRA and the Master Repurchase Agreement

Difference	GMRA	MRA
Governing law	English	New York
Repo coverage	Securities	Securities and other assets
Confirmation status	Prevails over Agreement	Agreement prevails over Confirmation
Basis of remedies post-Event of Default	Close-out netting	Sale or purchase of Securities or other assets in a commercially reasonable manner
Default Notice requirements	Needed for all Events of Default except for two Acts of Insolvency	Not required except for non-payment of Income, when one business day's notice required ⟫→

212

Exhibit 5.1 *continued* Difference	GMRA	MRA
Failure to deliver securities an Event of Default	Optional Event of Default or mini close-out	Yes
Expulsion from an exchange or self-regulatory organisation and Event of Default	Yes	No
Default remedies limited to those under the Agreement	Yes	No, such remedies extend to those available under the law too
Minimum margin delivery period	Needs to be stated in Annex I	Same day or next business day
Particular margin assets proposable	Yes	No
Securities transferred free of liens	Yes	Not mentioned
Recharacterisation risk	Not covered	Covered in Paragraph 6
Hold-in-custody repo provisions	No	Yes
Specific US counterparty provisions	No	Yes
Late payment interest penalty	Yes	No
Non-reliance provision	Yes	No

Source: Based upon Supplemental Guidance Notes issued by The Bond Market Association in June 1997

Annex I

As with the ISDA Master Agreement, it is market practice not to make edits, amendments or changes directly to the pre-printed form of the Master Repurchase Agreement (the "Agreement"), other than the addition of the parties' names. Instead, any changes or amendments are made as part of Annex I (the equivalent of the Schedule in the ISDA Master Agreement).

Few changes, however, are typically added to Annex I. As opposed to the ISDA Master Agreement, where amendments or changes can run on for pages, additions to Annex I are usually limited to a standard few. The difference between the Master Repurchase Agreement and the ISDA Master Agreement stems primarily from the credit risk taken under the respective documents. Under the ISDA Master Agreement the exposure to a counterparty is often unsecured and there can be great volatility with respect to different transactions. In contrast there tends to be little if any unsecured exposure in a repurchase transaction that is short-term and the transactions are relatively stable in comparison. In addition there appears to have been greater unanimity among the dealers using the Master Repurchase Agreement with respect to the terms found in the pre-printed form compared with the ISDA Master Agreement.

> **Annex I**
> **Supplemental Terms and Conditions**
> This Annex I forms of the Master Repurchase Agreement dated as of _____,_____(the
> "Agreement") between_____ and _____. Capitalized terms used but not defined in this Annex I shall form a part of this Agreement and shall be applicable thereunder:

This paragraph clarifies that this Annex I is a part of the Master Repurchase Agreement executed by the parties.

> Other Applicable Annexes. In addition to this Annex I and Annex II, the following Annexes and any Schedules thereto shall form a part of this Agreement and shall be applicable thereunder:
> [Annex III (International Transactions)]
> [Annex IV (Party Acting As Agent)]
> [Annex V (Margin for Forward Transactions)]
> [Annex VI (Buy/Sell Back Transactions)]
> [Annex VII (Transactions Involving Registered Investment Companies)]

In this part of Annex I the parties identify which, if any, of the Annexes are to be made a part of the Master Repurchase Agreement. Since publication of Annex I, Annex VIII (Transactions in Equity Securities) and Annex IX (Transactions Involving Certain Japanese Financial Institutions) should also be added to the list of applicable annexes.

Additional provisions appearing in Annex I negotiations

The BMA has provided a schedule of Optional Provisions that could be added to Annex I. Although some parties may add even more provisions, these sample ones cover the vast majority of changes or amendments that parties find necessary for Annex I. The Optional Provisions are set forth below and are shaded in grey. Commentary with respect to each provision follows immediately after.

Schedule of Optional Provisions for Annex I

In an effort to provide consistency with respect to certain common amendments to the Master Repurchase Agreement, the BMA drafted the following provisions:

> **Definitions.** For purposes of the Agreement and this Annex I, the following terms shall have the following meanings:

Definition of Margin Notice Deadline

> "Margin Notice Deadline", _____ ([relevant city] time).

The definition of Margin Notice Deadline in the Agreement provides that the parties may designate a specific time before which a Buyer may call, pursuant to Paragraph 4, for Additional Purchased Securities if there is a Margin Deficit, or a Seller may call for a return of Purchased Securities if there is Margin Excess. Parties generally designate 10.00 a.m. (Eastern US time zone) as the Margin Notice Deadline.

Definition of Business Day

> "Business Day" or "business day", with respect to any Transaction (other than an International Transaction) hereunder, a day on which regular trading [may] occur in the principal market for the Purchased Securities subject to such Transaction[, which includes shortened trading days, days on which trades are permitted to occur but do not in fact occur and days on which the Purchased Securities are subject to percentage of movement or volume limitations]; provided, however, that for purposes of calculating Market Value, such term shall mean a day on which regular trading occurs in the principal market for the assets the value of which is being determined. Notwithstanding the foregoing, (i) for purposes of Paragraph 4 of the Agreement, "business day" shall mean any day on which regular trading occurs in the principal market for any Purchased Securities or for any assets constituting Additional Purchased Securities under any outstanding Transaction hereunder and "next business day" shall mean the next day on which a transfer of Additional Purchased Securities may be effected in accordance with Paragraph 7 of the Agreement, and (ii) in no event shall a Saturday or Sunday be considered a business day.

The Agreement expressly references the term "business day" in the following paragraphs:

- Paragraph 3(c): A party must give notice one business day prior to termination for a Transaction terminable upon demand.
- Paragraph 4(c): A party must give notice to exercise the margin maintenance provisions on a business day. If notice is given after the Margin Notice Deadline, the party is obligated to transfer margin on the next business day.
- Paragraph 11(iv): A Buyer must comply within one business day after notice with the Income transfer provisions of Paragraph 5.

In addition, however, the term is also important with respect to obtaining price quotations and determining Market Value.

In contrast to many definitions of the term "business day" in other finance agreements, this definition does not reference when banks are open for business. Instead, this definition focuses specifically on when regular trading occurs for the particular Purchased Security.

Margin Maintenance

> **Margin Maintenance.** Notwithstanding Paragraph 4 of the Agreement, with respect to any International Transaction [in which the Purchase Price and the Repurchase Price are denominated in the official currency of] [cleared and settled in] one of the following countries, transfers required to be made by Seller of cash or Additional Purchased Securities and Buyer of cash or Purchased Securities pursuant to Paragraph 4 of the Agreement shall be made by the close of business on the next business day following the business day on which notice is given, in the case of notice given at or before the Margin Notice Deadline, or by the close of business on the second business day following the business day on which notice is given, in the case of notice given after the Margin Notice Deadline:
>
> _____
> _____
> _____

This clause would generally be incorporated only if the parties were incorporating Annex III (International Transactions) into the Agreement. Because of differences in time zones, and the use of non-US markets and clearing organisations, the margin maintenance provisions in Paragraph 4 require additional time periods for making required transfers.

Income and Purchase Price

> **Purchase Price Maintenance.**
> (a) The parties agree that in any Transaction hereunder whose term extends over an Income payment date for the Securities subject to such Transaction, Buyer shall on the date such Income is paid transfer to or credit to the account of Seller an amount equal to such Income payment or payments pursuant to Paragraph 5(i) and shall not apply the Income payment or payments to reduce the amount to be transferred to Buyer or Seller upon termination of the Transaction pursuant to Paragraph 5(ii) of the Agreement.

The Agreement in Paragraph 5(ii) provides that a Buyer may elect not to transfer an amount equal to any Income payments received by the Buyer. Instead, the Buyer may reduce the amount to be transferred by the Seller on the Repurchase Date, typically a reduction in the Repurchase Price (see the discussion of Income Payment on page 191). Many parties, however, believe that such practice will result in potential confusion and may affect the anticipated yield or Price Differential on the Repurchase Date.

The above provision has the effect of deleting the election found in Paragraph 5(ii), requiring the Buyer always to transfer the Income Payments as provided in Paragraph 5(i).

Purchase Price Adjustments Under Paragraph 4

> (b) Notwithstanding the definition of Purchase Price in Paragraph 2 of the Agreement, and the provisions of Paragraph 4 of the Agreement, the parties agree (i) that the Purchase Price will not be increased or decreased by the amount of any cash transferred by one party to the other pursuant to Paragraph 4 of the Agreement and (ii) that transfer of such cash shall be treated as if it constituted a transfer of Securities (with a Market Value equal to the U.S. dollar amount of such cash) pursuant to Paragraph 4(a) or (b), as the case may be (including for purposes of the definition of "Additional Purchased Securities").

Clause (b) ensures consistency with the effect of clause (a). Parties often do not want the Purchase Price to vary for the reasons expressed above. Accordingly, clause (b) provides that transfers of cash between the parties pursuant to Paragraph 4 to eliminate either a Margin Deficit or a Margin Excess are deemed not to affect the Purchase Price. For example, the Seller will be obligated to transfer the same Repurchase Price (the Purchase Price plus the Price Differential) as the parties originally agreed to, regardless of how much cash was transferred to eliminate a Margin Deficit. The Seller, in turn, would transfer the original Purchased Securities plus any additional Purchased Securities or cash transferred by the Buyer pursuant to Paragraph 4(a).

In a Margin Excess scenario the Seller will be obligated to transfer the same Repurchase Price as the parties agreed to, regardless of any securities or cash that were transferred by the Buyer to the Seller to eliminate such Margin Excess. The Buyer, in turn, would be required to return the Purchased Securities, less any Securities previously transferred to the Seller.

Market Value

> **Market Value.**
> [Notwithstanding Paragraph 2(j) of the Agreement, the parties agree that in determining Market Value for purposes of Paragraph 4 of the Agreement, the price obtained pursuant to Paragraph 2(j) of the Agreement for the following types of Securities shall be reduced by the applicable percentage:
>
> | Security | Percentage Reduction |
> |---|---|
> | _____ | _____ |
> | _____ | _____ |
> | _____ | _____ |
>
> [Notwithstanding Paragraph 2(j) of the Agreement, the parties agree that in determining Market Value for purposes of Paragraph 4 of the Agreement, the price obtained pursuant to Paragraph 2(j) of the Agreement shall be reduced by a percentage agreed to by Buyer and Seller.]

This amendment is typically referred to as a security-specific haircut provision. This provision requires the party to determine an additional discount to the Market Value of Purchased Securities. Such a haircut would primarily benefit a Buyer. A Buyer may want additional protections to minimise the consequences of a default by the Seller on its repurchase obligations. By further discounting the Market Value of the Purchased Securities, a Margin Deficit would occur more quickly and would thus permit a Buyer to call for Additional Purchased Securities if the Purchased Securities went down in value.

The amendment provides that the haircut can occur on a security-by-security basis or as a uniform percentage. The security-specific haircuts are probably more accurate, given that a US Treasury Security would have a lower haircut than that applied to an agency or mortgage-backed Security.

Designated Offices

> **Designated Offices.**
> (a) The parties agree that Seller may act through the following branches or offices when entering into Transactions governed by the Agreement:
>
> _____
> _____
> _____
>
> (b) The parties agree that Buyer may act through the following branches or offices when entering into Transactions governed by the Agreement:
>
> _____
> _____
> _____

Parties normally enter into repurchase transactions through only one office. A large bank or investment bank, however, may have repo desks in multiple branches or offices throughout the world. By designating the offices that are eligible to trade, a party can limit its exposure to possible time zone differences, currency restrictions and other issues that stem from trading through foreign offices.

Use of New York Law and New York Courts

> **Submission to Jurisdiction and Waiver of Immunity.**
> (a) Each party irrevocably and unconditionally (i) submits to the non-exclusive jurisdiction of any United States Federal or New York State court sitting in Manhattan and any appellate court from any such court, solely for the purpose of any suit, action or proceeding brought to enforce its obligations under the Agreement or relating in any way to the Agreement or any Transaction under the Agreement and (ii) waives, to the
> ⟫→

COMMENTARY ON THE MASTER REPURCHASE AGREEMENT

> fullest extent it may effectively do so, any defense of an inconvenient forum to the maintenance of such action or proceeding in any such court and any right of jurisdiction on account of its place of residence or domicile.

As discussed in Chapter 2 (page 19), New York State courts or United States federal courts sitting in the State of New York (collectively "New York Courts") are required to apply New York State law if the parties have designated that New York State law is to govern the Agreement, as required by Paragraph 16 (NY General Obligation Law §5-1401(1)).

New York Courts must also take jurisdiction over a dispute filed in their courts. A New York Court must take jurisdiction even if it would normally have dismissed the action because the parties did not have any relationship with New York. For the statutory provisions to apply, however, the parties must agree to submit to the non-exclusive jurisdiction of the New York Courts. The above clause would be sufficient to satisfy that requirement (NY General Obligation Law §5-1402(1)).

Care should be taken in reviewing the submission to the jurisdiction clause. Many parties located in New York want their counterparties to agree to exclusive jurisdiction in the State of New York, meaning that the party would be unable to take legal action anywhere else but the State of New York.

Sovereign Immunity

> (b) To the extent that either party has or hereafter may acquire any immunity (sovereign or otherwise) from any legal action, suit or proceeding, from jurisdiction of any court or from set off or any legal process (whether service or notice, attachment prior to judgment, attachment in aid of execution of judgment, execution of judgment or otherwise) with respect to itself or any of its property, such party hereby irrevocably waives and agrees not to plead or claim such immunity in respect of any action brought to enforce its obligations under the Agreement or relating in any way to the Agreement or any Transaction under the Agreement.

Certain parties, such as foreign governments, often have immunity from legal actions in the United States. In order to ensure that a party may enforce its rights against such a party, the above clause should be added to the Agreement. Such a provision, however, may not be enforceable, depending upon public policy. If a party is concerned about its counterparty using immunity as a defence, it may want to obtain a legal opinion from its counterparty that opines that the clause would be enforceable against immunity claims.

Sovereign Action Event of Default

> **Additional Event of Default.** In addition to the Events of Default set forth in Paragraph 11 of the Agreement, it shall be an additional "Event of Default" if, as a

> result of sovereign action or inaction (directly or indirectly), Buyer or Seller becomes unable to perform any absolute or contingent obligation to make a payment or transfer or to receive a payment or transfer in respect of any Transaction under the Agreement or to comply with any other material provision of the Agreement relating to such Transaction.

This clause allows a party to declare an Event of Default and to terminate the Agreement in the event that a party is unable to perform because of the action or inaction of a sovereign or government. The defaulting party is presumably the party prevented from performing because of the sovereign action. This amendment clarifies how to treat a sovereign action that might otherwise have been treated as a *force majeure* or an impossibility.

Regulatory Netting Treatment Under Capital Adequacy Directive

Due to peculiarities of English law, when a UK party has agreed to use Annex III, certain provisions of the Master Repurchase Agreement must be amended and modified if the UK party is to receive regulatory netting treatment under the EU Capital Adequacy Directive. The BMA prepared the following lengthy language that amends Paragraph 11 so as to assist a UK party in receiving the desired regulatory netting treatment.

> **Alternative Termination Provision for U.K. and Certain Other Counterparties Seeking Regulatory Netting Treatment Under Capital Adequacy Directive.** The parties agree that a nondefaulting party that exercises or is deemed to exercise its right to declare an Event of Default under Paragraph 11(a) of the Agreement may elect, in lieu of application of subparagraphs (b) through (e) of Paragraph 11, to exercise its remedies through application of the following provisions:
> (b) Upon the nondefaulting party's exercise or deemed exercise of the option referred to in subparagraph (a) of this Paragraph (and the deemed occurrence of the Repurchase Date as provided therein), the performance of the respective obligations of the parties with respect to Transactions shall be effected only in accordance with the provisions of subparagraphs (c) through (i) of this Paragraph
> (c) The value of the Purchased Securities to be transferred and the aggregate Repurchase Prices to be paid by each party, and any other amounts owed or owing in connection with Transactions under this Agreement, shall be established by the nondefaulting party for all outstanding Transactions as at the Repurchase Date determined in accordance with subparagraph (a) of this Paragraph (and for this purpose, the value of Purchased Securities transferable by the nondefaulting party shall be the price therefor, obtained from a generally recognized source or the most recent closing bid from such source and the value of Purchased Securities transferable by the defaulting party shall be the price therefor, obtained from a generally recognized source or the most recent closing offer quotation from such source, in each case as determined by the nondefaulting party).

COMMENTARY ON THE MASTER REPURCHASE AGREEMENT

(d) On the basis of the values and other amounts established in accordance with subparagraph (c) of this Paragraph, an account shall be taken (as at the Repurchase Date determined in accordance with subparagraph (a) of this Paragraph) of the amounts owing by each party to the other under this Agreement (which amounts shall be equal, in the case of each party's claims against the other in respect of transfers of Securities, to the value of such Securities established in accordance with subparagraph (c) of this Paragraph) and the amounts owing by one party shall be set off and applied against the amounts owing by the other, and only the balance of the account shall become immediately due and payable (by the party owing the greater amount pursuant to the foregoing). For purposes of this calculation, all sums not denominated in the Base Currency shall be converted into the Base Currency on the relevant date at the Spot Rate prevailing at the relevant time.

(e) Unless otherwise provided in Annex I. the parties acknowledge and agree that (1) the Securities subject to any Transaction hereunder are instruments traded in a recognized market. (2) in the absence of a generally recognized source for prices or bid or offer quotations for any Security, the nondefaulting party may establish the source therefor in its sole discretion and (3) all prices, bids and offers shall be determined together with accrued Income (except to the extent contrary to market practice with respect to the relevant Securities).

FAS 125 Annex

The following provision has been referred to as the FAS 125 Annex. It was prepared as Supplemental Terms and Conditions to Annex I.

Although parties may find the provision useful, it is no longer needed for accounting reasons and is considered optional by The Bond Market Association.

7. Substitutions

(a) In the case of any Transaction for which the Repurchase Date is other than the business day immediately following the Purchase Date and with respect to which Seller does not have any existing right to substitute substantially the same Securities for Purchased Securities, Seller shall have the right, subject to the proviso to this sentence, upon notice to Buyer, which notice shall be given at or prior to 10 A.M. New York time on such business day, to substitute substantially the same Securities for any Purchased Securities; provided, however, that Buyer may elect by the close of business on the business day notice is received, or by the close of the next business day if notice is given after 10 A.M. New York time on such day, not to accept such substitution. In the event such substitution is accepted by Buyer, such substitution shall be made by Seller's transfer to Buyer of such other Securities and Buyer's transfer to Seller of such Purchased Securities, and after substitution, the substituted Securities

> shall be deemed to be Purchased Securities. In the event Buyer elects not to accept such substitution, Buyer shall offer Seller the right to terminate the Transaction.
> (b) In the event Seller exercises its right to substitute or terminate under subparagraph (a), Seller shall be obligated to pay to Buyer, by the close of the business day of such substitution or termination, as the case may be, an amount equal to (A) Buyer's actual cost (including all fees, expenses and commissions) of (i) entering into replacement transactions; (ii) entering into or terminating hedge transactions; and/or (iii) terminating transactions or substituting securities in like transactions with third parties in connection with or as a result of such substitution or termination, and (B) to the extent Buyer determines not to enter into replacement transactions, the loss incurred by Buyer directly arising or resulting from such substitution or termination. The foregoing amounts shall be solely determined and calculated by Buyer in good faith.

In 1996 the FASB promulgated Statement No. 125, *Accounting for Transfers and Servicing of Financial Assets and Extinguishments of Liabilities*. FAS 125 created accounting problems for US parties that were using the Master Repurchase Agreement. In June 1996 The Bond Market Association issued supplemental guidance and prepared a revised Annex I, which contained language to eliminate and ameliorate the accounting issues raised by the treatment of the substitution and termination provisions of the Master Repurchase Agreement.

In September 2000 the FASB issued Financial Accounting Statement No. 140, *Accounting for Transfers and Servicing of Financial Assets and Extinguishments of Liabilities*. This Statement replaced FAS 125. Shortly after the issuance of FAS 140 The Bond Market Association issued a notice stating that the FAS 125 Annex was no longer necessary for accounting, but may still be useful for non-accounting reasons (Notice Of Publication Of Optional Right Of Substitution/Termination Language For The Master Repurchase Agreement, Replacing Existing "FAS 125 Annex" (2000)).

Other Annexes

Annex II

> **Annex II**
> **Names and Addresses for Communications Between Parties**

Although they are relatively mundane, the importance of notice provisions cannot be overstated. Instructions, transfers and notices of Events of Default cannot be made properly unless the parties have provided their appropriate contact information.

Annex III

Annex III should be used when the Buyer and Seller are using the Master Repurchase Agreement and any of the following are applicable:

- The Purchased Securities are International Securities. These are Securities that are not denominated in US dollars; are capable of being cleared outside the United States; or are issued by a non-US issuer.
- A party is not organised under the laws of the United States (or a political subdivision thereof).
- A party (organised under the laws of the United States or a political subdivision thereof) has designated that it will enter into transactions through a branch or office located outside the United States.

The Annex supplies provisions and additions to the Master Repurchase Agreement to deal with concerns over entering into Transactions with non-US parties and cross-border payments and securities transfers.

Although Annex III is available, The Bond Market Association has recommended that parties use the TBMA/ISMA Global Master Repurchase Agreement if the parties intend to enter into International Transactions. A party may, however, still prefer to use the Master Repurchase Agreement and Annex III, because they are governed by New York law and a party may be more familiar and comfortable with it.

> **Annex III**
> **International Transactions**
> This Annex III (including any Schedules hereto) forms a part of the Master Repurchase Agreement dated as of _____ (the "Agreement") between _____ and _____. Capitalized terms used but not defined in this Annex III shall have the meanings ascribed to them in the Agreement.

This paragraph clarifies that this Annex III is a part of the Master Repurchase Agreement executed by the parties.

Paragraph 1

> **1. Definitions.** For purposes of the Agreement and this Annex III:

Paragraph 1 of Annex III contains an extensive listing of definitions. As with other typical finance agreements, each reference in the Agreement that is capitalised will have a corresponding definition either in Paragraph 1 of Annex III, Paragraph 2 (Definitions) of the Agreement or where it is first defined elsewhere in the Agreement's or the Annex's text.

> (a) The following terms shall have the following meanings:
> "Base Currency", United States dollars or such other currency as Buyer and Seller may agree in the Confirmation with respect to any International Transaction or otherwise in writing;

Assuming that the Purchased Securities are denominated or paid in a currency other than US dollars, the parties must agree to a Base Currency in order to calculate the margin maintenance provisions pursuant to Paragraph 4 of the Agreement. Because the margin maintenance calculation is made on an aggregate or net basis, the different currencies need to be translated into a Base Currency. If the parties have not agreed on a Base Currency, US dollars will be used.

> "Business Day" or "business day":
> (i) in relation to any International Transaction which (A) involves an International Security and (B) is to be settled through CEDEL or Euroclear, a day on which CEDEL or, as the case may be, Euroclear is open to settle business in the currency in which the Purchase Price and the Repurchase Price are denominated;
> (ii) in relation to any International Transaction which (A) involves an International Security and (B) is to be settled through a settlement system other than CEDEL or Euroclear, a day on which that settlement system is open to settle such International Transaction;
> (iii) in relation to any International Transaction which involves a delivery of Securities not falling within (i) or (ii) above, a day on which banks are open for business in the place where delivery of the relevant Securities is to be effected; and
> (iv) in relation to any International Transaction which involves an obligation to make a payment not falling within (i) or (ii) above, a day other than a Saturday or Sunday on which banks are open for business in the principal financial center of the country of which the currency in which the payment is denominated is the official currency and, if different, in the place where any account designated by the parties for the making or receipt of the payment is situated (or, in the case of ECU, a day on which ECU clearing operates);

The definition of Business Day provided in the Supplemental Provisions to Annex I would be inadequate for International Transactions in that it references only markets and exchanges in the United States. In order to ensure that transfers of Securities can be made on the appropriate day, the definition needed to be modified to the above.

> "CEDEL", CEDEL Bank, société anonyme;

Cedel Bank merged with Deutsche Börse AG to create what is now Clearstream Banking, société anonyme. Clearstream provides securities settlement and custody services for internationally traded bonds and equity securities.

> "Contractual Currency", the currency in which the International Securities subject to any International Transaction are denominated or such other currency as may be specified in the Confirmation with respect to any International Transaction;

International Securities are often denominated in a currency other than US dollars. This non-US denominated currency is referred to as the Contractual Currency.

COMMENTARY ON THE MASTER REPURCHASE AGREEMENT

> "Euroclear", Morgan Guaranty Trust Company of New York, Brussels Branch, as operator of the Euroclear System;

Euroclear provides securities settlement and custody services for internationally traded bonds and equity securities. Since 2000 Euroclear has been known as Euroclear Bank SA/NV.

> "International Security", any Security that (i) is denominated in a currency other than United States dollars or (ii) is capable of being cleared through a clearing facility outside the United States or (iii) is issued by an issuer organized under the laws of a jurisdiction other than the United States (or any political subdivision thereof);

Annex III should be used if the Purchased Securities are International Securities. An International Security has at least one of the three following characteristics:

- it is not denominated in US dollars;
- it can be cleared through a clearing facility outside the United States; or
- it is issued by a non-US issuer.

> "International Transaction", any Transaction involving (i) an International Security or (ii) a party organized under the laws of a jurisdiction other than the United States (or any political subdivision thereof) or having its principal place of business outside the United States or (iii) a branch or office outside the United States designated in Annex I by a party organized under the laws of the United States (or any political subdivision thereof) as an office through which that party may act;

Annex III should be used if the repurchase transaction is an International Transaction. An International Transaction has at least one of the following characteristics:

- the Purchased Security is an International Security;
- at least one of the parties under the Agreement is not organised under the laws of the United States (or any political subdivision thereunder); or
- at least one of the US parties intends to trade through a branch or office outside the United States.

> "LIBOR", in relation to any sum in any currency, the offered rate for deposits for such sum in such currency for a period of three months which appears on the Reuters Screen LIBO page as of 11:00 A.M., London time, on the date on which it is to be determined (or, if more than one such rate appears, the arithmetic mean of such rates);

LIBOR, an interest rate that is quoted in London, is more commonly referenced for non-US transactions than the Prime Rate. LIBOR (plus a spread) is used instead of the Prime Rate for International Transactions.

> "Spot Rate", where an amount in one currency is to be converted into a second currency on any date, the spot rate of exchange of a comparable amount quoted by a major money-center bank in the New York interbank market, as agreed by Buyer and Seller, for the sale by such bank of such second currency against a purchase by it of such first currency.

The Spot Rate is essentially the price for the sale of a foreign currency on a particular day on the interbank market. The interbank market is a market composed primarily of large international financial institutions for the trading of foreign currency on a daily basis.

> (b) Notwithstanding Paragraph 2 of the Agreement, the term "Prime Rate" shall mean, with respect to any International Transaction, LIBOR plus a spread, as may be specified in the Confirmation with respect to any International Transaction or otherwise in writing.

The Prime Rate is not typically used as an interest rate for transactions entered into outside the United States. Accordingly, Annex III provides that the term LIBOR (plus a spread) is to be used as the Interest Rate each time that the Prime Rate is specified in the Agreement. LIBOR is almost always quoted at a rate less than the Prime Rate, which is why a spread should be added. The spread is specified by the parties in the Confirmation.

Paragraph 2

> **2. Manner of Transfer.** All transfers of International Securities (i) shall be in suitable form for transfer and accompanied by duly executed instruments of transfer or assignment in blank (where required for transfer) and such other documentation as the transferee may reasonably request, or (ii) shall be transferred through the book-entry system of Euroclear or CEDEL, or (iii) shall be transferred through any other agreed securities clearing system or (iv) shall be transferred by any other method mutually acceptable to **Seller** and **Buyer**.

International Securities are transferred and cleared in a different manner from that applicable for US Treasury or Agency Securities set forth in Paragraph 7 of the Agreement. Paragraph 7 assumes that most Purchased Securities will be cleared in book-entry through the US Federal Reserve. Paragraph 2 of the Annex provides that they are to be transferred and cleared through Euroclear or Clearstream (as successor to CEDEL under the Agreement). Nonetheless, both Paragraph 7 of the Agreement and Annex III provide that Purchased Securities can also be cleared through "any other agreed securities system" or through "any other method mutually acceptable".

Because International Securities often will not be denominated in US dollars, Annex III provides rules as to how payments are to be made and in which currency.

Paragraph 3

> **3. Contractual Currency.**
> (a) Unless otherwise mutually agreed, all funds transferred in respect of the Purchase Price or the Repurchase Price in any International Transaction shall be in the Contractual Currency.

Annex III assumes that the parties will want the Purchase Price and Repurchase Price to be denominated in the Contractual Currency. The assumption is based on the fact that a party may not want to be subject to foreign exchange gains and losses from converting the Contractual Currency into US dollars, or that a party does not enter into transactions in US dollars.

> (b) Notwithstanding subparagraph (a) of this Paragraph 3, the payee of any payment may, at its option, accept tender thereof in any other currency; provided, however, that, to the extent permitted by applicable law, the obligation of the payor to make such payment will be discharged only to the extent of the amount of the Contractual Currency that such payee may, consistent with normal banking procedures, purchase with such other currency (after deduction of any premium and costs of exchange) for delivery within the customary delivery period for spot transactions in respect of the relevant currency.

Notwithstanding the rule that the Purchase Price and Repurchase Price are to be made in the Contractual Currency, a payee may agree to accept payment in a different currency. Paragraph 3(b) of the Annex provides the methodology as to how that payment is to be converted into the other currency. That amount will equal what the payee would have paid for the Contractual Currency (after deducting any premium and cost of exchange) within the market's standard delivery time period.

> (c) If for any reason the amount in the Contractual Currency so received, including amounts received after conversion of any recovery under any judgment or order expressed in a currency other than the Contractual Currency, falls short of the amount in the Contractual Currency due in respect of the Agreement, the party required to make the payment shall (unless an Event of Default has occurred and such party is the non-defaulting party) as a separate and independent obligation (which shall not merge with any judgment or any payment or any partial payment or enforcement of payment) and to the extent permitted by applicable law, immediately pay such additional amount in the Contractual Currency as may be necessary to compensate for the shortfall.

The most common application of clause (c) involves a situation where the payee is required to litigate in a foreign jurisdiction to recover the amounts that are owed in the Contractual Currency. Foreign judgements, however, are often rendered in the foreign jurisdiction's local currency, as opposed to the Contractual Currency. This can result in the payee receiving less than the full amount of the Contractual Currency required under the repurchase transaction because of the payment of a premium or other exchange costs. The payer is required to make the payee whole in such a situation by transferring additional amounts of Contractual Currency to the payee to compensate for any shortfall.

> (d) If for any reason the amount of the Contractual Currency received by one party hereto exceeds the amount in the Contractual Currency due such party in respect of the Agreement, then (unless an Event of Default has occurred and such party is the nondefaulting party) the party receiving the payment shall refund promptly the amount of such excess.

As explained in clause (c), a payee is entitled to be made whole in the event that it receives less than the amount of Contractual Currency because of exchange losses upon a currency conversion. A payee is also not entitled to receive more than the amount of Contractual Currency owed because of any exchange gains upon a currency conversion. A payee is required promptly to refund such excess in those circumstances.

Paragraph 4

> **4. Notices.** Any and all notices, statements, demands or other communications with respect to International Transactions shall be given in accordance with Paragraph 13 of the Agreement and shall be in the English language.

To avoid confusion and foreign language issues, all communications between the parties are still required to be made in English under Annex III.

Paragraph 5

Paragraph 5 deals with a possible, albeit unlikely, event in which the US or a foreign jurisdiction will impose a tax (such as a withholding tax, transfer tax, stamp tax or similar tax) on fund transfers between the parties with respect to the repurchase transaction.

> **5. Taxes.**
> (a) Transfer taxes, stamp taxes and all similar costs with respect to the transfer of Securities shall be paid by Seller.

The default rule is that the Seller bears the risk of the imposition of any taxes on the transfer of Securities. The Seller would bear this risk even if the taxes were imposed on the Buyer.

This would be logical given that the repurchase transaction is motivated by a Seller's desire to use its Securities as a financing tool.

> (b) (i) Unless otherwise agreed, all money payable by one party (the "Payor") to the other (the "Payee") in respect of any International Transaction shall be paid free and clear of, and without withholding or deduction for, any taxes or duties of whatsoever nature imposed, levied, collected, withheld or assessed by any authority having power to tax (a "Tax"), unless the withholding or deduction of such Tax is required by law. In that event, unless otherwise agreed, Payor shall pay such additional amounts as will result in the net amounts receivable by Payee (after taking account of such withholding or deduction) being equal to such amounts as would have been received by Payee had no such Tax been required to be withheld or deducted; provided that for purposes of Paragraphs 5 and 6 the term "Tax" shall not include any Tax that would not have been imposed but for the existence of any present or former connection between Payee and the jurisdiction imposing such Tax other than the mere receipt of payment from Payor or the performance of Payee's obligations under an International Transaction. The parties acknowledge and agree, for the avoidance of doubt, that the amount of Income required to be transferred, credited or applied by Buyer for the benefit of Seller under Paragraph 5 of the Agreement shall be determined without taking into account any Tax required to be withheld or deducted from such Income, unless otherwise agreed.

Paragraph 5(b)(i) of the Annex is commonly referred to as a gross up provision. The payor is required to "gross up" any cross-border payments to the foreign payee to the extent that any tax was withheld. The most likely cause for withholding would be where the payor's jurisdiction imposes a withholding tax on the Price Differential (typically characterised as an interest payment). The policy behind the provision in the Annex is that the foreign payee should receive the amount calculated under the terms of the Confirmation (the "Confirmation Payment") without any reduction for tax withholding.

The amount of the gross up as a percentage of the Confirmation Payment will be greater than the statutory withholding rate in the event that there would be additional tax withholding on any gross up payments made to the foreign payee. Under such a scenario, the formula used to determine the total payment to be made to the foreign payee (including the withholding tax) is equal to the Confirmation Payment divided by the difference of one and the withholding tax rate, which is expressed mathematically as follows:

(Confirmation Payment)/(1 − withholding tax rate) = Grossed up Payment

For example, assume that the payor is required to pay a foreign payee a Price Differential of US$1,000,000 under the terms of the Confirmation. Assume further that the statutory withholding rate is 20 per cent and that the payor is required to gross up the payment for the withholding tax imposed. The payor's total grossed up payment would equal US$1,250,000 calculated as follows: US$1,000,000 divided by (1 - 20 per cent). Out of the total payment, US$1,000,000 would be payable to the foreign payee, as required under the terms of the Confirmation, and US$250,000 would be the amount of withholding tax payable to the payor's taxing jurisdiction.

The gross up payment under the Annex is required only if the withholding tax is imposed by the payor's taxing jurisdiction solely because the payee entered into the Transaction. Therefore, if the foreign payee had subjected itself to the jurisdiction of the payor's tax authority for some reason other than engaging in the Transaction at issue, the tax would not be subject to the gross up provisions. A foreign payee might subject itself to the payor's tax authority jurisdiction, for example, by incorporating itself in the payor's jurisdiction or by conducting other business there on which it would pay local income or corporation tax. The ISDA Master Agreement contains a similar concept, which is referred to as an Indemnifiable Tax.

It is unlikely that there would be any withholding by the US Internal Revenue Service on a cross-border payment made by a US payor to a foreign payee. If such withholding were to occur, it would be imposed on the portion of the Repurchase Price referred to as the Price Differential (see the definition of Price Differential on page 182). Under US tax law the Price Differential is characterised as an interest payment by the Seller to the Buyer (see Revenue Rulings 74-27, 77-59; *Nebraska Department of Revenue v. Lowenstein*, 513 U.S. 123 (1994); *Union Planters National Bank of Memphis v. United States*, 426 F.2d 115 (6th Cir. 1970)). Although the United States has a 30 per cent withholding tax on cross-border payments, such tax is rarely, if ever, imposed, for several reasons (see IRC §§871(a) and 881).

First, the interest payments may be effectively connected to the US business of the foreign payee and thus would not be subject to withholding (see IRC 871(a), last sentence). Second, there may be reduced or no withholding on interest payments because of a tax treaty between the United States and the relevant foreign counterparty's country of residence. Third, most interest payments made under the Agreement will qualify for the portfolio interest exception, exempting the interest from withholding (see IRC §§871(h) and 881(c)). The portfolio interest exception applies because the Agreement is considered to be in registered form. This generally means that the foreign payee's identity is known at the time of the payment.

The portfolio interest exception unfortunately does not apply in two circumstances. First, it does not apply if the foreign payee is a 10 per cent or greater shareholder of the US payor. Second, it does not apply if a foreign payee is a bank that has actually made a disguised loan to the US payor in the ordinary course of its trade or business. If a US payor is concerned about these two exceptions, it may insist that a foreign payee represent that it is not a 10 per cent shareholder or a bank making a loan.

A discussion of potential withholding taxes imposed on non-US payors by the payor's taxing jurisdiction is beyond the scope of this section.

It is worth noting that the gross up obligation is not imposed on transfer payments involving Income.

> (ii) In the case of any Tax required to be withheld or deducted from any money payable to a party hereto acting as Payee by the other party hereto acting as Payor, Payee agrees to deliver to Payor (or, if applicable, to the authority imposing the Tax) any certificate or document reasonably requested by Payor that would entitle Payee to an exemption from, or reduction in the rate of, withholding or deduction of Tax from money payable by Payor to Payee.

COMMENTARY ON THE MASTER REPURCHASE AGREEMENT

Clause (ii) imposes on the payee an obligation to co-operate with the payor by delivering any certificates or documents needed by the payor. For example, where a foreign payee delivers a US Form W-8BEN or W-8ECI, potentially it would reduce the amount that a US payor would have to withhold if the Price Differential were later considered to be subject to withholding.

> (iii) Each party hereto agrees to notify the other party of any circumstance known or reasonably known to it (other than a Change of Tax Law, as defined in Paragraph 6 hereof) that causes a certificate or document provided by it pursuant to subparagraph (b)(ii) of this Paragraph to fail to be true.

Clause (iii) imposes a duty on the payee to notify the payor if any documents or certificates delivered as required by clause (ii) prove to be false. The ISDA Master Agreement imposes a similar obligation.

It is important that the payor understands if it can no longer rely upon such documents or certificates that permitted it to not withhold. If the payor is now required to begin withholding, it may instead decide no longer to enter into repurchase transactions with the foreign payee.

> (iv) Notwithstanding subparagraph (b)(i) of this Paragraph, no additional amounts shall be payable by Payor to Payee in respect of an International Transaction to the extent that such additional amounts are payable as a result of a failure by Payee to comply with its obligations under subparagraph (b)(ii) or (b)(iii) of this Paragraph with respect to such International Transaction.

Although the risk of withholding is imposed on the payor, it may still be willing to enter into repurchase transactions with a foreign payee if it believes that withholding will not be required if the payee delivers the appropriate documents or certificates. If the payor relied in good faith upon the covenant of the payee to deliver such documents or certificates, it should not be subject to the gross up provisions if the payee fails to perform or delivers incorrect documents or certificates. In those circumstances the payee would receive its payment net. The ISDA Master Agreement also provides similar protections for a payor.

Paragraph 6

Paragraph 6 of the Annex is intended to deal with a scenario in which a new tax or a new obligation to withhold is imposed by a taxing jurisdiction (a "Tax Event") after the parties have entered into an International Transaction. Because the parties may not have otherwise entered into such an International Transaction if the Tax Event was in force beforehand, the Annex provides a way for the parties either to terminate the problematic International Transaction or otherwise to limit the effect of the Tax Event. A similar right and procedure also exists in the ISDA Master Agreement.

> **6. Tax Event.**
> (a) This Paragraph 6 shall apply if either party notifies the other, with respect to a Tax required to be collected by withholding or deduction, that –
> (i) any action taken by a taxing authority or brought in a court of competent jurisdiction after the date an International Transaction is entered into, regardless of whether such action is taken or brought with respect to a party to the Agreement; or
> (ii) a change in the fiscal or regulatory regime after the date an International Transaction is entered into, (each, a "Change of Tax Law") has or will, in the notifying party's reasonable opinion, have a material adverse effect on such party in the context of an International Transaction.

A Tax Event is triggered only if the event occurs after the International Transaction has been entered into. It results from a tax change resulting from (i) action taken by a taxing authority or judicial authority or (ii) a statutory or regulatory change; in other words, events beyond the contracting parties' control.

> (b) If so requested by the other party, the notifying party will furnish the other party with an opinion of a suitably qualified adviser that an event referred to in subparagraph (a)(i) or (a)(ii) of this Paragraph 6 has occurred and affects the notifying party.

If a party asserts that a Tax Event has occurred, the other party can request a legal or similar opinion opining that the Tax Event has occurred and affects the other party.

> (c) Where this Paragraph 6 applies, the party giving the notice referred to in subparagraph (a) above may, subject to subparagraph (d) below, terminate the International Transaction effective from a date specified in the notice, not being earlier (unless so agreed by the other party) than 30 days after the date of such notice, by nominating such date as the Repurchase Date.

Upon occurrence of a Tax Event, the party adversely affected by the Tax Event may terminate the International Transaction by giving at least 30 days' notice. There is no restriction on a date longer than 30 days given that only the party wanting to terminate the International Transaction is affected by delaying the termination.

The termination date is deemed to be a Repurchase Date. The parties, of course, can agree to bring forward the termination date.

> (d) If the party receiving the notice referred to in subparagraph (a) of this Paragraph 6 so elects, it may override such notice by giving a counter-notice to the other party.

COMMENTARY ON THE MASTER REPURCHASE AGREEMENT

> If a counter-notice is given, the party which gives such counter-notice will be deemed to have agreed to indemnify the other party against the adverse effect referred to in subparagraph (a) of this Paragraph 6 so far as it relates to the relevant International Transaction and the original Repurchase Date will continue to apply.

The party not affected by the Tax Change can object to the termination by sending a counter-notice to the affected party. This counter-notice overrides the termination notice and reinstates the original Repurchase Date. However, the objecting party will be required to indemnify the affected party for adverse tax consequences incurred between the date that the termination would have been effective and the original Repurchase Date.

> (e) Where an International Transaction is terminated as described in this Paragraph 6, the party which has given the notice to terminate shall indemnify the other party against any reasonable legal and other professional expenses incurred by the other party by reason of the termination, but the other party may not claim any sum constituting consequential loss or damage in respect of a termination in accordance with this Paragraph 6.

Although the affected party is permitted to terminate the International Transaction, it is required to indemnify the non-affected party for any legal or professional expenses incurred as a result of the termination. The indemnification, however, does not include any consequential loss or damages.

> (f) This Paragraph 6 is without prejudice to Paragraph 5 of this Annex III; but an obligation to pay additional amounts pursuant to Paragraph 5 of this Annex III may, where appropriate, be a circumstance which causes this Paragraph 6 to apply.

Paragraph 6 of the Annex does not affect the non-affected party's obligation to gross up a payment under Paragraph 5 of the Annex, although it may permit terminating a Transaction that requires such gross up. However, such gross up may create a circumstance that justifies the application of Paragraph 6 of the Annex.

Paragraph 7

> **7. Margin.** In the calculation of "Margin Deficit" and "Margin Excess" pursuant to Paragraph 4 of the Agreement, all sums not denominated in the Base Currency shall be deemed to be converted into the Base Currency at the Spot Rate on the date of such calculation.

Paragraph 7 of the Annex describes the methodology for applying the margin maintenance provisions of Paragraph 4 of the Agreement in the event that the margin payments are to be made in different currencies. As explained above, the parties will convert the different payments into a Base Currency for purposes of measuring the amount of the margin payment.

233

Paragraph 8

> **8. Events of Default.**
> (a) In addition to the Events of Default set forth in Paragraph 11 of the Agreement, it shall be an additional "Event of Default" if either party fails, after one business day's notice, to perform any covenant or obligation required to be performed by it under this Annex III, including, without limitation, the payment of taxes or additional amounts as required by Paragraph 5 of this Annex III.

It is an Event of Default for purposes of Paragraph 11 of the Agreement for a party to fail to perform any covenant or obligation under the Annex, the most important of which are related to the payment of taxes. There is a one-day cure period after notice, however, before it becomes an Event of Default.

> (b) In addition to the other rights of a nondefaulting party under Paragraph 11 of the Agreement, following an Event of Default, the nondefaulting party may, at any time at its option, effect the conversion of any currency into a different currency of its choice at the Spot Rate on the date of the exercise of such option and offset obligations of the defaulting party denominated in different currencies against each other.

To facilitate netting of obligations under the Agreement, the nondefaulting party is allowed to effect the conversion of a currency into another currency of its choice. This would be necessary, of course, in order to exercise its right of offset if the obligations were denominated in different currencies.

Schedule 111.A

> **Schedule III.A**
> **International Transactions Relating to [Relevant Country]**
> This Schedule III.A forms a part of Annex III to the Master Repurchase Agreement dated as of_____, _____ (the "Agreement") between_____ and_____. Capitalized terms used but not defined in this Schedule III.A shall have the meanings ascribed to them in Annex III.

This paragraph clarifies that this Annex III.A is a part of the Master Repurchase Agreement executed by the parties.

> [Insert provisions applicable to relevant country.]

Based upon the particular laws of a foreign jurisdiction, there may be additional provisions that should be inserted to facilitate executing International Transactions.

Annex IV

A party executing an Agreement with an agent acting on behalf of a principal should have concerns about the role of the agent with respect to the respective rights and obligations of the agent and the principal under the Agreement. A party entering into transactions with an agent may subject itself to unanticipated credit and legal risk if the role of the agent and identity of the principal are not properly disclosed and understood. A party will often have concerns about the identity of all principals in order to determine whether it is doing business with a counterparty that may have particular regulatory, legal or competitive implications for it. The Bond Market Association modelled Annex IV after an agency annex developed for its Master Securities Loan Agreement (May 1993 version).

> **Annex IV**
> **Party Acting as Agent**
> This Annex IV forms a part of the Master Repurchase Agreement dated as of _____, ____ (the "Agreement") between _____ and _____.
> This Annex IV sets forth the terms and conditions governing all transactions in which a party selling securities or buying securities, as the case may be ("Agent") in a Transaction is acting as agent for one or more third parties (each, a "Principal"). Capitalized terms used but not defined in this Annex IV shall have the meanings ascribed to them in the Agreement.

This paragraph clarifies that this Annex IV is a part of the Master Repurchase Agreement executed by the parties.

Paragraph 1

> **1. Additional Representations.** In addition to the representations set forth in Paragraph 10 of the Agreement, Agent hereby makes the following representations, which shall continue during the term of any Transaction: Principal has duly authorized Agent to execute and deliver the Agreement on its behalf, has the power to so authorize Agent and to enter into the Transactions contemplated by the Agreement and to perform the obligations of Seller or Buyer, as the case may be, under such Transactions, and has taken all necessary action to authorize such execution and delivery by Agent and such performance by it.

Paragraph 1 of the Annex requires the Agent to represent that it is duly authorized and empowered to act and perform on behalf of its Principal. This representation is considered to be part of the representations made pursuant to Paragraph 10 of the Agreement. Accordingly, a misrepresentation under Paragraph 1 of the Annex will constitute an Event of Default under Paragraph 11 of the Agreement. This would permit the Agent's counterparty to terminate the Agreement.

Paragraph 2

> **2. Identification of Principals.** Agent agrees (a) to provide the other party, prior to the date on which the parties agree to enter into any Transaction under the Agreement, with a written list of Principals for which it intends to act as Agent (which list may be amended in writing from time to time with the consent of the other party), and (b) to provide the other party, before the close of business on the next business day after orally agreeing to enter into a Transaction, with notice of the specific Principal or Principals for whom it is acting in connection with such Transaction.

The Agent is required to disclose not only the identities of the Principals that it is representing, but also the identity of the Principal for whom it is acting with respect to a particular Transaction. This information is important for a party because it may be willing to enter into a particular Transaction with one of the principals but not with another, because of credit, legal or other issues.

> If (i) Agent fails to identify such Principal or Principals prior to the close of business on such next business day or (ii) the other party shall determine in its sole discretion that any Principal or Principals identified by Agent are not acceptable to it, the other party may reject and rescind any Transaction with such Principal or Principals, return to Agent any Purchased Securities or portion of the Purchase Price, as the case may be, previously transferred to the other party and refuse any further performance under such Transaction, and Agent shall immediately return to the other party any portion of the Purchase Price or Purchased Securities, as the case may be, previously transferred to Agent in connection with such Transaction; provided, however, that (A) the other party shall promptly (and in any event within one business day) notify Agent of its determination to reject and rescind such Transaction and (B) to the extent that any performance was rendered by any party under any Transaction rejected by the other party, such party shall remain entitled to any Price Differential or other amounts that would have been payable to it with respect to such performance if such Transaction had not been rejected.

The "other party" (the party not acting as Agent) has significant additional rights under Paragraph 2 that are not otherwise available to a party under the Agreement. The other party may reject and rescind the Transaction in two situations:

- the Agent has failed to identify the Principal; or
- the other party determines, in its sole discretion, that the Principal identified is not acceptable.

Upon such rejection, however, the other party is required to return any Purchased Securities if it were acting as the Buyer. If it were acting as the Seller, it is required to return the Purchase Price. The Agent, of course, has a corresponding duty to return the Purchase Price or Purchased Securities, depending on whether it was acting as the Seller or Buyer.

The other party is required to give notice of such rejection with respect to a particular Transaction within one business day of (i) the Agent's failure to identify the principal or (ii) the Agent's identification of the Principal with respect to that Transaction.

Although the Transaction was rejected and rescinded, to the extent that any performance was rendered by the Buyer (ie, the Securities were transferred in exchange for the Purchase Price), the Buyer would be entitled to any Price Differential that was earned prior to the rejection.

> The other party acknowledges that Agent shall not have any obligation to provide it with confidential information regarding the financial status of its Principals; Agent agrees, however, that it will assist the other party in obtaining from Agent's Principals such information regarding the financial status of such Principals as the other party may reasonably request.

The Agent is not obligated to provide any confidential financial information about the Principal to the other party. The Agent does covenant, however, that it will assist the other party in obtaining such information. The other party should be able to insist on obtaining such information before entering into a Transaction; otherwise it can refuse to deal with the Agent. However, obtaining such information may be more problematic once the Purchased Securities and Purchase Price are exchanged at the start of the Transaction.

Paragraph 3

> **3. Limitation of Agent's Liability.** The parties expressly acknowledge that if the representations of Agent under the Agreement, including this Annex IV, are true and correct in all material respects during the term of any Transaction and Agent otherwise complies with the provisions of this Annex IV, then (a) Agent's obligations under the Agreement shall not include a guarantee of performance by its Principal or Principals and (b) the other party's remedies shall not include a right of setoff in respect of rights or obligations, if any, of Agent arising in other transactions in which Agent is acting as principal.

The Agent has no liability to perform as if it were a party under the Agreement, so long as the representations provided under Paragraph 2 of the Annex are true and correct, and the Agent has complied with the provisions of the Annex. A misrepresentation or failure to comply, however, may subject the Agent to liability under the Agreement as if it were a principal under it, pursuant to general principles of agency law.

Paragraph 4

> **4. Multiple Principals.**
> (a) In the event that Agent proposes to act for more than one Principal hereunder, Agent and the other party shall elect whether (i) to treat Transactions under the Agreement as transactions entered into on behalf of separate Principals or (ii) to aggregate such Transactions as if they were transactions by a single Principal. Failure to make such an election in writing shall be deemed an election to treat Transactions under the Agreement as transactions on behalf of separate Principals.

The Agent may act for more than one Principal under the Agreement. If it is acting for more than one Principal, the Agent and the other party may elect either to:
(i) treat the Transactions as entered into on behalf of separate Principals, or
(ii) treat the aggregate Transactions as if they were entered into on behalf of a single Principal.

If no such election is made, the Transactions shall be treated as made on behalf of separate Principals.

> (b) In the event that Agent and the other party elect (or are deemed to elect) to treat Transactions under the Agreement as transactions on behalf of separate Principals, the parties agree that (i) Agent will provide the other party, together with the notice described in Paragraph 2(b) of this Annex IV, notice specifying the portion of each Transaction allocable to the account of each of the Principals for which it is acting (to the extent that any such Transaction is allocable to the account of more than one Principal); (ii) the portion of any individual Transaction allocable to each Principal shall be deemed a separate Transaction under the Agreement: (iii) the margin maintenance obligations of Buyer and Seller under Paragraph 4 of the Agreement shall be determined on a Transaction-by-Transaction basis (unless the parties agree to determine such obligations on a Principal-by-Principal basis); and (iv) Buyer's and Seller's remedies under the Agreement upon the occurrence of an Event of Default shall be determined as if Agent had entered into a separate Agreement with the other party on behalf of each of its Principals.

Subparagraph 4(b) of the Annex clarifies that, even though the different Principals are entering into a single Agreement through the Agent, each Principal shall be treated as having entered into a Transaction separately from the other Principals. Because of that the margin maintenance and events of default and remedies provisions are applied separately to each Principal with respect to the individual repurchase transactions that it has executed. It is also assumed under the subparagraph that the Agreement permits that only a portion of a Transaction may be allocable to a particular Principal, as opposed to the entire Transaction. This could enable a group of Principals to take advantage of economies of scale and enter into a large repurchase transaction where they could not do so individually.

> (c) In the event that Agent and the other party elect to treat Transactions under the Agreement as if they were transactions by a single Principal, the parties agree that (i) Agent's notice under Paragraph 2(b) of this Annex IV need only identify the names of its Principals but not the portion of each Transaction allocable to each Principal's account; (ii) the margin maintenance obligations of Buyer and Seller under Paragraph 4 of the Agreement shall, subject to any greater requirement imposed by applicable law, be determined on an aggregate basis for all Transactions entered into by Agent on behalf of any Principal; and (iii) Buyer's and Seller's remedies upon the occurrence of an Event of Default shall be determined as if all Principals were a single Seller or Buyer, as the case may be.

Subparagraph 4(c) provides that, if the other party and the Agent elect to treat Transactions as if they were entered into by a single Principal, the parties are to apply the margin maintenance, events of default and remedies provisions as if there were only a single Principal. The ability to net as a single Principal any amounts payable may be helpful, for example, in the event that the other party became insolvent.

> (d) Notwithstanding any other provision of the Agreement (including, without limitation, this Annex IV), the parties agree that any Transactions by Agent on behalf of an employee benefit plan under ERISA shall be treated as Transactions on behalf of separate Principals in accordance with Paragraph 4(b) of this Annex IV (and all margin maintenance obligations of the parties shall be determined on a Transaction-by-Transaction basis).

Paragraph 4(d) provides a special rule in the event that the Agent is acting on behalf of an employee benefit plan under ERISA. An employee benefit plan may not be aggregated with other Principals for purposes of applying the margin maintenance and other provisions.

Paragraph 5

> **5. Interpretation of Terms.** All references to "Seller" or "Buyer", as the case may be, in the Agreement shall, subject to the provisions of this Annex IV (including, among other provisions, the limitations on Agent's liability in Paragraph 3 of this Annex IV), be construed to reflect that (i) each Principal shall have, in connection with any Transaction or Transactions entered into by Agent on its behalf, the rights, responsibilities, privileges and obligations of a "Seller" or "Buyer", as the case may be, directly entering into such Transaction or Transactions with the other party under the Agreement, and (ii) Agent's Principal or Principals have designated Agent as their sole agent for performance of Seller's obligations to Buyer or Buyer's obligations to Seller, as the case may be, and for receipt of performance by Buyer of its obligations to Seller or Seller of its obligations to Buyer, as the case may be, in connection with any Transaction or Transactions under the Agreement (including, among other things, as Agent for each Principal in connection with transfers of Securities, cash or other property and as agent for giving and receiving all notices under the Agreement). Both Agent and its Principal or Principals shall be deemed "parties" to the Agreement and all references to a "party" or "either party" in the Agreement shall be deemed revised accordingly (and any Act of Insolvency with respect to Agent or any other Event of Default by Agent under Paragraph 11 of the Agreement shall be deemed an Event of Default by Seller or Buyer, as the case may be).

Paragraph 5 provides rules as to how to construe references to the Buyer and the Seller when there is an Agent acting for a Principal or Principals.

Annex V

Annex V was prepared by The Bond Market Association in order to modify the margin maintenance provisions of Paragraph 4 of the Agreement to govern Forward Transactions. Forward Transactions are defined as "any Transaction agreed to by the parties as to which the Purchase Date has not yet occurred". Although the provisions are useful, executing forward transactions through the Agreement is relatively uncommon in the United States (see discussion of Forward Transactions in Chapter 3, pages 95–96).

Annex V
Margin for Forward Transactions
This Annex V forms a part of the Master Repurchase Agreement dated as of _____, ___ (the "Agreement") between_____and _____.Capitalized terms used but not defined in this Annex V shall have the meanings ascribed to them in the Agreement.

1. Definitions. For purposes of the Agreement and this Annex V, the following terms shall have the following meanings:

"Forward Exposure", the amount of loss a party would incur upon canceling a Forward Transaction and entering into a replacement transaction, determined in accordance with market practice or as otherwise agreed by the parties;

"Forward Transaction", any Transaction agreed to by the parties as to which the Purchase Date has not yet occurred;

"Net Forward Exposure", the aggregate amount of a party's Forward Exposure to the other party under all Forward Transactions hereunder reduced by the aggregate amount of any Forward Exposure of the other party to such party under all Forward Transactions hereunder;

"Net Unsecured Forward Exposure", a party's Net Forward Exposure reduced by the Market Value of any Forward Collateral transferred to such party (and not returned) pursuant to Paragraph 2 of this Annex V.

2. Margin Maintenance.
(a) If at any time a party (the "In-the-Money Party") shall have a Net Unsecured Forward Exposure to the other party (the "Out-of-the-Money Party") under one or more Forward Transactions, the In-the-Money Party may by notice to the Out-of-the-Money Party require the Out-of-the-Money Party to transfer to the In-the-Money Party Securities or cash reasonably acceptable to the In-the-Money-Party (together with any Income thereon and proceeds thereof, "Forward Collateral") having a Market Value sufficient to eliminate such Net Unsecured Forward Exposure. The Out-of-the-Money Party may by notice to the In-the-Money Party require the In-the-Money Party to transfer to the Out-of-the-Money Party Forward Collateral having a Market Value that exceeds the In-the-Money Party's Net Forward Exposure ("Excess Forward Collateral Amount"). The rights of the parties under this subparagraph shall be in addition to their rights under subparagraphs (a) and (b) of Paragraph 4 and any other provisions of the Agreement.

(b) The parties may agree, with respect to any or all Forward Transactions hereunder, that the respective rights of the parties under subparagraph (a) of this Paragraph may be exercised only where a Net Unsecured Forward Exposure or Excess Forward Collateral Amount, as the case may be, exceeds a specified dollar amount or other specified threshold for such Forward Transactions (which amount or threshold shall be agreed to by the parties prior to entering into any such Forward Transactions).

(c) The parties may agree, with respect to any or all Forward Transactions hereunder, that the respective rights of the parties under subparagraph (a) of this Paragraph to require the elimination of a Net Unsecured Forward Exposure or Excess Forward Collateral Amount, as the case may be, may be exercised whenever such a Net Unsecured Forward Exposure or Excess Forward Collateral Amount exists with respect to any single Forward Transaction hereunder (calculated without regard to any other Forward Transaction outstanding hereunder).

(d) The parties may agree, with respect to any or all Forward Transactions hereunder, that (i) one party shall transfer to the other party Forward Collateral having a Market Value equal to a specified dollar amount or other specified threshold no later than the Margin Notice Deadline on the day such Forward Transaction is entered into by the parties or (ii) one party shall not be required to make any transfer otherwise required to be made under this Paragraph if, after giving effect to such transfer, the Market Value of the Forward Collateral held by such party would be less than a specified dollar amount or other specified threshold (which amount or threshold shall be agreed to by the parties prior to entering into any such Forward Transactions).

(e) If any notice is given by a party to the other under subparagraph (a) of this Paragraph at or before the Margin Notice Deadline on any business day, the party receiving such notice shall transfer Forward Collateral as provided in such subparagraph no later than the close of business in the relevant market on such business day. If any such notice is given after the Margin Notice Deadline, the party receiving such notice shall transfer such Forward Collateral no later than the close of business in the relevant market on the next business day.

(f) Upon the occurrence of the Purchase Date for any Forward Transaction and the performance by the parties of their respective obligations to transfer cash and Securities on such date, any Forward Collateral in respect of such Forward Transaction, together with any Income thereon and proceeds thereof, shall be transferred by the party holding such Forward Collateral to the other party; provided, however, that neither party shall be required to transfer such Forward Collateral to the other if such transfer would result in the creation of a Net Unsecured Forward Exposure of the transferor.

(g) The Pledgor (as defined below) of Forward Collateral may, subject to agreement with and acceptance by the Pledgee (as defined below) thereof, substitute other Securities reasonably acceptable to the Pledgee for any Securities Forward Collateral. Such substitution shall be made by transfer to the Pledgee of such other Securities and transfer to the Pledgor of such Securities Forward Collateral. After substitution, the substituted Securities shall constitute Forward Collateral.

3. Security Interest.

(a) In addition to the rights granted to the parties under Paragraph 6 of the Agreement, each party ("Pledgor") hereby pledges to the other party ("Pledgee") as security for the performance of its obligations hereunder, and grants Pledgee a security interest in and right of setoff against, any Forward Collateral and any other cash, Securities or property, and all proceeds of any of the foregoing, transferred by or on behalf of Pledgor to Pledgee or due from Pledgee to Pledgor in connection with the Agreement and the Forward Transactions hereunder.

(b) Unless otherwise agreed by the parties, a party to whom Forward Collateral has been transferred shall have the right to engage in repurchase transactions with Forward Collateral or otherwise sell, transfer, pledge or hypothecate Forward Collateral, including in respect of loans or other extensions of credit to such party that may be in amounts greater than the Forward Collateral such party is entitled to as security for obligations hereunder, and that may extend for periods of time longer than the periods during which such party is entitled to Forward Collateral as security for obligations hereunder; provided, however, that no such transaction shall relieve such party of its obligations to transfer Forward Collateral pursuant to Paragraph 2 or 4 of this Annex V or Paragraph 11 of the Agreement.

4. Events of Default.

(a) In addition to the Events of Default set forth in Paragraph 11 of the Agreement, it shall be an additional "Event of Default" if either party fails, after one business day's notice, to perform any covenant or obligation required to be performed by it under Paragraph 2 or any other provision of this Annex.

(b) In addition to the other rights of a nondefaulting party under Paragraphs 11 and 12 of the Agreement, if the nondefaulting party exercised or is deemed to have exercised the option referred to in Paragraph 11 (a) of the Agreement:

(i) The nondefaulting party, without prior notice to the defaulting party, may (A) immediately sell, in a recognized market (or otherwise in a commercially reasonable manner) at such price or prices as the nondefaulting party may reasonably deem satisfactory, any or all Forward Collateral subject to any or all Forward Transactions hereunder and apply the proceeds thereof to any amounts owing by the defaulting party hereunder or (B) in its sole discretion elect, in lieu of selling all or a portion of such Forward Collateral, to give the defaulting party credit for such Forward Collateral in an amount equal to the price therefore on such date, obtained from a generally recognized source or the most recent closing bid quotation from such a source, against any amounts owing by the defaulting party hereunder.

(ii) Any Forward Collateral held by the defaulting party, together with any Income thereon and proceeds thereof, shall be immediately transferred by the defaulting party to the nondefaulting party. The nondefaulting party may, at its option (which option shall be deemed to have been exercised immediately upon the occurrence of an Act of Insolvency), and without prior notice to the defaulting party, (i) immediately purchase, in a recognized market (or otherwise in a commercially reasonable manner) at such price or prices as the nondefaulting party may reasonably deem satisfactory, securities ("Replacement Securities") of the same class and amount as any Securities Forward Collateral that is not delivered by the defaulting party to the nondefaulting party as required hereunder or (ii) in its sole discretion elect, in lieu of purchasing Replacement Securities, to be deemed to have purchased Replacement Securities at the price therefor on such date, obtained from a generally recognized source or the most recent closing offer quotation from such a source, whereupon the defaulting party shall be liable for the price of such Replacement Securities together with the amount of any cash Forward Collateral not delivered by the defaulting party to the nondefaulting party as required hereunder.

Unless otherwise provided in Annex I, the parties acknowledge and agree that (1) the Forward Collateral subject to any Forward Transaction hereunder are instruments traded in a recognized market, (2) in the absence of a generally recognized source for prices or bid quotations for any Forward Collateral, the nondefaulting party may establish the source therefore in its sole discretion and (3) all prices and bids shall be determined together with accrued Income (except to the extent contrary to market practice with respect to the relevant Forward Collateral).

5. No Waivers, Etc. Without limitation of the provisions of Paragraph 17 of the Agreement. The failure to give a notice pursuant to subparagraph (a) (b) (c) or (d) of Paragraph 2 of this Annex V will not constitute a waiver of any right to do so at a later date.

Annex VI

Although Buy/Sell Back Transactions are relatively common in Europe and other foreign markets, they are still an anomaly in the United States. To further complicate their use in the United States, Buy/Sell Back Transactions resemble secured financings even more closely than do classic repurchase transactions. Because of the difference in terms between a Buy/Sell Back Transaction and a classic repurchase transaction, parties should take particular care that there are no unanticipated authority, accounting or recordkeeping issues that may cause problems.

The Bond Market Association closely modelled this technical Annex VI on the PSA/ISMA Global Master Repurchase Agreement Buy/Sell Back Annex. One principal difference between the two annexes, however, is how accrued interest is treated with respect to the Purchase Price. An explanation of the TBMA/ISMA GMRA Buy/Sell Back Annex can be found on page 112. Experienced legal counsel should be consulted when negotiating Annex VI and Buy/Sell Back

Annex VI
Buy/Sell Back Transactions
This Annex VI forms a part of the Master Repurchase Agreement dated as of _____, _____(the "Agreement") between _____ and_____. Capitalized terms used but not defined in this Annex VI shall have the meanings ascribed to them in the Agreement.

1. In the event of any conflict between the terms of this Annex VI and any other term of the Agreement, the terms of this Annex VI shall prevail.

2. Each Transaction shall be identified at the time it is entered into and in the relevant Confirmation as either a Repurchase Transaction or a Buy/Sell Back Transaction.

3. In the case of a Buy/Sell Back Transaction, the Confirmation delivered in accordance with Paragraph 3 of the Agreement may consist of a single document in respect of both of the transfers of funds against Securities which together form the Buy/Sell Back Transaction or separate Confirmations may be delivered in respect of each such transfer.

4. Definitions. The following definitions shall apply to Buy/Sell Back Transactions:
(a) "Accrued Interest", with respect to any Purchased Securities subject to a Buy/Sell Back Transaction, unpaid Income that has accrued during the period from (and including) the issue date or the last Income payment date (whichever is later) in respect of such Purchased Securities to (but excluding) the date of calculation. For these purposes unpaid Income shall be deemed to accrue on a daily basis from (and including) the issue date or the last Income payment date (as the case may be) to (but excluding) the next Income payment date or the maturity date (whichever is earlier);
(b) "Sell Back Differential", with respect to any Buy/Sell Back Transaction as of any date, the aggregate amount obtained by daily application of the Pricing Rate for such Buy/Sell Back Transaction to the Purchase Price for such Buy/Sell Back Transaction on a 360 day per year basis (unless otherwise agreed by the parties for the Transaction) for the actual number of days during the period commencing on (and including) the Purchase Date for such Buy/Sell Back Transaction and ending on (but excluding) the date of determination;
(c) "Sell Back Price", with respect to any Buy/Sell Back Transaction:

(i) in relation to the date originally specified by the parties as the Repurchase Date pursuant to Paragraph 2(q) of the Agreement, the price agreed by the Parties in relation to such Buy/Sell Back Transaction, and

(ii) in any other case (including for the purposes of the application of Paragraph 4 or Paragraph 11 of the Agreement), the product of the formula $(P + D) - (IR + C)$, where—

P=the Purchase Price
D=the Sell Back Differential

IR=the amount of any Income in respect of the Purchased Securities paid by the issuer on any date falling between the Purchase Date and the Repurchase Date

C=the aggregate amount obtained by daily application of the Pricing Rate for such Buy/Sell Back Transaction to any such Income from (and including) the date of payment by the issuer to (but excluding) the date of calculation.

5. When entering into a Buy/Sell Back Transaction the parties shall also agree on the Sell Back Price and the Pricing Rate to apply in relation to such Buy/Sell Back Transaction on the scheduled Repurchase Date. The parties shall record the Pricing Rate in at least one Confirmation applicable to such Buy/Sell Back Transaction.

6. Termination of a Buy/Sell Back Transaction shall be effected on the Repurchase Date by transfer to Seller or its agent of Purchased Securities against the payment by Seller of (i) in a case where the Repurchase Date is the date originally agreed to by the parties pursuant to Paragraph 2(q) of the Agreement, the Sell Back Price referred to in Paragraph 4(c)(i) of this Annex; and (ii) in any other case, the Sell Back Price referred to in Paragraph 4(c)(ii) of this Annex.

7. For the avoidance of doubt, the parties acknowledge and agree that the Purchase Price and the Sell Back Price in Buy/Sell Back Transactions shall include Accrued Interest (except to the extent contrary to market practice with respect to the Securities subject to such Buy/Sell Back Transaction, in which event (i) an amount equal to the Purchase Price plus Accrued Interest to the Purchase Date shall be paid to Seller on the Purchase Date and shall be used, in lieu of the Purchase Price, for calculating the Sell Back Differential, (ii) an amount equal to the Sell Back Price plus the amount of Accrued Interest to the Repurchase Date shall be paid to Buyer on the Repurchase Date, and (iii) the formula in Paragraph 4(c) (ii) of this Annex VI shall be replaced by the formula "(P + AI + D) -(IR + C)", where "AI" equals Accrued Interest to the Purchase Date).

8. Unless the parties agree in Annex I to the Agreement that a Buy/Sell Back Transaction is not to be repriced, they shall at the time of repricing agree on the Purchase Price, the Sell Back Price and the Pricing Rate applicable to such Transaction.

9. Paragraph 5 of the Agreement shall not apply to Buy/Sell Back Transactions. Seller agrees, on the date such Income is received, to pay to Buyer any Income received by Seller in respect of Purchased Securities that is paid by the issuer on any date falling between the Purchase Date and the Repurchase Date.

10. References to "Repurchase Price" throughout the Agreement shall be construed as references to "Repurchase Price or the Sell Back Price, as the case may be."

11. In 11 of the Agreement, references to the "Repurchase Prices" shall be construed as references to "Repurchase Prices and Sell Back Prices."

Annex VII

Registered Investment Companies are unique financial institutions that are subject to special securities law regulation. Registered Investment Companies ("Funds") can take the form of a mutual fund, a money market fund or a unit investment trust. Because of the special rules and regulations involving Funds, Annex VII should always be used with such parties. The provisions below were drafted by The Bond Market Association in consultation with the Investment Company Institute. The Investment Company Institute is the national trade group for mutual funds, close-end funds, exchange-traded funds and several sponsors of unit investment trusts.

> **Annex VII**
> **Transactions Involving Registered Investment Companies**
> This Annex VII (including any Schedules hereto) forms a part of the Master Repurchase Agreement dated as of, _____, ____ (the "Agreement") between _____ ("Counterparty") and each investment company identified on Schedule VII.A hereto (as such schedule may be amended from time to time) acting on behalf of its respective series or portfolios identified on such Schedule VII.A, or in the case of those investment companies for which no separate series or portfolios are identified on such Schedule VII.A, acting for and on behalf of itself (each such series, portfolio or investment company, as the case may be, hereinafter referred to as a "Fund"). In the event of any conflict between the terms of this Annex VII and any other term of the Agreement, the terms of this Annex VII shall prevail. Capitalized terms used but not defined in this Annex VII shall have the meanings ascribed to them in the Agreement.

This paragraph clarifies that this Annex VII is a part of the Master Repurchase Agreement executed by the parties.

Funds such as mutual funds and money market funds are often part of a family of funds sponsored by a particular company, such as Morgan Stanley, Fidelity or Charles Schwab. Often a family of funds will have one investment adviser that is responsible for the repurchase transaction trading activity of each of the funds within that particular family. Because of this, the investment adviser will often have each of the Funds that it advises enter into a single joint Agreement with a particular counterparty. Entering into only one Agreement may be more efficient and easier to administer than entering into multiple Agreements. Although the Funds are entering the Agreement jointly, each Fund is not jointly and severally liable for the liabilities of the other Funds party thereto.

Because of this, the block identifying the parties to the Agreement at the beginning of the master form will not reference a particular Fund, but will instead reference that each of the Funds that are party to the Agreement are identified on Schedule VII.A. of Annex VII.

Paragraph 1

> **1. Multiple Funds.** For any Transaction in which a Fund is acting as Buyer (or Seller, as the case may be), each reference in the Agreement and this Annex VII to Buyer (or Seller, as the case may be) shall be deemed a reference solely to the particular Fund to which such Transaction relates, as identified to Seller (or Buyer, as the case may be) by the Fund and as may be specified in the Confirmation therefor. In no circumstances shall the rights, obligations or remedies of either party with respect to a particular Fund constitute a right, obligation or remedy applicable to any other Fund. Specifically, and without otherwise limiting the scope of this Paragraph: (a) the margin maintenance obligations of Buyer and Seller specified in Paragraph 4 or any other provisions of the Agreement and the single agreement provisions of Paragraph 12 of the Agreement shall be applied based solely upon Transactions entered into by a particular Fund, (b) Buyer's and Seller's remedies under the Agreement upon the occurrence of an Event of Default shall be determined as if each Fund had entered into a separate Agreement with Counterparty, and (c) Seller and Buyer shall have no right to set off claims related to Transactions entered into by a particular Fund against claims related to Transactions entered into by any other Fund.

Paragraph 1 of Annex VII clarifies that, even though the different Funds are entering jointly into a single Agreement, each Fund shall be treated as having entered into the Agreement solely on its own with respect to each repurchase transaction executed by it pursuant to the Agreement. Because of that, the margin maintenance, events of default and remedies provisions are applied separately to each Fund with respect to the individual repurchase transactions that it has executed.

Paragraph 1 of this Annex also clarifies that there is no right to set off amounts owing under Transactions entered into with one Fund with those of another Fund.

Paragraph 2

> **2. Margin Percentage.** For any Transaction in which a Fund is acting as Buyer, the Buyer's Margin Percentage shall always be equal to at least _%, or such other percentage as the parties hereto may from time to time mutually determine; provided, that in no event shall such percentage be less than 100%. For any Transaction in which a Fund is acting as Seller, the Buyer's Margin Percentage shall be such percentage as the parties hereto may from time to time mutually determine; provided, that in no event shall such percentage be less than 100%.

Because of rules governing the margin that must be maintained by a Fund, Paragraph 2 of the Annex provides that the Margin percentage can never be below 100 per cent, meaning that a Fund, acting as a Buyer, should also be holding Purchased Securities with a Buyer's Margin Amount equal to at least 100 per cent of the Repurchase Price.

Paragraph 3

> **3. Confirmations.** Unless otherwise agreed, Counterparty shall promptly issue a Confirmation to the Fund pursuant to Paragraph 3 of the Agreement. Upon the transfer of substituted or Additional Purchased Securities by either party, Counterparty shall promptly provide notice to the Fund confirming such transfer.

Paragraph 3 provides that the counterparty will issue a Confirmation to the individual Fund that entered into a repurchase transaction. Where margin transfers and substitutions occur, these will be notified promptly to the Fund concerned.

Paragraph 4

> **4. Financial Condition.** Each party represents that it has delivered the following financial information to the other party to the Agreement: in the case of a party that is a registered broker-dealer, its most recent statements required to be furnished to customers by Rule 17a-5(c) under the 1934 Act; in the case of a party that is a Fund, its most recent audited or unaudited financial statements required to be furnished to its shareholders by Rule 30d-1 under the Investment Company Act of 1940; in the case of any other party, its most recent audited or unaudited statements of financial condition or other comparable information concerning its financial condition.

> Each party represents that the financial statements or information so delivered fairly reflect its financial condition and, if applicable, its net capital ratio, on the date as of which such financial statements or information were prepared. Each party agrees that it will make available and deliver to the other party, promptly upon request, all such financial statements that subsequently are required to be delivered to its customers or shareholders pursuant to Rule 17 a-5 (c) or Rule 30d-1, as the case may be, or, in the case of a party that is neither a registered broker-dealer nor a Fund, all such financial information that subsequently becomes available to the public.
>
> Each Fund acknowledges and agrees that it has made an independent evaluation of the creditworthiness of the other party that is required pursuant to the Investment Company Act of 1940 or the regulations thereunder. Each Fund agrees that its agreement to enter into each Transaction hereunder shall constitute an acknowledgment and agreement that it has made such an evaluation.

Because of specific securities regulations governing Funds, the Annex provides for specific deliveries of financial information as required by those regulations.

Paragraph 5

> **5. Segregation of Purchased Securities.** Unless otherwise agreed by the parties, any transfer of Purchased Securities to a Fund shall be effected by delivery or other transfer (in the manner agreed upon pursuant to Paragraph 7 of the Agreement) to the custodian or subcustodian designated for such Fund in Schedule VII.A hereto ("Custodian") for credit to the Fund's custodial account with such Custodian. If the party effecting such transfer is the Fund's Custodian, such party shall, unless otherwise directed by the Fund, (a) transfer and maintain such Purchased Securities to and in the Fund's custodial account with such party and (b) so indicate in a notice to the Fund.

Each Fund will generally have a Custodian or subcustodian responsible for the safekeeping of a Fund's securities. Paragraph 5 provides for the required segregation of Purchased Securities into the account of a Custodian or subcustodian.

Schedule VII.A

> **Schedule VII.A**
> **Supplemental Terms and Conditions of Transactions Involving Registered Investment Companies**
> This Schedule VII.A forms a part of Annex VII to the Master Repurchase Agreement dated as of_____, _____ (the "Agreement") between_____ and_____. Capitalized terms used but not defined in this Schedule VII.A shall have the meanings ascribed to them in Annex VII.

COMMENTARY ON THE MASTER REPURCHASE AGREEMENT

This paragraph clarifies that this Annex VII.A is a part of the Master Repurchase Agreement executed by the parties.

> **1.** This Agreement is entered into by or on behalf of the following Funds, and unless otherwise indicated by the appropriate Fund in connection with a Transaction, the following Custodians are designated to receive transfers of Purchased Securities on behalf of such Funds for credit to the appropriate Fund's custodial account:
>
> Name of Fund   Custodian

Paragraph 5 of Annex VII requires that the Custodian for each Fund party to the Agreement be listed in this section of Annex VIIA.

> Limitation of Liability: If the Fund is organized as a business trust (or a series thereof), the parties agree as follows: [insert appropriate language limiting liability of trustees, officers and others].

Market practice provides that certain limitation of liability provisions are often added for Funds that are organized as business trusts. Experienced legal counsel should be consulted as to the drafting of these provisions.

Schedule of Optional Provisions for Annex VII

The Bond Market Association has drafted the following optional boilerplate provisions for Annex VII in an effort to ensure uniformity with respect to the more popular alternatives.

> **Financial Condition. [Alternative 1]** [Each of the parties acknowledges that its agreement to enter into each Transaction under the agreement shall constitute a representation and warranty that there has been no material adverse change in its financial condition that such party has not disclosed to the other party in writing since the date of the latest statement provided by such party to the other party pursuant to Paragraph 4 of Annex VII.]
>
> **[Alternative 2]** [Each of the parties acknowledges that its agreement to enter into each Transaction under the Agreement shall constitute a representation and warranty that there has been no change in its financial condition that would materially adversely affect its ability to perform its obligations under the Agreement that such party has not disclosed to the other party in writing since the date of the latest statement provided by such party to the other party pursuant to Paragraph 4 of Annex VII.]

Additional Representations. In addition to the representations and warranties set forth in Paragraph 10 of the Agreement, (a) Seller represents and warrants to Buyer that with respect to each Transaction, it will have the right to transfer the Purchased Securities (including any substituted or Additional Purchased Securities) to Buyer in accordance with the terms of the Agreement and that, upon such transfer, such Securities will be free and clear of any prior lien, claim, security interest or other encumbrance on the Purchase Date, and (b) Buyer represents and warrants to Seller that, with respect to each Transaction, it will have the right to transfer the Purchased Securities (after adjustment for any substituted or Additional Purchased Securities) to Seller in accordance with the terms of the Agreement and that, upon such transfer, such Securities will be free and clear of any prior lien, claim, security interest or other encumbrance on the Repurchase Date.

Authorized Persons. [Alternative 1] [The following persons, and such other persons as are designated by such persons, are authorized to act for Seller (or Buyer, as the case may be) under the Agreement, until notice to the Fund by Seller (or Buyer, as the case may be):

_____
_____
_____

The following persons, and such other persons as are designated by such persons, are authorized to act for the Fund under the Agreement, until notice to Seller (or Buyer, as the case may be) by such Fund:

_____
_____
_____

[Alternative 2] [Each party shall provide the other with a list of persons authorized to act for such party under the Agreement which list of authorized persons may be supplemented or amended from time to time.]

Limitation of Liability. For any Transaction involving a Fund organized as a business trust (or a series thereof) where the trustees, officers, employees or interestholders of such business trust (or series thereof) may be held personally liable for its obligations. Seller (or Buyer, as the case may be) acknowledges and agrees that, to the extent such trustees are regarded as entering into the Agreement, they do so only as trustees and not individually and that the obligations of the Agreement are not binding upon any such trustee, officer, employee or interestholder individually, but are binding only upon the assets and property of said Fund (or series thereof). Seller (or Buyer, as the case may be) hereby agrees that such trustees, officers, employees or interestholders shall not be personally liable under the Agreement and that Seller (or Buyer, as the case may be) shall look solely to the property of the Fund (or series thereof) for the performance of the Agreement or payment of any claim under the Agreement.

COMMENTARY ON THE MASTER REPURCHASE AGREEMENT

> **Additional Event of Default.** In addition to the Events of Default set forth in Paragraph 11 of the Agreement, it shall be an additional "Event of Default" if a revocation or suspension of any authorization obtained by Buyer or Seller pursuant to Paragraph 10(iv) of the Agreement occurs.
>
> [**Payment and Transfer.** In accordance with Paragraph 7 of the Agreement, the parties agree that (i) Buyer shall pay the Purchase Price and Seller shall pay the Repurchase Price only against delivery or transfer of the Purchased Securities (after adjustment for any substituted or Additional Purchased Securities) ; (ii) any transfer of Securities or cash required by Paragraph 4 of the Agreement shall be made free to the other party; and (iii) any release of Purchased Securities permitted by Paragraph 9 of the Agreement shall be made only against delivery or transfer of the substituted Securities. Any transfer on a book-entry system shall be made in compliance with the rules of such system and applicable law.

Annex VIII

Prior to 1996, there were various legal issues that inhibited the growth of the repo market for Equity Securities. Congress, however, passed the National Securities Market Improvement Act of 1996, which eliminated many of the legal and regulatory rules that were limiting such growth. The Bond Market Association developed Annex VIII in 1998 in order to make it easier for parties to enter into repurchase transactions involving Equity Securities. Annex VIII is needed because the Agreement was drafted principally to facilitate repurchase transactions involving debt Securities.

The equity repo market is still relatively young in comparison with the traditional repo market involving debt Securities. Because of the market's relative youth and complexity, The Bond Market Association itself advises that a party should obtain experienced legal, tax and accounting advice prior to entering into equity repo transactions.

> **Annex VIII**
> **Transactions in Equity Securities**
> This Annex VIII (including any Schedules hereto) forms a part of the Master Repurchase Agreement dated as of_____, 19__ (the "Agreement") between_____ and _____. This Annex VIII sets forth supplemental terms and conditions governing all Transactions in U.S. and non-U.S. Equity Securities. In the event of any conflict between the terms of this Annex VIII and any other term of the Agreement, the terms of this Annex VIII shall prevail. Capitalized terms used but not defined in this Annex VIII shall have the meanings ascribed to them in the Agreement.

This paragraph clarifies that Annex VIII is a part of the Master Repurchase Agreement executed by the parties. It also clarifies that it is applicable to Transactions utilizing U.S., as well as non-U.S., Equity Securities.

Because of the complexity of U.S. securities laws and the equity market, the terms of

Annex VIII are deemed to prevail over any other terms found in another Annex or in the Agreement itself.

Paragraph 1

> **1. Definitions.** For the purposes of the Agreement and this Annex VIII, the following terms shall have the following meanings:

Paragraph 1 of Annex VIII contains a listing of definitions. As with other typical finance agreements, each reference in the Agreement that is capitalized will have a corresponding definition either in Paragraph 1 of Annex VIII, Paragraph 2 (Definitions) of the Agreement or where it is first defined elsewhere in the Agreement's or the Annex's text.

> "Equity Security", any stock or similar security; or any security convertible, with or without consideration, into such a security; or carrying any warrant or right to subscribe to or purchase such a security; or any such warrant or right: or any other "equity security" within the meaning of Section 3(a)(11) of the Exchange Act and the rules thereunder;

The definition of "Equity Security" helps to determine the scope of the Annex. The definition is relatively broad and, as discussed above, includes both U.S. and non-U.S. Securities. The definition of "Equity Security" expressly includes the following:

- any stock or similar security;
- any Security convertible into an Equity Security;
- any Security that carries a warrant or right to subscribe to or purchase an Equity Security;
- any warrant or similar right; and
- any Equity Security within the meaning of Section 3(a)(11) of the Securities Exchange Act of 1934.

> "Exchange Act", the Securities Exchange Act of 1934, as amended, and all rules and regulations promulgated thereunder;

The Securities Exchange Act of 1934, which created the Securities and Exchange Commission, governs the securities markets and requires periodical disclosures for public securities.

> "Market Value", with respect to Equity Securities, the meaning given in Paragraph 9 of this Annex;

See discussion below in Paragraph 9.

> "Purchased Securities" (including any "Additional Purchased Securities"), the meaning specified in the Agreement, except that if any new or different Security or other consideration shall be exchanged for any Purchased Security by recapitalization, merger, consolidation or other corporate action, such new or different Security or other consideration shall, effective upon such exchange, be deemed to become a Purchased Security, in substitution for the former Purchased Security for which such exchange is made;

The definition of Purchased Securities is expanded to include any new Securities or other consideration received by the Buyer that is exchanged for a Purchased Security, such as new Equity Securities received pursuant to a recapitalisation, merger, consolidation or other corporate action.

> "Securities Act", the Securities Act of 1933, as amended, and all rules and regulations promulgated thereunder;

The Securities Act of 1933 regulates the issuance of new securities issues. The Securities Act requires the registration of securities and disclosures of information.

> "Standard Settlement Date", the standard date for settlement of transactions in an Equity Security, established in accordance with Rule 15c6-1 under the Exchange Act, where applicable. or otherwise in accordance with customary market practice for such Equity Security, unless the parties agree to the contrary.

The standard date for settlement of transactions in Equity Securities is determined by Rule 15c6-1 (Settlement Cycle) (codified at 17 CFR 240.15c6–1(a)).

Paragraph 2

> **2. Termination.** Notwithstanding Paragraph 3(c) of the Agreement, in the case of Transactions in respect of Equity Securities terminable upon demand, the termination date specified in any notice by Seller shall be a business day no earlier than the Standard Settlement Date for trades of Purchased Securities entered into at the time of such notice.

In contrast to a termination involving debt securities, a termination of a Transaction involving Equity Securities can be no earlier than the Standard Settlement Date. With debt securities, the termination could be on the same or following business day on which notice is given. This is because a Buyer of the Purchased Securities may not have possession of the Equity Securities on the termination date and may need additional time to acquire them.

Paragraph 3

> **3. Margin Maintenance.** In addition to any agreement by the parties under Paragraph 4(f) of the Agreement, Buyer and Seller may agree, with respect to any or all Transactions under the Agreement, that the respective rights of Buyer and Seller under subparagraphs (a) and (b) of Paragraph 4 of the Agreement to require the elimination of a Margin Deficit or a Margin Excess, as the case may be, may be exercised whenever such a Margin Deficit or a Margin Excess exists with respect to any class of Transactions under the Agreement (calculated without regard to any other class of Transactions outstanding under the Agreement). The classes designated by the parties under this Paragraph may include, without limitation, Transactions in Equity Securities and Transactions in non-Equity Securities.

Paragraph 4 of the Agreement permits the margin maintenance payments to be computed on an aggregate or a net basis. There was some concern that parties might not have the operational ability to compute an aggregate or net margin maintenance payment for both Equity and non-Equity Securities. This Paragraph of the Annex permits the parties to make aggregate or net calculations for classes of Transactions, such as Equity versus non-Equity Securities.

Paragraph 4

> **4. Dividends, Distributions, etc.**
> (a) In accordance with Paragraph 5 of the Agreement, Seller shall be entitled to receive an amount equal to all Income paid or distributed on or in respect of Purchased Securities that is not otherwise received by Seller, to the full extent it would be so entitled if Purchased Securities had not been sold to Buyer. The parties expressly acknowledge and agree, for the avoidance of doubt, that such Income shall include, but not be limited to: (i) cash and all other property, (ii) stock dividends, (iii) Securities received as a result of split ups of Purchased Securities and distributions in respect thereof, (iv) interest payments and (v) all rights to purchase additional Securities (except to the extent that any amounts included in the foregoing clauses (i) through (v) would be deemed to be Purchased Securities under Paragraph 1 of this Annex).

Subparagraph 4(a) clarifies that Income includes cash as well as non-cash Income payments, such as stock dividends. Equity Securities receive distributions of non-cash Income payments much more frequently than do debt Securities.

> (b) Cash Income paid or distributed on or in respect of Purchased Securities, which Seller is entitled to receive pursuant to subparagraph (a) of this Paragraph, shall be treated in accordance with Paragraph 5 of the Agreement. Notwithstanding Paragraph 5 of the Agreement, non-cash Income received by Buyer shall be added to the Purchased Securities on the date of distribution and shall be considered such for all purposes, subject to Buyer's obligation to transfer Purchased Securities to Seller upon termination of the relevant Transaction in accordance with the terms of the Agreement.

Rather than require the non-cash Income to be distributed, any non-cash Income is added to the Purchased Securities. The non-cash Income will be distributed to the Seller on the Repurchase Date.

Paragraph 5

> **5. Payment and Transfer.** In addition to the transfer methods set forth in Paragraph 7 of the Agreement, Equity Securities transferred by one party hereto to the other party may be transferred through The Depository Trust Company.

The Depository Trust Company ("DTC") is a member of the US Federal Reserve system, a limited-purpose trust company under New York State banking law and a registered clearing agency with the SEC. The DTC provides clearing services for Equity Securities and, as a Custodian, retains custody of approximately 2 million securities issues.

Paragraph 6

> **6. Additional Representations.** In addition to the representations and warranties set forth in Paragraph 10 of the Agreement, the following representations and warranties shall apply, unless otherwise agreed by the parties:

Paragraph 6 of this Annex requires each party to make certain representations that it is duly authorised and empowered to act and perform on behalf of its Principal. These representations are considered to be part of the representations made pursuant to Paragraph 10 of the Agreement. Accordingly, a misrepresentation under Paragraph 6 of the Annex will constitute an Event of Default under Paragraph 11 of the Agreement. This would permit the non-defaulting party to terminate the Agreement.

> (a) on the Purchase Date for any Transaction and again on each date that Additional Purchased Securities that are Equity Securities are transferred pursuant to Paragraph 4(a) of the Agreement, Seller represents and warrants that (i) Seller is familiar with the provisions of Rule 144 under the Securities Act, (ii) Seller is not, and within the preceding three months has not been, an "affiliate" of the issuer of any Purchased Securities or Additional Purchased Securities as that term is used in Rule 144, and (iii) any Purchased Securities or Additional Purchased Securities transferred to Buyer by Seller are not "restricted securities" within the meaning of Rule 144 or otherwise subject to any legal, regulatory or contractual restrictions on transfer; and
> (b) on the Repurchase Date for any Transaction and on each date that Purchased Securities that are Equity Securities are transferred pursuant to Paragraph 4(b) of the Agreement, Buyer represents and warrants that (i) Buyer is familiar with the provisions of Rule 144 under the Securities Act. (ii) Buyer is not, and within the preceding three months has not been an "affiliate" of the issuer of any Purchased Securities as that term is used in Rule 144, and (iii) assuming the accuracy and completeness of Seller's representations under subparagraph (a) of this Paragraph, any Purchased Securities transferred to Seller by Buyer are not "restricted securities" within the meaning of Rule 144 or otherwise subject to any legal regulatory or contractual restrictions on transfer.

US securities laws place limitations on the transfer of restricted securities, such as securities acquired in unregistered private sales or from an affiliate of an issuer. Rule 144 allows public resale of restricted securities if certain conditions are met. The rules governing restricted securities and their public sale are complex. This representation is intended to ensure that these rules are followed as the Seller and Buyer transfer Purchased Securities at the inception of the Transaction and pursuant to margin maintenance payments under Paragraph 4 of the Agreement. Subparagraph 6(a) of Annex VIII is the representation made by the Seller and subparagraph 6(b) is the representation made by the Buyer.

Paragraph 7

> **7. Rights of Buyer in Purchased Securities.** Except as otherwise agreed by the parties, Seller waives the right to vote, or to provide any consent or to take any similar action with respect to, Purchased Securities that are Equity Securities in the event that the record date or deadline for such vote, consent or other action falls during the term of a Transaction.

Although Income is passed through to the Seller, the Buyer retains the right to vote, consent to, or take any similar action with respect to Purchased Securities that are Equity Securities.

Paragraph 8

> **8. Events of Default.** In addition to the Events of Default set forth in Paragraph 11 of the Agreement, it shall be an additional "Event of Default" if either party fails to perform any covenant or obligation required to be performed by it under this Annex VIII. Provided, however, that to the extent that Paragraphs 3 and 4 hereof supplement and amend, respectively, Paragraphs 4 and 5 of the Agreement, any such failure under Paragraphs 3 or 4 hereof shall constitute an "Event of Default" only after the expiration of the notice period, if any, specified in the Agreement with respect to the occurrence of an Event of Default for such a failure under such Paragraph 4 or 5 of the Agreement, as applicable.

It is an Event of Default for purposes of Paragraph 11 of the Agreement for a party to fail to perform any covenant or obligation under the Annex. Paragraph 8 of the Annex also provides that any cure or notice periods provided pursuant to Annex VIII shall be incorporated into Paragraph 11.

Paragraph 9

Paragraph 9 of the Annex provides additional methodologies and rules for valuing Equity Securities. As mentioned above, the Agreement was drafted primarily for repurchase transactions utilising debt securities and provides insufficient guidance, without Annex VIII, to properly determine the Market Value of Equity Securities.

9. Market Value

(a) Unless otherwise agreed, if the principal market for the Equity Securities to be valued is a national securities exchange in the United States, their Market Value shall be determined by their last sale price on such exchange on the preceding business day or, if there was no sale on that day, by the last sale price on the next preceding business day on which there was a sale on such exchange, all as quoted on the Consolidated Tape or, if not quoted on the Consolidated Tape, then as quoted by such exchange.

Subparagraph 9(a) provides for determining the Market Value for Equity Securities traded on a national securities exchange in the United States. The Consolidated Tape refers to the reporting of transactions for New York Stock Exchange listed Equity Securities that are executed on the New York Stock Exchange, a regional stock exchange (such as the Chicago Stock Exchange) or other particular markets.

(b) Except as provided in subparagraph (c) of this Paragraph or as otherwise agreed, if the principal market for the Equity Securities to be valued is the over-the-counter market, their Market Value shall be determined as follows. If the Equity Securities are quoted on The Nasdaq Stock Market ("Nasdaq"), their Market Value shall be the closing sale price on Nasdaq on the preceding business day or, if the Equity Securities are issues for which last sale prices are not quoted on Nasdaq, the closing bid price on such day. If the Equity Securities to be valued are not quoted on Nasdaq, their Market Value shall be the highest bid quotation as quoted in any of The Wall Street Journal, the OTC Bulletin Board service, quotations sheets of registered market makers and, if necessary, dealers telephone quotations on the preceding business day. In each case, if the relevant quotation did not exist on such day, then the relevant quotation on the next preceding business day in which there was such a quotation shall be the Market Value.

Subparagraph 9(b) provides for determining the Market Value for Equity Securities traded on the over-the-counter market in the United States, particularly the Nasdaq Stock Market. The subparagraph also provides a methodology for how to obtain a Market Value for Equity Securities that are not quoted on Nasdaq.

(c) Unless otherwise agreed, if the Equity Securities to be valued are principally cleared and settled outside the United States, their Market Value shall be determined as of the close of business on the preceding business day in accordance with market practice in the principal market for such Equity Securities.

Subparagraph 9(c) provides for determining the Market Value for Equity Securities that are cleared and settled outside the United States. The definition is purposefully flexible in order to deal with the myriad of exchanges or markets in which a non-U.S. Equity Security may be cleared and settled.

> (d) All determinations of Market Value under subparagraphs (a), (b) and (c) of this Paragraph shall include, where applicable, accrued Income to the extent not already included therein (other than any Income transferred to the other party pursuant to Paragraph 4 of this Annex), unless market practice with respect to the valuation of such Equity Securities in connection with repurchase agreements is to the contrary.

Subparagraph 9(d) clarifies that Market Value is to include accrued income for Equity Securities.

Paragraph 10

> **10. Additional Covenant.** Except to the extent required by applicable law or regulation or as otherwise agreed, Seller and Buyer agree that Transactions hereunder shall in no event be "exchange contracts" for purposes of the rules of any securities exchange and that Transactions hereunder shall not be governed by the buy-in or other rules of any such Exchange, registered national securities association or other self-regulatory organization.

Paragraph 10 clarifies that any Transactions involving Equity Securities will not be characterised as an exchange contract nor subject to the rules and regulations of a particular exchange.

Schedule VIII.A

Due to the complexity of equity repo transactions, The Bond Market Association drafted Scheduled VIII.A as a placeholder for any potential additional provisions that parties may want to add.

> **Schedule VIII.A**
> **Additional Provisions Regarding Transactions in Equity Securities**
> This Schedule VIII.A forms a part of Annex VIII to the Master Repurchase Agreement dated as of _____, 19___ (the "Agreement") between _____ and _____. Capitalized terms used but not defined in this Schedule VIII.A shall have the meanings ascribed to them in Annex VIII.

Annex IX

Due to the passage of Japanese tax legislation in 2002, there was the possibility that Transactions between a Japanese financial institution and a non-Japanese financial institution might be subject to a withholding tax on the Price Differential paid by the Japanese Seller. In order to qualify for certain exemptions from this withholding tax, The Bond Market Association prepared Annex IX. For the benefit of its members, The Bond Market Association also obtained a Japanese legal opinion opining on the efficacy of Annex IX.

> **Annex IX**
> **Transactions Involving Certain Japanese Financial Institutions**
> This Annex IX forms part of the Master Repurchase Agreement dated as of _____ (the "Agreement") between _____ and _____.
> Capitalized terms used but not defined in this Annex IX shall have the meanings ascribed to them in the Agreement. Paragraph references are to paragraphs in the Agreement unless otherwise set out herein.

This paragraph clarifies that Annex IX is a part of the Master Repurchase Agreement executed by the parties.

Paragraph 1

> 1. This Annex IX shall apply only to those Transactions where (a) one of the parties is, and the other party is not, resident in Japan for tax purposes and (b) where the parties have agreed that the Securities (whether Purchased Securities or Additional Purchased Securities) utilized in Transactions conducted pursuant to the Agreement will comprise or include Exempt Securities. For the purposes of this Annex IX, "Exempt Securities" means Securities which are specified in the Tax Special Measurement Law (sozei tokubetsu sochi hou) of Japan (Law No.26 of 1957), as amended (the "Tax Special Measurement Law"), and the Cabinet Order of the Tax Special Measurement Law (Cabinet Order No.43 of 1957), as amended (the "Cabinet Order"), for the purpose of the exemption from the withholding of the interests received from certain Japanese financial institutions as specified in the Tax Special Measurement Law and the Cabinet Order, with respect to the transactions of sale and repurchase of, or those of the sale and purchase with buy/sell back conditions of, Securities; provided that such transactions meet the requirements as provided in the relevant laws and regulations.

Paragraph 1 of the Annex provides the scope or the applicability of the Annex in different situations. Understanding the scope is important because only those Transactions identified in Paragraph 1 will qualify for the special exemptions from Japanese withholding tax on the Price Differential.

    First, it is applicable only if one of the parties is a resident of Japan for tax purposes and the other is not.

    Second, it is applicable only if the Purchased Securities are "Exempt Securities" under applicable Japanese law. These include foreign debt securities (ie, Securities issued by the US Treasury); debt issued by the political subdivisions of a foreign government (ie, municipal bonds); and government-sponsored agency debt (such as debt issued by Fannie Mae and Freddie Mac).

> Notwithstanding the above, this Annex IX shall not apply to any Transactions which utilize Securities (whether Purchased Securities or Additional Purchased Securities) issued in Japan (including, for example, Securities issued by a private entity organized under the laws of Japan, or those issued by public or Japanese government entities, such as Japanese Government Bonds).

Annex IX does not apply to Transactions where the Securities are issued in Japan. In other words, Annex IX will not enable the parties to such Transactions to qualify for an exemption from the tax withholding concern described above. In addition, there may be other tax issues that the Annex does not address as well.

Paragraph 2

> 2. In the event of any conflict between the terms and conditions of this Annex IX and any other term of the Agreement or any Annex to the Agreement, the terms in this Annex shall prevail to the extent of such inconsistency.

Because of the necessity to qualify for the exemption from withholding, the terms of Annex IX prevail over any other terms found in another Annex or in the Agreement itself.

Paragraphs 3, 4, 5 and 6

Paragraphs 3, 4, 5 and 6 are all technical provisions needed in order for a party to qualify for the exemption from Japanese tax withholding. As opposed to other legal issues discussed with respect to the Agreement, this Annex was prepared specifically to meet exemptions provided under Japanese tax law. Because of the technical nature of the Annex, the complexity of the issue and the proper interpretation of Japanese tax law, The Bond Market Association itself advises that a party should obtain experienced legal, tax and accounting advice prior to entering into Transactions and Annex IX with Japanese financial institutions.

> 3. Delete "or other assets" between the word "securities" and "("Securities")" in the second line of Paragraph 1.
> 4. Notwithstanding Paragraph 2, clauses (a)(i) and (a)(ii) in the Master Repurchase Agreement, "Act of Insolvency" shall occur with respect to any party hereto immediately upon the voluntary or involuntary filing of a petition in respect of it (including by the counterparty to the Agreement in respect of any obligation under the Agreement) with any court in Japan for the bankruptcy (hasan), corporate reorganization (kaisha kosei) or civil rehabilitation (minji saisei) of such party (the "Close-out Netting Event").

5. For the avoidance of doubt, and in addition to any other remedies available to the parties under Paragraph 11, immediately upon the occurrence of a Close-out Netting Event, regardless of the intent of the parties, without taking any procedure or entering into any arrangement, such as a notice or demand from one party to the other or any agreement between the parties, the sum due from one party in respect of all Transactions under the Agreement shall be set off against the sum due from the other in respect of all Transactions under the Agreement and only the balance shall be due and payable and constitute a single obligation or claim; provided that the conversion or valuation of the currency or the Securities for the purpose of the set-off shall be made in accordance with the Enforcement Regulations for the Law concerning Close-out Netting of Specified Transactions Entered into by Financial Institutions, etc. (The joint Ministerial Ordinance of the Prime Minister's Office and Ministry of Finance No.48 of 1998). In the event that (a) Annex III to the Agreement has been executed and made part of the Agreement, and (b) the conversion or valuation described in the prior sentence conflicts with the Contractual Currency, the conversion or valuation described in the prior sentence will prevail.

6. Add the following clause to Paragraph 19:

(e) It is understood that this Agreement is intended to constitute a "Master Agreement" as defined in the Law concerning Close-out Netting of Specified Financial Transactions Entered into by Financial Institutions, etc. (Law No.108 of 1998), as amended (the "Close-out Netting Law") and if any provision concerning the netting or set-off contained in the Agreement or Annexes is inconsistent with or conflicts with the provisions of the Close-out Netting Law, the Enforcement Regulations for the Close-out Netting Law (the "Enforcement Regulations"), or the Enforcement Order for the Close-out Netting Law (the "Close-out Cabinet Order"), then the provisions of the Close-out Netting Law, Enforcement Regulations or the Close-out Cabinet Order shall prevail.

Except as amended herein, the Agreement shall continue to have full force and effect in all respects.

---

* Within chapters, terms used in the commentaries may have capitalisation or minor spelling differences to match the corresponding documentation.

Chapter 6

Tri-party Custodial Agreements

Introduction

Tri-party custodial agreements ensure effective, secure, safe and efficient transfer of Securities between the Buyer and the Seller in a repurchase transaction through the use of a respected third-party Custodian. Transferring Securities between the Buyer and the Seller is possible without the use of a Custodian, but it can be expensive, difficult and subject to credit risk. Transferring title to Securities requires careful attention to ensure that the Securities are valued and transferred properly, whether it involves certificated Securities or Securities held through book-entry systems or clearing corporations. A tri-party custodial arrangement can greatly simplify and improve the repo trading relationship between a Buyer and a Seller, for the following reasons:

- A Custodian brings considerable expertise in transferring and valuing Securities, greatly reducing such transfer and custodial costs for the Buyer and the Seller.
- A Custodian can eliminate credit risk by ensuring the simultaneous transfer of cash in exchange for Securities at the inception of a repurchase transaction.
- Having a Custodian hold the Securities ensures that the Seller cannot transfer the same Securities to a third party.
- Finally, a Custodian ensures that the purchased Securities will be available for repurchase on the Repurchase Date.

There are two forms of custodial agreements that are used by the vast majority of repo market participants in the United States. The first is The Bank of New York's (BONY) standard form of Custodial Undertaking in Connection with Master Repurchase Agreement (the "BONY Custodial Agreement"). The other is the Custodial Agreement used by J.P. Morgan Chase (the "Chase Custodial Agreement").

This chapter will annotate the BONY Custodial Agreement. Although the two agreements are different in style, they are substantively similar, so the analysis below should also aid a party in understanding the Chase Custodial Agreement.

Paragraph-by-paragraph commentary

CUSTODIAL UNDERTAKING IN CONNECTION

WITH MASTER REPURCHASE AGREEMENT

****

TRI-PARTY CUSTODIAL AGREEMENTS

> BY AND AMONG
>
> _____
>
> (Buyer)
>
> AND
>
> _____
>
> (Seller)
>
> AND
>
> **THE BANK OF NEW YORK**
>
> (Custodian)

Because there are three parties to the Custodial Agreement, the Custodial Agreement is often referred to as a tri-party custodial agreement. The legal names of the parties will be entered here at the beginning of the Custodial Agreement. Parties will often add descriptive language, such as including where a party is incorporated or organised. The BONY Custodial Agreement is dated at the bottom of the agreement.

> **THIS CUSTODIAL UNDERTAKING** is made and entered into as of the date set forth below by and among Buyer, Seller, and Custodian.

As opposed to the Master Repurchase Agreement, a party will only act in the capacity as either one or the other – a Buyer or a Seller – pursuant to the Custodial Agreement. Typically, the Seller is a dealer of securities. This is because the dealer generally has a large inventory of Securities and needs financing. The Buyer typically holds a large amount of cash that it needs to invest in a safe and liquid investment.

> ## RECITALS
>
> **WHEREAS**, Buyer and Seller have entered into a TBMA Master Repurchase Agreement dated as of _____ (as it may be amended by the parties thereto, the "Master Repurchase Agreement"), and may from time to time enter into Transactions with respect to Eligible Securities (as hereinafter defined); and

Although the Custodial Agreement dictates how the Purchased Securities are to be held, the Master Repurchase Agreement still controls the relationship between the Buyer and the Seller.

> **WHEREAS**, Custodian has agreed to act as agent for Buyer and Seller in order to effect Transactions on their behalf, all as more particularly set forth herein;

Although the Seller typically pays the expenses of the custodial arrangement, the Custodian is the agent for both the Buyer and the Seller, owing duties to both parties.

> **NOW, THEREFORE**, in consideration of the mutual promises hereinafter set forth, the parties hereto agree as follows:

Paragraph 1

> **1. DEFINITIONS**
> Whenever used in this Custodial Undertaking, the following words shall have the meanings set forth below. Capitalized terms used but not defined herein shall have the meanings given them in the Master Repurchase Agreement.

Consistent with the style of other finance contracts, if a party encounters a capitalised term in the Custodial Agreement that is not defined therein, the definition of the term should be found in the Master Repurchase Agreement. As will be described below, there may be instances, such as with the term "Business Day", where the term is defined differently in the Custodial Agreement and the Master Repurchase Agreement.

> **A. "Authorized Person"** shall mean any person, whether or not any such person is an officer or employee of Buyer or Seller, as the case may be, duly authorized to give Oral Instructions and Written Instructions on behalf of Buyer or Seller, such persons and their specimen signatures to be designated in Schedule II attached hereto; as such Schedule II may be amended from time to time.

The individual entitled to give the Custodian instructions on behalf of a party is referred to as an "Authorized Person". If an individual is an Authorized Person, it is understood that the party may give oral or written instructions to the Custodian. It is not necessary that the individual be an officer or even an employee of such party.

An individual becomes an Authorized Person by being designated as such on Schedule II (as it may be amended).

> **B. "Book-Entry Securities"** shall mean Book-entry Securities as defined in 31 C.F.R. Part 357.2 and any other securities registered in the form of an entry on the records of the Book-Entry System.

Treasury Regulation 31 C.F.R. Part 357.2 defines a "Book-entry Security" as a Treasury Security maintained in "TRADES". It also refers to a Treasury Security maintained in "TREASURY DIRECT".

"TRADES" is defined in the regulation as the "Treasury/Reserve Automated Debt Entry System". The Custodial Agreement refers to the Treasury/Reserve Automated Debt Entry System as the "Book-Entry System" (see the immediately following definition).

"TREASURY DIRECT" is defined in the regulation as the "TREASURY DIRECT Book-Entry Securities System".

> **C. "Book-Entry System"** shall mean the Treasury/Reserve Automated Debt Entry System maintained at The Federal Reserve Bank of New York ("FRBNY").

TRADES is the Book-Entry System maintained at the Federal Reserve Bank of New York. The system provides for "issuance, principal and interest payment processing, custody and transfer and settlement services for Securities of the U.S. Treasury and certain federal agencies, government-sponsored enterprises, and international institutions".[1] (A complete list of these entities is attached as Exhibit 6.1 at the end of this chapter.)

> **D. "Business Day"** shall mean any day on which Custodian, Seller, the Book-Entry System and appropriate Clearing Corporation(s) are open for business.

This definition is substantively equivalent to the definition found in supplemental provisions to Annex I of the Master Repurchase Agreement (see discussion on page 215).

Note that the definition does not require that the Buyer be open for business on a Business Day. Because the Custodian generally looks only to the Buyer for instructions upon the occurrence of an Event of Default with respect to the Seller, it should not make much difference whether the Buyer is open for business. However, the Custodian would need the Buyer's instructions under Paragraph 5C if the Custodian were unable to complete a Transaction because of transfer and payment delays related to the Buyer not being open for business.

> **E. "Buyer's Account"** shall mean each custodial account maintained by Custodian on behalf of Buyer for the deposit of Eligible Securities with respect to Transactions and, for such purpose, Buyer's Account shall be deemed to be a "securities account" within the meaning of the UCC. For purposes of this Custodial Undertaking, Buyer's Account shall include any account for the deposit of cash in connection therewith.

The Custodian maintains an account for the Buyer for both the Purchased Securities and for any cash held with the Custodian.

Although the parties intend to treat the repurchase transaction as a sale, Paragraph 6 of

---

[1] *The Federal Reserve's Fedwire Book-Entry Securities Transfer Service* (revised December 1998).

the Master Repurchase Agreement provides that, in the event that a repurchase transaction is deemed to be a loan, the Seller shall be deemed to have a security interest in the Purchased Securities. To establish such a security interest, it is important that the Buyer's Account be characterised as a securities account for purposes perfecting a security interest in Securities held by a Custodian pursuant to Article 8 (see UCC §§8-102, 8-106, 8-501) and Article 9 (see UCC §§9-105, 106, 314) of the Uniform Commercial Code.

> **F. "Clearing Corporation"** shall mean The Depository Trust Company, Fixed Income Clearing Corporation, and any other clearing corporation within the meaning of Section 8-102 of the UCC or otherwise authorized to act as a securities depository or clearing agency.

Clearing Corporations are an integral part of the clearing, settling and holding of Book-Entry Securities. The Custodian may use the services of a Clearing Corporation, pursuant to its obligations under the Custodial Agreement, to clear, settle and hold Purchased Securities on behalf of the Buyer and the Seller. The Agreement specifically lists the Depository Trust Company ("DTC") and its subsidiary, the Fixed Income Clearing Corporation, as Clearing Corporations under the Agreement. The definition also includes any entity that would be considered to be a Clearing Corporation under Section 8-102 of the UCC, as well as any other entity that is authorised to act as a securities depository or a clearing agency.

DTC is one of the largest Clearing Corporations in the world. As part of its business DTC is also a member of the Federal Reserve System, a limited-purpose trust company under New York State banking law, and is a registered clearing agency with the Securities and Exchange Commission. The Fixed Income Clearing Corporation is a subsidiary of DTC that deals with US government and agency Securities and mortgage-backed Securities.

An entity is a Clearing Corporation under Section 8-102 if it (i) is registered as a clearing agency for federal securities law purposes; (ii) is a federal reserve bank; or (iii) an entity that clears or settles Securities, but is exempted or excluded from a registration requirement.

> **G. "Clearing Corporation Securities"** shall mean securities which are registered in the name of Custodian or its nominee in the form of an entry on the records of a Clearing Corporation.

The Custodian has title to Securities that it is holding on behalf of a Seller or Buyer through a Clearing Corporation.

> **H. "Eligible Securities"** shall mean those types of Securities which Buyer, Seller and Custodian have agreed shall be eligible for Transactions by inclusion on a Schedule of Eligible Securities substantially in the form of Schedule I hereto, as such Schedule of Eligible Securities may be amended from time to time, and cash.

TRI-PARTY CUSTODIAL AGREEMENTS

When using a Custodial Agreement, the Buyer and Seller will agree in advance of any trading what Securities the Buyer will accept. These Securities are then designated as Eligible Securities and are listed on Schedule I of the Custodial Agreement. As the parties enter into repurchase transactions, the Custodian will credit to the Buyer's Account Eligible Securities designated by the Seller.

> **I. "Margin Percentage"** shall mean the percentage indicated on Schedule I with respect to specific types of Eligible Securities, as Schedule I may be amended from time to time.

The Buyer and Seller negotiate and designate the Margin Percentage in Schedule I. The Margin Percentage is typically greater than 100 per cent, in order to provide the Buyer with an additional cushion against fluctuations in the Securities' Market Value. For US Treasury and Agency Securities it is typically 102 per cent. The Margin Percentage should be the same as the Buyer's Margin Percentage, as defined in the Master Repurchase Agreement, in order for the Margin Maintenance provisions in Paragraph 4 of the Master Repurchase Agreement to work consistently with the Custodial Agreement.

> **J. "Margin Value"** shall mean the amount obtained by dividing the Market Value of Securities by the applicable Margin Percentage.

Margin Value is equal to the Market Value of the Purchased Securities divided by the applicable Margin Percentage. For example, assume that the Purchased Securities have a Market Value of US$10,000,000 and the Margin Percentage is 102 per cent. The Margin Value for those Purchased Securities would be US$9,803,921.57.

The equivalent term for Margin Value under the Master Repurchase Agreement is either the Buyer's Margin Amount or the Seller's Margin Amount, although the numbers will differ because they are calculated using different methodologies (see the discussion of Paragraph 6A below).

> **K. "Market Value of Securities"** shall mean with respect to any Security as of any date, the sum of (i) the market value of such Security based on the most recently available closing bid price (usually from the previous Business Day) for the particular Security as made available to Custodian by pricing information services which Custodian uses generally for pricing such Securities, and (ii) accrued but unpaid Income, if any, on the particular Security (to the extent not included therein). In the case of cash and certificates of deposit, the face amount shall be deemed the Market Value. In the event that Custodian is unable to obtain the price of a particular Security from such pricing information services on any Business Day, the Market Value shall be as determined by Custodian in the reasonable exercise of its discretion based on information furnished to Custodian by one or more brokers (excluding Seller) in such Security or Custodian may price such Security using a formula utilized by Custodian for such purpose in the ordinary course of its business.

The Market Value of a Security is generally determined by referencing a recognised source such as Bloomberg, Reuters or *The Wall Street Journal*. The price is based on a bid quotation, meaning the price at which a broker would purchase the Security. Because accrued Income (generally accrued interest) will eventually be paid on a Purchased Security (and thus increase the amount of cash held by the Buyer), the amount of such accrued Income is added to the price of the Security. The Custodial Agreement provides that, if the Custodian is unable to obtain a price, the Custodian may obtain the information directly from outside brokers. The Custodian is also allowed to use its own valuation models for a Security if it is unable to obtain a price for that particular Security.

> **L. "Notice of Default"** shall mean a written notice delivered by Buyer to Custodian and Seller, or by Seller to Custodian and Buyer, informing Custodian and the defaulting party of an Event of Default pursuant to Paragraph 11 of the Master Repurchase Agreement and setting forth the specific Event of Default thereunder.

To exercise its remedies under the Custodial Agreement upon the occurrence of an Event of Default under the Master Repurchase Agreement, the non-defaulting party is required to give written notice to the Custodian and to the defaulting party. Because the Custodian may not allow the exercise of such remedies until after receipt of such notice, it is important that the parties clearly understand the notice procedures.

> **M. "Oral Instructions"** shall mean verbal communications received by Custodian from an Authorized Person.

The Custodian is permitted to rely upon Oral Instructions from a party, provided that such instructions come from an Authorized Person.

> **N. "Physical Securities"** shall mean securities and money market instruments issued in definitive form which are not Book-Entry Securities or Clearing Corporation Securities.

"Physical Securities" refers to certificated securities that are not in book-entry form. As a practical matter the use of Physical Securities is a rare event in the repo market. First, there are few, if any, large issuances of Securities that are not in book-entry form. Second, Physical Securities are difficult and costly to transfer, and do not lend themselves to use in the current repo market.

> **O. "Purchased Securities"** shall mean Eligible Securities transferred to Buyer's Account in connection with Transactions.

TRI-PARTY CUSTODIAL AGREEMENTS

The definition of "Purchased Securities" in the Custodial Agreement is substantively identical to the definition of the same term in the Master Repurchase Agreement. Both definitions provide that any Securities, whether they are transferred at the inception of the Transaction or pursuant to Paragraph 4 of the Master Repurchase Agreement or Paragraph 6 of the Custodial Agreement, are considered to be Purchased Securities.

> **P. "Securities"** shall mean Book-Entry Securities, Clearing Corporation Securities, Physical Securities and cash.

Similar to the definition in the Master Repurchase Agreement, this definition of "Securities" includes any form of Securities, whether in book-entry or certificated form. This definition is narrower, however, because it does not include "other assets", which do not necessarily need to be Securities under the Master Repurchase Agreement.

> **Q. "Seller's Account"** shall mean Seller's clearing account on Custodian's Government Securities Clearance System ("GSCS"), any other account in which Securities are held by Custodian on behalf of Seller pursuant to the terms of this Custodial Undertaking and any account for the deposit of cash maintained in connection therewith.

The Custodian maintains an account for the Seller for both the Purchased Securities and for any cash held with the Custodian.

There is no reference in this definition to the Uniform Commercial Code as there is in the definition of "Buyer's Account". This is because only the Buyer is concerned about having a security interest in Securities and cash pledged to it.

> **R. "UCC"** shall mean the Uniform Commercial Code of the State of New York (as may be amended from time to time).

"UCC" is defined to be the New York Uniform Commercial Code, which is codified at Mckinney's Consolidated Laws of New York Annotated, Chapter 38 (Uniform Commercial Code).

> **S. "Written Instructions"** shall mean written communications received by Custodian from an Authorized Person by telex, facsimile, through GSCS or any other electronic system whereby the receiver of such communications is able to verify by codes, passwords or otherwise with a reasonable degree of certainty the identity of the sender of such communications.

A Seller or Buyer under the Custodial Agreement may give Oral Instructions or Written Instructions to the Custodian for almost all purposes of the Custodial Agreement, with three narrow exceptions:

- A Buyer must give Written Instructions to the Custodian if it does not want the Custodian to accept Trust Receipts under Paragraph 5.
- A Custodian must receive Written Instructions before it is required to take actions with respect to a Security that is in default under Paragraph 5.
- Upon termination of the Custodial Agreement the Buyer must give the Custodian Written Instructions to change the Custodian under Paragraph 10.

It appears from the definition of Written Instructions that any written communication must also be sent electronically to the Custodian.

> All references to time in this Custodial Undertaking shall mean the time in effect on that day in New York, New York. Except as may otherwise apply for Income payable on particular Securities or as otherwise may be agreed to in writing by the parties hereto, all provisions in this Custodial Undertaking for the transfer, payment or receipt of funds or cash shall mean transfer of, payment in, or receipt of, United States dollars in immediately available funds.

Parties should be aware that all references to an hour refer to New York time (Eastern US time zone).

All transfers, payments and receipts under the Custodial Agreement are to be made in US dollars, except Income payments from Securities not payable in US dollars.

Paragraph 2

Paragraph 2 is an operative section that appoints and empowers the Custodian to act under the Agreement.

> **2. APPOINTMENT OF CUSTODIAN; AUTHORIZATION**
> **A.** Buyer and Seller hereby appoint Custodian as custodian of all Securities and cash at any time delivered to Custodian in connection with Transactions subject to this Custodial Undertaking and as their agent to effect Transactions. Custodian hereby accepts appointment as custodian and agent.

The Custodian is to act as a custodian for both the Buyer and the Seller. A Custodian is generally understood to be an entity that manages or administers the safekeeping of property or assets on behalf of another. The Custodian is to undertake custodial duties (as set out in the Custodial Agreement) with respect to Securities and cash that are delivered to the Custodian in connection with repurchase transactions.

In addition the Custodian is also an agent for both the Buyer and the Seller. An agent is generally understood to be someone who has the power to act on behalf of another. Periodically both the Buyer and the Seller give instructions to the Custodian about transferring Securities and cash between them. Because the Custodian is an agent for both parties (although compensated only by the Seller), there is always a tension with respect to an agent's relationship between the two parties in the event of conflicting instructions to the Custodian from the Buyer and the Seller.

> **B.** Buyer and Seller each authorizes and instructs Custodian to utilize the Book-Entry System, Clearing Corporations and the receipt and delivery of physical certificates or any combination thereof in connection with its performance hereunder. Book-Entry Securities and Clearing Corporation Securities credited to Buyer's Account and Seller's Account will be represented in accounts at the Book-Entry System and the appropriate Clearing Corporation in the name of Custodian or its nominee which include only assets held by Custodian for its customers and shall not include any assets held by Custodian in its individual capacity. Transactions with respect to Book-Entry Securities and Clearing Corporation Securities will be effected in accordance with, and subject to, the rules, regulations, operating procedures and custody arrangements of the Book-Entry System and each Clearing Corporation, respectively.

As the evidence of an ownership interest in Securities has evolved from certificated to book-entry form, it is important to set forth how such Book-Entry Securities are to be held. Paragraph 2B expressly authorises the Custodian to utilise the Book-Entry System and Clearing Corporations.

An important concern when using a Custodian is that the Custodian does not commingle its own assets with those of its customers. Such segregation is particularly important if the Custodian were to become insolvent. Unless such assets were segregated, it would be more difficult for a customer to prove that certain Securities held by the Custodian were the customer's property. Paragraph 2B requires that any Securities held by the Custodian, in its capacity as a Custodian, be held in accounts that contain only Securities of the Custodian's customers. Note that the Custodian is not required to hold the Securities in an account that contains just the Buyer's or Seller's Securities. Instead the Custodian is obligated to hold Securities in an account that has only customers' Securities in it. The Custodian would identify which Securities are the customer's from its books and records.

Paragraph 3

> **3. REPRESENTATIONS AND WARRANTIES**
> **A. <u>Buyer, Seller and Custodian</u>.** Buyer, Seller and Custodian each represents and warrants, which representations and warranties shall be deemed to be repeated on each Purchase Date and each Repurchase Date, that:

All three parties to the Custodial Agreement are required to make the representations in Paragraph 3. These representations are typical of a finance contract. The representations are important for three reasons:

- If a representation proves to be incorrect or untrue in any material respect, it is likely to constitute an Event of Default under Paragraph 11(vi) of the Master Repurchase Agreement and would permit the non-defaulting party to terminate the Master Repurchase Agreement or the Custodial Agreement.
- Requiring a party to make a representation should limit its right to assert later that it did not have the authority or power for conducting such business, or to raise similar issues that would render the agreement unenforceable.
- The representations are a form of due diligence that serve as a checklist for a party to ensure that there are no problems or issues that would prevent it from entering into the agreement with the other party.

The parties not only make the representations upon execution of the Custodial Agreement, but are also deemed to repeat them on each Purchase Date and Repurchase Date. This can be problematic if a party's situation has changed to such a degree that it can no longer make a particular representation.

> (i) It is duly organized and existing under the laws of the jurisdiction of its organization with full power and authority to execute and deliver this Custodial Undertaking and to perform all of the duties and obligations to be performed by it hereunder;

The first representation is used to determine whether the parties have the necessary corporate authority and power to enter into the Transactions. If there is any concern about this issue, a party may also want its counterparty to deliver a secretary's certificate verifying board resolutions that authorised the agreement.

> (ii) This Custodial Undertaking is, and each Transaction (with respect to Buyer and Seller only) will be, legally and validly entered into, does not, and will not, violate any ordinance, charter, by-law, rule or statute applicable to it, and is enforceable in accordance with its terms, except as may be limited by bankruptcy, insolvency or similar laws, or by equitable principles relating to or limiting creditors' rights generally; and

This representation is important if a party is doing business with a highly regulated entity, such as a utility or a broker-dealer. Many regulated entities have restrictions regarding the type and volume of business that they can conduct. The representation also covers other restrictions that may affect a party's right to enter into the agreement. For example, there may be restrictions in the company's by-laws or charter against engaging in such a transaction. There may be particular statutes or ordinances that prohibit engaging in such transactions, particularly for a government entity, such as a municipality.

> (iii) The person executing this Custodial Undertaking on its behalf has been duly and properly authorized to do so.

This representation affirms the authority of the party signing. A party may want to require its counterparty to deliver an incumbency certificate (with a specimen signature), which certifies that the signatory has authority to execute the agreement. The secretary's certificate, of course, should be checked against the executed agreement as additional due diligence.

> **B. Further Representations of Custodian.** Custodian further represents and warrants, which representations and warranties shall be deemed to be repeated on each Purchase Date and each Repurchase Date, that:
> (i) It is a New York trust company with its principal office at One Wall Street, New York, New York 10286;
> (ii) It will maintain Buyer's Account as a custody account and shall administer Buyer's Account in the same manner it administers similar accounts established for the same purpose; and
> (iii) It maintains a book-entry securities account with FRBNY and each Clearing Corporation in which it holds Securities hereunder.

These further representations from the Custodian are particularly important, given the unique corporate nature and business of the Custodian. Because they are deemed to be repeated upon each Purchase and Repurchase Date, they ensure that the Custodian will continue to maintain the necessary approvals and accounts.

Paragraph 4

> **4. DEPOSIT OF CASH AND ELIGIBLE SECURITIES**
> **A. Seller's Instructions.** On each Business Day that Seller and Buyer agree to enter into a Transaction subject to this Custodial Undertaking, Seller shall deliver to Custodian, prior to 2:00 p.m., Oral or Written Instructions containing the following information:
> (i) the Purchase Date and Purchase Price;
> (ii) the Repurchase Date and Repurchase Price (or rate); and
> (iii) name of Buyer.

The Seller is the only party that gives instructions to initiate a transfer of Eligible Securities. The Oral or Written Instructions delivered to the Custodian under Paragraph 4 are the functional equivalent of the Confirmation required under Paragraph 2 of the Master Repurchase Agreement. The Written Instructions contain information identical to that required in Paragraph 2 of the Master Repurchase Agreement for a Confirmation, with the exception that the instructions may not necessarily contain details about the Security to be transferred, or payment and delivery instructions. The Custodian will never see a copy of the Confirmation.

If the transfer is to be consummated on the same day on which the instructions are given, the Oral or Written Instructions must be provided by 2.00 p.m. In addition the Seller will need to identify by close of business the Eligible Securities to be transferred (as required under Paragraph 4B below).

> **B. Seller's Tender of Securities.** By the close of business on the Purchase Date, Seller shall transfer, or cause to be transferred, to Seller's Account sufficient Eligible Securities to complete Transactions on such Purchase Date. In connection therewith, Seller shall either deliver to Custodian Oral or Written Instructions identifying the Eligible Securities to be sold by Seller to Buyer, including a description setting forth the face amount of each Eligible Security and, where applicable, the CUSIP number for each such Eligible Security or instruct Custodian to identify Eligible Securities in Seller's Account to be transferred to Buyer's Account.

Although instructions for an initial transfer need to be given to the Custodian by 2.00 p.m., the Seller is not required to transfer Eligible Securities into the Seller's Account until close of business on the Purchase Date.

The Seller has two options with respect to the identification of the Eligible Securities to be transferred to the Buyer:

- It can identify in the instructions to the Custodian the specific Eligible Securities (with CUSIP numbers) to be transferred to the Buyer; or
- It can instruct the Custodian to determine which Eligible Securities (that are already held in the Seller's Account) to transfer to the Buyer. Under this alternative the Seller presumably has several different holdings of Eligible Securities. It may be more efficient for the Seller, once it has deposited a number of Eligible Securities into its account, to allow the Custodian to make the allocation decisions.

Note that Paragraph 4B does not permit the Buyer to identify, or to object to, the Eligible Securities to be transferred. Presumably such agreement between the Buyer and Seller with respect to the identification of the Eligible Securities was done expressly in the Confirmation or in Schedule I (where the Buyer may designate Eligible Securities that it would accept).

> **C. Buyer's Purchase Price.** Prior to 4:00 p.m. on the Purchase Date, Buyer shall transfer, or cause to be transferred, to Buyer's Account sufficient cash such that the total cash balance in Buyer's Account after such transfer equals or exceeds the Purchase Price contained in Seller's Oral or Written Instructions.

The Buyer must transfer the Purchase Price to its Account by 4.00 p.m. on the Purchase Date. The Custodial Agreement does not require either the Seller or the Custodian to notify the Buyer of the required cash transfer. Presumably the Buyer is aware of the required transfer through the Confirmation, or through an understanding that it has with the Seller.

TRI-PARTY CUSTODIAL AGREEMENTS

The Buyer and Seller may also have agreed that the Buyer would deposit a certain amount of cash in its Buyer's Account in anticipation of conducting a repurchase transaction in the future with the Seller.

Paragraph 5

> **5. EFFECTING TRANSACTIONS**
> **A. <u>Purchase Date</u>.** On the Purchase Date for any Transaction subject to this Custodial Undertaking, Custodian shall transfer to Seller's Account cash from Buyer's Account in an amount equal to the Purchase Price and transfer from Seller's Account to Buyer's Account Eligible Securities in accordance with Seller's Oral or Written Instructions with respect to such Transaction, subject to the following provisions:
> **(i) <u>Determination of Eligible Securities; Negotiability</u>.** Custodian shall determine that Securities to be transferred to Buyer's Account are Eligible Securities and that Physical Securities are in negotiable form. Any Securities which are not Eligible Securities and any Physical Securities which are not in negotiable form shall not be included in the calculations set forth below and shall not be transferred to Buyer's Account.

Based upon Schedule I, the Custodian determines whether the Securities that the Seller has instructed it to transfer are Eligible Securities. Although using Physical Securities in a repurchase transaction is unusual, if they are to be used, the Custodian must determine that the Physical Securities are in negotiable form, meaning that the Custodian has the necessary endorsements, stock powers or other documents necessary to transfer Physical Securities. The Custodian's experience and expertise in identifying Eligible Securities from one of the reasons parties enter into a Custodial Agreement.

Paragraph 5A(i) prohibits the Custodian from transferring to the Buyer Securities that are not Eligible Securities. Such a prohibition is important, given that a Buyer may not have the necessary credit and other approvals to purchase the non-Eligible Securities. Due to market conditions a Buyer may also be unable to liquidate non-Eligible Securities in the event that the Seller defaulted.

> **(ii) <u>Determination of Margin Value</u>.** Custodian shall determine the Margin Value of Eligible Securities to be transferred to Buyer's Account.

The Custodian is responsible for determining Margin Value for any Eligible Securities to be transferred. The calculation of Margin Value is relatively mechanical and equals the Market Value of the Eligible Securities divided by the Margin Percentage.

> **(iii) <u>Payment of Purchase Price</u>.** Provided the Margin Value of Eligible Securities to be transferred to Buyer's Account equals or exceeds the Purchase Price with respect to such Transaction, Custodian shall transfer such Eligible Securities from Seller's Account to Buyer's Account and shall disburse from Buyer's Account to Seller's Account cash in an amount equal to the Purchase Price.

A condition precedent for the Custodian to transfer cash from the Buyer's Account to the Seller's Account is that the Eligible Securities must have a Margin Value that at least equals the Purchase Price. Such a condition precedent helps to limit the credit risk that a Buyer assumes, by ensuring that Eligible Securities will be transferred to the Buyer's Account simultaneously with the transfer of the Buyer's cash to the Seller's Account.

> **(iv) Maintenance of Buyer's Account.**
> **(a) Physical Securities.** Custodian shall take possession of each Eligible Security which is a Physical Security at a secure facility at one of its offices in New York City and, during the term of a particular Transaction, shall identify such Physical Securities on its books and records as belonging to Buyer.
> **(b) Book-Entry Securities.** Each Eligible Security which is either (i) a Book-Entry Security, or (ii) a part of a fungible bulk of Book-Entry Securities shall be continuously maintained by Custodian in the Book-Entry System. During the term of a particular Transaction, Custodian shall identify such Book-Entry Securities on its books and records as belonging to Buyer.
> **(c) Clearing Corporation Securities.** Each Eligible Security which is either (i) a Clearing Corporation Security, or (ii) part of a fungible bulk of Clearing Corporation Securities shall be continuously maintained by Custodian in an account with the appropriate Clearing Corporation. During the term of a particular Transaction, Custodian shall continuously identify such Clearing Corporation Securities on its books and records as belonging to Buyer.

The focus in Paragraph 5A(iv) is on properly identifying on the Custodian's books and records the Buyer's Securities. Such identification is important because a Custodian could hold Securities not only on behalf of its customers, but also for its own account – both for trading purposes and as inventory. In the event that the Securities were commingled, or not properly identified, it would be difficult in an insolvency of the Custodian for the customer to identify which Securities were its property and which were part of the insolvent Custodian's estate.

> **(v) Intent of Buyer and Seller.** Buyer and Seller agree that it is intended that Custodian act as a "securities intermediary" as such term is defined in the UCC with respect to Transactions hereunder. In addition, the parties intend that all Securities in Buyer's Account and Seller's Account (excluding cash) shall be treated as "financial assets" as such term is defined in the UCC.

As explained above, although the parties intend to treat the repurchase transaction as a sale, Paragraph 6 of the Master Repurchase Agreement provides that, in the event that a repurchase transaction is deemed to be a loan, the Seller shall be deemed to have a security interest in the Purchased Securities. To establish such a security interest, it is important that the Custodian be characterised as a "securities intermediary", and that the Securities in the Buyer's and Seller's Accounts be treated as "financial assets" for purposes of perfecting a security interest in Securities held by a Custodian pursuant to Article 8 (see UCC §§8-102, 8-106, 8-501) and Article 9 (see UCC §§9-105, 106, 314) of the Uniform Commercial Code.

> **B. Trust Receipts.** Custodian is hereby authorized and directed to accept trust receipts as may be set forth in Schedule I hereto (each, a "Trust Receipt") evidencing either the holding by the issuer of such Trust Receipt (a "Trust Receipt Issuer") of Eligible Securities subject to Transactions or the crediting by the Trust Receipt Issuer to the account of Custodian of Eligible Securities subject to Transactions. Any Trust Receipt may be accompanied by an electronic file sent by Seller to Custodian containing information concerning the Eligible Securities represented by such Trust Receipts, including CUSIP number, par amount, maturity date and interest rates, upon which Custodian shall be entitled to rely without inquiry in performing its duties hereunder. Buyer may by Written Instructions direct Custodian not to accept Trust Receipts from particular Trust Receipt Issuers. Custodian shall hold Trust Receipts at a secure facility at one of its offices in New York City and, during the term of a particular Transaction, shall identify the Eligible Securities represented by Trust Receipts on its books and records as belonging to Buyer.

An issuer can issue trust receipts that represent a beneficial ownership interest in the securities held in trust. One common situation in which trust receipts are issued involves a custodian holding physical securities certificates on behalf of the owner. Custodians such as The Bank of New York will, as part of their custodial business, provide full-scale document custody and warehouse administration services for Physical Securities. Upon receipt of Physical Securities a custodian will provide certification of the Physical Securities that they are holding and safeguarding, in the form of Trust Receipts. The Trust Receipts are evidence (ie, a receipt from a custodian) of the Physical Securities that they are holding in trust. The Trust Receipts can also be used to transfer ownership of the underlying Physical Securities held in trust. Because of the pass-through nature of the trust arrangement, holding the Trust Receipts is substantively equivalent to holding the Physical Securities themselves.

Any issuer can issue trust receipts, however, whether the underlying securities are Physical Securities, Book-Entry Securities or Clearing Corporation Securities. The Trust Receipts are accompanied by a statement that describes the trust property, in this case Eligible Securities. The statement will identify the Eligible Securities, CUSIP number(s), par amount, maturity date and the interest rates payable. Under the Custodial Agreement the Custodian is entitled to rely upon such receipts and descriptions as evidence that they constitute Eligible Securities. The Custodian is obligated to safeguard the Trust Receipts. The Custodian, however, would not be able to verify that the securities identified in the Trust Receipts were actually being held by the issuer of the Trust Receipts, or if they even existed.

If the Buyer does not want the Custodian to hold Eligible Securities in the form of Trust Receipts, it must provide the Custodian with Written Instructions not to do so.

> **C. Custodian's Inability to Complete a Transaction.** If Custodian is unable to complete a Transaction because Seller has failed to provide complete Oral or Written Instructions as required by Paragraphs 4A and 4B or either Buyer or Seller has failed to arrange for the transfer of sufficient cash or Eligible Securities to Buyer's Account or Seller's Account, respectively, Custodian shall promptly notify Seller and Buyer and await the receipt of such Oral or Written Instructions, cash or Eligible Securities.

The intent of the Custodial Agreement is to complete a Transaction if at all possible. The Custodial Agreement has procedures for the Custodian to follow upon the occurrence of unforeseen contingencies.

A Custodian may be unable to complete a Transaction for several reasons:
(i) the Seller may have failed to deliver "complete" instructions, as required by Paragraphs 4A and 4B;
(ii) the Seller may not have transferred sufficient Eligible Securities into the Seller's Account; or
(iii) the Buyer may not have transferred sufficient cash into the Buyer's Account.
Upon any of the above occurrences (each a "Failure") the Custodian is promptly to notify the Seller and the Buyer of such Failure as a priority.

> If Custodian has not received Oral or Written Instructions from Seller by 4:30 p.m., sufficient cash from Buyer by the close of the FRBNY money wire or sufficient Eligible Securities by the close of GSCS or the appropriate Clearing Corporation or such time as Custodian may designate with respect to particular types of Physical Securities, Buyer and Seller irrevocably agree and instruct Custodian to effect the Transaction as follows: (i) if the cash balance in Buyer's Account shall be less than the Purchase Price set forth in Seller's Instructions, the cash balance in Buyer's Account shall be deemed to be the Purchase Price, the remaining terms of the Transaction shall be determined in accordance with Paragraph 5A, and Seller shall provide Custodian with further Oral or Written Instructions with respect to a recalculated Repurchase Price for such Transaction;

The Custodial Agreement provides specific instructions to the Custodian as to how to deal with each of the above Failures. The Custodian is to follow such instructions after one or more of the following specified time markers has passed:

- with respect to incomplete instructions, 4.30 p.m.;
- with respect to the failure by the Buyer to transfer sufficient cash, the close of FRBNY money wire (typically 5.00 p.m. New York time);
- with respect to the failure of the Seller to transfer Eligible Securities, either the close of the Custodian's GSCS (BONY's Global Securities Clearance System), which is typically 5.00 p.m. New York time, or the close of business for the appropriate Clearing Corporation;

TRI-PARTY CUSTODIAL AGREEMENTS

- with respect to the failure of the Seller to transfer Physical Securities, such time as the Custodian may designate with respect to that type of Physical Security; and
- with respect to the failure of the Buyer to transfer sufficient cash, the cash balance in the Buyer's Account shall be deemed to be the Purchase Price. Pursuant to the terms of Paragraph 5A the Custodian would transfer sufficient Eligible Securities to equal the Margin Value for such Purchase Price. This Margin Value, of course, would be less than what it would have been if the Buyer had transferred sufficient cash to the Buyer's Account as required by the terms of the Transaction. Any Eligible Securities remaining in the Seller's Account could be returned to the Seller.

> (ii) if the cash in Buyer's Account exceeds the Margin Value of Eligible Securities in Seller's Account, Custodian shall credit to Seller's Account cash in an amount equal to the Margin Value of the Eligible Securities, and the difference between the amount credited to Seller's Account and the Purchase Price shall be retained by Buyer and held by Custodian in Buyer's Account. In any event, Buyer and Seller shall remain obligated to each other pursuant to the original terms of each Transaction.

There are two possibilities in clause (ii) that would concern a Custodian. First, with respect to a failure of the Seller to transfer sufficient Eligible Securities as required by the instructions, the Custodian shall transfer only cash equal to the Margin Value of the Eligible Securities in the Seller's Account. Although not expressly stated, pursuant to Paragraph 5A the Purchase Price would be adjusted to equal the amount of cash transferred to the Seller's Account. Second, the Buyer may have a surplus of cash in the Buyer's Account greater than the amount needed for the Purchase Price. Clause (ii) clarifies that only the amount of the Purchase Price would be transferred.

The last sentence in Paragraph 5C clarifies that the execution of the Transaction by the Custodian on other than the express terms of the Transaction does not affect the obligations of the Buyer and Seller to each other under the original terms of the Transaction. For example, such a Failure may constitute an Event of Default under the Master Repurchase Agreement. A party may also have a claim for damages based upon such Failure.

> **D. Simultaneous Transaction.** Buyer and Seller agree that in effecting Transactions transfers between Buyer's Account and Seller's Account are intended to be, and shall be deemed to be, simultaneous.

The simultaneous transfer of cash for Eligible Securities is one of the motivating reasons for parties to enter into a tri-party custodial agreement. The simultaneous transfer, of course, eliminates the credit risk that one party will make its required transfer while the other does not. Note that such transfer does not have to be literally simultaneous in order for it to be deemed simultaneous under the Custodial Agreement.

> **E. Ownership of Securities.** (i) Upon the transfer of cash to Seller's Account and the transfer of Eligible Securities to Buyer's Account, it is agreed by Seller and Buyer that, subject to Seller's right of substitution pursuant to Paragraph 6B and notwithstanding the credit of Income to Seller's Account pursuant to Paragraph 5G, the Purchased Securities shall be for all purposes the property of Buyer. Buyer agrees, however, that, subject to Paragraph 8 hereof and Paragraph 11 of the Master Repurchase Agreement, it will resell to Seller on the Repurchase Date the Purchased Securities at the Repurchase Price.

Clause 5E(i) expressly states the key characteristic of a repurchase transaction: the actual sale (and title transfer) of the Eligible Securities from the Seller to the Buyer for all purposes. Also, the Buyer is obligated to resell the Securities on the Repurchase Date to the Seller, regardless of the Purchased Securities Market Value at that time.

It is worth noting, however, that the Seller retains (i) the right of substitution of Securities pursuant to Paragraph 6B (below); and (ii) the right to receive Income with respect to the Purchased Securities.

> (ii) Buyer, Seller and Custodian agree that all Purchased Securities and cash held in Buyer's Account from time to time will be held by Custodian as agent of Buyer, that Custodian will take such actions with respect to Buyer's Account and any Purchased Securities and cash therein as Buyer shall direct, and that in no event shall any consent of Seller be required for the taking of any such action by Custodian. Buyer hereby covenants that Buyer will not instruct Custodian to deliver any Securities to any person other than Seller until an Event of Default has occurred as to which Seller is the defaulting party. The foregoing covenant is for Seller's benefit only and shall not constitute a limitation on Buyer's right at any time to instruct Custodian and Custodian's obligation to act upon such instructions. Custodian shall not be liable for any Losses (as defined in paragraph 9A) incurred or sustained by Buyer, Seller or any third party as a result of Custodian transferring any Purchased Securities or cash in Buyer's Account pursuant to Buyer's instructions (whether or not subsequent to receipt of a Notice of Default) and shall have no further obligation or responsibility to Seller or Buyer under this Custodial Undertaking with respect to any Purchased Securities or cash transferred from Buyer's Account.

Paragraph 5E(ii) states that the Custodian is the agent of the Buyer with respect to the Purchased Securities and cash held in the Buyer's Account, and thus the Buyer and the Custodian have an agency relationship. Accordingly the Buyer may instruct the Custodian to take certain actions with respect to the Buyer's Account. The Buyer covenants, however, that it will not instruct the Custodian to take out any of the Purchased Securities for anyone (including the Buyer) other than to the Seller pursuant to the Instructions.

It is important to recognise that, even though the Buyer has covenanted not to instruct the Custodian to transfer the Purchased Securities, the Custodian is still obligated to follow the directions of the Buyer and to transfer the Purchased Securities if directed by the Buyer to do so. The Buyer would be in breach of his covenant, however, and the Seller would have a cause of action against the Buyer for damages.

TRI-PARTY CUSTODIAL AGREEMENTS

The Custodian also has no future duties to either the Buyer or the Seller once the Purchased Securities or cash have been transferred from the Buyer's Account to the Buyer or a third party. This is logical, because there are now no securities to hold by the Custodian. The Custodian is not liable for any Losses suffered by any party due to the Custodian following the Buyer's Instructions, except where such Losses arise out of the Custodian's gross negligence, bad faith or wilful misconduct.

> (iii) Any instruction to Custodian to transfer Purchased Securities or cash from Buyer's Account during the term of a Transaction shall be set forth in a written notice in substantially the form attached hereto as Appendix I. Buyer shall deliver such notice to a Vice President or above in Custodian's Broker Dealer Services Division and shall send Seller a copy of same. Custodian shall, as promptly as practicable under the circumstances, act in accordance with such instructions; it being understood and agreed that Custodian shall have no liability for its inability to comply with Buyer's instructions if the rules or systems of the Book-Entry System and/or applicable Clearing Corporation prevent Custodian from transferring Purchased Securities from Buyer's Account. Buyer shall pay to Custodian all applicable fees, costs and charges associated with such transfer from Buyer's Account.

Transfers of Eligible Securities from the Buyer's Account, other than as part of a repurchase or margin maintenance transfer, are unusual and should take place only upon the occurrence of an Event of Default with respect to the Seller. The Custodial Agreement requires the Buyer to provide instructions of such a transfer in substantially the same form as Appendix I and to copy the Seller.

Although the Seller is normally liable for any fees and expenses of the Custodian, the Buyer is required to pay any fees, costs or charges required with a transfer made at the Buyer's direction.

> **F. No Lien or Pledge by Custodian.** Custodian agrees that Purchased Securities shall not be subject to any security interest, lien or right of setoff by Custodian or any third party claiming through Custodian and Custodian shall not pledge, encumber, hypothecate, transfer, dispose of, or otherwise grant any third party an interest in, any Purchased Securities.

Although the Custodian has custody and possession of the Purchased Securities, it is not permitted to use the Purchased Securities in any manner. For example, the Custodian is not permitted to lend, sell, rehypothecate or use the Purchased Securities in any way. Although this clause would appear to be self-evident, broker-dealers typically have such rights with respect to Securities that they hold on behalf of their customers.

> **G. Payment of Income.** Until such time that Custodian shall receive a Notice of Default from Buyer pursuant to Paragraph 8, Custodian shall credit to Seller's Account

> Income received by Custodian. After receipt of such Notice of Default from Buyer, Custodian shall credit to Buyer's Account Income received by Custodian.

Under Paragraph 5 of the Master Repurchase Agreement Income is required to be passed through by the Seller to the Buyer. Paragraph 5G of the Custodial Agreement has a substantively similar provision. The Seller is assured of receiving the Income, because of the Custodian's control over receipt of the Income. In fact, the Custodian's receipt and control of the Income (ensuring that such Income is passed through to the Seller) is one of the reasons parties enter into a Custodial Agreement. However, where the Custodian receives a Notice of Default from the Buyer, the Custodian will credit the Buyer's Account with the Income that it receives.

> **H. Confirmations.** Custodian shall provide Buyer and Seller with confirmation statements reflecting Purchased Securities and cash positions in Buyer's Account on each Business Day or as otherwise may be requested by Buyer. Buyer and Seller shall promptly review all such confirmation statements and shall promptly advise Custodian of any error, omission or inaccuracy in such statements. Custodian shall undertake to correct any errors, failures or omissions that are reported to Custodian by Buyer or Seller. Any such corrections shall be reflected on subsequent confirmation statements.

The Custodian is obligated to provide confirmation statements to both the Buyer and the Seller on every Business Day that reflect the Purchased Securities in the Buyer's Account. The Custodian is also obligated to provide a confirmation statement every Business Day to the Buyer showing the cash positions in the Buyer's accounts.

The Buyer and Seller are promptly to review the confirmation statements, and report any errors, omissions or inaccuracies. As opposed to issuing a revised confirmation statement upon correction of any errors, the Custodian will make sure that corrections and adjustments appear on future confirmation statements.

> **I. Deliveries by Custodian.** Subject to this Custodial Undertaking, all transfers of Securities or cash by Custodian to Buyer from Buyer's Account shall be made to Buyer by delivery to the account(s) designated in Schedule III, as may be amended from time to time by delivery to and receipt by Custodian of a new Schedule III.

Although Paragraph 5I is self-evident, it is important that the Buyer maintains an accurate Schedule III. Because of the high use of computer technology and automation in the custodial process, delays in the transfer of Purchased Securities and cash can occur if the Buyer does not keep the information in Schedule III up to date.

TRI-PARTY CUSTODIAL AGREEMENTS

The margin maintenance and substitution provisions of the Master Repurchase Agreement are the most difficult provisions to apply. The Custodian's experience in executing the substitution and margin maintenance provisions is one of the prime reasons the parties enter into a Custodial Agreement.

For purposes of illustrating the margin maintenance and substitution provisions below, assume that there is only one repurchase transaction outstanding between the Buyer and the Seller. The Seller is selling US Treasury Securities with a Market Value on the Purchase Date of US$10,000,000. The Purchase Price is US$9,800,000. The Price Rate is 5 per cent and the Repurchase Date is 30 days later. The Repurchase Price is US$9,840,833.

Paragraph 6

> **6. VALUATION AND SUBSTITUTIONS OF SECURITIES**
> **A. Valuation of Securities.** At the opening of each Business Day during which a Transaction subject to this Custodial Undertaking shall remain outstanding, Custodian shall determine the Margin Value of all Purchased Securities in Buyer's Account.

The daily calculation of Margin Value is an important duty of the Custodian, in order to ensure that the margin maintenance provisions are followed. In fact, Paragraph 6 of the Custodial Agreement and Paragraphs 4 and 9 of the Master Repurchase Agreement should yield the same transfers of Purchased Securities. Margin Value is equal to the Market Value of the Purchased Securities divided by the applicable Margin Percentage. For example, assume that the Purchased Securities have a Market Value of US$10,000,000 and the Margin Percentage is 102 per cent. The Margin Value for those Purchased Securities would be US$9,803,921.57.

> **(i) Margin Deficit.** In the event the Purchase Price of outstanding Transactions is greater than the aggregate Margin Value of all Purchased Securities in Buyer's Account, Custodian shall so notify Seller prior to 2:00 p.m. On the date of any such notice, Seller shall promptly transfer to Buyer's Account additional Eligible Securities ("Additional Eligible Securities") such that, after transfer to Buyer's Account, the aggregate Margin Value of all Purchased Securities (including Additional Eligible Securities) in Buyer's Account equals or exceeds the Purchase Price of outstanding Transactions. If Seller fails to transfer an appropriate amount of Additional Eligible Securities on the date of any such notice, Custodian shall notify Buyer and Seller and await further instructions from Buyer. All Additional Eligible Securities transferred to Buyer's Account shall be deemed to be Purchased Securities.

Paragraph 6A(i) is substantively similar to Paragraph 4(a) of the Master Repurchase Agreement, although the formula for calculating a margin transfer is different. In the event that the Purchase Price is greater than the aggregate Margin Value of the Purchased Securities in the Buyer's Account, a margin deficit exists under the Custodial Agreement. Where this happens, the Custodian is to notify the Seller of such deficit by 2.00 p.m. The Seller is obligated to transfer Additional Eligible Securities equal to the deficit by close of business on the date that the notice is given. If the Seller fails to make such transfer, the Custodian is to notify the Buyer and await additional instructions. Note that the Buyer may not even be aware of such a margin deficit and is relying upon the Custodian to correct such deficit. Also, the Seller is prohibited from transferring cash to eliminate the deficit, although it would have been permitted to do so under the Master Repurchase Agreement. Instead, the Seller may transfer only Additional Eligible Securities.

The calculations for a margin transfer under the Custodial Agreement will yield a different transfer than calculations under the Master Repurchase Agreement because the formulas for the two are different. For example, under the Custodial Agreement, if the Purchase Price of the Securities were US$9,800,000 and the Market Value is US$10,000,000, the Seller would not be obligated to make a margin transfer because the Purchase Price is less than the Margin Value of US$9,803,921.57. In contrast, under the Master Repurchase Agreement the margin transfer would have been US$37,649.66 under the same facts (see sample calculation on page 188). This difference is due primarily to the Master Repurchase Agreement utilising the Repurchase Price rather than the Purchase Price, which is used in the Custodial Agreement. If the calculation in the Custodial Agreement had used the Repurchase Price instead, then the margin transfer would have been US$36,912 (Repurchase Price of US$9,840,833 less the Margin Value of US$9,803,921), much closer to the margin transfer of US$37,649.66 under the Master Repurchase Agreement.

> **(ii) Margin Excess.** In the event the then aggregate Margin Value of Purchased Securities in Buyer's Account shall exceed the Purchase Price of outstanding Transactions (such excess amount, the "Margin Excess"), Custodian shall so notify Seller and, upon Oral or Written Instructions from Seller, Custodian shall transfer Purchased Securities from Buyer's Account to Seller's Account having a Market Value equal to the Margin Excess. Buyer hereby irrevocably authorizes Custodian to accept the Oral or Written Instructions of Seller identifying the specific Purchased Securities to be released from Buyer's Account pursuant hereto. Upon transfer from Buyer's Account, released Securities shall cease to be Purchased Securities for all purposes hereunder.

Paragraph 6A(ii) is substantively similar to Paragraph 4(b) of the Master Repurchase Agreement, although the formula for calculating a margin transfer is different. In the event that the Purchase Price is less than the aggregate Margin Value of the Purchased Securities in the Buyer's Account, a margin excess exists under the Custodial Agreement and the Custodian must notify the Seller. Note that there is no express deadline to notify the Seller and that the Buyer is not notified of the margin excess.

The Seller is to instruct the Custodian to make a transfer of Purchased Securities from the Buyer's Account to the Seller's Account equal to such margin excess. The Buyer is deemed to have authorised the Custodian to make this transfer. Upon receipt of instructions from the Seller the Custodian is to make the transfer. Note that, in contrast to the Master Repurchase Agreement, the margin excess cannot be satisfied by the Buyer transferring cash.

The calculations for a margin transfer under the Custodial Agreement will yield slightly different transfers because the formula for making the calculations are different. For example, assume that the Market Value of the Purchase Securities were US$10,137,649.33, leading to a Margin Value of 9,938,871.89. Assuming a Purchase Price of US$9,800,000 the Buyer would make a margin transfer of Purchased Securities equal to US$138,871.89 to the Seller.

In contrast, under the Master Repurchase Agreement, the margin transfer would have been US$100,000 using the same facts. The difference is due primarily to the Master Repurchase Agreement utilising the Repurchase Price under Paragraph 4(b) instead of the Purchase Price, which is used in the Custodial Agreement. If the calculation in the Custodial Agreement had used the Repurchase Price, then the margin transfer would have been US$98,038 (Margin Value of US$9,938,871 less the Repurchase Price of US$9,840,833), much closer to the margin transfer of US$100,000 under the Master Repurchase Agreement.

> **B. <u>Substitutions of Purchased Securities</u>.** Buyer hereby authorizes Custodian, upon Oral or Written Instructions from Seller, to transfer Purchased Securities to Seller against transfer to Buyer's Account of substitute Eligible Securities ("Substitute Eligible Securities") provided that Custodian determines that the aggregate Margin Value of Purchase Securities (including Substitute Eligible Securities) in Buyer's Account after such substitution equals or exceeds the Purchase Price of outstanding Transactions. All Substitute Eligible Securities transferred to Buyer's Account shall be deemed to be Purchased Securities.

The Buyer expressly authorises the Custodian to substitute Purchased Securities upon the instruction by the Seller to the Custodian to do so. The only caveat, of course, is that the aggregate Margin Value of the Securities after the substitution must be equal to, or greater than, the Purchase Price.

The consent and substitution requirements are substantively similar to those found in Paragraph 9(b) of the Master Repurchase Agreement. Although the protections afforded to the Buyer are the same, they are determined differently. In the Master Repurchase Agreement the Market Values of the Securities substituted are compared with the Market Value of the Purchased Securities. In contrast, the Margin Values of the Securities are compared with the Custodial Agreement.

Paragraph 7

> **7. REPURCHASE DATE**
>
> On the Repurchase Date for any Transaction, subject to Paragraph 8 hereof and Paragraph 11 of the Master Repurchase Agreement, Buyer hereby irrevocably instructs Custodian to tender to Seller the Purchased Securities with respect to such Transaction and to transfer such Purchased Securities from Buyer's Account to Seller's Account. Seller hereby irrevocably instructs Custodian at the time Purchased Securities are

> transferred to Seller's Account to make payment to Buyer of the Repurchase Price by debiting cash from Seller's Account and crediting cash to Buyer's Account. If on the Repurchase Date Seller's Account does not contain sufficient cash available to repurchase all Purchased Securities with respect to any Transactions, Custodian shall notify Seller and Buyer and Seller shall give Custodian Oral or Written Instructions identifying which Purchased Securities, if any, are to be repurchased and the Repurchase Price.

The Buyer in Paragraph 7 irrevocably authorises the Custodian to transfer the Purchased Securities from the Buyer's Account to the Seller's Account on the Repurchase Date. The Seller also irrevocably authorises the Custodian to transfer the Repurchase Price from the Seller's Account to the Buyer's Account.

In the event that the cash in the Seller's Account is less than the Repurchase Price, the Custodian is to notify the Buyer and the Seller of the shortfall. The Seller is then to direct the Custodian to complete the repurchase by designating which Purchased Securities, if any, are to be repurchased and the revised Repurchase Price. As a practical matter such a shortfall would not occur. Although the Custodian is not obligated to do so, the Custodian would typically advance funds to the Seller sufficient to allow the Seller to repurchase the Purchased Securities at the Repurchase Price if there was insufficient cash in the Seller's Account.

It is worth noting that the Buyer may prefer not to complete the Transaction and may want to retain the Purchased Securities. The Custodial Agreement, however, does give the Buyer the right partially to execute the repurchase transaction.

Even though the Custodial Agreement authorises both the Seller and the Custodian partially to execute the repurchase, if necessary, the Seller's failure to tender the entire Repurchase Price would constitute an Event of Default under the Master Repurchase Agreement.

Paragraph 8

> **8. DEFAULT**
> In the event that Buyer or Seller delivers a Notice of Default to Custodian, Custodian shall notify the defaulting party of its receipt of such Notice of Default and act in accordance with the instructions of the non-defaulting party with respect to such non-defaulting party's rights pursuant to Paragraph 11 of the Master Repurchase Agreement. Custodian may fully rely without further inquiry on the statements set forth in such Notice of Default. In addition, Buyer and Seller acknowledge and agree that the provisions of Paragraph 11 of the Master Repurchase Agreement shall be fully effective with respect to all Transactions entered into between them, irrespective of whether such Transactions are entered into in connection with this Custodial Undertaking, directly between Buyer and Seller or otherwise.

Upon the occurrence of an Event of Default under the Master Repurchase Agreement the non-defaulting party is to deliver a Notice of Default to the Custodian. Although the Agreement does not provide a form to be used, the Notice of Default should detail the specific Event of Default that has occurred under Paragraph 11 of the Master Repurchase

Agreement. It is important that a non-defaulting party can give a Notice of Default without necessarily exercising its remedies under Paragraph 11.

Upon delivering a Notice of Default to the Custodian the Custodian is required to act in accordance with instructions from the non-defaulting party with respect to the non-defaulting party's rights under Paragraph 11 of the Master Repurchase Agreement. The non-defaulting party is thus free to exercise its rights under the Master Repurchase Agreement as if it had not entered into the Custodial Agreement.

For the Seller this would mean that it could compel the Custodian to deliver the Purchased Securities upon tender of the Repurchase Price. Because the Purchased Securities are in the possession of the Custodian, the Seller will be assured of being able to repurchase the Securities by tendering the Repurchase Price. Without the Custodian the Seller would be dependent upon the goodwill of the Buyer to tender the Purchased Securities against the Repurchase Price.

For a non-defaulting Buyer this would mean that it could take possession and control of the Purchased Securities in order to retain or liquidate them pursuant to Paragraph 11 of the Master Repurchase Agreement. Upon delivery of the Notice of Default the Buyer, as a non-defaulting party, is given additional rights under the Custodial Agreement in order to take possession of the Purchased Securities in its Account. First and most importantly, if the Buyer is the non-defaulting party, the Buyer may give instructions to the Custodian to transfer the Purchased Securities from the Buyer's Account to the Buyer or to a third party (see Paragraph 5E(ii)). Second, the Buyer can request that the Custodian make payments of Income to the Buyer's Account instead of the Seller's Account (see Paragraph 5G). Third, upon termination of the Custodial Agreement the Buyer can request that the Seller transfer the Purchased Securities to the Buyer or a third party (see Paragraph 10).

Unfortunately, the Custodial Agreement does not give the Buyer the right to compel the Custodian to deliver the Repurchase Price to the Buyer upon tender of the Purchased Securities. The Custodian does not have rights to cash or any Eligible Securities in the Seller's Account. In fact, the Custodial Agreement provides no restrictions on the Seller's right to transfer cash or Eligible Securities out of the Seller's Account.

There are no express Events of Default with respect to the Custodian's performance under the Custodial Agreement. Presumably, a Seller or Buyer could exercise its common law rights under the laws of the State of New York with respect to pursuing its rights and collecting damages from the Custodian under the Custodial Agreement.

Paragraph 9

9. CONCERNING CUSTODIAN
A. Limitation of Liability; Indemnification. Custodian shall not be liable for any costs, expenses, damages, liabilities or claims, including reasonable fees of counsel (collectively, "Losses"), resulting from its action or inaction in connection with this Custodial Undertaking, including Losses which are incurred by reason of any action or inaction by the Book-Entry System, any Clearing Corporation or Trust Receipt Issuer, or their successors or nominees, except for those Losses arising out of Custodian's gross negligence, bad faith or wilful misconduct. In no event shall Custodian be liable to Buyer, Seller or any third party for special, indirect or consequential damages, or lost profits or loss of business, arising under or in connection with this Custodial Undertaking.

Because of the high volume of Transactions and relatively low fees involved in being a custodian, the Custodian insists that it will not be liable for any costs, expenses, damages, liabilities or claims based upon its acting negligently or incorrectly in its role as a Custodian. The Custodian also insists that it will not be liable for Losses caused by the Book-Entry System, a Clearing Corporation or a Trust Receipt Issuer. For a Custodian to incur any liability for Losses a party would be required to prove that the Losses occurred as a result of the Custodian's gross negligence, bad faith or wilful misconduct, an extremely high threshold to establish liability. In addition, even if the Custodian is held liable for Losses under the Custodial Agreement, the Custodian cannot be held liable for special, indirect or consequential damages, or lost profits or loss of business.

> Custodian may, with respect to questions of law, apply for and obtain the advice and opinion of counsel, and shall be fully protected with respect to anything done or omitted by it in good faith in conformity with such reasonable advice or opinion. Buyer and Seller agree, jointly and severally, to indemnify Custodian and to hold it harmless against any and all Losses (including claims by Buyer or Seller) which are sustained by Custodian as a result of Custodian's action or inaction in connection with this Custodial Undertaking, except those Losses arising out of Custodian's gross negligence, bad faith or wilful misconduct.

In particularly difficult, complex or ambiguous situations with respect to questions of law under the Custodial Agreement, the Custodian is permitted to obtain legal advice. Following such advice will further insulate the Custodian from liability for Losses, because it would be evidence that the Losses did not result from the Custodian's gross negligence, bad faith or wilful misconduct. To add insult to injury, the Custodian, pursuant to Paragraph 9E, is probably entitled to reimbursement by the Seller for any legal costs incurred under Paragraph 9A, assuming that the Custodian's legal costs are characterised as "out of pocket" expenses under the Custodial Agreement.

In addition to not being liable for Losses suffered by others, the Buyer and Seller also agree jointly and severally to indemnify the Custodian for any Losses that the Custodian suffers. The only exception is if such Losses were incurred as a result of the Custodian's gross negligence, bad faith or wilful misconduct. Many parties are willing to indemnify the Custodian for any Losses that the Custodian causes itself; they are extremely reluctant, however, to be liable for Losses caused by their counterparty. Yet parties may find that attempting to negotiate almost any clause of the Custodial Agreement with the Custodian will prove to be slow, expensive, and probably futile, given the Custodian's strong negotiating position.

> It is expressly understood and agreed that Custodian's right to indemnification hereunder shall be enforceable against Buyer and Seller directly, without any obligation to first proceed against any third party for whom they may act, and irrespective of any rights or recourse that Buyer or Seller may have against any such third party. This indemnity shall be a continuing obligation of Buyer and Seller notwithstanding the termination of any Transactions or of this Custodial Undertaking.

Paragraph 9A clarifies that the Seller and Buyer are required to indemnify the Custodian with respect to Losses that occurred under the Custodial Agreement, even if such Losses were caused by third parties for whom the Buyer or Seller was acting.

The last sentence in Paragraph 9A is a survivability clause. The indemnification provided to the Custodian will continue even after termination of the Custodial Agreement. Even if the Custodian suffers Losses several years after termination of the Custodial Agreement, the obligation of the Seller and the Buyer to indemnify the Custodian will still be applicable.

> **B. No Guaranty by Custodian.** It is expressly agreed and acknowledged by Buyer and Seller that Custodian has made no determination regarding Buyer's or Seller's ability to perform their respective obligations in connection with Transactions and is not guaranteeing performance of or assuming any liability for the obligations of Buyer or Seller hereunder nor is it assuming any credit risk associated with Transactions hereunder, which liabilities and risks are the responsibility of Buyer and Seller; further, it is expressly agreed that Custodian is not undertaking to make credit available to Seller or Buyer to enable it to complete Transactions hereunder.

By executing the Custodial Agreement some parties may assume that its counterparty must have the wherewithal to perform, or the Custodian, a large and sophisticated participant in the repo market, would not have executed the Custodial Agreement. Paragraph 9B clarifies, however, that the Custodian has made no such determination.

The Custodian also clarifies in Paragraph 9B that (i) it is not guaranteeing the performance of either the Seller or the Buyer; (ii) it is not assuming any credit risk associated with the Transactions; and (iii) it is not undertaking to extend credit to either the Buyer or the Seller to complete a Transaction. Although these clarifications would appear to be self-evident, they reflect concerns of the Custodian to reduce its risk of Losses.

> **C. No Duty of Inquiry.** Without limiting the generality of the foregoing, Custodian shall be under no obligation to inquire into, and shall not be liable for:
> (i) The validity of the issue of any Securities purchased or sold by or for Buyer or Seller, the legality of the purchase or sale or the validity or enforceability of any Trust Receipt received by Custodian hereunder;
> (ii) The due authority of any Authorized Person to act on behalf of Buyer or Seller with respect to cash or Securities held in Buyer's Account or Seller's Account; or
> (iii) The due authority of Buyer, Seller or any entities for which Buyer acts to purchase, sell or hold any particular Security hereunder.

In an effort to limit its liability for Losses further, the Custodian disclaims a duty of inquiry with respect to several key concerns. First, it not responsible for inquiring as to whether an issue of Securities was valid. Although the Custodian would appear to be the party best able to make such a determination, given its activity in the securities markets, such a duty goes beyond the nature and scope of the custodial relationship.

Second, the Custodian is permitted to rely on Schedule II in relation to Authorized Persons. Requiring the Custodian to inquire into the actual due authority of an individual listed as an Authorized Person would impose an unreasonable burden on the Custodian.

Finally, the Custodian is not required to inquire into a Buyer's (whether as principal or agent) or a Seller's authority to enter into a particular Transaction. Again, such a duty would be onerous on the Custodian.

> **D. Securities in Default.** Custodian shall not be under any duty or obligation to take action to effect collection of any amount if the Securities upon which such amount is payable are in default, or if payment is refused after due demand or presentation, unless and until (i) it shall be directed to take such action by Written Instructions and (ii) it shall be assured to its satisfaction of reimbursement of its costs and expenses in connection with any such action.

It is possible that an Eligible Security held by a Buyer in the Buyer's Account may go into default. (Given the creditworthiness of the US Treasury and Agency Securities that are typically transferred under the Custodial Agreement, such defaults are probably unlikely.) The Custodian, however, is under no duty on its own to pursue collection of any amounts owing under the Eligible Security. The Custodian can pursue collection, however, provided that it has received Written Instructions to do so and that the Buyer or the Seller has assured the Custodian that it will be reimbursed for any costs or expenses incurred in pursuing collection.

> **E. Custodian Fee.** Custodian shall be entitled to receive and Seller agrees to pay to Custodian such compensation as may be agreed upon from time to time between Custodian and Seller and Custodian's out-of-pocket expenses.

The Seller is responsible for the Custodian's fees and out-of-pocket expenses. The Buyer, in fact, is probably unaware as to how much those expenses are. If the relationship between the Buyer, the Seller and the Custodian becomes contentious, it is likely that the Custodian will begin to incur additional out-of-pocket expenses, such as legal fees, as it attempts to meet its custodial and agency duties. If such contention results in litigation, these out-of-pocket expenses incurred by the Custodian can quickly dwarf any fees payable to it.

> **F. Reliance on Oral/Written Instructions.** Custodian shall be entitled to rely upon any Written Instruction or Oral Instruction received by Custodian and reasonably believed by Custodian to be delivered by an Authorized Person. Buyer and Seller agree to forward to Custodian Written Instructions confirming any and all Oral Instructions in such manner that such Written Instructions are received by Custodian by the close of business of the same day that such Oral Instructions are given to Custodian. Buyer and Seller agree that the fact that [if] such confirming Written Instructions are not received or that contrary Written Instructions are received by Custodian shall in no way affect the validity or enforceability of the transactions previously authorized and effected by Custodian.

Because business in the repo market is frequently and regularly entered into over the telephone, Paragraph 9F clarifies that the Custodian is permitted to rely upon either Written or Oral Instructions given by the parties. Paragraph 9F requires the relevant party to follow up with Written Instructions confirming any earlier Oral Instructions. The paragraph further clarifies, however, that failure to provide such Written Instructions will not affect the validity or enforceability of the Custodian's reliance on the earlier Oral Instructions.

> **G. Reliance on Pricing Services.** Custodian is authorized to utilize any generally recognized pricing information service (including brokers and dealers of Securities) in order to perform its valuation responsibilities hereunder, and Seller and Buyer agree to hold Custodian harmless from and against any Losses incurred as a result of errors or omissions of any such pricing information service, broker or dealer.

Failure to value Purchased Securities properly can result in serious problems. For example, the margin maintenance provisions may be improperly applied if there are errors in valuations, resulting in a party having fewer or more Securities than it is otherwise entitled to hold. Because of the possibility of Losses suffered due to inaccurate valuations, the Custodian is authorised under Paragraph 9G to rely on third-party pricing information that comes from a generally recognised pricing information service, such as Bloomberg, Reuters or Dow Jones, without incurring any liability for valuation errors caused by third parties.

> **H. Force Majeure.** Custodian shall not be responsible or liable for any failure or delay in the performance of its obligations under this Custodial Undertaking arising out of or caused, directly or indirectly, by circumstances beyond its reasonable control, including without limitation, acts of God, earthquakes, fires, floods, wars, civil or military disturbances, sabotage, epidemics, riots, loss or malfunctions of utilities, computer (hardware or software) or communications service, labor disputes, acts of civil or military authority, or governmental, judicial or regulatory actions; provided however, that Custodian shall use its best efforts to resume performance as promptly as practicable under the circumstances.

Although generally considered unlikely, a *force majeure* event can clearly affect the performance of a Custodian under the Custodial Agreement. For example, Custodians had serious difficulties in performing their custodial duties in the aftermath of the September 11 tragedy in 2001. The *force majeure* clause in Paragraph 9H is fairly typical of those found in finance contracts and protects the Custodian from liability for Losses incurred by others as a result of any delay or failure of the Custodian to perform because of a *force majeure* event.

> **I. No Additional Duties.** Custodian shall have no duties or responsibilities except such duties and responsibilities as are specifically set forth in this Custodial Undertaking, and no covenant or obligation shall be implied in this Custodial Undertaking against Custodian.

Although it may perhaps be viewed as overkill, Paragraph 9I reinforces the principle that a Custodian shall have no other duties and responsibilities than those expressly set out. It is also states that there are no implied covenants or obligations of the Custodian under the Custodial Agreement.

> **J. No Duty Regarding Derivatives.** If Buyer and Seller have selected Eligible Securities which derive all or a portion of their value from changes in the value of underlying securities, mortgages or other obligations, or one or more currencies, commodities, indices or other factors (hereinafter referred to as "Derivative Securities"), the parties understand that Custodian shall have no obligation to monitor whether any such Eligible Securities are also Derivative Securities. Accordingly, the parties agree that anything in the Custodial Undertaking to the contrary notwithstanding, it shall be Buyer's and Seller's responsibility to ensure that Eligible Securities do not include Derivative Securities unless they have otherwise agreed. Custodian shall have no liability whatsoever for any loss, damage or expense arising out of the ineligibility of Derivative Securities which are the subject of Transactions pursuant to this Custodial Undertaking.

There have been substantial disputes and litigation involving Derivative Securities. Derivative Securities often tend to perform in a volatile manner in the market, and such volatility and complexity have led to substantial losses being incurred by their holders. Paragraph 9J sets out that the Custodian has no special obligation to monitor or review the performance or price fluctuations of Purchased Securities that may also be characterised as Derivative Securities.

Paragraph 10

> **10. TERMINATION**
> Any of the parties hereto may terminate this Custodial Undertaking by giving to the other parties a notice in writing specifying the date of such termination, which shall be not less than thirty (30) days after the date of giving of such notice. Upon termination hereof, Seller shall pay to Custodian such compensation as may be due to Custodian as of the date of such termination, and shall likewise reimburse Custodian for any disbursements and expenses made or incurred by Custodian and payable or reimbursable hereunder. If Buyer does not provide Written Instructions designating a successor custodian prior to the termination date, Custodian shall, at Buyer's expense, continue to hold Purchased Securities and cash in Buyer's Account until the Repurchase Date with respect to each outstanding Transaction, or until it has received a Notice of Default in connection therewith, and Written Instructions with respect to delivery of such Purchased Securities. If Custodian has not received delivery instructions with respect to Purchased Securities and/or cash in Buyer's Account, Custodian may, in its sole discretion, hold Book-Entry Securities and Clearing Corporation Securities in escrow for the benefit of and at the expense of Buyer and deliver Physical Securities and cash to Buyer at the address provided below.

It is possible that either the Buyer, the Seller or the Custodian may want to terminate the

Custodial Agreement due to disagreements or dissatisfaction with the performance of one of the other parties under the Custodial Agreement. For example, a party may become dissatisfied with a Custodian's Margin Value calculations or its efficiency in processing Instructions. A party terminates the Custodial Agreement by giving no less than 30 days' notice to the other parties. The Seller, of course, is required to pay on the termination date any fees or expenses owing to the Custodian.

The principal issue that must be resolved upon the termination of the Custodial Agreement relates to the Buyer's Account. Permitting the Custodian to transfer the Purchased Securities to the Buyer upon termination of the Custodian Agreement by the Buyer would violate the purpose of the Custodial Agreement and could result in the Seller not being able to repurchase the Purchased Securities, because the Buyer has otherwise disposed of them. The concerns of the Seller are resolved by requiring that the Buyer designate a successor Custodian to hold the Buyer's Account. If the Buyer does not designate a new Custodian, the current Custodian, at the Buyer's expense, shall continue to hold each of the Purchased Securities until each of the Repurchase Dates has passed.

Paragraph 11

Paragraph 11 provides standard boilerplate provisions found in most finance contracts.

> **11. MISCELLANEOUS**
> **A. Authorized Persons.** Buyer and Seller each agrees to furnish to Custodian a new Schedule II in the event that any Authorized Person ceases to be an Authorized Person or in the event that other or additional Authorized Persons are appointed and authorized. Until such new Schedule II is received, Custodian shall be fully protected in acting under the provisions of this Custodial Undertaking upon Oral Instructions or Written Instructions from a person reasonably believed to be an Authorized Person as set forth in the last delivered Schedule II.

Paragraph 11A permits the Custodian to follow instructions provided by an Authorized Person until a revised Schedule II is received from a party. Because an Authorized Person can direct the transfer and disposition of Securities and cash, the Buyer and the Seller should be diligent in keeping Schedule II current.

> **B. Access to Books and Records.** Upon reasonable request, Buyer and Seller shall have access to Custodian's books and records maintained in connection with this Custodial Undertaking during Custodian's normal business hours. Upon reasonable request, copies of any such books and records shall be provided to Buyer or Seller at its expense.

To resolve disputes with both the Custodian and the other party, a party may need more than the information delivered periodically by the Custodian. Paragraph 11B provides a Buyer or a Seller the right to review the Custodian's books and records, and to obtain copies of any relevant portions. The requester of such information, however, will be required to pay for any expenses incurred by the Custodian to provide copies of the relevant information.

> **C. Invalidity of any Provision.** In case any provision in or obligation under this Custodial Undertaking shall be invalid, illegal or unenforceable in any jurisdiction, the validity, legality and enforceability of the remaining provisions or obligations shall not in any way be affected or impaired thereby, and if any provision is inapplicable to any person or circumstances, it shall nevertheless remain applicable to all other persons and circumstances.

Paragraph 11C is typically referred to as a severability or separability provision. It is possible that a court may find a certain provision to be unenforceable, for example, because such provision violates public policy. Some courts have invalidated an entire agreement or contract based on finding only one clause to be unenforceable. The severability clause is intended to clarify that the parties want the court to enforce the remainder of the Custodial Agreement, regardless of the unenforceability of a single provision.

> **D. Parties, Entire Agreement, Amendments.**
> (i) **The Custodial Undertaking.** Buyer, Seller, and Custodian agree that this Custodial Undertaking constitutes the entire agreement among the parties hereto with respect to Transactions subject to this Custodial Undertaking and may not be amended or modified in any manner except by a written agreement executed by the parties hereto.

Paragraph 11D(i) is a form of "integration" or "merger" clause. It provides that the Custodial Agreement will supersede any other arrangements with respect to Transactions subject to any Custodial Undertaking that the parties have entered into previously. The clause is intended to preclude disputes by providing that the Custodial Agreement is the controlling document with respect to any transfers of cash or Securities between the Buyer and the Seller, in the absence of any subsequent agreement between the parties to the contrary.

The clause also requires that any amendment or modification to the Custodial Agreement be in writing and executed by all three parties.

> (ii) **The Custodial Undertaking and the Master Repurchase Agreement.** Buyer and Seller acknowledge and agree that the Master Repurchase Agreement in conjunction with this Custodial Undertaking represents the entire agreement between Buyer and Seller with respect to Transactions. Buyer and Seller acknowledge and agree that Custodian is not party to the Master Repurchase Agreement.

Paragraph 11D(ii) is another form of integration or merger clause. The clause protects the Custodian from any liability under the Master Repurchase Agreement by expressly stating that the Custodian is not a party to that agreement.

> **E. Binding Agreement.** This Custodial Undertaking shall extend to and shall be binding upon the parties hereto, and their respective successors and assigns; provided however, that this Custodial Undertaking shall not be assignable by any party without the written consent of the other parties.

The parties may not assign the Custodial Agreement to a third party without the consent of the other two non-transferring parties. The prohibition against assignments is important, because a non-transferring party may have concerns about the third-party transferee. For example, a non-transferring party may not have the necessary credit approvals to engage in repurchase transactions with the third party. It may even be precluded by statute from dealing with certain types of entities.

> **F. Applicable Law/Jurisdiction.** This Custodial Undertaking shall be construed in accordance with the laws of the State of New York without regard to the conflict of laws principles thereof. The parties hereby consent to the jurisdiction of a state or federal court situated in New York City, New York, in connection with any dispute arising hereunder. The parties hereby waive their right to trial by jury in any proceeding involving, directly or indirectly, any matter in any way arising out of, related to, or connected with, this Custodial Undertaking.

The Custodial Agreement is to be governed by New York law. New York law (including the case law interpreting its provisions) is considered to be the most sophisticated and relevant for enforcing and interpreting finance contracts such as the Custodial Agreement. As explained in Chapter 2 (page 19), New York courts will enforce the selection of New York law. If both parties agree in advance to submit to New York jurisdiction (which is the case here in this clause), New York courts will also agree to adjudicate disputes, even if the Transactions and the parties have no relationship with the State of New York. The parties also waive trial by jury, because large financial institutions believe that juries are not appropriate for deciding legal disputes with their customers or counterparties. They believe that a judge will have a better grasp of the sophisticated arguments involved in financial agreement litigation than a jury. In addition, they understand that a judge will apply the relevant law, however sympathetic he or she might feel toward the plaintiff. A jury might be tempted to downgrade legal precedents in order to reach a verdict that they think is just.

> **G. Waiver of Immunity.** To the extent that in any jurisdiction any party may now or hereafter be entitled to claim, for itself or its assets, immunity from suit, execution, attachment (before or after judgment) or other legal process, each party irrevocably agrees not to claim, and it hereby waives, such immunity in connection with this Custodial Undertaking.

Foreign jurisdictions and even US municipalities may try to claim immunity from a lawsuit upon suffering Losses under the Custodial Agreement, thus arguing, for example, that they did not have to make a large margin maintenance payment because the agreement was not enforceable. Each party agrees not to claim sovereign immunity and waives any such rights. Although a party may waive such rights, a court may consider such a waiver to be a violation of public policy and refuse to enforce the provision. If a party is worried about such a result, it should consider obtaining a legal opinion from the party at the execution of the Custodial Agreement, opining that such a waiver is enforceable.

> **H. Headings and References.** The headings and captions in this Custodial Undertaking are for reference only and shall not affect the construction or interpretation of any of its provisions.

Headings and other non-operative references are added to assist in reading the Custodial Agreement. In construing or interpreting the Custodial Agreement Paragraph 11H provides that parties may not interpret a particular provision by referencing any heading or other non-operative references in the Custodial Agreement.

> **I. Counterparts.** This Custodial Undertaking may be executed in any number of counterparts, each of which shall be deemed to be an original, but such counterparts shall, together, constitute only one instrument.

Historically, there has been concern that the execution of an agreement might not be valid if parties signed different signature pages, meaning that the signatures of both parties did not end up on the same page. Because of Paragraph 11I, however, parties may agree to execute an agreement on different signature pages, making it simpler to obtain all the necessary signatures. This often happens when execution takes place by fax or by courier.

> **J. Inconsistency with Master Repurchase Agreement.** In the event of any inconsistency between the terms and conditions of the Master Repurchase Agreement and this Custodial Undertaking with respect to the rights, duties or obligations of Custodian and Transactions subject to this Custodial Undertaking, the terms and conditions of this Custodial Undertaking shall govern.

Although this clause appears among the miscellaneous boilerplate provisions, its importance cannot be overemphasised. Theoretically, the transfer of Purchased Securities between the parties should be identical, regardless of whether a Custodial Agreement is entered into. However, as shown in Paragraph 6 with respect to the margin maintenance provisions, there will probably be inconsistencies between the two agreements. Because of these potential inconsistencies the parties agree that the terms of the Custodial Agreement will prevail. This would prevent a party from declaring an Event of Default, for example under the Master

Repurchase Agreement, which was caused by an inconsistency between the Master Repurchase Agreement and the Custodial Agreement.

> **K. Notices.** Any notice authorized or required by this Custodial Undertaking shall be sufficiently given if addressed to the receiving party and hand delivered or sent by mail, telex or facsimile to the individuals at the addresses specified in Schedule IV or to such other person or persons as the receiving party may from time to time designate in writing. Such notice shall be effective upon receipt.

Notice provisions are generally underrated in importance. Failure to understand how – or to whom – notice is to be given can compromise a party's rights under the Custodial Agreement. For example, failure to deliver a Notice of Default properly to a Custodian may result in the non-defaulting party being unable to exercise its remedies. This can result in several days' delays as the parties determine when proper notice was given, if at all.

> **L. Confidentiality.** The parties hereto agree not to disclose to any other party and to keep confidential the terms and conditions of this Custodial Undertaking (including fee arrangements) and any amendment, supplement or Schedule hereto. In the event that any party hereto breaches any provision of this section, any other party shall be entitled to temporary and permanent injunctive relief against the breaching party without the necessity of proving actual damages. Notwithstanding the foregoing, Custodian may disclose Buyer's or Seller's name, address, securities position and other information to the extent required by law, the rules of any stock exchange or regulatory or self-regulatory organization or any order or decree of any court or administrative body that is binding on Custodian or any Clearing Corporation or the terms of the organizational documents of the issuer of any Security or the terms of any Security itself.

It is unclear why the terms of the Custodial Agreement should be confidential, given that such terms have nothing to do with what would seem to be the important part of the relationship, that is, the terms of a particular Transaction. The Custodian, however, may be concerned that it will be requested or required to provide the same negotiated provisions to other parties that it agreed to with the Buyer and the Seller. The Custodian may also have different fee scales that it charges customers, depending upon a party's size, creditworthiness and the amount of business that it does with the Custodian. Disclosing fee information may weaken a Custodian's negotiating position on other Custodial Agreement negotiations.

> **M. Parties Deemed Principals.** Unless the parties hereto execute and deliver a Custodial Agency Annex, attached as Exhibit II, pursuant to which the identity of all principals for whom any party may act in connection with this Custodial Undertaking is disclosed, each

> party shall be responsible for the performance of its obligations hereunder as a principal. However, the execution and delivery of a Custodial Agency Annex shall not relieve any party of its obligations hereunder except as provided by applicable law.

The Buyer and Seller are required to identify any parties in which the Buyer and Seller are acting as an agent; otherwise the Buyer and the Seller shall be deemed to be the principal when such party is acting on behalf of an undisclosed principal.

> IN WITNESS WHEREOF, the parties hereto have caused this Custodial Undertaking to be executed by their respective corporate officers, thereunto duly authorized, as of the _____ day of _____, 20___.
>
> By:_____   By:_____
> Title: Title:
>   **THE BANK OF NEW YORK**
>
> By:_____
> Title:

Upon execution of the Custodial Agreement a party should verify that the person executing the Custodial Agreement on behalf of its counterparty was authorised to do so. Generally, a party establishes such authorisation by providing an incumbency certificate or a signature page from its signature book.

The incumbency certificate is verification from the party's company secretary that the person executing the Custodial Agreement was authorised to do so. Often the certificate will also contain a specimen signature of the person signing the Custodial Agreement.

Typically, a bank will provide an extract from its signature book or a list of authorised signatories for the bank. The signature book will provide a specimen signature of each signatory plus a description of the types of documents that such person is authorised to sign.

Schedule I

> **SCHEDULE I**
>
> **ELIGIBLE SECURITIES**

The list of Eligible Securities can be done in several different ways. The following are three examples of how a list of Eligible Securities could be presented. The descriptions of Eligible Securities are much more cryptic than what one would normally see, for example, in the ISDA Credit Support Annex.

TRI-PARTY CUSTODIAL AGREEMENTS

EXAMPLE 1
SCHEDULE I
SCHEDULE OF ELIGIBLE SECURITIES

Custodial Undertaking in Connection with Master Repurchase Agreement dated as of _____, among _____ ("Buyer"), _____ ("Seller") and The Bank of New York.

	Yes/No	Margin		Yes/No	Margin		Yes/No	Margin
U.S. TREASURIES			**GNMA**			**PRIVATE LABELS MBS & CMOS**		
BILLS	___	___	TRUST RECEIPTS	___	___	MBS PASS THROUGHS	___	___
BONDS	___	___	GNMA I/II-SINGLE FAMILY	___	___	***CMO TYPES:***		
NOTES	___	___	GNMA I/II-OTHERS-FIXED RATE	___	___	RESIDUALS	___	___
STRIPS	___	___	GNMA I/II OTHERS-ADJUST. RATE	___	___	INVERSE IO FLOATERS	___	___
SYNTHETIC TREASURIES						IOETTES	___	___
(e.g.CATS,COUGRS,TIGRS)	___	___	**AGENCY MORTGAGE BACKS**			INTEREST ONLY (IO)	___	___
			TRUST RECEIPTS	___	___	PRINCIPAL ONLY (PO)	___	___
AGENCY DEBENTURES			PASS THROUGHS-FIXED RATE	___	___	INVERSE FLOATERS	___	___
FAMC (Fed Agriculture Mtge Corp)	___	___	PASS THROUGHS-ADJUST. RATE	___	___	SUPER FLOATERS	___	___
FCFAC (Farm Credit Finan. Asst.)	___	___	MBS STRIPS (IO,PO,RECOMB)	___	___	COMPANION FLOATERS	___	___
FFCB (Farm Credit System Banks)	___	___				SEQUENTIAL AND OTHER FLOATERS	___	___
FmHA (Farmers Home Admin.)	___	___	**AGENCY REMICS/CMOS**			PAC & OTHER SCHEDULED FLOATERS	___	___
FHLB (Federal Home Loan Banks)	___	___	***REMIC TYPES:***			Z BONDS	___	___
FHLMC (Federal Home Loan Mtge)	___	___	RESIDUALS	___	___	COMPANION BONDS	___	___
FICO (Financing Corporation)	___	___	INVERSE IO FLOATERS	___	___	SEQUENTIAL BONDS	___	___
FLBB (Federal Land Bank Bonds)	___	___	IOETTES	___	___	TAC BONDS	___	___
FNMA (Federal Nat'l Mtge Corp)	___	___	INTEREST ONLY (IO)	___	___	PAC & OTHER SCHEDULED BONDS	___	___
REFCO (Resolution Funding Corp)	___	___	PRINCIPAL ONLY (PO)	___	___			
SLMA (Student Loan Mtge Corp)	___	___	INVERSE FLOATERS	___	___	**ASSET BACKED SECURITIES**	___	___

A PRACTICAL GUIDE TO USING REPO MASTER AGREEMENTS

	Yes/No	Margin		Yes/No	Margin		Yes/No	Margin
TVA (Tennessee Valley Authority)			SUPER FLOATERS			CREDIT CARD & OTHER ASSET BACKS		
USPS (U.S. States Postal Service)			COMPANION FLOATERS					
AGENCY *STRUCTURED NOTES*			SEQUENTIAL AND OTHER FLOATERS			**CORPORATES**		
			PAC & OTHER SCHEDULED FLOATERS			CORPORATE BOND (≥**BBB-**)		
INTERNATIONAL AGENCIES			Z BONDS			CORPORATE BOND (≤**BB+**)		
ADBB (Asian Development Bank)			COMPANION BONDS			MEDIUM-TERM NOTE (≥**BBB-**)		
AFDB (African Development Bank)			SEQUENTIAL BONDS			MEDIUM-TERM NOTE (≤**BB+**)		
IADB (Inter-American Dev. Bank)			TAC BONDS					
IFCO (International Finance Corp)			PAC & OTHER SCHEDULED BONDS			**MONEY MARKETS**		
WLDB (World Bank)						COMMERCIAL PAPER (≥**A1/P1**)		
			MUNICIPAL BOND			COMMERCIAL PAPER (≤**A2/P2**)		
CASH	YES		MUNICIPAL BONDS			BANKERS ACCEPTANCE		
						CD (DOMESTIC & EURO)		
						BANK NOTES		

BUYER ACKNOWLEDGES AND AGREES THAT IF A CLASS OF SECURITY CONTAINS NEW ISSUES OF SECURITIES, SUCH NEW ISSUES OF SECURITIES SHALL BE DEEMED TO BE ELIGIBLE SECURITIES.

[BUYER] [SELLER] ACCEPTED:
_____ _____ THE BANK OF NEW YORK

By: By: By:
Title: Title: Title:
Date: Date: Date:

THE BANK OF NEW YORK

1/2003

TRI-PARTY CUSTODIAL AGREEMENTS

Example 1 is a comprehensive form provided by The Bank of New York. Example 2 is a simplified example of the form provided by The Bank of New York. Finally, Example 3 is a highly simplified example that would still be acceptable.

EXAMPLE 2
(Schedule I)

Security Type	Credit Rating**	Margin (%)***
Debt Securities*		
U.S. Treasury Securities	AAA	102
Federal National Mortgage Association	AAA	102
Federal Home Loan Bank	AAA	102
Federal Home Loan Mortgage Corporation	AAA	102
Mortgage-Backed Securities**		
GNMA-Pass Throughs	AAA	102
GNMA-REMICS	AAA	102
FNMA- Pas Throughs	AAA	102
FNMA-REMICs	AAA	102
FHLMC-Pass Throughs	AAA	102
FHLMC-REMICS	AAA	102
Private Label Pass Throughs	AAA	102
Private label CMO	AAA	102

*   No principal- or interest-only securities. No callable or structured Notes.
**   Custodian may rely upon a recognized credit rating service in determining the credit ratings of securities and shall in no circumstances be liable for any errors made by such service.
***   Market valuations must be available on Bloomberg.
**** All Mortgage-Backed Securities must pass FFIEC test.
        Exclusions for REMIC & CMO Tranches:
        No Interest-Only
        No Residual
        No IOETTE
        No Principal-Only
        No Inverse Floater
        No Zero Coupon

EXAMPLE 3
(Schedule I)

Types of Securities	Margin (%)
(1) Agency Mortgage-Backed Securities (which pass FFIEC Test)	102
(2) AAA-rated Private Label Mortgage Backed Securities (which pass FFIEC Test)	102
(3) Cash	100
(4) AAA-rated privately-issued asset-backed securities backed by home equity or manufactured housing loans that are either (i) loans with a floating rate of interest or (ii) loans with a fixed rate of interest and a weighted average life of no more than four years based upon Bloomberg's default prepayment speed	102

301

Schedule II

SCHEDULE II
Authorized Persons

The following individuals have been designated as Authorized Persons of Buyer and Seller, respectively, in connection with the Custodial Undertaking In Connection With Master Repurchase Agreement dated as of _____.

BUYER

Name	Signature
_____	_____
_____	_____
_____	_____
_____	_____

SELLER

Name	Signature
_____	_____
_____	_____
_____	_____

An Authorized Person is defined in Paragraph 1A as "any person, whether or not any such person is an officer or employee of Buyer or Seller, as the case may be, duly authorized to give Oral Instructions and Written Instructions on behalf of Buyer or Seller, such persons and their specimen signatures to be designated in Schedule II attached hereto; as such Schedule II may be amended from time to time".

Both Oral and Written Instructions under the Custodial Agreement are required to be given by an Authorized Person of the party that is giving the instructions.

Care should be taken in updating Schedule II because the Custodian, under Paragraph 9F, is entitled to rely upon the names provided in Schedule II when acting upon Written or Oral Instructions. The parties' obligation to update the schedule is also imposed by Paragraph 11A.

Schedule III

SCHEDULE III

Account Information for Delivery of Buyer's Securities and Cash

ABA:_____
Bank Name:_____
City:_____
Account Name:_____
Account Number:_____

The Buyer is required to provide the information in Schedule III pursuant to Paragraph 5I so that the Custodian will know where to transfer Securities and cash for the Buyer.

TRI-PARTY CUSTODIAL AGREEMENTS

Schedule IV

SCHEDULE IV
ADDRESS FOR NOTICES
TO SELLER:

_____
_____
_____
_____

TO BUYER:

_____
_____
_____
_____

TO CUSTODIAN:

The Bank of New York
One Wall Street, 4th Floor
New York, New York 10286
Attn: Tri-Party Services
Government Securities Clearance Division
Telephone: (212) 635-4857
Fax: (212) 635-1190

Paragraph 11K requires that notices be directed to the parties at the addresses and telephone numbers provided in Schedule III.

Appendix I

APPENDIX I

Buyer's Instructions

To: The Bank of New York
     Broker Dealer Services
     One Wall Street, 4th Floor
     New York, New York 10286
     Attention: Vice President

This notice is given pursuant to Paragraph 5E of the Custodial Undertaking in Connection With Master Repurchase Agreement by and among _____ ("Buyer"), _____ ("Seller") and The Bank of New York ("Custodian") dated as of _____ (the "Custodial Undertaking"). Buyer hereby instructs Custodian to transfer the Purchased Securities and cash in Buyer's Account (as defined in the Custodial Undertaking) to:

ABA:_____

Bank or Depository: _____

303

> City: _____
> Account Name: _____
> Account Number: _____
>
> Date: _____
>
> _____
> [Buyer]
> By: _____
> Title: _____

A Buyer is required to deliver instructions pursuant to Paragraph 5E(iii) in the form of Appendix I.

Appendix II

The Buyer and the Seller are required to identify any parties in which the Buyer and the Seller are acting as an agent; otherwise the Buyer and the Seller shall be deemed to be the principal when such party is acting on behalf of an undisclosed principal. The following is the form provided by The Bank of New York to disclose the principals:

> **APPENDIX II**
> **CUSTODIAL AGENCY ANNEX**
>
> This Annex forms a part of the Custodial Undertaking In Connection With Master Repurchase Agreement dated as of _____ (the "Custodial Undertaking") by and among _____ ("Agent"), as agent for the principal(s) identified on Appendix A attached hereto (each, a "Buyer"), _____ ("Seller") and The Bank of New York ("Custodian"). Capitalized terms used but not defined shall have the meanings ascribed to them in the Custodial Undertaking.
>
> **1. Representations and Warranties of Agent**
>
> In addition to the representations set forth in Section 3.A of the Custodial Undertaking, Agent hereby represents and warrants, which representations and warranties shall be deemed to be continuing during the term of any Transaction, that:
> (a) Each Buyer has duly authorized Agent to execute and deliver the Custodial Undertaking on its behalf, has the power to so authorize Agent and to enter into the Transactions contemplated by the Master Repurchase Agreement and otherwise perform its obligations pursuant to the Master Repurchase Agreement and the Custodial Undertaking, and has taken all necessary action to authorize such execution and delivery by Agent and such performance by it; and

(b) No Transaction effected hereunder shall be for the account of any third party not listed on Appendix A hereto.

(c) Agent is subject to a rule implementing 31 U.S.C. §5318(h) and maintains an anti-money laundering program compliant with the requirements of the USA PATRIOT Act (the "Act") and the rules thereunder; (2) Agent is regulated by a federal functional regulator as that term is defined under 31.C.F.R. §103.120(a)(2); (3) Agent has implemented a customer identification program compliant with Section 326 of the Act that enables Agent to form a reasonable belief that it knows the true identity of its customers (including each Buyer), including procedures to obtain information from and verify the identity of customers, maintain records of the information used to verify identity, determine whether any customer appears on any government list of known or suspected terrorists or terrorist organizations, and provide customers with adequate notice that the institution is requesting information to verify their identities; (4) Agent is in compliance with its anti-money laundering program and its customer identification program; and (5) Agent will certify annually that it has implemented its anti-money laundering program and that it (or its agent) will perform all aspects of its customer identification program with respect to each Buyer.

2. Multiple Buyers

(a) **Choice of Account(s).** In the event that Agent proposes to act for more than one Buyer hereunder, Agent and Seller shall, subject to Custodian's prior consent, elect whether (i) to treat Transactions under the Custodial Undertaking as transactions entered into on behalf of separate Buyers, or (ii) to aggregate such Transactions as if they were transactions by a single Buyer. Failure to make such an election shall be deemed an election to treat Transactions under the Custodial Undertaking as transactions by a single Buyer.

(b) **Separate Accounts for Buyers.** In the event that Agent and Seller (with Custodian's prior consent) elect to treat Transactions under the Custodial Undertaking as transactions on behalf of separate Buyers, the parties agree that (i) Custodian shall establish a separate Buyer's Account in the name of each Buyer, (ii) Agent will provide Seller and Custodian with Written Instructions specifying the portion of each Transaction allocable to the account of each of the Buyers for which it is acting (to the extent that any such Transaction is allocable to the account of more than one Buyer); (iii) Custodian shall perform its obligations pursuant to Section 6 of the Custodial Undertaking on a Transaction-by-Transaction basis; and (iv) the parties' respective remedies under the Custodial Undertaking shall be determined as if Agent had entered into a separate Custodial Undertaking with the other party on behalf of each of its Buyers.

(c) **Omnibus Account for Buyer(s).** In the event that Agent and Seller elect to treat Transactions under the Custodial Undertaking as if they were transactions by a single Buyer or Custodian's consent to establish separate Buyer's Accounts is not obtained, the parties agree that (i) Custodian shall establish one omnibus Buyer's Account in which all Buyers' interests with respect to Transactions shall be commingled,

(ii) Custodian shall perform its obligations pursuant to Section 6 on a Transaction-by-Transaction basis; and (iii) the parties' respective remedies under the Custodial Undertaking shall be determined as if all Buyers were a single Buyer.

3. Custodian Not Responsible for Buyer Confirmations. Notwithstanding any provision in the Custodial Undertaking to the contrary, all confirmation statements prepared by Custodian pursuant to the Custodial Undertaking shall be delivered to Agent and Custodian shall have no responsibility for providing any Buyer with confirmation statements reflecting Purchased Securities or cash positions in a Buyer's Account.

4. Rescinded Authority. Agent shall provide Seller and Custodian promptly with a revised Appendix A whenever a Buyer rescinds Agent's authority to perform its obligations pursuant to the Custodial Undertaking.

5. Inconsistency with Agency Annex to Master Repurchase Agreement. In the event of any inconsistency between the terms and conditions of any agency annex to the Master Repurchase Agreement and this Custodial Agency Annex, the terms and conditions of this Custodial Agency Annex shall govern.

IN WITNESS WHEREOF, the parties have caused this Annex to be executed by their respective officers, thereunto duly authorized, as of the _____ day of _____, 20__.

AGENT:

_____
_____

In its Individual Capacity

By:_____   By:_____
Title: Title:

THE BANK OF NEW YORK

By:_____
Title:

APPENDIX A
LIST OF BUYERS

Exhibit 6.1
Securities eligible for deposit in Federal Reserve's Book-Entry Securities System[2]

United States Treasury

Farm Credit Financial Assistance Corporation
Farmers Home Administration
Federal Agricultural Mortgage Corporation (Farmer Mac)
Federal Farm Credit Banks Funding Corporation
Federal Home Loan Banks
Federal Home Loan Mortgage Corporation (Freddie Mac)
Federal National Mortgage Association (Fannie Mae)
Financing Corporation
Student Loan Marketing Association (Sallie Mae)
United States Postal Service
Tennessee Valley Authority
Resolution Funding Corporation

African Development Bank
Asian Development Bank
Inter-American Development Bank
International Bank for Reconstruction and Development
International Finance Corporation

Source: *The Federal Reserve's Fedwire Book-Entry Securities Transfer Service* (revised December 1998).

* Within chapters, terms used in the commentaries may have capitalisation or minor spelling differences to match the corresponding documentation.

Chapter 7

New developments

The repo market, of course, is well established in many countries and, in general, has evolved more steadily than the derivatives market. However, new developments regularly occur. Those of note in the past two years have been outlined below.

European Repo Council half-yearly survey

The above survey of the European repo market's volume, product and tenor spread is now well established. It is published in mid-March and mid-September each year, and shows a snapshot of the market at the close of business on a particular day in the previous December and June. The latest version of this survey may be found on ISMA's website (www.isma.org).

Form of mini close-out notice

Again in relation to settlement failures, in March 2003 ISMA published a form of mini close-out notice that can be used where a Buyer fails to deliver Securities on the Repurchase Date. Previously a Seller composed its own notice for this purpose, but the ISMA form, which is available on its website (www.isma.org), has brought some harmonisation to the market in this respect. In the notice the Seller has the choice of demanding Equivalent Securities by a stated deadline or of terminating the individual transaction.

Shaping of deal tickets for settlement purposes

The term "shaping" means splitting transactions into appropriate maximum ticket sizes for individual deals. One of the problems in the European market is the frequency of settlement failures and ISMA has attributed this, in part, to unwieldy ticket sizes. Consequently, with effect from 1 January 2004, ISMA's board has recommended that its members should split their transactions into the following maximum ticket sizes:

(i) for transactions in euro-denominated securities, €50 million and multiples thereof, if applicable;

(ii) for transactions in US dollar-denominated securities, US$50 million and multiples thereof, if applicable;

(iii) for transactions in sterling-denominated securities, £50 million and multiples thereof, if applicable;

(iv) for transactions in yen-denominated securities, ¥5 billion and multiples thereof, if applicable;

(v) for transactions in securities denominated in currencies other than those referred to in (i) to (iv) above, the equivalent (appropriately rounded, if necessary) of €50 million and multiples thereof, if applicable.

The aim is for the settlement process to operate more smoothly in the market.

ISMA's buy-in rules

These buy-in rules are contained in section 450 of ISMA's rules and recommendations. Under them a buyer must serve a buy-in pre-advice notice (which cannot be served until five business days after the value date), followed by a buy-in notice, which much be served two business days after the buy-in pre-advice notice. The rules then prescribe that the buyer has to execute the buy-in five business days after the date of the buy-in notice. Therefore, the total period between the value date and earliest date the buy-in can be completed is, under current ISMA rules, 12 business days.

The buy-in rules do not actually apply to repos transacted under the TBMA/ISMA GMRA, where, under paragraph 10(h), the failure of a Buyer to deliver Equivalent Securities on the Repurchase Date provides the Seller with three remedies, including closing out the relevant Transaction.

If the Seller wishes to close out the Transaction, it must deliver a notice to the Buyer, after which it has five business days in which to buy the Securities in the market. It can claim the cost of these Securities and reasonable expenses from the Buyer. If it does not buy in the Securities, their value at the end of the five business days is taken.

Market players considered there to be a major mismatch between a party's position when exercising a buy-in under ISMA's rules or under paragraph 10(h) of the TBMA/ISMA GMRA.

After much discussion it was ultimately decided by ISMA's board in December 2003 that, with effect from 1 January 2004, the minimum time period in ISMA's buy-in rules between a failure to deliver and the completion of the buy-in should be reduced from 12 to five business days, in order to harmonise the position and eliminate basis risk. It was also agreed that the buy-in pre-advice notice should be issued immediately after a failure to deliver and be followed by the buy-in notice after a period of two business days, and that the buy-in should take place three business days after that.

Bibliography

Websites

www.bondmarkets.com. The Bond Market Association website contains extensive amounts of information on the repo industry, markets and standard forms.

www.isma.org

Books

Choudhury, Moorad, *The REPO Handbook* (London, Butterworth Heinemann, 2002).

Fabozzi, Frank J., *Securities Lending and Repurchase Agreements* (New York, Frank J. Fabozzi Associates, 1997).

Georgiou, Christopher, *NatWest User's Guide to the PSA/ISMA Global Master Repurchase Agreement (1995 version)* (London, IFR Publishing, 1998).

Nat West Markets Handbook of International Repo (London, IFR Publishing, 1995).

Stigum, Marcia, *The Money Market*, 3rd edition (New York, Irwin, 1990), Chapter 13.

Stigum, Marcia, *The Repo and Reverse Markets* (New York, Dow Jones–Irwin, 1989).

Tyson-Quah, Kathleen, *Cross-Border Securities: Repo, Lending and Collateralisation* (London, Sweet & Maxwell, 1997).

Reports

Bank for International Settlements: Implications of Repo Markets for Central Banks (CGFS Publications No 10, March 1999).

The Bond Market Association and the International Securities Market Association: *Guidance Notes for Use with the TBMA/ISMA Global Master Repurchase Agreement* (October 2000).

International Securities Market Association: European Repo Market Survey Number 6 – conducted December 2003 (Zurich, March 2004).

Technical Committee of the International Organization of Securities Commission, Committee on Payment and Settlement Systems, Securities Lending Transactions: Market Development and Implications (July 1999).

Articles

Bowsher, Norman N., 'Repurchase Agreements', *61 Fed. Res. Bank of St. Louis 17–22* (No. 9 - Sept. 1979).

Brown, Claude, 'Similar but Different: Repos and Buy/Sellbacks Compared' (*International Financial Law Review*, March 1996)

Burnham, James B., 'The Government Securities Act of 1986 – A Case Study of the Demand for Regulation', *Regulation: The Cato Review of Bus. And Gov.* at www.cato.org/pubs/regulations1 regv13n2/13n2-burnham.html

Fleming, Michael J., and Garbade, Kenneth D., 'When the Back Office Moved to the Front Burner: Settlement Fails in the Treasury Market After 9/11', *Economic Policy Review*, 35 (November 2002).

Fleming, Michael J., and Garbade, Kenneth D., 'The Repurchase Agreement Refined: GCF Repo', *Current Issues in Economics and Finance*, Vol. 9, No. 6 (June 2003).

Fleming, Michael J., and Garbade, Kenneth D., 'Repurchase Agreements with Negative Interest Rates', *Current Issues in Economics and Finance*, Vol. 10, No.5 (April 2004).

Hagerty, William F., 'Lifting the Cloud of Uncertainty over the Repo Market: Characterization of Repos as Separate Purchases and Sales of Securities', 37 *Vanderbilt Law Review* 401 (March, 1984).

Lumpkin, Stephen A., *Repurchase and Reverse Purchase Agreements*, 73 *Federal Reserve Bank of Richmond Economic Review*, 15-23 (Jan-Feb 1987). Available at www.blfconseil.com/pages/web/us/blffinancial/repurchaseandreverse.htm

Lumpkin, Stephen A., 'Repurchase and Reverse Purchase Agreements', *Instruments of the Money Market*, Chapter 6 (last updated 1993), available at www.rich.frb.org/pubs/instruments/ch6.html

Morton, Guy, 'International Coverage of the PSA/ISMA Global Master Repurchase Agreement', *Journal of International Banking and Financial Law* (Butterworths, March 1997).

Schatz, Howard A., 'The Characterization of Repurchase Agreements in the Context of the Federal Securities Laws', 61 *St. John's Law Review* 290 (Winter 1987).

Schroeder, Jeanne L., 'Is Article 8 Finally Ready This Time?: The Radical Reform of Secured Lending on Wall Street', *1994 Columbus Business Law Review*, 291 (1994).

Schroeder, Jeanne L., 'Repo Madness: The Characterization of Repurchase Agreements under the Bankruptcy Code and the U.C.C.', 46 *Syracuse Law Review*, 999 (1996).

Schroeder, Jeanne L., 'A Repo Opera: How Criimi Mae Got Repos Backwards', 76 *Am. Bankr. L.J.* 565 (Fall 2002).

Smith, Wayne, 'Repurchase Agreements and Federal Funds', 64 *Federal Reserve Bulletin*, pp.353–360 (May 1978).

Sumrow, Shad E., 'State Taxation of Income from "Repurchase Agreements": Loewenstein v. Dept. of Revenue', 28 *Creighton Law Review*, 275 (December 1994).

'U.S. Repo Market', 335 *Euromoney*, 14 (March 1997 Supp.).

Walters, Gary, 'Repurchase Agreements and the Bankruptcy Code: The Need for Legislative Action', 52 *Fordham Law Review*, 828 (April 1984).

Cases

Cohen, 67 B.R. at 557.

Cohen v. Savings Bldg. & Loan Co. (In re Bevill, Bresler & Schulman Asset Management Corp.), 896 F.2d 54, 55 (3d Cir. 1981).

Cosmopolitan Credit & Inv. Corp. v. Blyth Eastman Dillon & Co., Inc., 507 F.Supp. 954 (S.D. Fla. 1981).

Gilmore v. State Bd. Of Admin., 382 So. 2d. 861 (Fla. Dist. Ct. App. 1980).

Granite Partners, L.P. v. Bear, Stearns & Co. Inc., 17 F.Supp.2d 275 (S.D.N.Y., 1998).

In re Criimi May, Inc., et al., 251 B.R. 796 (2000).

In re Lombard-Wall, Inc., 23 B.R. 165 (Bankr. S.D.N.Y. 1982).

In re Lombard-Wall, Inc. 44 B.R. 928 (Bkrtcy.N.Y., 1984).

Jonas v. Farmer Bros. Co. (In re Comark), 145 B.R. 47, 53 (Bankr. 9th Cir. 1992).

King v. Pope, 91 S.W.3d 314 (2002).

Lombard-Wall, Inc. v. Bankers Trust Co., 23 B.R. 165 (1982).

Main Street Assoc. v. Manko, 179 F.Supp.2d 339 (2002).

Manufacturers Hanover Trust Co. v. Drysdale Securities Corp., 801 F.2d 13 (1986).

McDow v. Off. Comm. of Equity Sec. Holders of Criimi Mae Inc., 247 B.R. 146 (1999).

Resolution Trust Corp. v. Aetna Casualty & Sur. Co. 25 F.3d 570, 571-573 (7th Cir. 1994).

Securities and Exchange Comm. v. Drysdale Securities Corp., 785 F.2d 38 (1986).

Securities and Exchange Comm. v. Miller, 495 F.Supp. 465 (1980).

Securities and Exchange Comm v. W.J. Howey Co. 328 U.S. 293, 66 S.Ct. 1100 (1946).

Appendix 1

TBMA/ISMA Global Master Repurchase Agreement

Reproduced with the kind permission of the
International Securities Market Association
and
The Bond Market Association

The Bond Market Association
New York • Washington • London
www.bondmarkets.com

International Securities Market Association
Rigistrasse 60, P.O. Box, CH-8033, Zürich
www.isma.org

2000 VERSION

TBMA/ISMA

GLOBAL MASTER REPURCHASE AGREEMENT

Dated as of _____

Between:

_____ ("Party A")

and

_____ ("Party B")

1. **Applicability**

(a) From time to time the parties hereto may enter into transactions in which one party, acting through a Designated Office, ("Seller") agrees to sell to the other, acting through a Designated Office, ("Buyer") securities and financial instruments ("Securities") (subject to paragraph 1(c), other than equities and Net Paying Securities) against the payment of the purchase price by Buyer to Seller, with a simultaneous agreement by Buyer to sell to Seller Securities equivalent to such Securities at a date certain or on demand against the payment of the repurchase price by Seller to Buyer.

(b) Each such transaction (which may be a repurchase transaction ("Repurchase Transaction") or a buy and sell back transaction ("Buy/Sell Back Transaction")) shall be referred to herein as a "Transaction" and shall be governed by this Agreement, including any supplemental terms or conditions contained in Annex I hereto, unless otherwise agreed in writing.

October 2000

(c) If this Agreement may be applied to -

(i) Buy/Sell Back Transactions, this shall be specified in Annex I hereto, and the provisions of the Buy/Sell Back Annex shall apply to such Buy/Sell Back Transactions;

(ii) Net Paying Securities, this shall be specified in Annex I hereto and the provisions of Annex I, paragraph 1(b) shall apply to Transactions involving Net Paying Securities.

(d) If Transactions are to be effected under this Agreement by either party as an agent, this shall be specified in Annex I hereto, and the provisions of the Agency Annex shall apply to such Agency Transactions.

2. **Definitions**

(a) "Act of Insolvency" shall occur with respect to any party hereto upon -

(i) its making a general assignment for the benefit of, entering into a reorganisation, arrangement, or composition with creditors; or

(ii) its admitting in writing that it is unable to pay its debts as they become due; or

(iii) its seeking, consenting to or acquiescing in the appointment of any trustee, administrator, receiver or liquidator or analogous officer of it or any material part of its property; or

(iv) the presentation or filing of a petition in respect of it (other than by the counterparty to this Agreement in respect of any obligation under this Agreement) in any court or before any agency alleging or for the bankruptcy, winding-up or insolvency of such party (or any analogous proceeding) or seeking any reorganisation, arrangement, composition, re-adjustment, administration, liquidation, dissolution or similar relief under any present or future statute, law or regulation, such petition (except in the case of a petition for winding-up or any analogous proceeding, in respect of which no such 30 day period shall apply) not having been stayed or dismissed within 30 days of its filing; or

(v) the appointment of a receiver, administrator, liquidator or trustee or analogous officer of such party or over all or any material part of such party's property; or

(vi) the convening of any meeting of its creditors for the purposes of considering a voluntary arrangement as referred to in section 3 of the Insolvency Act 1986 (or any analogous proceeding);

(b) "Agency Transaction", the meaning specified in paragraph 1 of the Agency Annex;

(c) "Appropriate Market", the meaning specified in paragraph 10;

(d) "Base Currency", the currency indicated in Annex I hereto;

(e) "Business Day" -

(i) in relation to the settlement of any Transaction which is to be settled through Clearstream or Euroclear, a day on which Clearstream or, as the case may be, Euroclear is open to settle business in the currency in which the Purchase Price and the Repurchase Price are denominated;

(ii) in relation to the settlement of any Transaction which is to be settled through a settlement system other than Clearstream or Euroclear, a day on which that settlement system is open to settle such Transaction;

(iii) in relation to any delivery of Securities not falling within (i) or (ii) above, a day on which banks are open for business in the place where delivery of the relevant Securities is to be effected; and

(iv) in relation to any obligation to make a payment not falling within (i) or (ii) above, a day other than a Saturday or a Sunday on which banks are open for business in the principal financial centre of the country of which the currency in which the payment is denominated is the official currency and, if different, in the place where any account designated by the parties for the making or receipt of the payment is situated (or, in the case of a payment in euro, a day on which TARGET operates);

(f) "Cash Margin", a cash sum paid to Buyer or Seller in accordance with paragraph 4;

(g) "Clearstream", Clearstream Banking, société anonyme, (previously Cedelbank) or any successor thereto;

(h) "Confirmation", the meaning specified in paragraph 3(b);

(i) "Contractual Currency", the meaning specified in paragraph 7(a);

(j) "Defaulting Party", the meaning specified in paragraph 10;

(k) "Default Market Value", the meaning specified in paragraph 10;

(l) "Default Notice", a written notice served by the non-Defaulting Party on the Defaulting Party under paragraph 10 stating that an event shall be treated as an Event of Default for the purposes of this Agreement;

(m) "Default Valuation Notice", the meaning specified in paragraph 10;

(n) "Default Valuation Time", the meaning specified in paragraph 10;

(o) "Deliverable Securities", the meaning specified in paragraph 10;

(p) "Designated Office", with respect to a party, a branch or office of that party which is

(q) specified as such in Annex I hereto or such other branch or office as may be agreed to by the parties;

(q) "Distributions", the meaning specified in sub-paragraph (w) below;

(r) "Equivalent Margin Securities", Securities equivalent to Securities previously transferred as Margin Securities;

(s) "Equivalent Securities", with respect to a Transaction, Securities equivalent to Purchased Securities under that Transaction. If and to the extent that such Purchased Securities have been redeemed, the expression shall mean a sum of money equivalent to the proceeds of the redemption;

(t) Securities are "equivalent to" other Securities for the purposes of this Agreement if they are: (i) of the same issuer; (ii) part of the same issue; and (iii) of an identical type, nominal value, description and (except where otherwise stated) amount as those other Securities, provided that -

   (A) Securities will be equivalent to other Securities notwithstanding that those Securities have been redenominated into euro or that the nominal value of those Securities has changed in connection with such redenomination; and

   (B) where Securities have been converted, subdivided or consolidated or have become the subject of a takeover or the holders of Securities have become entitled to receive or acquire other Securities or other property or the Securities have become subject to any similar event, the expression "equivalent to" shall mean Securities equivalent to (as defined in the provisions of this definition preceding the proviso) the original Securities together with or replaced by a sum of money or Securities or other property equivalent to (as so defined) that receivable by holders of such original Securities resulting from such event;

(u) "Euroclear", Morgan Guaranty Trust Company of New York, Brussels office, as operator of the Euroclear System or any successor thereto;

(v) "Event of Default", the meaning specified in paragraph 10;

(w) "Income", with respect to any Security at any time, all interest, dividends or other distributions thereon, but excluding distributions which are a payment or repayment of principal in respect of the relevant securities ("Distributions");

(x) "Income Payment Date", with respect to any Securities, the date on which Income is paid in respect of such Securities or, in the case of registered Securities, the date by reference to which particular registered holders are identified as being entitled to payment of Income;

(y) "LIBOR", in relation to any sum in any currency, the one month London Inter Bank Offered Rate in respect of that currency as quoted on page 3750 on the Bridge

Telerate Service (or such other page as may replace page 3750 on that service) as of 11:00 a.m., London time, on the date on which it is to be determined;

(z) "Margin Ratio", with respect to a Transaction, the Market Value of the Purchased Securities at the time when the Transaction was entered into divided by the Purchase Price (and so that, where a Transaction relates to Securities of different descriptions and the Purchase Price is apportioned by the parties among Purchased Securities of each such description, a separate Margin Ratio shall apply in respect of Securities of each such description), or such other proportion as the parties may agree with respect to that Transaction;

(aa) "Margin Securities", in relation to a Margin Transfer, Securities reasonably acceptable to the party calling for such Margin Transfer;

(bb) "Margin Transfer", any, or any combination of, the payment or repayment of Cash Margin and the transfer of Margin Securities or Equivalent Margin Securities;

(cc) "Market Value", with respect to any Securities as of any time on any date, the price for such Securities at such time on such date obtained from a generally recognised source agreed to by the parties (and where different prices are obtained for different delivery dates, the price so obtainable for the earliest available such delivery date) (provided that the price of Securities that are suspended shall (for the purposes of paragraph 4) be nil unless the parties otherwise agree and (for all other purposes) shall be the price of those Securities as of close of business on the dealing day in the relevant market last preceding the date of suspension) plus the aggregate amount of Income which, as of such date, has accrued but not yet been paid in respect of the Securities to the extent not included in such price as of such date, and for these purposes any sum in a currency other than the Contractual Currency for the Transaction in question shall be converted into such Contractual Currency at the Spot Rate prevailing at the relevant time;

(dd) "Net Exposure", the meaning specified in paragraph 4(c);

(ee) the "Net Margin" provided to a party at any time, the excess (if any) at that time of (i) the sum of the amount of Cash Margin paid to that party (including accrued interest on such Cash Margin which has not been paid to the other party) and the Market Value of Margin Securities transferred to that party under paragraph 4(a) (excluding any Cash Margin which has been repaid to the other party and any Margin Securities in respect of which Equivalent Margin Securities have been transferred to the other party) over (ii) the sum of the amount of Cash Margin paid to the other party (including accrued interest on such Cash Margin which has not been paid by the other party) and the Market Value of Margin Securities transferred to the other party under paragraph 4(a) (excluding any Cash Margin which has been repaid by the other party and any Margin Securities in respect of which Equivalent Margin Securities have been transferred by the other party) and for this purpose any amounts not denominated in the Base Currency shall be converted into the Base Currency at the Spot Rate

(ff) "Net Paying Securities", Securities which are of a kind such that, were they to be the subject of a Transaction to which paragraph 5 applies, any payment made by Buyer under paragraph 5 would be one in respect of which either Buyer would or might be required to make a withholding or deduction for or on account of taxes or duties or Seller might be required to make or account for a payment for or on account of taxes or duties (in each case other than tax on overall net income) by reference to such payment;

(gg) "Net Value", the meaning specified in paragraph 10;

(hh) "New Purchased Securities", the meaning specified in paragraph 8(a);

(ii) "Price Differential", with respect to any Transaction as of any date, the aggregate amount obtained by daily application of the Pricing Rate for such Transaction to the Purchase Price for such Transaction (on a 360 day basis or 365 day basis in accordance with the applicable ISMA convention, unless otherwise agreed between the parties for the Transaction), for the actual number of days during the period commencing on (and including) the Purchase Date for such Transaction and ending on (but excluding) the date of calculation or, if earlier, the Repurchase Date;

(jj) "Pricing Rate", with respect to any Transaction, the per annum percentage rate for calculation of the Price Differential agreed to by Buyer and Seller in relation to that Transaction;

(kk) "Purchase Date", with respect to any Transaction, the date on which Purchased Securities are to be sold by Seller to Buyer in relation to that Transaction;

(ll) "Purchase Price", on the Purchase Date, the price at which Purchased Securities are sold or are to be sold by Seller to Buyer;

(mm) "Purchased Securities", with respect to any Transaction, the Securities sold or to be sold by Seller to Buyer under that Transaction, and any New Purchased Securities transferred by Seller to Buyer under paragraph 8 in respect of that Transaction;

(nn) "Receivable Securities", the meaning specified in paragraph 10;

(oo) "Repurchase Date", with respect to any Transaction, the date on which Buyer is to sell Equivalent Securities to Seller in relation to that Transaction;

(pp) "Repurchase Price", with respect to any Transaction and as of any date, the sum of the Purchase Price and the Price Differential as of such date;

(qq) "Special Default Notice", the meaning specified in paragraph 14;

(rr) "Spot Rate", where an amount in one currency is to be converted into a second currency on any date, unless the parties otherwise agree, the spot rate of exchange quoted by Barclays Bank PLC in the London inter-bank market for the sale by it of such second currency against a purchase by it of such first currency;

(ss) "TARGET", the Trans-European Automated Real-time Gross Settlement Express Transfer System;

(tt) "Term", with respect to any Transaction, the interval of time commencing with the Purchase Date and ending with the Repurchase Date;

(uu) "Termination", with respect to any Transaction, refers to the requirement with respect to such Transaction for Buyer to sell Equivalent Securities against payment by Seller of the Repurchase Price in accordance with paragraph 3(f), and reference to a Transaction having a "fixed term" or being "terminable upon demand" shall be construed accordingly;

(vv) "Transaction Costs", the meaning specified in paragraph 10;

(ww) "Transaction Exposure", with respect to any Transaction at any time during the period from the Purchase Date to the Repurchase Date (or, if later, the date on which Equivalent Securities are delivered to Seller or the Transaction is terminated under paragraph 10(g) or 10(h)), the difference between (i) the Repurchase Price at such time multiplied by the applicable Margin Ratio (or, where the Transaction relates to Securities of more than one description to which different Margin Ratios apply, the amount produced by multiplying the Repurchase Price attributable to Equivalent Securities of each such description by the applicable Margin Ratio and aggregating the resulting amounts, the Repurchase Price being for this purpose attributed to Equivalent Securities of each such description in the same proportions as those in which the Purchase Price was apportioned among the Purchased Securities) and (ii) the Market Value of Equivalent Securities at such time. If (i) is greater than (ii), Buyer has a Transaction Exposure for that Transaction equal to that excess. If (ii) is greater than (i), Seller has a Transaction Exposure for that Transaction equal to that excess; and

(xx) except in paragraphs 14(b)(i) and 18, references in this Agreement to "written" communications and communications "in writing" include communications made through any electronic system agreed between the parties which is capable of reproducing such communication in hard copy form.

3. **Initiation; Confirmation; Termination**

(a) A Transaction may be entered into orally or in writing at the initiation of either Buyer or Seller.

(b) Upon agreeing to enter into a Transaction hereunder Buyer or Seller (or both), as shall have been agreed, shall promptly deliver to the other party written confirmation

of such Transaction (a "Confirmation").

The Confirmation shall describe the Purchased Securities (including CUSIP or ISIN or other identifying number or numbers, if any), identify Buyer and Seller and set forth -

(i) the Purchase Date;

(ii) the Purchase Price;

(iii) the Repurchase Date, unless the Transaction is to be terminable on demand (in which case the Confirmation shall state that it is terminable on demand);

(iv) the Pricing Rate applicable to the Transaction;

(v) in respect of each party the details of the bank account[s] to which payments to be made hereunder are to be credited;

(vi) where the Buy/Sell Back Annex applies, whether the Transaction is a Repurchase Transaction or a Buy/Sell Back Transaction;

(vii) where the Agency Annex applies, whether the Transaction is an Agency Transaction and, if so, the identity of the party which is acting as agent and the name, code or identifier of the Principal; and

(viii) any additional terms or conditions of the Transaction;

and may be in the form of Annex II hereto or may be in any other form to which the parties agree.

The Confirmation relating to a Transaction shall, together with this Agreement, constitute prima facie evidence of the terms agreed between Buyer and Seller for that Transaction, unless objection is made with respect to the Confirmation promptly after receipt thereof. In the event of any conflict between the terms of such Confirmation and this Agreement, the Confirmation shall prevail in respect of that Transaction and those terms only.

(c) On the Purchase Date for a Transaction, Seller shall transfer the Purchased Securities to Buyer or its agent against the payment of the Purchase Price by Buyer.

(d) Termination of a Transaction will be effected, in the case of on demand Transactions, on the date specified for Termination in such demand, and, in the case of fixed term Transactions, on the date fixed for Termination.

(e) In the case of on demand Transactions, demand for Termination shall be made by Buyer or Seller, by telephone or otherwise, and shall provide for Termination to occur after not less than the minimum period as is customarily required for the settlement or delivery of money or Equivalent Securities of the relevant kind.

(f) On the Repurchase Date, Buyer shall transfer to Seller or its agent Equivalent

Securities against the payment of the Repurchase Price by Seller (less any amount then payable and unpaid by Buyer to Seller pursuant to paragraph 5).

4. **Margin Maintenance**

(a) If at any time either party has a Net Exposure in respect of the other party it may by notice to the other party require the other party to make a Margin Transfer to it of an aggregate amount or value at least equal to that Net Exposure.

(b) A notice under sub-paragraph (a) above may be given orally or in writing.

(c) For the purposes of this Agreement a party has a Net Exposure in respect of the other party if the aggregate of all the first party's Transaction Exposures plus any amount payable to the first party under paragraph 5 but unpaid less the amount of any Net Margin provided to the first party exceeds the aggregate of all the other party's Transaction Exposures plus any amount payable to the other party under paragraph 5 but unpaid less the amount of any Net Margin provided to the other party; and the amount of the Net Exposure is the amount of the excess. For this purpose any amounts not denominated in the Base Currency shall be converted into the Base Currency at the Spot Rate prevailing at the relevant time.

(d) To the extent that a party calling for a Margin Transfer has previously paid Cash Margin which has not been repaid or delivered Margin Securities in respect of which Equivalent Margin Securities have not been delivered to it, that party shall be entitled to require that such Margin Transfer be satisfied first by the repayment of such Cash Margin or the delivery of Equivalent Margin Securities but, subject to this, the composition of a Margin Transfer shall be at the option of the party making such Margin Transfer.

(e) Any Cash Margin transferred shall be in the Base Currency or such other currency as the parties may agree.

(f) A payment of Cash Margin shall give rise to a debt owing from the party receiving such payment to the party making such payment. Such debt shall bear interest at such rate, payable at such times, as may be specified in Annex I hereto in respect of the relevant currency or otherwise agreed between the parties, and shall be repayable subject to the terms of this Agreement.

(g) Where Seller or Buyer becomes obliged under sub-paragraph (a) above to make a Margin Transfer, it shall transfer Cash Margin or Margin Securities or Equivalent Margin Securities within the minimum period specified in Annex I hereto or, if no period is there specified, such minimum period as is customarily required for the settlement or delivery of money, Margin Securities or Equivalent Margin Securities of the relevant kind.

(h) The parties may agree that, with respect to any Transaction, the provisions of sub-paragraphs (a) to (g) above shall not apply but instead that margin may be provided

October 2000

separately in respect of that Transaction in which case -

(i) that Transaction shall not be taken into account when calculating whether either party has a Net Exposure;

(ii) margin shall be provided in respect of that Transaction in such manner as the parties may agree; and

(iii) margin provided in respect of that Transaction shall not be taken into account for the purposes of sub-paragraphs (a) to (g) above.

(i) The parties may agree that any Net Exposure which may arise shall be eliminated not by Margin Transfers under the preceding provisions of this paragraph but by the repricing of Transactions under sub-paragraph (j) below, the adjustment of Transactions under sub-paragraph (k) below or a combination of both these methods.

(j) Where the parties agree that a Transaction is to be repriced under this sub-paragraph, such repricing shall be effected as follows -

(i) the Repurchase Date under the relevant Transaction (the "Original Transaction") shall be deemed to occur on the date on which the repricing is to be effected (the "Repricing Date");

(ii) the parties shall be deemed to have entered into a new Transaction (the "Repriced Transaction") on the terms set out in (iii) to (vi) below;

(iii) the Purchased Securities under the Repriced Transaction shall be Securities equivalent to the Purchased Securities under the Original Transaction;

(iv) the Purchase Date under the Repriced Transaction shall be the Repricing Date;

(v) the Purchase Price under the Repriced Transaction shall be such amount as shall, when multiplied by the Margin Ratio applicable to the Original Transaction, be equal to the Market Value of such Securities on the Repricing Date;

(vi) the Repurchase Date, the Pricing Rate, the Margin Ratio and, subject as aforesaid, the other terms of the Repriced Transaction shall be identical to those of the Original Transaction;

(vii) the obligations of the parties with respect to the delivery of the Purchased Securities and the payment of the Purchase Price under the Repriced Transaction shall be set off against their obligations with respect to the delivery of Equivalent Securities and payment of the Repurchase Price under the Original Transaction and accordingly only a net cash sum shall be paid by one party to the other. Such net cash sum shall be paid within the period specified in sub-paragraph (g) above.

October 2000

(k) The adjustment of a Transaction (the "Original Transaction") under this sub-paragraph shall be effected by the parties agreeing that on the date on which the adjustment is to be made (the "Adjustment Date") the Original Transaction shall be terminated and they shall enter into a new Transaction (the "Replacement Transaction") in accordance with the following provisions -

    (i) the Original Transaction shall be terminated on the Adjustment Date on such terms as the parties shall agree on or before the Adjustment Date;

    (ii) the Purchased Securities under the Replacement Transaction shall be such Securities as the parties shall agree on or before the Adjustment Date (being Securities the aggregate Market Value of which at the Adjustment Date is substantially equal to the Repurchase Price under the Original Transaction at the Adjustment Date multiplied by the Margin Ratio applicable to the Original Transaction);

    (iii) the Purchase Date under the Replacement Transaction shall be the Adjustment Date;

    (iv) the other terms of the Replacement Transaction shall be such as the parties shall agree on or before the Adjustment Date; and

    (v) the obligations of the parties with respect to payment and delivery of Securities on the Adjustment Date under the Original Transaction and the Replacement Transaction shall be settled in accordance with paragraph 6 within the minimum period specified in sub-paragraph (g) above.

5. **Income Payments**

Unless otherwise agreed -

    (i) where the Term of a particular Transaction extends over an Income Payment Date in respect of any Securities subject to that Transaction, Buyer shall on the date such Income is paid by the issuer transfer to or credit to the account of Seller an amount equal to (and in the same currency as) the amount paid by the issuer;

    (ii) where Margin Securities are transferred from one party ("the first party") to the other party ("the second party") and an Income Payment Date in respect of such Securities occurs before Equivalent Margin Securities are transferred by the second party to the first party, the second party shall on the date such Income is paid by the issuer transfer to or credit to the account of the first party an amount equal to (and in the same currency as) the amount paid by the issuer;

and for the avoidance of doubt references in this paragraph to the amount of any Income paid by the issuer of any Securities shall be to an amount paid without any

 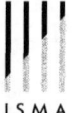

withholding or deduction for or on account of taxes or duties notwithstanding that a payment of such Income made in certain circumstances may be subject to such a withholding or deduction.

6. **Payment and Transfer**

(a) Unless otherwise agreed, all money paid hereunder shall be in immediately available freely convertible funds of the relevant currency. All Securities to be transferred hereunder (i) shall be in suitable form for transfer and shall be accompanied by duly executed instruments of transfer or assignment in blank (where required for transfer) and such other documentation as the transferee may reasonably request, or (ii) shall be transferred through the book entry system of Euroclear or Clearstream, or (iii) shall be transferred through any other agreed securities clearance system or (iv) shall be transferred by any other method mutually acceptable to Seller and Buyer.

(b) Unless otherwise agreed, all money payable by one party to the other in respect of any Transaction shall be paid free and clear of, and without withholding or deduction for, any taxes or duties of whatsoever nature imposed, levied, collected, withheld or assessed by any authority having power to tax, unless the withholding or deduction of such taxes or duties is required by law. In that event, unless otherwise agreed, the paying party shall pay such additional amounts as will result in the net amounts receivable by the other party (after taking account of such withholding or deduction) being equal to such amounts as would have been received by it had no such taxes or duties been required to be withheld or deducted.

(c) Unless otherwise agreed in writing between the parties, under each Transaction transfer of Purchased Securities by Seller and payment of Purchase Price by Buyer against the transfer of such Purchased Securities shall be made simultaneously and transfer of Equivalent Securities by Buyer and payment of Repurchase Price payable by Seller against the transfer of such Equivalent Securities shall be made simultaneously.

(d) Subject to and without prejudice to the provisions of sub-paragraph 6(c), either party may from time to time in accordance with market practice and in recognition of the practical difficulties in arranging simultaneous delivery of Securities and money waive in relation to any Transaction its rights under this Agreement to receive simultaneous transfer and/or payment provided that transfer and/or payment shall, notwithstanding such waiver, be made on the same day and provided also that no such waiver in respect of one Transaction shall affect or bind it in respect of any other Transaction.

(e) The parties shall execute and deliver all necessary documents and take all necessary steps to procure that all right, title and interest in any Purchased Securities, any Equivalent Securities, any Margin Securities and any Equivalent Margin Securities shall pass to the party to which transfer is being made upon transfer of the same in accordance with this Agreement, free from all liens, claims, charges and encumbrances.

(f) Notwithstanding the use of expressions such as "*Repurchase Date*", "*Repurchase Price*", "*margin*", "*Net Margin*", "*Margin Ratio*" and "*substitution*", which are used to reflect terminology used in the market for transactions of the kind provided for in this Agreement, all right, title and interest in and to Securities and money transferred or paid under this Agreement shall pass to the transferee upon transfer or payment, the obligation of the party receiving Purchased Securities or Margin Securities being an obligation to transfer Equivalent Securities or Equivalent Margin Securities.

(g) Time shall be of the essence in this Agreement.

(h) Subject to paragraph 10, all amounts in the same currency payable by each party to the other under any Transaction or otherwise under this Agreement on the same date shall be combined in a single calculation of a net sum payable by one party to the other and the obligation to pay that sum shall be the only obligation of either party in respect of those amounts.

(i) Subject to paragraph 10, all Securities of the same issue, denomination, currency and series, transferable by each party to the other under any Transaction or hereunder on the same date shall be combined in a single calculation of a net quantity of Securities transferable by one party to the other and the obligation to transfer the net quantity of Securities shall be the only obligation of either party in respect of the Securities so transferable and receivable.

(j) If the parties have specified in Annex I hereto that this paragraph 6(j) shall apply, each obligation of a party under this Agreement (other than an obligation arising under paragraph 10) is subject to the condition precedent that none of those events specified in paragraph 10(a) which are identified in Annex I hereto for the purposes of this paragraph 6(j) (being events which, upon the serving of a Default Notice, would be an Event of Default with respect to the other party) shall have occurred and be continuing with respect to the other party.

7. **Contractual Currency**

(a) All the payments made in respect of the Purchase Price or the Repurchase Price of any Transaction shall be made in the currency of the Purchase Price (the "Contractual Currency") save as provided in paragraph 10(c)(ii). Notwithstanding the foregoing, the payee of any money may, at its option, accept tender thereof in any other currency, provided, however, that, to the extent permitted by applicable law, the obligation of the payer to pay such money will be discharged only to the extent of the amount of the Contractual Currency that such payee may, consistent with normal banking procedures, purchase with such other currency (after deduction of any premium and costs of exchange) for delivery within the customary delivery period for spot transactions in respect of the relevant currency.

(b) If for any reason the amount in the Contractual Currency received by a party, including amounts received after conversion of any recovery under any judgment or

order expressed in a currency other than the Contractual Currency, falls short of the amount in the Contractual Currency due and payable, the party required to make the payment will, as a separate and independent obligation, to the extent permitted by applicable law, immediately transfer such additional amount in the Contractual Currency as may be necessary to compensate for the shortfall.

(c) If for any reason the amount in the Contractual Currency received by a party exceeds the amount of the Contractual Currency due and payable, the party receiving the transfer will refund promptly the amount of such excess.

8. **Substitution**

(a) A Transaction may at any time between the Purchase Date and Repurchase Date, if Seller so requests and Buyer so agrees, be varied by the transfer by Buyer to Seller of Securities equivalent to the Purchased Securities, or to such of the Purchased Securities as shall be agreed, in exchange for the transfer by Seller to Buyer of other Securities of such amount and description as shall be agreed ("New Purchased Securities") (being Securities having a Market Value at the date of the variation at least equal to the Market Value of the Equivalent Securities transferred to Seller).

(b) Any variation under sub-paragraph (a) above shall be effected, subject to paragraph 6(d), by the simultaneous transfer of the Equivalent Securities and New Purchased Securities concerned.

(c) A Transaction which is varied under sub-paragraph (a) above shall thereafter continue in effect as though the Purchased Securities under that Transaction consisted of or included the New Purchased Securities instead of the Securities in respect of which Equivalent Securities have been transferred to Seller.

(d) Where either party has transferred Margin Securities to the other party it may at any time before Equivalent Margin Securities are transferred to it under paragraph 4 request the other party to transfer Equivalent Margin Securities to it in exchange for the transfer to the other party of new Margin Securities having a Market Value at the time of transfer at least equal to that of such Equivalent Margin Securities. If the other party agrees to the request, the exchange shall be effected, subject to paragraph 6(d), by the simultaneous transfer of the Equivalent Margin Securities and new Margin Securities concerned. Where either or both of such transfers is or are effected through a settlement system in circumstances which under the rules and procedures of that settlement system give rise to a payment by or for the account of one party to or for the account of the other party, the parties shall cause such payment or payments to be made outside that settlement system, for value the same day as the payments made through that settlement system, as shall ensure that the exchange of Equivalent Margin Securities and new Margin Securities effected under this sub-paragraph does not give rise to any net payment of cash by either party to the other.

October 2000

APPENDIX 1

9. **Representations**

Each party represents and warrants to the other that -

(a) it is duly authorised to execute and deliver this Agreement, to enter into the Transactions contemplated hereunder and to perform its obligations hereunder and thereunder and has taken all necessary action to authorise such execution, delivery and performance;

(b) it will engage in this Agreement and the Transactions contemplated hereunder (other than Agency Transactions) as principal;

(c) the person signing this Agreement on its behalf is, and any person representing it in entering into a Transaction will be, duly authorised to do so on its behalf;

(d) it has obtained all authorisations of any governmental or regulatory body required in connection with this Agreement and the Transactions contemplated hereunder and such authorisations are in full force and effect;

(e) the execution, delivery and performance of this Agreement and the Transactions contemplated hereunder will not violate any law, ordinance, charter, by-law or rule applicable to it or any agreement by which it is bound or by which any of its assets are affected;

(f) it has satisfied itself and will continue to satisfy itself as to the tax implications of the Transactions contemplated hereunder;

(g) in connection with this Agreement and each Transaction -

  (i) unless there is a written agreement with the other party to the contrary, it is not relying on any advice (whether written or oral) of the other party, other than the representations expressly set out in this Agreement;

  (ii) it has made and will make its own decisions regarding the entering into of any Transaction based upon its own judgment and upon advice from such professional advisers as it has deemed it necessary to consult;

  (iii) it understands the terms, conditions and risks of each Transaction and is willing to assume (financially and otherwise) those risks; and

(h) at the time of transfer to the other party of any Securities it will have the full and unqualified right to make such transfer and that upon such transfer of Securities the other party will receive all right, title and interest in and to those Securities free of any lien, claim, charge or encumbrance.

On the date on which any Transaction is entered into pursuant hereto, and on each day on which Securities, Equivalent Securities, Margin Securities or Equivalent Margin Securities are to be transferred under any Transaction, Buyer and Seller shall each be

October 2000

deemed to repeat all the foregoing representations. For the avoidance of doubt and notwithstanding any arrangements which Seller or Buyer may have with any third party, each party will be liable as a principal for its obligations under this Agreement and each Transaction.

10. **Events of Default**

(a) If any of the following events (each an "Event of Default") occurs in relation to either party (the "Defaulting Party", the other party being the "non-Defaulting Party") whether acting as Seller or Buyer -

(i) Buyer fails to pay the Purchase Price upon the applicable Purchase Date or Seller fails to pay the Repurchase Price upon the applicable Repurchase Date, and the non-Defaulting Party serves a Default Notice on the Defaulting Party; or

(ii) if the parties have specified in Annex I hereto that this sub-paragraph shall apply, Seller fails to deliver Purchased Securities on the Purchase Date or Buyer fails to deliver Equivalent Securities on the Repurchase Date, and the non-Defaulting Party serves a Default Notice on the Defaulting Party; or

(iii) Seller or Buyer fails to pay when due any sum payable under sub-paragraph (g) or (h) below, and the non-Defaulting Party serves a Default Notice on the Defaulting Party; or

(iv) Seller or Buyer fails to comply with paragraph 4 and the non-Defaulting Party serves a Default Notice on the Defaulting Party; or

(v) Seller or Buyer fails to comply with paragraph 5 and the non-Defaulting Party serves a Default Notice on the Defaulting Party; or

(vi) an Act of Insolvency occurs with respect to Seller or Buyer and (except in the case of an Act of Insolvency which is the presentation of a petition for winding-up or any analogous proceeding or the appointment of a liquidator or analogous officer of the Defaulting Party in which case no such notice shall be required) the non-Defaulting Party serves a Default Notice on the Defaulting Party; or

(vii) any representations made by Seller or Buyer are incorrect or untrue in any material respect when made or repeated or deemed to have been made or repeated, and the non-Defaulting Party serves a Default Notice on the Defaulting Party; or

(viii) Seller or Buyer admits to the other that it is unable to, or intends not to, perform any of its obligations hereunder and/or in respect of any Transaction and the non-Defaulting Party serves a Default Notice on the Defaulting Party; or

October 2000

(ix) Seller or Buyer is suspended or expelled from membership of or participation in any securities exchange or association or other self regulating organisation, or suspended from dealing in securities by any government agency, or any of the assets of either Seller or Buyer or the assets of investors held by, or to the order of, Seller or Buyer are transferred or ordered to be transferred to a trustee by a regulatory authority pursuant to any securities regulating legislation and the non-Defaulting Party serves a Default Notice on the Defaulting Party; or

(x) Seller or Buyer fails to perform any other of its obligations hereunder and does not remedy such failure within 30 days after notice is given by the non-Defaulting Party requiring it to do so, and the non-Defaulting Party serves a Default Notice on the Defaulting Party;

then sub-paragraphs (b) to (f) below shall apply.

(b) The Repurchase Date for each Transaction hereunder shall be deemed immediately to occur and, subject to the following provisions, all Cash Margin (including interest accrued) shall be immediately repayable and Equivalent Margin Securities shall be immediately deliverable (and so that, where this sub-paragraph applies, performance of the respective obligations of the parties with respect to the delivery of Securities, the payment of the Repurchase Prices for any Equivalent Securities and the repayment of any Cash Margin shall be effected only in accordance with the provisions of sub-paragraph (c) below).

(c) (i) The Default Market Values of the Equivalent Securities and any Equivalent Margin Securities to be transferred, the amount of any Cash Margin (including the amount of interest accrued) to be transferred and the Repurchase Prices to be paid by each party shall be established by the non-Defaulting Party for all Transactions as at the Repurchase Date; and

(ii) on the basis of the sums so established, an account shall be taken (as at the Repurchase Date) of what is due from each party to the other under this Agreement (on the basis that each party's claim against the other in respect of the transfer to it of Equivalent Securities or Equivalent Margin Securities under this Agreement equals the Default Market Value therefor) and the sums due from one party shall be set off against the sums due from the other and only the balance of the account shall be payable (by the party having the claim valued at the lower amount pursuant to the foregoing) and such balance shall be due and payable on the next following Business Day. For the purposes of this calculation, all sums not denominated in the Base Currency shall be converted into the Base Currency on the relevant date at the Spot Rate prevailing at the relevant time.

(d) For the purposes of this Agreement, the "Default Market Value" of any Equivalent Securities or Equivalent Margin Securities shall be determined in accordance with

October 2000

sub-paragraph (e) below, and for this purpose -

(i) the "Appropriate Market" means, in relation to Securities of any description, the market which is the most appropriate market for Securities of that description, as determined by the non-Defaulting Party;

(ii) the "Default Valuation Time" means, in relation to an Event of Default, the close of business in the Appropriate Market on the fifth dealing day after the day on which that Event of Default occurs or, where that Event of Default is the occurrence of an Act of Insolvency in respect of which under paragraph 10(a) no notice is required from the non-Defaulting Party in order for such event to constitute an Event of Default, the close of business on the fifth dealing day after the day on which the non-Defaulting Party first became aware of the occurrence of such Event of Default;

(iii) "Deliverable Securities" means Equivalent Securities or Equivalent Margin Securities to be delivered by the Defaulting Party;

(iv) "Net Value" means at any time, in relation to any Deliverable Securities or Receivable Securities, the amount which, in the reasonable opinion of the non-Defaulting Party, represents their fair market value, having regard to such pricing sources and methods (which may include, without limitation, available prices for Securities with similar maturities, terms and credit characteristics as the relevant Equivalent Securities or Equivalent Margin Securities) as the non-Defaulting Party considers appropriate, less, in the case of Receivable Securities, or plus, in the case of Deliverable Securities, all Transaction Costs which would be incurred in connection with the purchase or sale of such Securities;

(v) "Receivable Securities" means Equivalent Securities or Equivalent Margin Securities to be delivered to the Defaulting Party; and

(vi) "Transaction Costs" in relation to any transaction contemplated in paragraph 10(d) or (e) means the reasonable costs, commission, fees and expenses (including any mark-up or mark-down) that would be incurred in connection with the purchase of Deliverable Securities or sale of Receivable Securities, calculated on the assumption that the aggregate thereof is the least that could reasonably be expected to be paid in order to carry out the transaction;

(e) (i) If between the occurrence of the relevant Event of Default and the Default Valuation Time the non-Defaulting Party gives to the Defaulting Party a written notice (a "Default Valuation Notice") which –

(A) states that, since the occurrence of the relevant Event of Default, the non-Defaulting Party has sold, in the case of Receivable Securities, or purchased, in the case of Deliverable Securities, Securities which form

part of the same issue and are of an identical type and description as those Equivalent Securities or Equivalent Margin Securities, and that the non-Defaulting Party elects to treat as the Default Market Value -

(aa) in the case of Receivable Securities, the net proceeds of such sale after deducting all reasonable costs, fees and expenses incurred in connection therewith (provided that, where the Securities sold are not identical in amount to the Equivalent Securities or Equivalent Margin Securities, the non-Defaulting Party may either (x) elect to treat such net proceeds of sale divided by the amount of Securities sold and multiplied by the amount of the Equivalent Securities or Equivalent Margin Securities as the Default Market Value or (y) elect to treat such net proceeds of sale of the Equivalent Securities or Equivalent Margin Securities actually sold as the Default Market Value of that proportion of the Equivalent Securities or Equivalent Margin Securities, and, in the case of (y), the Default Market Value of the balance of the Equivalent Securities or Equivalent Margin Securities shall be determined separately in accordance with the provisions of this paragraph 10(e) and accordingly may be the subject of a separate notice (or notices) under this paragraph 10(e)(i)); or

(bb) in the case of Deliverable Securities, the aggregate cost of such purchase, including all reasonable costs, fees and expenses incurred in connection therewith (provided that, where the Securities purchased are not identical in amount to the Equivalent Securities or Equivalent Margin Securities, the non-Defaulting Party may either (x) elect to treat such aggregate cost divided by the amount of Securities sold and multiplied by the amount of the Equivalent Securities or Equivalent Margin Securities as the Default Market Value or (y) elect to treat the aggregate cost of purchasing the Equivalent Securities or Equivalent Margin Securities actually purchased as the Default Market Value of that proportion of the Equivalent Securities or Equivalent Margin Securities, and, in the case of (y), the Default Market Value of the balance of the Equivalent Securities or Equivalent Margin Securities shall be determined separately in accordance with the provisions of this paragraph 10(e) and accordingly may be the subject of a separate notice (or notices) under this paragraph 10(e)(i));

(B) states that the non-Defaulting Party has received, in the case of Deliverable Securities, offer quotations or, in the case of Receivable

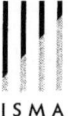

Securities, bid quotations in respect of Securities of the relevant description from two or more market makers or regular dealers in the Appropriate Market in a commercially reasonable size (as determined by the non-Defaulting Party) and specifies -

(aa) the price or prices quoted by each of them for, in the case of Deliverable Securities, the sale by the relevant market marker or dealer of such Securities or, in the case of Receivable Securities, the purchase by the relevant market maker or dealer of such Securities;

(bb) the Transaction Costs which would be incurred in connection with such a transaction; and

(cc) that the non-Defaulting Party elects to treat the price so quoted (or, where more than one price is so quoted, the arithmetic mean of the prices so quoted), after deducting, in the case of Receivable Securities, or adding, in the case of Deliverable Securities, such Transaction Costs, as the Default Market Value of the relevant Equivalent Securities or Equivalent Margin Securities; or

(C) states –

(aa) that either (x) acting in good faith, the non-Defaulting Party has endeavoured but been unable to sell or purchase Securities in accordance with sub-paragraph (i)(A) above or to obtain quotations in accordance with sub-paragraph (i)(B) above (or both) or (y) the non-Defaulting Party has determined that it would not be commercially reasonable to obtain such quotations, or that it would not be commercially reasonable to use any quotations which it has obtained under sub-paragraph (i)(B) above; and

(bb) that the non-Defaulting Party has determined the Net Value of the relevant Equivalent Securities or Equivalent Margin Securities (which shall be specified) and that the non-Defaulting Party elects to treat such Net Value as the Default Market Value of the relevant Equivalent Securities or Equivalent Margin Securities,

then the Default Market Value of the relevant Equivalent Securities or Equivalent Margin Securities shall be an amount equal to the Default Market Value specified in accordance with (A), (B)(cc) or, as the case may be, (C)(bb) above.

October 2000

(ii) If by the Default Valuation Time the non-Defaulting Party has not given a Default Valuation Notice, the Default Market Value of the relevant Equivalent Securities or Equivalent Margin Securities shall be an amount equal to their Net Value at the Default Valuation Time; provided that, if at the Default Valuation Time the non-Defaulting Party reasonably determines that, owing to circumstances affecting the market in the Equivalent Securities or Equivalent Margin Securities in question, it is not possible for the non-Defaulting Party to determine a Net Value of such Equivalent Securities or Equivalent Margin Securities which is commercially reasonable, the Default Market Value of such Equivalent Securities or Equivalent Margin Securities shall be an amount equal to their Net Value as determined by the non-Defaulting Party as soon as reasonably practicable after the Default Valuation Time.

(f) The Defaulting Party shall be liable to the non-Defaulting Party for the amount of all reasonable legal and other professional expenses incurred by the non-Defaulting Party in connection with or as a consequence of an Event of Default, together with interest thereon at LIBOR or, in the case of an expense attributable to a particular Transaction, the Pricing Rate for the relevant Transaction if that Pricing Rate is greater than LIBOR.

(g) If Seller fails to deliver Purchased Securities to Buyer on the applicable Purchase Date Buyer may -

(i) if it has paid the Purchase Price to Seller, require Seller immediately to repay the sum so paid;

(ii) if Buyer has a Transaction Exposure to Seller in respect of the relevant Transaction, require Seller from time to time to pay Cash Margin at least equal to such Transaction Exposure;

(iii) at any time while such failure continues, terminate the Transaction by giving written notice to Seller. On such termination the obligations of Seller and Buyer with respect to delivery of Purchased Securities and Equivalent Securities shall terminate and Seller shall pay to Buyer an amount equal to the excess of the Repurchase Price at the date of Termination over the Purchase Price.

(h) If Buyer fails to deliver Equivalent Securities to Seller on the applicable Repurchase Date Seller may -

(i) if it has paid the Repurchase Price to Buyer, require Buyer immediately to repay the sum so paid;

(ii) if Seller has a Transaction Exposure to Buyer in respect of the relevant Transaction, require Buyer from time to time to pay Cash Margin at least equal to such Transaction Exposure;

(iii) at any time while such failure continues, by written notice to Buyer declare that that Transaction (but only that Transaction) shall be terminated immediately in accordance with sub-paragraph (c) above (disregarding for this purpose references in that sub-paragraph to transfer of Cash Margin and delivery of Equivalent Margin Securities and as if references to the Repurchase Date were to the date on which notice was given under this sub-paragraph).

(i) The provisions of this Agreement constitute a complete statement of the remedies available to each party in respect of any Event of Default.

(j) Subject to paragraph 10(k), neither party may claim any sum by way of consequential loss or damage in the event of a failure by the other party to perform any of its obligations under this Agreement.

(k) (i) Subject to sub-paragraph (ii) below, if as a result of a Transaction terminating before its agreed Repurchase Date under paragraphs 10(b), 10(g)(iii) or 10(h)(iii), the non-Defaulting Party, in the case of paragraph 10(b), Buyer, in the case of paragraph 10(g)(iii), or Seller, in the case of paragraph 10(h)(iii), (in each case the "first party") incurs any loss or expense in entering into replacement transactions, the other party shall be required to pay to the first party the amount determined by the first party in good faith to be equal to the loss or expense incurred in connection with such replacement transactions (including all fees, costs and other expenses) less the amount of any profit or gain made by that party in connection with such replacement transactions; provided that if that calculation results in a negative number, an amount equal to that number shall be payable by the first party to the other party.

(ii) If the first party reasonably decides, instead of entering into such replacement transactions, to replace or unwind any hedging transactions which the first party entered into in connection with the Transaction so terminating, or to enter into any replacement hedging transactions, the other party shall be required to pay to the first party the amount determined by the first party in good faith to be equal to the loss or expense incurred in connection with entering into such replacement or unwinding (including all fees, costs and other expenses) less the amount of any profit or gain made by that party in connection with such replacement or unwinding; provided that if that calculation results in a negative number, an amount equal to that number shall be payable by the first party to the other party.

(l) Each party shall immediately notify the other if an Event of Default, or an event which, upon the serving of a Default Notice, would be an Event of Default, occurs in relation to it.

11. **Tax Event**

(a) This paragraph shall apply if either party notifies the other that -

   (i) any action taken by a taxing authority or brought in a court of competent jurisdiction (regardless of whether such action is taken or brought with respect to a party to this Agreement); or

   (ii) a change in the fiscal or regulatory regime (including, but not limited to, a change in law or in the general interpretation of law but excluding any change in any rate of tax),

   has or will, in the notifying party's reasonable opinion, have a material adverse effect on that party in the context of a Transaction.

(b) If so requested by the other party, the notifying party will furnish the other with an opinion of a suitably qualified adviser that an event referred to in sub-paragraph (a)(i) or (ii) above has occurred and affects the notifying party.

(c) Where this paragraph applies, the party giving the notice referred to in sub-paragraph (a) may, subject to sub-paragraph (d) below, terminate the Transaction with effect from a date specified in the notice, not being earlier (unless so agreed by the other party) than 30 days after the date of the notice, by nominating that date as the Repurchase Date.

(d) If the party receiving the notice referred to in sub-paragraph (a) so elects, it may override that notice by giving a counter-notice to the other party. If a counter-notice is given, the party which gives the counter-notice will be deemed to have agreed to indemnify the other party against the adverse effect referred to in sub-paragraph (a) so far as relates to the relevant Transaction and the original Repurchase Date will continue to apply.

(e) Where a Transaction is terminated as described in this paragraph, the party which has given the notice to terminate shall indemnify the other party against any reasonable legal and other professional expenses incurred by the other party by reason of the termination, but the other party may not claim any sum by way of consequential loss or damage in respect of a termination in accordance with this paragraph.

(f) This paragraph is without prejudice to paragraph 6(b) (obligation to pay additional amounts if withholding or deduction required); but an obligation to pay such additional amounts may, where appropriate, be a circumstance which causes this paragraph to apply.

12. **Interest**

   To the extent permitted by applicable law, if any sum of money payable hereunder or under any Transaction is not paid when due, interest shall accrue on the unpaid sum

October 2000   - 23 -

as a separate debt at the greater of the Pricing Rate for the Transaction to which such sum relates (where such sum is referable to a Transaction) and LIBOR on a 360 day basis or 365 day basis in accordance with the applicable ISMA convention, for the actual number of days during the period from and including the date on which payment was due to, but excluding, the date of payment.

13. **Single Agreement**

Each party acknowledges that, and has entered into this Agreement and will enter into each Transaction hereunder in consideration of and in reliance upon the fact that all Transactions hereunder constitute a single business and contractual relationship and are made in consideration of each other. Accordingly, each party agrees (i) to perform all of its obligations in respect of each Transaction hereunder, and that a default in the performance of any such obligations shall constitute a default by it in respect of all Transactions hereunder, and (ii) that payments, deliveries and other transfers made by either of them in respect of any Transaction shall be deemed to have been made in consideration of payments, deliveries and other transfers in respect of any other Transactions hereunder.

14. **Notices and Other Communications**

(a) Any notice or other communication to be given under this Agreement -

   (i) shall be in the English language, and except where expressly otherwise provided in this Agreement, shall be in writing;

   (ii) may be given in any manner described in sub-paragraphs (b) and (c) below;

   (iii) shall be sent to the party to whom it is to be given at the address or number, or in accordance with the electronic messaging details, set out in Annex I hereto.

(b) Subject to sub-paragraph (c) below, any such notice or other communication shall be effective -

   (i) if in writing and delivered in person or by courier, at the time when it is delivered;

   (ii) if sent by telex, at the time when the recipient's answerback is received;

   (iii) if sent by facsimile transmission, at the time when the transmission is received by a responsible employee of the recipient in legible form (it being agreed that the burden of proving receipt will be on the sender and will not be met by a transmission report generated by the sender's facsimile machine);

   (iv) if sent by certified or registered mail (airmail, if overseas) or the equivalent (return receipt requested), at the time when that mail is delivered or its delivery is attempted;

(v) if sent by electronic messaging system, at the time that electronic message is received;

except that any notice or communication which is received, or delivery of which is attempted, after close of business on the date of receipt or attempted delivery or on a day which is not a day on which commercial banks are open for business in the place where that notice or other communication is to be given shall be treated as given at the opening of business on the next following day which is such a day.

(c) If -

(i) there occurs in relation to either party an event which, upon the service of a Default Notice, would be an Event of Default; and

(ii) the non-Defaulting Party, having made all practicable efforts to do so, including having attempted to use at least two of the methods specified in sub-paragraph (b)(ii), (iii) or (v), has been unable to serve a Default Notice by one of the methods specified in those sub-paragraphs (or such of those methods as are normally used by the non-Defaulting Party when communicating with the Defaulting Party),

the non-Defaulting Party may sign a written notice (a "Special Default Notice") which -

(aa) specifies the relevant event referred to in paragraph 10(a) which has occurred in relation to the Defaulting Party;

(bb) states that the non-Defaulting Party, having made all practicable efforts to do so, including having attempted to use at least two of the methods specified in sub-paragraph (b)(ii), (iii) or (v), has been unable to serve a Default Notice by one of the methods specified in those sub-paragraphs (or such of those methods as are normally used by the non-Defaulting Party when communicating with the Defaulting Party);

(cc) specifies the date on which, and the time at which, the Special Default Notice is signed by the non-Defaulting Party; and

(dd) states that the event specified in accordance with sub-paragraph (aa) above shall be treated as an Event of Default with effect from the date and time so specified.

On the signature of a Special Default Notice the relevant event shall be treated with effect from the date and time so specified as an Event of Default in relation to the Defaulting Party, and accordingly references in paragraph 10 to a Default Notice shall be treated as including a Special Default Notice. A Special Default Notice shall be given to the Defaulting Party as soon as practicable after it is signed.

October 2000

(d) Either party may by notice to the other change the address, telex or facsimile number or electronic messaging system details at which notices or other communications are to be given to it.

15. **Entire Agreement; Severability**

This Agreement shall supersede any existing agreements between the parties containing general terms and conditions for Transactions. Each provision and agreement herein shall be treated as separate from any other provision or agreement herein and shall be enforceable notwithstanding the unenforceability of any such other provision or agreement.

16. **Non-assignability; Termination**

(a) Subject to sub-paragraph (b) below, neither party may assign, charge or otherwise deal with (including without limitation any dealing with any interest in or the creation of any interest in) its rights or obligations under this Agreement or under any Transaction without the prior written consent of the other party. Subject to the foregoing, this Agreement and any Transactions shall be binding upon and shall inure to the benefit of the parties and their respective successors and assigns.

(b) Sub-paragraph (a) above shall not preclude a party from assigning, charging or otherwise dealing with all or any part of its interest in any sum payable to it under paragraph 10(c) or (f) above.

(c) Either party may terminate this Agreement by giving written notice to the other, except that this Agreement shall, notwithstanding such notice, remain applicable to any Transactions then outstanding.

(d) All remedies hereunder shall survive Termination in respect of the relevant Transaction and termination of this Agreement.

(e) The participation of any additional member State of the European Union in economic and monetary union after 1 January 1999 shall not have the effect of altering any term of the Agreement or any Transaction, nor give a party the right unilaterally to alter or terminate the Agreement or any Transaction.

17. **Governing Law**

This Agreement shall be governed by and construed in accordance with the laws of England. Buyer and Seller hereby irrevocably submit for all purposes of or in connection with this Agreement and each Transaction to the jurisdiction of the Courts of England.

Party A hereby appoints the person identified in Annex I hereto as its agent to receive on its behalf service of process in such courts. If such agent ceases to be its agent,

Party A shall promptly appoint, and notify Party B of the identity of, a new agent in England.

Party B hereby appoints the person identified in Annex I hereto as its agent to receive on its behalf service of process in such courts. If such agent ceases to be its agent, Party B shall promptly appoint, and notify Party A of the identity of, a new agent in England.

Each party shall deliver to the other, within 30 days of the date of this Agreement in the case of the appointment of a person identified in Annex I or of the date of the appointment of the relevant agent in any other case, evidence of the acceptance by the agent appointed by it pursuant to this paragraph of such appointment.

Nothing in this paragraph shall limit the right of any party to take proceedings in the courts of any other country of competent jurisdiction.

18. **No Waivers, etc.**

   No express or implied waiver of any Event of Default by either party shall constitute a waiver of any other Event of Default and no exercise of any remedy hereunder by any party shall constitute a waiver of its right to exercise any other remedy hereunder. No modification or waiver of any provision of this Agreement and no consent by any party to a departure herefrom shall be effective unless and until such modification, waiver or consent shall be in writing and duly executed by both of the parties hereto. Without limitation on any of the foregoing, the failure to give a notice pursuant to paragraph 4(a) hereof will not constitute a waiver of any right to do so at a later date.

19. **Waiver of Immunity**

   Each party hereto hereby waives, to the fullest extent permitted by applicable law, all immunity (whether on the basis of sovereignty or otherwise) from jurisdiction, attachment (both before and after judgment) and execution to which it might otherwise be entitled in any action or proceeding in the Courts of England or of any other country or jurisdiction, relating in any way to this Agreement or any Transaction, and agrees that it will not raise, claim or cause to be pleaded any such immunity at or in respect of any such action or proceeding.

20. **Recording**

   The parties agree that each may electronically record all telephone conversations between them.

21. **Third Party Rights**

   No person shall have any right to enforce any provision of this Agreement under the Contracts (Rights of Third Parties) Act 1999.

THE BOND MARKET ASSOCIATION

ISMA

[Name of Party]

By_____

Title_____

Date_____

[Name of Party]

By_____

Title_____

Date_____

APPENDIX 1

ANNEX I

Supplemental Terms or Conditions

Paragraph references are to paragraphs in the Agreement.

1. The following elections shall apply -

[(a)   paragraph 1(c)(i). Buy/Sell Back Transactions [may/may not] be effected under this Agreement, and accordingly the Buy/Sell Back Annex [shall/shall not] apply.]*

[(b)   paragraph 1(c)(ii). Transactions in Net Paying Securities [may/may not] be effected under this Agreement, and accordingly the provisions of sub-paragraphs (i) and (ii) below [shall/shall not] apply.

   (i)   The phrase "other than equities and Net Paying Securities" shall be replaced by the phrase "other than equities".

   (ii)   In the Buy/Sell Back Annex the following words shall be added to the end of the definition of the expression "IR": "and for the avoidance of doubt the reference to the amount of Income for these purposes shall be to an amount paid without withholding or deduction for or on account of taxes or duties notwithstanding that a payment of such Income made in certain circumstances may be subject to such a withholding or deduction".]*

[(c)   paragraph 1(d). Agency Transactions [may/may not] be effected under this Agreement, and accordingly the Agency Annex [shall/shall not] apply.]*

(d)   paragraph 2(d). The Base Currency shall be: _____.

(e)   paragraph 2(p). [list Buyer's and Seller's Designated Offices]

(f)   paragraph 2(cc). The pricing source for calculation of Market Value shall be: _____.

(g)   paragraph 2(rr). Spot rate to be: _____.

(h)   paragraph 3(b). [Seller/Buyer/both Seller and Buyer]* to deliver Confirmation.

(i)   paragraph 4(f). Interest rate on Cash Margin to be [ ]% for _____ currency.
                                                          [ ]% for _____ currency.

   Interest to be payable [payment intervals and dates].

(j)   paragraph 4(g). Delivery period for margin calls to be: _____.

.

* Delete as appropriate

October 2000   - 29 -

[(k)] paragraph 6(j). Paragraph 6(j) shall apply and the events specified in paragraph 10(a) identified for the purposes of paragraph 6(j) shall be those set out in sub paragraphs [   ] of paragraph 10(a) of the Agreement.]*

[(l)] paragraph 10(a)(ii). Paragraph 10(a)(ii) shall apply.]*

(m) paragraph 14. For the purposes of paragraph 14 of this Agreement -

    (i) Address for notices and other communications for Party A -

        Address:
        Attention:
        Telephone:
        Facsimile:
        Telex:
        Answerback:
        Other:

    (ii) Address for notices and other communications for Party B -

        Address:
        Attention:
        Telephone:
        Facsimile:
        Telex:
        Answerback:
        Other:

[(n)] paragraph 17. For the purposes of paragraph 17 of this Agreement -

    (i) Party A appoints [   ] as its agent for service of process;

    (ii) Party B appoints [   ] as its agent for service of process.]*

* Delete as appropriate

APPENDIX 1

2. The following supplemental terms and conditions shall apply -

[Existing Transactions

(a) The parties agree that this Agreement shall apply to all transactions which are subject to the PSA/ISMA Global Master Repurchase Agreement between them dated _____ and which are outstanding as at the date of this Agreement so that such transactions shall be treated as if they had been entered into under this Agreement, and the terms of such transactions are amended accordingly with effect from the date of this Agreement.]*

[Forward Transactions

(b) The parties agree that Forward Transactions (as defined in sub-paragraph (i)(A) below) may be effected under this Agreement and accordingly the provisions of sub-paragraphs (i) to (iv) below shall apply.

    (i) The following definitions shall apply -

        (A) "Forward Transaction", a Transaction in respect of which the Purchase Date is at least [three] Business Days after the date on which the Transaction was entered into and has not yet occurred;

        (B) "Forward Repricing Date", with respect to any Forward Transaction the date which is such number of Business Days before the Purchase Date as is equal to the minimum period for the delivery of margin applicable under paragraph 4(g).

    (ii) The Confirmation relating to any Forward Transaction may describe the Purchased Securities by reference to a type or class of Securities, which, without limitation, may be identified by issuer or class of issuers and a maturity or range of maturities. Where this paragraph applies, the parties shall agree the actual Purchased Securities not less than two Business Days before the Purchase Date and Buyer or Seller (or both), as shall have been agreed, shall promptly deliver to the other party a Confirmation which shall describe such Purchased Securities.

    (iii) At any time between the Forward Repricing Date and the Purchase Date for any Forward Transaction the parties may agree either –

        (A) to adjust the Purchase Price under that Forward Transaction; or

        (B) to adjust the number of Purchased Securities to be sold by Seller to Buyer under that Forward Transaction.

* Delete as appropriate

October 2000

(iv) Where the parties agree to an adjustment under paragraph (iii) above, Buyer or Seller (or both), as shall have been agreed, shall promptly deliver to the other party a Confirmation of the Forward Transaction, as adjusted under paragraph (iii) above.

(c) Where the parties agree that this paragraph shall apply, paragraphs 2 and 4 of the Agreement are amended as follows.

(i) Paragraph 2(ww) is deleted and replaced by the following -

"(ww) "Transaction Exposure" means -

(i) with respect to any Forward Transaction at any time between the Forward Repricing Date and the Purchase Date, the difference between (A) the Market Value of the Purchased Securities at the relevant time and (B) the Purchase Price;

(ii) with respect to any Transaction at any time during the period (if any) from the Purchase Date to the date on which the Purchased Securities are delivered to Buyer or, if earlier, the date on which the Transaction is terminated under paragraph 10(g), the difference between (A) the Market Value of the Purchased Securities at the relevant time and (B) the Repurchase Price at the relevant time;

(iii) with respect to any Transaction at any time during the period from the Purchase Date (or, if later, the date on which the Purchased Securities are delivered to Buyer or the Transaction is terminated under paragraph 10(g)) to the Repurchase Date (or, if later, the date on which Equivalent Securities are delivered to Seller or the Transaction is terminated under paragraph 10(h)), the difference between (A) the Repurchase Price at the relevant time multiplied by the applicable Margin Ratio (or, where the Transaction relates to Securities of more than one description to which different Margin Ratios apply, the amount produced by multiplying the Repurchase Price attributable to Equivalent Securities of each such description by the applicable Margin Ratio and aggregating the resulting amounts, the Repurchase Price being for this purpose attributed to Equivalent Securities of each such description in the same proportions as those in which the Purchase Price was apportioned among the Purchased Securities) and (B) the Market Value of Equivalent Securities at the relevant time.

In each case, if (A) is greater than (B), Buyer has a Transaction Exposure for that Transaction equal to the excess, and if (B) is greater than (A), Seller has a Transaction Exposure to Buyer equal to the excess."

    (ii)   In paragraph 4(c) -

        (aa)   the words "any amount payable to the first party under paragraph 5 but unpaid" are deleted and replaced by "any amount which will become payable to the first party under paragraph 5 during the period after the time at which the calculation is made which is equal to the minimum period for the delivery of margin applicable under paragraph 4(g) or which is payable to the first party under paragraph 5 but unpaid"; and

        (bb)   the words "any amount payable to the other party under paragraph 5 but unpaid" are deleted and replaced by "any amount which will become payable to the other party under paragraph 5 during the period after the time at which the calculation is made which is equal to the minimum period for the delivery of margin applicable under paragraph 4(g) or which is payable to the other party under paragraph 5 but unpaid".]*

* Delete as appropriate

ANNEX II

Form of Confirmation

To: _____

From: _____

Date: _____

Subject: [Repurchase][Buy/Sell Back]* Transaction
            (Reference Number:)

Dear Sirs,

The purpose of this [letter]/[facsimile]//[telex], a "Confirmation" for the purposes of the Agreement, is to set forth the terms and conditions of the above repurchase transaction entered into between us on the Contract Date referred to below.

This Confirmation supplements and forms part of, and is subject to, the Global Master Repurchase Agreement as entered into between us as of [ ] as the same may be amended from time to time (the "Agreement"). All provisions contained in the Agreement govern this Confirmation except as expressly modified below. Words and phrases defined in the Agreement and used in this Confirmation shall have the same meaning herein as in the Agreement.

1. Contract Date:

2. Purchased Securities [state type[s] and nominal value[s]]:

3. CUSIP, ISIN or other identifying number[s]:

4. Buyer:

5. Seller:

6. Purchase Date:

7. Purchase Price:

8. Contractual Currency:

[9. Repurchase Date]:*

[10. Terminable on demand]:*

11. Pricing Rate:

---

* Delete as appropriate

[12. Sell Back Price:]*

13. Buyer's Bank Account[s] Details:

14. Seller's Bank Account[s] Details:

[15. The Transaction is an Agency Transaction. [Name of Agent] is acting as agent for [name or identifier of Principal]]:*

[16. Additional Terms]:*

Yours faithfully,

* Delete as appropriate

Appendix 2

Amendment Agreement to a PSA/ISMA Global Master Repurchase Agreement

Reproduced with the kind permission of the
International Securities Market Association
and
The Bond Market Association

The Bond Market Association
New York • Washington • London
www.bondmarkets.com

International Securities Market Association
Rigistrasse 60, P.O. Box, CH-8033, Zürich
www.isma.org

AMENDMENT AGREEMENT TO A
PSA/ISMA GLOBAL MASTER REPURCHASE AGREEMENT

Dated as of _____

Between:

_____ _____ _____ of _____ _____ _____ ("**Party A**");

and

_____ _____ _____ of _____ _____ _____ ("**Party B**")

WHEREAS the parties have entered into the 1995 version of the PSA/ISMA Global Master Repurchase Agreement on _____ (the "GMRA 1995") and now wish to enter into transactions on the terms of the 2000 version of the TBMA/ISMA Global Master Repurchase Agreement published by The Bond Market Association and the International Securities Market Association (the "GMRA 2000").

NOW IT IS AGREED as follows:

1. Interpretation

In this Agreement –

"Agency Annex" means the Agency Annex to the GMRA 2000 published by The Bond Market Association and the International Securities Market Association; and

"Buy/Sell Back Annex" means the Buy/Sell Back Annex to the GMRA 2000 published by The Bond Market Association and the International Securities Market Association.

2. Amendment

(a) The heading and paragraphs 1 to 20 of the GMRA 1995 are deleted and replaced by the heading and paragraphs 1 to 21 of the GMRA 2000.

(b) Annexes III and IV to the GMRA 1995 are deleted and replaced by the Buy/Sell Back Annex and the Agency Annex.

October 2000

(c) Annexes V to VIII to the GMRA 1995 are deleted.

3. Annex I

Annex I to the GMRA 1995 is deleted and replaced by Annex I in the form set out in the Schedule to this Agreement.

4. Governing Law

Paragraph 17 of the GMRA 2000 shall apply to this Agreement as if that paragraph and paragraph 1(n) of Annex I to the GMRA 2000 were expressly set out herein.

[Name of Party]   [Name of Party]

By _____   By _____

Title _____   Title _____

Date _____   Date _____

APPENDIX 2

SCHEDULE

ANNEX I

Supplemental Terms or Conditions

Paragraph references are to paragraphs in the Agreement.

1. The following elections shall apply -

[(a) paragraph 1(c)(i). Buy/Sell Back Transactions [may/may not] be effected under this Agreement, and accordingly the Buy/Sell Back Annex [shall/shall not apply.]*

[(b) paragraph 1. Transactions in Net Paying Securities [may/may not] be effected under this Agreement, and accordingly the provisions of sub-paragraphs (i) and (ii) below [shall/shall not] apply.

(i) The phrase "other than equities and Net Paying Securities" shall be replaced by the phrase "other than equities".

(ii) In the Buy/Sell Back Annex the following words shall be added to the end of the definition of the expression "IR": "and for the avoidance of doubt the reference to the amount of Income for these purposes shall be to an amount paid without withholding or deduction for or on account of taxes or duties notwithstanding that a payment of such Income made in certain circumstances may be subject to such a withholding or deduction".]*

[(c) paragraph 1(d). Agency Transactions [may/may not] be effected under this Agreement, and accordingly the Agency Annex [shall/shall not apply.]*

(d) paragraph 2(d). The Base Currency shall be: _____.

(e) paragraph 2(p). [list Buyer's and Seller's Designated Offices]

(f) paragraph 2(cc). The pricing source for calculation of Market Value shall be: _____.

(g) paragraph 2(rr). Spot rate to be _____.

(h) paragraph 3(b). [Seller/Buyer/both Seller and Buyer]* to deliver Confirmation.

(i) paragraph 4(f). Interest rate on Cash Margin to be [ ]% for _____ currency.
[ ]% for _____ currency.

Interest to be payable [payment intervals and dates].

---

* Delete as appropriate

October 2000

(j) paragraph 4(g). Delivery period for margin calls to be _____.

[(k) paragraph 6(j). Paragraph 6(j) shall apply and the events specified in paragraph 10(a) identified for the purposes of paragraph 6(j) shall be those set out in sub-paragraphs [   ] of paragraph 10(a) of the Agreement.]*

[(l) paragraph 10(a)(ii). Paragraph 10(a)(ii) shall apply.]*

(m) paragraph 14. For the purposes of paragraph 14 of this Agreement –

    (i) Address for notices and other communications for Party A -

        Address:
        Attention:
        Telephone:
        Facsimile:
        Telex:
        Answerback:
        Other:

    (ii) Address for notices and other communications for Party B -

        Address:
        Attention:
        Telephone:
        Facsimile:
        Telex:
        Answerback:
        Other:

[(n) paragraph 17. For the purposes of paragraph 17 of this Agreement –

    (i) Party A appoints [   ] as its agent for service of process;

    (ii) Party B appoints [   ] as its agent for service of process.]*

2. The following supplemental terms and conditions shall apply -

[Existing Transactions

(a) The parties agree that this Agreement shall apply to all transactions which are subject to the PSA/ISMA Global Master Repurchase Agreement between them dated _____ and which are outstanding as at the date of this Agreement so that such transactions shall be treated as if they had been entered into under this Agreement, and the terms of such transactions are amended accordingly with effect from the date of this Agreement.]*

---

* Delete as appropriate

[Forward Transactions

(b) The parties agree that Forward Transactions (as defined in sub-paragraph (i)(A) below) may be effected under this Agreement and accordingly the provisions of sub-paragraphs (i) to (iv) below shall apply.

    (i) The following definitions shall apply –

        (A) "Forward Transaction", a Transaction in respect of which the Purchase Date is at least [three] Business Days after the date on which the Transaction was entered into and has not yet occurred;

        (B) "Forward Repricing Date", with respect to any Forward Transaction the date which is such number of Business Days before the Purchase Date as is equal to the minimum period for the delivery of margin applicable under paragraph 4(g).

    (ii) The Confirmation relating to any Forward Transaction may describe the Purchased Securities by reference to a type or class of Securities, which, without limitation, may be identified by issuer or class of issuers and a maturity or range of maturities. Where this paragraph applies, the parties shall agree the actual Purchased Securities not less than two Business Days before the Purchase Date and Buyer or Seller (or both), as shall have been agreed, shall promptly deliver to the other party a Confirmation which shall describe such Purchased Securities.

    (iii) At any time between the Forward Repricing Date and the Purchase Date for any Forward Transaction the parties may agree either –

        (A) to adjust the Purchase Price under that Forward Transaction; or

        (B) to adjust the number of Purchased Securities to be sold by Seller to Buyer under that Forward Transaction.

    (iv) Where the parties agree to an adjustment under paragraph (iii) above, Buyer or Seller (or both), as shall have been agreed, shall promptly deliver to the other party a Confirmation of the Forward Transaction, as adjusted under paragraph (iii) above.

(c) Where the parties agree that this paragraph shall apply, paragraphs 2 and 4 of the Agreement are amended as follows.

    (i) Paragraph 2(ww) is deleted and replaced by the following -

    "(ww) "Transaction Exposure" means -

 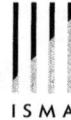

(i) with respect to any Forward Transaction at any time between the Forward Repricing Date and the Purchase Date, the difference between (A) the Market Value of the Purchased Securities at the relevant time and (B) the Purchase Price;

(ii) with respect to any Transaction at any time during the period (if any) from the Purchase Date to the date on which the Purchased Securities are delivered to Buyer or, if earlier, the date on which the Transaction is terminated under paragraph 10(g), the difference between (A) the Market Value of the Purchased Securities at the relevant time and (B) the Repurchase Price at the relevant time;

(iii) with respect to any Transaction at any time during the period from the Purchase Date (or, if later, the date on which the Purchased Securities are delivered to Buyer or the Transaction is terminated under paragraph 10(g)) to the Repurchase Date (or, if later, the date on which Equivalent Securities are delivered to Seller or the Transaction is terminated under paragraph 10(h)), the difference between (A) the Repurchase Price at the relevant time multiplied by the applicable Margin Ratio (or, where the Transaction relates to Securities of more than one description to which different Margin Ratios apply, the amount produced by multiplying the Repurchase Price attributable to Equivalent Securities of each such description by the applicable Margin Ratio and aggregating the resulting amounts, the Repurchase Price being for this purpose attributed to Equivalent Securities of each such description in the same proportions as those in which the Purchase Price was apportioned among the Purchased Securities) and (B) the Market Value of Equivalent Securities at the relevant time.

In each case, if (A) is greater than (B), Buyer has a Transaction Exposure for that Transaction equal to the excess, and if (B) is greater than (A), Seller has a Transaction Exposure to Buyer equal to the excess."

(ii) In paragraph 4(c) -

(aa) the words "any amount payable to the first party under paragraph 5 but unpaid" are deleted and replaced by "any amount which will become payable to the first party under paragraph 5 during the period after the time at which the calculation is made which is equal to the minimum period for the delivery of margin applicable under paragraph 4(g) or which is payable to the first party under paragraph 5 but unpaid"; and

(bb) the words "any amount payable to the other party under paragraph 5 but unpaid" are deleted and replaced by "any amount which will become payable to the other party under paragraph 5 during the period after the time at which the calculation is made which is equal to the minimum period for the delivery of margin applicable under paragraph 4(g) or which is payable to the other party under paragraph 5 but unpaid".]*

* Delete as appropriate

Appendix 3

The European Master Agreement

Reproduced with the kind permission of the
European Banking Federation

APPENDIX 3

FEDERATION BANCAIRE DE L'UNION EUROPEENNE
BANKING FEDERATION OF THE EUROPEAN UNION
BANKENVEREINIGUNG DER EUROPÄISCHEN UNION

in co-operation with

EUROPEAN SAVINGS BANKS GROUP   EUROPEAN ASSOCIATION OF COOPERATIVE BANKS
GROUPEMENT EUROPEEN DES CAISSES D'EPARGNE   GROUPEMENT EUROPEEN DES BANQUES COOPERATIVES
EUROPÄISCHE SPARKASSENVEREINIGUNG   EUROPÄISCHE VEREINIGUNG DER GENOSSENSCHAFTSBANKEN

MASTER AGREEMENT
FOR FINANCIAL TRANSACTIONS

GENERAL PROVISIONS
Edition 2004

1. Purpose, Structure, Interpretation

(1) *Purpose, Applicability.* The provisions set out in this document (the "General Provisions") are intended to govern financial transactions (each a "Transaction") under any Master Agreement for Financial Transactions (each a "Master Agreement") based on the form published by the Banking Federation of the European Union ("FBE"). The provisions of a Master Agreement shall apply to the extent that they are incorporated by the parties into the terms of a Transaction or type of Transactions between them.

(2) *Structure.* A Master Agreement consists of (i) an agreement between the parties thereto providing a basis for Transactions between them (the "Special Provisions"), (ii) these General Provisions, (iii) any annexes thereto (each an "Annex"), being Annexes concerning particular types of Transactions ("Product Annexes") or concerning other matters and (iv) any supplements to the Product Annexes (each a "Supplement"). If no Special Provisions have been agreed, these General Provisions (together with, if applicable, any Annexes and any Supplements thereto) shall constitute a Master Agreement governing all Transactions into the terms of which they have been incorporated. Each Master Agreement and the terms agreed in respect of all Transactions there under shall collectively be referred to herein as the "Agreement".

(3) *Interpretation.* In the event of any conflict between different parts of the Agreement, (i) any Annex shall prevail over the General Provisions, (ii) the Special Provisions shall prevail over the General Provisions and any Annex and (iii) the terms agreed in respect of an individual Transaction shall, in respect of that Transaction only, prevail over all other terms of the Agreement. Unless otherwise specified, all references herein or in any Annex to Sections are to Sections of these General Provisions or such Annex, respectively. Certain expressions used in the Agreement are defined at the places indicated in the Index of Defined Terms published by the FBE in connection with these General Provisions.

(4) *Single Agreement.* The Agreement constitutes a single contractual relationship. Accordingly, (i) each obligation of a party under any Transaction is incurred and performed in consideration of the obligations incurred and to be performed by the other party under all Transactions, and (ii) unless otherwise agreed, a failure by a party to perform an obligation under any Transaction shall constitute a failure to perform under the Agreement as a whole.

The parties enter into the Master Agreement between them and each Transaction there under in reliance on these principles, which they consider fundamental to their risk assessment.

(5) *Modifications.* Any modification of these General Provisions or any modified or new Annex which the FBE may promulgate in the future may become effective between the parties to a Master Agreement by each party notifying its acceptance in the manner designated by the FBE.

2. Transactions

(1) *Form.* A Transaction may be entered into orally or by any other means of communication.

Copyright © 2004 FBE   General Provisions - 2004

(2) *Confirmation.* Upon the parties having agreed on a Transaction each party shall promptly send to the other a confirmation (a "Confirmation") of such Transaction in the manner specified in Section 8(1). The absence of either or both Confirmations shall not affect the validity of the Transaction.

3. Payments, Deliveries and Related Definitions

(1) *Date, Place, Manner.* Each party shall make the payments and deliveries to be made by it at the time, date and place and to the account agreed in respect of the Transaction concerned and in the manner customary for payments or deliveries of the relevant kind. Each payment shall be made in the currency agreed in respect thereof (the "Contractual Currency"), free of all costs and in funds which are freely available on the due date. Each party may change its account for receiving a payment or delivery by giving notice to the other at least ten Business Days prior to the scheduled date for the relevant payment or delivery, unless the other party reasonably objects to such change and gives timely notice thereof.

(2) *Transfer of Title. Retransfer of Securities.*

(a) *Transfer of Title.* Unless otherwise agreed, any delivery or transfer of securities or other financial instruments ("Securities") or any other assets (including, in respect of Derivative Transactions, any other underlying assets of such Transactions) by a party to the other pursuant to the Agreement shall constitute a transfer to such other party of the unrestricted title to such Securities and/or assets or, if customary in the place where delivery is to be effected, of a legal position (such as a co-ownership interest in a collective holding of Securities, the position as beneficiary of a trust or another form of beneficial ownership) which is the functional equivalent of such title (including, in each case, an unrestricted right to dispose of such Securities and/or assets) and not the creation of a security interest; the use of the terms "margin" or "substitution" shall not be construed as indicating an agreement to the contrary. The transferor of any Securities and/or assets shall, accordingly, (i) not retain in respect of those Securities and/or assets any ownership interest, security interest or right to dispose and (ii) execute all documents reasonably required to effect such full transfer. As far as transfer of Securities is concerned, if registered Securities are to be transferred, the transferee may dispose of the Securities received before the transfer is entered into the relevant register; if the entry depends upon a circumstance beyond the transferor's reasonable control, the transferor does not warrant that such entry will be effected.

(b) *Retransfer of Securities.* An obligation to return or retransfer any Securities is an obligation to transfer Securities of the same kind as such Securities. Securities are "of the same kind" as other Securities if they are of the same issuer and the same type and nominal value and represent identical rights as such other Securities; if all such other Securities have been redeemed, redenominated, exchanged, converted, subdivided, consolidated or been the subject of a capital increase, capital reduction, call on partly paid securities or event similar to any of the foregoing, Securities "of the same kind" means the amount of Securities, money and other property (together "Substitute Assets") received in respect of such other Securities as a result of such event (provided that if any sum had to be paid in order to receive such Substitute Assets, an obligation to transfer them shall be conditional upon payment by the transferee of such sum to the transferor).

(3) *Conditions Precedent.* Each payment or delivery obligation of a party is subject to the conditions precedent that (i) no Event of Default or event which by the lapse of time or the giving of notice (or both) may become an Event of Default with respect to the other party has occurred and is continuing and (ii) no notice of termination has been given in respect of the relevant Transaction because of a Change of Circumstances.

(4) *Payment Netting.* If on any date both parties would otherwise be required to make payments in the same currency in respect of the same Transaction, the mutual payment obligations shall automatically be set off against each other and the party owing the higher amount shall pay to the other the difference between the amounts owed. The parties may agree that this principle shall apply in respect of two or more Transactions or one or more types of Transactions or that it shall apply also in respect of mutual obligations to deliver assets which are fungible with each other. If and so long as a single currency can be expressed in different currency units (such as the euro unit and national currency units under the principles governing the transition to European Economic and Monetary Union), the principle set forth in the first sentence of this subsection shall apply only if both payments are to be made in the same unit.

(5) *Late Payment.* If in respect of a Transaction a party fails to make a payment to the other when due (and, for the avoidance of doubt, without being entitled to withhold such payment), interest, payable on demand, shall accrue (before and after judgment) at the Default Rate on the amount outstanding, calculated for the period from (and including) the due date to (but excluding) the day on which such payment is received. "Default Rate" means the higher of (a) the Interbank Rate and (b) the cost to the other party, as certified by it, of funding the relevant amount, in each case plus any interest surcharge which may be agreed in the Special Provisions. "Interbank Rate" means the interbank offered interest rate charged by prime banks to each other for overnight deposits at the place of payment and in the currency of the amount outstanding for each day on which interest is to be charged (being, if an amount in euros is outstanding, the Euro Overnight Index Average ("EONIA") Rate calculated by the European Central Bank).

(6) *Business Day Convention.* If any payment or delivery date, any determination or valuation date, any commencement or termination date or any exercise date agreed between the parties which is deemed to be a Business Day is not a Business Day, payments, deliveries, determinations or valuations shall be made or, as the case may be, the commencement date, the termination date or the exercise date shall be deemed to occur, as elected in respect of the relevant Transaction, on (a) the immediately preceding Business Day ("Preceding"), (b) the immediately following Business Day ("Following"), or (c) the immediately following Business Day, unless such day falls in the next calendar month, in which case the relevant

Copyright © 2004 FBE

General Provisions - 2004

payment, delivery, determination or valuation shall be made or, as the case may be, the relevant commencement date, termination date or exercise date shall be deemed to occur on the immediately preceding Business Day ("Modified Following" or "Modified"), provided that failing such election, (b) shall apply.

(7) *Business Day Definition*. "Business Day" means (a) in relation to any payment in euros a day on which all relevant parts of TARGET are operational to effect such a payment, (b) in relation to any payment in any other currency a day (other than a Saturday or a Sunday) on which commercial banks are open for business (including payments in the currency concerned as well as dealings in foreign exchange and foreign currency deposits) in the place(s) agreed in relation to the relevant Transaction or, if not so agreed, in the place where the relevant account is located and, if different, in the principal financial centre, if any, of the currency of such payment, (c) in relation to any delivery of Securities, (i) where a Transaction is to be settled through a securities settlement system, a day on which such securities settlement system is open for business in the place where delivery of the Securities is to be effected, and (ii) where a Transaction is to be settled in a way other than (i), a day (other than a Saturday or a Sunday) on which commercial banks are open for business in the place where delivery of the Securities is to be effected, (d) in relation to any delivery of any assets other than Securities, a day (other than a Saturday or a Sunday) on which commercial banks are open for business in the place where delivery of the relevant assets is to be effected or any other day agreed between the parties in the Confirmation of the relevant Transactions or otherwise, (e) in relation to any valuation, a day on which an up-to-date valuation based on the agreed price sources can reasonably be carried out, and (f) in relation to any notice or other communication, a day (other than a Saturday or Sunday) on which commercial banks are open for business in the city specified in the address provided by the recipient pursuant to Section 8(1).

(8) *Market Value*. "Market Value" means in respect of any Securities as of any time on any date, (a) the price for such Securities then quoted through and obtainable from a generally recognised source agreed to by the parties and (b) failing such agreement or such quotation (i) if the Securities are listed on a stock exchange and not then suspended, their price last quoted on such exchange; (ii) if the Securities are not so listed, but have, on the main market on which they are traded, the price published or made public by a central bank or an entity of undisputed authority on such day, such price last published or made public; and (iii) in any other case, the average of the bid and offer prices for such Securities, as of such time on such date, as established by two leading market participants other than the parties, in each of the cases listed in (a) and (b) together with (if not included in such price) any interest accrued on such Securities as of that date.

4.   Taxes

(1)   *Withholding Tax*. If a party is or will be obliged to deduct or withhold an amount for or on account of any tax or other duty from a payment which it is to make, it shall pay to the other party such additional amounts as are necessary to ensure that such other party receives the full amount to which it would have been entitled at the time of such payment if no deduction or withholding had been required. This shall not apply if the tax or duty concerned is imposed or levied (a) by or on behalf or for the account of the jurisdiction (or a tax authority of or resident in the jurisdiction) in which the Booking Office of the payee (or its place of residence, if the payee is an individual) is located, (b) pursuant to (directly or indirectly) an obligation imposed by a treaty to which such jurisdiction is a party, or by a regulation or directive enacted under such treaty, or (c) because the payee has failed to perform its obligation under Section l0(4)(b).

(2)   *Documentary Tax*. Subject to Section 10(2), each party shall pay any stamp, documentary or similar tax or duty payable with respect to the Agreement (a "Documentary Tax") and imposed upon it in the jurisdiction in which its Booking Office or place of residence is located and shall indemnify the other party for any Documentary Tax payable in such jurisdiction and imposed upon the other party, unless the Booking Office of such other party (or its place of residence, if the other party is an individual) is also located in such jurisdiction.

5.   Representations

(1)   *Representations*. Each party represents to the other, as of the date on which it enters into a Master Agreement and as of each date on which a Transaction is entered into, that:

(a)   *Status*. It is validly existing under the laws of its organisation or incorporation;

(b)   *Corporate Action*. It is duly authorised to execute and deliver, and perform its obligations under, the Agreement;

(c)   *No Violation or Conflict*. The execution, delivery and performance of the Agreement do not violate or conflict with any provision of law, judgment or government or court order applicable to it, or any provision of its constitutional documents;

(d)   *Consents*. All governmental and other consents which are required to be obtained by it with respect to the Agreement have been obtained and are in full force and effect;

(e)   *Obligations Binding*. Its obligations under the Agreement are legal, valid and binding;

(f)   *Absence of Certain Events*. No Event of Default or event which by the lapse of time or the giving of notice (or both) may become an Event of Default and, to its knowledge, no Change of Circumstances with respect to it has occurred and is continuing;

(g)   *Absence of Litigation*. There is not pending or, to its knowledge, threatened against it any action, suit or proceeding before any court, tribunal, arbitrator or governmental or other authority that is likely to affect the legality, validity, binding effect or enforceability against it of the Agreement or its ability to perform its obligations under the Agreement;

(h) *No Reliance*. It has the necessary knowledge and experience to assess the benefits and risks incurred in each Transaction and has not relied for such purpose on the other party;

(i) *Margin*. It has full title to the Securities transferred, as margin or collateral, to the other party under the Agreement and that such Securities shall be free and clear of any lien, security interest or any other right which may affect the right of the other party to dispose freely of such Securities.

(2) *Applicability to Guarantor*. If a third person specified in the Special Provisions or in a Confirmation as Guarantor (a "Guarantor") has, in an instrument specified in the Special Provisions or otherwise agreed between the parties, given a guarantee or other credit support in respect of any obligations of either party under the Agreement (a "Guarantee"), then the representations of such party in respect of itself and the Agreement pursuant to subsection 1(a) through (i) shall *mutatis mutandis* apply also to the Guarantor and the Guarantee.

6. Termination

(1) *Termination due to an Event of Default*.

(a) *Event of Default*. The occurrence of any of the following events in respect of a party shall constitute an event of default ("Event of Default"):

(i) *Failure to Pay or Deliver*. The party fails to make, when due, any payment or delivery under the Agreement and such failure continues for three Business Days after the day on which notice of such failure is given to the party;

(ii) *Failure to Provide or Return Margin or Collateral*. The party fails to provide or return, when due, margin or collateral required to be provided or returned by it under the Agreement;

(iii) *Other Breach of Agreement*. The party fails to perform, when due, any other obligation under the Agreement and such failure continues for thirty days after the day on which notice of such failure is given to the party;

(iv) *Misrepresentation* Any representation by the party in the Agreement proves to have been incorrect on the date as of which it was made and the other party determines in good faith that, as a result thereof (or of the matters of fact or law which were not correctly stated), the balance of its risks and benefits under the Agreement is materially adversely affected;

(v) *Default under Specified Transactions*. If the parties have, in the Special Provisions, specified any Transactions ("Specified Transactions") to which this Section 6(l)(a)(v) will apply, the party fails to make a payment or a delivery under any such Specified Transaction and such failure (A) results in the liquidation or early termination of, or an acceleration of obligations under, such Specified Transaction or (B) continues beyond any applicable grace period (or, if there is no such period, for at least three Business Days) after the last payment or delivery date of such Specified Transaction, provided, in either case, that such failure is not caused by circumstances which, if occurring under the Agreement, would constitute a Change of Circumstances as described in subsection 2(a)(ii);

(vi) *Cross Default*. Any payment obligation of the party in respect of borrowed money (whether incurred by it as primary or secondary obligor and whether arising from one or more contracts or instruments) in an aggregate amount of not less than the applicable Default Threshold (A) has become, or may be declared, due and payable prior to the stated maturity thereof as a result of any default or similar event (however described) which has occurred in respect of the party or (B) has not been performed for more than seven days after its due date and, in either case, the other party has reasonable grounds to conclude that the financial obligations of the party under the Agreement may not be performed. "Default Threshold" means the amount specified as such in the Special Provisions in respect of a party or, in the absence of such specification, 1 per cent. of such party's equity (meaning the sum of its capital, disclosed reserves and retained earnings, determined in accordance with generally accepted accounting principles applicable to that party, as reported in its most recent published audited financial statements);

(vii) *Restructuring Without Assumption*. The party is subject to a Corporate Restructuring and the Successor Entity fails to assume all obligations of such party under the Agreement. "Corporate Restructuring" means, with respect to such party, any consolidation or amalgamation with, or merger into, or demerger, or transfer of all or substantially all assets to, another person, or an agreement providing for any of the foregoing, and "Successor Entity" means the person which results from, survives or is the transferee in, such Corporate Restructuring;

(viii) *Insolvency Events*. (1) The party is dissolved or has a resolution passed for its dissolution (other than, in either case, pursuant to a Corporate Restructuring resulting in a solvent Successor Entity); (2) the party commences an Insolvency Proceeding against itself or takes any corporate action to authorize such Insolvency Proceeding; (3) a governmental or judicial authority or self-regulatory organisation having jurisdiction over the party in a Specified Jurisdiction (a "Competent Authority") commences an Insolvency Proceeding with respect to the party; (4) a Competent Authority takes any action under any bankruptcy, insolvency or similar law or any banking, insurance or similar law governing the operation of the party which is likely to prevent the party from performing when due its payment or delivery obligations under the Agreement; (5) a person other than a Competent Authority commences an Insolvency Proceeding against the party in a Specified Jurisdiction and such action (A) results in a Judgment of Insolvency, or (B) is not dismissed or stayed within thirty days following the action or event commencing the Insolvency Proceeding, unless the commencement of such Proceedings by such person or under the given circumstances is obviously inadmissible or frivolous; (6) the party is bankrupt or insolvent as defined under any bankruptcy or insolvency law applicable to it in a Specified Jurisdiction; (7) the party makes a general assignment for the benefit of, or enters into a composition or amicable settlement with, its creditors generally; (8) the party is generally unable to pay its debts as they fall due; or (9) the party causes or is subject to any event which, under the laws of the Specified Jurisdiction, has an effect which is analogous to any of the events specified in Nos. (1) to (8). "Insolvency Proceeding" means a mandatory or voluntary proceeding seeking a judgment, order or arrangement of insolvency, bankruptcy, composition, amicable settlement, rehabilitation, reorganisation, administration, dissolution or liquidation with respect to a party or its assets or seeking the appointment of a receiver, liquidator, administrator or similar official for such party or for all or any substantial part its assets under any bankruptcy, insolvency or similar law or any banking, insurance or similar law governing the operation of the party; the expression does not include a solvent corporate reorganisation. An Insolvency Proceeding is "commenced" if a petition to conduct such proceeding is presented to or filed with, or (where no such petition is required) a decision to conduct such proceeding is taken by, a competent court, authority, corporate body or person. "Judgment of Insolvency" means any judgment, order or arrangement instituting an Insolvency Proceeding. "Specified Jurisdiction" in relation to a party means the jurisdiction of that party's organisation, incorporation, principal office or residence and any additional jurisdiction that may be specified with respect to that party in the Special Provisions;

(ix) *Repudiation of Obligations*. The party declares that it will not perform any material obligation under the Agreement or under any Specified Transaction (otherwise than as part of a bona fide dispute as to the existence, nature or extent of such obligation);

(x) *Guarantee Ineffective*. A Guarantee given with respect to the party is not in full force and effect, except if it has ceased to be in effect (i) in accordance with its terms, (ii) upon satisfaction of all of the party's obligations secured by such Guarantee or (iii) with the consent of the other party.

(b) *Termination*. If an Event of Default occurs with respect to a party (the "Defaulting Party") and is continuing, the other party (the "Non-Defaulting Party") may, by giving not more than twenty days' notice specifying the relevant Event of Default, terminate all outstanding Transactions, but not part thereof only, with effect as from a date (the "Early Termination Date") to be designated by it in such notice. Notwithstanding the foregoing, unless otherwise specified in the Special Provisions, all Transactions shall terminate, and the Early Termination Date shall occur, automatically in the case of an Event of Default mentioned in paragraph (a)(viii)(l), (2), (3), (5)(A) or, to the extent analogous thereto, (9) as of the time immediately preceding the relevant event or action.

(2) *Termination due to Change of Circumstances*.

(a) *Change of Circumstances*. The occurrence of any of the following events or circumstances in respect of a party shall constitute a change of circumstances ("Change of Circumstances"):

(i) *Tax Event*. As a result of the entry into force of any new law or regulation or of any change in law or any other provision of mandatory effect or change in the application or official interpretation thereof occurring after the date on which a Transaction is entered into, or as a result of a Corporate Restructuring of either party not falling under subsection 1(a)(vii), the party would, on or before the next due date relating to such Transaction, (A) be required to pay additional amounts pursuant to Section 4(1) with regard to a payment which it is obliged to make, other than a payment of interest pursuant to Section 3(5), or (B) receive a payment, other than a payment of interest pursuant to Section 3(5), from which an amount is required to be deducted for or on account of a tax or duty and no additional amount is required to be paid in respect of such tax or duty under Section 4(1), other than by reason of Section 4(l)(c);

(ii) *Illegality, Impossibility*. As a result of the entry into force of any new law or regulation or of any change in law or any other provision of mandatory effect or change in the application or official interpretation thereof or, if so specified in the Special Provisions, as a result of an Impossibility Event, in each case occurring after the date on which a Transaction is entered into,

it becomes, or is likely to become, unlawful or impossible for the party (A) to make, or receive, a payment or delivery in respect of such Transaction when due or to punctually comply with any other material obligation under the Agreement relating to such Transaction or (B) to perform any obligation to provide margin or collateral as and when required to be provided by it under the Agreement; "Impossibility Event" means any catastrophe, armed conflict, act of terrorism, riot or any other circumstance beyond the party's reasonable control affecting the operations of the party;

(iii) *Credit Event upon Restructuring*. If the party is subject to a Corporate Restructuring, the creditworthiness of the Successor Entity is materially weaker than that of the party immediately before the Corporate Restructuring.

(b) *Termination*. If a Change of Circumstances occurs with respect to a party (the "Affected Party"), the Affected Party in the case of paragraph (a)(i) or (ii), and the other party (the "Non-Affected Party") in the case of paragraph (a)(ii) or (iii) may, subject to the limitations set forth below, by giving not more than twenty days' notice, terminate the Transaction(s) affected by such change, with effect as from a date (the "Early Termination Date") to be designated by it in such notice, it being understood that, in the case of paragraph (a)(iii), all Transactions will be deemed so affected. If, without prejudice to any agreement between the parties on the provision of margin or collateral, either party determines that as a result of such termination its credit exposure to the other party is significantly increased, it may, not later than one week after the effective date of the notice of termination, by giving notice to the other party require such other party to provide, within one week after receipt of such last-mentioned notice, margin or collateral reasonably acceptable to it in such amount as to be at least equal to the increase in credit exposure under the Agreement, as determined by it. In the cases of paragraph (a)(i) and (ii), the right to terminate shall be subject to the following limitations: (i) the Early Termination Date may not be earlier than thirty days before the date on which the Change of Circumstances becomes effective, and (ii) the Affected Party may, unless it would otherwise be required to pay additional amounts as contemplated by paragraph

(a)(i)(A), give notice of termination only after a period of thirty days has expired following a notice by it informing the other party of such event and if the situation (if capable of remedy) has not been remedied within such period (by way of an agreed transfer of the affected Transactions to another Booking Office or otherwise).

(3)   *Applicability to Guarantor* If a Guarantee has been given with respect to a party and any of the events described in subsections l(a)(iii) through (ix) and 2(a) occurs with respect to the relevant Guarantor or such Guarantee, the occurrence of such event shall have the same effect as if it had occurred with respect to such party or the Agreement, respectively.

(4)   *Effect of Termination* In the event of a termination pursuant to this Section 6, neither party shall be obliged to make any further payment or delivery under the terminated Transaction(s) which would have become due on or after the Early Termination Date or to provide or return margin or collateral which would otherwise be required to be provided or returned under the Agreement and related to the terminated Transaction(s). These obligations shall be replaced by an obligation of either party to pay the Final Settlement Amount in accordance with Section 7.

(5)   *Event of Default and Change of Circumstances*. If an event or circumstance which would otherwise constitute or give rise to an Event of Default also constitutes a Change of Circumstances as referred to in subsection 2(a)(ii), it will be treated as a Change of Circumstances and will not constitute an Event of Default, except that any event as described in subsection 1(a)(viii) will always be treated as an Event of Default and not as a Change of Circumstances.

7.   Final Settlement Amount

(1)   Calculation.

(a)   Procedure and Bases of Calculation. Upon termination pursuant to Section 6, the Non-Defaulting Party or, as the case may be, the Non-Affected Party or, if there are two Affected Parties, each party (each the "Calculation Party") shall as soon as reasonably possible calculate the Final Settlement Amount.

"Final Settlement Amount" means, subject to subsection 2(b)(i), the amount determined by the Calculation Party to be equal to, as of the Early Termination Date, (A) the sum of all Transaction Values which are positive for it, the Amounts Due owed to it and its Margin Claims less (B) the sum of the absolute amounts of all Transaction Values which are negative for it, the Amounts Due owed by it and the Margin Claims of the other party;

"Amounts Due" owed by a party means the sum of (i) any amounts that were required to be paid by such party under any Transaction, but not paid, (ii) the Default Value, as of the agreed delivery date, of each asset that was required to be delivered by such party under any Transaction, but not delivered (in either case regardless of whether or not the party was entitled to withhold such payment or delivery, by virtue of Section 3(3) or for any other reason) and (iii) interest on the amounts specified in (i) and (ii) from (and including) the due date of the relevant payment or delivery to (but excluding) the Early Termination Date at the Interbank Rate or, if Section 3(5) is applicable, the Default Rate; Margin Claims shall be disregarded for the determination of Amounts Due;

"Default Value" means, in respect of any assets (including Securities or, in respect of Derivative Transactions, any other underlying assets of such Transactions) on any given date, an amount equal to (A) if the assets are or were to be delivered by the Calculation Party, the net proceeds (after deducting fees and expenses) which the Calculation Party has or could have reasonably received when selling assets of the same kind and quantity in the market on such date, (B) if the assets are or were to be delivered to the Calculation Party, the cost (including fees and expenses) which the Calculation Party has or would have reasonably incurred in purchasing assets of the same kind and quantity in the market on such date, and (C) if a market price for such assets cannot be determined, an amount which the Calculation Party determines in good faith to be its total losses and costs (or gains, in which case expressed as a negative number) in connection with such assets;

"Margin Claims" means, as of the Early Termination Date, the aggregate of the amount of cash paid and the Default Value of Securities transferred, as margin or collateral, by a party and not repaid or retransferred to it, plus any interest accrued on such cash at the rate agreed in respect thereof;

"Transaction Value" means, with respect to any Transaction or group of Transactions, an amount equal to, at the option of the Calculation Party, (i) the loss incurred (expressed as a positive number) or gain realized (expressed as a negative number) by the Calculation Party as a result of the termination of such Transaction(s), or (ii) the arithmetic mean of the quotations for replacement or hedge transactions on the Quotation Date obtained by the Calculation Party from not less than two leading market participants. In the case of (ii), each such quotation shall be expressed as the amount which the market participant would pay or receive on the Quotation Date if such market participant were to assume, as from the Quotation Date, the rights and obligations of the other party (or their economic equivalent) under the relevant Transaction(s); the resulting amount shall be expressed as a positive number if it would be payable to the market participant, and shall otherwise be expressed as a negative number. If, in such case, no or only one quotation can reasonably be obtained, the Transaction Value shall be determined pursuant to (i).

"Quotation Date" means the Early Termination Date, except that in the event of an automatic termination as provided in Section 6(1)(b), the Quotation Date shall be the date designated as such by the Non-Defaulting Party, which shall be not later than the fifth Business Day after the day on which the Non-Defaulting Party became aware of the event which caused such automatic termination.

(b)   Conversion. Any Amounts Due, Default Value, Margin Claims and Transaction Value not denominated in the Base Currency shall be converted into the Base Currency at the Applicable Exchange Rate. "Base Currency" means the euro, unless otherwise agreed. "Applicable Exchange Rate" means the arithmetic mean of the respective rates at which the person calculating or

converting an amount pursuant to the Agreement is reasonably able to (i) purchase the relevant other currency with, and (ii) sell such currency for, the Base Currency on the date as of which such amount is calculated or converted.

(2) *Payment Obligations.*

(a) *One Calculation Party.* If one party only acts as Calculation Party, the Final Settlement Amount, as calculated by it, shall be paid (i) to that party by the other party if it is a positive number and (ii) by that party to the other party if it is a negative number; in the latter case the amount payable shall be the absolute value of the Final Settlement Amount.

(b) *Two Calculation Parties.* If both parties act as Calculation Party and their calculations of the Final Settlement Amount differ from each other, the Final Settlement Amount shall (i) be equal to one-half of the difference between the amounts so calculated by both parties (such difference being, for the avoidance of doubt, the sum of the absolute values of such amounts if one is positive and the other negative) and (ii) be paid by the party which has calculated a negative or the lower positive amount.

(3) *Notification and Due Date*

(a) *Notification.* The Calculation Party shall notify as soon as reasonably possible the other party of the Final Settlement Amount calculated by it and provide to such other party a statement setting forth in reasonable detail the basis upon which the Final Settlement Amount was determined.

(b) *Due Date.* The Final Settlement Amount shall be payable immediately upon receipt of the notification mentioned in paragraph (a) if termination occurs as a result of an Event of Default, and otherwise within two Business Days following such receipt, but in either case not before the Early Termination Date. It shall bear interest as from the Early Termination Date to the date on which the payment is due at the Interbank Rate and thereafter at the Default Rate.

(4) *Set-Off.* The Non-Defaulting Party may set off its obligation (if any) to pay the Final Settlement Amount against any actual or contingent claims ("Counterclaims") which it has against the Defaulting Party on any legal grounds whatsoever (including by virtue of any financing or other contract). For the purpose of calculating the value of the Counterclaims, the Non-Defaulting Party shall, (i) to the extent that they are not payable in the Base Currency, convert them into the Base Currency at the Applicable Exchange Rate, (ii) to the extent that they are contingent or unascertained, take into account for such calculation their potential amount, if ascertainable, or otherwise a reasonable estimate thereof, (iii) to the extent that they are claims other than for the payment of money, determine their value in money and convert them into a money claim expressed in the Base Currency and (iv) to the extent that they are not yet due and payable, determine their present value (also having regard to interest claims). The provisions of this subsection 4 relating to Counterclaims against a Defaulting Party shall apply *mutatis mutandis* to Counterclaims against an Affected Party if termination occurred pursuant to Section 6(2)(a)(ii) or (iii).

8. Notices

(1) *Manner of Giving Notices.* Unless otherwise specified in the Agreement, any notice or other communication under the Agreement shall be made by letter, telex, telefax or any electronic messaging system agreed to by the parties in the Special Provisions to the address (if any) previously specified by the addressee.

(2) *Effectiveness.* Every notice or other communication made in accordance with subsection 1 shall be effective (a) if made by letter or telefax, upon receipt by the addressee, (b) if made by telex, upon receipt by the sender of the addressee's answerback at the end of transmission, and (c) if made by an electronic messaging system, upon receipt of that electronic message, provided that if, in any such case, such notice or other communication is not received on a Business Day or is received after the close of business on a Business Day, it shall take effect on the first following day that is a Business Day.

(3) *Change of Address.* Either party may by notice to the other change the address, telex or telefax number or electronic messaging system details at which notices or other communications are to be given to it.

9. Booking Offices

(1) *Extent of Obligations.* If a party enters into a Transaction through a Booking Office other than its principal office, its obligations in respect of that Transaction shall constitute obligations of such party as a whole, to the same extent as if they had been entered through such party's principal office. Such party shall not be obliged, however, to perform such obligations through any of its other offices if performance through that Booking Office is unlawful or impossible by virtue of any of the events described in Section 6(2)(a)(ii).

(2) *Change of Booking Office.* Neither party may change a Booking Office without the prior written consent of the other party.

(3) *Definition.* "Booking Office" of a party means the office agreed by the parties through which such party is acting for the relevant Transaction, provided that if no such office is agreed in respect of a party, such party's principal office (or, in the absence of a principal office, such party's registered office or place of residence) shall be deemed to be the Booking Office.

10. Miscellaneous

(1) *Transfer of Rights and Obligations.* No rights or obligations under the Agreement may be transferred, charged or otherwise disposed of to or in favour of any third person without the prior consent of the other party given in the manner specified in Section 8(1), except that no such consent shall be required in the case of a transfer of all or substantially all assets of a party in connection with a

Corporate Restructuring which does not involve a change of the tax status relevant to the Agreement and does not otherwise adversely affect the interests of the other party to any significant extent.

The limitation provided in the preceding sentence shall not apply to a party's right to receive the Final Settlement Amount or to be indemnified pursuant to subsection 2.

(2)   *Expenses*. A Defaulting Party and a party failing to make a payment or delivery when due shall on demand indemnify the other party for all reasonable expenses, including legal fees, incurred by the other party for the enforcement or protection of its rights under the Agreement in connection with an Event of Default or such failure.

(3)   *Recording*. Each party (i) may electronically or otherwise record telephone conversations of the parties in connection with the Agreement or any potential Transaction, (ii) shall give notice of such potential recording to its relevant personnel and obtain any consent that may be legally required before permitting such personnel to conduct such telephone conversations and (iii) agrees that recordings may be submitted in evidence in any Proceedings relating to the Agreement or any potential Transaction.

(4)   *Documents*. So long as either party has or may have any obligation under the Agreement, each party shall, if it is reasonably able and legally in a position to do so and would not thereby materially prejudice its legal or commercial position, promptly make available to the other or to any appropriate government or taxing authority any form, certificate or other document (properly completed and, where appropriate, certified) that is either (a) specified in the Agreement, or (b) reasonably requested in writing in order to allow the other party to make a payment under the Agreement without any deduction or withholding for or on account of any tax or other duty, or with such deduction or withholding at a reduced rate.

(5)   *Remedies*. The rights and remedies provided in the Agreement are cumulative and not exclusive of any rights and remedies provided by law.

(6)   *No Waiver*. A failure or delay in exercising (and any partial exercise of) any right or remedy under the Agreement shall not operate as a waiver (or partial waiver) of, and accordingly not preclude or limit any future exercise of, that right or remedy.

(7)   *Termination*. The Agreement may be terminated by either party upon the giving of not less than twenty days' notice to the other party. Notwithstanding such notice, any Transaction then outstanding shall continue to be subject to the provisions of the Agreement and to that extent the effect of the termination shall occur only when all obligations under the last such Transaction shall have been performed.

(8)   *Contractual Currency*. If for any reason a payment is made in a currency other than the Contractual Currency and the amount so paid, converted into the Contractual Currency at the exchange rate prevailing at the time of such payment for the sale of such other currency against the Contractual Currency, as reasonably determined by the payee, falls short of the amount in the Contractual Currency payable under the Agreement, the party owing such amount shall, as a separate and independent obligation, immediately compensate the other party for the shortfall.

(9)   *Previous Transactions*. Transactions entered into prior to the effective date of a Master Agreement will be subject to such Master Agreement, individually or by category, to the extent provided in the Special Provisions.

(10)   *Agency Transactions*.

(a)   *Conditions*. A party may enter into a Transaction (an "Agency Transaction") as agent (the "Agent") for a third person (a "Principal") only if (i) the party has authority on behalf of that Principal to enter into the Transaction, to perform on behalf of that Principal all of that Principal's obligations and to accept performance of the obligations of the other party and receive all notices and other communications under the Agreement and (ii) when entering into the Transaction and in the relevant Confirmation the party specifies that it is acting as Agent in respect of the Transaction and discloses to the other party the identity of the Principal. If these conditions are not fully satisfied, the party shall be deemed to act as principal.

(b)   *Information on Certain Events*. Each party undertakes that, if it enters as Agent into an Agency Transaction, forthwith upon becoming aware (i) of any event or circumstance which constitutes an event as described in Section 6(l)(a)(viii) with respect to the relevant Principal or (ii) of any breach of any of the representations given in Section 5 and paragraph (f) below or of any event or circumstance which has the result that any such representation would be incorrect on the date as of which it was made, it will inform the other party of that fact and will, if so required by the other party, furnish the other party with such additional information as the other party may reasonably request.

(c)   *Parties*. Each Agency Transaction shall be a transaction solely between the relevant Principal and the other party. All provisions of the Agreement shall apply separately as between the other party and each Principal for whom the Agent has entered into an Agency Transaction, as if each such Principal were a party to a separate Agreement with the other party, except as provided in paragraph (d) below. A Process Agent appointed by the Agent shall be a Process Agent also for each Principal.

(d)   *Notice of Termination*. If an Event of Default or a Change of Circumstances as described in Section 6(2)(a)(ii) or (iii) occurs with respect to the Agent, the other party may give notice pursuant to Section 6(l)(b) or 6(2)(b), respectively, to the Principal with the same effect as if an Event of Default or Change of Circumstances, respectively, had occurred with respect to the Principal.

(e)   *Own Account Transactions*. The foregoing provisions do not affect the operation of the Agreement between the parties hereto in respect of any Transactions into which the Agent may enter on its own account as a principal.

(f)   *Representation*. Each party acting as Agent represents to the other in its own name and in the name of

9

the Principal that it will, on each occasion on which it enters or purports to enter into an Agency Transaction, have the authority as described in subsection 10(a)(i) on behalf of the person whom it specifies as the Principal in respect of that Agency Transaction.

(11) *Severability* In the event that any provision of the Agreement is invalid, illegal or unenforceable under the law of any jurisdiction, the validity, legality and enforceability of the remaining provisions in the Agreement under the law of such jurisdiction, and the validity, legality and enforceability of such and any other provisions under the law of any other jurisdiction shall not in any way be affected thereby. The parties shall, in such event, in good faith negotiate a valid provision the economic effect of which comes as close as possible to that of the invalid, illegal or unenforceable provisions.

11. Governing Law, Settlement of Disputes, Jurisdiction, Arbitration

(1) *Governing Law*. The Agreement shall be governed by and construed in accordance with the law specified in the Special Provisions or, failing such specification, the law of the country, if identical, in which both parties' principal offices are located when the Master Agreement between them is entered into.

(2) *Settlement of Disputes, Jurisdiction, Arbitration*. Each party irrevocably agrees that in respect of any dispute arising under or related to the Agreement (i) the courts specified in the Special Provisions shall have non-exclusive jurisdiction and each party irrevocably submits to such non-exclusive jurisdiction, or (ii) if so specified in the Special Provisions, any such dispute shall be finally settled by one or more arbitrators appointed and proceeding in accordance with the rules of arbitration specified in the Special Provisions, each party agreeing to comply with such rules.

Failing either of such specifications, the courts having jurisdiction in the principal financial centre or, in the absence of a generally recognized financial centre, the capital city of the country whose law governs the Agreement shall have non-exclusive jurisdiction with respect to any suit, action or other proceeding relating to the Agreement (the "Proceedings") and each party irrevocably submits to such non-exclusive jurisdiction.

(3) *Service of Process*. If so specified in the Special Provisions, each party appoints a process agent (the "Process Agent") to receive, for it and on its behalf, service of process in any Proceedings. If for any reason a party's Process Agent is unable to act as such, such party shall promptly notify the other party and within thirty days appoint a substitute process agent which is acceptable to the other party.

(4) *Waiver of Immunity*. The Agreement constitutes a commercial agreement. To the fullest extent permitted by applicable law, each party waives, with respect to itself and its assets (irrespective of their use or intended use), all immunity on the grounds of sovereignty or otherwise from suit, execution or other legal process and agrees that it will not claim any such immunity in any Proceedings.

Copyright © 2004 FBE

General Provisions - 2004

FEDERATION BANCAIRE DE L'UNION EUROPEENNE
BANKING FEDERATION OF THE EUROPEAN UNION
BANKENVEREINIGUNG DER EUROPÄISCHEN UNION

in co-operation with

EUROPEAN SAVINGS BANKS GROUP   EUROPEAN ASSOCIATION OF COOPERATIVE BANKS
GROUPEMENT EUROPEEN DES CAISSES D'EPARGNE   GROUPEMENT EUROPEEN DES BANQUES COOPERATIVES
EUROPÄISCHE SPARKASSENVEREINIGUNG   EUROPÄISCHE VEREINIGUNG DER GENOSSENSCHAFTSBANKEN

MASTER AGREEMENT
FOR FINANCIAL TRANSACTIONS

dated as of _____

between

_____ and _____
("Party A")   ("Party B")

SPECIAL PROVISIONS
Edition 2004

1. Nature of Agreement

This contractual arrangement (the "Special Provisions"), together with the General Provisions (the "General Provisions") and any annex (each an "Annex") referred to below, constitutes a master agreement (the "Master Agreement") under which the parties may enter into financial transactions.

2. Incorporation of Documents

The following documents, all in the _____ language, published by the FBE are hereby incorporated into and shall accordingly form part of the Master Agreement:

(a) the General Provisions, Edition 2004
(b) the following Annex[es][1]

Product Annex[es] for :
Repurchase Transactions, Edition January 2001
Securities Loans, Edition January 2001
Derivative Transactions, Edition 2004
Supplement for Foreign Exchange Transactions, Edition 2004
Supplement for Interest Rate Transactions, Edition 2004
Supplement for Option Transactions, Edition 2004
Margin Maintenance Annex, Edition 2004
Other Supplements (give details)

---

[1] Delete and/or complete the references in this paragraph (b) as appropriate

Copyright © 2004 FBE   Special provisions - 2004

3. **Addresses for notices (Section 8(1) of the General Provisions)**

The addresses for notices and other communications between the parties are: ...

4. **Governing law, Settlement of Disputes, Jurisdiction, Arbitration (Section 11(1) and (2) of the General Provisions)**

The law governing the Agreement is _____ law.

Settlement of Disputes:

Jurisdiction[2]: The court(s) referred to in Section 11(2) is/are _____.

Arbitration[3]: The rules of arbitration referred to in Section 11(2) are the Rules of Arbitration of[4] [Euro Arbitration – European Center for Financial Dispute Resolution] [the International Chamber of Commerce][§§] [other][§§] [with which each party agrees to comply].

The parties agree to submit those disputes to [a single] [three] arbitrator[s].

Such arbitration shall take place in _____.

The language[s] in which arbitration shall be conducted [is] [are] _____.

5. **Other provisions**

_____[5]

_____   _____
(Name of Party A)   (Name of Party B)

By: By:

_____   _____
Name(s):   Name(s):
Title(s):   Title(s):

---

[2] Delete if not applicable
[3] Delete if not applicable
[4] If arbitration is selected, specify which rules apply
[5] Insert amendments (which may be provisions from the attached Appendix) or state "None"

Copyright © 2004 FBE   Special provisions - 2004

Appendix (Checklist)
Elections and Amendments[6]

I. General Provisions

(1) Section 3(4) (Payment Netting)

The principle set forth in Section 3(4), first sentence, of the General Provisions is hereby extended so as to apply also to:

- mutual payments in the same currency in respect of [the following types of Transactions: ...][all types of Transactions] and

- mutual deliveries of assets that are fungible with each other and are due in respect of [the same Transaction] [the following types of Transactions: ...] [all types of Transactions].

(2) Section 3(5) (Late Payment)

The interest surcharge referred to in Section 3(5) shall be ... per cent per annum.

(3) Section 3(8) (Market Value)

The price source for determining the Market Value of Securities shall be...

(4) Section 5(2) (Guarantor/Guarantee)

Guarantor means

    in relation to Party A: ... (whose jurisdiction of organisation/incorporation is ...)
    in relation to Party B: ... (whose jurisdiction of organisation/incorporation is ...).

Guarantee means

    in relation to Party A: ...
    in relation to Party B: ...

(5) Section 6(1)(a)(v) (Default under Specified Transactions)

Section 6(1)(a)(v) will apply to [Party A][Party B][both parties] and "Specified Transactions" are ..... (e.g.: derivative and other trading transactions (to be specified) entered into with the other party to the Agreement and/or with any third party).

(6) Section 6(1)(a)(vi) (Cross Default)

Section 6(1)(a)(vi) shall not apply/apply only to Party [A] [B] and not to the other party/apply with the following modifications:

The Default Threshold is:

    in relation to Party A: ...
    in relation to Party B: ...

(7) Section 6(1)(a)(viii) (Insolvency Events)

The following shall, in addition to each party's country of organisation, incorporation, principal office or residence, be a Specified Jurisdiction:

    in relation to Party A: ...
    in relation to Party B: ...

Sub-paragraph (viii) (5) (B) shall not apply/shall apply with a period of ... days instead of thirty days/shall apply only to Party [A] [B].

---

[6] These provisions refer to clauses of the Master Agreement contemplating possible choices or modifications to be made in the Special Provisions. When any such provision is not inserted, the relevant fall back provision specified in the Master Agreement will apply. Parties may insert these provisions (or any other clause amending the terms of the Master Agreement) in paragraph no 5 (Other provisions) of the Special Provisions

Copyright © 2004 FBE   Special provisions - 2004

(8) Section 6(1)(b) (Automatic Termination)

Section 6(1)(b), second sentence, shall not apply/shall apply only in relation to Party [A][B].

(9) Section 6(2)(a) (Change of Circumstances)

Section 6(2)(a)(ii) shall extend to an Impossibility Event.

(10) Section 7(1)(b) (Conversion)

"Base Currency" means...

(11) Section 8(1) (Manner of Giving Notices)

The electronic messaging system(s) for purposes of Section 8(1) is/are: ...

(12) Section 9(1) (Booking Offices)

Booking Offices may be

    in relation to Party A: - for Repurchase Transactions: ...
                                           - for Securities Loans: ...
                                           - for Derivative Transactions.....

    in relation to Party B: - for Repurchase Transactions: ...
                                           - for Securities Loans: ...
                                           - for Derivative Transactions.....

(13) Section 10(4) (Documents)

The following documents shall be delivered by Party A and Party B, respectively, by the dates specified below:

	Type of document	To be delivered by (date)
Party A:	......	......
Party B:	......	......

(14) Section 10(9) (Previous Transactions)

[Specify relevant transactions (if any) and further details (e.g. effect/cessation of effect of contractual terms governing previous transactions)]

(15) Section 11(3) (Service of Process)

The Process Agent (Section 11(3)) is

        in relation to Party A: ...
        in relation to Party B: ...

II. Margin Maintenance Annex

(1) Transactions and groups of Transactions covered

Net Exposure shall be calculated, and Margin transferred, in respect of the following Booking Offices and types of Transactions:

(i)   [all Booking Offices in the aggregate]
        [each Booking Office of Party A/B][7]
        [each pair of Booking Offices of Party A and Party B][8]
        [other arrangement]

---

[7] If one Party acts through more than one office
[8] If both parties act through more than one office

(ii) [the aggregate of all Repurchase Transactions, Securities Loans and Derivative Transactions],
[the aggregate of all Repurchase Transactions, of all Securities Loans and of all Derivative Transactions in each case separately],
[the aggregate of all Transactions relating to fixed income Securities, of all Transactions relating to equity Securities and of Derivative Transactions, in each case separately],
[each Transaction separately],
[other arrangement].

(2) Eligible Margin

Cash Margin: eligible currencies (other than the Base Currency):

Currency	Valuation Percentage	Transferring party	
[ ]	[ ]%	[Party A]	[Party B]

Interest payable on Cash Margin: ...

Margin Securities:

	Eligible Securities	Valuation Percentage	Transferring party	
(i)	Negotiable debt obligations issued by the Government of [ ] having an original maturity at issuance of not more than [one year]	[ ]%	[Party A]	[Party B]
(ii)	Negotiable debt obligations issued by the Government of [ ] having an original maturity at issuance of more than [one year] but not more than 10 years	[ ]%	[Party A]	[Party B]
(iii)	Other:		[Party A]	[Party B]

(3) "Valuation Agent" means: ...

(4) Valuation Procedure

   (a) "Valuation Date" means each [Business Day/Monday...]

   (b) "Independent Amount" means
       - with respect to Party A: ...
       - with respect to Party B: ...

   (c) "Exposure Threshold" means:
       - in relation to the Net Exposure of Party B to Party A: ...
       - in relation to the Net Exposure of Party A to Party B: ...

   (d) "Minimum Transfer Amount" means: ...

(5) Margin Transfer Deadline

The date by which transfers of Margin have to be effected pursuant to Section 2(2) of the Margin Maintenance Annex shall be...

III. Other Annexes

Repurchase Annex

   Section 2(7)(v) shall apply.

Securities Lending Annex

   Section 2(6)(v) shall apply.

Copyright © 2004 FBE   Special provisions - 2004

Derivatives Annex

Section 1(2)(b)

The provisions of Section 1(2)(b) of the Derivatives Annex shall not apply to foreign exchange transactions settling within two Business Days following the date/one Business Day following the date/on the same Business Day[9] on which the transaction is concluded.

Section 1(2)(c)

The provisions of Section 1(2)(c) of the Derivatives Annex shall apply to the following types of Derivative Transactions:

types of Derivative Transactions
[   ].

Section 2

The Market Standard Documentation(s) set out below shall be incorporated into the terms of the following types of Derivative Transactions:

Market Standard Documentation(s)	types of Derivative Transactions
[ ]	[ ].

The terms in the Market Standard Documentation(s) which have been incorporated into the terms of a Derivative Transaction shall be construed in accordance with the following law(s) as set out below:

Market Standard Documentation(s)	law
[ ]	[ ].

---

[9] Delete where not applicable

Copyright © 2004 FBE

Special provisions - 2004

FEDERATION BANCAIRE DE L'UNION EUROPEENNE
BANKING FEDERATION OF THE EUROPEAN UNION
BANKENVEREINIGUNG DER EUROPÄISCHEN UNION

in co-operation with

EUROPEAN SAVINGS BANKS GROUP
GROUPEMENT EUROPEEN DES CAISSES D'EPARGNE
EUROPÄISCHE SPARKASSENVEREINIGUNG

EUROPEAN ASSOCIATION OF COOPERATIVE BANKS
GROUPEMENT EUROPEEN DES BANQUES COOPERATIVES
EUROPÄISCHE VEREINIGUNG DER GENOSSENSCHAFTSBANKEN

MASTER AGREEMENT
FOR FINANCIAL TRANSACTIONS

MARGIN MAINTENANCE ANNEX
Edition 2004

This Annex supplements the General Provisions which form part of any Master Agreement for Financial Transactions based on the form published by the FBE.

1. Net Exposure

(1) General Principles. If, at any time when Net Exposure is calculated pursuant to subsection 2, one party (the "Margin Provider") has an Adjusted Net Exposure to the other (the "Margin Recipient") resulting from any Transactions and/or from transfers of Margin pursuant to this Annex, the Margin Recipient may by notice to the Margin Provider require the same to transfer to it cash ("Cash Margin") or Securities ("Margin Securities") acceptable to the Margin Recipient and whose aggregate Market Value, when multiplied by the valuation percentage, if any, agreed between the parties ("Valuation Percentage"), shall be at least equal to the Adjusted Net Exposure. "Adjusted Net Exposure" means the sum of the Net Exposure and any supplementary amount ("Independent Amount") agreed in favour of the Margin Recipient less any Independent Amount agreed in favour of the Margin Provider. Such notice may be given orally or as provided in Section 8(1) of the General Provisions. The Net Exposure will be determined, and accordingly Margin will be required to be transferred, in respect of (a) all such Transactions, (b) specified groups of Transactions, (c) each individual Transaction or (d) otherwise, as agreed by the parties (in the Special Provisions or otherwise), provided that failing such agreement, (b) shall apply in such a manner that all Repurchase Transactions, all Securities Loans and all Derivative Transactions shall each form a separate group of Transactions to which this Annex applies. The "Market Value" of cash shall be the nominal amount thereof, converted, if not denominated in the Base Currency, in accordance with subsection 2. Any reference in this Annex to Transactions shall be construed as a reference to Repurchase Transactions and/or Securities Loans and/or Derivative Transactions.

(2) Calculation. The person designated by the parties for this purpose or, failing such designation, each party (each the "Valuation Agent") shall calculate the Net Exposure on each Valuation Date by 11 a.m. Brussels time. The Net Exposure shall be expressed as a positive number if the Valuation Agent would, pursuant to its calculation, be the Margin Recipient, and shall otherwise be expressed as a negative number. All calculations shall be made in the Base Currency; any amount not denominated in the Base Currency shall be converted into the Base Currency at the Applicable Exchange Rate.

(3) Definitions. "Net Exposure" means (I) in relation to Repurchase Transactions and Securities Loans the excess (if any), calculated pursuant to subsection 2, of the Liabilities of the Margin Provider over the Liabilities of the Margin Recipient, and (II) in relation to Derivative Transactions the Potential Final Settlement Amount, provided that (a) if the calculation is to be made pursuant to both (I) and (II), the Net Exposure shall be the aggregate of the amounts so calculated, (b) the amount of any prior Adjusted Net Exposure in respect of which a transfer of Margin has already been required, but not completed, shall be subtracted from any Net Exposure subsequently calculated and (c) if both parties act as Valuation Agent and their calculations of Net Exposure differ from each other, (i) the Net Exposure shall be one-half of the difference of the amounts so calculated by both parties (such difference being, for the avoidance of doubt, the sum of the absolute values of such amounts if one is positive and the other negative) and (ii) the Margin Provider shall be the party which has calculated a negative or the lower positive amount; "Liabilities" means, with respect to a party, the aggregate of

(a) the Market Values of any Securities transferred to that party under a Transaction or pursuant to this Annex and not yet returned to the other party, multiplied (i) in the case of Loaned Securities, by the applicable Margin Ratio and (ii) in the case of Margin Securities, by any applicable Valuation Percentage;

(b) a cash amount equal to the sum of (i) the amount, multiplied by the applicable Margin Ratio, of that party's obligation(s) to pay the Repurchase Price in respect of any Repurchase Transaction if the relevant Valuation Date were the Repurchase Date, and (ii) the Market Value, multiplied by any applicable Valuation Percentage, of any Cash Margin transferred to and not repaid by that party (including unpaid accrued interest on such Cash Margin); and

(c) the cash amount or cash equivalent in respect of any Distribution to be paid or transferred by such party to the other party, but not yet paid or transferred;

"Margin" means either Cash Margin or Margin Securities;

"Margin Ratio" (also called "Haircut") means, with respect to each Repurchase Transaction or Securities Loan, the percentage agreed by the parties by which the Liabilities of the Seller or the Borrower in relation to the Repurchase Price and the Loaned Securities, respectively, are multiplied, as provided under "Liabilities" above, in order to determine the Net Exposure; failing an agreement to that effect, the Margin Ratio shall be equal to (a) with respect to a Repurchase Transaction, the Market Value of the Purchased Securities on the date on which the Transaction was entered into, divided by the Purchase Price, and (b) with respect to a Securities Loan (i) the Market Value, on the date on which the Transaction was entered into, of any Margin to be provided at the commencement of such Securities Loan, multiplied by the applicable Valuation Percentage and divided by the Market Value of the Loaned Securities as of such date, and (ii) if no Margin is provided at the commencement of such Securities Loan, 100 per cent., unless the parties have expressly excluded the provision of Margin for the entire term of the Transaction, in which case the Margin Ratio shall be zero until the Return Date;

"Potential Final Settlement Amount" means the amount which, at the time on each Valuation Date when Net Exposure is calculated in respect of Derivative Transactions pursuant to subsection 2, the Valuation Agent, acting as if it were the Calculation Party (as defined in Section 7(1)(a) of the General Provisions), determines to be equal to the Final Settlement Amount calculated in respect of Derivative Transactions (but excluding Repurchase Transactions and Securities Loans), if the same had to be calculated as of such time and date, such determination to be made in accordance with Section 7(1)(a) of the General Provisions, except that (a) if the determination can be made on the basis of bid and offered quotations, the arithmetic mean of such quotations shall be used for such determination, and (b) the amount of Margin Claims shall be adjusted so as to take into account the applicable Valuation Percentages;

"Valuation Date" means, in respect of calculation of the Net Exposure, each of the dates agreed as such between the parties, and failing such agreement each Business Day.

2. Notification of Adjusted Net Exposure and Transfer of Margin

(1) Notification. Promptly after determining the Net Exposure, the Valuation Agent shall notify each relevant party of the Adjusted Net Exposure and upon request of a party provide such party with a statement setting forth in reasonable detail the calculation basis of the Adjusted Net Exposure. The notice may be given orally or as provided in Section 8(1) of the General Provisions.

(2) Transfer. The Margin Provider shall, upon receipt of the notice referred to in the first sentence of Section 1(1), transfer to the Margin Recipient Margin with an aggregate Market Value at least equal to the Adjusted Net Exposure no later than the date agreed for such transfer, and failing such agreement on the Business Day immediately following receipt of such notice, if such notice is received on a Business Day prior to 11.00 a. m., and otherwise on the second Business Day following such receipt.

(3) Composition of Margin. The Margin Provider is entitled to determine the composition of the Margin to be transferred, unless the Margin Recipient has previously paid Cash Margin which has not been repaid or transferred Margin Securities which have not been returned to it, in which case the Margin Provider shall first repay such Cash Margin or return such Margin Securities.

(4) Cash Margin. Cash Margin shall be acceptable for the purpose of Section 1 (1) if transferred in the Base Currency or such other currency as the parties may have specified as eligible (in the Special Provisions or otherwise). A payment of Cash Margin shall give rise to a debt owing from the Margin Recipient to the Margin Provider and shall bear interest at such rate, and payable at such times, as agreed by the parties. In the absence of such agreement, that rate shall be equal to the Interbank Rate less 0.10 per cent. per annum, and the interest shall be payable at the end of each calendar month and on each date when the Margin Recipient is required to provide or return Margin.

(5) Margin Securities. Margin Securities shall be acceptable for the purpose of Section 1(1) if Securities of the relevant kind have been specified by the parties as eligible (in the Special Provisions or otherwise) or (b) have an original maturity of not more than five years and are issued by the central government of the country in which the Margin Recipient has its principal office or in which it is organised, incorporated or resident. A transfer of Margin Securities shall give rise to an obligation of the Margin Recipient to the Margin Provider to return such Securities as provided in this Annex.

(6) Margin Thresholds. Except in the case of a return of Margin pursuant to subsection 7, a transfer of Margin will take place only (a) to the extent that the Adjusted Net Exposure exceeds the threshold amount, if any, agreed by the parties ("Exposure Threshold") in relation to the Margin Recipient's Net Exposure and (b) if the Market Value of the Margin to be transferred exceeds the minimum amount, if any, agreed for such transfer (the "Minimum Transfer Amount"). In the absence of an agreement on either or both such amounts, such amount, or both, respectively, shall be zero.

(7) Return of Margin. Upon satisfaction by a party of all its obligations under Transactions in respect of which Margin is required to be transferred as provided in the fourth sentence of Section 1(1), any Margin

previously transferred and not returned shall be returned to the party which transferred it.

3.   Provisions Applicable to Margin Securities

The provisions of Section 3 of the Repurchase Annex (regarding substitution of Purchased Securities) and Sections 2(3), 2(5)(b)(ii) and (d), 2(6) and 3 of the Securities Lending Annex (regarding interpretation, failure to return Loaned Securities, special events, Distributions and subscription rights) shall apply *mutatis mutandis* to Margin Securities transferred pursuant to this Annex, provided that (a) the consent of the Margin Recipient shall not be required for a substitution by the Margin Provider of new Margin Securities acceptable pursuant to Section 2(5) of this Annex for Margin Securities previously transferred and (b) if any of the special events referred to in Section 2(6) of the Securities Lending Annex occurs in relation to Margin Securities, the relevant Transaction shall not be modified or terminated, but Margin acceptable pursuant to Section 2(4) or (5) of this Annex shall be substituted for such Securities upon request of either party.

FEDERATION BANCAIRE DE L'UNION EUROPEENNE
BANKING FEDERATION OF THE EUROPEAN UNION
BANKENVEREINIGUNG DER EUROPÄISCHEN UNION

in co-operation with

EUROPEAN SAVINGS BANKS GROUP
GROUPEMENT EUROPEEN DES CAISSES D'EPARGNE
EUROPÄISCHE SPARKASSENVEREINIGUNG

EUROPEAN ASSOCIATION OF COOPERATIVE BANKS
GROUPEMENT EUROPEEN DES BANQUES COOPERATIVES
EUROPÄISCHE VEREINIGUNG DER GENOSSENSCHAFTSBANKEN

MASTER AGREEMENT FOR FINANCIAL TRANSACTIONS

PRODUCT ANNEX FOR SECURITIES LOANS

Edition January 2001

This Annex supplements the General Provisions which form part of any Master Agreement for Financial Transactions based on the form published by the Banking Federation of the European Union.

1. Purpose, Applicability

(1) Purpose. The purpose of this Annex ("Securities Lending Annex") is to govern Transactions ("Securities Loans") in which one party (the "Lender") lends to the other (the "Borrower") Securities (the "Loaned Securities") for a determined or initially undetermined period of time. Any reference in this Annex to a Transaction shall be construed as a reference to a Securities Loan.

(2) Applicability. If this Annex forms part of a Master Agreement between any two parties, such Master Agreement (including this Annex) shall apply to any Securities Loan between such parties which is to be conducted by each party through a Booking Office specified in such Master Agreement in respect of Securities Loans.

2. Deliveries and Returns

(1) Initial Delivery. On the date agreed for the delivery of the Loaned Securities (the "Delivery Date"), the Lender shall transfer such Loaned Securities to the Borrower.

(2) Return. On the date agreed for the return of the Loaned Securities (the "Return Date"), the Borrower shall transfer to the Lender Securities of the same kind and quantity as the Loaned Securities.

(3) Interpretation. Any reference in this Annex to the Loaned Securities or other Securities in the context of the return or retransfer thereof, or to any rights or other assets to be transferred pursuant to Section 3(4), shall be construed so as to mean a reference to Securities, rights or assets of the same kind and quantity as (also referred to below as the "Equivalent" of) such Loaned Securities or other Securities, rights or assets, respectively.

(4) On Demand Transactions. The parties may agree that Securities Loans are terminable on demand, in which case the Return Date shall be the date specified in the demand notice sent by either party to the other, provided that the period between the taking effect of such notice and the Return Date so specified shall be not less than the minimum period customarily required for the delivery of Securities of the relevant kind. In the absence of a demand notice, the Return Date for a Transaction terminable on demand shall be the day which falls 364 days after the Delivery Date.

(5) Late Delivery

(a) *Failure by Lender.* If the Lender fails to transfer the Loaned Securities to the Borrower on the applicable Delivery Date, the Borrower may, at any time while such failure continues:

(i) require the Lender to pay to the Borrower an amount equal to the excess, if any, of the Borrower's Alternative Borrowing Cost over the pro rata portion of the Lending Fee attributable to the period of the delay, each calculated for the period from (and including) the Delivery Date to

Copyright © 2001 FBE

Product Annex for Securities Loans - 2001

(but excluding) the earlier of the date on which the Loaned Securities are transferred to the Borrower and the Return Date (which in the case of a Transaction terminable on demand shall be deemed to be the earliest date on which the Loaned Securities would be required to be returned following a demand by the Lender); "Alternative Borrowing Cost" of a party means the cost (including fees and expenses), as determined by such party, which such party has or would have reasonably incurred in borrowing the Equivalent of the Loaned Securities in the market for the relevant period; and

(ii) if the parties have not agreed on measures to promptly remedy the failure, give notice to the Lender that the Return Date shall be advanced so as to occur immediately, whereupon the obligations of the parties to lend or return the Loaned Securities (respectively) shall cease and no deliveries or payments shall be due between them other than, if applicable, pursuant to (i).

(b) *Failure by Borrower*. If the Borrower fails to return the Loaned Securities on the applicable Return Date, the Lender may, at any time while such failure continues:

(i) require the Borrower to pay to the Lender an amount equal to the higher of (a) the Lender's Alternative Borrowing Cost and (b) the Lending Fee, each calculated for the period from (and including) the Return Date to (but excluding) the date of actual return of the Loaned Securities or, if earlier, the date specified in the notice, if any, given pursuant to (ii); and

(ii) if the parties have not agreed on measures to promptly remedy the failure, give notice to the Borrower requiring cash settlement in lieu of delivery on a date to be specified in such notice, whereupon the obligation of the Borrower to return the Loaned Securities shall cease and the Borrower shall pay to the Lender an amount equal to the Acquisition Cost for such Securities; "Acquisition Cost" means the cost (including fees and expenses), as determined by the Lender, which the Lender has or would have reasonably incurred in purchasing the Equivalent of the Loaned Securities in the market on the date so specified for cash settlement.

(c) *Partial Delivery*. If the Lender or the Borrower transfers some, but not all, of the Loaned Securities on the date specified in sub-paragraph (a) or (b), respectively, the respective other party may, at its option, either accept such transfer and exercise its rights under those sub-paragraphs with respect to the residual Loaned Securities or decline such acceptance and exercise its rights with respect to all Loaned Securities.

(d) *Remedies*. Beyond the remedies provided in this subsection 5, neither party shall in the event of any failure by the other party to transfer or return Loaned Securities, be entitled to recover any additional damage as a consequence of such failure, and such failure shall not constitute an Event of Default under Section 6(1)(a)(iii) of the General Provisions. This paragraph (d) is without prejudice to any remedy available in the event of a failure by a party to perform any other obligation (including any obligation to make a payment under this subsection 5).

(6) *Special Events*. If, during the term of a Transaction and in respect of some or all of the Loaned Securities:

(i) a payment of any interest or dividend or any other distribution of money or other property by the issuer of the Loaned Securities (collectively a "Distribution", which term shall include a repayment of principal and a payment in the case of a capital reduction) would, as a result of any change in law or in the application or official interpretation thereof occurring after the date on which such Transaction is entered into, be subject to any deduction or withholding in respect of a tax or other duty or would give rise to a tax credit,

(ii) a notice of early redemption has been validly given;

(iii) a public redemption, exchange, conversion or compensation offer or a public purchase bid is made or announced;

(iv) subscription or other preferential rights which are not freely transferable are granted, or non-fungible property is distributed, to the holders; or

(v) if specified in the Special Provisions, a tax credit or tax entitlement is attached to any interest or dividend paid to the holders (whether or not subparagraph (i) would otherwise apply)

then, subject to any other agreement between the parties, the Return Date for such Securities shall, automatically in the case of (v) and otherwise upon demand by either party, be advanced to the third Business Day before, in the case of (i), (ii) and (v), the expected payment or redemption date or before, in the case of (iii) and (iv), the last day on which such bid or offer may be accepted or the day on which such rights or assets are granted or distributed.

3.   Distributions, Subscription Rights

(1) Cash Distributions. If during the term of a Securities Loan any Distribution of money is made by the issuer to the holders of the Loaned Securities, the Borrower shall pay to the Lender, on the date of such Distribution, an amount in the same currency as, and equal to, the amount received by the holders in respect of such Distribution.

(2) Withholding Taxes Tax Credits If a Distribution is subject to withholding tax and/or gives rise to a tax credit, the amount payable by the Borrower under subsection 1 shall be equal to the full amount to which the Lender would be entitled, as previously notified by it, in respect of such Distribution if it were the owner of the Loaned Securities, including the amount of (a) any applicable withholding tax to the extent that the Lender would be entitled to apply for an exemption from, or a refund of, such tax and (b) any tax credit available to the Lender.

(3) Subscription Rights. If subscription rights which are freely transferable are granted with respect to the Loaned Securities, the Borrower shall transfer to the Lender not later than on the third day on which such rights are traded, the Equivalent of the subscription rights attributable to such Loaned Securities. If the rights are not so transferred by such date, the Lender may purchase their Equivalent in the market for the account of the Borrower. Should the Lender be unable so to purchase the rights, it may require the Borrower to pay to it an amount equal to the Market Value

of such rights prevailing on the next following trading day for such rights.

(4) Non-cash Distributions Any freely transferable bonus shares, non-cash Distributions and ancillary rights (other than subscription rights) which are issued, made or allotted with respect to the Loaned Securities during the term of a Securities Loan shall be transferred to the Lender on the Return Date.

(5) Transfer Obligations For the avoidance of doubt, the provisions of subsections 1 through 4 shall apply whether or not the Borrower retains the ownership of the Loaned Securities during the term of the Transaction.

4.   Lending Fee

The Borrower shall pay to the Lender for each Securities Loan a fee (the "Lending Fee") equal to the rate per annum agreed in respect of such Securities Loan and calculated on the value of the Loaned Securities agreed by the parties for this purpose. The Lending Fee shall be calculated for the period from (and including) the Delivery Date or, if later, the date of actual transfer of the Loaned Securities to the Borrower, to (but excluding) the Return Date or, if later, the date of actual return of the Loaned Securities to the Lender, based on the actual number of days in such period and a 360-day year. Unless otherwise agreed, the Lender shall calculate the Lending Fee at the beginning of each month for the preceding month or, if earlier, on the Return Date, and send the Borrower a statement setting forth such Lending Fee. The Lending Fee shall be payable on the second Business Day following the receipt of such statement sent by the Lender.

5.   Margin Provisions

Any obligations of the parties to transfer cash or Securities as Margin under certain circumstances shall be performed in accordance with the provisions of the applicable Margin Maintenance Annex published by the FBE, or with any other rules to be separately agreed.

Suggested form of Confirmation

To:

From:

Date:

We refer to our telephone conversation and hereby confirm our agreement to enter into a Securities Loan Transaction [which shall be subject to the FBE Master Agreement for Financial Transactions between us]. The terms of the Transaction are as follows:

Reference Number:
Transaction Date:

Lender:
Borrower:

Delivery Date:
Return Date: […..(date)] [on demand]

Loaned Securities (designation, type):
Securities Code:
Amount/Number of Loaned Securities:

Lending Fee Rate: … % p.a.
Value of the Loaned Securities for purposes
of Lending Fee calculation:
[Distribution amount payable to Lender:] [Gross without deduction] [plus ... % tax credit] [net after deduction of... % withholding tax]

[Margin:][1] [Cash Margin: ... (specify currency and amount)]
[Margin Securities: ... (specify type and amount); applicable Valuation Percentage: %]
[other: ... (specify details)]

[Margin Ratio (Haircut)[2]:

Borrower's account:

Lender's account:

Delivery system:
[Agency: The Transaction is an Agency Transaction. [Name of Agent] is acting as agent for [name or identifier of Principal]].

[Additional provisions:]

Please confirm that the foregoing correctly sets forth the terms of our agreement by countersigning this Confirmation and returning it to [   ] or by sending us a confirmation substantially similar to this Confirmation, which confirmation sets forth the material terms of the Securities Loan to which this Confirmation relates and indicates agreement to those terms.

Yours sincerely

---

[1] Relevant if Margin is to be provided in respect of the relevant individual Transaction
[2] The terms "Margin Ratio" and "Haircut" have the same meaning; either or both may be used

Copyright © 2001 FBE   Product Annex for Securities Loans - 2001

APPENDIX 3

FEDERATION BANCAIRE DE L'UNION EUROPEENNE
BANKING FEDERATION OF THE EUROPEAN UNION
BANKENVEREINIGUNG DER EUROPÄISCHEN UNION

in co-operation with

EUROPEAN SAVINGS BANKS GROUP
GROUPEMENT EUROPEEN DES CAISSES D'EPARGNE
EUROPÄISCHE SPARKASSENVEREINIGUNG

EUROPEAN ASSOCIATION OF COOPERATIVE BANKS
GROUPEMENT EUROPEEN DES BANQUES COOPERATIVES
EUROPÄISCHE VEREINIGUNG DER GENOSSENSCHAFTSBANKEN

MASTER AGREEMENT
FOR FINANCIAL TRANSACTIONS

PRODUCT ANNEX
FOR
REPURCHASE TRANSACTIONS

Edition January 2001

This Annex supplements the General Provisions which form part of any Master Agreement for Financial Transactions based on the form published by the Banking Federation of the European Union.

1. Purpose, Applicability

(1) Purchase. The purpose of this Annex ("Repurchase Annex") is to govern Transactions ("Repurchase Transactions") in which one party (the "Seller") sells to the other (the "Buyer") Securities against payment of an agreed price (the "Purchase Price") and in which the Buyer sells to the Seller Securities of the same kind and quantity as such Securities against payment of another agreed price for delivery and payment at a specified later date or on demand. Any reference in this Annex to a Transaction shall be construed as a reference to a Repurchase Transaction.

(2) Applicability. If this Annex forms part of a Master Agreement between any two parties, such Master Agreement (including this Annex) shall apply to any Repurchase Transaction between such parties which is to be conducted by each party through a Booking Office specified in such Master Agreement in respect of Repurchase Transactions.

2. Deliveries and Payments

(1) Purchase. On the settlement date agreed for the purchase of Securities by the Buyer under a Transaction (the "Purchase Date"), the Seller shall transfer to the Buyer the Securities sold in that Transaction (the "Purchased Securities") against simultaneous payment of the Purchase Price.

(2) Repurchase. On the settlement date agreed for the repurchase of the Purchased Securities (the "Repurchase Date"), the Buyer shall transfer to the Seller Securities of the same kind and quantity as the Purchased Securities against simultaneous payment of the Repurchase Price.

(3) Definitions, Interpretation. "Repurchase Price" means the sum of the Purchase Price and the Price Differential. "Price Differential" means for any Transaction the aggregate amount obtained by applying the pricing rate agreed for such Transaction and expressed as a percentage per annum (the "Pricing Rate") to the Purchase Price for the actual number of days during the period from (and including) the Purchase Date to (but excluding) the Repurchase Date, on a 360-day or 365-day basis in accordance with market practice or on any other basis agreed between the parties. A payment shall be "simultaneous" if it occurs as part of a delivery versus-payment system or, should the use of such system in the given circumstances not be customary, if it occurs on the same day as the transfer of the relevant Securities. Any reference in this Annex to the Purchased Securities or other Securities in the context of the return or retransfer thereof, or to any rights or other assets to be transferred pursuant to Section 4(4), shall be construed so as to mean a reference to Securities, rights or assets of the same kind and quantity as (also referred to below as the "Equivalent" of) such Purchased Securities or other Securities, rights or assets, respectively.

(4) On Demand Transactions. The parties may agree that Transactions are terminable on demand, in which case the Repurchase Date shall be the date specified in the demand notice sent by either party to the other, provided that the

Copyright © 2001 FBE

Product Annex for Repurchase Transactions - 2001

period between the taking effect of such notice and the Repurchase Date so specified shall be not less than the minimum period customarily required for the payment of money and the delivery of Securities of the relevant kind. In the absence of a demand notice, the Repurchase Date for a Transaction terminable on demand shall be the day which falls 364 days after the Purchase Date.

(5) Late Payment. If the Purchase Price or the Repurchase Price is not paid when due, the interest payable pursuant to Section 3(5) of the General Provisions shall be calculated at the higher of the Default Rate and the Pricing Rate, without prejudice to the application of Section 6(l)(a)(i) of the General Provisions.

(6)   *Late Delivery*

(a) *Failure by Seller* If the Seller fails to transfer the Purchased Securities to the Buyer on the applicable Purchase Date, the Buyer may, at any time while such failure continues:

(i) if it has paid the Purchase Price to the Seller, require the Seller immediately to repay the sum so paid;

(ii) require the Seller to pay to the Buyer an amount equal to the excess, if any, of the Buyer's Borrowing Cost over the pro rata portion of the Price Differential attributable to the period of the delay, each calculated for the period from (and including) the Purchase Date to (but excluding) the earlier of the date on which the Purchased Securities are transferred to the Buyer and the Repurchase Date (which in the case of a Transaction terminable on demand shall be deemed to be the earliest date on which the Purchased Securities would be required to be returned following a demand by the Seller); "Borrowing Cost" of a party means the cost (including fees and expenses), as determined by such party, which such party has or would have reasonably incurred in borrowing the Equivalent of the Purchased Securities in the market for the relevant period; and

(iii) if the parties have not agreed on measures to promptly remedy the failure, give notice that the Repurchase Date shall be advanced so as to occur immediately, whereupon the mutual obligations originally agreed by the parties under the relevant Transaction shall be netted, so that no payments or deliveries are due except that the Seller shall pay to the Buyer (in addition to complying with its obligations pursuant to (i) and (ii), if applicable) an amount equal to the Price Differential for the period from (and including) the Purchase Date to (but excluding) the Repurchase Date so advanced.

(b) *Failure by Buyer*. If the Buyer fails to return the Purchased Securities to the Seller on the applicable Repurchase Date, the Seller may, at any time while such failure continues:

(i) if it has paid the Repurchase Price to the Buyer, require the Buyer immediately to repay the sum so paid;

(ii) require the Buyer to pay to the Seller an amount equal to the excess, if any, of the Seller's Borrowing Cost over the amount receivable if the Repurchase Price were placed on deposit at the Interbank Rate, each calculated for the period from (and including) the Repurchase Date to (but excluding) the date of actual return of the Purchased Securities or, if earlier, the date specified in the notice, if any, given pursuant to (iii); and

(iii) if the parties have not agreed on measures to promptly remedy the failure, give notice requiring cash settlement in lieu of delivery on a date to be specified in such notice, whereupon the obligations of the parties originally agreed in respect of the Repurchase Date shall cease, and the Buyer shall (A) pay to the Seller (in addition to complying with its obligations pursuant to (i) and (ii), if applicable) an amount equal to the excess, if any, of the Alternative Purchase Cost for such Securities over the Repurchase Price or, as the case may be, (B) be entitled to receive from the Seller the excess, if any, of the Repurchase Price over such Alternative Purchase Cost; "Alternative Purchase Cost" means the cost (including fees and expenses), as determined by the Seller, which the Seller has or would have reasonably incurred in purchasing the Equivalent of the Purchased Securities in the market on the date so specified for cash settlement.

(c) *Remedies* Beyond the remedies provided in this subsection 6, neither party shall, in the event of any failure by the other party to transfer or return Purchased Securities, be entitled to recover any additional damage as a consequence of such failure, and such failure shall not constitute an Event of Default under Section 6(l)(a)(iii) of the General Provisions. This paragraph (c) is without prejudice to any remedy available in the event of any failure by a party to perform any other obligation (including any obligation to make a payment under this subsection 6) when due.

(7) Special Events If, during the term of a Transaction and in respect of some or all of the Purchased Securities:

(i) a payment of any interest or dividend or any other distribution of money or other property by the issuer of the Purchased Securities (collectively a "Distribution", which term shall include a repayment of principal and a payment in the case of a capital reduction) would, as a result of any change in law or in the application or official interpretation thereof occurring after the date on which such Transaction is entered into, be subject to any deduction or withholding in respect of a tax or other duty or would give rise to a tax credit;

(ii) a notice of early redemption has been validly given;

(iii) a public redemption, exchange, conversion or compensation offer or a public purchase bid is made or announced;

(iv) subscription or other rights or assets which are not freely transferable are granted or distributed to the holders; or

(v) if specified in the Special Provisions, a tax credit or tax entitlement is attached to any interest or dividend paid to the holders (whether or not subparagraph (i) would otherwise apply) then, subject to any other agreement between the parties, the Repurchase Date for such Securities shall, automatically in the case of (v) and otherwise upon demand by either party, be advanced to the third Business Day before, in the case of (i), (ii) and (v), the expected payment or redemption date or before, in the case of (iii) and (iv), the last day on which such bid or offer may be accepted or the day on which such rights or assets are granted or distributed.

3. Substitution

(1) General Principle The Seller may, at its cost and with the consent of the Buyer, substitute for any Purchased Securities other Securities ("New Securities") which at the time at which the parties agree to such substitution have a Market Value at least equal to the Market Value of the Purchased Securities for which they are substituted.

(2) No Novation. The substitution shall have no novation effect on the relevant Transaction, and the Transaction shall continue in effect, except that the New Securities will be deemed to be Purchased Securities instead of the Securities that are replaced.

(3) Simultaneous Retransfer. The substitution will be carried out by simultaneous transfer of the New Securities in exchange for the Purchased Securities to be replaced.

4. Distributions, Subscription Rights

(1) Cash Distributions. If during the term of a Transaction any Distribution of money is made by the issuer to the holders of the Purchased Securities, the Buyer shall pay to the Seller, on the date of such Distribution, an amount in the same currency as, and equal to, the amount received by the holders in respect of such Distribution.

(2) Withholding Taxes Tax Credits If a Distribution is subject to withholding tax and/or gives rise to a tax credit, the amount payable by the Buyer under subsection 1 shall be equal to the full amount to which the Seller would be entitled, as previously notified by it, in respect of such Distribution if it were the owner of the Purchased Securities, including the amount of (a) any applicable withholding tax to the extent that the Seller would be entitled to apply for an exemption from, or a refund of, such tax and (b) any tax credit available to the Seller.

(3) Subscription Rights if subscription rights which are freely transferable are granted with respect to the Purchased Securities, the Buyer shall transfer to the Seller, not later than on the third day on which such rights are traded, the Equivalent of the subscription rights attributable to such Purchased Securities. If the rights are not so transferred by such date, the Seller may purchase their Equivalent in the market for the account of the Buyer. Should the Seller be unable so to purchase the rights, it may require the Buyer to pay to it an amount equal to the Market Value of such rights prevailing on the next following trading day for such rights.

(4) Non-cash Distributions Any freely transferable bonus shares, non-cash Distributions and ancillary rights (other than subscription rights) which are issued, made or allotted with respect to the Purchased Securities during the term of a Transaction shall be transferred to the Seller on the Repurchase Date.

(5) Transfer Obligations For the avoidance of doubt, the provisions of subsections 1 through 4 shall apply whether or not the Buyer retains the ownership of the Purchased Securities during the term of the Transaction.

5. Specific Terms for Buy/Sell Back Transactions

(1) Applicability, Definitions Transactions shall be subject to this Section 5 if they are identified as Buy/Sell Back Transactions. "Buy/Sell Back Transactions" are Repurchase Transactions for which the Purchase Price and the Repurchase Price are each composed of (a) a price quoted exclusive of Accrued Interest (being the "Clean Price", payable on the Purchase Date, and the "Forward Price", also called "Sell Back Price", payable on the Repurchase Date) and (b) Accrued Interest, calculated as of the Purchase Date when payable together with the Clean Price and calculated as of the Repurchase Date when payable together with the Forward Price. "Accrued Interest" means the accrued portion, as of the relevant date of calculation, of the interest (if any) payable by the issuer of the Purchased Securities in respect of such Securities.

(2) Interpretation In the event of any conflict, this Section 5 shall, with respect to Buy/Sell Back Transactions, prevail over any other terms of this Annex. For Buy/Sell Back Transactions, (a) any reference in the Agreement to the Purchase Price shall be construed as referring to the Clean Price plus Accrued Interest paid or payable on the Purchase Date and (b) any reference in the Agreement to the Repurchase Price shall, notwithstanding the definition of that term in Section 2 (3), be construed as referring to the agreed Forward Price plus Accrued Interest paid or payable on the Repurchase Date or, as the case may be, to the adjusted Forward Price calculated pursuant to subsection 5 (to which no Accrued Interest shall be added).

(3) Confirmation the Confirmation of a Buy/Sell Back Transaction shall specify), the Forward Price and the Pricing Rate.

(4) Distributions Section 4(1) shall apply to Buy/Sell Back Transactions only if specifically so agreed.

(5) Adjusted Forward Price In relation to a date other than the originally agreed Repurchase Date, for example in relation to a Repurchase Date advanced in accordance with Section ^{2}(6)(a)(iii) or Section 2(7), the Forward Price shall be equal to:

(a) the Repurchase Price as defined in Section 2(3), less (except if the parties have agreed that Section 4 (1) shall apply)

(b) the sum of (i) the amount of any Distribution in respect of the Purchased Securities made by the issuer on a date falling between the Purchase Date and the Repurchase Date, and (ii) the aggregate amount obtained by daily application of the Pricing Rate for the relevant Transaction to such amount from (and including) the date of the Distribution to (but excluding) such advanced or postponed Repurchase Date.

6. Margin Maintenance, Repricing

(1) Margin Provisions any obligations of the parties to transfer cash or Securities as Margin under certain circumstances shall be performed in accordance with the provisions of the applicable Margin Maintenance Annex

4

published by the FBE, or with any other rules to be separately agreed.

(2) Repricing If the parties agree on the repricing of one or more Transactions (the "Original Transactions") instead of a transfer of Margin, then

(a) the Repurchase Date of each Original Transaction shall be deemed advanced to the date as of which the repricing is to occur (the "Repricing Date"),

(b) a new Transaction (the "New Transaction") shall be deemed entered into under which (i) Purchased Securities shall be the Equivalent of those purchased under the Original Transaction, (ii) the Purchase Date shall be the Repricing Date, (iii) the Purchase Price shall be equal to the Market Value of such Securities on the Repricing Date divided by the Margin Ratio, if any, applicable to the Original Transaction, as agreed pursuant to the applicable Margin Maintenance Annex, and (iv) the Repurchase Date, the Pricing Rate, the Margin Ratio and, subject to the above, the other terms shall be identical to the ones of the Original Transaction, and

(c) the obligations to pay the Purchase Price and to transfer the Purchased Securities under the New Transaction shall be discharged by setting them off against the obligations to pay the Repurchase Price and to retransfer the Equivalent of the Purchased Securities under the Original Transaction, so that only a net cash amount shall be payable by one party to the other on the Repricing Date or, if that is not practicable, on the next Business Day.

APPENDIX 3

5

Suggested form of Confirmation

To:
From:
Date:

We refer to our telephone conversation and hereby confirm our agreement to enter into a Repurchase Transaction [in the form of a Buy/Sell Back Transaction] [which shall be subject to the FBE Master Agreement for Financial Transactions between us]. The terms of the Transaction are as follows:

Reference Number:
Transaction Date

Seller:
Buyer:

Purchase Date:
Repurchase Date: [(date)][on demand]

Purchased Securities (designation, type):
Securities Code:
Amount/Number of Purchased Securities:

Purchase Price:
[Clean Price:]
[Accrued Interest payable on Purchase Date:]
Pricing Rate: % p.a.
[Forward Price (Sell Back Price):]
[Accrued Interest payable on
Repurchase Date:]
[Distribution amount payable to Seller:]   [Gross without deduction][plus % tax credit][net after deduction of... % withholding tax]

[Eligible Margin:]   [Cash Margin: (specify currency)]
                                                     [Margin Securities: (specify type)]
                                                     [other: (specify details)]

[Margin Ratio (Haircut)[6]

Buyer's account:
Seller's account:
Delivery system:

[Agency: The Transaction is an Agency Transaction. [Name of Agent] is acting as agent for [name or identifier of Principal]]

[Additional provisions:]

Please confirm that the foregoing correctly sets forth the terms of our agreement by countersigning this Confirmation and returning it to [ ] or by sending us a confirmation substantially similar to this Confirmation, which confirmation sets forth the material terms of the Transaction to which this Confirmation relates and indicates agreement to those terms.

Yours sincerely,

1,2,3,4   Relevant only for Buy/Sell Back Transactions. The terms "Forward Price" and Sell Back Price" (note 3) have the same meaning; either or both may be used.
5   Relevant if eligible Margin is not specified in the Special Provisions.
6   The terms "Margin Ratio" and "Haircut" have the same meaning; either or both may be used.

Copyright © 2001 FBE   Product Annex for Repurchase Transactions - 2001

FEDERATION BANCAIRE DE L'UNION EUROPEENNE
BANKING FEDERATION OF THE EUROPEAN UNION
BANKENVEREINIGUNG DER EUROPÄISCHEN UNION

in co-operation with

EUROPEAN SAVINGS BANKS GROUP
GROUPEMENT EUROPEEN DES CAISSES D'EPARGNE
EUROPÄISCHE SPARKASSENVEREINIGUNG

EUROPEAN ASSOCIATION OF COOPERATIVE BANKS
GROUPEMENT EUROPEEN DES BANQUES COOPERATIVES
EUROPÄISCHE VEREINIGUNG DER GENOSSENSCHAFTSBANKEN

MASTER AGREEMENT
FOR FINANCIAL TRANSACTIONS

PRODUCT ANNEX FOR DERIVATIVE TRANSACTIONS
Edition 2004

This Annex, together with any Supplement thereto, supplements the General Provisions which form part of any Master Agreement for Financial Transactions based on the form published by the FBE.

1. Purpose, Applicability

(1) Purpose. The purpose of this Annex ("Derivatives Annex") is to govern Transactions ("Derivative Transactions") which are (a) over-the-counter market transactions, including, but not limited to, forward, swap, option, cap, floor, and collar transactions, any combination of these and any other similar transactions, the object of which is (i) the exchange of amounts of money denominated in different currencies, (ii) the delivery or transfer of currencies, securities, financial instruments, commodities, precious metals, energy (including but not limited to gas and electricity) or any other assets, (iii) the payment of money, if either the obligation to make such payment, or the amount thereof, is contingent upon market-related, credit-related or other events or circumstances, (including, but not limited to, the level of interest or exchange rates, credit spreads, prices, market or economic indices, statistics, weather conditions, economic conditions or any other measurement), (iv) any combination of the foregoing, or (b) any transaction referred to in Section 1(2)(a) of this Annex.

(2) Applicability. If this Annex forms part of a Master Agreement between any two parties, such Master Agreement (including this Annex) shall apply to any Derivative Transaction between such parties which is to be conducted by each party through a Booking Office specified in such Master Agreement in respect of Derivative Transactions and which either (a) has been entered into subject to the terms of such Master Agreement (whether or not the transaction is of a type referred to in Section 1(1)(a) of this Annex), or (b) is a Foreign Exchange Transaction if the parties have specified in Section 2 of the Special Provisions that the Foreign Exchange Supplement shall be incorporated into this Annex, or (c) is of a type specified in the Special Provisions as being a type to which this Annex shall apply.

2. Other Market Standard Documentation

If the parties have, in the Special Provisions, a Confirmation or otherwise, incorporated into the terms of a Transaction any Market Standard Documentation, in whole or in part, such documentation (or parts thereof) so incorporated shall apply to such Transaction. For the avoidance of doubt, the terms of such Market Standard Documentation shall, unless the parties have agreed otherwise, be construed in accordance with the law agreed by the parties in Section 4 of the Special Provisions to govern the Master Agreement. "Market Standard Documentation" means a documentation (including, but not limited to, any documentation published by a member association of the FBE or by an industry association) which sets out for different types of Transactions the terms and technical characteristics relating to such Transactions and which may include one or more definitions, lists of definitions, addenda (including, but not limited to, samples of Confirmation) or provisions for use in connection with other market standard master agreements.

3. Margin Provisions

Any obligations of the parties to transfer cash or Securities as Margin under certain circumstances shall be performed in accordance with the provisions of the applicable Margin Maintenance Annex or with any other rules to be separately agreed.

4. Definitions common to Supplements to this Annex

"Calculation Agent" means the party or any other third person specified as such in respect of the relevant Transaction; the Calculation Agent shall make all calculations, adjustments, determinations, estimates, anticipations or selections in good faith and in a reasonable manner;

Copyright © 2004 FBE

Product Annex for Derivative Transactions - 2004

"Cash Settlement Currency" means the euro, unless otherwise agreed;

"Effective Date" means the date agreed as such between the parties in respect of the relevant Transaction or, failing such agreement, the Trade Date; the Effective Date is the first day of the term of the Transaction and shall not be subject to adjustments in accordance with Section 3(6) of the General Provisions, unless otherwise specified by the parties;

"Exchange" means the regulated or organised exchange(s) or the quotation system(s) for any underlying asset or any underlying measurement of a Transaction, agreed as such between the parties. This definition shall be subject to any modification which may be agreed in any Confirmation or agreed between the parties in a separate document (including any applicable Supplement) or otherwise;

"Exchange Business Day" means a day on which the Exchange(s) is/are open for trading. If any payment or delivery date, any determination or valuation date, any commencement or termination date or any exercise date agreed between the parties which is deemed to be an Exchange Business Day is not an Exchange Business Day, the provisions of Section 3(6) of the General Provisions shall be applicable provided that for purposes of application of those provisions, references to a "Business Day" shall be deemed to be references to an "Exchange Business Day";

"Market Disruption Convention" means any provisions incorporated in any Confirmation or agreed between the parties in a separate document (including any applicable Supplement) or otherwise, providing for the consequences of a Market Disruption Event occurring and continuing at the Valuation Time on any Valuation Date;

"Market Disruption Event" means in respect of any underlying asset or measurement of a Transaction and to the extent such underlying asset or measurement is subject to quotations, the situation where the Calculation Agent ascertains during the one-half hour period that ends at the relevant Valuation Time any suspension of quotations or any material limitation of trading (in particular by reason of movements in prices exceeding the limits allowed by any relevant exchange(s), or any relevant central bank or any market undertaking or otherwise) on the relevant exchange(s), of the underlying asset or measurement or, as the case may be, of any future or option contract relating to the underlying asset or measurement. This definition shall be subject to any modification which may be agreed in any Confirmation or agreed between the parties in a separate document (including any applicable Supplement) or otherwise;

"Settlement Date" means, subject to any modifications made in an applicable Supplement and to adjustments in accordance with Section 3(6) of the General Provisions, each date agreed between the parties upon which payments, deliveries or transfers shall be made in respect of the relevant Transaction;

a payment shall be "simultaneous" if it occurs as part of a delivery-versus-payment system or, should such system not exist or the use of such system in the given circumstances not be customary, if it occurs on the same day as the delivery or transfer of currencies, securities, financial instruments, commodities, precious metals, energy or any other assets;

"Termination Date" means the date agreed as such between the parties in respect of the relevant Transaction or, failing such agreement, the last Settlement Date of the Transaction; the Termination Date is the last day of the term of the Transaction and shall not be subject to adjustments in accordance with Section 3(6) of the General Provisions, unless otherwise specified by the parties;

"Trade Date" means the date on which the parties enter into the relevant Transaction;

"Valuation Date" means, subject to adjustments in accordance with the applicable Market Disruption Convention or Section 3(6) of the General Provisions, (i) the date agreed as such between the parties on which the relevant prices, interest rates, exchange rates, credit spreads, market or economic indices, statistics, weather conditions, economic conditions or any other measurement are to be determined in respect of the relevant Transaction or, failing such agreement, (ii) the date so specified in the applicable Supplement;

"Valuation Time" means the time agreed as such between the parties in respect of the relevant Transaction or, failing such agreement, the close of business on the Valuation Date.

FEDERATION BANCAIRE DE L'UNION EUROPEENNE
BANKING FEDERATION OF THE EUROPEAN UNION
BANKENVEREINIGUNG DER EUROPÄISCHEN UNION

in co-operation with

EUROPEAN SAVINGS BANKS GROUP
GROUPEMENT EUROPEEN DES CAISSES D'EPARGNE
EUROPÄISCHE SPARKASSENVEREINIGUNG

EUROPEAN ASSOCIATION OF COOPERATIVE BANKS
GROUPEMENT EUROPEEN DES BANQUES COOPERATIVES
EUROPÄISCHE VEREINIGUNG DER GENOSSENSCHAFTSBANKEN

MASTER AGREEMENT
FOR FINANCIAL TRANSACTIONS

SUPPLEMENT TO THE
DERIVATIVES ANNEX

FOREIGN EXCHANGE TRANSACTIONS
Edition 2004

This Supplement complements the General Provisions and the Derivatives Annex which form part of a Master Agreement for Financial Transactions based on the form published by the FBE.

1. Purpose, Interpretation

(1) *Purpose.* The purpose of this Supplement ("Foreign Exchange Supplement") is to govern Foreign Exchange Transactions, which means a Foreign Exchange Spot, Foreign Exchange Forward, Non-Deliverable Foreign Exchange Forward, Foreign Exchange Option, Non-Deliverable Foreign Exchange Option or any other Transaction so agreed by the parties in respect of the individual Transaction or in the Special Provisions.

(2) *Interpretation.* This Supplement forms an integral part of the Derivatives Annex. The term "Annex" as used in Section 1(3) of the General Provisions should be construed as to include this Supplement. In the event of any conflict between different parts of the Derivatives Annex and this Supplement, this Supplement shall prevail.

2. Foreign Exchange Transactions

"Foreign Exchange Spot" means a Transaction in which one party (the "Seller") sells to the other (the "Buyer") a specified amount of a specified currency (the "Reference Currency") against payment of an agreed amount of a specified different currency (the "Settlement Currency"), and both obligations are settled on a spot basis.

"Foreign Exchange Forward" means a Transaction in which the Seller sells to the Buyer a specified amount of the Reference Currency against payment of an agreed amount of the Settlement Currency, and both obligations are settled on a specified later date.

"Non-Deliverable Foreign Exchange Forward" means a Transaction in which the Seller sells to the Buyer a specified amount of the Reference Currency, which is a non-convertible, non-transferable or thinly traded currency, against payment of an agreed amount of the Settlement Currency, and both obligations are settled by the payment by the Seller or, as the case may be, the Buyer of the Settlement Currency Amount based on the difference between the agreed price for the Settlement Currency and the price for the Settlement Currency on a specified later date.

"Foreign Exchange Option" means an Option Transaction in which the Seller grants to the Buyer against payment of the Premium the right to purchase, in the case of a Call, or sell, in the case of a Put, a specified amount of the Reference Currency (the "Call Currency" in the case of a Call and the "Put Currency" in the case of a Put) against payment of an agreed amount of the Settlement Currency (the "Put Currency" in the case of a Call and the "Call Currency" in the case of a Put). The Option Transaction may be settled by (i), in the case of a Foreign Exchange Option to which "Physical Settlement" applies (the "Physically Settled Foreign Exchange Option"), delivering or transferring a specified amount of the Reference Currency against payment of an agreed amount of the Settlement Currency or (ii), in the case of a Foreign Exchange Option to which "Cash Settlement" applies (the "Cash Settled Foreign Exchange Option"), paying the Cash Settlement Amount based on the difference between the agreed price for the Settlement Currency and the price for the Settlement Currency on the Valuation Date.

"Non-Deliverable Foreign Exchange Option" means an Option Transaction in which the Seller grants to the Buyer against payment of the Premium the right to purchase, in the case of a Call, or sell, in the case of a

Copyright © 2004 FBE

Foreign Exchange Transactions - 2004

Put, a specified amount of the Reference Currency, which is a non-convertible, non-transferable or thinly traded currency, (the "Call Currency" in the case of a Call and the "Put Currency" in the case of a Put) against payment of an agreed amount of the Settlement Currency (the "Put Currency" in the case of a Call and the "Call Currency" in the case of a Put), and both obligations are settled by paying the Cash Settlement Amount based on the difference between the agreed price for the Settlement Currency and the price for the Settlement Currency on the Valuation Date.

3. Deliveries and Payments

(1) *Foreign Exchange Spot and Foreign Exchange Forward*. On the agreed Settlement Date for the Foreign Exchange Spot or the Foreign Exchange Forward the Seller shall deliver or transfer to the Buyer the specified amount of the Reference Currency and the Buyer shall deliver or transfer to the Seller the agreed amount of the Settlement Currency.

(2) *Non-Deliverable Foreign Exchange Forward*. On the agreed Settlement Date for the Non-Deliverable Foreign Exchange Forward, the Seller shall pay to the Buyer the absolute value of the Settlement Currency Amount, if such amount is a negative number, and the Buyer shall pay to the Seller the Settlement Currency Amount, if such amount is a positive number.

"Settlement Currency Amount" means an amount expressed in the Settlement Currency calculated on the basis of the following formula:

$$\left[\text{AgreedAmount of the Settlement Currency} \times \left(1 - \frac{\text{Forward Rate}}{\text{Settlement Currency Rate}}\right) \right]$$

(3) *Physically Settled Foreign Exchange Option*. On the agreed Premium Payment Date for the Physically Settled Foreign Exchange Option the Buyer shall pay to the Seller the Premium. If the Physically Settled Foreign Exchange Option is exercised or deemed to be exercised, on the agreed Settlement Date of the Option Transaction, the Seller shall deliver or transfer to the Buyer the specified amount of the Reference Currency against simultaneous payment of the agreed amount of the Settlement Currency.

(4) *Non-Deliverable Foreign Exchange Option and Cash Settled Foreign Exchange Option*. On the agreed Premium Payment Date for the Non-Deliverable Foreign Exchange Option or the Cash Settled Foreign Exchange Option the Buyer shall pay to the Seller the Premium. If the Option Transaction is exercised or deemed to be exercised, on the agreed Settlement Date for the Non-Deliverable Foreign Exchange Option or the Cash Settled Foreign Exchange Option, the Seller shall pay to the Buyer the Cash Settlement Amount, if such amount is a positive number.

"Cash Settlement Amount" means an amount expressed in the Settlement Currency and calculated as follows, (i) in the case of an Option Transaction where the Reference Currency is the Put Currency and the Settlement Currency is the Call Currency:

$$\left[\text{Agreed Amount of the Call Currency} \times \left(\frac{\text{Settlement Currency Rate} - \text{Strike Price}}{\text{Settlement Currency Rate}} \right) \right]$$

and (ii) in the case of an Option Transaction where the Reference Currency is the Call Currency and the Settlement Currency is the Put Currency:

$$\left[\text{Agreed Amount of the Put Currency} \times \left(\frac{\text{Strike Price} - \text{Settlement Currency Rate}}{\text{Settlement Currency Rate}} \right) \right]$$

(5) *Definitions.* "Forward Rate" means the forward foreign exchange rate agreed as such between the parties, such rate shall be expressed as an amount of the Reference Currency per one unit of the Settlement Currency.

"Settlement Currency Rate" means the foreign exchange rate expressed as an amount of the Reference Currency per one unit of the Settlement Currency as determined by the Calculation Agent on the Valuation Date for the Valuation Time based on the currency exchange rate for the Reference Currency and the Settlement Currency (the "Currency Pair") (i) quoted through and obtainable from the Price Source specified in the agreed Currency Rate Option or, failing such agreement, (ii) determined by the Calculation Agent. "Currency Rate Option" means the foreign exchange rate agreed by the parties by reference to the publication, screen or web page of an information vendor or any other price source (the "Price Source").

"Strike Price" means the foreign exchange rate agreed between the parties at which the Currency Pair shall be exchanged if an Option Transaction is exercised or deemed to be exercised; such rate shall be expressed as an amount of the Reference Currency per one unit of the Settlement Currency.

4. Provisions applicable to Option Transactions

Unless otherwise defined in this Supplement, any term relating to Option Transactions is to be construed in accordance with the applicable Options Supplement published by the FBE.

Copyright © 2004 FBE   Foreign Exchange Transactions - 2004

FEDERATION BANCAIRE DE L'UNION EUROPEENNE
BANKING FEDERATION OF THE EUROPEAN UNION
BANKENVEREINIGUNG DER EUROPÄISCHEN UNION

in co-operation with

EUROPEAN SAVINGS BANKS GROUP
GROUPEMENT EUROPEEN DES CAISSES D'EPARGNE
EUROPÄISCHE SPARKASSENVEREINIGUNG

EUROPEAN ASSOCIATION OF COOPERATIVE BANKS
GROUPEMENT EUROPEEN DES BANQUES COOPERATIVES
EUROPÄISCHE VEREINIGUNG DER GENOSSENSCHAFTSBANKEN

MASTER AGREEMENT
FOR FINANCIAL TRANSACTIONS

SUPPLEMENT TO THE
DERIVATIVES ANNEX

OPTION TRANSACTIONS
Edition 2004

This Supplement complements the General Provisions, the Derivatives Annex and each Supplement to such Annex which form part of a Master Agreement for Financial Transactions based on the form published by the FBE.

1. Purpose, Interpretation

(1) *Purpose.* The purpose of this Supplement ("Options Supplement") is to govern Transactions ("Option Transactions") in which one party (the "Seller") grants to the other party (the "Buyer"), against payment of an agreed premium (the "Premium") or any other consideration, the right (the "Option") to

(a) purchase, in the case of a Call, or sell, in the case of a Put, a specified amount, quantity or number of currencies, securities, financial instruments, commodities, precious metals, energy or any other assets (an "Underlying Asset") against payment of an agreed price, whereby both obligations are to be settled (i) by delivering or transferring the specified amount, quantity or number of the Underlying Asset against payment of the agreed price, in the case of an Option Transaction to which "Physical Settlement" applies, or (ii) in the case of an Option Transaction to which "Cash Settlement" applies, by paying a Cash Settlement Amount based on the difference of the agreed price (the "Strike Price") for the Underlying Asset and the price (the "Settlement Price") for such Underlying Asset on the Valuation Date,

(b) request the payment of a Cash Settlement Amount based on the difference of an agreed level (the "Strike Level") of interest or exchange rates, credit spreads, prices, market or economic indices, statistics, weather conditions, economic conditions or any other measurement (an "Underlying Measurement") and the level (the "Settlement Level") of such Underlying Measurement on the Valuation Date,

(c) cause an underlying Transaction (the "Underlying Transaction") to become effective, whereby the Underlying Transaction is to be settled (i) by making all payments and deliveries or transfers to be made by the parties in accordance with the terms of the Underlying Transaction, in the case of an Option Transaction to which "Physical Settlement" applies or (ii), in the case of an Option Transaction to which "Cash Settlement" applies, by paying a Cash Settlement Amount based on the value of the Underlying Transaction on the Valuation Date, if such value, from the Buyer's perspective, is a positive number, or

(d) terminate a specified Transaction to the effect that all obligations under the terminated Transaction or under the Agreement related to the terminated Transaction, which otherwise would have become due on or after the Exercise Date shall be replaced by an obligation to pay a Cash Settlement Amount based on the value of the terminated Transaction and owed by the Seller if such amount is a positive number and by the Buyer if such amount is a negative number.

(2) *Interpretation.* This Supplement forms an integral part of the Derivatives Annex. The term "Annex" as used in Section 1(3) of the General Provisions should be construed as to include this Supplement. In the event of any conflict between different parts of the Derivatives Annex and this Supplement, this Supplement shall prevail.

2. Option Transactions

(1) *Styles.* "American Option" means an Option Transaction in which the Option is exercisable on each Exercise Business Day during a period from (and including) the Commencement Date to (and including) the Expiration Date.

Copyright © 2004 FBE

Option Transactions - 2004

"Bermuda Option" means an Option Transaction in which the Option is exercisable on each Exercise Business Day so agreed to between the parties (each a "Scheduled Exercise Date") and on the Expiration Date, subject to adjustments in accordance with Section 3(6) of the General Provisions. "European Option" means an Option Transaction in which the Option is exercisable on the Expiration Date.

"Asian Option" means an American Option, Bermuda Option or European Option in which the Settlement Price or the Settlement Level is calculated on the Valuation Date as the average of prices or levels determined for the Underlying Asset or Underlying Measurement on each Averaging Date.

(2) *Types*. "Call" means an Option Transaction that, upon exercise (i), in case of Section 1(1)(a)(i) of this Supplement, obliges the Seller to deliver or transfer the specified amount, quantity or number of the Underlying Asset against payment of the agreed price, or (ii), in case of Section 1(1)(a)(ii) or 1(1)(b) of this Supplement, entitles the Buyer to request payment of the Cash Settlement Amount if the Settlement Price exceeds the Strike Price or the Settlement Level exceeds the Strike Level.

"Put" means an Option Transaction that, upon exercise (i), in case of Section 1(1)(a)(i) of this Supplement, obliges the Buyer to deliver or transfer the specified amount, quantity or number of the Underlying Asset against payment of the agreed price, or (ii), in case of Section 1(1)(a)(ii) or 1(1)(b) of this Supplement, entitles the Buyer to request payment of the Cash Settlement Amount if the Strike Price exceeds the Settlement Price or the Strike Level exceeds the Settlement Level.

(3) *Definitions of Dates*. "Expiration Date" means the Exercise Business Day agreed between the parties beyond which an Option can not be exercised any more, subject to adjustments in accordance with Section 3(6) of the General Provisions.

"Commencement Date" means the Exercise Business Day agreed as such between the parties (subject to adjustments in accordance with Section 3(6) of the General Provisions) or, failing such agreement, the Trade Date.

"Averaging Date" means each date agreed as such between the parties (subject to adjustments in accordance with Section 3(6) of the General Provisions) or, failing any agreement, each Exercise Business Day from (and including) the Commencement Date to (and including) the Expiration Date.

"Exercise Date" means each Exercise Business Day on which an Option is exercised or deemed to be exercised.

"Exercise Business Day" means each day during the Exercise Period on which an Option may be exercised, that is either (a) a Business Day (as defined in Section 3(7) of the General Provisions) in (i) the place(s) agreed between the parties or, failing such agreement, (ii) the place(s) determined pursuant to the terms of any applicable Supplement or, failing such terms (iii) the city specified in the address of the Seller's Office or (b) an Exchange Business Day.

"Valuation Date" means the Exercise Business Day agreed as such between the parties (subject to adjustments in accordance with Section 3(6) of the General Provisions) or failing such agreement, the Exercise Date.

3. Premium

The Buyer shall pay to the Seller the Premium on the date or dates (each a "Premium Payment Date") agreed between the parties (subject to adjustments in accordance with Section 3(6) of the General Provisions) or, failing such agreement, the date that is two Business Days immediately following the Trade Date.

4. Exercise

(1) *Exercise by Notice*. The Buyer is entitled to exercise an Option by giving notice (the "Exercise Notice"), which may be given orally, including by telephone, to the Seller's Office during the Exercise Period. An Exercise Notice is irrevocable. If an Exercise Notice is given orally, the Buyer shall promptly send to the Seller a confirmation of such notice in the manner specified in Section 8(1) of the General Provisions. The absence of such confirmation shall not affect the validity of the exercise of the Option.

"Seller's Office" means the office and contact details specified as such in the terms of an Option Transaction or, if none is specified, the office through which the Seller enters into the relevant Option Transaction.

(2) *Exercise Period*. "Exercise Period" means the period from (and including) the Earliest Exercise Time to (and including) the Latest Exercise Time on a day that is, (i) in the case of an European Option, the Expiration Date, (ii) in the case of an American Option, each Exercise Business Day from (and including) the Commencement Date to (and including) the Expiration Date and (iii) in the case of a Bermuda Option the Expiration Date and each Scheduled Exercise Date.

"Earliest Exercise Time" means the time agreed as such pursuant to the terms of an Option Transaction or, failing such agreement, 11:00 a.m. local time in the city specified in the address of the Seller's Office.

"Latest Exercise Time" means the time agreed as such pursuant to the terms of an Option Transaction or, failing such agreement, close of business in the city specified in the address of the Seller's Office.

(3) *Exercise Time*. An Exercise Notice which is received by the Seller at any time other than on an Exercise Business Day during the Exercise Period shall be invalid, unless such notice is received (i) prior to the Earliest Exercise Time on an Exercise Business Day, in which case it shall be deemed to be received at the Earliest Exercise Time, (ii) in respect of an European Option only, on any Exercise Business Day prior to the Expiration Date, in which case such notice shall be deemed to be received at the Earliest Exercise Time on the Expiration Date or (iii) in respect of an American Option only, after the Latest Exercise Time on an Exercise Business Day other than the Expiration Date, in which case it shall be deemed received at the Earliest Exercise Time on the following Exercise Business Day.

(4) *Automatic Exercise*. If the parties agree to apply "Automatic Exercise" to an Option Transaction, then the unexercised amount or number of the Underlying Asset or the unexercised number of Options under such Option Transaction ("Unexercised Quantity") shall be deemed to be automatically exercised at the Latest Exercise Time on the Expiration Date if at such time the Buyer would be entitled to request payment of the Cash Settlement Amount, unless the Buyer notifies the Seller prior to such time at the Seller's Office, orally, including by telephone, or in writing, that it does not wish Automatic Exercise to apply.

(5) *Conditional Exercise.* The parties may specify in relation to an Option Transaction that the Option may only be exercised if a specified event has occurred ("Knock-in Event") or not occurred ("Knock-out Event") or if the price of the Underlying Asset or the level of the Underlying Measurement agreed as such between the parties ("Barrier") has been reached or crossed or not.

(6) *Partial Exercise.* If the parties agree to apply "Partial Exercise" to an Option Transaction, then the Buyer shall be entitled to exercise less than the entire amount or number of Options, provided that the Exercise Notice specifies the amount or number (the "Exercise Quantity") of Options exercised. Any Exercise Quantity must be (i) equal to or greater than the minimum quantity agreed between the parties (the "Minimum Exercise Quantity") and (ii) equal to or an integral multiple of the number agreed between the parties (the "Integral Multiple") in respect of the relevant Option Transaction. Any exercise (i) which does not specify an Exercise Quantity will be deemed to be an exercise of the Unexercised Quantity, (ii) of less than the Minimum Exercise Quantity is invalid, (iii) which refers to an Exercise Quantity which is not equal to or an integral multiple of the Integral Multiple will be deemed to be an exercise of a number of Options equal to the nearest smaller integral multiple of the Integral Multiple.

(7) *Multiple Exercise.* If the parties agree to apply "Multiple Exercise" to an American Option or Bermuda Option, then the Buyer shall be entitled to exercise parts of or the entire Unexercised Quantity once or several times during the Exercise Period, provided that any Exercise Notice specifies the Exercise Quantity. Except for the exercise of the entire Unexercised Quantity on the Expiration Date, any Exercise Quantity must be (i) equal to or greater than the Minimum Exercise Quantity, (ii) equal to or less than the maximum quantity agreed between the parties (the "Maximum Exercise Quantity") and (iii) equal to or an integral multiple of the Integral Multiple, each as agreed in respect of the relevant Option Transaction. Any exercise (i) which does not specify an Exercise Quantity will be deemed to be an exercise of the Unexercised Quantity, (ii) of more than the Maximum Exercise Quantity will be deemed to be an exercise of the Maximum Exercise Quantity, (iii) of less than the Minimum Exercise Quantity is invalid and (iv) which refers to an Exercise Quantity which is not equal to or an integral multiple of the Integral Multiple will be deemed to be an exercise of a number of Options equal to the nearest smaller integral multiple of the Integral Multiple. As a consequence of any such exercise of Options in a quantity of less than the Unexercised Quantity the Unexercised Quantity shall be reduced accordingly.

5. Cash Settlement

(1) *Cash Settlement Amount.* "Cash Settlement Amount" means the amount agreed between the parties or, failing such agreement, an amount in the Cash Settlement Currency determined by the Calculation Agent on the Valuation Date in accordance with the applicable Cash Settlement Method.

"Cash Settlement Method" means (a) the methodology or formula agreed between the parties in respect of the individual Option Transaction or defined in any applicable Supplement or, failing such agreement or Supplement, (b), in case of Section 1(1)(a)(ii) or 1(1)(b) of this Supplement, the following method: the Cash Settlement Amount shall be calculated by the Calculation Agent on the Valuation Date based on the Settlement Price or Settlement Level determined on such date or, in case of Asian Options, on each Averaging Date; the Cash Settlement Amount shall be equal to the product of (i) the difference between the Settlement Price and the Strike Price or, as the case may be, the Settlement Level and the Strike Level and (ii), in case of Section 1(1)(b) of this Supplement, the agreed amount per unit of the Underlying Measurement, (iii) the Exercise Quantity and (iv) the agreed factor, if any, (c), in case of Section 1(1)(c) or 1(1)(d) of this Supplement, the method specified in Section 7(1)(a) of the General Provisions and applied as if the Buyer were the Calculation Party.

(2) *Payment of the Cash Settlement Amount.* The Cash Settlement Amount shall be paid on the Settlement Date agreed as such between the parties or, failing such agreement, two Business Days following the Valuation Date.

6. Taxes and Duties.

If "Physical Settlement" applies to an Option Transaction, the Buyer shall bear all taxes and duties necessarily falling due in connection with the delivery or transfer of the Underlying Asset.

FEDERATION BANCAIRE DE L'UNION EUROPEENNE
BANKING FEDERATION OF THE EUROPEAN UNION
BANKENVEREINIGUNG DER EUROPÄISCHEN UNION

in co-operation with

EUROPEAN SAVINGS BANKS GROUP
GROUPEMENT EUROPEEN DES CAISSES D'EPARGNE
EUROPÄISCHE SPARKASSENVEREINIGUNG

EUROPEAN ASSOCIATION OF COOPERATIVE BANKS
GROUPEMENT EUROPEEN DES BANQUES COOPERATIVES
EUROPÄISCHE VEREINIGUNG DER GENOSSENSCHAFTSBANKEN

MASTER AGREEMENT FOR FINANCIAL TRANSACTIONS

SUPPLEMENT TO THE DERIVATIVES ANNEX

INTEREST RATE TRANSACTIONS
Edition 2004

This Supplement complements the General Provisions and the Derivatives Annex which form part of a Master Agreement for Financial Transactions based on the form published by the FBE.

1. Purpose, Interpretation

(1) Purpose. The purpose of this Supplement ("Interest Rate Supplement") is to govern Interest Rate Transactions, which means an Interest Rate Swap, Cross Currency Rate Swap, Forward Rate Agreement, Interest Rate Cap, Interest Rate Floor, Interest Rate Swaption or any other Transaction so agreed by the parties in respect of an individual Transaction or in the Special Provisions.

(2) Interpretation This Supplement forms an integral part of the Derivatives Annex. The term "Annex" as used in Section 1(3) of the General Provisions should be construed as to include this Supplement. In the event of any conflict between different parts of the Derivatives Annex and this Supplement, this Supplement shall prevail.

2. Interest Rate Transactions

"Interest Rate Swap" means a Transaction in which (a) one party pays, once or periodically, amounts of money (the "Floating Amounts") in a specified currency calculated on a specified notional amount (the "Notional Amount") in such currency and a specified Floating Rate, and (b) the other party pays, once or periodically, either (i) amounts of money (the "Fixed Amounts") in the same currency calculated on the same Notional Amount and a specified Fixed Rate or (ii) Floating Amounts in the same currency calculated on the same Notional Amount and a different Floating Rate.

"Cross Currency Rate Swap" means a Transaction in which (a) one party pays, once or periodically, Floating Amounts or Fixed Amounts in a specified currency calculated on a specified notional amount (the "Currency Amount") in such currency, and (b) the other party pays, once or periodically, Floating Amounts or Fixed Amounts in a different currency calculated on a Currency Amount in such different currency.

"Forward Rate Agreement" or "FRA" means a Transaction in which one party (the "Seller") or the other party (the "Buyer") pays, once or periodically, Floating Amounts in a specified currency calculated on a Notional Amount in such currency and the difference between the Floating Rate and the Fixed Rate.

"Interest Rate Cap" means a Transaction in which the Seller pays to the Buyer against payment of an agreed premium, once or periodically, Floating Amounts in a specified currency calculated on a Notional Amount in such currency and the difference between the Floating Rate and the Fixed Rate, if such amount is a positive number.

"Interest Rate Floor" means a Transaction in which the Seller pays to the Buyer against payment of an agreed premium, once or periodically, Floating Amounts in a specified currency calculated on a Notional Amount in such currency and the difference between the Floating Rate and the Fixed Rate, if such amount is a negative number.

"Interest Rate Swaption" means an Option Transaction in which the Seller grants to the Buyer against payment of a Premium the right to cause the underlying Interest Rate Transaction (the "Underlying Transaction") to become effective, whereby the Underlying Transaction is to be settled (i) by making all payments and deliveries or transfers to be made by the parties in accordance with the terms of the Underlying Transaction, in the case of an Interest Rate Swaption to which "Physical Settlement" applies (the "Physically Settled Interest Rate Swaption") or (ii), in the case of an Interest Rate Swaption to which "Cash Settlement" applies (the "Cash Settled Interest

Copyright © 2004 FBE

Interest Rate Transactions - 2004

Rate Swaption"), by paying the Cash Settlement Amount based on the value of the Underlying Transaction on the Valuation Date, if such value, from the Buyer's perspective, is a positive number.

3. **Deliveries and Payments**

(1) *Interest Rate Swap and Cross Currency Rate Swap*. On each agreed Settlement Date for the payment of a Floating Amount, the party (the "Floating Amount Payer") that owes such amount shall pay the Floating Amount and on each Settlement Date for the payment of a Fixed Amount, the party (the "Fixed Amount Payer") that owes such amount shall pay the Fixed Amount.

(2) *Forward Rate Agreement*. On each agreed Settlement Date for the payment of a Floating Amount, the Seller shall pay to the Buyer the Floating Amount if such amount is a positive number and the Buyer shall pay to the Seller the Floating Amount if such amount is a negative number.

(3) *Interest Rate Cap and Interest Rate Floor*. On each agreed Settlement Date for the payment of a premium, the Buyer shall pay to the Seller the agreed premium. On each agreed Settlement Date for the payment of a Floating Amount, the Seller under an Interest Rate Cap shall pay to the Buyer the Floating Amount if such amount is a positive number and the Seller under an Interest Rate Floor shall pay to the Buyer the Floating Amount if such amount is a negative number.

(4) *Physically Settled Interest Rate Swaption*. On each agreed Premium Payment Date for a Physically Settled Interest Rate Swaption, the Buyer shall pay to the Seller the Premium. If a Physically Settled Interest Rate Swaption is exercised or deemed to be exercised, on each agreed Settlement Date for the payment of a Floating Amount under the Underlying Transaction, the Floating Amount Payer shall pay the Floating Amount and on each Settlement Date agreed for the payment of a Fixed Amount under the Underlying Transaction, the Fixed Amount Payer shall pay the Fixed Amount.

(5) *Cash Settled Interest Rate Swaption.* On each agreed Premium Payment Date for a Cash Settled Interest Rate Swaption, the Buyer shall pay to the Seller the Premium. If a Cash Settled Interest Rate Swaption is exercised or deemed to be exercised, on the Settlement Date for the Cash Settled Interest Rate Swaption, the Seller shall pay to the Buyer the Cash Settlement Amount, if such amount is a positive number. The Cash Settlement Amount is (a) the amount agreed as such between the parties or, failing such agreement, (b) an amount in the Cash Settlement Currency equal to the value of the Underlying Transaction as determined by the Calculation Agent on the Valuation Date in accordance with (i) the Cash Settlement Method agreed between the parties in respect of the relevant Option Transaction or, failing such agreement, (ii) Section 7(1)(a) of the General Provisions and applied as if the Buyer were the Calculation Party.

4. **Calculation of Fixed Amounts and Floating Amounts**

(1) *Fixed Amounts*. The Fixed Amount payable on a Settlement Date of a Fixed Amount is the amount (a) agreed to by the parties in respect of that Settlement Date or the Calculation Period relating to that Settlement Date or, failing such agreement, (b) equal to the product of (i) the Calculation Amount (ii) the Fixed Rate, and (iii) the Day Count Fraction elected by the parties in respect of the Fixed Amounts.

(2) *Floating Amounts*. The Floating Amount payable on a Settlement Date of a Floating Amount is the amount (a), if neither "Compounding" nor "Flat Compounding" is elected in respect of the relevant Transaction, equal to the product of (i) the Calculation Amount, (ii) the Floating Rate (plus or minus a spread), and (iii) the Day Count Fraction elected by the parties in respect of Floating Amounts; or (b), if "Compounding" is elected in respect of the relevant Transaction, equal to the sum of the Compounding Period Amounts calculated for each Compounding Period in the Calculation Period relating to that Settlement Date; or (c), if "Flat Compounding" is elected in respect of the relevant Transaction, equal to the sum of (i) the Basic Compounding Period Amounts and (ii) the Additional Compounding Period Amounts, each calculated for each Compounding Period in the Calculation Period relating to that Settlement Date. For the purposes of the calculation of the Floating Amount and where "Compounding" or "Flat Compounding" is elected in respect of the relevant Transaction:

"Compounding Period" means, in relation to a Calculation Period, each period beginning with, and including, the Effective Date or a Compounding Date and ending with, but excluding, the next following Compounding Date or Termination Date.

"Compounding Date" means each day during the term of the relevant Transaction agreed as such by the parties, subject to adjustments in accordance with Section 3(6) of the General Provisions applicable to Period End Dates in respect of the Transaction.

"Compounding Period Amount" means, for each Compounding Period, an amount equal to the product of (i) the Adjusted Calculation Amount, (ii) the Floating Rate (plus or minus a spread), and (iii) the Day Count Fraction elected by the parties in respect of Floating Amounts.

"Adjusted Calculation Amount" means (i) in relation to the first Compounding Period in the Calculation Period, the Calculation Amount for this Calculation Period and (ii) in relation to each succeeding Compounding Period in this Calculation Period, an amount equal to the sum of the Calculation Amount for this Calculation Period and the Compounding Period Amounts for each of the preceding Compounding Periods in this Calculation Period.

"Basic Compounding Period Amount" means, for each Compounding Period, an amount calculated in accordance with the method indicated in subsection 2(a) above.

"Additional Compounding Period Amount" means, for each Compounding Period, an amount equal to the product of (i) the Flat Compounding Amount, (ii) the Floating Rate, and (iii) the Day Count Fraction elected by the parties in respect of Floating Amounts.

"Flat Compounding Amount" means (i) in relation to the first Compounding Period in the Calculation Period, zero and (ii) in relation to each succeeding Compounding Period in this Calculation Period, an amount equal to the sum of the Basic Compounding Period Amounts and the Additional Compounding Period Amounts for each of the preceding Compounding Periods in this Calculation Period.

(3) *Calculation Amount*. "Calculation Amount" means the Notional Amount or, as the case may be, the Currency Amount expressed in a specified currency agreed to by the parties in respect of the relevant Settlement Date or the Calculation Period relating to that Settlement Date.

(4) *Fixed Rate*. "Fixed Rate" means the interest rate expressed as a decimal figure equal to a per annum rate agreed by the parties in respect of the relevant Settlement Date or the Calculation Period relating to that Settlement Date.

(5) *Floating Rate*. "Floating Rate" means
(a) in respect of a Forward Rate Agreement, Interest Rate Cap and Interest Rate Floor, the difference between (i) the interest rate determined in the manner described in (b) below and (ii) the Fixed Rate, in each case expressed as a decimal figure equal to a per annum rate, and (b) in respect of all other Interest Rate Transactions (i) the interest rate expressed as a decimal figure equal to a per annum rate agreed by the parties in respect of the relevant Settlement Date or the Calculation Period or Compounding Period relating to that Settlement Date, or, failing such agreement, (ii) if the parties agreed to a specified Floating Rate Option and either (x) only one Reset Date has been agreed by the parties in respect of the relevant Settlement Date or the Calculation Period or Compounding Period relating to that Settlement Date, the Settlement Interest Rate on that Reset Date, or (y) more than one Reset Date has been agreed by the parties in respect of the relevant Settlement Date or the Calculation Period or Compounding Period relating to that Settlement Date, the arithmetic mean of the Settlement Interest Rates for each of those Reset Dates, or (z) more than one Reset Date and "Weighted Average" has been agreed by the parties in respect of the relevant Settlement Date or the Calculation Period or Compounding Period relating to that Settlement Date, the weighted arithmetic mean of the Settlement Interest Rates for each of those Reset Dates calculated by (x) multiplying each Settlement Interest Rate by the number of days such Settlement Interest Rate is in effect, (y) determining the sum of those products, and (z) dividing such sum by the number of days in the relevant Calculation Period or Compounding Period.

"Settlement Interest Rate" means the interest rate expressed as a decimal figure equal to a per annum rate as determined on or in respect of the relevant Reset Date on the basis of the interest rate (i) quoted through and obtained from the Price Source specified in the agreed Floating Rate Option or, failing such agreement, (ii) determined by the Calculation Agent.

"Floating Rate Option" means the interest rate agreed by the parties by reference to the publication, screen or web page of an information vendor or any other price source (the "Price Source").

"Reset Date" means, subject to adjustments in accordance with Section 3(6) of the General Provisions, each day (i) agreed as such by the parties in respect of the relevant Transaction or (ii) determined by applying the agreed Floating Rate Option, subject to the provisions of paragraph 8 below.

(6) *Rounding.* Any interest rate used for calculating a Floating Amount or Fixed Amount shall, if not already an integral number, be rounded up or down to the nearest fifth decimal place. If the sixth decimal place is equal to five, the fifth decimal place shall be rounded up.

(7) *Day Count Fraction*. "Day Count Fraction" means, as elected by the parties in respect of calculating the Fixed Amounts or Floating Amounts or Compounding Period Amounts:

(a) "1/1" means the fraction whose numerator is 1 and whose denominator is 1.

(b) "Actual/360" means the fraction whose numerator is the actual number of days elapsed during the Calculation Period or Compounding Period and whose denominator is 360.

(c) "30E/360" means the fraction whose numerator is the number of days elapsed during the Calculation Period or Compounding Period, calculated on the basis of a year comprising 12 months of 30 days and whose denominator is 360. If the last day of the Calculation Period or Compounding Period is the last day of the month of February, the number of days elapsed during such month shall be taken as the actual number of days.

(d) "30/360" means the fraction whose numerator is the number of days elapsed during the Calculation Period or Compounding Period, calculated on the basis of a year comprising 12 months of 30 days and whose denominator is 360. If the last day of the Calculation Period or Compounding Period is the 31st day of a month and the first day of the Calculation Period or Compounding Period is a day other than the 30th or 31st day of a month, the last month of the period shall be deemed to be a month of 31 days. If the last day of the Calculation Period or Compounding Period is the last day of the month of February, the number of days elapsed during such month shall be taken as the actual number of days.

(e) "360/360 (German Master)" means the fraction whose numerator is the number of days elapsed during the Calculation Period or Compounding Period, calculated on the basis of 360-day year with 12 months of 30 days and whose denominator is 360.

(f) "Actual/365" means the fraction whose numerator is the actual number of days elapsed during the Calculation Period or Compounding Period and whose denominator is 365 or 366 in the case of a leap year. If part of the Calculation Period or Compounding Period should fall in a leap year, Actual/365 shall mean the sum of (i) the fraction whose numerator is the actual number of days elapsed during the non-leap year and whose denominator is 365 and (ii) the fraction whose numerator is the number of actual days elapsed during the leap year and whose denominator is 366.

(g) "Actual/Fixed 365" means the fraction whose numerator is the actual number of days elapsed during the Calculation Period or Compounding Period and whose denominator is 365.

(h) "365/365 (German Master)" means the fraction whose numerator is the number of days elapsed during the Calculation Period or Compounding Period and whose denominator is 365 or 366 in the case of a leap year.

Copyright © 2004 FBE

Interest Rate Transactions - 2004

(i) "Actual/Actual AFB/FBF Master Agreement)" means the fraction whose numerator is the actual number of days elapsed during the Calculation Period or Compounding Period and whose denominator is 365 (or 366 if 29 February falls within the Calculation Period or Compounding Period). If the Calculation Period or Compounding Period is a term of more than one year, the basis shall be calculated as follows: (a) the number of complete years shall be counted back from the last day of the Calculation Period or Compounding Period and (b) this number shall be increased by the fraction for the relevant period calculated as shown above.

(8) *Determination of the Settlement Interest Rate.* Where a Floating Rate is to be determined by reference to a specified Floating Rate Option, the Calculation Agent shall notify the other party or, as the case may be, each party the Settlement Interest Rate and the Floating Rate calculated therefrom on the Reset Date or promptly thereafter. If on a Reset Date a Price Source Disruption Event occurs and the Calculation Agent determines that such event is material, (a) if only one Reset Date has been agreed by the parties in respect of the relevant Settlement Date or the Calculation Period or Compounding Period relating to that Settlement Date, the Reset Date shall be postponed to the first succeeding Business Day on which there is no Price Source Disruption Event, unless there is a Price Source Disruption Event relating to the relevant Floating Rate Option on each of the five Business Days immediately following the Reset Date, in which case such fifth Business Day shall be deemed to be the Reset Date and the Calculation Agent shall determine the Settlement Interest Rate on that fifth Business Day; or (b) if more than one Reset Date has been agreed by the parties in respect of the relevant Settlement Date or the Calculation Period or Compounding Period relating to that Settlement Date, that Reset Date should be omitted and deemed to be not a relevant Reset Date, provided that if through operation of this provision there would not be a Reset Date, then (a) above will apply.

(9) *Price Source Disruption and Price Source Conversion.* "Price Source Disruption Event" means any failure of the relevant Price Source to announce, display or publish the interest rate for the relevant Floating Rate Option or any other information necessary for determining the interest rate or a temporary or permanent discontinuance or unavailability of the Price Source. If the relevant Price Source has ceased to announce, display or publish the interest rate for the relevant Floating Rate Option and (i) if an alternative price source (the "Successor Price Source") has been agreed by the parties for the relevant Transaction or, failing such agreement, (ii) if a Successor Price Source is officially designated in the information vendor's publication, screen or web page or by the sponsor of the Floating Rate Option, the Calculation Agent will determine the Settlement Interest Rate by reference to that Successor Price Source. If no such Successor Price Source has been agreed or designated, the Calculation Agent will determine the Settlement Interest Rate by reference to a new Floating Rate Option agreed by the parties.

(10) *Correction of Published Interest Rates.* Where a Floating Rate is to be determined by reference to a specified Floating Rate Option, in the event that an interest rate announced, displayed or published by the relevant information vendor and used by the Calculation Agent for determining the Settlement Interest Rate is subsequently corrected and announced, displayed or published within thirty Business Days after the relevant Reset Date, the Calculation Agent shall notify the other party or, as the case may be, each party of the Settlement Interest Rate, the Floating Rate calculated there from and the Floating Amount payable as a result of that correction.

(11) *Calculation Period, Period End Date.*
"Calculation Period" means each period beginning with, and including, the Effective Date or a Period End Date and ending with, but excluding, the next following Period End Date or Termination Date. "Period End Date" means (a) each day during the term of the Transaction agreed as such by the parties, or (b) if "Eurodollar Convention" has been agreed by the parties, each day during the term of the Transaction that numerically corresponds with the preceding applicable Period End Date or Effective Date in the calendar month that is the specified number of months after the month in which such preceding applicable Period End Date or Effective Date occurred, provided that if there is no numerically corresponding day in the calendar month in which such Period End Date should occur, Period End Date will be the last Business Day of that calendar month and all subsequent Period End Dates will be the last Business Day of the calendar month that is the specified number of months after the month in which the preceding applicable Period End Date occurred and, failing such agreements, (c) each Settlement Date, in each case subject to adjustments in accordance with Section 3(6) of the General Provisions which shall apply accordingly, provided that no such adjustment applies if "No Adjustment" has been agreed by the parties.

(12) *Settlement Date.* "Settlement Date" means in respect of the payment of a Floating Amount or Fixed Amount either (a) each day during the term of the Transaction agreed by the parties upon which the payment of a Floating Amount or a Fixed Amount shall be made, or (b) if "Delayed Payment" is agreed between the parties, each date that is the specified number of days after the applicable Period End Date or Termination Date, or (c) if "Early Payment" is agreed between the parties, each date that is the specified number of days prior to the applicable Period End Date or Termination Date or, failing such agreements, (d) each Period End Date, in each case subject to adjustments in accordance with Section 3(6) of the General Provisions.

5. Provisions applicable to Option Transactions

Unless otherwise defined in this Supplement, any term relating to Option Transactions is to be construed in accordance with the applicable Options Supplement published by the FBE.

APPENDIX 3

FEDERATION BANCAIRE DE L'UNION EUROPEENNE
BANKING FEDERATION OF THE EUROPEAN UNION
BANKENVEREINIGUNG DER EUROPÄISCHEN UNION

in co-operation with

EUROPEAN SAVINGS BANKS GROUP
GROUPEMENT EUROPEEN DES CAISSES D'EPARGNE
EUROPÄISCHE SPARKASSENVEREINIGUNG

EUROPEAN ASSOCIATION OF COOPERATIVE BANKS
GROUPEMENT EUROPEEN DES BANQUES COOPERATIVES
EUROPÄISCHE VEREINIGUNG DER GENOSSENSCHAFTSBANKEN

**MASTER AGREEMENT
FOR FINANCIAL TRANSACTIONS**

INDEX OF DEFINED TERMS
Edition 2004

This index sets forth the documents and sections in which the terms listed below are defined.

As used in this index,
SP means Special Provisions,
GP means General Provisions,
REPO means Product Annex for Repurchase Transactions,
SL means Product Annex for Securities Loans,
D means Product Annex for Derivative Transactions,
MMA means Margin Maintenance Annex,
SIR means Supplement to the Derivatives Annex - Interest Rate Transactions,
SFX means Supplement to the Derivatives Annex - Foreign Exchange Transactions,
SO means supplement to the Derivatives Annex - Option Transactions.

Numbers not in parentheses are references to sections of the relevant document; numbers and letters in parentheses are references to subsections and paragraphs.

A.
Accrued Interest REPO 5(1)
Acquisition Cost SL 2(5)(b)(ii)
Additional Compounding Period Amount SIR 4(2)
Adjusted Calculation Amount SIR 4(2)
Adjusted Net Exposure MMA 1(1)
Affected Party GP 6(2)(b)
Agency Transaction GP 10(10)(a)
Agent GP l0(I0)(a)
Agreement GP 1(2)
Alternative Borrowing Cost SL 2(5)(a)(i)
Alternative Purchase Cost REPO 2(6)(b)(iii)
American Option SO 2(1)
Amounts Due GP 7(1)(a)
Annex SP1; GP1(2)
Applicable Exchange Rate GP 7(l)(b)
Asian Option SO 2(1)
Automatic Exercise SO 4(4)
Averaging Date SO 2(3)

B.
Barrier SO 4(5)
Base Currency GP 7(l)(b)
Basic Compounding Period Amount SIR 4(2)
Bermuda Option SO 2(1)
Booking Office GP 9(3)
Borrower SL 1(1)
Borrowing Cost REPO 2(6)(a)(ii)
Business Day GP 3(7)
Buyer REPO 1(1); SO 1(1); SFX 2; SIR 2
Buy/Sell Back Transactions REPO 5(1)

C.
Calculation Agent D 4
Calculation Amount SIR 4(3)
Calculation Party GP 7(1)(a)
Calculation Period SIR 4(11)
Call SO 2(2)
Call Currency SFX 2
Cash Margin MMA 1(1)
Cash Settled Foreign Exchange Option SFX 2
Cash Settled Interest Rate Swaption SIR 2
Cash Settlement SO 1(1)(a)(ii); SO 1(1)(c)(ii); SFX 2; SIR 2
Cash Settlement Amount SO 5(1); SFX 3(4)
Cash Settlement Currency D 4
Cash Settlement Method SO 5(1)
Change of Circumstances GP 6(2)(a)
Clean Price REPO 5(1)
Commence GP 6(1)(a)(viii)
Commencement Date SO 2(3)
Competent Authority GP 6(1)(a)(viii)(3)
Compounding SIR 4(2)
Compounding Date SIR 4(2)
Compounding Period SIR 4(2)
Compounding Period Amount SIR 4(2)
Confirmation GP 2(2)
Contractual Currency GP 3(1)
Corporate Restructuring GP 6(1)(a)(vii)
Counterclaims GP 7(4)
Cross Currency Rate Swap SIR 2
Currency Amount SIR 2
Currency Pair SFX 3(5)
Currency Rate Option SFX 3(5)

Copyright © 2004 FBE   Index of Defined Terms - 2004

D.

Day Count Fraction (1/1; Actual/360; 30E/360; 30/360; 360/360 (German Master); Actual/365; Actual/Fixed 365; 365/365 (German Master); Actual/Actual (AFB / FBF Master Agreement)) SIR 4(7)
Default Rate GP 3(5)
Default Threshold GP 6(1)(a)(vi)
Default Value GP 7(l)(a)
Defaulting Party GP 6(1)(b)
Delayed Payment SIR 4(12)
Delivery Date SL 2(1)
Derivative Transactions D 1(1)
Derivatives Annex D 1(1)
Distribution REPO 2(7)(i); SL 2(6)(i)
Documentary Tax GP 4(2)

E.

Earliest Exercise Time SO 4(2)
Early Payment SIR 4(12)
Early Termination Date GP 6(l)(b); GP 6(2)(b)
Effective Date D 4
EONIA GP 3(5)
Equivalent REPO 2(3); SL 2(3)
Eurodollar Convention SIR 4(11)
European Option SO 2(1)
Event of Default GP 6(l)(a)
Exchange D 4
Exchange Business Day D 4
Exercise Business Day SO 2(3)
Exercise Date SO 5(2)
Exercise Notice SO 4(1)
Exercise Period SO 4(2)
Exercise Quantity SO 4(6)
Expiration Date SO 2 (3)
Exposure Threshold MMA 2(6)

F.

FBE GP 1(1)
Flat Compounding Amount SIR 4(2)
Final Settlement Amount GP 7(l)(a)
Fixed Amount Payer SIR 3(1)
Fixed Amounts SIR 2
Fixed Rate SIR 4(4)
Flat Compounding SIR 4(2)
Floating Amount Payer SIR 3(1)
Floating Amounts SIR 2
Floating Rate SIR 4(5)
Floating Rate Option SIR 4(5)
Following GP 3(6)(b)
Foreign Exchange Forward SFX 2
Foreign Exchange Option SFX 2
Foreign Exchange Spot SFX 2
Foreign Exchange Supplement SFX 1(1)
Foreign Exchange Transactions SFX 1(1)
Forward Price REPO 5(1)
Forward Rate SFX 3(5)
Forward Rate Agreement (FRA) SIR 2

G.

General Provisions SP 1; GP 1(1)
Guarantee GP 5(2)
Guarantor GP 5(2)

H.

Haircut MMA 1(3)

Copyright © 2004 FBE   Index of Defined Terms - 2004

I.
Impossibility Event GP 6(2)(a)(ii)
Independent Amount MMA 1(1)
Insolvency Proceeding GP 6(1)(a)(viii)
Integral Multiple SO 4(6)
Interbank Rate GP 3(5)
Interest Rate Cap SIR 2
Interest Rate Floor SIR 2
Interest Rate Supplement SIR 1(1)
Interest Rate Transactions SIR 1(1)
Interest Rate Swap SIR 2
Interest Rate Swaption SIR 2

J.
Judgment of Insolvency GP 6(1)(a)(viii)

K.
Kind ("of the same kind") GP 3(2)(b)
Knock-in Event SO 4(5)
Knock-out Event SO 4(5)

L.
Latest Exercise Time SO 4(2)
Lender SL 1(1)
Lending Fee SL 4
Liabilities MMA 1(3)
Loaned Securities SL 1(1)

M.
Margin MMA 1(3)
Margin Claim GP 7(l)(a)
Margin Ratio MMA 1(3)
Margin Provider MMA 1(1)
Margin Recipient MMA 1(1)
Margin Securities MMA 1(1)
Market Disruption Convention D 4
Market Disruption Event D 4
Market Standard Documentation D 2
Market Value GP 3(8); MMA 1(1)
Master Agreement SP 1; GP 1(1)
Maximum Exercise Quantity SO 4(7)
Minimum Exercise Quantity SO 4(6)
Minimum Transfer Amount MMA 2(6)
Modified, Modified Following GP 3(6)(c)
Multiple Exercise SO 4(7)

N.
Net Exposure MMA 1(3)
New Securities REPO 3(1)
New Transaction REPO 6(2)(b)
No Adjustment SIR 4(11)
Non-Affected Party GP 6(2)(b)
Non-Defaulting Party GP 6(l)(b)
Non-Deliverable Foreign Exchange Forward SFX 2
Non-Deliverable Foreign Exchange Option SFX 2
Notional Amount SIR 2

0.
Option SO 1(1)
Option Transactions SO 1(1)
Options Supplement SO 1(1)
Original Transactions REPO 6(2)

P.
Partial Exercise SO 4(6)
Period End Date SIR 4(11)
Physical Settlement SO 1(1)(a)(i); SO 1(1)(c)(i); SFX 2; SIR 2
Physically Settled Foreign Exchange Option SFX 2
Physically Settled Interest Rate Swaption SIR 2
Potential Final Settlement Amount MMA 1(3)
Preceding GP 3(6)(a)
Premium SO 1(1)
Premium Payment Date SO 3
Price Differential REPO 2(3)
Price Source SFX 3(5); SIR 4(5)
Price Source Disruption Event SIR 4(9)
Pricing Rate REPO 2(3)
Principal GP 10(10)(a)
Proceedings GP 11(2)
Process Agent GP 11(3)
Product Annexes GP 1(2)
Purchase Date REPO 2(1)
Purchase Price REPO 1(1)
Purchased Securities REPO 2(1)
Put SO 2(2)
Put Currency SFX 2

Q.
Quotation Date GP 7(1)(a)

R.
Reference Currency SFX 2
Repricing Date REPO 6(2)(a)
Repurchase Annex REPO 1(1)
Repurchase Date REPO 2(2)
Repurchase Price REPO 2(3)
Repurchase Transactions REPO 1(1)
Reset Date SIR 4(5)
Return Date SL 2(2)

S.
Scheduled Exercise Date SO 2(1)
Securities GP 3(2)(a)
Securities Lending Annex SL 1(1)
Securities Loans SL 1(1)
Sell Back Price REPO 5(1)
Seller REPO 1(1); SO 1(1); SFX 2; SIR 2
Seller's Office SO 4(1)
Settlement Currency SFX 2
Settlement Currency Amount SFX 3(2)
Settlement Currency Rate SFX 3(5)
Settlement Date D 4; SIR 4(12)
Settlement Interest Rate SIR 4(5)
Settlement Level SO 1(1)(b)
Settlement Price SO 1(1)(a)(ii)
simultaneous REPO 2(3); D 4
Special Provisions GP 1(2); SP I
Specified Jurisdiction GP 6(l)(a)(viii)
Specified Transactions GP 6(l)(a)(v)
Strike Level SO 1(1)(b)
Strike Price SO 1(1)(a); SFX 3(5)
Substitute Assets GP 3(2)(b)
Successor Entity GP 6(l)(a)(vii)
Successor Price Source SIR 4(9)

T.
Termination Date D 4
Trade Date D 4
Transaction GP 1(1)
Transaction Value GP 7(1)(a)

U.
Underlying Asset SO 1(1)(a)
Underlying Measurement SO 1(1)(b)
Underlying Transaction SO 1(1)(c); SIR 2
Unexercised Quantity SO 4(4)

V.
Valuation Agent MMA 1(2);
Valuation Date MMA 1(3); D 4; SO 5(2)
Valuation Percentage MMA 1(1)
Valuation Time D 4

W.
Weighted Average SIR 4(5)

Appendix 4

Master Repurchase Agreement

Reproduced with the kind permission of
The Bond Market Association

Master Repurchase Agreement

September 1996 Version

Dated as of _____

Between: _____

and _____

1. Applicability

From time to time the parties hereto may enter into transactions in which one party ("Seller") agrees to transfer to the other ("Buyer") securities or other assets ("Securities") against the transfer of funds by Buyer, with a simultaneous agreement by Buyer to transfer to Seller such Securities at a date certain or on demand, against the transfer of funds by Seller. Each such transaction shall be referred to herein as a "Transaction" and, unless otherwise agreed in writing, shall be governed by this Agreement, including any supplemental terms or conditions contained in Annex I hereto and in any other annexes identified herein or therein as applicable hereunder.

2. Definitions

(a) "Act of Insolvency", with respect to any party, (i) the commencement by such party as debtor of any case or proceeding under any bankruptcy, insolvency, reorganization, liquidation, moratorium, dissolution, delinquency or similar law, or such party seeking the appointment or election of a receiver, conservator, trustee, custodian or similar official for such party or any substantial part of its property, or the convening of any meeting of creditors for purposes of commencing any such case or proceeding or seeking such an appointment or election, (ii) the commencement of any such case or proceeding against such party, or another seeking such an appointment or election, or the filing against a party of an application for a protective decree under the provisions of the Securities Investor Protection Act of 1970, which (A) is consented to or not timely contested by such party, (B) results in the entry of an order for relief, such an appointment or election, the issuance of such a protective decree or the entry of an order having a similar effect, or (C) is not dismissed within 15 days, (iii) the making by such party of a general assignment for the benefit of creditors, or (iv) the admission in writing by such party of such party's inability to pay such party's debts as they become due;

(b) "Additional Purchased Securities", Securities provided by Seller to Buyer pursuant to Paragraph 4(a) hereof;

(c) "Buyer's Margin Amount", with respect to any Transaction as of any date, the amount obtained by application of the Buyer's Margin Percentage to the Repurchase Price for such Transaction as of such date;

(d) "Buyer's Margin Percentage", with respect to any Transaction as of any date, a percentage (which may be equal to the Seller's Margin Percentage) agreed to by Buyer and Seller or, in the absence of any such agreement, the percentage obtained by dividing the Market Value of the Purchased Securities on the Purchase Date by the Purchase Price on the Purchase Date for such Transaction;

(e) "Confirmation", the meaning specified in Paragraph 3(b) hereof;

(f) "Income", with respect to any Security at any time, any principal thereof and all interest, dividends or other distributions thereon;

(g) "Margin Deficit", the meaning specified in Paragraph 4(a) hereof;

(h) "Margin Excess", the meaning specified in Paragraph 4(b) hereof;

(i) "Margin Notice Deadline", the time agreed to by the parties in the relevant Confirmation, Annex I hereto or otherwise as the deadline for giving notice requiring same-day satisfaction of margin maintenance obligations as provided in Paragraph 4 hereof (or, in the absence of any such agreement, the deadline for such purposes established in accordance with market practice);

(j) "Market Value", with respect to any Securities as of any date, the price for such Securities on such date obtained from a generally recognized source agreed to by the parties or the most recent closing bid quotation from such a source, plus accrued Income to the extent not included therein (other than any Income credited or transferred to, or applied to the obligations of, Seller pursuant to Paragraph 5 hereof) as of such date (unless contrary to market practice for such Securities);

(k) "Price Differential", with respect to any Transaction as of any date, the aggregate amount obtained by daily application of the Pricing Rate for such Transaction to the Purchase Price for such Transaction on a 360 day per year basis for the actual number of days during the period commencing on (and including) the Purchase Date for such Transaction and ending on (but excluding) the date of determination (reduced by any amount of such Price Differential previously paid by Seller to Buyer with respect to such Transaction);

(l) "Pricing Rate", the per annum percentage rate for determination of the Price Differential;

(m) "Prime Rate", the prime rate of U.S. commercial banks as published in The Wall Street Journal (or, if more than one such rate is published, the average of such rates);

(n) "Purchase Date", the date on which Purchased Securities are to be transferred by Seller to Buyer;

(o) "Purchase Price", (i) on the Purchase Date, the price at which Purchased Securities are transferred by Seller to Buyer, and (ii) thereafter, except where Buyer and Seller agree otherwise, such price increased by the amount of any cash transferred by Buyer to Seller pursuant to Paragraph 4(b) hereof and decreased by the amount of any cash transferred by Seller to Buyer pursuant to Paragraph 4(a) hereof or applied to reduce Seller's obligations under clause (ii) of Paragraph 5 hereof;

(p) "Purchased Securities", the Securities transferred by Seller to Buyer in a Transaction hereunder, and any Securities substituted therefor in accordance with Paragraph 9 hereof. The term "Purchased Securities" with respect to any Transaction at any time also shall include Additional Purchased Securities delivered pursuant to Paragraph 4(a) hereof and shall exclude Securities returned pursuant to Paragraph 4(b) hereof;

(q) "Repurchase Date", the date on which Seller is to repurchase the Purchased Securities from Buyer, including any date determined by application of the provisions of Paragraph 3(c) or 11 hereof;

(r) "Repurchase Price", the price at which Purchased Securities are to be transferred from Buyer to Seller upon termination of a Transaction, which will be determined in each case (including Transactions terminable upon demand) as the sum of the Purchase Price and the Price Differential as of the date of such determination;

(s) "Seller's Margin Amount", with respect to any Transaction as of any date, the amount obtained by application of the Seller's Margin Percentage to the Repurchase Price for such Transaction as of such date;

(t) "Seller's Margin Percentage", with respect to any Transaction as of any date, a percentage (which may be equal to the Buyer's Margin Percentage) agreed to by Buyer and Seller or, in the absence of any such agreement, the percentage obtained by dividing the Market Value of the Purchased Securities on the Purchase Date by the Purchase Price on the Purchase Date for such Transaction.

3. Initiation; Confirmation; Termination

(a) An agreement to enter into a Transaction may be made orally or in writing at the initiation of either Buyer or Seller. On the Purchase Date for the Transaction, the Purchased Securities shall be transferred to Buyer or its agent against the transfer of the Purchase Price to an account of Seller.

(b) Upon agreeing to enter into a Transaction hereunder, Buyer or Seller (or both), as shall be agreed, shall promptly deliver to the other party a written confirmation of each Transaction (a "Confirmation"). The Confirmation shall describe the Purchased Securities (including CUSIP number, if any), identify Buyer and Seller and set forth (i) the Purchase Date, (ii) the Purchase Price, (iii) the Repurchase Date, unless the Transaction is to be terminable on demand, (iv) the Pricing Rate or Repurchase Price applicable to the Transaction, and (v) any additional terms or conditions of the Transaction not inconsistent with this Agreement. The Confirmation, together with this Agreement, shall constitute conclusive evidence of the terms agreed between Buyer and Seller with respect to the Transaction to which the Confirmation relates, unless with respect to the Confirmation specific objection is made promptly after receipt thereof. In the event of any conflict between the terms of such Confirmation and this Agreement, this Agreement shall prevail.

(c) In the case of Transactions terminable upon demand, such demand shall be made by Buyer or Seller, no later than such time as is customary in accordance with market practice, by telephone or otherwise on or prior to the business day on which such termination will be effective. On the date specified in such demand, or on the date fixed for termination in the case of Transactions having a fixed term, termination of the Transaction will be effected by transfer to Seller or its agent of the Purchased Securities and any Income in respect thereof received by Buyer (and not previously credited or transferred to, or applied to the obligations of, Seller pursuant to Paragraph 5 hereof) against the transfer of the Repurchase Price to an account of Buyer.

4. **Margin Maintenance**

   (a) If at any time the aggregate Market Value of all Purchased Securities subject to all Transactions in which a particular party hereto is acting as Buyer is less than the aggregate Buyer's Margin Amount for all such Transactions (a "Margin Deficit"), then Buyer may by notice to Seller require Seller in such Transactions, at Seller's option, to transfer to Buyer cash or additional Securities reasonably acceptable to Buyer ("Additional Purchased Securities"), so that the cash and aggregate Market Value of the Purchased Securities, including any such Additional Purchased Securities, will thereupon equal or exceed such aggregate Buyer's Margin Amount (decreased by the amount of any Margin Deficit as of such date arising from any Transactions in which such Buyer is acting as Seller).

   (b) If at any time the aggregate Market Value of all Purchased Securities subject to all Transactions in which a particular party hereto is acting as Seller exceeds the aggregate Seller's Margin Amount for all such Transactions at such time (a "Margin Excess"), then Seller may by notice to Buyer require Buyer in such Transactions, at Buyer's option, to transfer cash or Purchased Securities to Seller, so that the aggregate Market Value of the Purchased Securities, after deduction of any such cash or any Purchased Securities so transferred, will thereupon not exceed such aggregate Seller's Margin Amount (increased by the amount of any Margin Excess as of such date arising from any Transactions in which such Seller is acting as Buyer).

   (c) If any notice is given by Buyer or Seller under subparagraph (a) or (b) of this Paragraph at or before the Margin Notice Deadline on any business day, the party receiving such notice shall transfer cash or Additional Purchased Securities as provided in such subparagraph no later than the close of business in the relevant market on such day. If any such notice is given after the Margin Notice Deadline, the party receiving such notice shall transfer such cash or Securities no later than the close of business in the relevant market on the next business day following such notice.

   (d) Any cash transferred pursuant to this Paragraph shall be attributed to such Transactions as shall be agreed upon by Buyer and Seller.

(e) Seller and Buyer may agree, with respect to any or all Transactions hereunder, that the respective rights of Buyer or Seller (or both) under subparagraphs (a) and (b) of this Paragraph may be exercised only where a Margin Deficit or Margin Excess, as the case may be, exceeds a specified dollar amount or a specified percentage of the Repurchase Prices for such Transactions (which amount or percentage shall be agreed to by Buyer and Seller prior to entering into any such Transactions).

(f) Seller and Buyer may agree, with respect to any or all Transactions hereunder, that the respective rights of Buyer and Seller under subparagraphs (a) and (b) of this Paragraph to require the elimination of a Margin Deficit or a Margin Excess, as the case may be, may be exercised whenever such a Margin Deficit or Margin Excess exists with respect to any single Transaction hereunder (calculated without regard to any other Transaction outstanding under this Agreement).

5. Income Payments

Seller shall be entitled to receive an amount equal to all Income paid or distributed on or in respect of the Securities that is not otherwise received by Seller, to the full extent it would be so entitled if the Securities had not been sold to Buyer. Buyer shall, as the parties may agree with respect to any Transaction (or, in the absence of any such agreement, as Buyer shall reasonably determine in its discretion), on the date such Income is paid or distributed either (i) transfer to or credit to the account of Seller such Income with respect to any Purchased Securities subject to such Transaction or (ii) with respect to Income paid in cash, apply the Income payment or payments to reduce the amount, if any, to be transferred to Buyer by Seller upon termination of such Transaction. Buyer shall not be obligated to take any action pursuant to the preceding sentence (A) to the extent that such action would result in the creation of a Margin Deficit, unless prior thereto or simultaneously therewith Seller transfers to Buyer cash or Additional Purchased Securities sufficient to eliminate such Margin Deficit, or (B) if an Event of Default with respect to Seller has occurred and is then continuing at the time such Income is paid or distributed.

6. Security Interest

Although the parties intend that all Transactions hereunder be sales and purchases and not loans, in the event any such Transactions are deemed to be loans, Seller shall be deemed to have pledged to Buyer as security for the performance by Seller of its obligations under each such Transaction, and shall be deemed to have granted to Buyer a security interest in, all of the Purchased Securities with respect to all Transactions hereunder and all Income thereon and other proceeds thereof.

7. Payment and Transfer

Unless otherwise mutually agreed, all transfers of funds hereunder shall be in immediately available funds. All Securities transferred by one party hereto to the other party (i) shall be in suitable form for transfer or shall be accompanied by duly executed instruments of transfer or assignment in blank and such other documentation as the party receiving possession may reasonably request, (ii) shall be transferred on the book-entry system of a Federal Reserve Bank, or (iii) shall be transferred by any other method mutually acceptable to Seller and Buyer.

8. Segregation of Purchased Securities

To the extent required by applicable law, all Purchased Securities in the possession of Seller shall be segregated from other securities in its possession and shall be identified as subject to this Agreement. Segregation may be accomplished by appropriate identification on the books and records of the holder, including a financial or securities intermediary or a clearing corporation. All of Seller's interest in the Purchased Securities shall pass to Buyer on the Purchase Date and, unless otherwise agreed by Buyer and Seller, nothing in this Agreement shall preclude Buyer from engaging in repurchase transactions with the Purchased Securities or otherwise selling, transferring, pledging or hypothecating the Purchased Securities, but no such transaction shall relieve Buyer of its obligations to transfer Purchased Securities to Seller pursuant to Paragraph 3, 4 or 11 hereof, or of Buyer's obligation to credit or pay Income to, or apply Income to the obligations of, Seller pursuant to Paragraph 5 hereof.

> **Required Disclosure for Transactions in Which the Seller Retains Custody of the Purchased Securities**
>
> Seller is not permitted to substitute other securities for those subject to this Agreement and therefore must keep Buyer's securities segregated at all times, unless in this Agreement Buyer grants Seller the right to substitute other securities. If Buyer grants the right to substitute, this means that Buyer's securities will likely be commingled with Seller's own securities during the trading day. Buyer is advised that, during any trading day that Buyer's securities are commingled with Seller's securities, they [will]* [may]** be subject to liens granted by Seller to [its clearing bank]* [third parties]** and may be used by Seller for deliveries on other securities transactions. Whenever the securities are commingled, Seller's ability to resegregate substitute securities for Buyer will be subject to Seller's ability to satisfy [the clearing]* [any]** lien or to obtain substitute securities.
>
> * Language to be used under 17 C.F.R. ß403.4(e) if Seller is a government securities broker or dealer other than a financial institution.
> ** Language to be used under 17 C.F.R. ß403.5(d) if Seller is a financial institution.

9. Substitution

(a) Seller may, subject to agreement with and acceptance by Buyer, substitute other Securities for any Purchased Securities. Such substitution shall be made by transfer to Buyer of such other Securities and transfer to Seller of such Purchased Securities. After substitution, the substituted Securities shall be deemed to be Purchased Securities.

(b) In Transactions in which Seller retains custody of Purchased Securities, the parties expressly agree that Buyer shall be deemed, for purposes of subparagraph (a) of this Paragraph, to have agreed to and accepted in this Agreement substitution by Seller of other Securities for Purchased Securities; provided, however, that such other Securities shall have a Market Value at least equal to the Market Value of the Purchased Securities for which they are substituted.

10. Representations

Each of Buyer and Seller represents and warrants to the other that (i) it is duly authorized to execute and deliver this Agreement, to enter into Transactions contemplated hereunder and to perform its obligations hereunder and has taken all necessary action to authorize such execution, delivery and performance, (ii) it will engage in such Transactions as principal (or, if agreed in writing, in the form of an annex hereto or otherwise, in advance of any Transaction by the other party hereto, as agent for a disclosed principal), (iii) the person signing this Agreement on its behalf is duly authorized to do so on its behalf (or on behalf of any such disclosed principal), (iv) it has obtained all authorizations of any governmental body required in connection with this Agreement and the Transactions hereunder and such authorizations are in full force and effect and (v) the execution, delivery and performance of this Agreement and the Transactions hereunder will not violate any law, ordinance, charter, by-law or rule applicable to it or any agreement by which it is bound or by which any of its assets are affected. On the Purchase Date for any Transaction Buyer and Seller shall each be deemed to repeat all the foregoing representations made by it.

11. Events of Default

In the event that (i) Seller fails to transfer or Buyer fails to purchase Purchased Securities upon the applicable Purchase Date, (ii) Seller fails to repurchase or Buyer fails to transfer Purchased Securities upon the applicable Repurchase Date, (iii) Seller or Buyer fails to comply with Paragraph 4 hereof, (iv) Buyer fails, after one business day's notice, to comply with Paragraph 5 hereof, (v) an Act of Insolvency occurs with respect to Seller or Buyer, (vi) any representation made by Seller or Buyer shall have been incorrect or untrue in any material respect when made or repeated or deemed to have been made or repeated, or (vii) Seller or Buyer shall admit to the other its inability to, or its intention not to, perform any of its obligations hereunder (each an "Event of Default"):

(a) The nondefaulting party may, at its option (which option shall be deemed to have been exercised immediately upon the occurrence of an Act of Insolvency), declare an Event of Default to have occurred hereunder and, upon the exercise or deemed exercise of such option, the Repurchase Date for each Transaction hereunder shall, if it has not already occurred, be deemed immediately to occur (except that, in the event that the Purchase Date for any Transaction has not yet occurred as of the date of such exercise or deemed exercise, such Transaction shall be deemed immediately canceled). The nondefaulting party shall (except upon the occurrence of an Act of Insolvency) give notice to the defaulting party of the exercise of such option as promptly as practicable.

(b) In all Transactions in which the defaulting party is acting as Seller, if the nondefaulting party exercises or is deemed to have exercised the option referred to in subparagraph (a) of this Paragraph, (i) the defaulting party's obligations in such Transactions to repurchase all Purchased Securities, at the Repurchase Price therefor on the Repurchase Date determined in accordance with subparagraph (a) of this Paragraph, shall thereupon become immediately due and payable, (ii) all Income paid after such exercise or deemed exercise shall be retained by the nondefaulting party and applied to the aggregate unpaid Repurchase Prices and any other amounts owing by the defaulting party hereunder, and (iii) the defaulting party shall immediately deliver to the nondefaulting party any Purchased Securities subject to such Transactions then in the defaulting party's possession or control.

(c) In all Transactions in which the defaulting party is acting as Buyer, upon tender by the nondefaulting party of payment of the aggregate Repurchase Prices for all such Transactions, all right, title and interest in and entitlement to all Purchased Securities subject to such Transactions shall be deemed transferred to the nondefaulting party, and the defaulting party shall deliver all such Purchased Securities to the nondefaulting party.

(d) If the nondefaulting party exercises or is deemed to have exercised the option referred to in subparagraph (a) of this Paragraph, the nondefaulting party, without prior notice to the defaulting party, may:

(i) as to Transactions in which the defaulting party is acting as Seller, (A) immediately sell, in a recognized market (or otherwise in a commercially reasonable manner) at such price or prices as the nondefaulting party may reasonably deem satisfactory, any or all Purchased Securities subject to such Transactions and apply the proceeds thereof to the aggregate unpaid Repurchase Prices and any other amounts owing by the defaulting party hereunder or (B) in its sole discretion elect, in lieu of selling all or a portion of such Purchased Securities, to give the defaulting party credit for such Purchased Securities in an amount equal to the price therefor on such date, obtained from a generally recognized source or the most recent closing bid quotation from such a source, against the aggregate unpaid Repurchase Prices and any other amounts owing by the defaulting party hereunder; and

(ii) as to Transactions in which the defaulting party is acting as Buyer, (A) immediately purchase, in a recognized market (or otherwise in a commercially reasonable manner) at such price or prices as the nondefaulting party may reasonably deem satisfactory, securities ("Replacement Securities") of the same class and amount as any Purchased Securities that are not delivered by the defaulting party to the nondefaulting party as required hereunder or (B) in its sole discretion elect, in lieu of purchasing Replacement Securities, to be deemed to have purchased Replacement Securities at the price therefor on such date, obtained from a generally recognized source or the most recent closing offer quotation from such a source.

Unless otherwise provided in Annex I, the parties acknowledge and agree that (1) the Securities subject to any Transaction hereunder are instruments traded in a recognized market, (2) in the absence of a generally recognized source for prices or bid or offer quotations for any Security, the nondefaulting party may establish the source therefor in its sole discretion and (3) all prices, bids and offers shall be determined together with accrued Income (except to the extent contrary to market practice with respect to the relevant Securities).

(e) As to Transactions in which the defaulting party is acting as Buyer, the defaulting party shall be liable to the nondefaulting party for any excess of the price paid (or deemed paid) by the nondefaulting party for Replacement Securities over the Repurchase Price for the Purchased Securities replaced thereby and for any amounts payable by the defaulting party under Paragraph 5 hereof or otherwise hereunder.

(f) For purposes of this Paragraph 11, the Repurchase Price for each Transaction hereunder in respect of which the defaulting party is acting as Buyer shall not increase above the amount of such Repurchase Price for such Transaction determined as of the date of the exercise or deemed exercise by the nondefaulting party of the option referred to in subparagraph (a) of this Paragraph.

(g) The defaulting party shall be liable to the nondefaulting party for (i) the amount of all reasonable legal or other expenses incurred by the nondefaulting party in connection with or as a result of an Event of Default, (ii) damages in an amount equal to the cost (including all fees, expenses and commissions) of entering into replacement transactions and entering into or terminating hedge transactions in connection with or as a result of an Event of Default, and (iii) any other loss, damage, cost or expense directly arising or resulting from the occurrence of an Event of Default in respect of a Transaction.

(h) To the extent permitted by applicable law, the defaulting party shall be liable to the nondefaulting party for interest on any amounts owing by the defaulting party hereunder, from the date the defaulting party becomes liable for such amounts hereunder until such amounts are (i) paid in full by the defaulting party or (ii) satisfied in full by the exercise of the nondefaulting party's rights hereunder. Interest on any sum payable by the defaulting party to the nondefaulting party under this Paragraph 11(h) shall be at a rate equal to the greater of the Pricing Rate for the relevant Transaction or the Prime Rate.

(i) The nondefaulting party shall have, in addition to its rights hereunder, any rights otherwise available to it under any other agreement or applicable law.

12. Single Agreement

Buyer and Seller acknowledge that, and have entered hereinto and will enter into each Transaction hereunder in consideration of and in reliance upon the fact that, all Transactions hereunder constitute a single business and contractual relationship and have been made in consideration of each other. Accordingly, each of Buyer and Seller agrees (i) to perform all of its obligations in respect of each Transaction hereunder, and that a default in the performance of any such obligations shall constitute a default by it in respect of all Transactions hereunder, (ii) that each of them shall be entitled to set off claims and apply property held by them in respect of any Transaction against obligations owing to them in respect of any other Transactions hereunder and (iii) that payments, deliveries and other transfers made by either of them in respect of any Transaction shall be deemed to have been made in consideration of payments, deliveries and other transfers in respect of any other Transactions hereunder, and the obligations to make any such payments, deliveries and other transfers may be applied against each other and netted.

13. Notices and Other Communications

Any and all notices, statements, demands or other communications hereunder may be given by a party to the other by mail, facsimile, telegraph, messenger or otherwise to the address specified in Annex II hereto, or so sent to such party at any other place specified in a notice of change of address hereafter received by the other. All notices, demands and requests hereunder may be made orally, to be confirmed promptly in writing, or by other communication as specified in the preceding sentence.

14. Entire Agreement; Severability

This Agreement shall supersede any existing agreements between the parties containing general terms and conditions for repurchase transactions. Each provision and agreement herein shall be treated as separate and independent from any other provision or agreement herein and shall be enforceable notwithstanding the unenforceability of any such other provision or agreement.

15. Non-assignability; Termination

(a) The rights and obligations of the parties under this Agreement and under any Transaction shall not be assigned by either party without the prior written consent of the other party, and any such assignment without the prior written consent of the other party shall be null and void. Subject to the foregoing, this Agreement and any Transactions shall be binding upon and shall inure to the benefit of the parties and their respective successors and assigns. This Agreement may be terminated by either party upon giving written notice to the other, except that this Agreement shall, notwithstanding such notice, remain applicable to any Transactions then outstanding.

(b) Subparagraph (a) of this Paragraph 15 shall not preclude a party from assigning, charging or otherwise dealing with all or any part of its interest in any sum payable to it under Paragraph 11 hereof.

16. Governing Law

This Agreement shall be governed by the laws of the State of New York without giving effect to the conflict of law principles thereof.

17. No Waivers, Etc.

No express or implied waiver of any Event of Default by either party shall constitute a waiver of any other Event of Default and no exercise of any remedy hereunder by any party shall constitute a waiver of its right to exercise any other remedy hereunder. No modification or waiver of any provision of this Agreement and no consent by any party to a departure herefrom shall be effective unless and until such shall be in writing and duly executed by both of the parties hereto. Without limitation on any of the foregoing, the failure to give a notice pursuant to Paragraph 4(a) or 4(b) hereof will not constitute a waiver of any right to do so at a later date.

18. Use of Employee Plan Assets

(a) If assets of an employee benefit plan subject to any provision of the Employee Retirement Income Security Act of 1974 ("ERISA") are intended to be used by either party hereto (the "Plan Party") in a Transaction, the Plan Party shall so notify the other party prior to the Transaction. The Plan Party shall represent in writing to the other party that the Transaction does not constitute a prohibited transaction under ERISA or is otherwise exempt therefrom, and the other party may proceed in reliance thereon but shall not be required so to proceed.

(b) Subject to the last sentence of subparagraph (a) of this Paragraph, any such Transaction shall proceed only if Seller furnishes or has furnished to Buyer its most recent available audited statement of its financial condition and its most recent subsequent unaudited statement of its financial condition.

(c) By entering into a Transaction pursuant to this Paragraph, Seller shall be deemed (i) to represent to Buyer that since the date of Seller's latest such financial statements, there has been no material adverse change in Seller's financial condition which Seller has not disclosed to Buyer, and (ii) to agree to provide Buyer with future audited and unaudited statements of its financial condition as they are issued, so long as it is a Seller in any outstanding Transaction involving a Plan Party.

19. Intent

(a) The parties recognize that each Transaction is a "repurchase agreement" as that term is defined in Section 101 of Title 11 of the United States Code, as amended (except insofar as the type of Securities subject to such Transaction or the term of such Transaction would render such definition inapplicable), and a "securities contract" as that term is defined in Section 741 of Title 11 of the United States Code, as amended (except insofar as the type of assets subject to such Transaction would render such definition inapplicable).

(b) It is understood that either party's right to liquidate Securities delivered to it in connection with Transactions hereunder or to exercise any other remedies pursuant to Paragraph 11 hereof is a contractual right to liquidate such Transaction as described in Sections 555 and 559 of Title 11 of the United States Code, as amended.

(c) The parties agree and acknowledge that if a party hereto is an "insured depository institution," as such term is defined in the Federal Deposit Insurance Act, as amended ("FDIA"), then each Transaction hereunder is a "qualified financial contract," as that term is defined in FDIA and any rules, orders or policy statements thereunder (except insofar as the type of assets subject to such Transaction would render such definition inapplicable).

(d) It is understood that this Agreement constitutes a "netting contract" as defined in and subject to Title IV of the Federal Deposit Insurance Corporation Improvement Act of 1991 ("FDICIA") and each payment entitlement and payment obligation under any Transaction hereunder shall constitute a "covered contractual payment entitlement" or "covered contractual payment obligation", respectively, as defined in and subject to FDICIA (except insofar as one or both of the parties is not a "financial institution" as that term is defined in FDICIA).

20. Disclosure Relating to Certain Federal Protections

The parties acknowledge that they have been advised that:

(a) in the case of Transactions in which one of the parties is a broker or dealer registered with the Securities and Exchange Commission ("SEC") under Section 15 of the Securities Exchange Act of 1934 ("1934 Act"), the Securities Investor Protection Corporation has taken the position that the provisions of the Securities Investor Protection Act of 1970 ("SIPA") do not protect the other party with respect to any Transaction hereunder;

(b) in the case of Transactions in which one of the parties is a government securities broker or a government securities dealer registered with the SEC under Section 15C of the 1934 Act, SIPA will not provide protection to the other party with respect to any Transaction hereunder; and

(c) in the case of Transactions in which one of the parties is a financial institution, funds held by the financial institution pursuant to a Transaction hereunder are not a deposit and therefore are not insured by the Federal Deposit Insurance Corporation or the National Credit Union Share Insurance Fund, as applicable.

[Name of Party]   [Name of Party]

By: _____   By: _____

Title: _____   Title: _____

Date: _____   Date: _____

Annex I

Supplemental Terms and Conditions

This Annex I forms a part of the Master Repurchase Agreement dated as of _____, ___ (the "Agreement") between _____ and _____. Capitalized terms used but not defined in this Annex I shall have the meanings ascribed to them in the Agreement.

1. Other Applicable Annexes. In addition to this Annex I and Annex II, the following Annexes and any Schedules thereto shall form a part of this Agreement and shall be applicable thereunder:

    [Annex III (International Transactions)]

    [Annex IV (Party Acting as Agent)]

    [Annex V (Margin for Forward Transactions)]

    [Annex VI (Buy/Sell Back Transactions)]

    [Annex VII (Transactions Involving Registered Investment Companies)]

Annex II

Names and Addresses for Communications Between Parties

Annex III

International Transactions

This Annex III (including any Schedules hereto) forms a part of the Master Repurchase Agreement dated as of _____ (the "Agreement") between _____ and _____ . Capitalized terms used but not defined in this Annex III shall have the meanings ascribed to them in the Agreement.

1. **Definitions.** For purposes of the Agreement and this Annex III:
   (a) The following terms shall have the following meanings:

    "Base Currency", United States dollars or such other currency as Buyer and Seller may agree in the Confirmation with respect to any International Transaction or otherwise in writing;

    "Business Day" or "business day":

    (i) in relation to any International Transaction which (A) involves an International Security and (B) is to be settled through CEDEL or Euroclear, a day on which CEDEL or, as the case may be, Euroclear is open to settle business in the currency in which the Purchase Price and the Repurchase Price are denominated;

    (ii) in relation to any International Transaction which (A) involves an International Security and (B) is to be settled through a settlement system other than CEDEL or Euroclear, a day on which that settlement system is open to settle such International Transaction;

    (iii) in relation to any International Transaction which involves a delivery of Securities not falling within (i) or (ii) above, a day on which banks are open for business in the place where delivery of the relevant Securities is to be effected; and

    (iv) in relation to any International Transaction which involves an obligation to make a payment not falling within (i) or (ii) above, a day other than a Saturday or Sunday on which banks are open for business in the principal financial center of the country of which the currency in which the payment is denominated is the official currency and, if different, in the place where any account designated by the parties for the making or receipt of the payment is situated (or, in the case of ECU, a day on which ECU clearing operates);

    "CEDEL", CEDEL Bank, société anonyme;

    "Contractual Currency", the currency in which the International Securities subject to any International Transaction are denominated or such other currency as may be specified in the Confirmation with respect to any International Transaction;

    "Euroclear", Morgan Guaranty Trust Company of New York, Brussels Branch, as operator of the Euroclear System;

"International Security", any Security that (i) is denominated in a currency other than United States dollars or (ii) is capable of being cleared through a clearing facility outside the United States or (iii) is issued by an issuer organized under the laws of a jurisdiction other than the United States (or any political subdivision thereof);

"International Transaction", any Transaction involving (i) an International Security or (ii) a party organized under the laws of a jurisdiction other than the United States (or any political subdivision thereof) or having its principal place of business outside the United States or (iii) a branch or office outside the United States designated in Annex I by a party organized under the laws of the United States (or any political subdivision thereof) as an office through which that party may act;

"LIBOR", in relation to any sum in any currency, the offered rate for deposits for such sum in such currency for a period of three months which appears on the Reuters Screen LIBO page as of 11:00 A.M., London time, on the date on which it is to be determined (or, if more than one such rate appears, the arithmetic mean of such rates);

"Spot Rate", where an amount in one currency is to be converted into a second currency on any date, the spot rate of exchange of a comparable amount quoted by a major money-center bank in the New York interbank market, as agreed by Buyer and Seller, for the sale by such bank of such second currency against a purchase by it of such first currency.

(b) Notwithstanding Paragraph 2 of the Agreement, the term "Prime Rate" shall mean, with respect to any International Transaction, LIBOR plus a spread, as may be specified in the Confirmation with respect to any International Transaction or otherwise in writing.

2. **Manner of Transfer.** All transfers of International Securities (i) shall be in suitable form for transfer and accompanied by duly executed instruments of transfer or assignment in blank (where required for transfer) and such other documentation as the transferee may reasonably request, or (ii) shall be transferred through the book-entry system of Euroclear or CEDEL, or (iii) shall be transferred through any other agreed securities clearing system or (iv) shall be transferred by any other method mutually acceptable to Seller and Buyer.

3. **Contractual Currency.**
   (a) Unless otherwise mutually agreed, all funds transferred in respect of the Purchase Price or the Repurchase Price in any International Transaction shall be in the Contractual Currency.

   (b) Notwithstanding subparagraph (a) of this Paragraph 3, the payee of any payment may, at its option, accept tender thereof in any other currency; provided, however, that, to the extent permitted by applicable law, the obligation of the payor to make such payment will be discharged only to the extent of the amount of the Contractual Currency that such payee may, consistent with normal banking procedures, purchase with such other currency (after deduction of any premium and costs of exchange) for delivery within the customary delivery period for spot transactions in respect of the relevant currency.

(c) If for any reason the amount in the Contractual Currency so received, including amounts received after conversion of any recovery under any judgment or order expressed in a currency other than the Contractual Currency, falls short of the amount in the Contractual Currency due in respect of the Agreement, the party required to make the payment shall (unless an Event of Default has occurred and such party is the nondefaulting party) as a separate and independent obligation (which shall not merge with any judgment or any payment or any partial payment or enforcement of payment) and to the extent permitted by applicable law, immediately pay such additional amount in the Contractual Currency as may be necessary to compensate for the shortfall.

(d) If for any reason the amount of the Contractual Currency received by one party hereto exceeds the amount in the Contractual Currency due such party in respect of the Agreement, then (unless an Event of Default has occurred and such party is the nondefaulting party) the party receiving the payment shall refund promptly the amount of such excess.

4. **Notices.** Any and all notices, statements, demands or other communications with respect to International Transactions shall be given in accordance with Paragraph 13 of the Agreement and shall be in the English language.

5. **Taxes.**
   (a) Transfer taxes, stamp taxes and all similar costs with respect to the transfer of Securities shall be paid by Seller.

   (b) (i) Unless otherwise agreed, all money payable by one party (the "Payor") to the other (the "Payee") in respect of any International Transaction shall be paid free and clear of, and without withholding or deduction for, any taxes or duties of whatsoever nature imposed, levied, collected, withheld or assessed by any authority having power to tax (a "Tax"), unless the withholding or deduction of such Tax is required by law. In that event, unless otherwise agreed, Payor shall pay such additional amounts as will result in the net amounts receivable by Payee (after taking account of such withholding or deduction) being equal to such amounts as would have been received by Payee had no such Tax been required to be withheld or deducted; provided that for purposes of Paragraphs 5 and 6 the term "Tax" shall not include any Tax that would not have been imposed but for the existence of any present or former connection between Payee and the jurisdiction imposing such Tax other than the mere receipt of payment from Payor or the performance of Payee's obligations under an International Transaction. The parties acknowledge and agree, for the avoidance of doubt, that the amount of Income required to be transferred, credited or applied by Buyer for the benefit of Seller under Paragraph 5 of the Agreement shall be determined without taking into account any Tax required to be withheld or deducted from such Income, unless otherwise agreed.

   (ii) In the case of any Tax required to be withheld or deducted from any money payable to a party hereto acting as Payee by the other party hereto acting as Payor, Payee agrees to deliver to Payor (or, if applicable, to the authority imposing the Tax) any certificate or document reasonably requested by Payor that would entitle Payee to an exemption from, or reduction in the rate of, withholding or deduction of Tax from money payable by Payor to Payee.

(iii) Each party hereto agrees to notify the other party of any circumstance known or reasonably known to it (other than a Change of Tax Law, as defined in Paragraph 6 hereof) that causes a certificate or document provided by it pursuant to subparagraph (b)(ii) of this Paragraph to fail to be true.

(iv) Notwithstanding subparagraph (b)(i) of this Paragraph, no additional amounts shall be payable by Payor to Payee in respect of an International Transaction to the extent that such additional amounts are payable as a result of a failure by Payee to comply with its obligations under subparagraph (b)(ii) or (b)(iii) of this Paragraph with respect to such International Transaction.

6. **Tax Event.**

    (a) This Paragraph 6 shall apply if either party notifies the other, with respect to a Tax required to be collected by withholding or deduction, that —

    (i) any action taken by a taxing authority or brought in a court of competent jurisdiction after the date an International Transaction is entered into, regardless of whether such action is taken or brought with respect to a party to the Agreement; or

    (ii) a change in the fiscal or regulatory regime after the date an International Transaction is entered into,

    (each, a "Change of Tax Law") has or will, in the notifying party's reasonable opinion, have a material adverse effect on such party in the context of an International Transaction.

    (b) If so requested by the other party, the notifying party will furnish the other party with an opinion of a suitably qualified adviser that an event referred to in subparagraph (a)(i) or (a)(ii) of this Paragraph 6 has occurred and affects the notifying party.

    (c) Where this Paragraph 6 applies, the party giving the notice referred to in subparagraph (a) above may, subject to subparagraph (d) below, terminate the International Transaction effective from a date specified in the notice, not being earlier (unless so agreed by the other party) than 30 days after the date of such notice, by nominating such date as the Repurchase Date.

    (d) If the party receiving the notice referred to in subparagraph (a) of this Paragraph 6 so elects, it may override such notice by giving a counter-notice to the other party. If a counter-notice is given, the party which gives such counter-notice will be deemed to have agreed to indemnify the other party against the adverse effect referred to in subparagraph (a) of this Paragraph 6 so far as it relates to the relevant International Transaction and the original Repurchase Date will continue to apply.

    (e) Where an International Transaction is terminated as described in this Paragraph 6, the party which has given the notice to terminate shall indemnify the other party against any reasonable legal and other professional expenses incurred by the other party by reason of the termination, but the other party may not claim any sum constituting consequential loss or damage in respect of a termination in accordance with this Paragraph 6.

(f) This Paragraph 6 is without prejudice to Paragraph 5 of this Annex III; but an obligation to pay additional amounts pursuant to Paragraph 5 of this Annex III may, where appropriate, be a circumstance which causes this Paragraph 6 to apply.

7. **Margin.** In the calculation of "Margin Deficit" and "Margin Excess" pursuant to Paragraph 4 of the Agreement, all sums not denominated in the Base Currency shall be deemed to be converted into the Base Currency at the Spot Rate on the date of such calculation.

8. **Events of Default.**
    (a) In addition to the Events of Default set forth in Paragraph 11 of the Agreement, it shall be an additional "Event of Default" if either party fails, after one business day's notice, to perform any covenant or obligation required to be performed by it under this Annex III, including, without limitation, the payment of taxes or additional amounts as required by Paragraph 5 of this Annex III.

    (b) In addition to the other rights of a nondefaulting party under Paragraph 11 of the Agreement, following an Event of Default, the nondefaulting party may, at any time at its option, effect the conversion of any currency into a different currency of its choice at the Spot Rate on the date of the exercise of such option and offset obligations of the defaulting party denominated in different currencies against each other.

Schedule III.A

International Transactions Relating to [Relevant Country]

This Schedule III.A forms a part of Annex III to the Master Repurchase Agreement dated as of _____ , _____ (the "Agreement") between _____ and _____ . Capitalized terms used but not defined in this Schedule III.A shall have the meanings ascribed to them in Annex III.

[Insert provisions applicable to relevant country.]

Annex IV

Party Acting as Agent

This Annex IV forms a part of the Master Repurchase Agreement dated as of
_____ , _____ (the "Agreement") between _____ and
_____ . This Annex IV sets forth the terms and conditions governing all transactions in which a party selling securities or buying securities, as the case may be ("Agent"), in a Transaction is acting as agent for one or more third parties (each, a "Principal"). Capitalized terms used but not defined in this Annex IV shall have the meanings ascribed to them in the Agreement.

1. **Additional Representations.** In addition to the representations set forth in Paragraph 10 of the Agreement, Agent hereby makes the following representations, which shall continue during the term of any Transaction: Principal has duly authorized Agent to execute and deliver the Agreement on its behalf, has the power to so authorize Agent and to enter into the Transactions contemplated by the Agreement and to perform the obligations of Seller or Buyer, as the case may be, under such Transactions, and has taken all necessary action to authorize such execution and delivery by Agent and such performance by it.

2. **Identification of Principals.** Agent agrees (a) to provide the other party, prior to the date on which the parties agree to enter into any Transaction under the Agreement, with a written list of Principals for which it intends to act as Agent (which list may be amended in writing from time to time with the consent of the other party), and (b) to provide the other party, before the close of business on the next business day after orally agreeing to enter into a Transaction, with notice of the specific Principal or Principals for whom it is acting in connection with such Transaction. If (i) Agent fails to identify such Principal or Principals prior to the close of business on such next business day or (ii) the other party shall determine in its sole discretion that any Principal or Principals identified by Agent are not acceptable to it, the other party may reject and rescind any Transaction with such Principal or Principals, return to Agent any Purchased Securities or portion of the Purchase Price, as the case may be, previously transferred to the other party and refuse any further performance under such Transaction, and Agent shall immediately return to the other party any portion of the Purchase Price or Purchased Securities, as the case may be, previously transferred to Agent in connection with such Transaction; provided, however, that (A) the other party shall promptly (and in any event within one business day) notify Agent of its determination to reject and rescind such Transaction and (B) to the extent that any performance was rendered by any party under any Transaction rejected by the other party, such party shall remain entitled to any Price Differential or other amounts that would have been payable to it with respect to such performance if such Transaction had not been rejected. The other party acknowledges that Agent shall not have any obligation to provide it with confidential information regarding the financial status of its Principals; Agent agrees, however, that it will assist the other party in obtaining from Agent's Principals such information regarding the financial status of such Principals as the other party may reasonably request.

3. **Limitation of Agent's Liability.** The parties expressly acknowledge that if the representations of Agent under the Agreement, including this Annex IV, are true and correct in all material respects during the term of any Transaction and Agent otherwise complies with the provi-

sions of this Annex IV, then (a) Agent's obligations under the Agreement shall not include a guarantee of performance by its Principal or Principals and (b) the other party's remedies shall not include a right of setoff in respect of rights or obligations, if any, of Agent arising in other transactions in which Agent is acting as principal.

4. **Multiple Principals.**
    (a) In the event that Agent proposes to act for more than one Principal hereunder, Agent and the other party shall elect whether (i) to treat Transactions under the Agreement as transactions entered into on behalf of separate Principals or (ii) to aggregate such Transactions as if they were transactions by a single Principal. Failure to make such an election in writing shall be deemed an election to treat Transactions under the Agreement as transactions on behalf of separate Principals.

    (b) In the event that Agent and the other party elect (or are deemed to elect) to treat Transactions under the Agreement as transactions on behalf of separate Principals, the parties agree that (i) Agent will provide the other party, together with the notice described in Paragraph 2(b) of this Annex IV, notice specifying the portion of each Transaction allocable to the account of each of the Principals for which it is acting (to the extent that any such Transaction is allocable to the account of more than one Principal); (ii) the portion of any individual Transaction allocable to each Principal shall be deemed a separate Transaction under the Agreement; (iii) the margin maintenance obligations of Buyer and Seller under Paragraph 4 of the Agreement shall be determined on a Transaction-by-Transaction basis (unless the parties agree to determine such obligations on a Principal-by-Principal basis); and (iv) Buyer's and Seller's remedies under the Agreement upon the occurrence of an Event of Default shall be determined as if Agent had entered into a separate Agreement with the other party on behalf of each of its Principals.

    (c) In the event that Agent and the other party elect to treat Transactions under the Agreement as if they were transactions by a single Principal, the parties agree that (i) Agent's notice under Paragraph 2(b) of this Annex IV need only identify the names of its Principals but not the portion of each Transaction allocable to each Principal's account; (ii) the margin maintenance obligations of Buyer and Seller under Paragraph 4 of the Agreement shall, subject to any greater requirement imposed by applicable law, be determined on an aggregate basis for all Transactions entered into by Agent on behalf of any Principal; and (iii) Buyer's and Seller's remedies upon the occurrence of an Event of Default shall be determined as if all Principals were a single Seller or Buyer, as the case may be.

    (d) Notwithstanding any other provision of the Agreement (including, without limitation, this Annex IV), the parties agree that any Transactions by Agent on behalf of an employee benefit plan under ERISA shall be treated as Transactions on behalf of separate Principals in accordance with Paragraph 4(b) of this Annex IV (and all margin maintenance obligations of the parties shall be determined on a Transaction-by-Transaction basis).

5. **Interpretation of Terms.** All references to "Seller" or "Buyer", as the case may be, in the Agreement shall, subject to the provisions of this Annex IV (including, among other provisions, the limitations on Agent's liability in Paragraph 3 of this Annex IV), be construed to

reflect that (i) each Principal shall have, in connection with any Transaction or Transactions entered into by Agent on its behalf, the rights, responsibilities, privileges and obligations of a "Seller" or "Buyer", as the case may be, directly entering into such Transaction or Transactions with the other party under the Agreement, and (ii) Agent's Principal or Principals have designated Agent as their sole agent for performance of Seller's obligations to Buyer or Buyer's obligations to Seller, as the case may be, and for receipt of performance by Buyer of its obligations to Seller or Seller of its obligations to Buyer, as the case may be, in connection with any Transaction or Transactions under the Agreement (including, among other things, as Agent for each Principal in connection with transfers of Securities, cash or other property and as agent for giving and receiving all notices under the Agreement). Both Agent and its Principal or Principals shall be deemed "parties" to the Agreement and all references to a "party" or "either party" in the Agreement shall be deemed revised accordingly (and any Act of Insolvency with respect to Agent or any other Event of Default by Agent under Paragraph 11 of the Agreement shall be deemed an Event of Default by Seller or Buyer, as the case may be).

Annex V

Margin for Forward Transactions

This Annex V forms a part of the Master Repurchase Agreement dated as of _____, ____ (the "Agreement") between _____ and _____. Capitalized terms used but not defined in this Annex V shall have the meanings ascribed to them in the Agreement.

1. **Definitions.** For purposes of the Agreement and this Annex V, the following terms shall have the following meanings:

   "Forward Exposure", the amount of loss a party would incur upon canceling a Forward Transaction and entering into a replacement transaction, determined in accordance with market practice or as otherwise agreed by the parties;

   "Forward Transaction", any Transaction agreed to by the parties as to which the Purchase Date has not yet occurred;

   "Net Forward Exposure", the aggregate amount of a party's Forward Exposure to the other party under all Forward Transactions hereunder reduced by the aggregate amount of any Forward Exposure of the other party to such party under all Forward Transactions hereunder;

   "Net Unsecured Forward Exposure", a party's Net Forward Exposure reduced by the Market Value of any Forward Collateral transferred to such party (and not returned) pursuant to Paragraph 2 of this Annex V.

2. **Margin Maintenance.**
   (a) If at any time a party (the "In-the-Money Party") shall have a Net Unsecured Forward Exposure to the other party (the "Out-of-the-Money Party") under one or more Forward Transactions, the In-the-Money Party may by notice to the Out-of-the-Money Party require the Out-of-the-Money Party to transfer to the In-the-Money Party Securities or cash reasonably acceptable to the In-the-Money-Party (together with any Income thereon and proceeds thereof, "Forward Collateral") having a Market Value sufficient to eliminate such Net Unsecured Forward Exposure. The Out-of-the-Money Party may by notice to the In-the-Money Party require the In-the-Money Party to transfer to the Out-of-the-Money Party Forward Collateral having a Market Value that exceeds the In-the-Money Party's Net Forward Exposure ("Excess Forward Collateral Amount"). The rights of the parties under this subparagraph shall be in addition to their rights under subparagraphs (a) and (b) of Paragraph 4 and any other provisions of the Agreement.

   (b) The parties may agree, with respect to any or all Forward Transactions hereunder, that the respective rights of the parties under subparagraph (a) of this Paragraph may be exercised only where a Net Unsecured Forward Exposure or Excess Forward Collateral Amount, as the case may be, exceeds a specified dollar amount or other specified threshold for such Forward Transactions (which amount or threshold shall be agreed to by the parties prior to entering into any such Forward Transactions).

(c) The parties may agree, with respect to any or all Forward Transactions hereunder, that the respective rights of the parties under subparagraph (a) of this Paragraph to require the elimination of a Net Unsecured Forward Exposure or Excess Forward Collateral Amount, as the case may be, may be exercised whenever such a Net Unsecured Forward Exposure or Excess Forward Collateral Amount exists with respect to any single Forward Transaction hereunder (calculated without regard to any other Forward Transaction outstanding hereunder).

(d) The parties may agree, with respect to any or all Forward Transactions hereunder, that (i) one party shall transfer to the other party Forward Collateral having a Market Value equal to a specified dollar amount or other specified threshold no later than the Margin Notice Deadline on the day such Forward Transaction is entered into by the parties or (ii) one party shall not be required to make any transfer otherwise required to be made under this Paragraph if, after giving effect to such transfer, the Market Value of the Forward Collateral held by such party would be less than a specified dollar amount or other specified threshold (which amount or threshold shall be agreed to by the parties prior to entering into any such Forward Transactions).

(e) If any notice is given by a party to the other under subparagraph (a) of this Paragraph at or before the Margin Notice Deadline on any business day, the party receiving such notice shall transfer Forward Collateral as provided in such subparagraph no later than the close of business in the relevant market on such business day. If any such notice is given after the Margin Notice Deadline, the party receiving such notice shall transfer such Forward Collateral no later than the close of business in the relevant market on the next business day.

(f) Upon the occurrence of the Purchase Date for any Forward Transaction and the performance by the parties of their respective obligations to transfer cash and Securities on such date, any Forward Collateral in respect of such Forward Transaction, together with any Income thereon and proceeds thereof, shall be transferred by the party holding such Forward Collateral to the other party; provided, however, that neither party shall be required to transfer such Forward Collateral to the other if such transfer would result in the creation of a Net Unsecured Forward Exposure of the transferor.

(g) The Pledgor (as defined below) of Forward Collateral may, subject to agreement with and acceptance by the Pledgee (as defined below) thereof, substitute other Securities reasonably acceptable to the Pledgee for any Securities Forward Collateral. Such substitution shall be made by transfer to the Pledgee of such other Securities and transfer to the Pledgor of such Securities Forward Collateral. After substitution, the substituted Securities shall constitute Forward Collateral.

3. **Security Interest.**
    (a) In addition to the rights granted to the parties under Paragraph 6 of the Agreement, each party ("Pledgor") hereby pledges to the other party ("Pledgee") as security for the performance of its obligations hereunder, and grants Pledgee a security interest in and right of setoff against, any Forward Collateral and any other cash, Securities or property, and all proceeds of any of the foregoing, transferred by or on behalf of Pledgor to Pledgee or due from Pledgee to Pledgor in connection with the Agreement and the Forward Transactions hereunder.

(b) Unless otherwise agreed by the parties, a party to whom Forward Collateral has been transferred shall have the right to engage in repurchase transactions with Forward Collateral or otherwise sell, transfer, pledge or hypothecate Forward Collateral, including in respect of loans or other extensions of credit to such party that may be in amounts greater than the Forward Collateral such party is entitled to as security for obligations hereunder, and that may extend for periods of time longer than the periods during which such party is entitled to Forward Collateral as security for obligations hereunder; provided, however, that no such transaction shall relieve such party of its obligations to transfer Forward Collateral pursuant to Paragraph 2 or 4 of this Annex V or Paragraph 11 of the Agreement.

4. **Events of Default.**
   (a) In addition to the Events of Default set forth in Paragraph 11 of the Agreement, it shall be an additional "Event of Default" if either party fails, after one business day's notice, to perform any covenant or obligation required to be performed by it under Paragraph 2 or any other provision of this Annex.

   (b) In addition to the other rights of a nondefaulting party under Paragraphs 11 and 12 of the Agreement, if the nondefaulting party exercised or is deemed to have exercised the option referred to in Paragraph 11(a) of the Agreement:

   (i) The nondefaulting party, without prior notice to the defaulting party, may (A) immediately sell, in a recognized market (or otherwise in a commercially reasonable manner) at such price or prices as the nondefaulting party may reasonably deem satisfactory, any or all Forward Collateral subject to any or all Forward Transactions hereunder and apply the proceeds thereof to any amounts owing by the defaulting party hereunder or (B) in its sole discretion elect, in lieu of selling all or a portion of such Forward Collateral, to give the defaulting party credit for such Forward Collateral in an amount equal to the price therefor on such date, obtained from a generally recognized source or the most recent closing bid quotation from such a source, against any amounts owing by the defaulting party hereunder.

   (ii) Any Forward Collateral held by the defaulting party, together with any Income thereon and proceeds thereof, shall be immediately transferred by the defaulting party to the nondefaulting party. The nondefaulting party may, at its option (which option shall be deemed to have been exercised immediately upon the occurrence of an Act of Insolvency), and without prior notice to the defaulting party, (i) immediately purchase, in a recognized market (or otherwise in a commercially reasonable manner) at such price or prices as the nondefaulting party may reasonably deem satisfactory, securities ("Replacement Securities") of the same class and amount as any Securities Forward Collateral that is not delivered by the defaulting party to the nondefaulting party as required hereunder or (ii) in its sole discretion elect, in lieu of purchasing Replacement Securities, to be deemed to have purchased Replacement Securities at the price therefor on such date, obtained from a generally recognized source or the most recent closing offer quotation from such a source, whereupon the defaulting party shall be liable for the price of such Replacement Securities together with the amount of any cash Forward Collateral not delivered by the defaulting party to the nondefaulting party as required hereunder.

Unless otherwise provided in Annex I, the parties acknowledge and agree that (1) the Forward Collateral subject to any Forward Transaction hereunder are instruments traded in a recognized market, (2) in the absence of a generally recognized source for prices or bid quotations for any Forward Collateral, the nondefaulting party may establish the source therefor in its sole discretion and (3) all prices and bids shall be determined together with accrued Income (except to the extent contrary to market practice with respect to the relevant Forward Collateral).

5. **No Waivers, Etc.** Without limitation of the provisions of Paragraph 17 of the Agreement, the failure to give a notice pursuant to subparagraph (a), (b), (c) or (d) of Paragraph 2 of this Annex V will not constitute a waiver of any right to do so at a later date.

Annex VI

Buy/Sell Back Transactions

This Annex VI forms a part of the Master Repurchase Agreement dated as of
_____ , ____ (the "Agreement") between _____
and _____ . Capitalized terms used but not defined in this Annex VI shall have the meanings ascribed to them in the Agreement.

1. In the event of any conflict between the terms of this Annex VI and any other term of the Agreement, the terms of this Annex VI shall prevail.

2. Each Transaction shall be identified at the time it is entered into and in the relevant Confirmation as either a Repurchase Transaction or a Buy/Sell Back Transaction.

3. In the case of a Buy/Sell Back Transaction, the Confirmation delivered in accordance with Paragraph 3 of the Agreement may consist of a single document in respect of both of the transfers of funds against Securities which together form the Buy/Sell Back Transaction or separate Confirmations may be delivered in respect of each such transfer.

4. **Definitions.** The following definitions shall apply to Buy/Sell Back Transactions:

    (a) "Accrued Interest", with respect to any Purchased Securities subject to a Buy/Sell Back Transaction, unpaid Income that has accrued during the period from (and including) the issue date or the last Income payment date (whichever is later) in respect of such Purchased Securities to (but excluding) the date of calculation. For these purposes unpaid Income shall be deemed to accrue on a daily basis from (and including) the issue date or the last Income payment date (as the case may be) to (but excluding) the next Income payment date or the maturity date (whichever is earlier);

    (b) "Sell Back Differential", with respect to any Buy/Sell Back Transaction as of any date, the aggregate amount obtained by daily application of the Pricing Rate for such Buy/Sell Back Transaction to the Purchase Price for such Buy/Sell Back Transaction on a 360 day per year basis (unless otherwise agreed by the parties for the Transaction) for the actual number of days during the period commencing on (and including) the Purchase Date for such Buy/Sell Back Transaction and ending on (but excluding) the date of determination;

    (c) "Sell Back Price", with respect to any Buy/Sell Back Transaction:

    (i) in relation to the date originally specified by the parties as the Repurchase Date pursuant to Paragraph 2(q) of the Agreement, the price agreed by the Parties in relation to such Buy/Sell Back Transaction, and

    (ii) in any other case (including for the purposes of the application of Paragraph 4 or Paragraph 11 of the Agreement), the product of the formula $(P + D) - (IR + C)$, where —

    P = the Purchase Price

D = the Sell Back Differential

IR = the amount of any Income in respect of the Purchased Securities paid by the issuer on any date falling between the Purchase Date and the Repurchase Date

C = the aggregate amount obtained by daily application of the Pricing Rate for such Buy/Sell Back Transaction to any such Income from (and including) the date of payment by the issuer to (but excluding) the date of calculation.

5. When entering into a Buy/Sell Back Transaction the parties shall also agree on the Sell Back Price and the Pricing Rate to apply in relation to such Buy/Sell Back Transaction on the scheduled Repurchase Date. The parties shall record the Pricing Rate in at least one Confirmation applicable to such Buy/Sell Back Transaction.

6. Termination of a Buy/Sell Back Transaction shall be effected on the Repurchase Date by transfer to Seller or its agent of Purchased Securities against the payment by Seller of (i) in a case where the Repurchase Date is the date originally agreed to by the parties pursuant to Paragraph 2(q) of the Agreement, the Sell Back Price referred to in Paragraph 4(c)(i) of this Annex; and (ii) in any other case, the Sell Back Price referred to in Paragraph 4(c)(ii) of this Annex.

7. For the avoidance of doubt, the parties acknowledge and agree that the Purchase Price and the Sell Back Price in Buy/Sell Back Transactions shall include Accrued Interest (except to the extent contrary to market practice with respect to the Securities subject to such Buy/Sell Back Transaction, in which event (i) an amount equal to the Purchase Price plus Accrued Interest to the Purchase Date shall be paid to Seller on the Purchase Date and shall be used, in lieu of the Purchase Price, for calculating the Sell Back Differential, (ii) an amount equal to the Sell Back Price plus the amount of Accrued Interest to the Repurchase Date shall be paid to Buyer on the Repurchase Date, and (iii) the formula in Paragraph 4(c)(ii) of this Annex VI shall be replaced by the formula "$(P + AI + D) - (IR + C)$", where "AI" equals Accrued Interest to the Purchase Date).

8. Unless the parties agree in Annex I to the Agreement that a Buy/Sell Back Transaction is not to be repriced, they shall at the time of repricing agree on the Purchase Price, the Sell Back Price and the Pricing Rate applicable to such Transaction.

9. Paragraph 5 of the Agreement shall not apply to Buy/Sell Back Transactions. Seller agrees, on the date such Income is received, to pay to Buyer any Income received by Seller in respect of Purchased Securities that is paid by the issuer on any date falling between the Purchase Date and the Repurchase Date.

10. References to "Repurchase Price" throughout the Agreement shall be construed as references to "Repurchase Price or the Sell Back Price, as the case may be."

11. In 11 of the Agreement, references to the "Repurchase Prices" shall be construed as references to "Repurchase Prices and Sell Back Prices."

Annex VII

Transactions Involving Registered Investment Companies

This Annex VII (including any Schedules hereto) forms a part of the Master Repurchase Agreement dated as of _____ , ____ (the "Agreement") between _____ ("Counterparty") and each investment company identified on Schedule VII.A hereto (as such schedule may be amended from time to time) acting on behalf of its respective series or portfolios identified on such Schedule VII.A, or in the case of those investment companies for which no separate series or portfolios are identified on such Schedule VII.A, acting for and on behalf of itself (each such series, portfolio or investment company, as the case may be, hereinafter referred to as a "Fund"). In the event of any conflict between the terms of this Annex VII and any other term of the Agreement, the terms of this Annex VII shall prevail. Capitalized terms used but not defined in this Annex VII shall have the meanings ascribed to them in the Agreement.

1. **Multiple Funds.** For any Transaction in which a Fund is acting as Buyer (or Seller, as the case may be), each reference in the Agreement and this Annex VII to Buyer (or Seller, as the case may be) shall be deemed a reference solely to the particular Fund to which such Transaction relates, as identified to Seller (or Buyer, as the case may be) by the Fund and as may be specified in the Confirmation therefor. In no circumstances shall the rights, obligations or remedies of either party with respect to a particular Fund constitute a right, obligation or remedy applicable to any other Fund. Specifically, and without otherwise limiting the scope of this Paragraph: (a) the margin maintenance obligations of Buyer and Seller specified in Paragraph 4 or any other provisions of the Agreement and the single agreement provisions of Paragraph 12 of the Agreement shall be applied based solely upon Transactions entered into by a particular Fund, (b) Buyer's and Seller's remedies under the Agreement upon the occurrence of an Event of Default shall be determined as if each Fund had entered into a separate Agreement with Counterparty, and (c) Seller and Buyer shall have no right to set off claims related to Transactions entered into by a particular Fund against claims related to Transactions entered into by any other Fund.

2. **Margin Percentage.** For any Transaction in which a Fund is acting as Buyer, the Buyer's Margin Percentage shall always be equal to at least ___%, or such other percentage as the parties hereto may from time to time mutually determine; provided, that in no event shall such percentage be less than 100%. For any Transaction in which a Fund is acting as Seller, the Buyer's Margin Percentage shall be such percentage as the parties hereto may from time to time mutually determine; provided, that in no event shall such percentage be less than 100%.

3. **Confirmations.** Unless otherwise agreed, Counterparty shall promptly issue a Confirmation to the Fund pursuant to Paragraph 3 of the Agreement. Upon the transfer of substituted or Additional Purchased Securities by either party, Counterparty shall promptly provide notice to the Fund confirming such transfer.

4. **Financial Condition.** Each party represents that it has delivered the following financial information to the other party to the Agreement: in the case of a party that is a registered broker-dealer, its most recent statements required to be furnished to customers by Rule 17a-5(c) under the 1934 Act; in the case of a party that is a Fund, its most recent audited or unau-

dited financial statements required to be furnished to its shareholders by Rule 30d-1 under the Investment Company Act of 1940; in the case of any other party, its most recent audited or unaudited statements of financial condition or other comparable information concerning its financial condition.

Each party represents that the financial statements or information so delivered fairly reflect its financial condition and, if applicable, its net capital ratio, on the date as of which such financial statements or information were prepared. Each party agrees that it will make available and deliver to the other party, promptly upon request, all such financial statements that subsequently are required to be delivered to its customers or shareholders pursuant to Rule 17a-5(c) or Rule 30d-1, as the case may be, or, in the case of a party that is neither a registered broker-dealer nor a Fund, all such financial information that subsequently becomes available to the public.

Each Fund acknowledges and agrees that it has made an independent evaluation of the creditworthiness of the other party that is required pursuant to the Investment Company Act of 1940 or the regulations thereunder. Each Fund agrees that its agreement to enter into each Transaction hereunder shall constitute an acknowledgment and agreement that it has made such an evaluation.

5. **Segregation of Purchased Securities.** Unless otherwise agreed by the parties, any transfer of Purchased Securities to a Fund shall be effected by delivery or other transfer (in the manner agreed upon pursuant to Paragraph 7 of the Agreement) to the custodian or subcustodian designated for such Fund in Schedule VII.A hereto ("Custodian") for credit to the Fund's custodial account with such Custodian. If the party effecting such transfer is the Fund's Custodian, such party shall, unless otherwise directed by the Fund, (a) transfer and maintain such Purchased Securities to and in the Fund's custodial account with such party and (b) so indicate in a notice to the Fund.

Schedule VII.A

Supplemental Terms and Conditions of Transactions Involving Registered Investment Companies

    This Schedule VII.A forms a part of Annex VII to the Master Repurchase Agreement dated as of _____ , ____ (the "Agreement") between _____ and _____ . Capitalized terms used but not defined in this Schedule VII.A shall have the meanings ascribed to them in Annex VII.

1. This Agreement is entered into by or on behalf of the following Funds, and unless otherwise indicated by the appropriate Fund in connection with a Transaction, the following Custodians are designated to receive transfers of Purchased Securities on behalf of such Funds for credit to the appropriate Fund's custodial account:

   Name of Fund   Custodian

[ ]. <u>Limitation of Liability.</u> If the Fund is organized as a business trust (or a series thereof), the parties agree as follows: [insert appropriate language limiting liability of trustees, officers and others].

40 Broad Street
New York, NY 10004-2373
Telephone 212.440.9400
Fax 212.440.5260
www.bondmarkets.com

APPENDIX 4

Annex VIII

Transactions in Equity Securities

This Annex VIII (including any Schedules hereto) forms a part of the Master Repurchase Agreement dated as of _____, 19__ (the "Agreement") between _____ and _____. This Annex VIII sets forth supplemental terms and conditions governing all Transactions in U.S. and non-U.S. Equity Securities. In the event of any conflict between the terms of this Annex VIII and any other term of the Agreement, the terms of this Annex VIII shall prevail. Capitalized terms used but not defined in this Annex VIII shall have the meanings ascribed to them in the Agreement.

1. **Definitions**. For the purposes of the Agreement and this Annex VIII, the following terms shall have the following meanings:

    "Equity Security", any stock or similar security; or any security convertible, with or without consideration, into such a security; or carrying any warrant or right to subscribe to or purchase such a security; or any such warrant or right; or any other "equity security" within the meaning of Section 3(a)(11) of the Exchange Act and the rules thereunder;

    "Exchange Act", the Securities Exchange Act of 1934, as amended, and all rules and regulations promulgated thereunder;

    "Market Value", with respect to Equity Securities, the meaning given in Paragraph 9 of this Annex;

    "Purchased Securities" (including any "Additional Purchased Securities"), the meaning specified in the Agreement, except that if any new or different Security or other consideration shall be exchanged for any Purchased Security by recapitalization, merger, consolidation or other corporate action, such new or different Security or other consideration shall, effective upon such exchange, be deemed to become a Purchased Security, in substitution for the former Purchased Security for which such exchange is made;

    "Securities Act", the Securities Act of 1933, as amended, and all rules and regulations promulgated thereunder;

    "Standard Settlement Date", the standard date for settlement of transactions in an Equity Security, established in accordance with Rule 15c6-1 under the Exchange Act, where applicable, or otherwise in accordance with customary market practice for such Equity Security, unless the parties agree to the contrary.

2. **Termination**. Notwithstanding Paragraph 3(c) of the Agreement, in the case of Transactions in respect of Equity Securities terminable upon demand, the termination date specified in any notice by Seller shall be a business day no earlier than the Standard Settlement Date for trades of Purchased Securities entered into at the time of such notice.

February 1998 ■ Transactions in Equity Securities ■ 1

3. **Margin Maintenance.** In addition to any agreement by the parties under Paragraph 4(f) of the Agreement, Buyer and Seller may agree, with respect to any or all Transactions under the Agreement, that the respective rights of Buyer and Seller under subparagraphs (a) and (b) of Paragraph 4 of the Agreement to require the elimination of a Margin Deficit or a Margin Excess, as the case may be, may be exercised whenever such a Margin Deficit or a Margin Excess exists with respect to any class of Transactions under the Agreement (calculated without regard to any other class of Transactions outstanding under the Agreement). The classes designated by the parties under this Paragraph may include, without limitation, Transactions in Equity Securities and Transactions in non-Equity Securities.

4. **Dividends, Distributions, etc.**

    (a) In accordance with Paragraph 5 of the Agreement, Seller shall be entitled to receive an amount equal to all Income paid or distributed on or in respect of Purchased Securities that is not otherwise received by Seller, to the full extent it would be so entitled if Purchased Securities had not been sold to Buyer. The parties expressly acknowledge and agree, for the avoidance of doubt, that such Income shall include, but not be limited to: (i) cash and all other property, (ii) stock dividends, (iii) Securities received as a result of split ups of Purchased Securities and distributions in respect thereof, (iv) interest payments and (v) all rights to purchase additional Securities (except to the extent that any amounts included in the foregoing clauses (i) through (v) would be deemed to be Purchased Securities under Paragraph 1 of this Annex).

    (b) Cash Income paid or distributed on or in respect of Purchased Securities, which Seller is entitled to receive pursuant to subparagraph (a) of this Paragraph, shall be treated in accordance with Paragraph 5 of the Agreement. Notwithstanding Paragraph 5 of the Agreement, non-cash Income received by Buyer shall be added to the Purchased Securities on the date of distribution and shall be considered such for all purposes, subject to Buyerís obligation to transfer Purchased Securities to Seller upon termination of the relevant Transaction in accordance with the terms of the Agreement.

5. **Payment and Transfer.** In addition to the transfer methods set forth in Paragraph 7 of the Agreement, Equity Securities transferred by one party hereto to the other party may be transferred through The Depository Trust Company.

6. **Additional Representations.** In addition to the representations and warranties set forth in Paragraph 10 of the Agreement, the following representations and warranties shall apply, unless otherwise agreed by the parties:

    (a) on the Purchase Date for any Transaction and again on each date that Additional Purchased Securities that are Equity Securities are transferred pursuant to Paragraph 4(a) of the Agreement, Seller represents and warrants that (i) Seller is familiar with the provisions of Rule 144 under the Securities Act, (ii) Seller is not, and within the preceding three months has not been, an "affiliate" of the issuer of any Purchased Securities or Additional Purchased Securities as that term is used in Rule 144, and (iii) any Purchased Securities or Additional Purchased Securities transferred to Buyer by Seller are not "restricted securities" within the meaning of Rule 144 or otherwise subject to any legal, regulatory or contractual restrictions on transfer; and

(b) on the Repurchase Date for any Transaction and on each date that Purchased Securities that are Equity Securities are transferred pursuant to Paragraph 4(b) of the Agreement, Buyer represents and warrants that (i) Buyer is familiar with the provisions of Rule 144 under the Securities Act, (ii) Buyer is not, and within the preceding three months has not been, an "affiliate" of the issuer of any Purchased Securities as that term is used in Rule 144, and (iii) assuming the accuracy and completeness of Seller's representations under subparagraph (a) of this Paragraph, any Purchased Securities transferred to Seller by Buyer are not "restricted securities" within the meaning of Rule 144 or otherwise subject to any legal, regulatory or contractual restrictions on transfer.

7. **Rights of Buyer in Purchased Securities**. Except as otherwise agreed by the parties, Seller waives the right to vote, or to provide any consent or to take any similar action with respect to, Purchased Securities that are Equity Securities in the event that the record date or deadline for such vote, consent or other action falls during the term of a Transaction.

8. **Events of Default**. In addition to the Events of Default set forth in Paragraph 11 of the Agreement, it shall be an additional "Event of Default" if either party fails to perform any covenant or obligation required to be performed by it under this Annex VIII, provided, however, that to the extent that Paragraphs 3 and 4 hereof supplement and amend, respectively, Paragraphs 4 and 5 of the Agreement, any such failure under Paragraphs 3 or 4 hereof shall constitute an "Event of Default" only after the expiration of the notice period, if any, specified in the Agreement with respect to the occurrence of an Event of Default for such a failure under such Paragraph 4 or 5 of the Agreement, as applicable.

9. **Market Value**

   (a) Unless otherwise agreed, if the principal market for the Equity Securities to be valued is a national securities exchange in the United States, their Market Value shall be determined by their last sale price on such exchange on the preceding business day or, if there was no sale on that day, by the last sale price on the next preceding business day on which there was a sale on such exchange, all as quoted on the Consolidated Tape or, if not quoted on the Consolidated Tape, then as quoted by such exchange.

   (b) Except as provided in subparagraph (c) of this Paragraph or as otherwise agreed, if the principal market for the Equity Securities to be valued is the over-the-counter market, their Market Value shall be determined as follows. If the Equity Securities are quoted on The Nasdaq Stock Market ("Nasdaq"), their Market Value shall be the closing sale price on Nasdaq on the preceding business day or, if the Equity Securities are issues for which last sale prices are not quoted on Nasdaq, the closing bid price on such day. If the Equity Securities to be valued are not quoted on Nasdaq, their Market Value shall be the highest bid quotation as quoted in any of The Wall Street Journal, the OTC Bulletin Board service, quotations sheets of registered market makers and, if necessary, dealers' telephone quotations on the preceding business day. In each case, if the relevant quotation did not exist on such day, then the relevant quotation on the next preceding business day in which there was such a quotation shall be the Market Value.

   (c) Unless otherwise agreed, if the Equity Securities to be valued are principally cleared and settled outside the United States, their Market Value shall be determined as of the close of business on the preceding business day in accordance with market practice in the principal market for such Equity Securities.

(d) All determinations of Market Value under subparagraphs (a), (b) and (c) of this Paragraph shall include, where applicable, accrued Income to the extent not already included therein (other than any Income transferred to the other party pursuant to Paragraph 4 of this Annex), unless market practice with respect to the valuation of such Equity Securities in connection with repurchase agreements is to the contrary.

10. **Additional Covenant**. Except to the extent required by applicable law or regulation or as otherwise agreed, Seller and Buyer agree that Transactions hereunder shall in no event be "exchange contracts" for purposes of the rules of any securities exchange and that Transactions hereunder shall not be governed by the buy-in or other rules of any such exchange, registered national securities association or other self-regulatory organization.

Schedule VIII.A

Additional Provisions Regarding Transactions in Equity Securities

This Schedule VIII.A forms a part of Annex VIII to the Master Repurchase Agreement dated as of _____, 19__ (the "Agreement") between _____ and _____. Capitalized terms used but not defined in this Schedule VIII.A shall have the meanings ascribed to them in Annex VIII.

Annex IX

Transactions Involving Certain Japanese Financial Institutions

This Annex IX forms part of the Master Repurchase Agreement dated as of _____ (the "Agreement") between _____ and _____. Capitalized terms used but not defined in this Annex IX shall have the meanings ascribed to them in the Agreement. Paragraph references are to paragraphs in the Agreement unless otherwise set out herein.

1. This Annex IX shall apply only to those Transactions where (a) one of the parties is, and the other party is not, resident in Japan for tax purposes and (b) where the parties have agreed that the Securities (whether Purchased Securities or Additional Purchased Securities) utilized in Transactions conducted pursuant to the Agreement will comprise or include Exempt Securities. For the purposes of this Annex IX, "Exempt Securities" means Securities which are specified in the Tax Special Measurement Law (*sozei tokubetsu sochi hou*) of Japan (Law No.26 of 1957), as amended (the "Tax Special Measurement Law"), and the Cabinet Order of the Tax Special Measurement Law (Cabinet Order No.43 of 1957), as amended (the "Cabinet Order"), for the purpose of the exemption from the withholding of the interests received from certain Japanese financial institutions as specified in the Tax Special Measurement Law and the Cabinet Order, with respect to the transactions of sale and repurchase of, or those of the sale and purchase with buy/sell back conditions of, Securities; provided that such transactions meet the requirements as provided in the relevant laws and regulations. Notwithstanding the above, this Annex IX shall not apply to any Transactions which utilize Securities (whether Purchased Securities or Additional Purchased Securities) issued in Japan (including, for example, Securities issued by a private entity organized under the laws of Japan, or those issued by public or Japanese government entities, such as Japanese Government Bonds).

2. In the event of any conflict between the terms and conditions of this Annex IX and any other term of the Agreement or any Annex to the Agreement, the terms in this Annex shall prevail to the extent of such inconsistency.

3. Delete "or other assets" between the word "securities" and "("Securities")" in the second line of Paragraph 1.

4. Notwithstanding Paragraph 2, clauses (a)(i) and (a)(ii) in the Master Repurchase Agreement, "Act of Insolvency" shall occur with respect to any party hereto immediately upon the voluntary or involuntary filing of a petition in respect of it (including by the counterparty to the Agreement in respect of any obligation under the Agreement) with any court in Japan for the bankruptcy (*hasan*), corporate reorganization (*kaisha kosei*) or civil rehabilitation (*minji saisei*) of such party (the "Close-out Netting Event").

5. For the avoidance of doubt, and in addition to any other remedies available to the parties under Paragraph 11, immediately upon the occurrence of a Close-out Netting Event, regardless of the intent of the parties, without taking any procedure or entering into any arrangement, such as a notice or demand from one party to the other or any

August 2002 – Master Repurchase Agreement

agreement between the parties, the sum due from one party in respect of all Transactions under the Agreement shall be set off against the sum due from the other in respect of all Transactions under the Agreement and only the balance shall be due and payable and constitute a single obligation or claim; provided that the conversion or valuation of the currency or the Securities for the purpose of the set-off shall be made in accordance with the Enforcement Regulations for the Law concerning Close-out Netting of Specified Transactions Entered into by Financial Institutions, etc. (The joint Ministerial Ordinance of the Prime Minister's Office and Ministry of Finance No.48 of 1998). In the event that (a) Annex III to the Agreement has been executed and made part of the Agreement, and (b) the conversion or valuation described in the prior sentence conflicts with the Contractual Currency, the conversion or valuation described in the prior sentence will prevail.

6. Add the following clause to Paragraph 19:

"(e) It is understood that this Agreement is intended to constitute a "Master Agreement" as defined in the Law concerning Close-out Netting of Specified Financial Transactions Entered into by Financial Institutions, etc. (Law No.108 of 1998), as amended (the "Close-out Netting Law") and if any provision concerning the netting or set-off contained in the Agreement or Annexes is inconsistent with or conflicts with the provisions of the Close-out Netting Law, the Enforcement Regulations for the Close-out Netting Law (the "Enforcement Regulations"), or the Enforcement Order for the Close-out Netting Law (the "Close-out Cabinet Order"), then the provisions of the Close-out Netting Law, Enforcement Regulations or the Close-out Cabinet Order shall prevail."

Except as amended herein, the Agreement shall continue to have full force and effect in all respects.

Appendix 5

Custodial Undertaking in Connection with Master Repurchase Agreement

(April 2003 version)

The Bank of New York

Reproduced with the kind permission of
The Bank of New York

CUSTODIAL UNDERTAKING IN CONNECTION

WITH MASTER REPURCHASE AGREEMENT
[April 2003 version]

****

BY AND AMONG

_____

(Buyer)

AND

_____

(Seller)

AND

THE BANK OF NEW YORK

(Custodian)

APPENDIX 5

THIS **CUSTODIAL UNDERTAKING** is made and entered into as of the date set forth below by and among Buyer, Seller, and Custodian.

RECITALS

WHEREAS, Buyer and Seller have entered into a TBMA Master Repurchase Agreement dated as of _____ (as it may be amended by the parties thereto, the "Master Repurchase Agreement"), and may from time to time enter into Transactions with respect to Eligible Securities (as hereinafter defined); and

WHEREAS, Custodian has agreed to act as agent for Buyer and Seller in order to effect Transactions on their behalf, all as more particularly set forth herein;

NOW, THEREFORE, in consideration of the mutual promises hereinafter set forth, the parties hereto agree as follows:

1. DEFINITIONS

Whenever used in this Custodial Undertaking, the following words shall have the meanings set forth below. Capitalized terms used but not defined herein shall have the meanings given them in the Master Repurchase Agreement.

A. "Authorized Person" shall mean any person, whether or not any such person is an officer or employee of Buyer or Seller, as the case may be, duly authorized to give Oral Instructions and Written Instructions on behalf of Buyer or Seller, such persons and their specimen signatures to be designated in Schedule II attached hereto; as such Schedule II may be amended from time to time.

B. "Book-Entry Securities" shall mean Book-entry Securities as defined in 31 C.F.R. Part 357.2 and any other securities registered in the form of an entry on the records of the Book-Entry System.

C. "Book-Entry System" shall mean the Treasury/Reserve Automated Debt Entry System maintained at The Federal Reserve Bank of New York ("FRBNY").

D. "Business Day" shall mean any day on which Custodian, Seller, the Book-Entry System and appropriate Clearing Corporation(s) are open for business.

E. "Buyer's Account" shall mean each custodial account maintained by Custodian on behalf of Buyer for the deposit of Eligible Securities with respect to Transactions and, for such purpose, Buyer's Account shall be deemed to be a "securities account" within the meaning of the UCC. For purposes of this Custodial Undertaking, Buyer's Account shall include any account for the deposit of cash in connection therewith.

F. "Clearing Corporation" shall mean The Depository Trust Company, Fixed Income Clearing Corporation, and any other clearing corporation within the meaning of Section 8-102 of the UCC or otherwise authorized to act as a securities depository or clearing agency.

G. "Clearing Corporation Securities" shall mean securities which are registered in the name of Custodian or its nominee in the form of an entry on the records of a Clearing Corporation.

H. "Eligible Securities" shall mean those types of Securities which Buyer, Seller and Custodian have agreed shall be eligible for Transactions by inclusion on a Schedule of Eligible Securities substantially in the form of Schedule I hereto, as such Schedule of Eligible Securities may be amended from time to time, and cash.

I. "Margin Percentage" shall mean the percentage indicated on Schedule I with respect to specific types of Eligible Securities, as Schedule I may be amended from time to time.

J. "Margin Value" shall mean the amount obtained by dividing the Market Value of Securities by the applicable Margin Percentage.

K. "Market Value of Securities" shall mean with respect to any Security as of any date, the sum of (i) the market value of such Security based on the most recently available closing bid price (usually from the previous Business Day) for the particular Security as made available to Custodian by pricing information services which Custodian uses generally for pricing such Securities, and (ii) accrued but unpaid Income, if any, on the particular Security (to the extent not included therein). In the case of cash and certificates of deposit, the face amount shall be deemed the Market Value. In the event that Custodian is unable to obtain the price of a particular Security from such pricing information services on any Business Day, the Market Value shall be as determined by Custodian in the reasonable exercise of its discretion based on information furnished to Custodian by one or more brokers (excluding

Seller) in such Security or Custodian may price such Security using a formula utilized by Custodian for such purpose in the ordinary course of its business.

L. **"Notice of Default"** shall mean a written notice delivered by Buyer to Custodian and Seller, or by Seller to Custodian and Buyer, informing Custodian and the defaulting party of an Event of Default pursuant to Paragraph 11 of the Master Repurchase Agreement and setting forth the specific Event of Default thereunder.

M. **"Oral Instructions"** shall mean verbal communications received by Custodian from an Authorized Person.

N. **"Physical Securities"** shall mean securities and money market instruments issued in definitive form which are not Book-Entry Securities or Clearing Corporation Securities.

O. **"Purchased Securities"** shall mean Eligible Securities transferred to Buyer's Account in connection with Transactions.

P. **"Securities"** shall mean Book-Entry Securities, Clearing Corporation Securities, Physical Securities and cash.

Q. **"Seller's Account"** shall mean Seller's clearing account on Custodian's Government Securities Clearance System ("GSCS"), any other account in which Securities are held by Custodian on behalf of Seller pursuant to the terms of this Custodial Undertaking and any account for the deposit of cash maintained in connection therewith.

R. **"UCC"** shall mean the Uniform Commercial Code of the State of New York (as may be amended from time to time).

S. **"Written Instructions"** shall mean written communications received by Custodian from an Authorized Person by telex, facsimile, through GSCS or any other electronic system whereby the receiver of such communications is able to verify by codes, passwords or otherwise with a reasonable degree of certainty the identity of the sender of such communications.

All references to time in this Custodial Undertaking shall mean the time in effect on that day in New York, New York. Except as may otherwise apply for Income payable on particular Securities or as otherwise may be agreed to in writing by the parties hereto, all provisions in this Custodial Undertaking for the transfer, payment or receipt of funds or cash shall mean transfer of, payment in, or receipt of, United States dollars in immediately available funds.

2. APPOINTMENT OF CUSTODIAN; AUTHORIZATION

A. Buyer and Seller hereby appoint Custodian as custodian of all Securities and cash at any time delivered to Custodian in connection with Transactions subject to this Custodial Undertaking and as their agent to effect Transactions. Custodian hereby accepts appointment as custodian and agent.

B. Buyer and Seller each authorizes and instructs Custodian to utilize the Book-Entry System, Clearing Corporations and the receipt and delivery of physical certificates or any combination thereof in connection with its performance hereunder. Book-Entry Securities and Clearing Corporation Securities credited to Buyer's Account and Seller's Account will be represented in accounts at the Book-Entry System and the appropriate Clearing Corporation in the name of Custodian or its nominee which include only assets held by Custodian for its customers and shall not include any assets held by Custodian in its individual capacity. Transactions with respect to Book-Entry Securities and Clearing Corporation Securities will be effected in accordance with, and subject to, the rules, regulations, operating procedures and custody arrangements of the Book-Entry System and each Clearing Corporation, respectively.

3. REPRESENTATIONS AND WARRANTIES

A. **Buyer, Seller and Custodian.** Buyer, Seller and Custodian each represents and warrants, which representations and warranties shall be deemed to be repeated on each Purchase Date and each Repurchase Date, that:

(i) It is duly organized and existing under the laws of the jurisdiction of its organization with full power and authority to execute and deliver this Custodial Undertaking and to perform all of the duties and obligations to be performed by it hereunder;

(ii) This Custodial Undertaking is, and each Transaction (with respect to Buyer and Seller only) will be, legally and validly entered into, does not, and will not, violate any ordinance, charter, by-law, rule or statute applicable to it, and is enforceable in accordance with its terms, except as may be limited by bankruptcy, insolvency or similar laws, or by equitable principles relating to or limiting creditors' rights generally; and

(iii) The person executing this Custodial Undertaking on its behalf has been duly and properly authorized to do so.

APPENDIX 5

-3-

B. **Further Representations of Custodian.** Custodian further represents and warrants, which representations and warranties shall be deemed to be repeated on each Purchase Date and each Repurchase Date, that:

(i) It is a New York trust company with its principal office at One Wall Street, New York, New York 10286;

(ii) It will maintain Buyer's Account as a custody account and shall administer Buyer's Account in the same manner it administers similar accounts established for the same purpose; and

(iii) It maintains a book-entry securities account with FRBNY and each Clearing Corporation in which it holds Securities hereunder.

4. **DEPOSIT OF CASH AND ELIGIBLE SECURITIES**

A. **Seller's Instructions.** On each Business Day that Seller and Buyer agree to enter into a Transaction subject to this Custodial Undertaking, Seller shall deliver to Custodian, prior to 2:00 p.m., Oral or Written Instructions containing the following information:

(i) the Purchase Date and Purchase Price;

(ii) the Repurchase Date and Repurchase Price (or rate); and

(iii) name of Buyer.

B. **Seller's Tender of Securities.** By the close of business on the Purchase Date, Seller shall transfer, or cause to be transferred, to Seller's Account sufficient Eligible Securities to complete Transactions on such Purchase Date. In connection therewith, Seller shall either deliver to Custodian Oral or Written Instructions identifying the Eligible Securities to be sold by Seller to Buyer, including a description setting forth the face amount of each Eligible Security and, where applicable, the CUSIP number for each such Eligible Security or instruct Custodian to identify Eligible Securities in Seller's Account to be transferred to Buyer's Account.

C. **Buyer's Purchase Price.** Prior to 4:00 p.m. on the Purchase Date, Buyer shall transfer, or cause to be transferred, to Buyer's Account sufficient cash such that the total cash balance in Buyer's Account after such transfer equals or exceeds the Purchase Price contained in Seller's Oral or Written Instructions.

5. **EFFECTING TRANSACTIONS**

A. **Purchase Date.** On the Purchase Date for any Transaction subject to this Custodial Undertaking, Custodian shall transfer to Seller's Account cash from Buyer's Account in an amount equal to the Purchase Price and transfer from Seller's Account to Buyer's Account Eligible Securities in accordance with Seller's Oral or Written Instructions with respect to such Transaction, subject to the following provisions:

(i) **Determination of Eligible Securities; Negotiability.** Custodian shall determine that Securities to be transferred to Buyer's Account are Eligible Securities and that Physical Securities are in negotiable form. Any Securities which are not Eligible Securities and any Physical Securities which are not in negotiable form shall not be included in the calculations set forth below and shall not be transferred to Buyer's Account.

(ii) **Determination of Margin Value.** Custodian shall determine the Margin Value of Eligible Securities to be transferred to Buyer's Account.

(iii) **Payment of Purchase Price.** Provided the Margin Value of Eligible Securities to be transferred to Buyer's Account equals or exceeds the Purchase Price with respect to such Transaction, Custodian shall transfer such Eligible Securities from Seller's Account to Buyer's Account and shall disburse from Buyer's Account to Seller's Account cash in an amount equal to the Purchase Price.

(iv) **Maintenance of Buyer's Account.**

(a) **Physical Securities.** Custodian shall take possession of each Eligible Security which is a Physical Security at a secure facility at one of its offices in New York City and, during the term of a particular Transaction, shall identify such Physical Securities on its books and records as belonging to Buyer.

(b) **Book-Entry Securities.** Each Eligible Security which is either (i) a Book-Entry Security, or (ii) a part of a fungible bulk of Book-Entry Securities shall be continuously maintained by Custodian in the Book-Entry System. During the term of a particular Transaction, Custodian shall identify such Book-Entry Securities on its books and records as belonging to Buyer.

(c) **Clearing Corporation Securities.** Each Eligible Security which is either (i) a Clearing Corporation Security, or (ii) part of a fungible bulk of Clearing Corporation Securities shall be continuously maintained by Custodian in an account with the appropriate Clearing Corporation. During the term of a particular Transaction, Custodian shall continuously identify such Clearing Corporation Securities on its books and records as belonging to Buyer.

(v) **Intent of Buyer and Seller.** Buyer and Seller agree that it is intended that Custodian act as a "securities intermediary" as such term is defined in the UCC with respect to Transactions hereunder. In addition, the parties intend that all Securities in Buyer's Account and Seller's Account (excluding cash) shall be treated as "financial assets" as such term is defined in the UCC.

B. **Trust Receipts.** Custodian is hereby authorized and directed to accept trust receipts as may be set forth in Schedule I hereto (each, a "Trust Receipt") evidencing either the holding by the issuer of such Trust Receipt (a "Trust Receipt Issuer") of Eligible Securities subject to Transactions or the crediting by the Trust Receipt Issuer to the account of Custodian of Eligible Securities subject to Transactions. Any Trust Receipt may be accompanied by an electronic file sent by Seller to Custodian containing information concerning the Eligible Securities represented by such Trust Receipts, including CUSIP number, par amount, maturity date and interest rates, upon which Custodian shall be entitled to rely without inquiry in performing its duties hereunder. Buyer may by Written Instructions direct Custodian not to accept Trust Receipts from particular Trust Receipt Issuers. Custodian shall hold Trust Receipts at a secure facility at one of its offices in New York City and, during the term of a particular Transaction, shall identify the Eligible Securities represented by Trust Receipts on its books and records as belonging to Buyer.

C. **Custodian's Inability to Complete a Transaction.** If Custodian is unable to complete a Transaction because Seller has failed to provide complete Oral or Written Instructions as required by Paragraphs 4A and 4B or either Buyer or Seller has failed to arrange for the transfer of sufficient cash or Eligible Securities to Buyer's Account or Seller's Account, respectively, Custodian shall promptly notify Seller and Buyer and await the receipt of such Oral or Written Instructions, cash or Eligible Securities. If Custodian has not received Oral or Written Instructions from Seller by 4:30 p.m., sufficient cash from Buyer by the close of the FRBNY money wire or sufficient Eligible Securities by the close of GSCS or the appropriate Clearing Corporation or such time as Custodian may designate with respect to particular types of Physical Securities, Buyer and Seller irrevocably agree and instruct Custodian to effect the Transaction as follows: (i) if the cash balance in Buyer's Account shall be less than the Purchase Price set forth in Seller's Instructions, the cash balance in Buyer's Account shall be deemed to be the Purchase Price, the remaining terms of the Transaction shall be determined in accordance with Paragraph 5A, and Seller shall provide Custodian with further Oral or Written Instructions with respect to a recalculated Repurchase Price for such Transaction; or (ii) if the cash in Buyer's Account exceeds the Margin Value of Eligible Securities in Seller's Account, Custodian shall credit to Seller's Account cash in an amount equal to the Margin Value of the Eligible Securities, and the difference between the amount credited to Seller's Account and the Purchase Price shall be retained by Buyer and held by Custodian in Buyer's Account. In any event, Buyer and Seller shall remain obligated to each other pursuant to the original terms of each Transaction.

D. **Simultaneous Transaction.** Buyer and Seller agree that in effecting Transactions transfers between Buyer's Account and Seller's Account are intended to be, and shall be deemed to be, simultaneous.

E. **Ownership of Securities.** (i) Upon the transfer of cash to Seller's Account and the transfer of Eligible Securities to Buyer's Account, it is agreed by Seller and Buyer that, subject to Seller's right of substitution pursuant to Paragraph 6B and notwithstanding the credit of Income to Seller's Account pursuant to Paragraph 5G, the Purchased Securities shall be for all purposes the property of Buyer. Buyer agrees, however, that, subject to Paragraph 8 hereof and Paragraph 11 of the Master Repurchase Agreement, it will resell to Seller on the Repurchase Date the Purchased Securities at the Repurchase Price.

(ii) Buyer, Seller and Custodian agree that all Purchased Securities and cash held in Buyer's Account from time to time will be held by Custodian as agent of Buyer, that Custodian will take such actions with respect to Buyer's Account and any Purchased Securities and cash therein as Buyer shall direct, and that in no event shall any consent of Seller be required for the taking of any such action by Custodian. Buyer hereby covenants that Buyer will not instruct Custodian to deliver any Securities to any person other than Seller until an Event of Default has occurred as to which Seller is the defaulting party. The foregoing covenant is for Seller's benefit only and shall not constitute a limitation on Buyer's right at any time to instruct Custodian and Custodian's obligation to act upon such

APPENDIX 5

-5-

instructions. Custodian shall not be liable for any Losses (as defined in paragraph 9A) incurred or sustained by Buyer, Seller or any third party as a result of Custodian transferring any Purchased Securities or cash in Buyer's Account pursuant to Buyer's instructions (whether or not subsequent to receipt of a Notice of Default) and shall have no further obligation or responsibility to Seller or Buyer under this Custodial Undertaking with respect to any Purchased Securities or cash transferred from Buyer's Account.

(iii) Any instruction to Custodian to transfer Purchased Securities or cash from Buyer's Account during the term of a Transaction shall be set forth in a written notice in substantially the form attached hereto as Appendix I. Buyer shall deliver such notice to a Vice President or above in Custodian's Broker Dealer Services Division and shall send Seller a copy of same. Custodian shall, as promptly as practicable under the circumstances, act in accordance with such instructions; it being understood and agreed that Custodian shall have no liability for its inability to comply with Buyer's instructions if the rules or systems of the Book-Entry System and/or applicable Clearing Corporation prevent Custodian from transferring Purchased Securities from Buyer's Account. Buyer shall pay to Custodian all applicable fees, costs and charges associated with such transfer from Buyer's Account.

F. No Lien or Pledge by Custodian. Custodian agrees that Purchased Securities shall not be subject to any security interest, lien or right of setoff by Custodian or any third party claiming through Custodian and Custodian shall not pledge, encumber, hypothecate, transfer, dispose of, or otherwise grant any third party an interest in, any Purchased Securities.

G. Payment of Income. Until such time that Custodian shall receive a Notice of Default from Buyer pursuant to Paragraph 8, Custodian shall credit to Seller's Account Income received by Custodian. After receipt of such Notice of Default from Buyer, Custodian shall credit to Buyer's Account Income received by Custodian.

H. Confirmations. Custodian shall provide Buyer and Seller with confirmation statements reflecting Purchased Securities and cash positions in Buyer's Account on each Business Day or as otherwise may be requested by Buyer. Buyer and Seller shall promptly review all such confirmation statements and shall promptly advise Custodian of any error, omission or inaccuracy in such statements. Custodian shall undertake to correct any errors, failures or omissions that are reported to Custodian by Buyer or Seller. Any such corrections shall be reflected on subsequent confirmation statements.

I. Deliveries by Custodian. Subject to this Custodial Undertaking, all transfers of Securities or cash by Custodian to Buyer from Buyer's Account shall be made to Buyer by delivery to the account(s) designated in Schedule III, as may be amended from time to time by delivery to and receipt by Custodian of a new Schedule III.

6. VALUATION AND SUBSTITUTIONS OF SECURITIES

A. Valuation of Securities. At the opening of each Business Day during which a Transaction subject to this Custodial Undertaking shall remain outstanding, Custodian shall determine the Margin Value of all Purchased Securities in Buyer's Account.

(i) **Margin Deficit.** In the event the Purchase Price of outstanding Transactions is greater than the aggregate Margin Value of all Purchased Securities in Buyer's Account, Custodian shall so notify Seller prior to 2:00 p.m. On the date of any such notice, Seller shall promptly transfer to Buyer's Account additional Eligible Securities ("Additional Eligible Securities") such that, after transfer to Buyer's Account, the aggregate Margin Value of all Purchased Securities (including Additional Eligible Securities) in Buyer's Account equals or exceeds the Purchase Price of outstanding Transactions. If Seller fails to transfer an appropriate amount of Additional Eligible Securities on the date of any such notice, Custodian shall notify Buyer and Seller and await further instructions from Buyer. All Additional Eligible Securities transferred to Buyer's Account shall be deemed to be Purchased Securities.

(ii) **Margin Excess.** In the event the then aggregate Margin Value of Purchased Securities in Buyer's Account shall exceed the Purchase Price of outstanding Transactions (such excess amount, the "Margin Excess"), Custodian shall so notify Seller and, upon Oral or Written Instructions from Seller, Custodian shall transfer Purchased Securities from Buyer's Account to Seller's Account having a Market Value equal to the Margin Excess. Buyer hereby irrevocably authorizes Custodian to accept the Oral or Written Instructions of Seller identifying the specific Purchased Securities to be released from Buyer's Account pursuant hereto. Upon transfer from Buyer's Account, released Securities shall cease to be Purchased Securities for all purposes hereunder.

B. Substitutions of Purchased Securities. Buyer hereby authorizes Custodian, upon Oral or Written Instructions from Seller, to transfer Purchased Securities to Seller against transfer to Buyer's Account of substitute Eligible Securities ("Substitute Eligible Securities") provided that Custodian determines that the aggregate Margin Value of Purchase Securities (including Substitute Eligible Securities) in Buyer's Account after such substitution equals or exceeds the Purchase Price of outstanding Transactions. All Substitute Eligible Securities transferred to Buyer's Account shall be deemed to be Purchased Securities.

7. REPURCHASE DATE

-6-

On the Repurchase Date for any Transaction, subject to Paragraph 8 hereof and Paragraph 11 of the Master Repurchase Agreement, Buyer hereby irrevocably instructs Custodian to tender to Seller the Purchased Securities with respect to such Transaction and to transfer such Purchased Securities from Buyer's Account to Seller's Account. Seller hereby irrevocably instructs Custodian at the time Purchased Securities are transferred to Seller's Account to make payment to Buyer of the Repurchase Price by debiting cash from Seller's Account and crediting cash to Buyer's Account. If on the Repurchase Date Seller's Account does not contain sufficient cash available to repurchase all Purchased Securities with respect to any Transactions, Custodian shall notify Seller and Buyer and Seller shall give Custodian Oral or Written Instructions identifying which Purchased Securities, if any, are to be repurchased and the Repurchase Price.

8. DEFAULT

In the event that Buyer or Seller delivers a Notice of Default to Custodian, Custodian shall notify the defaulting party of its receipt of such Notice of Default and act in accordance with the instructions of the non-defaulting party with respect to such non-defaulting party's rights pursuant to Paragraph 11 of the Master Repurchase Agreement. Custodian may fully rely without further inquiry on the statements set forth in such Notice of Default. In addition, Buyer and Seller acknowledge and agree that the provisions of Paragraph 11 of the Master Repurchase Agreement shall be fully effective with respect to all Transactions entered into between them, irrespective of whether such Transactions are entered into in connection with this Custodial Undertaking, directly between Buyer and Seller or otherwise.

9. CONCERNING CUSTODIAN

A. Limitation of Liability; Indemnification. Custodian shall not be liable for any costs, expenses, damages, liabilities or claims, including reasonable fees of counsel (collectively, "Losses"), resulting from its action or inaction in connection with this Custodial Undertaking, including Losses which are incurred by reason of any action or inaction by the Book-Entry System, any Clearing Corporation or Trust Receipt Issuer, or their successors or nominees, except for those Losses arising out of Custodian's gross negligence, bad faith or willful misconduct. In no event shall Custodian be liable to Buyer, Seller or any third party for special, indirect or consequential damages, or lost profits or loss of business, arising under or in connection with this Custodial Undertaking. Custodian may, with respect to questions of law, apply for and obtain the advice and opinion of counsel, and shall be fully protected with respect to anything done or omitted by it in good faith in conformity with such reasonable advice or opinion. Buyer and Seller agree, jointly and severally, to indemnify Custodian and to hold it harmless against any and all Losses (including claims by Buyer or Seller) which are sustained by Custodian as a result of Custodian's action or inaction in connection with this Custodial Undertaking, except those Losses arising out of Custodian's gross negligence, bad faith or willful misconduct. It is expressly understood and agreed that Custodian's right to indemnification hereunder shall be enforceable against Buyer and Seller directly, without any obligation to first proceed against any third party for whom they may act, and irrespective of any rights or recourse that Buyer or Seller may have against any such third party. This indemnity shall be a continuing obligation of Buyer and Seller notwithstanding the termination of any Transactions or of this Custodial Undertaking.

B. No Guaranty by Custodian. It is expressly agreed and acknowledged by Buyer and Seller that Custodian has made no determination regarding Buyer's or Seller's ability to perform their respective obligations in connection with Transactions and is not guaranteeing performance of or assuming any liability for the obligations of Buyer or Seller hereunder nor is it assuming any credit risk associated with Transactions hereunder, which liabilities and risks are the responsibility of Buyer and Seller; further, it is expressly agreed that Custodian is not undertaking to make credit available to Seller or Buyer to enable it to complete Transactions hereunder.

C. No Duty of Inquiry. Without limiting the generality of the foregoing, Custodian shall be under no obligation to inquire into, and shall not be liable for:

(i) The validity of the issue of any Securities purchased or sold by or for Buyer or Seller, the legality of the purchase or sale or the validity or enforceability of any Trust Receipt received by Custodian hereunder;

(ii) The due authority of any Authorized Person to act on behalf of Buyer or Seller with respect to cash or Securities held in Buyer's Account or Seller's Account; or

(iii) The due authority of Buyer, Seller or any entities for which Buyer acts to purchase, sell or hold any particular Security hereunder.

D. Securities in Default. Custodian shall not be under any duty or obligation to take action to effect collection of any amount if the Securities upon which such amount is payable are in default, or if payment is refused after due demand or presentation, unless and

-7-

until (i) it shall be directed to take such action by Written Instructions and (ii) it shall be assured to its satisfaction of reimbursement of its costs and expenses in connection with any such action.

E. Custodian Fee. Custodian shall be entitled to receive and Seller agrees to pay to Custodian such compensation as may be agreed upon from time to time between Custodian and Seller and Custodian's out-of-pocket expenses.

F. Reliance on Oral/Written Instructions. Custodian shall be entitled to rely upon any Written Instruction or Oral Instruction received by Custodian and reasonably believed by Custodian to be delivered by an Authorized Person. Buyer and Seller agree to forward to Custodian Written Instructions confirming any and all Oral Instructions in such manner that such Written Instructions are received by Custodian by the close of business of the same day that such Oral Instructions are given to Custodian. Buyer and Seller agree that the fact that such confirming Written Instructions are not received or that contrary Written Instructions are received by Custodian shall in no way affect the validity or enforceability of the transactions previously authorized and effected by Custodian.

G. Reliance on Pricing Services. Custodian is authorized to utilize any generally recognized pricing information service (including brokers and dealers of Securities) in order to perform its valuation responsibilities hereunder, and Seller and Buyer agree to hold Custodian harmless from and against any Losses incurred as a result of errors or omissions of any such pricing information service, broker or dealer.

H. Force Majeure. Custodian shall not be responsible or liable for any failure or delay in the performance of its obligations under this Custodial Undertaking arising out of or caused, directly or indirectly, by circumstances beyond its reasonable control, including without limitation, acts of God, earthquakes, fires, floods, wars, civil or military disturbances, sabotage, epidemics, riots, loss or malfunctions of utilities, computer (hardware or software) or communications service, labor disputes, acts of civil or military authority, or governmental, judicial or regulatory actions; provided however, that Custodian shall use its best efforts to resume performance as promptly as practicable under the circumstances.

I. No Additional Duties. Custodian shall have no duties or responsibilities except such duties and responsibilities as are specifically set forth in this Custodial Undertaking, and no covenant or obligation shall be implied in this Custodial Undertaking against Custodian.

J. No Duty Regarding Derivatives. If Buyer and Seller have selected Eligible Securities which derive all or a portion of their value from changes in the value of underlying securities, mortgages or other obligations, or one or more currencies, commodities, indices or other factors (hereinafter referred to as "Derivative Securities"), the parties understand that Custodian shall have no obligation to monitor whether any such Eligible Securities are also Derivative Securities. Accordingly, the parties agree that anything in the Custodial Undertaking to the contrary notwithstanding, it shall be Buyer's and Seller's responsibility to ensure that Eligible Securities do not include Derivative Securities unless they have otherwise agreed. Custodian shall have no liability whatsoever for any loss, damage or expense arising out of the ineligibility of Derivative Securities which are the subject of Transactions pursuant to this Custodial Undertaking.

10. TERMINATION

Any of the parties hereto may terminate this Custodial Undertaking by giving to the other parties a notice in writing specifying the date of such termination, which shall be not less than thirty (30) days after the date of giving of such notice. Upon termination hereof, Seller shall pay to Custodian such compensation as may be due to Custodian as of the date of such termination, and shall likewise reimburse Custodian for any disbursements and expenses made or incurred by Custodian and payable or reimbursable hereunder. If Buyer does not provide Written Instructions designating a successor custodian prior to the termination date, Custodian shall, at Buyer's expense, continue to hold Purchased Securities and cash in Buyer's Account until the Repurchase Date with respect to each outstanding Transaction, or until it has received a Notice of Default in connection therewith, and Written Instructions with respect to delivery of such Purchased Securities. If Custodian has not received delivery instructions with respect to Purchased Securities and/or cash in Buyer's Account, Custodian may, in its sole discretion, hold Book-Entry Securities and Clearing Corporation Securities in escrow for the benefit of and at the expense of Buyer and deliver Physical Securities and cash to Buyer at the address provided below.

11. MISCELLANEOUS

A. Authorized Persons. Buyer and Seller each agrees to furnish to Custodian a new Schedule II in the event that any Authorized Person ceases to be an Authorized Person or in the event that other or additional Authorized Persons are appointed and authorized. Until such new Schedule II is received, Custodian shall be fully protected in acting under the provisions of this Custodial Undertaking upon Oral Instructions or Written Instructions from a person reasonably believed to be an Authorized Person as set forth in the last delivered Schedule II.

-8-

B. **Access to Books and Records**. Upon reasonable request, Buyer and Seller shall have access to Custodian's books and records maintained in connection with this Custodial Undertaking during Custodian's normal business hours. Upon reasonable request, copies of any such books and records shall be provided to Buyer or Seller at its expense.

C. **Invalidity of any Provision**. In case any provision in or obligation under this Custodial Undertaking shall be invalid, illegal or unenforceable in any jurisdiction, the validity, legality and enforceability of the remaining provisions or obligations shall not in any way be affected or impaired thereby, and if any provision is inapplicable to any person or circumstances, it shall nevertheless remain applicable to all other persons and circumstances.

D. **Parties, Entire Agreement, Amendments**.

(i) **The Custodial Undertaking**. Buyer, Seller, and Custodian agree that this Custodial Undertaking constitutes the entire agreement among the parties hereto with respect to Transactions subject to this Custodial Undertaking and may not be amended or modified in any manner except by a written agreement executed by the parties hereto.

(ii) **The Custodial Undertaking and the Master Repurchase Agreement**. Buyer and Seller acknowledge and agree that the Master Repurchase Agreement in conjunction with this Custodial Undertaking represents the entire agreement between Buyer and Seller with respect to Transactions. Buyer and Seller acknowledge and agree that Custodian is not party to the Master Repurchase Agreement.

E. **Binding Agreement**. This Custodial Undertaking shall extend to and shall be binding upon the parties hereto, and their respective successors and assigns; provided however, that this Custodial Undertaking shall not be assignable by any party without the written consent of the other parties.

F. **Applicable Law/Jurisdiction**. This Custodial Undertaking shall be construed in accordance with the laws of the State of New York without regard to the conflict of laws principles thereof. The parties hereby consent to the jurisdiction of a state or federal court situated in New York City, New York in connection with any dispute arising hereunder. The parties hereby waive their right to trial by jury in any proceeding involving, directly or indirectly, any matter in any way arising out of, related to, or connected with, this Custodial Undertaking.

G. **Waiver of Immunity**. To the extent that in any jurisdiction any party may now or hereafter be entitled to claim, for itself or its assets, immunity from suit, execution, attachment (before or after judgment) or other legal process, each party irrevocably agrees not to claim, and it hereby waives, such immunity in connection with this Custodial Undertaking.

H. **Headings and References**. The headings and captions in this Custodial Undertaking are for reference only and shall not affect the construction or interpretation of any of its provisions.

I. **Counterparts**. This Custodial Undertaking may be executed in any number of counterparts, each of which shall be deemed to be an original, but such counterparts shall, together, constitute only one instrument.

J. **Inconsistency with Master Repurchase Agreement**. In the event of any inconsistency between the terms and conditions of the Master Repurchase Agreement and this Custodial Undertaking with respect to the rights, duties or obligations of Custodian and Transactions subject to this Custodial Undertaking, the terms and conditions of this Custodial Undertaking shall govern.

K. **Notices**. Any notice authorized or required by this Custodial Undertaking shall be sufficiently given if addressed to the receiving party and hand delivered or sent by mail, telex or facsimile to the individuals at the addresses specified in Schedule IV or to such other person or persons as the receiving party may from time to time designate in writing. Such notice shall be effective upon receipt.

L. **Confidentiality**. The parties hereto agree not to disclose to any other party and to keep confidential the terms and conditions of this Custodial Undertaking (including fee arrangements) and any amendment, supplement or Schedule hereto. In the event that any party hereto breaches any provision of this section, any other party shall be entitled to temporary and permanent injunctive relief against the breaching party without the necessity of proving actual damages. Notwithstanding the foregoing, Custodian may disclose Buyer's or Seller's name, address, securities position and other information to the extent required by law, the rules of any stock exchange or regulatory or self-regulatory organization or any order or decree of any court or administrative body that is binding on Custodian or any Clearing Corporation or the terms of the organizational documents of the issuer of any Security or the terms of any Security itself.

M. **Parties Deemed Principals**. Unless the parties hereto execute and deliver a Custodial Agency Annex [in substantially the form attached hereto as Appendix II]. pursuant to which the identity of all principals for whom any party may act in connection with

-9-

this Custodial Undertaking is disclosed, each party shall be responsible for the performance of its obligations hereunder as a principal. However, the execution and delivery of a Custodial Agency Annex shall not relieve any party of its obligations hereunder except as provided by applicable law.

IN WITNESS WHEREOF, the parties hereto have caused this Custodial Undertaking to be executed by their respective corporate officers, thereunto duly authorized, as of the _____ day of _____, 20___.

_____   _____

By:_____   By:_____

Title: Title:

                                        THE BANK OF NEW YORK

                                        By:_____

                                        Title:

SCHEDULE I

ELIGIBLE SECURITIES

APPENDIX 5

SCHEDULE II

The following individuals have been designated as Authorized Persons of Buyer and Seller, respectively, in connection with the Custodial Undertaking In Connection With Master Repurchase Agreement dated as of _____.

BUYER

Name	Signature
_____	_____
_____	_____
_____	_____
_____	_____

SELLER

Name	Signature
_____	_____
_____	_____
_____	_____
_____	_____

APPENDIX 5

SCHEDULE III

Account Information for Delivery of Buyer's Securities and Cash

ABA: _____

Bank Name: _____

City: _____

Account Name: _____

Account Number: _____

APPENDIX 5

SCHEDULE IV

ADDRESS FOR NOTICES

TO SELLER:

_____
_____
_____
_____

TO BUYER:

_____
_____
_____
_____

TO CUSTODIAN:

The Bank of New York
One Wall Street, 4th Floor
New York, New York 10286
Attn: Tri-Party Services
Government Securities Clearance Division
Telephone: (212) 635-4857
Fax: (212) 635-1190

APPENDIX 5

APPENDIX I

To: The Bank of New York
      Broker Dealer Services
      One Wall Street, 4th Floor
      New York, New York 10286
      Attention: Vice President

This notice is given pursuant to Paragraph 5E of the Custodial Undertaking in Connection With Master Repurchase Agreement by and among _____ ("Buyer"), _____ ("Seller") and The Bank of New York ("Custodian") dated as of _____ (the "Custodial Undertaking"). Buyer hereby instructs Custodian to transfer the Purchased Securities and cash in Buyer's Account (as defined in the Custodial Undertaking) to:

    ABA: _____

    Bank or Depository: _____

    City: _____

    Account Name: _____

    Account Number: _____

Date: _____

_____
[Buyer]

By: _____

Title:

APPENDIX II

CUSTODIAL AGENCY ANNEX

This Annex forms a part of the Custodial Undertaking In Connection With Master Repurchase Agreement dated as of _____ (the "Custodial Undertaking") by and among _____ ("Agent"), as agent for the principal(s) identified on Appendix A attached hereto (each, a "Buyer"), _____ ("Seller") and The Bank of New York ("Custodian"). Capitalized terms used but not defined shall have the meanings ascribed to them in the Custodial Undertaking.

1. **Representations and Warranties of Agent**

In addition to the representations set forth in Section 3.A of the Custodial Undertaking, Agent hereby represents and warrants, which representations and warranties shall be deemed to be continuing during the term of any Transaction, that:

(a) Each Buyer has duly authorized Agent to execute and deliver the Custodial Undertaking on its behalf, has the power to so authorize Agent and to enter into the Transactions contemplated by the Master Repurchase Agreement and otherwise perform its obligations pursuant to the Master Repurchase Agreement and the Custodial Undertaking, and has taken all necessary action to authorize such execution and delivery by Agent and such performance by it; and

(b) No Transaction effected hereunder shall be for the account of any third party not listed on Appendix A hereto.

(c) Agent is subject to a rule implementing 31 U.S.C. 5318(h) and maintains an anti-money laundering program compliant with the requirements of the USA PATRIOT Act (the "Act") and the rules thereunder; (2) Agent is regulated by a federal functional regulator as that term is defined under 31.C.F.R. §103.120(a)(2); (3) Agent has implemented a customer identification program compliant with Section 326 of the Act that enables Agent to form a reasonable belief that it knows the true identity of its customers (including each Buyer), including procedures to obtain information from and verify the identity of customers, maintain records of the information used to verify identity, determine whether any customer appears on any government list of known or suspected terrorists or terrorist organizations, and provide customers with adequate notice that the institution is requesting information to verify their identities; (4) Agent is in compliance with its anti-money laundering program and its customer identification program; and (5) Agent will certify annually that it has implemented its anti-money laundering program and that it (or its agent) will perform all aspects of its customer identification program with respect to each Buyer.

2. **Multiple Buyers**

(a) **Choice of Account(s)**. In the event that Agent proposes to act for more than one Buyer hereunder, Agent and Seller shall, subject to Custodian's prior consent, elect whether (i) to treat Transactions under the Custodial Undertaking as transactions entered into on behalf of separate Buyers, or (ii) to aggregate such Transactions as if they were transactions by a single Buyer. Failure to make such an election shall be deemed an election to treat Transactions under the Custodial Undertaking as transactions by a single Buyer.

(b) **Separate Accounts for Buyers**. In the event that Agent and Seller (with Custodian's prior consent) elect to treat Transactions under the Custodial Undertaking as transactions on behalf of separate Buyers, the parties agree that (i) Custodian shall establish a separate Buyer's Account in the name of each Buyer, (ii) Agent will provide Seller and Custodian with Written Instructions specifying the portion of each Transaction allocable to the account of each of the Buyers for which it is acting (to the extent that any such Transaction is allocable to the account of more than one Buyer); (iii) Custodian shall perform its obligations pursuant to Section 6 of the Custodial Undertaking on a Transaction-by-Transaction basis; and (iv) the parties' respective remedies under the Custodial Undertaking shall be determined as if Agent had entered into a separate Custodial Undertaking with the other party on behalf of each of its Buyers.

(c) **Omnibus Account for Buyer(s)**. In the event that Agent and Seller elect to treat Transactions under the Custodial Undertaking as if they were transactions by a single Buyer or Custodian's consent to establish separate Buyer's Accounts is not obtained, the parties agree that (i) Custodian shall establish one omnibus Buyer's Account in which all Buyers' interests with respect to Transactions shall be commingled, (ii) Custodian shall perform its obligations pursuant to

Section 6 on a Transaction-by-Transaction basis; and (iii) the parties' respective remedies under the Custodial Undertaking shall be determined as if all Buyers were a single Buyer.

3. **Custodian Not Responsible for Buyer Confirmations**. Notwithstanding any provision in the Custodial Undertaking to the contrary, all confirmation statements prepared by Custodian pursuant to the Custodial Undertaking shall be delivered to Agent and Custodian shall have no responsibility for providing any Buyer with confirmation statements reflecting Purchased Securities or cash positions in a Buyer's Account.

4. **Rescinded Authority**. Agent shall provide Seller and Custodian promptly with a revised Appendix A whenever a Buyer rescinds Agent's authority to perform its obligations pursuant to the Custodial Undertaking.

5. **Inconsistency with Agency Annex to Master Repurchase Agreement**. In the event of any inconsistency between the terms and conditions of any agency annex to the Master Repurchase Agreement and this Custodial Agency Annex, the terms and conditions of this Custodial Agency Annex shall govern.

IN WITNESS WHEREOF, the parties have caused this Annex to be executed by their respective officers, thereunto duly authorized, as of the _____ day of _____, 20__.

AGENT:

In its Individual Capacity

By:_____

Title:

By:_____

Title:

THE BANK OF NEW YORK

By:_____

Title:

agencyan.doc
(3-04)

APPENDIX A

LIST OF BUYERS

APPENDIX 5

SCHEDULE I
SCHEDULE OF ELIGIBLE SECURITIES

Custodial Undertaking in Connection with Master Repurchase Agreement dated as of _____, among _____ ("Seller") and The Bank of New York. _____ ("Buyer"),

	Yes/No	Margin		Yes/No	Margin
U.S. TREASURIES			**GNMA**		
BILLS			TRUST RECEIPTS		
BONDS			GNMA I/II-SINGLE FAMILY		
NOTES			GNMA I/II-OTHERS-FIXED RATE		
STRIPS			GNMA I/II OTHERS-ADJUST. RATE		
SYNTHETIC TREASURIES					
(e.g. CATS,COUGRS,TIGRS)			**AGENCY MORTGAGE BACKS**		
			TRUST RECEIPTS		
AGENCY DEBENTURES			PASS THROUGHS-FIXED RATE		
FAMC (Fed Agriculture Mtge Corp)			PASS THROUGHS-ADJUST. RATE		
FCFAC (Farm Credit Finan. Asst.)			MBS STRIPS (IO,PO,RECOMB)		
FFCB (Farm Credit System Banks)					
FmHA (Farmers Home Admin.)			**AGENCY REMICS/CMOS**		
FHLB (Federal Home Loan Banks)			*REMIC TYPES:*		
FHLMC (Federal Home Loan Mtge)			RESIDUALS		
FICO (Financing Corporation)			INVERSE IO FLOATERS		
FLBB (Federal Land Bank Bonds)			IOETTES		
FNMA (Federal Nat'l Mtge Corp)			INTEREST ONLY (IO)		
REFCO (Resolution Funding Corp)			PRINCIPAL ONLY (PO)		
SLMA (Student Loan Mtge Corp)			INVERSE FLOATERS		
TVA (Tennessee Valley Authoriry)			SUPER FLOATERS		
USPS (U.S. States Postal Service)			COMPANION FLOATERS		
AGENCY STRUCTURED NOTES			SEQUENTIAL AND OTHER FLOATERS		
			PAC & OTHER SCHEDULED FLOATERS		
INTERNATIONAL AGENCIES			Z BONDS		
ADBB (Asian Development Bank)			COMPANION BONDS		
AFDB (African Development Bank)			SEQUENTIAL BONDS		
IADB (Inter-American Dev. Bank)			TAC BONDS		
IFCO (International Finance Corp)			PAC & OTHER SCHEDULED BONDS		
WLDB (World Bank)					
			MUNICIPAL BOND		
CASH	YES		MUNICIPAL BONDS		
			PRIVATE LABELS MBS & CMOS		
			MBS PASS THROUGHS		
			CMO TYPES:		
			RESIDUALS		
			INVERSE IO FLOATERS		
			IOETTES		
			INTEREST ONLY (IO)		
			PRINCIPAL ONLY (PO)		
			INVERSE FLOATERS		
			SUPER FLOATERS		
			COMPANION FLOATERS		
			SEQUENTIAL AND OTHER FLOATERS		
			PAC & OTHER SCHEDULED FLOATERS		
			Z BONDS		
			COMPANION BONDS		
			SEQUENTIAL BONDS		
			TAC BONDS		
			PAC & OTHER SCHEDULED BONDS		
			ASSET BACKED SECURITIES		
			CREDIT CARD & OTHER ASSET BACKS		
			CORPORATES		
			CORPORATE BOND (>**BBB-**)		
			CORPORATE BOND (<**BB+**)		
			MEDIUM-TERM NOTE (> **BBB-**)		
			MEDIUM-TERM NOTE (< **BB+**)		
			MONEY MARKETS		
			COMMERCIAL PAPER (>**A1/P1**)		
			COMMERCIAL PAPER (<**A2/P2**)		
			BANKERS ACCEPTANCE		
			CD (DOMESTIC & EURO)		
			BANK NOTES		

BUYER ACKNOWLEDGES AND AGREES THAT IF A CLASS OF SECURITY CONTAINS NEW ISSUES OF SECURITIES, SUCH NEW ISSUES OF SECURITIES SHALL BE DEEMED TO BE ELIGIBLE SECURITIES.

[BUYER]   [SELLER]   ACCEPTED:

                                                                       THE BANK OF NEW YORK

By: By: By:
Title: Title: Title:
Date: Date: Date:

1/2003

THE BANK OF NEW YORK

Index

Accrued Interest 161, 244
Act of Insolvency 35, 179
Additional Purchased Securities 188, 217
adjustment 56
Agency Annex and Addendum 110
Agency Transaction 102, 149
Agent 149, 235, 304
Appropriate Market 72
Article 8 . . . . .22, 177, 266, 277
Article 9 . . . . .22, 266, 277
Authorized Person 264
automatic stay 16, 24
avoiding power 25

Base Currency 90, 223, 142
Bills Annex 111
Book-Entry Securities 264, 276
Book-Entry System .265
Business Day 36, 128, 215, 224, 265
Buyer 8, 34, 153, 178, 239
Buyer's Account 265
Buyer's Margin Amount 180
Buyer's Margin Percentage 181
buy-in 157
Buy/Sell Back Annex 112
buy/sellbacks 9
Cabinet Order 259
Canadian Annex 109
Capital Adequacy Directive 220
Cash Margin 37, 169
Cedel 224

Central Gilts Office (CGO) 64
Change of Circumstances 137, 139
cherry picking 10, 71, 123
Clearing Corporation 266, 276
Clearing Corporation Securities 266, 276
Clearstream 37, 224
Close-out Cabinet Order 261
Close-out Netting Law 261
collateral 51
Confirmation 49, 124, 162, 186, 247, 282
Contractual Currency 62, 148, 224, 227
Counterparty 246
counterparty default 12
Credit Event Upon Restructuring 138
Crest 113
cross-currency repo 5
Cross Default 134
Custodial Undertaking 294, 262
Custodian 248, 262

DBV Transactions 114
Default Market Value 70
Default Notice 38
Default Under Specified Transactions 133
Default Valuation Notice 74
Default Valuation Time 72
Deliverable Securities 72
delivery versus payment 3
Designated Office 39, 218
Distributions 11, 159, 162, 254

477

Eligible Securities 266
emerging markets 103
Employment Retirement Income
Security Act (ERISA) 208, 239
Entire Agreement 85, 206, 294
Equities Annex 112
equity repo 6
Equity Security 252
Equivalent Margin Securities 39
Equivalent Securities 39
Euroclear 40, 225
European Repo Council 1, 308
Events of Default 67, 174, 197, 234, 242, 256
Exchange Act 211, 252

FASB 125/140 99
Federal Deposit Insurance Act
(FIDA) 23, 25–27, 210
Federal Deposit Insurance
Corporation (FIDC) 25–27
Federal Deposit Insurance Corporation
Improvement Act of 1991 (FDICIA)
.... 25–28, 210
Final Settlement Amount 140
flex repo 4
Forward Exposure 240
Forward Transactions 94
Fund 245–246

general collateral repo 4
General Provisions 119
Gilts Annex 113
governing law 51, 172, 207

hold-in custody repo 5

Illegality 137
Impossibility 137
Income 12, 41, 181, 216
Income Payment Date 41

International Security 225
International Transaction 225
In-the-Money Party 240
ISMA's buy-in rules 309
issuer risk 12
Italian Annex 109

Japanese Securities Annex 110

legal risk 13
LIBOR 41, 225

Margin Deficit 188, 283
Margin Excess 189, 284
margining 9
Margin Maintenance Annex 120, 165
Margin Notice Deadline 182, 215
Margin Percentage 247, 267
Margin Ratio 41
Margin Securities 42, 169
Margin Transfer 42
Margin Value 267
market risk 13
Market Value 42, 129, 182, 217, 257
Market Value of Securities 267
mini close-out 77–79

Net Exposure 165
Net Forward Exposure 240
Netherlands Annex 110
Net Margin 43
Net Paying Securities 44
Net Unsecured Forward Exposure 242
Net Value 73
New Purchased Securities 63
Notice of Default 268
NY General Obligation Law §5-1401 .... 20, 219
NY General Obligation Law §5-1402\ ... 20, 219

INDEX

open repo 5
operational risk 13
Oral Instructions 268
Orange County 28–29
Out-of-the-Money Party 240
overnight repo 5

Physical Securities 268, 276
Pledgor 242
Preference payments 25
Price Differential 45, 154, 182
Pricing Rate 45, 154, 183
Prime Rate 183, 226
Principal 149, 235
Process Agent 93, 152
Product Annex for Repurchase Transactions .. 152
Product Annex for Securities Loans 164
Purchase Date 45, 183, 275
Purchased Securities 46, 153, 184, 253, 268
Purchase Price 10, 46, 183, 216

Receivable Securities 73
recharacterisation 20
Recording 88
Registered Investment Companies .. 245–246, 248
Repricing 163
Repurchase Date 46, 184, 285, 268
Repurchase Price 46, 154, 185
Reverse Repo 4
Richard Sykes opinion 17
Rule 144 255–256

Scope of Agreement 98
secured party 21–22
Securities 34, 125, 178, 269
Securities Act 253
Securities Investor Protection
Act (SIPA) 24, 211
Securities Investor Protection
Corporation (SIPC) 23–24

securities loans 11
Security Interest 192, 242
Sell Back Differential 244
Sell Back Price 161, 244
Seller 7, 33, 153, 178, 239
Seller's Account 269
Seller's Margin Amount 185
Seller's Margin Percentage 185
set off 144
Severability 29, 85, 151, 206
shaping 308
Single Agreement 82, 123, 204
single branch margining 98
South African Annex 110
Special Default Notice 84
Special Provisions 120, 171
special repo 4
Spot Rate 47, 226
Standard Settlement Date 253
Substitution 11, 63, 159, 195, 221
Syndicated repo 6

TARGET 47
Tax Event 80, 137, 232
Tax Special Measurement Law 259
term repo 5
Thai Annex 110
Third Party Rights 88
TRADES Regulations 22
Transaction 34, 123, 178
Transaction Exposure 48, 94
tri-party repo 5

UCC 269
US Bankruptcy Code 23–27
US Treasury repo 101

Written Instructions 269

479